Go Solo 2

The Authorized Guide to Version 2 of the Single UNIX® Specification

The Open Group

Go Solo 2

The Authorized Guide to Version 2 of the Single UNIX® Specification

ISBN: 0-13-575689-8
Document Number: X909P

Published in the U.K. by The Open Group.

Any comments relating to the material contained in this document may be submitted to:

The Open Group
Apex Plaza
Forbury Road
Reading
Berkshire RG1 1AX

Or by email to:

OGspecs@opengroup.org

Contents

List of Examples

List of Figures

List of Tables

Acknowledgements

The Open Group gratefully acknowledges:

- the contributions of the authors (see **About the Authors** on page xv)
- the Space and Naval Warfare Systems Command, who gave permission for use of their original papers for Chapter 9 and Chapter 10
- DISA for its efforts in bringing the NGCR OSSWG document up-to-date
- members of the Aspen Group who contributed to the development of the Aspen threads extensions
- the POSIX 1387.2 working group and ballot group, plus the members of the X/Open Systems Management Technical Working Group devoted to extensions to POSIX 1387.2
- members of the Large File Summit
- Pierre Lewis and Ted Timar for permission to reproduce the Usenet FAQ material included on the Go Solo 2 CD-ROM
- SunSoft for permission to reproduce material relating to threads and large files included on the Go Solo 2 CD-ROM
- Derek Noonburg for permission to include the Xpdf viewer on the Go Solo 2 CD-ROM
- Adobe for permission to include the Adobe Acrobat Reader on the Go Solo 2 CD-ROM
- members of the review team: Chris Bamford, Graham Bird. Sean Eric Fagan, Francoise Miane, and Richard Wendland.

Trademarks

Adobe™ and Acrobat Reader™ are trademarks of Adobe Systems Incorporated.

AIX® is a registered trademark of IBM Corporation.

AT&T® is a registered trademark of AT&T in the U.S.A. and other countries.

Digital™ and DEC™ are trademarks of Digital Equipment Corporation.

HP® is a registered trademark of Hewlett-Packard.

IBM®, MVS/ESA®, and OpenEdition® are registered trademarks of IBM in the United States.

Macintosh® is a registered trademark of Apple Computer, Inc.

Microsoft® and Windows NT® are registered trademarks of Microsoft Corporation in the United States and/or other countries. NT is a trademark of Northern Telecom Limited.

Motif®, OSF/1®, and UNIX® are registered trademarks and the "X Device"™ and The Open Group™ are trademarks of The Open Group.

NetWare® is a registered trademark of Novell, Inc.

Novell® is a registered trademark of Novell, Inc.

OpenNT™ is a trademark of Softway Systems, Inc.

POSIX® is a registered trademark of the Institute of Electrical and Electronic Engineers, Inc.

SCO® and UnixWare® are registered trademarks of The Santa Cruz Operation, Inc. in the U.S.A. and other countries.

Sun® and Solaris® are registered trademarks of Sun Microsystems, Inc.

/usr/group® is a registered trademark of UniForum, the International Network of UNIX System Users.

XENIX® is a registered trademark of Microsoft Corporation.

This list represents, as far as possible, those products that are trademarked. The Open Group acknowledges that there may be other products that might be covered by trademark protection and advises the reader to verify them independently.

About the Authors

Barrie Archer is a Systems Designer working in ICL Enterprise Technology. He works on ICL's System Management Strategy and participated in the development of ICL's OPENframework Architecture for Systems Management. He was the ICL representative to, and a founding member of, The Open Group Systems Management Technical Working Group and POSIX 1387.2 working group.

Jay Ashford is a Senior Programmer working in AIX System Architecture and Standards, and is responsible for system management standards and liaison to the IEEE PASC development group. He was the Chair of the POSIX 1387.2 working group and continues to be active in the Software Administration extensions sub-group within The Open Group Systems Management Technical Working Group.

Don Ault joined IBM in 1974. He worked in MVS performance, test and development until 1990 when he joined the OpenEdition kernel development team, specializing in OpenEdition integration with MVS.

Werner Bachmann is a project leader at Siemens Nixdorf Informationssysteme AG working on the implementation of the UNIX 95 interfaces in BS2000, and acts as a consultant for porting projects of UNIX system software on BS2000 for several software companies.

Andre Bellotti is an engineering supervisor with Digital Equipment Corporation and a former member of The Open Group Base Technical Working Group.

Scott Bender joined IBM in 1981. He worked in DPCX system test and DPPX development until 1990 when he joined the OpenEdition kernel development team, specializing in signals and threading.

Dave Butenhof is a Principal Engineer with Digital Equipment Corporation and is a member of the POSIX.1c working group. He was a member of the Aspen working group that developed the Aspen threads extensions.

Karen Gordon is an Adjunct Associate Professor of Computer Science at Vanderbilt University. She was a member of the U.S. Navy's NGCR OSSWG and the IEEE POSIX Realtime Working Group.

Joseph M. Gwinn has been building, adapting, and using realtime embedded operating systems for 25 years, most recently for a large US defense contractor. Mr. Gwinn holds degrees in Electrical Engineering and Computer Science, and is the Vice-Chair of the POSIX System Services Working Group (SSWG) and is also the Chair of the Realtime subgroup of the SSWG.

Cathy Hughes is a Technical Editor with The Open Group. She has edited many X/Open and Open Group publications, including most recently the Single UNIX Specification, Version 2.

Andrew Josey is a Senior Test Development Manager with The Open Group and is Chair of The Open Group Base Technical Working Group. He is the IEEE PASC Functional Chair of Interpretations.

David Lindner is a Principal Engineer with Digital Equipment Corporation and a former member of The Open Group Internationalization Technical Working Group.

Finnbarr P. Murphy is a principal software engineer with Digital Equipment Corporation and is Vice-Chair of The Open Group Base Technical Working Group. He was a member of the working group that developed the Aspen threads extensions.

Jim Oblinger is a member of the technical staff at the Naval Undersea Warfare Center. He was the Chairman of the U.S. Navy's NGCR OSSWG and a member of the IEEE POSIX Realtime Working Group.

Frank Prindle is an independent consultant, recently retired from the Naval Air Warfare Center. He was a member of the U.S. Navy's NGCR OSSWG, the IEEE POSIX Realtime Working Group, and The Open Group Base Technical Working Group.

Mike Spiegel joined IBM in 1983. He worked in TSO development and performance analysis until 1990 when he joined the OpenEdition kernel development team, specializing in process management, threading and program execution/load.

Stephen R. Walli is Vice-president of Research and Development and a founder at Softway Systems (http://www.OpenNT.com). He is a long time participant and officer in the IEEE and ISO POSIX working groups, and has represented the USENIX technical community at these standards development meetings.

George Williams is a Technical Contributor working in HP Open Systems Software and is responsible for Software Management Architecture and Standards. He was a member of the POSIX 1387.2 working group and contributes to the ongoing Software Administration extensions in The Open Group Systems Management Technical Working Group.

About The Open Group

The Open Group

The Open Group is an international open systems organization that is leading the way in creating the infrastructure needed for the development of network-centric computing and the information superhighway. Formed in 1996 by the merger of the X/Open Company and the Open Software Foundation, The Open Group is supported by most of the world's largest user organizations, information systems vendors and software suppliers. By combining the strengths of open systems specifications and a proven branding scheme with collaborative technology development and advanced research, The Open Group is well positioned to assist user organizations, vendors and suppliers in the development and implementation of products supporting the adoption and proliferation of open systems.

With more than 300 member companies, The Open Group helps the IT industry to advance technologically while managing the change caused by innovation. It does this by:

- consolidating, prioritizing and communicating customer requirements to vendors
- conducting research and development with industry, academia and government agencies to deliver innovation and economy through projects associated with its Research Institute
- managing cost-effective development efforts that accelerate consistent multi-vendor deployment of technology in response to customer requirements
- adopting, integrating and publishing industry standard specifications that provide an essential set of blueprints for building open information systems and integrating new technology as it becomes available
- licensing and promoting the X/Open brand that designates vendor products which conform to X/Open Product Standards
- promoting the benefits of open systems to customers, vendors and the public.

The Open Group operates in all phases of the open systems technology lifecycle including innovation, market adoption, product development and proliferation. Presently, it focuses on seven strategic areas: open systems application platform development, architecture, distributed systems management, interoperability, distributed computing environment, security, and the information superhighway. The Open Group is also responsible for the management of the UNIX trade mark on behalf of the industry.

The X/Open Process

This description is used to cover the whole Process developed and evolved by X/Open. It includes the identification of requirements for open systems, development of CAE and Preliminary Specifications through an industry consensus review and adoption procedure (in parallel with formal standards work), and the development of tests and conformance criteria.

This leads to the preparation of a Product Standard which is the name used for the documentation that records the conformance requirements (and other information) to which a vendor may register a product. There are currently two forms of Product Standard, namely the

Profile Definition and the Component Definition, although these will eventually be merged into one.

The X/Open brand logo is used by vendors to demonstrate that their products conform to the relevant Product Standard. By use of the X/Open brand they guarantee, through the X/Open Trade Mark Licence Agreement (TMLA), to maintain their products in conformance with the Product Standard so that the product works, will continue to work, and that any problems will be fixed by the vendor.

Open Group Publications

The Open Group publishes a wide range of technical literature, the main part of which is focused on specification development and product documentation, but which also includes Guides, Snapshots, Technical Studies, Branding and Testing documentation, industry surveys and business titles.

There are several types of specification:

- *CAE Specifications*

  CAE (Common Applications Environment) Specifications are the stable specifications that form the basis for our product standards, which are used to develop X/Open branded systems. These specifications are intended to be used widely within the industry for product development and procurement purposes.

  Anyone developing products that implement a CAE Specification can enjoy the benefits of a single, widely supported industry standard. In addition, they can demonstrate product compliance through the X/Open brand. CAE Specifications are published as soon as they are developed, so enabling vendors to proceed with development of conformant products without delay.

- *Preliminary Specifications*

  Preliminary Specifications usually address an emerging area of technology and consequently are not yet supported by multiple sources of stable conformant implementations. They are published for the purpose of validation through implementation of products. A Preliminary Specification is not a draft specification; rather, it is as stable as can be achieved, through applying The Open Group's rigorous development and review procedures.

  Preliminary Specifications are analogous to the *trial-use* standards issued by formal standards organizations, and developers are encouraged to develop products on the basis of them. However, experience through implementation work may result in significant (possibly upwardly incompatible) changes before its progression to becoming a CAE Specification. While the intent is to progress Preliminary Specifications to corresponding CAE Specifications, the ability to do so depends on consensus among Open Group members.

- *Consortium and Technology Specifications*

  The Open Group publishes specifications on behalf of industry consortia. For example, it publishes the NMF SPIRIT procurement specifications on behalf of the Network Management Forum. It also publishes Technology Specifications relating to OSF/1, DCE, OSF/Motif and CDE.

  Technology Specifications (formerly AES Specifications) are often candidates for consensus review, and may be adopted as CAE Specifications, in which case the relevant Technology Specification is superseded by a CAE Specification.

In addition, The Open Group publishes:

- *Product Documentation*

  This includes product documentation — programmer's guides, user manuals, and so on — relating to the Pre-structured Technology Projects (PSTs), such as DCE and CDE. It also includes the Single UNIX Documentation, designed for use as common product documentation for the whole industry.

- *Guides*

  These provide information that is useful in the evaluation, procurement, development or management of open systems, particularly those that relate to the CAE Specifications. The Open Group Guides are advisory, not normative, and should not be referenced for purposes of specifying or claiming conformance to a Product Standard.

- *Technical Studies*

  Technical Studies present results of analyses performed on subjects of interest in areas relevant to The Open Group's Technical Program. They are intended to communicate the findings to the outside world so as to stimulate discussion and activity in other bodies and the industry in general.

- *Snapshots*

  These provide a mechanism to disseminate information on its current direction and thinking, in advance of possible development of a Specification, Guide or Technical Study. The intention is to stimulate industry debate and prototyping, and solicit feedback. A Snapshot represents the interim results of a technical activity.

Versions and Issues of Specifications

As with all *live* documents, CAE Specifications require revision to align with new developments and associated international standards. To distinguish between revised specifications which are fully backwards compatible and those which are not:

- A new *Version* indicates there is no change to the definitive information contained in the previous publication of that title, but additions/extensions are included. As such, it *replaces* the previous publication.

- A new *Issue* indicates there is substantive change to the definitive information contained in the previous publication of that title, and there may also be additions/extensions. As such, both previous and new documents are maintained as current publications.

Corrigenda

Readers should note that Corrigenda may apply to any publication. Corrigenda information is published on the World-Wide Web at **http://www.opengroup.org/public/pubs**.

Ordering Information

Full catalogue and ordering information on all Open Group publications is available on the World-Wide Web at **http://www.opengroup.org/public/pubs**.

The Business Case for Open Systems

Expectations for Open Systems in a Changing Marketplace

During the past decade, the concept of open systems changed dramatically. What began originally as a strategic imperative for vendors became a compelling supply/demand dynamic, as buyers began to flex their procurement muscles by specifying systems based on an "open" configuration.

The momentum for open systems began in the vendor community. Indeed, the original X/Open Company Ltd. was founded in 1984 to remedy the absence of standards in the area of open systems; under its auspices, the open systems product brand was introduced in 1988. For largely competitive reasons, the X/Open sponsors saw the need for, and the value to be gained from, open systems. Consequently, they assigned resources to create standards for the technologies that they considered important. The major role of the user community back then was quite fundamental: to buy the products based upon those standards.

In the subsequent years, however, the user's role expanded significantly. Like the vendors before them, organizations utilizing information technology (IT) began to recognize the power of an open systems procurement strategy. Their focus was on operational efficiencies, not supply-side technology requirements. But their influence was profound nonetheless. Rather than affiliating with the X/Open technical working groups, users worked together on the X/Open user requirements councils and in the Xtra business requirements surveys.

Research has recorded steady growth in the number of organizations using open systems, from 68% in 1991 to an expected 96% in 1997. Similarly, while sales of proprietary systems declined by 2% between 1990 and 1994, open systems sales rose by 37% worldwide in the same period. This growth in market share is expected to continue at more than double the rate for proprietary systems.

What do buyers expect from an open systems strategy? In 1996 EvansGroup Technology carried out research among computer system buyers in the United States, UK and Europe. When asked about the benefits of open systems, the key issues of *compatibility, flexibility* and *cost* emerged. The table below shows how respondents ranked the various benefits of open systems.

Benefits of Open Systems	%
Flexibility	70%
Freedom to choose IT from different vendors	67%
Products from different vendors work together	66%
Access across multi-vendor environments	65%
Protect investment in existing computer system	61%
Ability to use/share information anywhere in the world	59%
Cost savings	55%
Interoperability/portability across various platforms	54%
Organizational change not constrained by IT system	49%
Cost of ownership	49%

This study and others like it continue to reinforce that for an organization to become a buyer and user of open systems, it must be assured of, if not guaranteed, a solid return on investment. Again, their specific expectations are for interoperability, flexibility, freedom of choice and cost reduction. Interoperability, the capability for systems and applications to work together, is one of the key drivers in the move toward open systems. Buyers want to be able to interconnect any system or software from any vendor without concern for incompatibilities. Ultimately, interoperability provides a greater level of flexibility in the way end-users implement and operate their computing environments.

Customers also want choice. In a proprietary systems and software environment, the customer's choice is limited. The promise of open systems is a world in which a wide range of compatible products are available, enabling customers to make selections based on price, service, support and features, rather than vendor.

Like all consumers, information technology buyers want value when they purchase system or software products. Proprietary products are traditionally more costly and offer fewer alternatives. Open systems products offer a level playing field with competition focused on product quality, service, support and performance, as well as ensuring value pricing.

The Open Group Response: The X/Open Brand

One of The Open Group's core charters is to license and promote the X/Open product brand, which designates products that are guaranteed to conform to open systems standards. The Open Group develops test suites, ensuring that products claimed to comply with open systems standards actually do so. Vendors of products displaying this X/Open brand guarantee that their products comply with the relevant open systems specifications. The X/Open brand from The Open Group is the most widely used procurement tool for the purchase of open systems products.

The traditional definition of a "brand" is a set of values ascribed to a product. The X/Open brand has a clear set of values, the focal point of which is the guarantee. The brand constitutes a guarantee, offered by the vendor to the buyer, that the branded product conforms to the specified standard, and will continue to conform, for as long as the product carries the X/Open brand.

The use of the brand by the vendor is supported by a legal contract, actually a trademark license, between the vendor and The Open Group, and legally commits the vendor to correct any conformance deficiencies should they ever become evident throughout the life of the branded product. Customers find assurance in this guarantee, that the product does what the specification says, providing value to both buyers and vendors.

Also important for customers is the fact that the X/Open brand is deliberately neutral. The Open Group product standards favor no hardware or software technology or vendor. They intentionally make no assumptions or prerequisites of technology, hardware or architecture. This allows implementors to innovate in any way, providing they conform to the standard.

The X/Open brand — the embodiment of The Open Group — provides a market delivery mechanism for open systems products and services. The brand represents a benchmark for vendor selection, ensuring customers of quality, guaranteed products.

Identifying the Benefits for Buyers

As we approach the new millennium there is a growing conviction that information technology can, and should, make a significant contribution to the success of business and government. Users are increasingly vocal in their conviction that to achieve the benefits of improved management, customer service and profitability, information systems must enhance, rather than restrict, the flow of information.

In this regard, the users' collective voice is being heard in their purchasing policies. Increasingly, organizations are building IT strategies that promote compatibility, portability and interoperability as central components. Their open systems-based procurement policies address these requirements by allowing users to communicate and share data across different platforms. Thus, one of the most fundamental benefits of this strategy is the ability to select the products that best meet functional requirements from a variety of suppliers. By enabling organizations to accept bids from a range of vendors, an open systems strategy allows procurement professionals to evaluate suppliers on a wide range of criteria. With the issue of system compatibility largely eliminated, other issues such as functionality, price, support and service can then be given their due weight.

Government and commercial organizations worldwide increasingly look for the X/Open brand when selecting products because it assures them of the highest degree of standards conformance in IT products. For example, the purchase of a branded UNIX 95 product will automatically ensure that the following standards are implemented:

- IEEE Std 1003.1-1990 (POSIX.1)
- IEEE Std 1003.2-1992 (POSIX.2)
- FIPS 151-2
- FIPS 189
- ISO/IEC 9945-1: 1990 (POSIX-1)
- ISO/IEC 9945-2: 1993 (POSIX-2)
- ISO/IEC 9899: 1990, Programming Languages — C (ISO C).

No other mechanism available offers that guarantee to IT buyers.

Identifying the Benefits for Vendors

Vendors benefit from the X/Open branding program as well. The brand is a tangible mark that they can show to customers, demonstrating guaranteed conformance to open systems standards. It also demonstrates the vendor's commitment to stand behind its product and emphasizes the effort invested by the vendor to meet the stringent requirements of the brand. Additionally, the brand enables the vendor to compete in the market that requires the brand in its product procurements — to date worth over $20 billion — and sets vendors apart from those that are not prepared to guarantee their products.

Vendors seeking to brand their products must go through a stringent process. The Open Group offers an extensive set of tools and services to help vendors bring their products into conformance with the standards, from specifications on CD-ROM to test suites, guides and more. Once a product conforms to the standard, vendors enter into a trademark licensing agreement that commits the vendor to guarantee to buyers that branded products will continue to conform for the life of the product — even through product revisions and updates.

Documenting the Benefits

The open systems "movement" is far enough along that promotion of its purpose is no longer an issue. Rather, with maturity has come a new generation of measurements designed to justify the expenditures of implementation. In addition to standard metrics like cycle time, quality, and return on investment, managers are also employing measures of a more qualitative nature: How is the IT investment be aligned with the organization's overall strategic goals? To what degree is the new framework adaptable to future changes in the organization's business requirements?

On the adoption of open systems, there are a growing number of documented successes for organizations worldwide.

NASA

In the early 1990s the world's foremost scientific space organization — NASA — faced serious problems in its technology and procurement strategies. A review of its information system needs revealed a complex, protracted procurement cycle and dominance by a single supplier and architecture. For users this meant their work was constrained by sometimes inappropriate and dated systems that offered little choice or power to meet their varied and changing IT needs.

For procurement managers, reliance on proprietary technology caused an additional problem. Federal procurement regulations require agencies to secure multiple bids for all purchases over a certain value, but because NASA was so closely tied to a single vendor, this was not possible. Not only was IT constraining its business, effectively, NASA was breaking the law.

As David Howell, Chief of Data Systems of the Technology Division at NASA's Goddard Space Flight Center said:

> "We needed to break away from vendor-control and we needed solutions with high growth and networking capabilities. Open systems are best for that purpose."

Having realized that open systems were vital for its future, NASA's solution was the development of a set of open systems procurement contracts to provide high-performance UNIX operating system-based workstations and support equipment, including servers, printers and networking equipment.

Known as SEWP (Scientific and Engineering Workstation Procurement), these contracts provided NASA with a whole new procurement methodology. SEWP increased the availability of equipment to users, promoted an open computing environment, broke the cycle of reliance on proprietary technology and reduced the high cost of software conversion. In short, NASA's open systems strategy provides an effective future-proof platform to support change and innovation.

An important result of the program has been the shortening of NASA's procurement cycle from as much as two years to approximately 45 days.

The Boeing Company

The Boeing Company's migration to open systems began a decade ago. The cost of computing company-wide was doubling every two years. But that cost was not driven by increased functionality or increased capabilities; it was the lack of an open systems-based infrastructure.

Functions were isolated and pockets of computing existed throughout the company. Individual groups were making their own decisions about computing needs without regard to the need for connecting all users, applications and different business processes together, resulting in a nearly endless variety of systems and software. Older legacy systems with closed environments were posing similar challenges to communication and information flow among groups and departments.

Boeing's future depended on connecting people and systems. "The move to open systems was a straightforward business case," according to John Warner, president of Boeing's Information and Support Services Division. "We needed to put disparate systems together so that we could do projects like the 777 airplane, and we needed to make sure we could get the most value for our investment in computing systems."

Boeing developed a computing standard that defined the Boeing open systems direction for heterogeneous computing environments. A statement of direction was distributed; it included all aspects of providing a computing environment to support the business process of The Boeing Company.

The scope of the standard was company wide. All operating divisions incorporated the open system philosophy and developed vision statements that included elements unique to their products and customers. The specifications are now used for all requests for equipment throughout Boeing.

Open systems has removed many of the walls that added cost and slowed communication at Boeing. The 777 project became a real proving ground for open systems. Boeing's computing environment met the challenge, allowing unprecedented cooperation and communication between myriad teams of engineers, manufacturing planners, tool designers, suppliers, and others.

Open systems has helped streamline a number of processes. Once, maintenance manuals were laboriously produced, printed, and shipped to customers. Today, Boeing can provide maintenance information quickly and efficiently to customers electronically, eliminating the time and expense of manually producing and distributing mountains of paper.

The training and support functions within Boeing are sporting a more streamlined look as well. A plethora of proprietary systems and software requires more training and support than the more heterogeneous, open environment. The open systems environment has reduced duplication in these activities for both end-users and support personnel, leading to significant cost savings without reduced levels of support and training.

Boeing set out on the path to open systems to tie business processes together and to control costs. In the process, the company has become more competitive. The move to an open systems-based infrastructure is an ongoing process at Boeing. The transition from legacy systems to a new, distributed environment will continue as budgets allow, and open systems will play a major role in the procurement process. Boeing has not set specific goals or timetables, however, for achieving an open computing environment. Instead, it establishes goals based on capabilities and the related cost to provide those capabilities.

UK National Insurance Recording System

In 1996, the UK National Insurance Recording System, known as NIRS2, was commissioned by the Contributions Agency, part of the UK Department of Social Security (DSS). The project is seen as proof positive that a government-mandated open systems policy can indeed be justified on purely business and technical grounds.

National Insurance in the UK is an income-related payment collected by the Contributions Agency to pay social security and retirement benefits for UK residents. Payments are unique for each individual, so NIRS2 must record accurately the cumulative national insurance contributions of every single UK resident.

NIRS2 is the first major IT project being built under the British government's new financing policy, the Private Finance Initiative (PFI), under which suppliers plan and build IT systems at their own cost. The suppliers recoup their investments and running costs solely through charging for the system on a per-use basis; for example, charging for each transaction or query.

Under such schemes significant risks are transferred to the supplier, including development, financial and technology risks.

When it goes live in the first quarter of 1997, NIRS2 will have some 60 million national insurance accounts requiring a database of 400 gigabytes. The system will have approximately 5,000 users in the Contributions Agency at the National Insurance administrative headquarters in Newcastle, England, and in field offices around the UK. NIRS2 will have to cope with some 200 transactions a second, for both batch and on-line processing. By the time the initial seven-year operating contract ends in 2004, the database will contain an estimated 800 gigabytes of data.

In April 1995, the Contributions Agency awarded the NIRS2 contract to Andersen Consulting, after running a large procurement. For their part, Andersen Consulting considered a range of solutions including proprietary mainframes. In the end, they chose to build NIRS2 using an open systems architecture.

In the NIRS2 installation, central processing is based on a cluster of open application and database servers from Hewlett Packard. The eight application servers have four processors, and the four database servers have six processors, all running under the Single UNIX Specification. The client workstations are industry-standard PCs which communicate with the servers using the DCE communications standards.

HP and the relational database, Sybase, were chosen by Andersen Consulting after a competition with other vendors.

Security, which is often seen as a weakness for UNIX-based systems, is ensured using dedicated communication lines and secure communications protocols, along with strict authentication procedures.

The architecture designed by Andersen provides the processing capacity by partitioning the database across several database servers and by splitting the application load across several application servers, effectively creating a virtual mainframe. An open transaction processing monitor, Encina, is used to manage the transaction integrity between the application and the database servers.

"If you drew a line around the central processors, it would look like we had a mainframe. But we haven't paid mainframe prices for providing that functionality, and we have more control over the design and upgrading of the system by using this architecture," explained Guy Morgan, an associate partner at Andersen responsible for the NIRS2 architecture. "The architecture is very scaleable; we can add more disk, RAM, and processors to the individual servers; and if even more capacity is required, we can introduce another application or database server. This scalability is achieved at a much lower cost than if we were adding new mainframe nodes. The architecture was designed to be inherently scaleable to cope with the changing business volumes over the duration of the contract."

Andersen has taken the open systems approach a stage further by avoiding proprietary fourth-generation languages (4GLs) and instead using industry-standard third-generation languages (3GLs), such as C and C++, to develop the NIRS2 applications.

"When we looked at price performance, development effectiveness, flexibility, and scalability coupled with the skills available within the firm, open systems was a natural winner," adds Morgan. "We can provide the security, availability, and performance of traditional mainframe systems using an architecture based on UNIX and open systems."

LittonPRC

Litton/PRC, one of the leading U.S. systems integrators, has been building and reengineering information systems for its federal government and commercial customers based on open systems standards since 1984. PRC turned its open systems development skills to its own internal proprietary mainframe-based systems five years ago. Today, PRC's open client/server environment has streamlined the process of accessing information and empowered its employees.

The decision to migrate from a proprietary, centralized computing environment to one that was open and decentralized was the function of a combination of factors.

PRC had evolved from a highly centralized organization to one with a more departmental structure, reflecting the needs of its increasingly diverse customers. The mainframe environment had become awkward, inflexible and expensive. Hard-copy report distribution required the generation of volumes of paper that was physically shipped to various locations each week.

But it was federal accounting changes in the early '90s and continued growth in PRC's business that brought the need for change to a head. Rules governing timecards and payroll for federal contractors were undergoing dramatic changes, impacting PRC's accounting systems. To keep up with these changes, the company would have to add to the mainframe population — a significant capitalization cost. Because they had an older, proprietary "stovepipe" accounting system, the need was to replace, not upgrade. The cost of the physical hardware highly favored an open environment.

The highest priority for change involved those areas impacted by the new federal acquisition rules. PRC identified human resources and finance as the first systems to migrate to the new open client/server environment. The firm selected PeopleSoft's human resource and finance modules containing employee benefits, general ledger, and asset management applications.

As the HR and finance systems were being developed, the network was being prepared. High-speed fiber optic circuits were added and servers were put in place to handle the distributed computing.

The first operational release, consisting of time card and budget reporting, was prevalidated in the third quarter of 1994. The full operational release, which included the general accounting system, was introduced during the first quarter of 1995. The change-over from a mainframe-based system to a fully open environment was completed within a six-month period.

The changes were clearly worth the effort. Despite the fact that PC, Mac and UNIX platforms and HP, DEC Alpha, Sun and Silicon Graphics servers are connected to a hybrid network, communications and connectivity have been enhanced significantly. As noted by Cora Carmody, Chief Information Officer for PRC, "Because of open systems and the underlying standards, it is much easier to connect. Most of our users don't sense the hybrid network situation. It's transparent to them."

By replacing its accounting and human resource systems, PRC also sidestepped another concern — the Year-2000 problem. With so many older legacy systems subject to arithmetic paralysis when the year 1999 becomes 2000, thousands of corporations are expecting to spend millions of dollars to rewrite software code. PRC's new software was developed with the next century in mind.

Another benefit, PRC has greatly reduced the distribution of hard-copy documents, which are now printed only when and where they are needed. And a large percentage of "paperwork" is completed on-line without ever being printed out. That reduces cycle time.

Since implementation of the HR and finance systems, PRC has continued to enhance its open systems environment. In 1996, the firm migrated Microsoft Mail, PC Mail and cc:Mail users to Exchange mail to allow easier communication among employees and external clients worldwide.

Also in 1996, two electronic data interchange (EDI) connections were established with Staples, the office supplier, and FedEx to streamline the ordering of goods and services from these vendors. PRC is currently implementing another EDI link that will enable its federal government customers to access PRCs services more easily.

During 1997, Carmody plans to begin establishing standards for desktop platforms, and implementing PeopleSoft's Manufacturing module. Although PRC is not a manufacturer, as a system integrator it must bring together large numbers of components, track them, process orders and bill clients for them.

Other X/Open Brand Procurements

There are many other instances of open systems procurement policies, as evidenced by the increasing number of X/Open brand conformance requirements being issued by government and commercial entities worldwide.

For example, in 1996, after several years of study and system demonstration evaluations, the U.S. Internal Revenue Service published the comprehensive Open Systems Standards Profile, essentially a handbook on how to implement the standards and how to seek help in using them. The document includes a Target Standards List (standards obtainable within the next three to five years) and Interim Standards List (standards available today). The first resulting implementation, a U.S. Treasury Department distributed processing system contract, is scheduled to begin in July 1997.

Also in 1996, the U.S. Air Force announced its mandate of the X/Open brand in its $1.2 billion Desktop V procurement. This project comprises a number of systems, including notebooks, desktops and servers, with the total number amounting to 360,000 computers and 10,000 servers.

Other procurements that have named the X/Open brand as a minimum criteria for bid include the U.S. Air Force's ICARDS procurement for $932 million and Workstation procurement for an estimated $800 million, the UK National Health Service procurement for $375 million, and NASA's SEWP II procurement for an estimated $829 million.

Investing in the Future: Open Systems

The Open Group has worked diligently for over a decade to bring interoperability, freedom of choice, flexibility and greater value to buyers of open systems. The Open Group has succeeded in creating a broad range of product standards, under the X/Open brand, that guarantee to buyers that they are receiving absolute standards conformance in information technology products.

Through the brand, open systems vendors have been able to deliver tangible value to their customers, demonstrating their commitment to stand behind their product by investing the effort to meet stringent requirements of the brand. Vendors and buyers have benefited from this partnership between end-users, system and software suppliers and The Open Group.

The experiences of government agencies and commercial organizations worldwide, several of which were summarized here, reinforce the business return of an open systems strategy. Similarly, the current spate of emerging open systems procurement releases further confirms the long-term benefits of such a strategy.

Further Information

More information on procurement tools and procurements using the X/Open brand can be found at **http://www.opengroup.org**.

About This Document

This book is designed for users, developers, and implementors of open systems. It provides complete information on what's new in the Single UNIX Specification, Version 2 and comprehensive reference material on every aspect. Finally, it includes a CD-ROM with the complete 3000 page Single UNIX Specification, Version 2 in html and pdf formats.

This book is divided into five parts:

- **Part One** gives an overview of the Single UNIX Specification, describing the contents of the specifications.
  - Chapter 1 gives a brief history of the UNIX operating system, and its journey to becoming the Single UNIX Specification, Version 2.
  - Chapter 2 describes the formal X/Open "branding" processes and the UNIX 98 brand.
  - Chapter 3 describes how the Single UNIX Specification environment is organized and where to look for more detailed information in the Single UNIX Specification.
  - Chapter 4 covers System Interfaces and Headers, Issue 5 (XSH), describing the feature groups and groups the interfaces into categories to give the reader an understanding of what facilities are available.
  - Chapter 5 describes the contents of Commands and Utilities, Issue 5 (XCU) together with a description of the options.
  - Chapter 6 describes Networking Services, Issue 5. This includes a functional overview, together with migration information on the changes introduced in Networking Services, Issue 5.
  - Chapter 7 describes the contents of X/Open Curses, Issue 4, Version 2.
- **Part Two** describes what's new in the Single UNIX Specification, Version 2, with individual chapters giving detailed information on the new features.
  - Chapter 8 gives an overview of the new features of the Single UNIX Specification, Version 2. For each specification, a brief description of the changes is given. Subsequent chapters give more detailed information on the new features.
  - Chapter 9 offers a programmer's overview of POSIX.1b, which is included in the Single UNIX Specification, Version 2. It describes the application program interfaces specified under the realtime options, and it briefly explains why and how the interfaces may be used.
  - Chapter 10 offers a programmer's overview of POSIX.1c, which is included in the Single UNIX Specification, Version 2. It describes the application program interfaces specified under the eight threads-related options, and it briefly explains why and how the interfaces may be used.
  - Chapter 11 is an introduction to the X/Open Threads Extension developed by the Aspen group which is included in the Single UNIX Specification, Version 2.

— Chapter 12 gives a brief outline of the Dynamic Linking routines included in the Single UNIX Specification, Version 2. These changes were put forward by the Aspen group.

— Chapter 13 is a brief introduction to the Multibyte Support Extension introduced in the ISO C Amendment 1 (MSE).

— Chapter 14 introduces 64-bit programming models, data size neutrality, and application porting issues.

— Chapter 15 is an abridged version of the submission received by X/Open from the Large File Summit, an industry initiative to produce a common specification for support of files that are bigger than the current limit of 2GB on existing 32-bit systems. It details the modifications to the Single UNIX Specification to support large files with unlimited file offsets.

— Chapter 16 is about the Year 2000. It outlines the problem, gives some general advice on how to prepare, and gives practical advice on how to use interfaces within the Single UNIX Specification to cope with the millennium rollover.

— Chapter 17 is about the UNIX 98 Software Administration Component which provides software packagers with a common way to define software relationships which range from simple to complex, and to package that software into a single distribution for multiple platforms.

- **Part Three** includes guidance on using the Single UNIX Specification to develop new applications and to port existing applications to UNIX branded systems. Detailed migration reference information is included of the changes between Version 1 and Version 2 of the Single UNIX Specification. A comprehensive C-language migration guide detailing the difference between Common Usage C (K&R) and the ISO C standard is also included.

— Chapter 18 covers a general set of topics of interest to developers, including feature groups, the compilation environment and advice on portability issues.

— Chapter 19 gives quick reference tables of all the commands and function interfaces defined in UNIX 98, complete with an indication of their availability in UNIX 95, POSIX-1, POSIX-2, ISO C standard, SVID 3 and 4.3BSD.

— Chapter 20 provides migration information on the changes made in Issue 5 that might affect an application program.

— Chapter 21 provides migration information on the changes made to the header files in XSH, Issue 5. It describes the namespace issues that programmers should be aware of.

— Chapter 22 provides migration information on the changes made in XCU, Issue 5 that might affect an application program.

— Chapter 23 describes techniques for writing C-language code that conforms to the ISO C standard.

- **Part Four** include Case Studies of implementation experiences of aspects of the Single UNIX Specification:

— Chapter 24 describes the merging of UNIX and MVS and the Creation of OpenEdition MVS.

— Chapter 25 describes the implementation experience of integrating UNIX system interfaces into the Mainframe Operating System BS2000.

— Chapter 26 describes the implementation of open systems interfaces on Windows NT.

- **Part Five** contains the following appendices:
  - Appendix A covers a number of topics concerning installation and contents of the Go Solo 2 CD-ROM.
  - Appendix B contains the Go Solo 2 CD-ROM Terms and Conditions.
  - Appendix C contains the glossary of terms.
  - Appendix D contains the list of referenced documents.

Go Solo 2

Part 1:

Introduction

The Open Group

Chapter 1

The Single UNIX Specification

Many names have been applied to the work that has culminated in the Single UNIX Specification and the X/Open UNIX brand. It began as the *Common API Specification*, became *Spec 1170*, and is now the *Single UNIX Specification*, published in a number of The Open Group's Common Applications Environment (CAE) specifications.

This chapter describes the Single UNIX Specification. It gives a brief history of the UNIX operating system, and its journey to becoming the Single UNIX Specification, Version 2.

1.1 Introduction

Today, the cost of developing applications software is considerably greater than the cost of the hardware on which the applications run. Preserving this investment in an organization's critical applications, while freeing the organization to mix and match platforms as hardware costs fall, has led to the idea of "open systems". One of the cornerstones of open systems is portability — the ability to move an application's source code to another platform and rebuild the application without changing the source.

Software portability problems do not just affect an organization directly through its own applications. Hardware vendors often find their market limited by the applications that run on their platforms. Independent software vendors (ISVs) often limit themselves in the number of platforms on which they sell their products, due to the costs of maintaining multiple ports of the application for multiple platforms. Consumers are caught, often choosing hardware platforms based on the applications they need to purchase, but without the ability to know what new applications will be available on these platforms in the future.

The UNIX operating system has long been identified with the portability of applications. The operating system source code itself was developed for the most part in the C language, which had a fairly portable compiler.

In 1993, a group of vendors, under the auspices of the *Common Open Software Environment* (COSE) project, began to develop a single specification of the UNIX programming interface, to further enhance applications portability. This work became known as Spec 1170 and was published in late 1994 by X/Open as the first version of Single UNIX Specification.

Other events occurred during the same period to change the nature of UNIX systems. While UNIX system derivatives have long been identified with portability, *the* UNIX operating system was a licensed product developed at AT&T Bell Laboratories. AT&T licensed the source code to other vendors that wished to develop UNIX operating systems, and AT&T owned the registered trademark. AT&T created UNIX System Laboratories (USL), a separate majority-owned subsidiary which was purchased by Novell in 1993.

As the Spec 1170 work moved to X/Open for fast-track as an X/Open specification, the sole licensing rights to the UNIX trademark were transferred to X/Open by Novell.

In 1995, X/Open introduced the UNIX 95 brand for computer systems guaranteed to meet the Single UNIX Specification. The Single UNIX Specification brand program has now achieved critical mass; vendors whose products have met the demanding criteria for the UNIX 95 brand now account for the majority of UNIX systems sales by value.

Previously, the UNIX operating system had been a product with four elements (see Figure 1-1): the specification (for example, SVID), the technology (for example, SVR4), the registered trademark (UNIX), and the product (for example, UNIXWare).

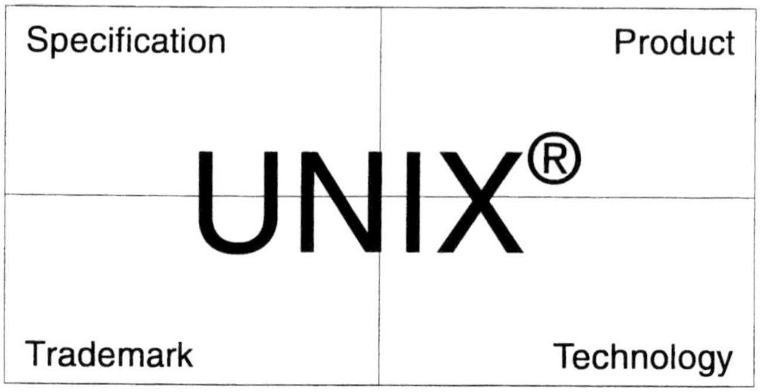

Figure 1-1 UNIX Operating System Elements

With the Single UNIX Specification, there is now a single, open, consensus specification that defines a product. There is also a mark, or brand, that is used to identify those products that conform to the Single UNIX Specification. Both the specification and the trademark are now managed and held in trust for the industry by The Open Group.

There are now many competing products, all guaranteeing to implement the Single UNIX Specification, ensuring competition and vendor choice. Buyers can expect each of these products to carry the X/Open UNIX brand as a guarantee of conformance to the specification and that the vendor stands behind a quality product.

The UNIX system is now no longer just the operating system product from AT&T (later, Novell), documented by the System V Interface Definition (SVID), controlled and licensed from a single vendor. Neither is it a collection of slightly different products from different vendors, each extended in slightly different ways. The UNIX specification has been separated from its licensed source-code product, and the UNIX system has become a single stable specification to be used to develop portable applications that run on systems conforming to the Single UNIX Specification.

The base is now in place to better support portable applications development by:

- providing a rich set of interfaces that cover a broad range of historical UNIX systems practice, simplifying the porting of existing applications, and protecting current application development investments
- providing a stable specification against which to write applications that will be portable to many platforms, and a stable methodology to evolve the specification in a manner that is not in the control of any single vendor
- ensuring that the portability model embodied in the specifications is based on consensus-based formal standards to encourage competition
- supporting the specification with the X/Open brand to provide both halves of the portability formula, where application developers can write source code to the specification and purchase products branded to the specification with the confidence that the application will

port in a very straightforward manner.

This document introduces the Single UNIX Specification, Version 2, providing a brief history of the work that led to its creation, complete information on what's new in Version 2, migration information on the changes between Version 1 and Version 2, what is covered in each part of the specification, and how to use the documents to advantage to develop portable applications. Chapter 2 on page 13 discusses the overall structure of the X/Open Common Applications Environment documentation, and covers the product standards and the X/Open brand.

1.2 History and Timeline

Since it first appeared from AT&T's Bell Laboratories in the early 1970s, the success of the UNIX operating system has been plagued by one major problem: recipients of the (at that time free) UNIX system code all began developing their own different versions in their own, different, ways for use and sale. Universities, research institutes, government bodies and computer companies all began using the powerful UNIX system to develop many of the technologies which today are part of a UNIX system.

Computer-aided design, manufacturing control systems, laboratory simulations, even the Internet itself, all began life with and because of UNIX systems.

By the late 1970s, a ripple effect had come into play. By now the under- and post-graduate students whose laboratory work had pioneered these new applications of technology were attaining management and decision-making positions inside the computer system suppliers and among its customers. And they wanted to continue using UNIX systems.

Soon all the large vendors, and many smaller ones, were marketing their own, diverging, versions of the UNIX system optimized for their own computer architectures and boasting many different strengths and features. Customers found that, although UNIX systems were available everywhere, they seldom were able to interwork or coexist without significant investment of time and effort to make them work effectively. The trademark UNIX was ubiquitous, but it was applied to a multitude of different, incompatible products.

In the early 1980s, the market for UNIX systems had grown enough to be noticed by industry analysts and researchers. Now the question was no longer "What is a UNIX system?" but "Is a UNIX system suitable for business and commerce?".

Throughout the early and mid-1980s, the debate about the strengths and weaknesses of UNIX systems raged, often fueled by the utterances of the vendors themselves who sought to protect their profitable proprietary system sales by talking UNIX systems down. And, in an effort to further differentiate their competing UNIX system products, they kept developing and adding features of their own.

In 1984, another factor brought added attention to UNIX systems. A group of vendors concerned about the continuing encroachment into their markets and control of system interfaces by the larger companies, developed the concept of open systems. Open systems were those that would meet agreed specifications or standards.

This resulted in the formation of X/Open Company Ltd. whose remit was, and today in the guise of The Open Group remains, to define a comprehensive open systems environment. Open systems, they declared, would save on costs, attract a wider portfolio of applications, and enable competition on equal terms. X/Open chose the UNIX system interfaces as the platform for the basis of open systems.

Although UNIX was still owned by AT&T, the company did little commercially with it until the mid-1980s. Then the spotlight of X/Open showed clearly that a single, standard version of the

UNIX system would be in the wider interests of the industry and its customers. The question now was "Which version?".

In a move intended to unify the market in 1987, AT&T announced an agreement with Sun Microsystems, the leading proponent of the Berkeley-derived strain of UNIX systems. However, the rest of the industry viewed the development with considerable concern. Believing that their own markets were under threat, they clubbed together to develop their own "new" open systems operating system. Their new organization was called the Open Software Foundation (OSF). In response to this, the AT&T/Sun faction formed UNIX International.

The ensuing "wars" divided the system vendors between these two camps clustered around the two dominant technologies: AT&T's System V and the OSF system called OSF/1. In the meantime, X/Open held the center ground. It continued the process of standardizing the APIs necessary for an open operating system specification.

In addition, it looked at areas of the system beyond the operating system level where a standard approach would add value for supplier and customer alike, developing or adopting specifications for languages, database connectivity, networking and mainframe interworking. The results of this work were published in successive X/Open Portability Guides.

XPG4 Base was released in October 1992. During this time, X/Open had put in place a brand program based on vendor guarantees and supported by testing. Since the publication of XPG4, X/Open has continued to broaden the scope of open systems specifications in line with market requirements. As the benefits of the X/Open brand became known and understood, many large organizations began using X/Open as the basis for system design and procurement. By 1993, over $7 billion had been spent on X/Open branded systems. By the start of 1997 that figure has risen to over $23 billion. To date, procurements referencing the Single UNIX Specification amount to over $5.2 billion.

In early 1993, AT&T sold UNIX System Laboratories to Novell which was looking for a heavyweight operating system to link to its NetWare product range. At the same time, the company recognized that vesting control of the definition (specification) and trademark with a vendor-neutral organization would further facilitate the value of the UNIX system as a foundation of open systems. In late 1993, Novell transferred rights to the UNIX trademark to X/Open. So, the constituent parts of the UNIX system, previously owned by a single entity, were now quite separate.

In 1995, SCO bought the UNIX systems business from Novell, and UNIX system source code and technology continues to be developed under the ownership of SCO.

In 1995, X/Open introduced the UNIX 95 brand for computer systems guaranteed to meet the Single UNIX Specification. The Single UNIX Specification brand program has now achieved critical mass: vendors whose products have met the demanding criteria for the UNIX 95 brand now account for the majority of UNIX systems by value.

For over ten years, since the inception of X/Open, UNIX had been closely linked with open systems. X/Open, now part of The Open Group, continues to develop and evolve the Single UNIX Specification and associated brand program on behalf of the IT community. The Single UNIX Specification, Version 2, published in early 1997, is the latest result of this industry initiative.

1.2.1 Timeline

1969	The Beginning	The history of UNIX starts back in 1969, when Ken Thompson, Dennis Ritchie, and others started working on the "little-used PDP-7 in a corner" at Bell Laboratories and what was to become the UNIX system.
1971	First Edition	It had an assembler for a PDP-11/20, filesystem, *fork*( ), *roff* and *ed*. It was used for text processing of patent documents.
1973	Fourth Edition	It was rewritten in C. This made it portable and changed the history of operating systems.
1975	Sixth Edition	The UNIX system leaves home. Also widely known as Version 6, this is the first to be widely available outside Bell Laboratories. The first BSD version (1.x) was derived from Version 6.
1979	Seventh Edition	It was an "improvement over all preceding and following Unices" [Bourne]. It had C, UUCP, and the Bourne shell. It was ported to the VAX and the kernel was more than 40 Kilobytes (K).
1980	Xenix	Microsoft introduces Xenix. 32V and 4BSD introduced.
1982	System III	AT&T's UNIX System Group (USG) releases System III, the first public release outside Bell Laboratories.
1983	System V	Computer Research Group (CRG), UNIX System Group (USG), and a third group merge to become the UNIX System Development Laboratories. AT&T announces System V, the first supported release.
1984	4.2BSD	University of California at Berkeley releases 4.2BSD.
1984	SVR2	System V Release 2 introduced. At this time there are 100,000 UNIX system installations around the world.
1987	SVR3	System V Release 3 including STREAMS, TLI, and RFS. At this time there are 750,000 UNIX system installations around the world.
1988	POSIX.1	POSIX.1 published. Open Software Foundation (OSF) and UNIX International formed.
1989	SVR4	System V Release 4 ships, unifying System V, BSD, and Xenix. AT&T UNIX Software Operation formed in preparation for a spinoff of USL.
1990	XPG3	X/Open launches the XPG3 Brand.
1991		UNIX System Laboratories (USL) becomes a company, majority-owned by AT&T.

1992	SVR4.2	USL releases System V Release 4.2 (Destiny). The XPG4 Brand is launched by X/Open in October, and Novell announces its intent to acquire USL on 22nd December.
1993	4.4BSD	4.4BSD, the final release from Berkeley. Novell acquires USL on 16th June.
Late 1993	SVR4.2MP	Novell transfers rights to the UNIX trademark and the Single UNIX Specification to X/Open. In December Novell releases SVR4.2MP, the final USL OEM release of System V.
1994	Single UNIX Specification	X/Open introduces the Single UNIX Specification.
1995	UNIX 95	X/Open introduces the UNIX 95 brand program.
1996		The Open Group forms as a merger of OSF and X/Open.
1997	Single UNIX Specification, Version 2	The Open Group introduces the Single UNIX Specification, Version 2, including support for realtime, threads, and 64-bit and larger processors.
1997	UNIX 98	The Open Group introduces the UNIX 98 brand program.

1.3 The Single UNIX Specification (1994)

The Common API Specification project started when several vendors (Sun Microsystems, IBM, Hewlett-Packard, Novell/USL, and OSF) joined together to provide a single unified specification of the UNIX system services. By implementing a single common definition of the UNIX system services, third-party independent software vendors (ISVs) would be able to more easily deliver strategic applications on all of these vendors' platforms at once.

The focus of this initiative was to deliver the core application interfaces used by current application programs. The economic driver that initiated the project was to ease the porting of existing successful applications. While the work was led by a central group of vendors, it received widespread support within the industry.

A two-pronged approach was used to develop the Common API Specification. First, a set of formal industry specifications was chosen to form the overall base for the work. This would provide stability, vendor neutrality, and lay a well charted course for future application development, taking advantage of the careful work that had gone into developing these specifications. It would also preserve the portability of existing applications already developed to these core models.

The X/Open XPG4 Base was chosen as the stable functional base from which to start. XPG4 Base supports the POSIX.1 system interface and the ANSI C/ISO C standard at its core. It also provides a rich set of 174 commands and utilities.

Many UNIX systems already conformed to this specification. To this base was added the traditional UNIX System V Interface Definition (SVID) Edition 3, Level 1 calls, and the OSF Application Environment Specification (AES) Full Use interface definitions. These represented the stable central core of the latter two specifications.

The second part of the approach was to incorporate interfaces that are acknowledged common practice but have not yet been incorporated into any formal specification or standard. The intent was to ensure that existing applications running on UNIX systems would port with relative ease to a platform supporting the Common API Specification. A survey of real-world applications was used to determine what additional interfaces would be required in the specification.

Fifty successful application packages were selected to be analyzed using the following criteria:

- ranked in International Data Corporation's *Survey of Leading UNIX Applications*, 1992
- the application's domain of applicability was checked to ensure that no single application type (for example, databases) was overly represented
- the application had to be available for analysis either as source code, or as a shared or dynamic linked library.

From the group of fifty, the top ten were selected carefully, ensuring that no more than two representative application packages in a particular problem space were chosen. The ten chosen applications were:

AutoCAD	FrameMaker	Island Write/Paint	SAS (4GL)	Teamwork
Cadence	Informix	Lotus 1-2-3	Sybase	WordPerfect

APIs used by the applications that were not part of the base specifications were analyzed:

- If an API was used by any of the top ten applications, it was considered for inclusion.
- If an API was not used by one of the top ten, but was used by any three of the remaining 40 applications, it was considered for inclusion.
- While the investigation of these 50 applications was representative of large complex applications, it was still not considered a broad enough survey, so an additional 3,500 modules were scanned. If an API was used at least seven times in modules that came from at least two platforms (to screen out vendor-specific libraries), then the interface was considered for inclusion.

The goal was to ensure that APIs in common use were included, even if they were not in the formal specifications that made up the base. Making the Common API Specification a superset of existing base specifications ensured that any existing applications should work unmodified. The sponsors of the work considered pruning the Common API Specification of interfaces from the base specifications that were not found to be in common use in the application survey.

This idea was rejected for two reasons. While some of the interfaces in the base specifications were not yet considered common practice, their inclusion in the overall specification meant there existed clear signposts for future applications development work. Also, it was recognized that the applications chosen for the survey were still only a representative sample, and that many other applications not surveyed may use these interfaces.

When the survey was complete, there were 130 interfaces that did not already appear in the base specification. These interfaces seemed to be predominantly Berkeley BSD calls that had never been covered in XPG4 Base, the SVID, or the OSF AES, but did represent common practice in UNIX system applications developed originally on BSD-derived platforms. Such things as sockets and the 4.3BSD memory management calls were commonly used in many applications.

The resulting Common API Specification was impressive in its coverage. The top ten applications surveyed were completely covered. Of the remaining 40 application packages, the next 25 were within 5% of complete coverage. The software vendors involved all acknowledged that it would be fairly straightforward for them to modify the 5% of applications to conform fully to the specification.

There were 1170 interfaces in the complete specification when the work was done (926 programming interfaces, 70 headers, 174 commands and utilities), and Spec 1170 was born.

Because of the breadth and origins of the specification, duplication of functionality existed. There were similar interfaces for doing the same thing in such areas as memory management (*bcopy*( ) versus *memmove*( )) and creating temporary filenames (*tmpnam*( ) versus *mktemp*( )). This duplication was allowed since it would increase the number of existing applications that would be portable in the new model. At the same time, certain functions were identified as the recommended practice for future development. There are cases where the duplicated functionality cannot coexist in the same application (for example, conflicting signals models), and it is important to ensure that the application is correctly configured if the expected behavior is to be observed.

In December 1993, Spec 1170 was delivered to X/Open for fast-track processing into a proper industry supported specification. This work progressed through 1994 and culminated in publication of the Single UNIX Specification in October 1994. There were then more than 1170 interfaces in the specification as the review process shaped the document.

1.4 The Single UNIX Specification, Version 2

Work commenced in late 1995 to revise the Single UNIX Specification. This revision incorporates standards for threads (which the ISVs have been seeking for some time), realtime (which is a key requirement of the federal government), removal of any architectural dependencies to permit 64-bit processing (which emerged from the Aspen Group), large file support, enhanced multibyte support, and some year 2000 issues.

Five CAE specifications make up the Single UNIX Specification, Version 2 as follows:

- System Interface Definitions, Issue 5 (XBD)

  XBD, Issue 5 outlines the common definitions used by both XSH, Issue 5 and XCU, Issue 5. Such items as locales and regular expression grammars appear here, along with a large glossary defining common terms and concepts.

- System Interfaces and Headers, Issue 5 (XSH)

  XSH, Issue 5 describes all of the programming interfaces and headers available, with the exception of the networking and terminal interfaces (contained in their own documents). The front section introduces general information concerning usage guidelines, the compilation environment, error numbers, types, standard streams, STREAMS, threads, and realtime. The rest of the document contains reference pages describing each interface (in alphabetical order) and its use, and each header and its contents.

- Commands and Utilities, Issue 5 (XCU)

  XCU, Issue 5 describes all of the commands and utilities available. The first section describes the syntax and functionality of the shell in depth. The rest of the document contains reference pages describing each command and utility (in alphabetical order) and its use.

- Networking Services, Issue 5

  Three sets of networking services are defined: X/Open Transport Interface (XTI), XPG4 Sockets, and IP Address Resolution interfaces. These services are described in the Networking Services, Issue 5, along with appendices containing useful additional protocol information and examples.

- X/Open Curses, Issue 4, Version 2

  The X/Open Curses interfaces are described in this document. It is an upwardly-compatible version of X/Open Curses, Issue 3, extended to support internationalization, enhanced character sets, and different writing directions.

1.5 The X/Open UNIX Brand

The X/Open UNIX brand is one of The Open Group's internationally recognized portfolio of open systems brands which represent the three primary ingredients required for open systems:

- widely accepted and available specifications describing the software interfaces between components of a computer system such as the operating system, networks, applications, and the desktop screen environment
- computer systems developed to meet The Open Group's specifications and marketed by vendors
- the assurance that products meet agreed specifications and conformance requirements by passing the rigorous tests developed by The Open Group.

The X/Open UNIX brand has created more choice in the market for computer system buyers. It also enables cost and time savings for suppliers and stimulates competition in a larger, unified market for UNIX system products clearly identified by the X/Open UNIX brand.

Since February 1995, computer systems have carried the X/Open UNIX brand if:

- they guarantee to support the services specified in the Single UNIX Specification.

Customers can identify X/Open UNIX branded products by the X/Open brand logo and the mandatory attribution declaring to which version of the specification the product complies:

- UNIX 93 applies to UNIX system products which pre-date the Single UNIX Specification.
- UNIX 95 applies to UNIX system products which conform to the Single UNIX Specification.
- UNIX 98 applies to UNIX system products which conform to the Single UNIX Specification, Version 2.

Vendors marketing products that carry the UNIX 93 logo guarantee to move their products to full UNIX 95 conformance.

In licensing the X/Open UNIX brand, a vendor warrants and represents that every branded product:

- conforms to the specification
- will continue to conform to the specification
- will be rectified within an agreed time should it be found to be non-conformant.

The X/Open brand is widely recognized as the international symbol of assurance in open systems. By early 1997, the value of procurements of open systems referencing the X/Open brand exceeds $23 billion.

1.6 Summary

The Single UNIX Specification offers benefits for all.

For users, products that support the Single UNIX Specification provide a powerful open platform for the development, implementation, and management of mission-critical computer systems. The specification facilitates freedom of choice across the widest possible range of systems, thereby protecting investment in existing software and data.

For software vendors, the Single UNIX Specification offers an opportunity to cut significantly the cost of developing and maintaining their products. It also expands the market opportunity by expanding the market itself, cutting time-to-market, and reducing product development costs.

For system vendors, the Single UNIX Specification unifies a previously fragmented market and offers the chance for all to compete on equal terms, while reducing the cost required to maintain technical incompatibilities.

From now on, system vendors have a standard specification and a brand program underpinning a widely recognized mark through which they can bring to market their UNIX system products.

Under the X/Open brand program, products that implement the services as specified in the Single UNIX Specification are able to carry the UNIX trademark.

As a result, customers will be assured that, by asking for an X/Open UNIX branded system, they will derive the associated business benefits of the guarantee. The development and quality assurance of X/Open UNIX branded systems is aided by the availability of a suite of software testing tools. These have been developed to cover all aspects of the Single UNIX Specification: core system calls, commands and utilities, terminal interfaces, and transport interfaces.

Chapter 2

Product Standards and Brands

2.1 The Brand

Branding is the process by which a vendor warrants that a product complies with a particular X/Open Product Standard. It is called branding because it is built around the right to use an X/Open trademark, with trademark law as its legal basis. Once a product is shown to comply with a particular Product Standard and has been registered as conformant, the vendor is entitled to use the designated trademark in relation to that product with respect to that Product Standard. That right continues for so long as the product remains compliant and registered.

A vendor wishing to brand must first sign the Trademark License Agreement, thereby accepting its terms and conditions. This confers the right to use the designated trademark on, or in relation to, registered products, and the licensee warrants that any registered product fully conforms, and will continue to conform, to one or more Product Standards, and commits to the speedy correction of any discrepancies.

Branding normally applies to computing system platforms and concerns the standards that apply to the interfaces they present to application programs (APIs), and where appropriate to the protocols used in communicating across networks. Application software written to use the APIs defined by an X/Open Product Standard should be portable to any platform registered as conformant to that Product Standard.

By calling for X/Open branded products in their procurements, purchasers can ensure that they acquire products that are guaranteed to conform to the required Product Standards.

This chapter describes branding in relation to UNIX 98. Complete definitive details of the branding process, and its full scope, are published in How to Brand — What to Buy, available from The Open Group.

2.2 Product Standards

There are currently two forms of Product Standard, namely Components and Profiles. The requirements for conformance to these Product Standards are specified in Component and Profile Definitions.

A component is the smallest element of functionality to which specific products may be separately branded under the X/Open brand program. It corresponds to a coherent set of system or product functionality which is implementable in a genuinely open manner by adherence to detailed technical specifications that are identified by the Component Definition. The technical specifications may be X/Open CAE Specifications, other industry standards, or formal (*de jure*) standards.

Profiles are normally collections of Components (although they can also refer directly to detailed technical specifications) integrated together to form functionally more complete entities (they are intended to define a product in the form in which the buyer would want to buy and use it). The ability to reference the combined functionality of several Components by means of a single Profile Definition greatly facilitates the use of the X/Open brand in procurement. Products that conform to a Profile Definition not only meet all the conformance requirements of the underlying Component Definitions, but also additional conformance requirements regarding the functionality concerned being provided in a fully harmonized and integrated way.

The following tables list Components and Profiles to which products can be registered as conformant (they are not necessarily complete lists as items are continually being added). Updated Versions of existing Components are identified by adding "Vn" (where n=2, 3, and so on) to the name, and new Versions of Profiles are identified by incrementing the year identifier. New versions do not imply that the older version is necessarily obsolete. The compatibility relationship with earlier versions is identified in the Component or Profile Definition itself.

2.2.1 Components

Area	Component
Operating System and Languages	XPG4 Internationalized System Calls and Libraries XPG4 Internationalized System Calls and Libraries Extended XPG4 Internationalized System Calls and Libraries Extended V2 XPG4 Commands and Utilities XPG4 Commands and Utilities V2 XPG4 Commands and Utilities V3 XPG4 C Language XPG4 COBOL Language XPG4 Pascal Language XPG4 FORTRAN Language XPG4 Ada Language
Data Management	XPG4 ISAM XPG4 Relational Database XPG4 Calendaring and Scheduling
User Interface	XPG4 X Window System Display XPG4 X Window System Application Interface XPG4 X Window System Application Interface V2 XPG4 Motif Toolkit XPG4 Terminal Interfaces XPG4 Internationalized Terminal Interfaces
General Interworking	XPG4 BSFT XPG4 X.400 Gateway XPG4 X.400 Message Access XPG4 Directory Access XPG4 Network File System XPG4 Sockets XPG4 Sockets V2 XPG4 Transport Service (XTI) XPG4 Transport Service (XTI) V2
Mainframe Interworking	XPG4 CPI-C
PC Interworking	XPG4 (PC)NFS Server XPG4 LMX Server
Security	Secure Communication Services
Systems Management	Software Administration
Media	XPG4 Magnetic Media

2.2.2 Profiles

Area	Profile
Operating System and Languages	XPG4 Base XPG4 Base 95 XPG4 UNIX (UNIX 95) UNIX 98 UNIX 98 Workstation
User Interface	XPG4 Common Desktop Environment
Security	Baseline Security 96

2.3 Conformance Statements

The detailed specifications referenced by a Component or Profile Definition may explicitly allow for alternative behaviors, or may allow support for certain interfaces or elements of protocol to be optional; that is, their support is at the discretion of the implementor. There are also cases where numerical limits are defined, with conformance being possible for a wide range of different values; for example, the length of a password.

It is important that the application writer or purchaser has a clear and concise document that describes the way in which a given product conforms to the specifications with respect to these implementation options. The way in which a particular branded product has responded to these implementation options is documented in the product's *Conformance Statement*.

The Conformance Statement also uniquely identifies the product, describes the environment in which conformance was demonstrated (that is, the testing environment), and gives any additional information called for by the Component or Profile Definition.

Conformance Statements are produced by completing a standard Questionnaire, one of which exists for each Component and Profile.

The Conformance Statement for a registered product has to be maintained by the vendor in an up-to-date state at all times. Organizations procuring X/Open branded products should request to see the Conformance Statements for products under consideration. This will allow the purchaser to clearly compare products from different vendors with respect to their conformance claims. It is planned to introduce a world wide web based system in late 1997 that will enable buyers to browse all Conformance Statements on-line.

2.4 Testing

It is a condition of the X/Open brand that conformance of the product must have been demonstrated in a test environment, and details of the environment used must be identified in the product's Conformance Statement. In addition, X/Open can at any time request an audit and require conformance to be demonstrated.

Where possible, X/Open provides stringent test suites that must be successfully executed, and a test report submitted, before the product can be registered as conformant to a Product Standard (Component or Profile). Such Test Suites are identified in the Product Standard document in a section headed *Indicator of Compliance*.

It should be noted, however, that the terms of the Trademark License Agreement are such that the vendor warrants that the product conforms and commits to speedy correction of any discrepancies that may appear in the field. This is independent of the requirement to have passed any designated test suite. The fact that a test suite may not have detected the discrepancy, or that there is no required test suite, does not reduce the commitment in any way.

Registration of branded products must be renewed annually. If a new test suite or new edition of a test suite is introduced as an indicator of compliance, a new test report is required as part of the renewal process at the first product renewal nine months after the introduction of the new or revised suite. This nine month period gives the vendor time to absorb the test suite into the product release cycle.

This nine month grace period applies only to existing releases of branded products. As new products or new product releases are brought to market, they must brand against the test suite criteria defined in the Product Standard at the time.

2.5 UNIX 98

UNIX 98 is the label applied to products that are guaranteed by the vendor to conform to the Single UNIX Specification, Version 2. The brand confers the right to associate the UNIX 98 name with the product, and implies a warranty of conformance and a commitment to the timely rectification of any discrepancies.

What constitutes the Single UNIX Specification, Version 2, and its relationship to the previous version, the Single UNIX Specification, is the main theme of this book, and is covered in detail by the foregoing chapters. This section describes how the various facilities are packaged into brandable entities — Components and Profiles — to which products can be registered.

The previous issue of Go Solo described the first version of the Single UNIX Specification, and the corresponding XPG4 UNIX (that is, UNIX 95) Product Standard. The focus of this issue of Go Solo is the Single UNIX Specification, Version 2, and the corresponding UNIX 98 Product Standard and constituent Components.

The following sections briefly describe the two new Single UNIX Specification, Version 2-based Product Standards — the UNIX 98 Product Standard itself and the UNIX 98 Workstation Product Standard. The Profiles and constituent Components are included on the accompanying CD-ROM.

Although a product must be registered for each of the constituent Component Definitions before it can be registered for the UNIX 98 or UNIX 98 Workstation Product Standard, it can be registered for the individual Component Definitions at any time and in any order. A product can, for example, follow a planned migration path from UNIX 95 to UNIX 98.

2.5.1 The UNIX 98 Product Standard

The UNIX 98 Product Standard calls for collective conformance to each of the following Component Definitions:

XPG4 Internationalized System Calls and Libraries Extended V2
XPG4 Commands and Utilities V3
XPG4 C Language
XPG4 Internationalized Terminal Interfaces
XPG4 Sockets V2
XPG4 Transport Service (XTI) V2

It also provides for optional conformance to the following Component Definition:

Software Administration

The Conformance Statement identifies whether the option is supported by a registered product.

Registration of conformance to these Component Definitions must be prior to or concurrent with the UNIX 98 registration.

2.5.2 The UNIX 98 Workstation Product Standard

The UNIX 98 Workstation Product Standard calls for collective conformance to the Components of the UNIX 98 Product Standard, together with conformance to the XPG4 Common Desktop Environment (CDE) Product Standard. It requires conformance to all the following Component Definitions:

XPG4 Internationalized System Calls and Libraries Extended V2
XPG4 Commands and Utilities V3
XPG4 C Language
XPG4 Internationalized Terminal Interfaces
XPG4 Sockets V2
XPG4 Transport Service (XTI) V2
XPG4 X Window System Application Interface V2
XPG4 Motif Toolkit
XPG4 Calendaring and Scheduling.

It also provides for optional conformance to the following Component Definition:

Software Administration

The Conformance Statement identifies whether the option is supported by a registered product.

Registration of conformance to these Component Definitions must be prior to or concurrent with the UNIX 98 Workstation registration.

Chapter 3

The Single UNIX Environment

The Single UNIX Specification programming environment provides a broad-based functional set of interfaces to support the porting of existing UNIX applications and the development of new applications. The environment also supports a rich set of tools for application development. This chapter describes the overall environment, programming, and utility considerations, and some of the global issues such as internationalization support, environment variables, and file access. It describes how the environment is organized and where to look for detailed information in the Single UNIX Specification. References give the name of the Single UNIX Specification document and section in which more detailed explanations and definitions can be found.

3.1 Introduction

The X/Open UNIX programming environment began as the desire of a group of system vendors to provide real-world portability platforms to encourage software vendors to deliver their existing applications across all such UNIX environments. The resultant X/Open UNIX environment has a much broader appeal than the original focus.

The Single UNIX Specification uses the CAE documentation as its base. The documentation is structured as follows:

- XSI (X/Open System Interface), composed of System Interface Definitions, Issue 5 (XBD), System Interfaces and Headers, Issue 5 (XSH), and Commands and Utilities, Issue 5 (XCU)
- Networking Services, Issue 5
- X/Open Curses, Issue 4, Version 2.

XBD starts with a Glossary (Chapter 2). Rather than being a simple compendium of acronyms and obscure references, this glossary describes all of the basic terminology and concepts used throughout the Single UNIX Specification. The differences between *character set* and *codeset*, how *file access permissions* work, and how *pathname resolution* is accomplished are all described.

One thing that becomes apparent working with the Single UNIX Specification is its focus on application development. The Single UNIX Specification is similar to the User's and Programmer's Reference Manuals on Berkeley or System V systems. Matters of system management are not part of this specification. Directory organization is not discussed beyond the simple few directories and devices that applications generally use. User management discussions do not appear. There is no discussion of such files as **/etc/passwd** or **/etc/groups**, since an application's access to the information traditionally kept in these files is through programmatic interfaces such as *getpwnam*( ) and *getgrnam*( ). Processes have *appropriate privileges*, and there is no concept of the "superuser" or "root".

3.2 Formal Standards Alignment

The Single UNIX Specification clearly supports formal standards developed for application portability. The following source-code portability standards lie at the core of the Single UNIX Specification:

- ISO/IEC 9945-1: 1996 (POSIX-1)
- ISO/IEC 9945-2: 1993 (POSIX-2)
- ISO/IEC 9899: 1990, Programming Languages — C (ISO C)
- ISO/IEC 9899:1990/Amendment 1:1995 (E)
- FIPS 151-2
- FIPS 189.

The Single UNIX Specification fully aligns with these standards. Where there are multiple interfaces to accomplish some task, the standards-based interfaces are clearly identified as the preferred way of doing things to support future portability.

There are sections in POSIX-1 where options may be implemented or not, and a system could still claim conformance to the standard. Likewise, certain minimal values for operating system limits are defined, but the actual values are not described. The National Institute of Standards and Technology (NIST), a United States federal government organization that prepares Federal Information Processing Standards (FIPS), used by other U.S. government agencies in procurements, has developed a FIPS for POSIX-1. FIPS 151-2 clearly identifies what options are to be implemented in a "FIPS"-conforming POSIX-1 system, and sets certain limits. The Single UNIX Specification aligns with the FIPS 151-2 view of POSIX-1.

Refer to XSH, Section 1.6, Relationship to Formal Standards, for more information.

3.3 Portability Codes

While great care has been taken to align the Single UNIX Specification with formal standards, it is still a superset specification that extends functionality or perhaps presents a more exact (and restrictive) definition. When this occurs, the text in the Single UNIX Specification is clearly marked by shading and a portability code appears in the margin.

A programmer needs to take care when using functionality that appears in a shaded area if they are developing applications that need to be maximally portable or portable beyond X/Open UNIX branded systems. For example, if functionality is marked with EX in the margin, it will be available on all X/Open UNIX branded systems, but may not be available on systems only supporting POSIX.1. Alternatively, an application may depend on the exact format of output from a particular utility whose output format is incompletely specified, as indicated by shading and OF marked in the margin. It is likely that an application is developed with a particular platform, or at least a well-defined set of platforms in mind. These codes are exceptionally useful to warn a developer of areas of potential problems.

The following codes are used in the Single UNIX Specification:

EC **Enhanced Curses**
The functionality is part of the X/Open Curses, Issue 4, Version 2 enhancement. This code only appears in X/Open Curses, Issue 4, Version 2. This code identifies functionality that is a mandatory part of the Single UNIX Specification, yet optional for XPG4 Base.

EX Extension
The functionality extends one of the core formal standards (POSIX.1, POSIX.2, the ISO C standard), or makes mandatory something that is optional in the formal standard. This functionality could be expected to be found on all X/Open UNIX branded systems. Certain specific extensions (for example, Job Control) have their own margin code.

FIPS FIPS Extension
Extensions to align with U.S. government FIPS 151-2 are so marked.

JC Job Control Extension
Job control is an optional feature of POSIX.1 and effects the behavior of a number of POSIX.2 utilities. It is mandatory in the Single UNIX Specification.

OB Obsolescent
Features marked as obsolescent are portable to all Single UNIX Specification platforms, but may be withdrawn in a future issue. This functionality should be avoided.

OF Output Format Incompletely Specified
The format of a utility's output is incompletely specified, and therefore cannot be processed consistently by another application across multiple platforms.

OH Optional Header
Certain headers are not required to be included in a source module on XSI-conforming systems, although one of the formal standards may require it. These headers are marked in the Synopsis sections.

OP Optional Service
Some functionality depends upon an optional service, and the functionality affected need not be supported if the optional service is not present.

PI Possibly Inconsistent
It is not possible to guarantee that an interface behaves consistently on all implementations. Certain features of *lp* are so marked.

RT Realtime
This identifies the interfaces and additional semantics in the Realtime Feature Group.

RTT Realtime Threads
This identifies the interfaces and additional semantics in the Realtime Threads Feature Group.

UN Unsupported Feature Permitted
The functionality need not be implemented on all X/Open UNIX branded systems. Certain features of *lp* are so marked.

If the Synopsis section of a reference page is shaded and marked with the two-letter portability code, then the entire interface is an extension. Refer to XBD, **Section 1.3**, **Portability**, for more information.

3.4 Common Directories and Devices

The Single UNIX Specification describes an application portability environment, and as such defines a certain minimal set of directories and devices that applications regularly use. The following directories are defined:

/ The root directory of the filesystem.

/dev Contains the devices **/dev/console**, **/dev/null**, **/dev/tty**.

/tmp A directory where applications can create temporary files.

The directory structure does not cross into such system management issues as where user accounts are organized or software packages are installed. Refer to XBD, **Section 8.1**, **Directory Structure and Files**, for more information.

XBD, **Chapter 8**, **Directory Structure and Devices**, also defines the mapping of control character sequences to real character values, and describes the actions an implementation must take when it cannot support certain terminal behavior.

3.5 Environment Variables

When a program begins, an environment is made available to it. The environment consists of strings of the form *name=value*, where *name* is the name associated with the environment variable, and its value is represented by the characters in *value*. UNIX systems traditionally pass information to programs through the environment variable mechanism. The Single UNIX Specification uses only upper-case characters and underscores to name environment variables, reserving for applications the name space of names containing lower-case characters.

A number of utilities and functions defined in the Single UNIX Specification use environment variables to modify their behavior. The Environment Variable section of a utility's reference page describes any appropriate environment variables. Quite a number of environment variables (listed below) modify the behavior of more than a single utility.

ARFLAGS
CC
CDPATH
CFLAGS
CHARSET
COLUMNS
DATEMSK
DEAD
EDITOR
ENV
EXINIT
FC
FCEDIT
FFLAGS
GET
GFLAGS
HISTFILE
HISTORY
HISTSIZE
HOME
IFS
LANG
LC_ALL
LC_COLLATE
LC_CTYPE
LC_MESSAGES
LC_MONETARY
LC_NUMERIC
LC_TIME
LDFLAGS
LEX
LFLAGS
LINENO
LINES
LISTER
LOGNAME
LPDEST
MAIL
MAILCHECK
MAILER
MAILPATH
MAILRC
MAKEFLAGS
MAKESHELL
MANPATH
MBOX
MORE
MSGVERB
NLSPATH
NPROC
OLDPWD
OPTARG
OPTERR
OPTIND
PAGER
PATH
PPID
PRINTER
PROCLANG
PROJECTDIR
PS1
PS2
PS3
PS4
PWD
RANDOM
SECONDS
SHELL
TERM
TERMCAP
TERMINFO
TMPDIR
TZ
USER
VISUAL
YACC
YFLAGS

3.6 YACC Grammars as Specifications

The Single UNIX Specification describes certain functionality and "little" languages with *yacc* grammars. The *yacc* utility (Yet-Another-Compiler-Compiler) is used to build language parsers, and the syntax of the *yacc* input language is designed for describing languages. Because of this, and its familiarity in the community, it has been used in the Single UNIX Specification to describe the shell (XCU, **Chapter 2**, **Shell Command Language**), the *awk* language (XCU, **Chapter 3**, **Utilities**, *awk*), the *bc* language (XCU, **Chapter 3**, **Utilities**,*bc*), the locale definition language (XBD, **Chapter 5**, **Locale**), basic and extended regular expressions (XBD, **Chapter 7**, **Regular Expressions**), and *terminfo* source format (X/Open Curses, Issue 4, Version 2, **Section 6.1.2**, **Formal Grammar**).

These grammars are representations of the languages they describe, and a number of caveats apply:

- They are not complete input grammars to *yacc* itself.
- They are not based on any existing implementations, nor have they been tested as such.
- Were these partial grammars to be completed, there are no guarantees that they are the most efficient method of defining the respective languages for *yacc* to process.

Refer to XCU, **Chapter 1**, **Introduction** for more information.

3.7 Regular Expressions

Both Basic Regular Expressions (BRE) and Extended Regular Expressions (ERE) are described in XBD, **Chapter 7**, **Regular Expressions**, and all of the utilities and interfaces that use regular expressions refer back to this definition.

Basic regular expressions:

> *csplit*, *ctags*, *ed*, *ex*, *expr*, *grep*, *more*, *nl*, *pax*, *pg*, *sed*, *vi*

Extended regular expressions:

> *awk*, *egrep*, *grep −E*, *lex*

The POSIX.2 functions *regcomp*( ) and *regexec*( ) implement regular expressions as defined in the Single UNIX Specification. There are other historical methods of handling regular expressions that appear in the Single UNIX Specification, but these exist strictly for porting existing applications and have all been marked LEGACY.

3.8 File Access

The Single UNIX Specification refers to two types of interactions that may effect file access in the filesystem, altering the behavior described in the specification. If the files are available on a network filesystem, the system interfaces for accessing files may behave differently. If that filesystem conforms to the XNFS, Issue 4 specification, then the behavior is defined by that specification. This restriction is described in XSH, **Chapter 2**, **General Information**.

The Single UNIX Specification also describes symbolic links. The behavior of symbolic links is fully specified with respect to their creation and use through the relevant XSH interfaces, such as *symlink*( ), *lstat*( ), *readlink*( ), *realpath*( ), and pathname resolution (XBD, **Chapter 2**, **Glossary**). The behavior is *not* specified with respect to the utilities described in XCU. See Section 3.10.2 on page 28 and XCU, **Chapter 1**, **Introduction** for more information.

3.9 Programming Environment

The Single UNIX Specification and X/Open UNIX branded systems are tools for developing portable applications and for porting existing applications that were originally developed to run on UNIX systems. XSH defines the C-language programming environment, and the syntax and semantics of the interfaces. Feature test macros, name space issues, and the program interaction with the operating system are all described in the opening chapters of the document. The following introductions to these topics include references and additional explanations to orient an application developer with the information presented in XSH.

3.9.1 C-language Support

The programming interfaces in XSH are described in C-language syntax, as defined in the ISO C standard, and presume a C-language compilation environment. (Implementations may make the functionality available through other programming languages, but this is not covered by the Single UNIX Specification.)

For an implementation to be a conforming X/Open UNIX branded system, it must support the XPG4 C Language component, which identifies the ISO C standard dialect. Implementations may additionally support the X/Open Common Usage C dialect as a migration strategy from previous XPG3 environments. X/Open Common Usage C is defined in Programming Languages, Issue 3, Chapters 1 to 4, and essentially refers to the C Language before the ISO C standard.

XCU defines both *c89* and *cc* as interfaces to a C compilation environment. The *c89* interface is preferable, as it is an interface to the standard C compiler, and is recommended for future work. The *cc* interface maps to an unspecified C compiler environment, and is marked LEGACY in Issue 5. Refer to XCU, **Chapter 3**, **Utilities**, *c89* and *cc*, and XSH, **Chapter 2**, **General Information** for more information.

3.9.2 Feature Test Macros and Name Space Issues

There are a number of tasks that must be done to effectively make the interface environment available to a program. A number of C-language macros, referred to as *feature test macros*, must be defined before any headers are included. These macros might more accurately be referred to as header configuration macros, as they control what symbols and prototypes will be exposed by the headers. The macro _XOPEN_SOURCE must be defined to a value of 500 to make available the functionality of the Single UNIX Specification, Version 2. With respect to POSIX functionality covered by the Single UNIX Specification, this is equivalent to defining the POSIX macro _POSIX_SOURCE, and defining _POSIX_C_SOURCE to be greater than zero and less than or equal to 199506L.

Use of the _XOPEN_SOURCE macro should not be confused with the other feature test macros associated with Feature Groups and functionality, such as _XOPEN_UNIX. These feature test macros are the implementation's way of announcing functionality to the application. (A complete list of feature test macros associated with Feature Groups appears in Table 18-1 on page 192.)

In the first case (implementation-dependent _XOPEN_SOURCE=500), the application program is announcing to the implementation its desire to have certain symbols and prototypes exposed. In the second case (implementation-dependent _XOPEN_UNIX), the application program is testing the implementation to determine whether the functionality exists. Refer to XSH, **Chapter 2**, **General Information** for more information.

The X/Open UNIX name space is well defined. All identifiers defined in the Single UNIX Specification appear in the headers described in XSH, **Chapter 4**, **Headers** (with the exception of *environ*). Tables in XSH, **Chapter 2**, **General Information** clearly describe which identifier prefixes and suffixes are reserved for the implementation, which identifier macro prefixes may be used by the application programmer providing appropriate **#undef** statements are used to prevent conflicts, and which identifiers are reserved for external linkage.

3.9.3 Error Numbers

Each interface reference page lists in the Errors section possible error returns that may be tested in *errno* upon the unsuccessful completion of a function call. Each error return has a symbolic name (defined as a manifest constant in **<errno.h>**) which should always be used by the portable application, as the actual error values are unspecified. All of the error names are listed in XSH, **Chapter 2**, **General Information** along with additional relevant information.

3.9.4 Standard I/O Streams

When a program starts, it has associated three I/O streams associated with it, namely *standard input* (the keyboard), *standard output*, and *standard error* (both associated with the display). These streams are already open for the process, and ready for I/O.

The mechanics of stream I/O, buffering, relationships to file descriptors, and inheritance across process creation are all discussed in XSH, **Chapter 2**, **General Information**.

3.9.5 STREAMS

STREAMS is a method of implementing network services and other character-based input/output mechanisms, with the STREAM being a full-duplex connection between a process and a device. STREAMS provides direct access to protocol modules, and optional protocol modules can be interposed between the process-end of the STREAM and the device-driver at the device-end of the STREAM. Pipes can be implemented using the STREAMS mechanism, so they can provide process-to-process as well as process-to-device communications.

XSH, **Chapter 2**, **General Information** introduces STREAMS I/O, the message types used to control them, an overview of the priority mechanism, and the interfaces used to access them.

3.9.6 Interprocess Communication

The Single UNIX Specification describes a set of interprocess communications (IPC) primitives, namely message queues, semaphores, and shared memory. These functions are all derived from the SVID.

General information that is shared by all three mechanisms is described in XSH, **Chapter 2**, **General Information**. There, the common permissions mechanism is briefly introduced, describing the mode bits, and how they are used to determine whether or not a process has access to read or write/alter the appropriate instance of one of the IPC mechanisms. All other relevant information is contained in the reference pages themselves.

3.9.7 Realtime

The Single UNIX Specification, Version 2 introduces realtime functionality to support the source portability of applications with realtime requirements. This is derived from the POSIX Realtime Extension. Realtime is discussed in XSH, **Chapter 2**, **General Information**. This section includes an overview of the functional areas: semaphores, process memory locking, memory mapped files and shared memory objects, priority scheduling, realtime signals, timers, interprocess communication, synchronous input/output, and asynchronous input/output.

3.9.8 Threads

The Single UNIX Specification, Version 2 introduces threads functionality to support multiple flows of control, called *threads*, within a process. These are derived from the POSIX Threads Extension, with additional X/Open extensions. Threads is discussed in XSH, **Chapter 2**, **General Information**, which includes an overview of the supported interfaces, threads implementation models, threads mutexes, threads attributes, thread scheduling, thread cancellation, and thread read-write locks.

3.9.9 General Terminal Interface

The general terminal interface defined in POSIX.1 is described in the Single UNIX Specification, providing a mechanism to control asynchronous communications ports. It is left to implementations as to whether or not they support network connections and synchronous communications ports. While the definition comes from POSIX.1, it has been extended in the X/Open UNIX environment to support additional input and output modes.

While all of the interface details are contained in XSH, the mechanics of the terminal interface with respect to process groups, controlling terminals, input and output processing, input, output and control modes, and special characters are described in XBD, **Chapter 9**, **General Terminal Interface**.

This interface should not be confused with the X/Open Curses interface that provides a terminal-independent way to update character screens.

3.9.10 How to Read an XSH Reference Page

Each reference page in XSH has a common layout of sections describing the interface. (Function interface descriptions in Networking Services, Issue 5 and X/Open Curses, Issue 4, Version 2 follow the same layout.) This layout is similar to the manual page or "man" page format shipped with most UNIX systems, and each interface has sections describing Synopsis, Description, Return Value, and Errors. These are the four sections that relate to conformance.

Additional sections contain considerable extra information for the application developer. Example sections provide source-code examples of how to use certain interfaces. Application Usage sections provide additional caveats, issues, and recommendations to the developer. See Also sections contain useful pointers to related interfaces and headers that a developer may wish to also read.

Future Directions sections act as pointers to related work that may impact on the interface in the future, and often cautions the developer to architect the code to account for a change in this area. (A Future Directions section expresses current thinking and should not be considered a commitment to adopt the feature or interface in the future.)

The Change History section describes when the interface was introduced, and how it has changed. This information can be useful when porting existing applications that may reflect earlier implementations of the interface.

Feature Group labels in the reference page headers, and portability shading and margin marks are features already described in this document; they appear on the reference pages to guide an application developer when deciding how best an interface should be used. Refer to XSH, **Section 1.8**, **Format of Entries**, for information on the exact layout.

3.10 Commands and Utilities Environment

The Single UNIX Specification describes 174 utilities supported on an X/Open UNIX branded system. These utilities provide a rich environment for building shell script applications, supporting program development (the C Language in particular), and providing a user portability environment.

XCU, along with the shell command language, symbolic links, file format notation, utility reference page layouts, and guidelines, are all introduced in this section. The following introductions to these topics include references and additional explanations to orient an application developer with the information presented in XCU.

3.10.1 X/Open Shell Command Language

The X/Open shell is a powerful and flexible programming language. A considerable number of utilities on early UNIX systems were actually shell programs.

The Single UNIX Specification shell fully conforms to the POSIX.2 shell. This shell is for the most part based on the Bourne shell with features from the KornShell, *ksh*. Traditional System V shell scripts may require some modification.

The shell command language is defined in its entirety in XCU, **Chapter 2**, **Shell Command Language**. This is a very strict definition of the shell. Token recognition, word expansions, simple and compound commands, the shell grammar, the execution environment, and special built-ins are a few of the topics covered. It is not a guide to writing or porting shell scripts.

3.10.2 Symbolic Links

The Single UNIX Specification adds support for symbolic links in the filesystem. The programmatic interfaces that manipulate symbolic links (or *symlinks*) are all well defined in XSH, and *symlink* concepts with respect to issues like pathname resolution are discussed in XBD. An X/Open UNIX branded system supports *symlinks*, and application programs may make use of them.

There is potential confusion when discussing *symlinks* with respect to the Single UNIX Specification commands and utilities:

- XCU conformance states that implementations need not support *symlinks*.
- XCU further states that the effects of using utilities that manipulate files are unspecified when the last component of the pathname is a symbolic link.

What this is saying is that symbolic link behavior and the means of manipulating symbolic links is not currently defined in XCU. A future edition of this part of the Single UNIX Specification will align with the POSIX.2b standards effort, a document which will amend ISO/IEC 9945-2: 1993 (POSIX-2), and specify the behavior of utilities with respect to symbolic links. Refer to XCU, **Chapter 1**, **Introduction** for additional details.

3.10.3 File Format Notation

Sections in the utility reference pages often require the expected input used by the utility or output it generates to be described. Additionally, information files used or created sometimes require description. The method used throughout XCU is a format description plus its arguments, similar to that used by the *printf*( ) function. These file format specifications are presented as:

```
"<format>" [ ,<arg1>, <arg2>, ..., <argn>]
```

The *format* specifier contains the format string a programmer might use to write the data. The specifiers should not be considered format strings that could be directly used in a call to *scanf*( ). The conversion specifications in the format string are what would be expected by a developer familiar with the *printf*( ) interface. Refer to XBD, **Chapter 3**, **File Format Notation**, for more information.

3.10.4 How to Read an XCU Reference Page

Each reference page in XCU has a common layout of sections describing the interface. This layout, while similar to the manual page or "man" page format shipped with most UNIX systems, offers a more detailed view of the utility's description.

As well as the Synopsis and Description sections, each interface has sections describing Options, Operands, stdin (standard input format), Input Files, Environment Variables, Asynchronous Events (what signals are caught and the consequence of receiving signals), stdout (standard output format), stderr, and Output Files.

An Extended Description will be used if the utility has a particularly long description; for example, if it supports its own language (*awk*), or provides a considerable number of subcommands (*mailx*).

Utilities generally return 0 upon successful completion, and a failed status as greater than 0. Exit Status sections specify this, but will also describe if particular values are returned in certain circumstances. In general, an application should be written to test for successful completion, rather than specific error returns.

The Consequence of Errors section describes what happens to such items as open files, process state, and the environment, should errors occur.

As with the XSH reference pages, additional sections contain considerable extra information for the application developer, and Examples, Application Usage, Future Directions, See Also, and Change History sections may all be present. The defaults for these sections, and additional detail about what each section specifies, is covered in XCU, **Chapter 1**, **Introduction**.

3.11 X/Open Networking Services

The X/Open Networking Services have traditionally consisted of simply the X/Open Transport Interface (XTI). With the introduction of X/Open UNIX, sockets and IP address resolution interfaces have been added. As with XSH, the application developer needs to define _XOPEN_SOURCE to be 500 prior to the inclusion of any Single UNIX Specification headers.

The *c89* and *cc* compiler utilities will recognize the additional **–l** operand for the **xnet** library. Furthermore, an X/Open UNIX branded system supporting the DEVELOPMENT utilities described in XCU will also recognize **–l xnet** for the *lint* utility.

3.12 X/Open Curses Interfaces

The Single UNIX Specification includes X/Open Curses, Issue 4, Version 2. These interfaces provide a terminal-independent character screen update method. X/Open Curses, Issue 4, Version 2 is an upwardly-compatible enhancement of X/Open Curses, Issue 3.

Note: X/Open Curses, Issue 4, Version 2 obsoletes X/Open Curses, Issue 4.

The enhanced functionality includes:

- multi-byte and wide-character support
- color terminal support
- wide and non-spacing character generalizations such that multi-column display characters and non-spacing characters are supported.

New interfaces over Issue 3 are marked with ENHANCED CURSES in the reference page header, and shading and a portability code is used (EC) to indicate in the introductory chapters and reference pages the extended features.

Applications using the interfaces from X/Open Curses, Issue 4, Version 2 need to define the _XOPEN_SOURCE macro to be 500 prior to including any headers. These feature test macros ensure the appropriate name space is exposed in the headers.

On X/Open UNIX branded systems supporting the functionality labelled ENHANCED CURSES, the *c89* and *cc* compiler front-ends will recognize the additional –**l** operand for the **curses** library.

3.13 Internationalization

There is a rich set of interfaces in the Single UNIX Specification to support internationalized applications development. Internationalization refers to developing an application without prior knowledge of the language, cultural information, or character set encoding scheme that will be used in the run-time environment. The application responds accordingly at run time for cultural or locale-specific conditions. The term "internationalization" is often shortened to simply "I18N", for "I" — 18 letters (nternationalizatio) — "N".

Localization is the process of establishing a base of cultural and codeset data on a system such that it can be accessed. It is the method by which *locales* are created in such a way that internationalized programs can access the relevant information.

There are a number of factors that need to be considered when structuring an application to support multiple cultures:

- Cultural-specific data (for example, date, number, and monetary formats) needs to be defined in a locale, with the appropriate tools and interfaces available for creating and accessing the information.
- Provision for handling text strings in programs, and managing catalogues of these strings for multiple natural languages, needs to be made.
- Multi-byte and wide-character handling interfaces are required to manage textual data that is not represented in single byte per character formats.
- Codeset conversion tools need to be supported.

All of these requirements are met in the Single UNIX Specification. Utilities exist to support the definition and display of locales (*localedef* and *locale*). Programming interfaces exist to access the locale-specific data, and others have been extended such that all the checking and manipulations done with characters and strings can be done with wide characters and wide-character strings. Interfaces to access message string catalogues (*catopen*( ), *catgets*( ), and *catclose*( )) and a tool to define them (*gencat*) exist. Codeset conversions can be done at the utility (*iconv*) and program level (*iconv_open*( ), *iconv*( ), and *iconv_close*( )).

Much of the I18N information is unfortunately spread throughout the Single UNIX Specification, with specific interface and utility descriptions appearing in XSH and XCU respectively. Introductions to character and codeset issues and the locale definition language appear in XBD, **Chapter 4**, **Character Set**, and **Chapter 5**, **Locale**, respectively.

Chapter 4

System Interfaces

The Single UNIX Specification covers a broad spectrum of functionality, providing a rich environment for applications portability and portable applications development. In this chapter, the XSH Feature Groups are described and the interfaces are grouped into categories to give the reader an understanding of what facilities are available. Some of these categories are well defined, being based on the Feature Groups or headers. Other category boundaries are more arbitrary. The Networking Services and Curses interfaces are described in their own chapters.

4.1 Feature Groups

XSH contains the Base interfaces and several Feature Groups. Interfaces that are part of a Feature Group have a Feature Group-specific label that appears in the Synopsis of the interface's reference page.

XSH contains the following Feature Groups:

- **Encryption** covering the functions *crypt*( ), *encrypt*( ), and *setkey*( ). The reference pages for these functions are marked CRYPT.
- **Realtime** covering the functions, derived from the POSIX Realtime Extension, in the Realtime Feature Group. The reference pages for these functions are marked REALTIME. Where additional semantics are added to existing pages, the new material is marked by the RT legend.
- **Realtime Threads** covering the functions, derived from the POSIX Threads Extension, which are related to the Realtime functionality. The reference pages for these functions are marked REALTIME THREADS. Where additional semantics are added to existing pages, the new material is marked by the RTT legend.
- The **Legacy** Feature Group includes the interfaces and headers which were mandatory in previous versions of the specification, but are optional in this version. The reference pages for these functions are marked LEGACY.

Anything that does not fall into the Feature Groups listed above is considered to be Base functionality. To conform to the Single UNIX Specification, only the Base interfaces are mandatory.

4.2 POSIX.1 System Interfaces

As has been stated, the Single UNIX Specification supports and is aligned with key consensus-based formal standards, of which POSIX.1 forms the core of the operating system service interface.

POSIX.1

- Process Primitives:

  _exit( ), *exec*( ), *fork*( ), *wait*( ), *waitpid*( )

- Signals:

  kill( ), *sigaction*( ), *sigaddset*( ), *sigdelset*( ), *sigemptyset*( ), *sigfillset*( ), *sigismember*( ), *sigpending*( ), *sigprocmask*( ), *sigsuspend*( )

- Timers:

  alarm( ), *pause*( ), *sleep*( )

- Process Environment Manipulation:

  ctermid( ), *getegid*( ), *getenv*( ), *geteuid*( ), *getgid*( ), *getgroups*( ), *getlogin*( ), *getpgrp*( ), *getpid*( ), *getppid*( ), *getuid*( ), *isatty*( ), *setgid*( ), *setpgid*( ), *setsid*( ), *setuid*( ), *sysconf*( ), *time*( ), *times*( ), *ttyname*( ), *uname*( )

- File and Directory Control:

  access( ), *chdir*( ), *chmod*( ), *chown*( ), *closedir*( ), *creat*( ), *fpathconf*( ), *fstat*( ), *getcwd*( ), *link*( ), *mkdir*( ), *mkfifo*( ), *open*( ), *opendir*( ), *pathconf*( ), *readdir*( ), *rename*( ), *rewinddir*( ), *rmdir*( ), *stat*( ), *umask*( ), *unlink*( ), *utime*( )

- Input/Output Processing:

  close( ), *dup*( ), *dup2*( ), *fcntl*( ), *lseek*( ), *pipe*( ), *read*( ), *write*( )

- Other C-language Functions:

  fdopen( ), *fileno*( ), *siglongjmp*( ), *sigsetjmp*( ), *tzset*( )

- General Terminal Interface:

  cfgetispeed( ), *cfgetospeed*( ), *cfsetispeed*( ), *cfsetospeed*( ), *tcdrain*( ), *tcflow*( ), *tcflush*( ), *tcgetattr*( ), *tcgetpgrp*( ), *tcsendbreak*( ), *tcsetattr*( ), *tcsetpgrp*( )

- User Database Access:

  getgrgid( ), *getgrnam*( ), *getpwnam*( ), *getpwuid*( )

POSIX.1b

The following interfaces derived from the POSIX Realtime Extension form the Realtime Feature Group within the Single UNIX Specification, Version 2:

> aio_cancel(), aio_error(), aio_fsync(), aio_read(), aio_return(), aio_suspend(), aio_write(), clock_getres(), clock_gettime(), clock_settime(), fdatasync(), lio_listio(), mlock(), mlockall(), mq_close(), mq_getattr(), mq_notify(), mq_open(), mq_receive(), mq_send(), mq_setattr(), mq_unlink(), munlock(), munlockall(), nanosleep(), sched_get_priority_max(), sched_get_priority_min(), sched_getparam(), sched_getscheduler(), sched_rr_get_interval(), sched_setparam(), sched_setscheduler(), sched_yield(), sem_close(), sem_destroy(), sem_getvalue(), sem_init(), sem_open(), sem_post(), sem_trywait(), sem_unlink(), sem_wait(), shm_open(), shm_unlink(), sigqueue(), sigtimedwait(), sigwaitinfo(), timer_create(), timer_delete(), timer_getoverrun(), timer_gettime(), timer_settime(), **<aio.h>**, **<mqueue.h>**, **<sched.h>**

POSIX.1c

The following interfaces derived from the POSIX Threads Extension are mandatory in the Single UNIX Specification, Version 2:

> asctime_r(), ctime_r(), flockfile(), ftrylockfile(), funlockfile(), getc_unlocked(), getchar_unlocked(), getgrgid_r(), getgrnam_r(), getpwnam_r(), getpwuid_r(), gmtime_r(), localtime_r(), pthread_addr_setstacksize(), pthread_atfork(), pthread_attr_destroy(), pthread_attr_getdetachstate(), pthread_attr_getstackaddr(), pthread_attr_getstacksize(), pthread_attr_init(), pthread_attr_setdetachstate(), pthread_attr_setschedparam(), pthread_attr_setstackaddr(), pthread_cancel(), pthread_cleanup_pop(), pthread_cleanup_push(), pthread_cond_broadcast(), pthread_cond_destroy(), pthread_cond_init(), pthread_cond_signal(), pthread_cond_timedwait(), pthread_cond_wait(), pthread_condattr_destroy(), pthread_condattr_getpshared(), pthread_condattr_init(), pthread_condattr_setpshared(), pthread_create(), pthread_detach(), pthread_equal(), pthread_exit(), pthread_getschedparam(), pthread_getspecific(), pthread_join(), pthread_key_create(), pthread_key_delete(), pthread_kill(), pthread_mutex_destroy(), pthread_mutex_init(), pthread_mutex_lock(), pthread_mutex_trylock(), pthread_mutex_unlock(), pthread_mutexattr_destroy(), pthread_mutexattr_getpshared(), pthread_mutexattr_init(), pthread_mutexattr_setpshared(), pthread_once(), pthread_self(), pthread_setcancelstate(), pthread_setcanceltype(), pthread_setspecific(), pthread_sigmask(), pthread_testcancel(), putc_unlocked(), putchar_unlocked(), rand_r(), readdir_r(), sigwait(), strtok_r(), **<pthread.h>**

The following interfaces derived from the POSIX Threads Extension are in the Realtime Threads Feature Group:

> pthread_attr_getinheritsched(), pthread_attr_getschedpolicy(), pthread_attr_getscope(), pthread_attr_setinheritsched(), pthread_attr_setschedpolicy(), pthread_attr_setscope(), pthread_getschedparam(), pthread_mutex_getprioceiling(), pthread_mutex_setprioceiling(), pthread_mutexattr_getprioceiling(), pthread_mutexattr_getprotocol(), pthread_mutexattr_setprioceiling(), pthread_mutexattr_setprotocol(), pthread_setschedparam()

The Single UNIX Specification is further aligned with the particular options and requirements of the U.S. Government FIPS 151-2. POSIX.1 presumes an ISO C standard environment and requires most of the ISO C standard library be present. POSIX.1 extends certain of these interfaces.

4.3 ISO C Standard Library

The Single UNIX Specification is aligned with the ISO C standard, and thus specifies all of the library interfaces. The library can be split along the lines of the standard headers defined by the ISO C standard.

See also ISO C Amendment 1 (MSE) in Section 4.7.0 on page 40.

- **<assert.h>**

  assert( )

- **<ctype.h>**

  isalnum( ), *isalpha*( ), *iscntrl*( ), *isdigit*( ), *isgraph*( ), *islower*( ), *isprint*( ), *ispunct*( ), *isspace*( ), *isupper*( ), *isxdigit*( ), *tolower*( ), *toupper*( )

- **<locale.h>**

  setlocale( ),† *localeconv*( )

- **<math.h>**

  acos( ), *asin*( ), *atan*( ), *atan2*( ), *cos*( ), *sin*( ), *tan*( ), *cosh*( ), *sinh*( ), *tanh*( ), *exp*( ), *frexp*( ), *ldexp*( ), *log*( ), *log10*( ), *modf*( ), *pow*( ), *sqrt*( ), *ceil*( ), *fabs*( ), *floor*( ), *fmod*( )

- **<setjmp.h>**

  setjmp( ), *longjmp*( )

- **<signal.h>**

  signal( ), *raise*( )

- **<stdarg.h>**

  va_start( ), *va_arg*( ), *va_end*( )

- **<stdio.h>**

  remove( ), *rename*( ),† *tmpfile*( ), *tmpnam*( ), *fclose*( ), *fflush*( ), *fopen*( ), *freopen*( ), *setbuf*( ), *setvbuf*( ), *fprintf*( ), *fscanf*( ), *printf*( ), *scanf*( ), *sprintf*( ), *sscanf*( ), *vfprintf*( ), *vprintf*( ), *vsprintf*( ), *fgetc*( ), *fgets*( ), *fputc*( ), *fputs*( ), *getc*( ), *getchar*( ), *gets*( ), *putc*( ), *putchar*( ), *puts*( ), *ungetc*( ), *fread*( ), *fwrite*( ), *fgetpos*( ), *fseek*( ), *fsetpos*( ), *ftell*( ), *rewind*( ), *clearerr*( ), *feof*( ), *ferror*( ), *perror*( ),

- **<stdlib.h>**

  atof( ), *atoi*( ), *atol*( ), *strtod*( ), *strtol*( ), *strtoul*( ), *rand*( ), *srand*( ), *calloc*( ), *free*( ), *malloc*( ), *realloc*( ), *abort*( ), *atexit*( ), *exit*( ), *getenv*( ),† *system*( ),† *bsearch*( ), *qsort*( ), *abs*( ), *div*( ), *labs*( ), *ldiv*( ), *mblen*( ), *mbtowc*( ), *wctomb*( ), *mbstowcs*( ), *wcstombs*( )

- **<string.h>**

  memcpy( ), *memmove*( ), *strcpy*( ), *strncpy*( ), *strcat*( ), *strncat*( ), *memcmp*( ), *strcmp*( ), *strcoll*( ), *strncmp*( ), *strxfrm*( ), *memchr*( ), *strchr*( ), *strcspn*( ), *strpbrk*( ), *strrchr*( ), *strspn*( ), *strstr*( ), *strtok*( ), *memset*( ), *strerror*( ), *strlen*( )

---

† The functions marked with † appear in POSIX.1 or POSIX.2 and may have additional requirements placed upon them by the POSIX standard, beyond their definition in the ISO C standard. POSIX.1 requires most, but not all, of the C library functions.

- **<time.h>**

  clock( ), *difftime*( ), *mktime*( ),† *time*( ),† *asctime*( ), *ctime*( ),† *gmtime*( ),† *localtime*( ),† *strftime*( )†

4.4 POSIX.2 C-language Interfaces

The POSIX.2 C-language Interfaces are part of the Base in the Single UNIX Specification, Version 2. These interfaces perform such shell-like functions as pathname wildcard pattern matching (*globbing*), filename matching, regular-expression matching, and shell-like word expansions.

confstr( ), *getopt*( ), *pclose*( ), *popen*( ), *system*( ), *fnmatch*( ), *regcomp*( ), *regexec*( ), *wordexp*( ), *glob*( ), *regerror*( ), *regfree*( ), *wordfree*( ), *globfree*( )

It should be noted that there are several different sets of interfaces for handling regular expressions in the Single UNIX Specification. The POSIX.2-derived interfaces functions are the recommended set, as the others are less functional and exist to allow applications that have been developed to traditional UNIX system regular expression models to be easily ported.

4.5 IPC Interfaces

There are a number of interprocess communications (IPC) mechanisms based on classical SVID interfaces in the Single UNIX Specification. These are part of the Base in the Single UNIX Specification, Version 2.

These include support for semaphores, message queues, and shared memory. The Shared Memory interfaces allow multiple processes to share data by having the memory containing the data appear in each process' address space.

Calls to support semaphores include:

semctl( ), *semget*( ), *semop*( )

Calls to support message queues include:

msgctl( ), *msgget*( ), *msgrcv*( ), *msgsnd*( )

The *ftok*( ) interface is also provided.

Calls to support shared memory include:

shmat( ), *shmctl*( ), *shmdt*( ), *shmget*( )

It is important to note that all three IPC mechanisms have counterparts in POSIX.1b that are different. Application developers may want to structure their applications such that modules using these IPC mechanisms could be easily replaced in the future.

4.6 General Base Interfaces

These interfaces are the CAE extensions, which allow allow existing applications developed for XPG4, UNIX, and UNIX system derivatives to be easily ported to X/Open UNIX branded systems:

- STREAMS (**<stropts.h>**):

  fattach(), *fdetach*(), *getmsg*(), *getpmsg*(), *ioctl*(), *isastream*(), *putmsg*(), *putpmsg*()

- Symbolic Links (**<unistd.h>**):

  lchown(), *lstat*(), *readlink*(), *symlink*()

- Memory-mapped Files (**<sys/mman.h>**):

  mmap(), *mprotect*(), *msync*(), *munmap*()

- Interval Timers and I/O Multiplexing (**<sys/time.h>**):

  getitimer(), *gettimeofday*(), *select*(), *setitimer*(), *utimes*()

- Priority Scheduling and Process Resource Limit Control (**<sys/resource.h>**):

  getpriority(), *getrlimit*(), *getrusage*(), *setpriority*(), *setrlimit*()

- Input/Output Multiplexing (**<poll.h>**):

  poll()

- Additional Directory Manipulation Routines (**<dirent.h>**):

  seekdir(), *telldir*()

- Additional Support for Non-local goto Control Flow (**<setjmp.h>**):

  _longjmp(), *_setjmp*()

- System Logging (**<syslog.h>**):

  closelog(), *openlog*(), *setlogmask*(), *syslog*()

- User and Groups Database Access (**<grp.h>**):

  endgrent(), *endpwent*(), *getgrent*(), *getpwent*(), *setgrent*(), *setpwent*()

- Historical Pattern Matching Functions (**<libgen.h>**):

  basename(), *dirname*()

- BSD String Operations (**<strings.h>**):

  bcmp(), *bcopy*(), *bzero*(), *ffs*(), *index*(), *rindex*(), *strcasecmp*(), *strncasecmp*()

- Ndbm Database Operations (**<ndbm.h>**):

  dbm_clearerr(), *dbm_close*(), *dbm_delete*(), *dbm_error*(), *dbm_fetch*(), *dbm_firstkey*(), *dbm_nextkey*(), *dbm_open*(), *dbm_store*()

- User Accounting Database Access (**<utmpx.h>**):

  endutxent(), *getutxent*(), *getutxid*(), *getutxline*(), *pututxline*(), *setutxent*()

  Also, *ttyslot*() has been added to **<stdlib.h>**.

- User Context Control (**<ucontext.h>**):

  getcontext( ), *makecontext*( ), *setcontext*( ), *swapcontext*( )

- VFS Filesystem Information Access (**<sys/statvfs.h>**):

  fstatvfs( ), *statvfs*( )

- Additional Math Library Functions (**<math.h>**):

  acosh( ), *asinh*( ), *atanh*( ), *cbrt*( ), *expm1*( ), *ilogb*( ), *log1p*( ), *logb*( ), *nextafter*( ), *remainder*( ), *rint*( ), *scalb*( )

- System V Signal Management Functions (**<signal.h>**):

  sighold( ), *sigignore*( ), *sigpause*( ), *sigrelse*( ), *sigset*( )

  And other historical signal management functions:

  killpg( ), *sigaltstack*( ), *siginterrupt*( ), *sigstack*( )

  So as not to conflict signal models provided on different historical systems, *bsd_signal*( ) has been added as a direct replacement for the *signal*( ) function found on BSD systems.

- Additional System Interfaces (**<unistd.h>**):

  fchdir( ), *fchown*( ), *ftruncate*( ), *gethostid*( ), *getpgid*( ), *getsid*( ), *getwd*( ), *lockf*( ), *setpgrp*( ), *setregid*( ), *setreuid*( ), *sync*( ), *truncate*( ), *ualarm*( ), *usleep*( ), *vfork*( )

- Additional stat( )-related Interfaces (**<sys/stat.h>**):

  fchmod( ), *mknod*( )

- Additional Process Waiting Interfaces (**<sys/wait.h>**):

  wait( ), *waitid*( )

- Additional General Terminal Control Interface (**<termios.h>**):

  tcgetsid( )

- Additional Search Functions (**<search.h>**):

  insque( ), *remque*( )

- Additional Standard Library Functions (**<stdlib.h>**):

  a64l( ), *ecvt*( ), *fcvt*( ), *gcvt*( ), *getsubopt*( ), *initstate*( ), *l64a*( ), *random*( ), *realpath*( ), *setstate*( ), *srandom*( )

- Page-aligned Memory Allocation Function (**<stdlib.h>**):

  valloc( )

- Historical Temporary File and Filename Creation (**<stdlib.h>**):

  mktemp( ), *mkstemp*( )

  Also, *tempnam*( ) is added to **<stdio.h>**.

- Additional String Manipulation Function (**<string.h>**):

  strdup( )

- Pseudo-terminal Device Control (**<stdlib.h>**):

  grantpt( ), *ptsname*( ), *unlockpt*( )

- Vectored File Read/Write Interfaces (**<sys/uio.h>**):

  readv( ), *writev*( )

- Standard Error Stream Message Format Interface (**<fmtmsg.h>**):

  fmtmsg( )

- Historical Date and Time Interfaces:

  ftime( ) (in **<sys/timeb.h>**), *getdate*( ) (in **<time.h>**).

- Additional System Interfaces (**<unistd.h>**):

  chroot( ), *cuserid*( ), *fsync*( ), *getpass*( ), *nice*( ), *swab*( )

- Additional Character Type Interfaces (**<ctype.h>**):

  isascii( ), *toascii*( )

- Additional Math Library Functions (**<math.h>**):

  erf( ), *erfc*( ), *gamma*( ), *hypot*( ), *isnan*( ), *j0*( ), *j1*( ), *jn*( ), *lgamma*( ), *y0*( ), *y1*( ), *yn*( )

- Hash Table and Binary Tree Functions (**<search.h>**):

  hcreate( ), *hdestroy*( ), *hsearch*( ), *lfind*( ), *lsearch*( ), *tdelete*( ), *tfind*( ), *tsearch*( ), *twalk*( )

- Additional Random Number Generation Functions (**<stdlib.h>**):

  drand48( ), *erand48*( ), *jrand48*( ), *lcong48*( ), *lrand48*( ), *mrand48*( ), *nrand48*( ), *seed48*( ), *srand48*( )

- Environment Manipulation Function (**<stdlib.h>**):

  putenv( )

- Additional Memory Manipulation Function (**<string.h>**):

  memccpy( )

- The User Limit Interface (**<ulimit.h>**):

  ulimit( )

- File-tree Walking Interface (**<ftw.h>**):

  ftw( ), *nftw*( )

- Dynamic Linking (**<dlfcn.h>**):

  dlclose( ), *dlerror*( ), *dlopen*( ), *dlsym*( )

X/Open Threads Extension

pread( ), *pthread_attr_getguardsize*( ), *pthread_attr_setguardsize*( ), *pthread_getconcurrency*( ), *pthread_mutexattr_gettype*( ), *pthread_mutexattr_settype*( ), *pthread_rwlock_destroy*( ), *pthread_rwlock_init*( ), *pthread_rwlock_rdlock*( ), *pthread_rwlock_tryrdlock*( ), *pthread_rwlock_trywrlock*( ), *pthread_rwlock_unlock*( ), *pthread_rwlock_wrlock*( ), *pthread_rwlockattr_destroy*( ), *pthread_rwlockattr_getpshared*( ), *pthread_rwlockattr_init*( ), *pthread_rwlockattr_setpshared*( ), *pthread_setconcurrency*( ), *pwrite*( )

Large File Support

fseeko( ), *ftello*( ), **<stdio.h>**

Data Size Neutral

<inttypes.h>

Miscellaneous

snprintf( ), *vsnprintf*( ), **<stdio.h>**

4.7 Application Internationalization Support

The CAE has traditionally supported a wealth of interfaces for application internationalization (I18N), allowing programs to manipulate and output data in locales other than the traditional English C locale. The Single UNIX Specification, as a simple superset of the XPG4 Base environment, still supports all of these functions. Interfaces exist to support:

- locale initialization
- character classification
- case conversion
- character collation
- language information
- date and time formatting
- printing and scanning
- number conversion
- string handling
- codeset conversion.

The Single UNIX Specification is also aligned with ISO/IEC 9899:1990/Amendment 1:1995 (E). The Internationalization Guide, Version 2 describes the use of these features, functions, and commands with examples, and is recommended if a developer is writing internationalized applications.

Locale Initialization and Information

The *setlocale*( ), interface, described in the ISO C standard and extended by POSIX.1, initializes a program's locale. The *nl_langinfo*( ) interface provides an application with a method of accessing key cultural information associated with the program's locale.

ISO C Amendment 1 (MSE)

Many of the character interfaces found in historical UNIX and C-language environments are byte-oriented, and they really should be wide-character-oriented to support the internationalization of applications. To overcome this problem, the set of wide-character equivalents to these interfaces derived from ISO C Amendment 1 (MSE) is mandatory in UNIX systems.

> *btowc*( ), *fgetwc*( ), *fgetws*( ), *fputwc*( ), *fputws*( ), *fwide*( ), *fwprintf*( ), *fwscanf*( ), *getwc*( ), *getwchar*( ), *iswalnum*( ), *iswalpha*( ), *iswcntrl*( ), *iswctype*( ), *iswdigit*( ), *iswgraph*( ), *iswlower*( ), *iswprint*( ), *iswpunct*( ), *iswspace*( ), *iswupper*( ), *iswxdigit*( ), *mbrlen*( ), *mbrtowc*( ), *mbsinit*( ), *mbsrtowcs*( ), *putwc*( ), *putwchar*( ), *swprintf*( ), *swscanf*( ), *towctrans*( ), *towlower*( ), *towupper*( ), *ungetwc*( ), *vfwprintf*( ), *vswprintf*( ), *vwprintf*( ), *wcrtomb*( ), *wcscat*( ), *wcschr*( ), *wcscmp*( ), *wcscpy*( ), *wcscspn*( ), *wcslen*( ), *wcsncat*( ), *wcsncmp*( ), *wcsncpy*( ), *wcspbrk*( ), *wcsrchr*( ), *wcsrtombs*( ), *wcsspn*( ), *wcsstr*( ), *wcstod*( ), *wcstok*( ), *wcstol*( ), *wcstoul*( ), *wcswcs*( ), *wcswidth*( ), *wctob*( ), *wctrans*( ), *wctype*( ), *wcwidth*( ), *wmemchr*( ), *wmemcmp*( ), *wmemcpy*( ), *wmemmove*( ), *wmemset*( ), *wprintf*( ), *wscanf*( ), **<iso646.h>**, **<wctype.h>**

Enhanced I18N Interfaces

The Enhanced I18N interfaces are extensions over the ISO C standard. They are part of the Base functionality.

> *strfmon*( ), *strptime*( ), *wcscoll*( ), *wcsftime*( ), *wcsxfrm*( )

Message Catalogs

These Base functions allow an application to build and coordinate catalogs of text strings in multiple languages, all keyed the same way, such that depending upon the program's locale, the appropriate catalog string is retrieved. This functionality allows applications to output prompts and messages in different languages.

> *catclose*( ), *catgets*( ), *catopen*( )

Character Set Conversions

These Base functions allow an application to convert character data between supported character sets.

> *iconv*( ), *iconv_close*( ), *iconv_open*( )

4.8 Encryption

The Encryption Feature Group (marked with CRYPT in the reference page headers) contains interfaces that encrypt and decrypt strings.

> *crypt*( ), *encrypt*( ), *setkey*( )

This Feature Group might not be implemented on some systems, as there are U.S. federal government export restrictions on this technology.

4.9 Legacy

The Legacy Feature Group includes the interfaces and headers which were mandatory in previous versions of the specification but are optional in this version.

These interfaces and headers are retained in the specification because of their widespread use. Application writers should not rely on the existence of these interfaces or headers in new applications, but should follow the migration path detailed in the Application Usage sections of the relevant pages.

The interfaces and headers which form this Feature Group are as follows:

> *advance*( ), *brk*( ), *chroot*( ), *compile*( ), *cuserid*( ), *gamma*( ), *getdtablesize*( ), *getpagesize*( ), *getpass*( ), *getw*( ), *putw*( ), *re_comp*( ), *re_exec*( ), *regcmp*( ), *regex*( ), *sbrk*( ), *sigstack*( ), *step*( ), *ttyslot*( ), *valloc*( ), *wait3*( ), **<regexp.h>**, **<varargs.h>**, **<re_comp.h>**

Chapter 5

Commands and Utilities

XCU, Issue 5 describes all of the utilities required in the Single UNIX Specification environment. In this chapter, the contents of XCU together with the options are described.

5.1 Options in XCU

Some of the utilities need not be present on a system conforming to the Single UNIX Specification. The optional utilities are as follows:

- DEVELOPMENT utilities are those required in a software development environment. The reference pages for these utilities are marked DEVELOPMENT.
- FORTRAN utilities are required in a FORTRAN-77 development environment, and essentially consist of the compiler, *fort77*. The reference page for this utility is marked FORTRAN.
- Legacy utilities need not be implemented. These include such commands as *lpstat* and *uulog*. The reference pages for these utilities are marked LEGACY. If a migration path exists, advice is given to application developers regarding alternative means of obtaining similar functionality. This information may be found in the Application Usage sections of the relevant pages

5.2 Functional Overview

The Single UNIX Specification supports a robust tool environment of 174 utilities, described in XCU. The Single UNIX Specification utilities are essentially identical to XPG4 Base, and provide a standards-based tool environment based on UNIX systems practice.

The X/Open UNIX utilities are a superset of POSIX.2, adding functionality that the POSIX working groups chose not to standardize at the time. This includes utilities such as:

- the *sccs* suite of tools for source code management:

  admin, delta, get, prs, rmdel, sact, sccs, unget, val, what

- the *uucp* suite of tools for UNIX-to-UNIX file copying:

  uucp, uulog, uuname, uupick, uustat, uuto, uux

- the compression utilities:

  compress, pack, pcat, uncompress, unpack, zcat

- additional C-language development tools:

  cc, cflow, cxref, lint, m4

- additional utilities:

  fuser, ipcrm, ipcs, link, unlink

- traditional archiving tools (whose archive formats are supported with the *pax* utility):

  cpio, tar

- almost 30 other miscellaneous tools and utilities. (These tools can be found in the table in Section 19.2 on page 232, without a mark in the POSIX.2 column.)

The Single UNIX Specification utilities include:

alias	*date*	*jobs*	*pcat*	*tsort*
ar	*dd*	*join*	*pr*	*tty*
asa	*df*	*kill*	*printf*	*type*
at	*diff*	*ln*	*ps*	*ulimit*
awk	*dirname*	*locale*	*pwd*	*umask*
basename	*du*	*localedef*	*read*	*unalias*
batch	*echo*	*logger*	*renice*	*uname*
bc	*ed*	*logname*	*rm*	*uncompress*
bg	*env*	*lp*	*rmdir*	*unexpand*
c89	*ex*	*ls*	*sed*	*uniq*
cal	*expand*	*mailx*	*sh*	*uucp*
cat	*expr*	*man*	*sleep*	*uudecode*
cc	*false*	*mesg*	*sort*	*uuencode*
cd	*fc*	*mkdir*	*split*	*uupack*
chgrp	*fg*	*mkfifo*	*strings*	*uustat*
chmod	*file*	*more*	*stty*	*uux*
chown	*find*	*mv*	*tabs*	*vi*
cksum	*fold*	*newgrp*	*tail*	*wait*
cmp	*gencat*	*nice*	*talk*	*wc*
comm	*getconf*	*nl*	*tee*	*who*
command	*getopts*	*nohup*	*test*	*write*
compress	*grep*	*od*	*time*	*xargs*
cp	*hash*	*paste*	*touch*	*zcat*
crontab	*head*	*patch*	*tput*	
csplit	*iconv*	*pathchk*	*tr*	
cut	*id*	*pax*	*true*	

There are two additional groups of utilities in XCU. The software development tools, marked with DEVELOPMENT in the Name section of their reference page, consist of:

admin, cflow, ctags, cxref, delta, dis, get, lex, lint, m4, make, nm, prs, rmdel, sact, sccs, strip, unget, val, what, yacc

It should be noted that both compiler front-ends, *c89* and *cc*, are not considered part of the DEVELOPMENT group. All X/Open UNIX branded systems must provide a way of compiling C-language programs. (Note that *cc* is marked LEGACY.) The rest of the tools are development tools.

The only tool that is part of the FORTRAN development environment is the compiler itself, *fort77*, marked with FORTRAN in the Name section of the reference page.

There are a set of utilities that applications should avoid using. These are denoted by LEGACY in the Synopsis section of their reference pages.

calendar, cancel, cc, col, cpio, cu, dircmp, dis, du, egrep, fgrep, line, lint, lpstat, mail, pack, pcat, pg, spell, sum, tar, unpack, uulog, uuname, uupick, uuto

The *dis* disassembler is an optional DEVELOPMENT utility, and marked OPTIONAL in its reference page Name section.

An X/Open UNIX branded system will provide all the tools in XCU, with the following provisions:

- The DEVELOPMENT utilities need not be provided.
- The FORTRAN compiler need not be provided.
- The LEGACY utilities need not be provided.
- The OPTIONAL utility, *dis*, need not be provided.

If the implementation claims to provide the DEVELOPMENT option, then all the tools in the group must be provided with the exception of *dis*.

Chapter 6

Networking Interfaces

The X/Open Networking interfaces were originally based on the X/Open Transport Interface (XTI). Sockets and the IP Address Resolution interfaces are included as part of Networking Services, Issue 5.

6.1 Functional Overview

The following sections give a functional overview of the Networking Services, Issue 5 specification.

6.1.1 X/Open Transport Interface (XTI)

The X/Open Transport Interface (XTI) defines a protocol-independent transport-service interface allowing multiple users to communicate at the OSI Reference Model transport layer. The transport layer characteristics described by the specification are supported by a variety of transport-layer protocols. XTI can be used with:

- OSI Transport Protocols
- Internet Protocols (IP)
- NetBIOS
- Minimum OSI ACSE and Presentation Protocols
- IBM SNA
- Novell IPX/SPX
- Asynchronous Transfer Mode (ATM).

The appendices for XTI over IPX/SPX Transport Providers and the broadband Asynchronous Transfer Mode (ATM) Transport Provider have been added in Networking Services, Issue 5.

t_accept( )	*t_free*( )	*t_optmgmt*( )	*t_rcvuderr*( )	*t_sndudata*( )
t_alloc( )	*t_getinfo*( )	*t_rcv*( )	*t_rcvv*( )	*t_sndv*( )
t_bind( )	*t_getprotaddr*( )	*t_rcvconnect*( )	*t_rcvvudata*( )	*t_sndvudata*( )
t_close( )	*t_getstate*( )	*t_rcvdis*( )	*t_snd*( )	*t_strerror*( )
t_connect( )	*t_listen*( )	*t_rcvrel*( )	*t_snddis*( )	*t_sync*( )
t_errno( )	*t_look*( )	*t_rcvreldata*( )	*t_sndrel*( )	*t_unbind*( )
t_error( )	*t_open*( )	*t_rcvudata*( )	*t_sndreldata*( )	

XTI is based on the SVID, Issue 2, Volume III, Networking Services Extensions that specify the Transport Level Interface (TLI). A number of refinements were made:

- After careful consideration, a minimum number of interface modifications were made to account for certain service and protocol problems.
- Dependencies on specific UNIX system versions and transport providers were removed.

An application that has been written to conform to XTI may not be immediately portable over a provider that was written to conform to TLI. Refer to Networking Services, Issue 5, **Appendix E**, **XTI and TLI**, for more information on the differences that exist between XTI and TLI.

6.1.2 Sockets Interfaces

The Sockets interfaces also provide a transport service. They were originally defined as part of the Berkeley Standard Distribution (BSD) UNIX, and now have a wide base of implementation and use. Networking Services, Issue 5 covers their use over local UNIX connections and Internet Protocols.

It should be noted that addendum reference pages appear for certain interfaces already defined in XSH. These are extensions to those interfaces to allow them to be used with sockets. For example, **<sys/stat.h>** must define a number of macros to work with sockets.

accept( )	*getsockname*( )	*recvfrom*( )	*sendto*( )	*socketpair*( )
bind( )	*getsockopt*( )	*recvmsg*( )	*setsockopt*( )	
connect( )	*listen*( )	*send*( )	*shutdown*( )	
getpeername( )	*recv*( )	*sendmsg*( )	*socket*( )	

6.1.3 IP Address Resolution Interface

The following address resolution interfaces are included as part of the Single UNIX Specification. The term *address resolution* refers to obtaining network information. These interfaces can be used in conjunction with both Sockets and XTI when using the Internet Protocol (IP).

endhostent( )	*gethostname*( )	*getservbyname*( )	*inet_lnaof*( )	*sethostent*( )
endnetent( )	*getnetbyaddr*( )	*getservbyport*( )	*inet_makeaddr*( )	*setnetent*( )
endprotoent( )	*getnetbyname*( )	*getservent*( )	*inet_netof*( )	*setprotoent*( )
endservent( )	*getnetent*( )	*h_errno*( )	*inet_network*( )	*setservent*( )
gethostbyaddr( )	*getprotobyname*( )	*htonl*( )	*inet_ntoa*( )	
gethostbyname( )	*getprotobynumber*( )	*htons*( )	*ntohl*( )	
gethostent( )	*getprotoent*( )	*inet_addr*( )	*ntohs*( )	

6.2 Networking Services, Issue 5 Migration

This section highlights the major changes in Networking Services, Issue 5 that might affect an application programmer.

6.2.1 Change of size_t to socklen_t

Many of the interfaces using **size_t** have a new abstract type, **socklen_t**, introduced as part of the data size neutrality changes in the Single UNIX Specification, Version 2.

This has been introduced due to the widespread use of **size_t** to represent lengths of various objects in the context of socket interfaces and the move to 64-bit architectures. While **size_t**, being the largest size abstract buffer length, needs to evolve so that interfaces can use 64 bits to their advantage, most of the objects it is used with do not need to evolve, as such. Thus continued use of **size_t** would have caused unnecessary evolution of the socket binary interface without any added benefit.

The interfaces affected are as follows:

- Network address length:

  accept( ), *bind*( ), *connect*( ), *getpeername*( ), *getsockname*( ), *recvfrom*( ), *sendto*( ), **<sys/socket.h>**

- Option buffer length:

  getsockopt( ), *setsockopt*( ) **<sys/socket.h>**

- **msghdr** data length:

  <sys/socket.h>

6.2.2 Introduction of t_scalar_t and t_uscalar_t for XTI

Instances of the types **unsigned long** and **long** have been changed to an abstract unsigned integral type, **t_uscalar_t**, and an abstract signed integral type, **t_scalar_t**, respectively.

t_scalar_t and **t_uscalar_t** are equal length and occupy at least 32 bits.

This has been introduced due to the use of type **long** in 64-bit environments causing a binary incompatibility problem. Since **long** in 64-bit environments is 64 bit and 32 bit in 32-bit environments, if the specification had remained as is, XTI providers would have had to provide two sets of XTI libraries and expensive conversion modules to convert structures of one form to another. XTI performance would have consequently suffered significant degradation.

This change is pervasive in Networking Services, Issue 5 XTI.

It also explicitly affects the following interfaces:

t_getinfo( ), *t_open*( ), *t_optmgmt*( ), *t_optmgmt*( ), **<xti.h>**

6.2.3 Introduction of uint16_t and uint32_t for Sockets

The instances of the types **in_addr_t** and **in_port_t** have been changed to unsigned integral types **uint32_t** and **uint16_t**, respectively. The change has been made since the functions *htons*( ), and so on, which make use of the **in_addr_t** and **in_port_t** types are, in practice, used with general 32 and 16-bit quantities, not just Internet addresses and port numbers.

The functions affected include:

htonl( ), *htons*( ), *ntohl*( ), *ntohs*( )

6.2.4 Thread-safety

Networking Services, Issue 5 has been updated to address thread-safety since the Single UNIX Specification, Version 2 includes threads. All interfaces defined by Networking Services, Issue 5 will be thread-safe, except for the following interfaces which need not be thread-safe:

gethostbyaddr( ), *gethostbyname*( ), *gethostent*( ), *getnetbyaddr*( ), *getnetbyname*( ), *getnetent*( ), *getprotobynumber*( ), *getprotobyname*( ), *getprotoent*( ), *getservbyname*( ), *getservbyport*( ), *getservent*( ), *inet_ntoa*( )

A portable multi-threaded application may only safely call these functions when access to the function is serialized.

6.2.5 Scatter/Gather Support

The following functions are new in Networking Services, Issue 5, added to support scatter/gather vectored input/output. These routines are analogous to *readv*( ) and *writev*( ) from the XSH specification.

t_rcvv( ), *t_rcvvudata*( ), *t_sndv*( ), *t_sndvudata*( )

Chapter 7

Terminal Interfaces

The Single UNIX Specification contains X/Open Curses, Issue 4, Version 2. These interfaces support a terminal-independent character screen update method. X/Open Curses, Issue 4, Version 2 is an upwardly-compatible enhancement of X/Open Curses, Issue 3, but adds considerable functionality supporting multi-byte and wide characters, color terminal devices, support for wide-spacing and non-spacing characters, color support, and modem and printer control via *terminfo*.

New interfaces are marked with ENHANCED CURSES in their reference page headers, and a portability code (EC), similar to those found in XSH, is used with shading to indicate the extended features throughout the specification.

A number of interfaces have been marked TO BE WITHDRAWN, as comments from the industry have clarified certain interfaces in the earlier X/Open Curses, Issue 3 model. These interfaces are all still available on X/Open UNIX branded systems, supporting existing applications portability, and the Application Usage section of the appropriate reference pages gives guidance to developers for how best to plan for future portability needs.

7.1 Functional Overview

X/Open Curses, Issue 4, Version 2, Chapters 1 to 3, provide all the introductory material needed to work with the X/Open Curses interfaces. These interfaces include:

add_wch( )
add_wchnstr( )
addch( )
addchstr( )
addnstr( )
addnwstr( )
attr_get( )
attr_get( )
attr_off( )
attr_on( )
attr_set( )
attroff( )
baudrate( )
beep( )
bkgd( )
bkgrnd( )
border( )
border_set( )
box( )
box_set( )
delwin( )
derwin( )
doupdate( )
dupwin( )
echo( )
echo_wchar( )
echochar( )
endwin( )
erase( )
erasechar( )
filter( )
flash( )
flushinp( )
get_wch( )
get_wstr( )
getbegyx( )
getbkgd( )
getbkgrnd( )
getcchar( )
getch( )
initscr( )
innstr( )
innwstr( )
ins_nwstr( )
ins_wch( )
ins_wstr( )
insch( )
insdelln( )
insertln( )
insnstr( )
insstr( )
instr( )
intrflush( )
inwstr( )
is_linetouched( )
isendwin( )
keyname( )
keypad( )
killchar( )
leaveok( )
pnoutrefresh( )
printw( )
putp( )
putwin( )
qiflush( )
raw( )
redrawwin( )
refresh( )
reset_prog_mode( )
resetty( )
restartterm( )
ripoffline( )
savetty( )
scanw( )
scr_dump( )
scrl( )
scrollok( )
set_curterm( )
set_term( )
setcchar( )
standend( )
start_color( )
stdscr( )
subpad( )
subwin( )
syncok( )
term_attrs( )
termattrs( )
termname( )
tgetent( )
tigetflag( )
timeout( )
touchline( )
tparm( )
tputs( )
typeahead( )
unctrl( )
ungetch( )
untouchwin( )
use_env( )

can_change_color()
cbreak()
chgat()
clear()
clearok()
clrtobot()
clrtoeol()
color_content()
color_set()
copywin()
cur_term()
curs_set()
curscr()
def_prog_mode()
del_curterm()
delay_output()
delch()
deleteln()
delscreen()
getmaxyx()
getn_wstr()
getnstr()
getparyx()
getstr()
getwin()
getyx()
halfdelay()
has_colors()
has_ic()
hline()
hline_set()
idcok()
immedok()
in_wch()
in_wchnstr()
inch()
inchnstr()
init_color()
longname()
meta()
move()
mvcur()
mvderwin()
mvprintw()
mvscanw()
mvwin()
napms()
newpad()
newterm()
newwin()
nl()
nodelay()
noqiflush()
notimeout()
overlay()
pair_content()
pechochar()
setscrreg()
setupterm()
slk_attr_off()
slk_attr_on()
slk_attr_set()
slk_attroff()
slk_attroff()
slk_attron()
slk_attrset()
slk_clear()
slk_color()
slk_init()
slk_label()
slk_nooutrefresh()
slk_refresh()
slk_restore()
slk_set()
slk_touch()
slk_wset()
vid_attr()
vid_puts()
vidattr()
vline()
vline_set()
vw_printw()
vw_scanw()
vwprintw()
vwscanw()
wattr_get()
wattr_off()
wattr_on()
wattr_set()
wcolor_set()
wunctrl()

Note that there are functions listed in the table that represent a set of related functions. For example, *addch()* represents the set of functions *addch()*, *mvaddch()*, *mvwaddch()*, and *waddch()*. A table in X/Open Curses, Issue 4, Version 2, **Section 3.6.2**, **Function Families Provided**, summarizes these families of related calls.

Go Solo 2

Part 2:

What's New in Version 2

The Open Group

Chapter 8

Overview

This chapter gives an overview of the new features in the Single UNIX Specification, Version 2. For each specification a brief description of the changes is given. Subsequent chapters in this part give more detailed information on the new features.

8.1 Introduction

The Single UNIX Specification, Version 2 incorporates and aligns with the following:

- ISO/IEC 9945-1:1996 (POSIX-1), which incorporates IEEE Std 1003.1b-1993 and IEEE Std 1003.1i-1995 (POSIX Realtime Extension), and IEEE Std 1003.1c-1995 (POSIX Threads Extension).

  The POSIX Realtime Extension is an Optional Feature Group, allowing procurement of X/Open realtime systems with predictable, bounded behavior.

  The POSIX Threads Extension permits development of applications to make significant performance gains.

- Extended threads interfaces (the X/Open Threads Extension) over POSIX threads, based on industry input from Sun, Digital, HP, and OSF DCE.
- Dynamic Linking Extensions to permit applications to share common object code across many applications, and ease maintenance of bug fixes and performance enhancements for applications.
- ISO/IEC 9899:1990/Amendment 1:1995 (E) (Multibyte support).

  This further enhances internationalized applications support.

- Data Size Neutrality and 64-bit Support (n-bit cleanup) to remove any architectural dependencies in the UNIX specification. This is of particular relevance with the ongoing move to 64-bit CPUs.
- Large File Support to permit UNIX systems to support files of arbitrary sizes. This is of particular relevance to database applications.
- Year 2000 Alignment to minimize the impact of the millennium rollover.

8.2 New Interfaces in XSH, Issue 5

New system interfaces have been originated as follows:

- POSIX Realtime Extension
- POSIX Threads Extension
- X/Open Threads Extension
- Dynamic Linking Extensions
- ISO C Amendment 1 (MSE)
- Data Size Neutrality and 64-bit Support
- Large File Support
- Miscellaneous, including Year 2000 Alignment.

8.2.1 POSIX Realtime Extension

The Single UNIX Specification, Version 2 incorporates POSIX.1b and POSIX.1i. These are organized as an Optional Feature Group within the Single UNIX Specification, Version 2, denoted by the symbol _XOPEN_REALTIME.

By organizing the majority of the POSIX.1b feature options into a single Feature Group, it is possible for applications running on an X/Open realtime system to reliably utilize a cohesive set of realtime features.

8.2.1.1 Functional Overview

The functionality introduced by the POSIX Realtime Extension includes:

- Realtime signals: A determinism improvement facility that augments the BASE signals mechanism to enable asynchronous signal notifications to an application to be queued.
- Synchronized input and output: A determinism and robustness improvement mechanism to enhance the data input and output mechanisms.
- Asynchronous input and output: A functionality enhancement to allow an application process to queue data input and output commands with asynchronous notification of completion.
- Semaphores: A minimum synchronization primitive to serve as a basis for more complex synchronization mechanisms.
- Memory locking: A performance improvement facility to bind application programs into the high-performance memory.
- Memory mapped files and shared memory: A performance improvement facility to allow for programs to access files as part of the address space and for separate application programs to have portions of their address space commonly accessible.
- Priority scheduling: A performance and determinism improvement facility to allow applications to determine the order in which threads that are ready to run are granted access to processor resources.
- High resolution clocks and timers: A functionality and determinism improvement facility to increase the resolution and capabilities of the time-base interface.
- Message passing: A functionality enhancement to add a high-performance, deterministic interprocess communication facility for local communication.

8.2.1.2 *Mandatory Functionality*

Some parts of the POSIX Realtime Extension are mandatory in the Single UNIX Specification, Version 2, since they were previously in the Single UNIX Specification. These are as follows:

Mandatory POSIX Realtime Extension interfaces:

mmap( )
munmap( )
mprotect( )
msync( )
fsync( )
fchmod( )
ftruncate( )

Mandatory POSIX Realtime Extension headers:

<sys/mman.h>

8.2.1.3 *Optional Functionality*

The majority of the rest of the POSIX Realtime Extension is mandatory when _XOPEN_REALTIME is set to a value other than −1. The exception to this is _POSIX_PRIORITIZED_IO which is always optional.

The interfaces in the Realtime Threads Feature Group are:

aio_cancel( )
aio_error( )
aio_fsync( )
aio_read( )
aio_return( )
aio_suspend( )
aio_write( )
clock_getres( )
clock_gettime( )
clock_settime( )
fdatasync( )
lio_listio( )
mlock( )
mlockall( )
mq_close( )
mq_getattr( )
mq_notify( )
mq_open( )
mq_receive( )
mq_send( )
mq_setattr( )
mq_unlink( )
munlock( )
munlockall( )
nanosleep( )
sched_get_priority_max( )
sched_get_priority_min( )
sched_getparam( )
sched_getscheduler( )
sched_rr_get_interval( )
sched_setparam( )
sched_setscheduler( )
sched_yield( )
sem_close( )
sem_destroy( )
sem_getvalue( )
sem_init( )
sem_open( )
sem_post( )
sem_trywait( )
sem_unlink( )
sem_wait( )
shm_open( )
shm_unlink( )
sigqueue( )
sigtimedwait( )
sigwaitinfo( )
timer_create( )
timer_delete( )
timer_getoverrun( )
timer_gettime( )
timer_settime( )

The headers are:

<aio.h>
<mqueue.h>
<sched.h>

See Chapter 9 on page 65 for more information.

8.2.2 POSIX Threads Extension

The Single UNIX Specification includes support for threads programming that allows multiple tasks to run concurrently within the same program.

Multi-threading capabilities give a large benefit to certain classes of applications, typically server or parallel processing applications, allowing them to:

- make significant performance gains
- increase application throughput, even on uni-processor hardware
- utilize efficient within-process communication between threads
- make efficient use of system resources.

The threads capabilities included in the Single UNIX Specification are built upon IEEE Std 1003.1c-1995, known as Pthreads, with additional X/Open Threads Extensions.

8.2.2.1 Functional Overview

Pthreads is a general threads API, specifiying a robust set of threads facilities, including new thread-specific APIs for the following:

- Thread management
- Thread-specific data
- Thread cancellation
- Thread synchronization
- Thread execution scheduling
- Thread synchronization scheduling.

The majority of the Pthreads functionality is mandatory in the Single UNIX Specification, Version 2, apart from the following interfaces covered by the Pthreads compile-time symbolic constants as defined in **<unistd.h>**:

_POSIX_THREAD_PRIO_INHERIT
_POSIX_THREAD_PRIO_PROTECT
_POSIX_THREAD_PRIORITY_SCHEDULING

These options collectively make up the Realtime Threads Feature Group.

See Chapter 10 on page 83 for more information.

8.2.2.2 Mandatory Functionality

On systems conforming to Single UNIX Specification, Version 2 the following symbols are always defined:

_POSIX_THREADS
_POSIX_THREAD_ATTR_STACKADDR
_POSIX_THREAD_SAFE_FUNCTIONS
_POSIX_THREAD_ATTR_STACKSIZE
_POSIX_THREAD_PROCESS_SHARED

Therefore, the following threads interfaces are always supported:

asctime_r( )
ctime_r( )
flockfile( )
ftrylockfile( )
funlockfile( )
getc_unlocked( )
getchar_unlocked( )
getgrgid_r( )
getgrnam_r( )
getpwnam_r( )
getpwuid_r( )
gmtime_r( )
localtime_r( )
pthread_atfork( )
pthread_attr_destroy( )
pthread_attr_getdetachstate( )
pthread_attr_getschedparam( )
pthread_attr_getstackaddr( )
pthread_attr_getstacksize( )
pthread_attr_init( )
pthread_attr_setdetachstate( )
pthread_attr_setschedparam( )
pthread_attr_setstackaddr( )
pthread_attr_setstacksize( )
pthread_cancel( )
pthread_cleanup_pop( )
pthread_cleanup_push( )
pthread_cond_broadcast( )
pthread_cond_destroy( )
pthread_cond_init( )
pthread_cond_signal( )
pthread_cond_timedwait( )
pthread_cond_wait( )
pthread_condattr_destroy( )
<pthread.h>
pthread_condattr_getpshared( )
pthread_condattr_init( )
pthread_condattr_setpshared( )
pthread_create( )
pthread_detach( )
pthread_equal( )
pthread_exit( )
pthread_getspecific( )
pthread_join( )
pthread_key_create( )
pthread_key_delete( )
pthread_kill( )
pthread_mutex_destroy( )
pthread_mutex_init( )
pthread_mutex_lock( )
pthread_mutex_trylock( )
pthread_mutex_unlock( )
pthread_mutexattr_destroy( )
pthread_mutexattr_getpshared( )
pthread_mutexattr_init( )
pthread_mutexattr_setpshared( )
pthread_once( )
pthread_self( )
pthread_setcancelstate( )
pthread_setcanceltype( )
pthread_setspecific( )
pthread_sigmask( )
pthread_testcancel( )
putc_unlocked( )
putchar_unlocked( )
rand_r( )
readdir_r( )
sigwait( )
strtok_r( )

8.2.2.3 *Optional Functionality*

The optional interfaces derived from Pthreads in the Realtime Threads Feature Group are:

pthread_attr_getinheritsched( )
pthread_attr_getschedpolicy( )
pthread_attr_getscope( )
pthread_attr_setinheritsched( )
pthread_attr_setschedpolicy( )
pthread_attr_setscope( )
pthread_getschedparam( )
pthread_setschedparam( )
pthread_mutexattr_setprotocol( )
pthread_mutexattr_getprotocol( )
pthread_mutexattr_setprioceiling( )
pthread_mutexattr_getprioceiling( )
pthread_mutex_getprioceiling( )
pthread_mutex_setprioceiling( )

8.2.3 X/Open Threads Extension

Threads support in the Single UNIX Specification adds new extensions to POSIX.1c. The threads extensions over POSIX came from the Aspen Group, and include extensions made by OSF DCE as well as Sun, HP, and Digital. The following extensions are made over POSIX.1c threads:

- extended mutex attribute types
- read-write locks and attributes — allowing simultaneous read-only access to data
- thread concurrency level — the ability to set and get levels of thread concurrency; this is an efficiency issue which can lead to better program performance
- thread stack guard size
- parallel I/O.

See Chapter 11 on page 103 for further information.

The mandatory interfaces in the X/Open Threads Extension are:

pread( )
pthread_attr_getguardsize( )
pthread_attr_setguardsize( )
pthread_getconcurrency( )
pthread_mutexattr_gettype( )
pthread_mutexattr_settype( )
pthread_rwlock_destroy( )
pthread_rwlock_init( )
pthread_rwlock_rdlock( )
pthread_rwlock_tryrdlock( )
pthread_rwlock_trywrlock( )
pthread_rwlock_unlock( )
pthread_rwlock_wrlock( )
pthread_rwlockattr_destroy( )
pthread_rwlockattr_getpshared( )
pthread_rwlockattr_init( )
pthread_rwlockattr_setpshared( )
pthread_setconcurrency( )
pwrite( )

8.2.4 Dynamic Linking Extensions

The Single UNIX Specification, Version 2 Dynamic Linking Extensions that came out of the Aspen Group comprises a set of four interfaces and a header file to provide a portable dynamic linking API.

New interfaces:

dlopen( )
dlsym( )
dlclose( )
dlerror( )

New headers:

<dlfcn.h>

See Chapter 12 on page 113 for more information.

8.2.5 ISO C Amendment 1 (MSE)

The Single UNIX Specification, Version 2 is fully aligned with ISO/IEC 9899:1990/Amendment 1:1995 (E), which adds extensive multibyte support to the ISO C standard. The value of __STDC__VERSION for this version of the specification is 199409L.

The Single UNIX Specification, Version 2 includes the following new interfaces and header files from the ISO C Amendment 1 (MSE):

New interfaces:

btowc( )	*mbsrtowcs*( )	*wcrtomb*( )	*wmemcpy*( )
fwide( )	*swprintf*( )	*wcsrtombs*( )	*wmemmove*( )
fwprintf( )	*swscanf*( )	*wcsstr*( )	*wmemset*( )
fwscanf( )	*towctrans*( )	*wctob*( )	*wprintf*( )
mbrlen( )	*vfwprintf*( )	*wctrans*( )	*wscanf*( )
mbrtowc( )	*vswprintf*( )	*wmemchr*( )	
mbsinit( )	*vwprintf*( )	*wmemcmp*( )	

New headers:

<iso646.h>
<wctype.h>

The **<iso646.h>** header contains alternative spellings for C-language tokens.

The **<wctype.h>** header contains the multibyte versions of the interfaces contained in **<ctype.h>**.

See Chapter 13 on page 115 for more information.

8.2.6 Data Size Neutrality and 64-bit Support

The following header file has been added to support new abstract types:

<inttypes.h>

8.2.7 Large File Support

The Single UNIX Specification, Version 2 includes changes submitted by the Large File Summit. See Chapter 15 on page 147. These include the following new interfaces:

fseeko( )
ftello( )

8.2.8 Miscellaneous

The following interfaces were added to address some generic problems of the form *sprintf*(*s*, *f*, *data*) or *vsprintf*(*s*, *f*, *args*) where the data written to the string is too long for the string. This can cause crashes or other security holes in vulnerable applications.

snprintf( )
vsnprintf( )

8.3 Major Changes in XCU, Issue 5

The major changes in XCU, Issue 5 are the introduction of the LEGACY class of utility and Large File Support.

8.3.1 Legacy

The commands and utilities in the table below are marked LEGACY. Support for these utilities is optional, and thus these may not be supported on all implementations. Application writers should not use functionality marked LEGACY. Many of these utilities were previously marked TO BE WITHDRAWN in XCU, Issue 4, Version 2.

To determine whether the LEGACY utilities are collectively supported use the *getconf* utility with the _XOPEN_LEGACY *system_var*.

calendar	*cpio*	*du*	*lint*	*pcat*	*tar*	*uupick*
cancel	*cu*	*egrep*	*lpstat*	*pg*	*unpack*	*uuto*
cc	*dircmp*	*fgrep*	*mail*	*spell*	*uulog*	
col	*dis*	*line*	*pack*	*sum*	*uuname*	

8.3.2 Large File Support

The following utilities support files of any size up to the maximum that can be created by the implementation.

basename	*chmod*	*cp*	*du*	*mkdir*	*rm*	*test*
cat	*chown*	*dd*	*find*	*mv*	*rmdir*	*touch*
cd	*cksum*	*df*	*ln*	*pathchk*	*sh*	*ulimit*
chgrp	*cmp*	*dirname*	*ls*	*pwd*	*sum*	

For more information on changes to XCU related to Large File Support see Chapter 15 on page 147.

8.3.3 New Utilities

The following utilities are new in XCU, Issue 5:

fuser
ipcrm
ipcs
link
unlink

8.4 New Interfaces in Networking Services, Issue 5

Networking Services, Issue 5 contains a number of new features.

The most important is the removal of implicit data length assumptions (for example, that an item of type **int** is 32 bits long). This enables the APIs to be used effectively on new computer architectures with 64-bit (or bigger) word lengths. There are other improvements too, including:

- Networking Services, Issue 5 now takes account of threads.
- Support for scatter/gather (vectored I/O, as in *readv*( ) and *writev*( )) has been added to both Sockets and XTI.
- XTI can now be used in a way that takes less of the application's name space.
- Use of XTI over IPX/SPX is now specified.
- Use of Sockets and XTI with the broadband Asynchronous Transfer Mode (ATM) protocol is now specified.

The following interfaces are new in Networking Services, Issue 5:

t_rcvv( )
t_rcvvudata( )
t_sndv( )
t_sndvudata( )

8.5 New Curses Interfaces

There are no changes to the Curses interfaces since the first version of the Single UNIX Specification. The specification remains X/Open Curses, Issue 4, Version 2, which superseded X/Open Curses, Issue 4 in July 1996.

X/Open Curses, Issue 4, Version 2 applies to both the UNIX 95 and UNIX 98 branding requirements.

X/Open Corrigenda U018 describes how to compile a curses application in a UNIX 98 branding environment. (This Corrigenda is included on the accompanying CD-ROM.)

X/Open Curses, Issue 4, Version 2 contains corrections and clarifications which have been suggested by industry feedback based on Version 1 of the specification. In particular the following changes were made:

- Many of the function prototypes are corrected.
- Color handling is further clarified.

The following interfaces are new in X/Open Curses, Issue 4, Version 2:

color_set( )
slk_color( )
term_attrs( )
wcolor_set( )

Chapter 9

POSIX Realtime

IEEE Std 1003.1b-1993 (POSIX.1b),[1] the POSIX Realtime Extension, introduces several realtime facilities to the POSIX family of standards. The realtime facilities include realtime signals, synchronized I/O, asynchronous I/O, semaphores, memory locking, memory mapped files, shared memory, priority scheduling, high-resolution clocks and timers, and message passing.

This chapter gives a programmer's overview of POSIX.1b, which is included in the Single UNIX Specification, Version 2. It describes the application programming interfaces specified under the realtime options, and it briefly explains why and how the interfaces may be used. For each option, an indication of its status within the Single UNIX Specification is given.

9.1 Introduction

POSIX.1 is the base standard upon which the POSIX family of standards is being built. In keeping with its UNIX heritage, POSIX.1 is aimed at interactive time-sharing computing environments. The IEEE PASC Realtime Working Group[2] is chartered to extend the applicability of the POSIX family of standards beyond interactive time-sharing computing to the challenging domain of realtime computing.

In the view of the IEEE PASC Realtime Working Group, the uniqueness of realtime applications stems from their requirement for predictable response times. The requirement for predictability means that traditional time-sharing operating systems cannot support realtime applications, because time-sharing operating systems are not designed to provide predictable response times. They are designed to meet other resource management objectives. In time-sharing systems, there is no overall system design binding a single, specific application to the system. Instead, there are multiple independent processes running on the system at any given time. The processes compete for system resources. Resources are managed by the operating system for the benefit of all processes; that is, the operating system serves as an "arbiter"

---

1. Copies of ISO/IEC 9945-1:1996 (POSIX-1) may be obtained by contacting:

   IEEE Customer Service
   445 Hoes Lane
   PO Box 1331
   Piscataway, NJ 08855-1331
   USA
   Tel: 1-800-678-IEEE (inside USA and Canada)
   Tel: 1-908-981-0060 (outside USA and Canada)
   Fax: 1-908-981-9667
   Email: customer.service@ieee.org

   Hereinafter, IEEE Std 1003.1-1990 (POSIX.1) is referred to as POSIX.1, IEEE Std 1003.1b-1993 is referred to as POSIX.1b, and IEEE Std 1003.1c-1995 is referred to as POSIX.1c.

2. This working group was originally designated the IEEE P1003.4 Working Group, and is now a subgroup of the larger IEEE PASC System Services Working Group (SSWG). It is sometimes referred to as SSWG-RT.

among competing processes, making sure that all processes get their fair share of system resources. In time-sharing operating systems, such as those conforming to POSIX.1, the resource management objectives are high throughput, fast average response time, and fairness of allocation of system resources to competing processes.

Realtime systems, on the other hand, are subject to an overall system design. They are dedicated to a single application, which may consist of one or more concurrent processes. Resources are still managed by the operating system, but at the direction of the application, and in accordance with the overall system design. Importantly, realtime operating systems must allow time-critical application processes to direct resource management so that the time-critical processes can control their own response times, keeping the times within established bounds, possibly resulting in delay or even total starvation of some non-time-critical application processes. In other words, realtime operating systems must support time-critical application processes in their efforts to achieve predictable response times. Fairness is not, and should not be, an objective of realtime resource management. POSIX.1b introduces preemptive, dynamic-priority-driven scheduling as its primary mechanism for enabling applications to direct the operating system in its management of resources. It also introduces memory locking interfaces, which give applications further control of resource usage.

Realtime operating systems must support predictability in other senses as well. To this end, POSIX.1b introduces interfaces for realtime signals, synchronized I/O and high-resolution clocks and timers. Realtime signals offer higher reliability than POSIX.1 signals, because the realtime signals are queued and not lost if they arrive too quickly. Synchronized I/O enables an application to ensure that critical data is actually recorded on the target storage medium and not just stored in a system buffer (that is, the file cache). High-resolution clocks and timers enable an application to more precisely monitor the system and the environment in which it is embedded, and to more accurately schedule its own actions. In other words, realtime signals offer predictability with respect to the receipt of signals; synchronized I/O offers predictability with respect to the disposition of data that has been "written" to disks or other non-volatile storage media; and high-resolution clocks and timers offer predictability with respect to the timing of events and actions.

In addition to predictability, realtime operating systems must offer high performance, because realtime applications must operate in a predictable and timely manner. In support of high performance, POSIX.1b introduces asynchronous I/O for increased concurrency; shared memory, message passing and semaphores for high-performance interprocess communication and synchronization; and memory mapped files for high-performance file access.

Altogether, POSIX.1b defines application program interfaces in nine functional areas, which are discussed in this paper in the order in which they are defined in the standard:

- Realtime signals (ISO/IEC 9945-1: 1996 (POSIX-1), §3)
- Synchronized input and output (ISO/IEC 9945-1: 1996 (POSIX-1), §5 and 6)
- Asynchronous input and output (ISO/IEC 9945-1: 1996 (POSIX-1), §6)
- Semaphores (ISO/IEC 9945-1: 1996 (POSIX-1), §11)
- Memory locking (ISO/IEC 9945-1: 1996 (POSIX-1), §12.1)
- Memory mapped files and shared memory (ISO/IEC 9945-1: 1996 (POSIX-1), §12.2 and 12.3)
- Priority scheduling (ISO/IEC 9945-1: 1996 (POSIX-1), §13)
- High-resolution clocks and timers (ISO/IEC 9945-1: 1996 (POSIX-1), §14)

- Message passing (ISO/IEC 9945-1: 1996 (POSIX-1), §15).

POSIX.1b specifies these interfaces as a series of fourteen options to POSIX.1, as illustrated below.

Option	Mandatory POSIX	Mandatory UNIX 98
_POSIX_REALTIME_SIGNALS	No	Realtime FG*
_POSIX_SYNCHRONIZED_IO	No	Realtime FG
_POSIX_FSYNC	No	Yes
_POSIX_ASYNCHRONOUS_IO	No	Realtime FG
_POSIX_PRIORITIZED_IO	No	No
_POSIX_SEMAPHORES	No	Realtime FG
_POSIX_MEMLOCK	No	Realtime FG
_POSIX_MEMLOCK_RANGE	No	Realtime FG
_POSIX_MAPPED_FILES	No	Yes
_POSIX_SHARED_MEMORY_OBJECTS	No	Realtime FG
_POSIX_MEMORY_PROTECTION	No	Yes
_POSIX_PRIORITY_SCHEDULING	No	Realtime FG
_POSIX_TIMERS	No	Realtime FG
_POSIX_MESSAGE_PASSING	No	Realtime FG

In general, an operating system implementation can choose to provide any combination of one or more of the options.[3] To guide vendors towards a small number of common, useful, and distinctive combinations, the IEEE PASC Realtime Working Group is currently developing application environment profiles capturing some of the combinations that are perceived to be the most significant. The profiles are documented in IEEE draft standard P1003.13.

With respect to the Single UNIX Specification, Version 2, the options fall into three categories, as shown in the following table. Three of the options — _POSIX_FSYNC, _POSIX_MAPPED_FILES, and _POSIX_MEMORY_PROTECTION — are mandatory for conformance to the Single UNIX Specification. All of the remaining options, except _POSIX_PRIORITIZED_IO, are grouped into a single UNIX option: the Realtime Feature Group. _POSIX_PRIORITIZED_IO remains optional.

The function mapping to POSIX.1b options is given in the table below.

Function	POSIX Option
aio_cancel( )	_POSIX_ASYNCHRONOUS_IO
aio_error( )	_POSIX_ASYNCHRONOUS_IO
aio_read( )	_POSIX_ASYNCHRONOUS_IO
aio_return( )	_POSIX_ASYNCHRONOUS_IO
aio_suspend( )	_POSIX_ASYNCHRONOUS_IO
aio_write( )	_POSIX_ASYNCHRONOUS_IO

* FG is an abbreviation for Feature Group.

3. There are some exceptions; that is, some combinations of POSIX.1b options are invalid. In particular, a few of the options cannot be provided unless certain other options are also provided. These exceptions are noted in the following sections of this chapter.

<table>
<tr><th>Function</th><th>POSIX Option</th></tr>
<tr><td>lio_listio( )</td><td>_POSIX_ASYNCHRONOUS_IO</td></tr>
<tr><td>aio_fsync( )</td><td>_POSIX_ASYNCHRONOUS_IO && _POSIX_SYNCHRONIZED_IO</td></tr>
<tr><td>fdatasync( )</td><td>_POSIX_SYNCHRONIZED_IO</td></tr>
<tr><td>fsync( )</td><td>_POSIX_FSYNC</td></tr>
<tr><td>msync( )</td><td>_POSIX_MAPPED_FILES && _POSIX_SYNCHRONIZED_IO</td></tr>
<tr><td>fchmod( )</td><td>_POSIX_MAPPED_FILES || _POSIX_SHARED_MEMORY_OBJECTS</td></tr>
<tr><td>ftruncate( )</td><td>_POSIX_MAPPED_FILES || _POSIX_SHARED_MEMORY_OBJECTS</td></tr>
<tr><td>mmap( )</td><td>_POSIX_MAPPED_FILES || _POSIX_SHARED_MEMORY_OBJECTS</td></tr>
<tr><td>munmap( )</td><td>_POSIX_MAPPED_FILES || _POSIX_SHARED_MEMORY_OBJECTS</td></tr>
<tr><td>mlockall( )</td><td>_POSIX_MEMLOCK</td></tr>
<tr><td>munlockall( )</td><td>_POSIX_MEMLOCK</td></tr>
<tr><td>mprotect( )</td><td>_POSIX_MEMORY_PROTECTION</td></tr>
<tr><td>mq_close( )</td><td>_POSIX_MESSAGE_PASSING</td></tr>
<tr><td>mq_getattr( )</td><td>_POSIX_MESSAGE_PASSING</td></tr>
<tr><td>mq_open( )</td><td>_POSIX_MESSAGE_PASSING</td></tr>
<tr><td>mq_receive( )</td><td>_POSIX_MESSAGE_PASSING</td></tr>
<tr><td>mq_send( )</td><td>_POSIX_MESSAGE_PASSING</td></tr>
<tr><td>mq_setattr( )</td><td>_POSIX_MESSAGE_PASSING</td></tr>
<tr><td>mq_unlink( )</td><td>_POSIX_MESSAGE_PASSING</td></tr>
<tr><td>mq_notify( )</td><td>_POSIX_MESSAGE_PASSING && _POSIX_REALTIME_SIGNALS</td></tr>
<tr><td>sched_get_priority_max( )</td><td>_POSIX_PRIORITY_SCHEDULING</td></tr>
<tr><td>sched_get_priority_min( )</td><td>_POSIX_PRIORITY_SCHEDULING</td></tr>
<tr><td>sched_getparam( )</td><td>_POSIX_PRIORITY_SCHEDULING</td></tr>
<tr><td>sched_getscheduler( )</td><td>_POSIX_PRIORITY_SCHEDULING</td></tr>
<tr><td>sched_rr_get_interval( )</td><td>_POSIX_PRIORITY_SCHEDULING</td></tr>
<tr><td>sched_setparam( )</td><td>_POSIX_PRIORITY_SCHEDULING</td></tr>
<tr><td>sched_setscheduler( )</td><td>_POSIX_PRIORITY_SCHEDULING</td></tr>
<tr><td>sched_yield( )</td><td>_POSIX_PRIORITY_SCHEDULING</td></tr>
<tr><td>sigqueue( )</td><td>_POSIX_REALTIME_SIGNALS</td></tr>
<tr><td>sigtimedwait( )</td><td>_POSIX_REALTIME_SIGNALS</td></tr>
<tr><td>sigwaitinfo( )</td><td>_POSIX_REALTIME_SIGNALS</td></tr>
<tr><td>sem_close( )</td><td>_POSIX_SEMAPHORES</td></tr>
<tr><td>sem_destroy( )</td><td>_POSIX_SEMAPHORES</td></tr>
<tr><td>sem_getvalue( )</td><td>_POSIX_SEMAPHORES</td></tr>
<tr><td>sem_init( )</td><td>_POSIX_SEMAPHORES</td></tr>
<tr><td>sem_open( )</td><td>_POSIX_SEMAPHORES</td></tr>
<tr><td>sem_post( )</td><td>_POSIX_SEMAPHORES</td></tr>
<tr><td>sem_trywait( )</td><td>_POSIX_SEMAPHORES</td></tr>
<tr><td>sem_unlink( )</td><td>_POSIX_SEMAPHORES</td></tr>
<tr><td>sem_wait( )</td><td>_POSIX_SEMAPHORES</td></tr>
<tr><td>shm_open( )</td><td>_POSIX_SHARED_MEMORY_OBJECTS</td></tr>
<tr><td>shm_unlink( )</td><td>_POSIX_SHARED_MEMORY_OBJECTS</td></tr>
<tr><td>clock_getres( )</td><td>_POSIX_TIMERS</td></tr>
<tr><td>clock_gettime( )</td><td>_POSIX_TIMERS</td></tr>
<tr><td>clock_settime( )</td><td>_POSIX_TIMERS</td></tr>
<tr><td>nanosleep( )</td><td>_POSIX_TIMERS</td></tr>
<tr><td>timer_create( )</td><td>_POSIX_TIMERS</td></tr>
</table>

Function	POSIX Option
timer_delete( )	_POSIX_TIMERS
timer_getoverrun( )	_POSIX_TIMERS
timer_gettime( )	_POSIX_TIMERS
timer_settime( )	_POSIX_TIMERS

9.2 Realtime Signals

Asynchronous events drive many realtime systems. For such systems, a reliable, deterministic, high-performance mechanism for notifying applications of asynchronous event occurrences is essential to the effective operation of the system. Examples of POSIX.1b asynchronous events include asynchronous I/O completion, timer expiration and message arrival, as well as user-defined events.

The POSIX.1 signal facilities are a mechanism for asynchronous event notification, but they suffer from some serious shortcomings:

1. Signals do not queue, so if a signal of a given type arrives before a previous signal of the same type is handled, then the first of the two signals will be lost.
2. Signals cannot pass data, so they cannot readily indicate specific sources of events or errors.
3. The number of user-defined signals is only two, so applications are often forced to either avoid them or to overload them; that is, to use them for multiple purposes.

POSIX.1b extends the POSIX.1 signal facilities to overcome these deficiencies. In addition, it provides new functionality that allows processes to receive signals synchronously via polling. For conformance to the Single UNIX Specification, Version 2, an implementation supports the POSIX.1b signal facilities, in their entirety, if it provides the Realtime Feature Group. POSIX.1b specifies an option (designated by the symbol[4] _POSIX_REALTIME_SIGNALS) that amends the POSIX.1 signal facilities in the following ways:

- A range of signal numbers (specified by the implementation, but of at least a certain POSIX.1b-specified minimum range) is reserved for application use. The signals falling within this range exhibit the realtime behavior cited below. They are referred to as *realtime signals*.
- Signal numbers in the reserved realtime range represent priority levels. In particular, if multiple (unblocked) signals within the realtime range are pending, they are delivered in order according to signal number (with low numbers corresponding to high priorities).
- Multiple occurrences of a specific realtime signal are queued in first-in-first-out (FIFO) order.
- When a signal is generated, an application-defined signal value — an integer or pointer — can be associated with it. The value is delivered along with the signal to the signal handler. The value can be used to distinguish between multiple occurrences of signals having the same signal number.

4. In this context, the term "symbol" denotes a C-language compile-time symbolic constant. Each POSIX option has a unique symbol associated with it. At compile time, an application can determine whether or not the symbol representing a given POSIX option is defined. If the symbol is defined, then the option is supported by the underlying POSIX implementation.

In addition, the _POSIX_REALTIME_SIGNALS option introduces the following functions:

- Sending a specified realtime signal, along with a specified signal value, to a specified process (*sigqueue*( )).
- Waiting (possibly subject to a specified timeout) for a signal from a specified set of signals to become pending (*sigwaitinfo*( ), *sigtimedwait*( )). The addition of this function enables an alternative (synchronous or polled) approach to the receiving of signals. POSIX.1 provides only an asynchronous approach; that is, signal handlers.

9.3 Synchronized Input and Output

Some realtime applications, as well as certain non-realtime applications such as database management systems, require assurance of I/O completion (for example, assurance that for a write operation to a disk, the data actually makes it to the disk and not just to a system buffer).[5] POSIX.1b provides a mechanism for obtaining such assurance. The mechanism is referred to as synchronized I/O[6] and is available under the option _POSIX_SYNCHRONIZED_IO. For conformance to the Single UNIX Specification, Version 2, an implementation supports POSIX.1b synchronized I/O if it provides the Realtime Feature Group.

Two levels of I/O synchronization are defined in POSIX.1b: synchronized I/O data integrity completion and synchronized I/O file integrity completion. Their definitions, preceded by one supporting definition, are quoted below (ISO/IEC 9945-1:1996 (POSIX-1), §2.2.2):

- *Successfully transferred*: Data is successfully transferred for a write operation to a regular file when the system ensures that all data written is readable on any subsequent open of the file (even one that follows a system or power failure) in the absence of a failure of the physical storage medium.

  Data is successfully transferred for a read operation when an image of the data on the physical storage medium is available to the requesting process.

- *Synchronized I/O data integrity completion*: Occurs when:

  1. For reads, the operation has been completed or diagnosed if unsuccessful. The read is complete only when an image of the data has been successfully transferred to the requesting process. If there were any pending write requests affecting the data to be read at the time that the synchronized read operation was requested, these write requests shall be successfully transferred prior to reading the data.

---

5. Some operating systems, such as traditional UNIX systems, perform buffered I/O for devices such as disks. In these cases, the operating system has a pool of internal buffers that serves as a file cache (often referred to as a buffer cache). For a user write operation, user data is copied from user buffers to the file cache before being written to the file on the disk. For a user read operation, file data is read from the file cache if possible (if the data is already present in the file cache); otherwise, file data is read into the file cache and then into the designated user buffer. The operating system may use various policies and mechanisms in managing the file cache. For example, to improve performance, some of the policies try to minimize the number of disk writes; they do so by delaying write operations from the file cache to the disk as long as they deem appropriate. When such policies are employed, a user write operation may return (as if "completed") after the user data has been copied to the file cache but before the data is actually written to the disk. The user has no way of determining when the data actually makes it to the disk.

6. Synchronized I/O should not be confused with synchronous I/O. It is synchronous I/O that is the complement of asynchronous I/O; the two differ in their blocking behavior. Synchronous I/O causes the caller to block until the I/O operation completes; asynchronous I/O is non-blocking: it allows the caller to continue processing in parallel with the I/O operation. Synchronized I/O, on the other hand, involves a redefinition of what it means for an I/O operation to "complete". Synchronized I/O operation can be executed synchronously or asynchronously (that is, in blocking or non-blocking mode).

2. For writes, the operation has been completed or diagnosed if unsuccessful. The write is complete only when the data specified in the write request is successfully transferred (to the physical storage medium), and all filesystem information necessary to retrieve the data is successfully transferred.

- *Synchronized I/O file integrity completion*: Identical to a synchronized I/O data integrity completion with the addition that all file attributes relative to the I/O operation (including access time, modification time, status change time) shall be successfully transferred prior to returning to the calling process.

By specifying synchronized I/O data integrity completion in addition to synchronized I/O file integrity completion, POSIX.1b is providing flexibility to application developers. File integrity offers a higher level of integrity, at the price of increased overhead; data integrity sacrifices the integrity of some file attributes, which are not essential to data access, for the sake of performance. Application developers can tradeoff integrity and performance according to the demands of their applications.

The POSIX.1b synchronized I/O facilities, available under the _POSIX_SYNCHRONIZED_IO option, provide the following capabilities:

- Specifying that I/O completion for a specified file is to be redefined as either synchronized I/O data integrity completion or synchronized I/O file integrity completion. A process can make this specification for a file that is being opened (as part of the POSIX.1 *open*( ) function) or for one that is already open (via the POSIX.1 *fcntl*( ) function).

- Requesting the operating system to "synchronize" a specified file; that is, to force all currently queued I/O operations for the file to be completed in accordance with the definition of either synchronized I/O data integrity completion or synchronized I/O file integrity completion (*fdatasync*( ) for data integrity completion and *fsync*( ) for file integrity completion).

  POSIX.1b makes the *fsync*( ) function available under a separate option, designated by the symbol _POSIX_FSYNC, as well as under the synchronized I/O option (_POSIX_SYNCHRONIZED_IO). This permits an operating system to implement the *fsync*( ) function without implementing the full complement of synchronized I/O facilities defined in POSIX.1b. For conformance to the Single UNIX Specification, Version 2, the *fsync*( ) function is required, regardless of whether or not the Realtime Feature Group is provided.

9.4 Asynchronous Input and Output

Realtime and other high-performance processes often cannot afford to suspend execution while waiting for I/O operations to be completed. They need to be able to perform I/O and computation concurrently. POSIX.1b provides asynchronous I/O (that is, non-blocking I/O) as a mechanism for obtaining such concurrency. For conformance to the Single UNIX Specification, Version 2, an implementation must support POSIX.1b asynchronous I/O if it provides the Realtime Feature Group; however, the implementation need not support the POSIX.1b prioritized I/O suboption (discussed below).

The POSIX.1b asynchronous I/O facilities, available under the _POSIX_ASYNCHRONOUS_IO option, provide the following functions:

- Asynchronously reading or writing a specified file or device (*aio_read*( ), *aio_write*( )). Control returns to the caller when the read or write operation has been initiated, or, at a minimum, queued to the specified file or device. The caller can request notification of completion[7] of the asynchronous I/O operation through the specification of a signal that is to be posted to the caller upon I/O completion. Alternatively, the caller can poll for completion, by retrieving the error status and return status of the operation from time to time.

The caller can also specify an asynchronous I/O request priority in the asynchronous I/O control block used to describe the operation. If the _POSIX_PRIORITIZED_IO and _POSIX_PRIORITY_SCHEDULING options are supported, then asynchronous I/O operations are queued in priority order (if the process's scheduling policy is SCHED_FIFO or SCHED_RR), with the priority of an operation being a function of the calling process' priority and the asynchronous I/O request priority specified in the asynchronous I/O control block associated with the operation.

- Initiating a list of asynchronous I/O operations with a single system call (*lio_listio*( )). The list-I/O operation can be designated as being either synchronous or asynchronous. For asynchronous operations, the caller can request notification of completion of the list-I/O operation through the specification of a signal.
- Retrieving the error status (*aio_error*( )) or return status (*aio_return*( )) of a specified asynchronous I/O operation (that is, asynchronous read, write, or file synchronization operation).
- Canceling either a specified asynchronous I/O operation or all asynchronous I/O operations to a specified file (*aio_cancel*( )).
- Waiting for at least one of a specified set of I/O operations to complete (*aio_suspend*( )). The caller can bound the duration of the wait through the specification of a timeout.
- Asynchronously synchronizing a file (*aio_fsync*( )), in accordance with the definition of either synchronized I/O data integrity completion or synchronized I/O file integrity completion. The caller can request notification of completion of the file synchronization operation through the specification of a signal.

9.5 Semaphores

Realtime applications typically consist of multiple concurrently executing tasks. When the tasks are implemented as processes, interprocess communication and synchronization mechanisms become critical. The mechanisms must be fast and efficient. POSIX.1b adopts the counting semaphore as its basic high-performance process synchronization mechanism. For conformance to the Single UNIX Specification, Version 2, an implementation supports POSIX.1b counting semaphores if it provides the Realtime Feature Group.

A counting semaphore is a synchronization object with a non-negative integer value. The value counts the number of available "locks" for a shared resource being protected by the semaphore. When zero, a (possibly empty) set of processes is blocked awaiting the availability of a lock.

Counting semaphores can be used for various types of synchronization. For example, a counting semaphore (namely, a binary semaphore, which is simply a special counting semaphore whose value alternates between zero and one) can be used to achieve mutual exclusion as follows:

7. At the completion of a read operation, file or device data is present in the designated user buffer. At the completion of a write operation, user data is present in the file cache (in the case of normal buffered I/O with delayed writes to physical storage), in physical storage (in the case of unbuffered I/O or synchronized I/O), or in both.

1. A process locks the semaphore associated with a given shared resource to acquire mutually exclusive use of the shared resource.
2. The process uses the shared resource.
3. The process unlocks the semaphore.

In this case, the semaphore is always unlocked by the process that locked it.

As another example, a counting semaphore can be used to synchronize producers and consumers of items such as slots in a buffer. In this case, three semaphores might be used: one to provide mutually exclusive use of the buffer and its associated indexes, one to represent the number of full slots, and one to represent the number of empty slots. The *buffer_lock* semaphore is initialized to one, the *full* semaphore is initialized to zero, and the *empty* semaphore is initialized to the total number of slots in the buffer. *Locking* a semaphore corresponds to *waiting* for a condition to become true, and *unlocking* a semaphore corresponds to *signaling* that a condition has become true. A producer executes the following sequence of actions when writing to the buffer:

1. Lock the *empty* semaphore (that is, wait for an empty slot).
2. Lock the *buffer_lock* semaphore.
3. Put a data item in the buffer, and increment the producer's index into the buffer.
4. Unlock the *buffer_lock* semaphore.
5. Unlock the *full* semaphore (that is, signal that at least one slot is full).

Similarly, a consumer executes the following sequence of actions when reading from the buffer:

1. Lock the *full* semaphore (that is, wait for a full slot).
2. Lock the *buffer_lock* semaphore.
3. Remove a data item from the buffer, and increment the consumer's index into the buffer.
4. Unlock the *buffer_lock* semaphore.
5. Unlock the *empty* semaphore (that is, signal that at least one slot is empty).

In this case, the *full* and *empty* semaphores are not unlocked by the processes that locked them. Instead, the *full* semaphore is locked by the consumer and unlocked by the producer, while the *empty* semaphore is locked by the producer and unlocked by the consumer.

The POSIX.1b semaphore facilities, available under the _POSIX_SEMAPHORES option, provide the following functions:

- Initializing or destroying a specified unnamed semaphore, identified by a pointer (*sem_init*( ), *sem_destroy*( )). Initializing the semaphore entails setting it to a specified non-negative value. Destroying the semaphore renders it unusable until it is reinitialized.

  The initialize and destroy operations do not allocate and de-allocate memory for the unnamed semaphore. Instead, they just "consecrate" and "deconsecrate" memory that has previously been allocated by the calling process. That is, the pointer used as an argument in the *sem_init*( ) call references memory in the address space of the calling process. If the semaphore is to be shared among a set of cooperating processes,[8] then the pointer must

8. If the application intends for the semaphore to be used only within a single process (for example, by POSIX.1c threads within the process), then the unnamed semaphore need not reside in shared memory.

reference memory that is shared among those same cooperating processes (that is, in a shared memory object, described in Section 9.7 on page 76).

Once the unnamed semaphore is initialized, all the processes that have access to the memory holding the semaphore can use the semaphore for synchronization until one of the processes destroys the semaphore. After the semaphore is destroyed, the application can either de-allocate the memory that held the semaphore, or it can later re-initialize (that is, *re-consecrate*) the memory for use as a "new" unnamed semaphore.

- Creating or deleting a named semaphore with a specified name (*sem_open*( ) with the O_CREAT flag, *sem_unlink*( )). At creation, the semaphore is initialized to a specified non-negative value.

  A named semaphore can be used by processes that do not share memory. A named semaphore is created by the operating system upon the request of a process (similarly to the way in which a file is created). The semaphore is identified by other processes through its name, which is globally accessible, as discussed below in the paragraph following this list of functions.

- Opening or closing a specified named semaphore (*sem_open*( ), *sem_close*( )). The open operation returns a pointer to the semaphore; the pointer is used to identify the semaphore in subsequent semaphore operations (that is, *sem_wait*( ), *sem_trywait*( ), *sem_post*( ), *sem_getvalue*( ), *sem_close*( )).

- Locking a specified (named or unnamed) semaphore (*sem_wait*( )).[9] If the initial semaphore value is positive, then the caller decrements the semaphore and proceeds with execution. If the initial semaphore value is zero, then the caller blocks and enters the queue of processes waiting on the semaphore.[10] The caller can conditionally invoke the lock operation to avoid blocking (*sem_trywait*( )); if invoked conditionally, the lock operation is performed only if the semaphore value is positive at the time of invocation and thus would be guaranteed not to block the caller.

- Unlocking a specified (named or unnamed) semaphore (*sem_post*( )). If there are processes blocked on the semaphore, then one of them is unblocked; if priority scheduling is enabled, the blocked processes are unblocked in priority order, with FIFO ordering for processes of equal priority. Otherwise, if there are no blocked processes, the semaphore is incremented.

- Getting the value of a specified (named or unnamed) semaphore (*sem_getvalue*( )).

Named semaphores, as well as shared memory objects and message queues, must have globally accessible names; they are all used for interprocess communication and synchronization, and therefore must be capable of being referenced by all the processes that are attempting to communicate or synchronize with one another. To achieve global accessibility, operating system implementations may choose to use pathnames within the filesystem name space[11] for the names of these communication and synchronization objects. However,

---

9. Regardless of whether it is named or unnamed, the semaphore is referenced through a pointer. This applies to the *sem_trywait*( ), *sem_post*( ) and *sem_getvalue*( ) functions, as well as to the *sem_wait*( ) function.

10. During system design, the application programmer should take into account the possibility of semaphore-related priority inversion. Priority inversion occurs, for example, when a high priority process locks a "busy" semaphore that is about to be unlocked by a low priority process, but the low priority process is preempted by a medium priority process. The application programmer can avoid semaphore-related priority inversion in a number of ways, such as by having critical sections that are guarded by semaphores execute at a high priority. The problem of priority inversion is addressed in the context of another synchronization primitive, the mutex, in POSIX.1c.

11. The filesystem name space is the conventional name space for global objects in POSIX systems.

POSIX.1b does not require the names to be pathnames, because of potential problems regarding some of the semantics associated with the filesystem name space (that is, the semantics associated with the many functions that take pathnames as arguments, and expect the pathnames to represent files). Instead, POSIX.1b requires the communication and synchronization objects to have names whose syntax is modeled on those for files as follows (ISO/IEC 9945-1: 1996 (POSIX-1), Change History):

> The naming of semaphore, shared memory, and message queue objects has been made consistent with filenames: global names must start with a slash character and must obey construction rules for a pathname; the semantics of extra slash characters are not specified.

Additionally, POSIX.1b requires semaphores, shared memory objects, and message queues to have protection features modeled on those for files. In particular, the objects have a user ID, a group ID, and permission bits.

9.6 Memory Locking

Realtime and other high-performance processes often cannot tolerate the response time indeterminacy and degradation that can result from memory paging or swapping. POSIX.1b provides memory locking facilities to enable a process to, in effect, turn off memory paging and swapping on its address space (or possibly a designated portion of its address space). For conformance to the Single UNIX Specification, Version 2, an implementation supports the POSIX.1b memory locking facilities, in their entirety, if it provides the Realtime Feature Group.

The POSIX.1b memory locking facilities provide the following functions:

- Locking[12] or unlocking the calling process' address space, in its entirety, into main memory (*mlockall*( ), *munlockall*( )). These functions are available under the _POSIX_MEMLOCK option.
- Locking or unlocking a specified range of the calling process' address space into main memory (*mlock*( ), *munlock*( )). These functions are available under the _POSIX_MEMLOCK_RANGE option (which can be provided only if the _POSIX_MEMLOCK option is also provided).

12. *Locking* is also referred to as *locking down* or *pinning down*.

9.7 Memory Mapped Files and Shared Memory

In addition to memory locking, the POSIX.1b memory management facilities include memory mapped files and shared memory. Memory mapped files are primarily used for high-performance file access. When a file is mapped into the address space of a process, the process no longer has to perform "read" I/O operations to bring file data into memory, and the costly buffering typically associated with read I/O operations can be avoided. Instead, the operating system's memory management facilities take over, paging portions of the file into memory as needed. For conformance to the Single UNIX Specification, Version 2, POSIX.1b memory mapped files are mandatory, regardless of whether or not an implementation provides the Realtime Feature Group.

Shared memory is used for high-performance interprocess communication. When two processes map the same *shared memory object* into their respective address spaces, they are sharing memory. When one process writes to shared memory, the changes become immediately visible to all processes sharing the memory. For conformance to the Single UNIX Specification, Version 2, POSIX.1b shared memory facilities are mandatory if and only if an implementation provides the Realtime Feature Group.

Memory mapped files can also be used for interprocess communication: when a file is mapped into the address spaces of multiple processes in MAP_SHARED mode, the processes are, in effect, sharing memory. Therefore, the processes can communicate by writing to the file.

A system may support shared memory objects without supporting memory mapped files and *vice versa*. In such a case, the mapping and unmapping functions, cited below, would apply only to the supported class of memory objects.

The POSIX.1b memory mapping and sharing facilities provide the following functions:

- Creating or deleting a shared memory object with a specified name (*shm_open*( ) with the O_CREAT flag, *shm_unlink*( )). The initial size of the shared memory object is zero.[13] Naming and protection are as described in Section 9.5 on page 72. These functions are available under the _POSIX_SHARED_MEMORY_OBJECTS option.

- Opening a specified shared memory object (*shm_open*( )). The open operation returns a file descriptor representing the shared memory object; the file descriptor is used to identify the shared memory object in subsequent memory mapping operations. This function is available under the _POSIX_SHARED_MEMORY_OBJECTS option.

  The POSIX.1 *close*( ) function can be used to close a shared memory object, since the object is represented by a file descriptor. However, POSIX.1b declares the results of several other POSIX.1 functions, such as *read*( ), *write*( ), and *lseek*( ), which also take file descriptors as arguments, to be unspecified for shared memory objects. This is to relieve certain operating systems (namely, those that do not implement shared memory objects as regular files) of the burden of implementing these file functions for shared memory objects.

- Changing the "file mode" (that is, access permissions) of an object identified by a file descriptor (*fchmod*( )). This function complements the POSIX.1 *chmod*( ) function, which operates on objects identified by pathnames. The function is available under each of the following options: _POSIX_SHARED_MEMORY_OBJECTS and _POSIX_MAPPED_FILES.

13. The file size is increased through the POSIX.1b *ftruncate*( ) function, described later in the list of functions.

- Setting the size of a specified open (possibly mapped) file or shared memory object to a specified length (*ftruncate*()). If the current size is larger than the specified length, then truncation occurs. If the current size is smaller, then extension is required to occur in the case of shared memory objects, and extension may occur in the case of files. When extension occurs, the added area is zero-filled. This function is available under each of the following options: _POSIX_SHARED_MEMORY_OBJECTS and _POSIX_MAPPED_FILES.
- Mapping or unmapping a specified portion of a specified memory object into a process' address space at a specified address (*mmap*( ), *munmap*( )). The memory object can be a file or a shared memory object. These functions are available under each of the following options: _POSIX_SHARED_MEMORY_OBJECTS and _POSIX_MAPPED_FILES.

  The caller can specify how the mapped memory can be accessed (that is, by specifying the permissions PROT_READ, PROT_WRITE, PROT_EXECUTE, PROT_NONE), but an operating system implementation is not bound to enforce access restrictions unless it supports the _POSIX_MEMORY_PROTECTION option. Even then, it is required to strictly enforce only two classes of access restriction:

  1. read/execute only (indicated by the absence of the PROT_WRITE permission)
  2. no access (indicated by the presence of the PROT_NONE permission).

     However, it is expected that many operating system implementations will enforce additional classes of access restriction (for example, read only, execute only), as they typically already do. The POSIX.1b memory protection feature is mandatory for conformance to the Single UNIX Specification, Version 2.

  In addition, for memory mapped files, the calling process can specify how its writes to the mapped data are to be handled. In one mode (MAP_SHARED), the writes are made to the underlying file itself, and the changes to the mapped data are shared with all the other processes that map the file in MAP_SHARED mode. In the other mode (MAP_PRIVATE), the writes are not made to the underlying file itself, and changes are seen only by the process doing the writes. The process, in effect, writes only to a local cached copy of the file.
- Changing the access protections (read, write, execute, none) of a specified range of the caller's address space (*mprotect*( )). This function is available under the _POSIX_MEMORY_PROTECTION option, which is mandatory for conformance to the Single UNIX Specification, Version 2.
- Requesting the operating system to synchronize the contents of a specified range of the caller's address space with its representation on permanent storage (*msync*( )), if such a representation exists, as it does for memory mapped files. The synchronization is achieved by writing modified data from memory to permanent storage. For memory mapped files, all write operations are completed in accordance with synchronized I/O data integrity completion. The caller can direct the system to invalidate all cached copies[14] of the mapped data that are inconsistent with the permanent storage representation of the data. This function is required when the following options are simultaneously present in an implementation: _POSIX_MAPPED_FILES and _POSIX_SYNCHRONIZED_IO.

  The caller can invoke the memory synchronization operation in synchronous or asynchronous mode.

14. The cached copies may be held by processes that mapped the file in MAP_PRIVATE mode.

9.8 Priority Scheduling

Realtime applications need to be able to manage their own resource usage in accordance with their mission needs. POSIX.1b provides preemptive, dynamic-priority-driven execution scheduling facilities for this purpose. Using these facilities, an application can control the execution scheduling of its constituent processes by dynamically setting and changing the priorities of the processes.[15] For conformance to the Single UNIX Specification, Version 2, an implementation supports POSIX.1b priority scheduling if it provides the Realtime Feature Group.

POSIX.1b defines two variants of preemptive, dynamic-priority-driven execution scheduling. The variants are distinguished by the way in which processes of equal priority are scheduled. In the first variant, ready processes of equal priority are scheduled according to a first-in-first-out (FIFO) policy. In the second variant, ready processes of equal priority are scheduled according to a round-robin (RR) policy, with a specified time slice, RR.

The POSIX.1b execution scheduling facilities, available under the _POSIX_PRIORITY_SCHEDULING option, provide the following functions:

- Setting or getting the scheduling parameters (in particular, the priority) of a specified process (*sched_setparam*( ), *sched_getparam*( )).
- Setting or getting the scheduling policy process of a specified process (*sched_setscheduler*( ), *sched_getscheduler*( )). The scheduling policy can be:
  1. preemptive, dynamic-priority-driven, using FIFO within a priority level (SCHED_FIFO)
  2. preemptive, dynamic-priority-driven, using RR within a priority level, with a specified time slice (SCHED_RR)
  3. implementation-dependent (SCHED_OTHER).

  The *sched_setscheduler*( ) function sets the scheduling parameters, in addition to the scheduling policy, all at once, "because a process must be able to atomically adjust its priority relative to other processes scheduled under that policy" (ISO/IEC 9945-1: 1996 (POSIX-1), §13.4.4). This is necessary due to the fact that "the current process priority may not be valid under the new scheduling policy" ISO/IEC 9945-1: 1996 (POSIX-1), §13.4.4).
- Voluntarily relinquishing control of the processor (*sched_yield*( )). In effect, the calling process moves to the end of the queue of ready processes for its priority level.
- Getting scheduling parameter limits, including:
  1. the minimum and maximum priorities that can be used with a specified policy (*sched_get_priority_min*( ), *sched_get_priority_max*( ))
  2. the duration of the round robin time slice, RR (*sched_rr_get_interval*( )).

15. Various policies, such as rate monotonic scheduling (Liu and Layland 73; Sha and Goodenough 90; Sha and Sathaye 93) and deadline monotonic scheduling (Audsley et al. 93; Leung and Whitehead 82), can be applied in setting the process priorities.

9.9 High-resolution Clocks and Timers

POSIX.1b defines interfaces to high-resolution clocks and timers, which are essential to realtime applications. These interfaces make time visible to processes and enable processes to schedule timer events in a variety of useful ways, including periodically. The **timespec** data structure that is used by these interfaces to represent time provides for nanosecond resolution.[16] For conformance to the Single UNIX Specification, Version 2, an implementation supports POSIX.1b clocks and timers if it provides the Realtime Feature Group.

The POSIX.1b clock and timer facilities, available under the _POSIX_TIMERS option, provide the following functions:

- Setting the value of, getting the value of, or getting the resolution of a specified clock (*clock_settime*( ), *clock_gettime*( ), *clock_getres*( )). The specified clock may be the system-wide realtime clock, which is designated by a standard identifier (that is, CLOCK_REALTIME).

  The purpose of allowing these functions, as well as the timer functions described below, to accept a clock ID as an argument is to make them extensible. That is, an implementation can define clocks in addition to CLOCK_REALTIME, and an application can use these same functions to access the clocks. As stated in ISO/IEC 9945-1: 1996 (POSIX-1), §14.3.1.1:

  > "This was done because of the observation that many realtime platforms support multiple clocks; and it was desired to fit this model within the standard interface. But, implementation-dependent clocks need not represent actual hardware devices, nor are they necessarily system wide. For example, the BSD process virtual and profiling timers could be implemented as *per-process* clocks.[17]"

- Creating or deleting a per-process timer, based upon a specified clock and a specified mechanism for notifying the calling process of timer expiration (*timer_create*( ), *timer_delete*( )). The notification mechanism can be either a POSIX.1 signal or a POSIX.1b realtime signal.

- Setting the value of or getting the value of a specified per-process timer (*timer_settime*( ), *timer_gettime*( )). The value of a timer consists of two parts:

  1. timer interval
  2. remaining time to the next timer expiration.

  The remaining time to the next timer expiration can be set to a given offset from the current time, or to a given absolute value. The timer interval, if non-zero, indicates that periodic timer expirations are to begin occurring after the initial timer expiration, where the period is equal to the specified timer interval.

- Getting the overrun count, timer of a specified per-process timer (*timer_getoverrun*( )). At any point in time, at most one expiration signal is queued to a process for any given timer. An overrun is said to occur when a timer expires while a previous expiration is still pending

16. The fact that the data structure can represent time in nanoseconds does not imply that the underlying clock has any particular resolution. POSIX.1b mandates a specific software representation of time (capable of storing time down to the nanosecond level) for application software portability purposes. Hardware clock resolution and software time representation are independent. It is incumbent upon the application programmer to investigate the hardware clock resolution if the application program is dependent on it.

17. IEEE PASC P1003.1d draft standard introduces per-process and per-thread CPU time clocks for execution time monitoring of processes and threads (which are introduced in POSIX.1c).

(that is, while the signal providing notification of the expiration is pending). If POSIX.1b realtime signals are supported, then a count of the overruns associated with the most recent timer expiration can be obtained.

- Suspending execution for a specified time interval (*nanosleep*( )).

9.10 Message Passing

Message passing is a crucial component of realtime systems. The constituent processes of a realtime application require high-performance, efficient message passing. To this end, POSIX.1b supports simple (primarily intra-system) message passing facilities.[18] The facilities allow processes within a system to exchange messages via message queues. For conformance to the Single UNIX Specification, Version 2, an implementation supports POSIX.1b message passing if it provides the Realtime Feature Group.

The POSIX.1b message passing facilities, available under the _POSIX_MESSAGE_PASSING option, provide the following functions:

- Creating or deleting a message queue with a specified name (*mq_open*( ) with the O_CREAT flag, *mq_unlink*( )). At creation, the caller specifies the maximum message size and the maximum number of messages that are to be held in the queue. Naming and protection are as described in Section 9.5 on page 72.
- Opening or closing a specified message queue (*mq_open*( ), *mq_close*( )). The open operation returns a message queue descriptor representing the message queue; the descriptor is used to identify the message queue in subsequent message passing operations. The message queue can be opened in different access modes (receive only, send only, receive and send). The message queue can also be opened in different blocking modes (blocking or non-blocking).[19]
- Sending a message to a specified message queue at a specified message priority (*mq_send*( )). The message to be sent is identified by a pointer (to a buffer in which the message is held) and a length. If the message queue has sufficient capacity, the message is added to the queue at a position dictated by the value of the message priority. If the message queue does not have sufficient capacity, then the caller proceeds according to the blocking mode of the message queue. If the mode is blocking, then the send operation is postponed until sufficient capacity becomes available, thus blocking the caller. (Calling processes are unblocked in order, according to their priorities.) If the mode is non-blocking, then the send operation fails and control is returned to the caller.
- Receiving a message from a specified message queue into a specified buffer (*mq_receive*( )). If the message queue is not empty, the oldest of the highest priority messages is received by the caller. If the message queue is empty, the caller proceeds according to the blocking mode of the message queue. If the mode is blocking, then the caller blocks, awaiting the arrival of a message to the queue. (Calling processes are unblocked in order according to their priorities.) If the mode is non-blocking, then the receive operation fails and control is returned to the caller.

---

18. IEEE PASC P1003.1g draft standard addresses general-purpose distributed system communication. IEEE PASC P1003.21 draft standard is addressing realtime distributed system communication.

19. Also referred to as synchronous and asynchronous, respectively.

- Registering for asynchronous notification of message arrival at a specified message queue via a specified signal (*mq_notify*( )). The notification occurs when a queue transitions from empty to non-empty. Note that the registration is for a single message arrival. The *mq_notify*( ) function must be re-invoked for each notification. A notification may be canceled by invoking *mq_notify*( ) with a null signal. The *mq_notify*( ) function is required when the following options are simultaneously present in an implementation: _POSIX_MESSAGE_PASSING and _POSIX_REALTIME_SIGNALS.
- Setting or getting the values of attributes of a specified message queue (*mq_setattr*( ), *mq_getattr*( )). The attributes that can be queried include *blocking-mode*, *maximum-message-size*, *maximum-number-of-messages*, and *number-of-currently-queued-messages*. The only one of these attributes that can actually be set dynamically is the *blocking-mode* attribute. The *maximum-message-size* attribute and the *maximum-number-of-messages* attribute are assigned static values at message queue creation. The *number-of-currently-queued-messages* attribute is a status value maintained by the operating system.

Chapter 10

POSIX Threads

POSIX.1c, the POSIX Threads Extension, introduces a robust set of thread facilities to the POSIX family of standards. These thread facilities enable programmers to create and manage multiple threads of control within a single POSIX process.

This chapter offers a programmer's overview of POSIX.1c, which is included in the Single UNIX Specification, Version 2. It describes the application programming interfaces specified under the eight threads-related options, and it briefly explains why and how the interfaces may be used. For each option, an indication of its status within the Single UNIX Specification is given.

10.1 Introduction

Many applications can be designed as a set of cooperating sequential tasks, or threads of control, each assigned to some specific aspect of the problem being solved. For example, in realtime control applications, a separate task may be assigned to each sensor and actuator. In producer-consumer applications, some tasks may be producers, and others may be consumers. In a file server, each request for service may be handled by a newly spawned task. In many applications, dedicated tasks may handle background processing, while the main task does the foreground processing. Other dedicated tasks may await asynchronous events, so that the main task does not have to be interrupted when the events occur. In parallel-programming applications, the parallel threads of execution correspond to cooperating sequential tasks, which may run simultaneously on different processors in a multiprocessor system. In all cases, effective management of the cooperating sequential tasks is vital to the success of the application.

In traditional POSIX and UNIX operating systems, a sequential task — that is, thread of control — corresponds to the process. The process is the basic programming abstraction in these operating systems. Each process has a distinct address space — access to specific files, I/O devices, and other computer system resources — and a single thread of control. Resources are not shared among processes, because the processes, in general, represent different programs that must be protected from one another. In other words, the process serves not only as a unit of concurrency, but also as a unit of resource allocation (that is, protection boundary). In these operating systems, the cooperating sequential task programming paradigm is implemented by dividing the application into multiple processes.

The problem with the POSIX process model is that the burden of being a unit of resource allocation makes the process a *heavyweight* unit of concurrency.[20] POSIX.1c addresses this problem by adding a second level of concurrency to the POSIX process model. In particular, an

20. Processes are relatively *heavyweight* in terms of the overhead incurred at process creation and at context switches, due to the amount of process context that must be established at creation and saved and restored at context switches. Processes are also heavyweight with respect to communication, since processes can share data only through the explicit use of interprocess communication mechanisms such as message passing.

application is allowed to establish concurrent threads of control within a single process. The threads of control — variously referred to as threads, C threads, pthreads, tasks, or lightweight processes — share process memory and other resources. Thus, they incur minimal overhead and can offer efficient, high-performance concurrency. The thread mechanism has been identified as being particularly important to realtime systems, multiprocessor systems, and Ada programs using the Ada tasking facility.

POSIX.1c specifies a robust set of thread facilities. In doing so, it introduces new application program interfaces in the following functional areas:

- Thread management (ISO/IEC 9945-1: 1996 (POSIX-1), §16)
- Thread-specific data (ISO/IEC 9945-1: 1996 (POSIX-1), §17)
- Thread cancellation (ISO/IEC 9945-1: 1996 (POSIX-1), §18)
- Thread synchronization (ISO/IEC 9945-1: 1996 (POSIX-1), §11)
- Thread execution scheduling (ISO/IEC 9945-1: 1996 (POSIX-1), §13.1-13.5)
- Thread synchronization scheduling (ISO/IEC 9945-1: 1996 (POSIX-1), §13.6).

POSIX.1c also amends certain interfaces in POSIX.1 and POSIX.1b:

- Process creation interfaces are amended to work in the presence of threads (ISO/IEC 9945-1: 1996 (POSIX-1), §3.1).
- Signal interfaces are amended to work in the presence of threads (ISO/IEC 9945-1: 1996 (POSIX-1), §3.3).
- Thread creation is introduced as an event notification mechanism (ISO/IEC 9945-1: 1996 (POSIX-1), §3.3).
- All POSIX.1 and POSIX.1b blocking functions are amended to suspend only the calling thread, instead of the entire process in which the thread is embedded (ISO/IEC 9945-1: 1996 (POSIX-1), §3.5, 6, 11, 14).
- The POSIX.1b blocking functions (that is, semaphore locking, message sending, message receiving) that were defined in POSIX.1b to use process priorities to resolve contention are amended to take thread priorities into account (ISO/IEC 9945-1: 1996 (POSIX-1), §11, 15).
- POSIX.1c establishes thread-safe versions of POSIX.1 and C-language functions (ISO/IEC 9945-1: 1996 (POSIX-1), §4, 5, 8, 9).
- POSIX.1c redefines *errno* in order to make it meaningful in the presence of threads (ISO/IEC 9945-1: 1996 (POSIX-1), §2.4).

POSIX.1c thread facilities are specified as a series of eight options to POSIX.1, as amended by POSIX.1b. The core facilities are part of the *threads* option, whose presence in an operating system implementation is indicated by definition of the symbol _POSIX_THREADS. The remaining facilities are placed under seven subsidiary options, as illustrated below.

Option	Mandatory POSIX	Mandatory UNIX 98
_POSIX_THREAD_SAFE_FUNCTIONS	Yes	Yes
_POSIX_THREAD_ATTR_STACKADDR	No	Yes
_POSIX_THREAD_ATTR_STACKSIZE	No	Yes
_POSIX_THREAD_PROCESS_SHARED	No	Yes
_POSIX_THREAD_PRIORITY_SCHEDULING	No	Realtime Threads FG*
_POSIX_THREAD_PRIO_INHERIT	No	Realtime Threads FG
_POSIX_THREAD_PRIO_PROTECT	No	Realtime Threads FG

One of these — _POSIX_THREAD_SAFE_FUNCTIONS — is required to be supported whenever the threads option is supported; the others need not be for POSIX threads conformance. For conformance to the Single UNIX Specification, Version 2, the threads options are split so that non-realtime functionality is mandatory, and realtime functionality is grouped into a single option: the Realtime Threads Feature Group. The facilities described in the following sections are part of the threads option, unless explicitly described as being part of one of the above options.

10.2 Thread Management

POSIX.1c introduces interfaces for creating, managing, and terminating threads, where a thread is defined as follows ISO/IEC 9945-1: 1996 (POSIX-1), §2.2.2):

> "A single flow of control within a process. Each thread has its own thread ID, scheduling priority and policy (if the thread priority scheduling option is used), errno value, thread-specific key/value bindings, and the required system resources to support a flow of control. Anything whose address may be determined by a thread ... shall be accessible to all threads in the same process."

Thus, threads share process state, including process address space, as well as other resources such as files. Threads are identified by thread IDs, which are guaranteed to be unique only within a process.

Threads have properties referred to as *thread attributes* associated with them. There is one mandatory attribute — *detachstate* — and several optional attributes. The *detachstate* attribute governs the lifetime of a thread ID. That is, if a thread is created in a *detached* state, then its thread ID loses significance upon termination of the thread; if a thread is created in a *joinable* state, then its thread ID can be used as a parameter of the *pthread_join*( ) function, discussed below in the list of interfaces.

POSIX.1c specifies two classes of optional thread attributes. The first class is associated with the POSIX.1c stack options _POSIX_THREAD_ATTR_STACKSIZE and _POSIX_THREAD_ATTR_STACKADDR, and the second class is associated with the POSIX.1c thread priority scheduling option _POSIX_THREAD_PRIORITY_SCHEDULING. The stack attributes are *stacksize*, which specifies a minimum size for the thread's stack, and *stackaddr*, which specifies the address to be used for the thread's stack. The stack attributes are mandatory for conformance to the Single UNIX Specification, Version 2. The scheduling attributes are discussed in Section 10.6 on page 92.

* FG is an abbreviation for Feature Group.

At thread creation, a thread can be assigned default attribute values, or it can be assigned attribute values as specified in a designated *thread attributes object*. Thread attributes objects, which hold the values of thread attributes, are of an *opaque* data type.[21] Accordingly, the standard defines functions for setting and getting the values of each of the attributes held in threads attributes objects. In addition, the standard defines functions for setting and getting the values of selected attributes dynamically. For example, there are functions defined to set and get the value of the thread *detachstate* attribute in a specified thread attributes object, but not to dynamically change the value of the attribute in an existing thread. On the other hand, the priority of a thread can be assigned a value at thread creation through a thread attributes object, and, in addition, the priority can be dynamically changed during the execution of a thread.

The *attributes object* concept is used not only for threads, but also for mutexes and condition variables. It is intended to support extensibility. Implementations, or future standards, can add attributes without modifying the interfaces defined in POSIX.1c. They simply add functions for setting and getting the values of the new attributes in the thread attributes object.

POSIX.1c defines the following specific functions for thread management:

- Initializing a thread attributes object (*pthread_attr_init*( )); that is, setting all attributes to default values.
- Destroying a thread attributes object (*pthread_attr_destroy*( )); that is, rendering it invalid for use until it is re-initialized. In the POSIX.1c model, a thread attributes object must be destroyed before it can be re-initialized. The effect of re-initializing a thread attributes object that has not been destroyed (and is thus still initialized) is undefined.
- Setting or getting the values of the following thread attributes in a specified thread attributes object: *detachstate*, *stacksize* and *stackaddr*. The functions are *pthread_attr_setdetachstate*( ), *pthread_attr_getdetachstate*( ), *pthread_attr_setstacksize*( ), *pthread_attr_getstacksize*( ), *pthread_attr_setstackaddr*( ), and *pthread_attr_getstackaddr*( ).
- Creating a new thread (*pthread_create*( )), with attributes having either default values or values given in a specified thread attributes object. Upon creation, the thread starts executing a specified start routine, with a specified argument. The signal mask of the newly created thread is inherited from the thread that created it.

  The same thread attributes object can be used multiple times to create multiple threads. An application programmer could also set up multiple thread attributes objects, each with different attribute values, to be used in creating different classes of threads.
- Obtaining the calling thread's ID (*pthread_self*( )).
- Comparing two specified thread IDs (*pthread_equal*( )).
- Waiting for another thread, specified by its thread ID, to terminate (*pthread_join*( )). This function represents one mechanism through which threads can synchronize their execution. Other synchronization mechanisms include mutexes, condition variables, and signals,

21. This means that the internal structure of the thread attributes object is purposely unspecified in the standard and, in effect, hidden from applications; an application can access individual attributes held in the attributes object in a portable way only through operating system functions. The standard specifies separate operating system functions for each attribute. Therefore, the addition of a new attribute entails the addition of new operating system functions for accessing the attribute in the thread attributes object, rather than the re-specification of the data type of the thread attributes object. From this viewpoint, the opaqueness of the data type is an extensibility mechanism: old applications that can safely ignore the new attribute are unaffected by the addition of the new functions, whereas they would be affected by a re-specification of the data type of the thread attributes object (that is, they would have to be recompiled).

described in Section 10.5 on page 90 and Section 10.9 on page 96.

- Terminating the calling thread (*pthread_exit*( )).

In addition, POSIX.1c defines a function, *pthread_once*( ), in support of dynamic package initialization. The function enables a package, such as a C library, to execute a specified initialization routine only once within a multi-threaded user process, upon the first invocation of the package by the process. The function, which would be called from within the package doing the initialization, is as follows.

Executing a specified initialization routine (*pthread_once*( )) only once within a process, at its first invocation. The *pthread_once*( ) function has two arguments: the initialization routine and a special-purpose flag. The flag is initialized to a special value in accordance with the standard's specification of the *pthread_once*( ) function.

The motivation, as described in ISO/IEC 9945-1:1996 (POSIX-1), §B.16.2.8, is that some C-library routines are set up to execute an initialization routine upon the first invocation of the library routine by a process. The library routine uses a flag, declared as a static variable, to indicate whether or not the initialization routine has been executed. The flag is initially set to a value indicating non-initialized. Then, when the library routine is first invoked by the process, the library routine checks the flag, finds it set to the non-initialized value, executes the initialization routine, and finally sets the flag to the initialized value. In subsequent invocations, the library routine finds the flag set to the initialized value and bypasses the call to the initialization routine.

The problem that arises when a multi-threaded process attempts to use a library routine set up in this way is that two threads might call the library routine at about the same time and both find it set to the non-initialized value. That is, the second thread might check the flag before the first has a chance to change the value to indicate initialized. The solution to this problem entails providing mutually exclusive access to the code that deals with the flag and the initialization routine. The *pthread_once*( ) function, through the use of a special-purpose flag, in effect implements this solution.

10.3 Thread-specific Data

POSIX.1c provides a mechanism that enables applications to maintain specified data on a per-thread basis. The mechanism is motivated by the need of some modules (that is, groups of related functions) to maintain selected data across function invocations (that is, to maintain static data in the C programming language). If such a module is being used by multiple threads of a multi-threaded process, then the module may need to maintain such data separately for each calling thread, depending on the particular application.

For example, consider a module consisting of push, pop, and clear stack functions. Suppose that the module declares the stack and stack pointer as static data, instead of as function parameters. If the module is being used in a multi-threaded process, in which each thread needs its own stack and stack pointer, the module must have a mechanism for maintaining per-thread stacks and stack pointers.

In the POSIX.1c model, per-thread data is maintained through a key/value mechanism, an approach designed for efficiency and ease of use.[22] A *key* is an opaque object of type

22. An application process could maintain thread-specific data in other ways. For example, it could use a hash function on thread ID as a means of access to an area of thread-specific data. Then the application process would have to manage the use of sub-areas of the thread-specific data. The POSIX.1c thread-specific data interfaces, on the other hand, provide threads more direct access to sub-areas of their thread-specific data. Moreover, the sub-areas are independent; different parts of the application process can use different sub-areas without any need for process-wide cooperation.

pthread_key_t. The *value* of a key is thread-specific; that is, each key that has been established for a multi-threaded process has a distinct value for each thread of the process. For this reason, the thread-specific data of a process is sometimes thought of as a matrix, with rows corresponding to keys and columns to threads, although implementations need not work this way. A process can have up to PTHREAD_KEYS_MAX keys (or rows), where PTHREAD_KEYS_MAX is at least 128.

Keys are of opaque data type so that operating system implementations can have freedom in setting them up to offer efficient access to thread-specific data. Instead of holding thread-specific values directly, keys may hold means of accessing thread-specific values. Conceptually, a key isolates a row of the thread-specific data matrix, and then the key uses the thread ID of the calling thread (the thread calling *pthread_getspecific*( ) or *pthread_setspecific*( )) to isolate an entry in the row, thus obtaining the desired key value.

Typically, the value associated with a given key for a given thread is a pointer to memory dynamically allocated for the exclusive use of the given thread (for example, per-thread stack and stack pointer). The scenario for establishment and use of thread-specific data can be described as follows. A module that needs to maintain static data on a per-thread basis creates a new thread-specific data key as a part of its initialization routine. At initialization, all threads of the process are assigned null values for the new key. Then, upon each thread's first invocation of the module (which can be determined by checking for a null key value), the module dynamically allocates memory for the exclusive use of the calling thread, and stores a pointer to the memory as the calling thread's value of the new key. Upon later invocations of the same module by the same thread, the module can access the thread's data through the new key (that is, the thread's value for the key). Other modules can independently create other thread-specific data keys for other per-thread data for their own use.

The interfaces for managing thread-specific data are as follows:

- Creating or deleting a process-wide key to thread-specific data (*pthread_key_create*( ), *pthread_key_delete*( )). At creation, the value of the key is initialized to NULL for all active threads in the process in which the calling thread is embedded.

  At creation, a *destructor function* optionally can be specified for the key. Upon thread termination, if the key has a non-NULL value for the terminating thread, the destructor function is invoked with the key value as its argument. It is envisioned that the destructor function would be used to release the memory identified by the key value.

- Setting or getting the calling thread's value of a specified key (*pthread_setspecific*( ), *pthread_getspecific*( )). Note that a thread can access only its own values of any keys, because there is no thread ID parameter in these functions. When a thread accesses a key, it implicitly accesses its own value of the key.

10.4 Thread Cancellation

POSIX.1c provides facilities for canceling threads. The facilities enable a thread to cancel another specified thread within the same process. The facilities are aimed at allowing applications to cancel *cooperating* threads.

A thread that is the target of cancellation must be cooperative in the following sense. Each thread controls its own cancelability state and type. The cancelability state can be *enabled* or *disabled*. For the enabled state, the type can be *asynchronous* (cancellation requests accepted at any time) or *deferred* (cancellation accepted only at designated cancellation points). By default, threads are initialized with state enabled and type deferred. An uncooperative thread could disable cancellation, and thus thwart cancellation requests.

An application is expected to make cancellation graceful by specifying cancellation cleanup handlers. The cleanup handlers perform actions such as unlocking mutexes owned by the target thread (the thread being canceled), signaling conditions that the target thread may have caused to become true, releasing resources, and so on. These actions enable other threads in the application to make progress after the cancellation occurs.

The thread cancellation facilities specified in POSIX.1c include the following functions:

- Canceling execution of a specified thread (*pthread_cancel*( )). The cancellation occurs in accordance with the target thread's cancelability state and type. If and when cancellation does occur, cancellation cleanup handlers are invoked in last-in-first-out (LIFO) order, followed by thread-specific data destructor functions in unspecified order. Then the thread is terminated.
- Setting the cancelability state of the calling thread (*pthread_setcancelstate*( )) to either enabled or disabled.
- Setting the cancelability type of the calling thread (*pthread_setcanceltype*( )) to either asynchronous or deferred.
- Creating a cancellation point (*pthread_testcancel*( )). To designate a point in its execution as a cancellation point, a thread simply makes a call to the *pthread_testcancel*( ) function at that point.
- Establishing cancellation cleanup handlers (*pthread_cleanup_push*( ) and *pthread_cleanup_pop*( )). The *pthread_cleanup_push*( ) function is used to identify a specified routine as a cleanup handler. Conceptually, the routine is pushed onto the top of the calling thread's cancellation cleanup stack. The *pthread_cleanup_pop*( ) function is used to remove and optionally execute the cleanup handler at the top of the cancellation cleanup stack.

  The *pthread_cleanup_push*( ) and *pthread_cleanup_pop*( ) functions are used in pairs within the same lexical scope. For example, a given routine of an application can begin by pushing a cleanup handler written for the routine onto the cancellation cleanup stack of a calling thread and end by popping the cleanup handler from the stack. If the routine calls another routine, the second routine can also begin by pushing a different cleanup handler onto the stack and end by popping the cleanup handler from the stack. Thus, the most recently called subroutines have their cleanup handlers at the top of the cancellation cleanup stack.

10.5 Thread Synchronization

POSIX.1c introduces mutexes and condition variables as inter-thread synchronization mechanisms. While POSIX.1b semaphores could be used,[23] mutexes and condition variables offer higher performance and enhanced robustness in many cases. As noted in POSIX.1c, semaphores have two distinct uses: locking and waiting. Mutexes take over the locking role of semaphores, while condition variables take over the waiting role. That is, the mutex (a term derived from "mutual exclusion") is a locking mechanism used by threads to ensure mutually exclusive use of shared data and critical sections of code.[24] The condition variable is a waiting mechanism used to synchronize the executions of threads with respect to higher level actions of one another.

A condition variable always has a mutex associated with it. The mutex provides mutually exclusive access to some shared data (for example, a bounded buffer). In a typical scenario, a thread locks the mutex and then uses a condition variable to wait for some condition (for example, buffer not full) to become true with respect to the shared data. After using the shared data, the thread uses another condition variable to signal that it has caused some other condition (for example, buffer not empty) to become true with respect to the shared data, and then unlocks the mutex.

Mutexes and condition variables can be applied to the producer-consumer problem as follows. Suppose a producer and consumer need to coordinate use of a bounded buffer. They can do so through the use of two condition variables, non-empty and non-full, and a mutex. The mutex protects the shared resources, namely, the buffer and its attributes (that is, count of unconsumed characters, producer's index, consumer's index). The producer's execution cycle is as follows:

1. Produce a data item.
2. Lock the mutex.
3. Check the condition that the count of unconsumed data items in the buffer is less than the number of slots in the buffer. If the condition is false, wait on the condition variable non-full (which unlocks the mutex for the duration of the wait) and then repeat the check upon return from the wait. When the condition is determined to be true, go to step 4.
4. Put a data item in the buffer, and increment both the producer's index into the buffer and the count of unconsumed data items in the buffer.
5. If the count of unconsumed data items is now equal to one, inform the consumer by signaling via the condition variable non-empty. If the consumer was blocked on non-empty, this signal unblocks it.
6. Unlock the mutex.

The consumer's execution cycle is complementary.

---

23. Mutexes and condition variables can be used only by entities that share memory. While they are introduced primarily as an inter-thread synchronization mechanism, they can also be used among processes that share memory. Semaphores, on the other hand, are primarily an interprocess synchronization mechanism, even though they can be used by threads within a process. Semaphores get around the need for shared memory through global names, which make them accessible to all processes.

24. Unlike semaphores, mutexes are always unlocked by the entity that locked them. Thus, during the time a mutex is locked, it is said to be owned by the entity that locked it. Because a mutex has an owner, priority inheritance can be applied to the use of the mutex as a means of overcoming priority inversion (see Section 10.7 on page 94).

Both mutexes and condition variables are opaque objects (of types **pthread_mutex_t** and **pthread_cond_t**, respectively), and they use the attributes object concept described above in Section 10.2 on page 85. Accordingly, the POSIX.1c mutex and condition variable facilities include the following functions:

- Initializing or destroying a mutex attributes object (*pthread_mutexattr_init*( ), *pthread_mutexattr_destroy*( )). These functions are similar to their counterparts for threads attributes objects (see Section 10.2 on page 85).
- Setting or getting the value of the mutex attribute *pshared* in a specified mutex attributes object. These functions (*pthread_mutexattr_setpshared*( ), and *pthread_mutexattr_getpshared*( )) and the attribute itself are optional. Their presence in an implementation is indicated by definition of the symbol _POSIX_THREAD_PROCESS_SHARED. They extend the boundaries within which a mutex can be used beyond the threads of a single process. In particular, they enable a mutex to be used by any threads of any processes sharing the memory in which the mutex resides. This functionality is mandatory for conformance to the Single UNIX Specification, Version 2.
- Initializing a specified mutex (*pthread_mutex_init*( )), with attributes having either default values or values given in a specified mutex attributes object. Upon initialization, the mutex is in an unlocked state.
- Destroying a specified mutex (*pthread_mutex_destroy*( )); that is, rendering it invalid for subsequent use in mutex operations other than mutex initialization.
- Initializing or destroying a condition variable attributes object. These functions (*pthread_condattr_init*( ), *pthread_condattr_destroy*( )) are similar to their counterparts for threads attributes objects and mutexes.
- Setting or getting the value of the condition variable attribute *pshared* in a specified condition variable attributes object. These optional functions (*pthread_condattr_setpshared*( ), *pthread_condattr_getpshared*( )) are similar to their counterparts for mutexes. This functionality is mandatory for conformance to the Single UNIX Specification, Version 2.
- Initializing or destroying a specified condition variable. These functions (*pthread_cond_init*( ), *pthread_cond_destroy*( )) are similar to their counterparts for mutexes.

The mutex functions defined by POSIX.1c are as follows:

- Locking a specified mutex. Two forms of interfaces are provided. The first, *pthread_mutex_lock*( ), causes the calling thread to block if the mutex is already locked. The second, *pthread_mutex_trylock*( ), is a conditional form. That is, it locks the mutex only if the mutex is currently unlocked; otherwise, it simply returns control to the calling thread. In no case does *pthread_mutex_trylock*( ) block the caller. In other words, *pthread_mutex_trylock*( ) *polls* the mutex.

  Contention for mutexes is resolved according to the scheduling attributes of the calling threads, described in Section 10.6 on page 92.

  When a thread acquires a lock on a mutex, it is said to become the owner of the mutex.
- Unlocking a specified mutex. This function (*pthread_mutex_unlock*( )) is called by the owner of a mutex to release the mutex.

The condition variable functions defined by POSIX.1c are:

- Blocking on a specified condition variable, under the protection of a specified mutex (*pthread_cond_wait*( )). Typically, prior to invoking the wait operation, the calling thread shall have locked the mutex, examined the condition associated with the condition variable by querying shared data, and found the condition to be false. The invocation of the wait operation then causes the calling thread both to release the mutex and to block on the condition variable, the release and block being done atomically.

Upon return from the wait operation, the calling thread owns the mutex and can check the condition. If the condition is true, the thread can unlock the mutex and proceed. If the condition is false, the thread can simply repeat the wait operation.

A timeout can be associated with the wait operation through the use of the *pthread_cond_timedwait*( ) function.

- Unblocking a thread or threads blocked on a specified condition variable. Two functions are provided: *pthread_cond_signal*( ) for unblocking at least one blocked thread (if any are blocked), and *pthread_cond_broadcast*( ) for unblocking all blocked threads.

  The order in which threads are unblocked depends on the scheduling attributes of the threads, particularly priority.

POSIX.1c also amends the POSIX.1b semaphore interfaces. As indicated in Section 10.11 on page 98, it amends the *sem_wait*( ) function to suspend only the calling thread, and it amends the *sem_wait*( ) and *sem_post*( ) functions to take thread priorities into account in the resolution of contention for semaphores. In addition, it introduces an optimization feature: if a semaphore is initialized with a *pshared* argument of zero, then the semaphore is to be used as an inter-thread (*versus* interprocess) synchronization mechanism, and the operating system implementation can potentially optimize its performance. If an application tries to use a semaphore whose *pshared* argument is zero for interprocess synchronization, the effect is undefined in the standard.

10.6 Thread Execution Scheduling

POSIX.1c defines thread priority scheduling facilities as an option, designated by the symbol _POSIX_THREAD_PRIORITY_SCHEDULING, modeled on the POSIX.1b process priority scheduling option. However, the thread scheduling facilities, unlike the process scheduling facilities, use the attributes object concept, previously described in Section 10.2 on page 85. For conformance to the Single UNIX Specification, Version 2, this functionality is supported if the implementation provides the Realtime Threads Feature Group.

In particular, the thread scheduling facilities add the following attributes to the thread attributes object:

- Scheduling contention scope (*contentionscope*). The contention scope may be *process-wide* or *system-wide*.[25] If a thread has process-wide contention scope, it directly contends for processor resources only with other threads in its same process. If a thread has system-wide contention scope, it contends for processor resources with all threads in the system, according to their system-level scheduling attributes.

  For threads with system-wide contention scope, their system-level scheduling attributes are equal to their thread scheduling attributes. For threads with process-wide contention scope, their system-level scheduling attributes are derived from their thread and process scheduling

25. System-wide means across an implementation of a POSIX operating system, which is generally assumed to reside on a uniprocessor or a multiprocessor. (System-wide does not mean across autonomous systems inter-connected by a local area network.)

attributes using an implementation-dependent mapping. Thus, a thread with process-wide contention scope indirectly contends for processor resources with threads of system-wide scheduling scope.

- Scheduling policy (*schedpolicy*). The policies are the same as those specified for processes in POSIX.1b:

  1. preemptive, dynamic-priority-driven, using FIFO contention resolution within a priority level (SCHED_FIFO)[26]
  2. preemptive, dynamic-priority-driven, using round robin contention resolution within a priority level (SCHED_RR)
  3. implementation-dependent (SCHED_OTHER).

  The SCHED_FIFO and SCHED_RR policies are affected by the scheduling allocation domains of threads, where the scheduling allocation domain (also known as *processor affinity*) of a thread is defined to be the set of processors on which the thread can be scheduled at any given time. In particular, these policies are guaranteed to resolve contention as described in the preceding paragraph only in the case of allocation domains of size one. For allocation domains of size greater than one, POSIX.1c does not mandate a standard definition of the operation of these policies; instead, these policies operate in an implementation-dependent manner.

- Scheduling parameters (*schedparam*, a pointer to a structure). The SCHED_FIFO and SCHED_RR policies have a single parameter (that is, priority); the SCHED_OTHER policy has implementation-dependent parameters.

- Scheduling attributes inheritance flag (*inheritsched*). This attribute indicates whether the other scheduling attributes of a thread should be inherited[27] from the creating thread, or set to the values specified in the thread attributes object being used to create the thread.

For each of the attributes, POSIX.1c defines functions for setting and getting the value of the attribute in a specified thread attributes object (that is, *pthread_attr_setscope*( ), *pthread_attr_getscope*( ), *pthread_attr_setschedpolicy*( ), *pthread_attr_getschedpolicy*( ), *pthread_attr_setschedparam*( ), *pthread_attr_getschedparam*( ), *pthread_attr_setinheritsched*( ), *pthread_attr_getinheritsched*( )). For selected attributes — that is, the scheduling policy and associated parameters — the standard also defines functions for dynamically setting and getting the value of the attribute in a specified thread (*pthread_setschedparam*( ), *pthread_getschedparam*( )).[28] The values of the other attributes (*contentionscope* and *inheritsched*) cannot be changed after thread creation. POSIX.1c also introduces a function modeled on the POSIX.1b *sched_yield*( ) function. The function, *pthread_yield*( ), causes the calling thread to relinquish control of the processor. Additionally, the *sched_yield*( ) function itself is amended to refer to the calling thread, as opposed to the calling process. The

26. The rate monotonic scheduling policy [Liu and Layland 73; Sha and Goodenough 90; Sha and Sathaye 93] can be used as the method of assigning priorities to periodic threads in a periodic system. It assigns higher priorities to threads with shorter periods.

27. Here, the priority of a thread can be inherited from its creating thread. It should be noted that the term *priority inheritance* is not used in reference to this type of inheritance. As described in Section 10.7 on page 94, priority inheritance refers to the case in which a given thread inherits the priority of a higher-priority thread that the given thread is blocking by holding a resource such as a mutex, the intention being to prevent priority inversion.

28. This function changes the scheduling policy and parameters atomically, so that threads always maintain a consistent state with respect to scheduling. Changing the policy alone, or changing some but not all parameters, would leave the thread in an incomplete, incoherent, or undesired state. For example, suppose that a (valid) priority scheduling policy is specified, but an invalid scheduling priority is specified. Then, the *pthread_setschedparam*( ) function should fail.

pthread_yield( ) function is added, because the _POSIX_THREAD_PRIORITY_SCHEDULING option may be supported in the absence of _POSIX_PRIORITY_SCHEDULING, in which case the *sched_yield*( ) function would not be available.

10.7 Thread Synchronization Scheduling

POSIX.1c addresses priority inversion (a thread of high priority being blocked by one or more threads of lower priority), through optional synchronization scheduling facilities.[29] For conformance to the Single UNIX Specification, Version 2, this functionality is supported if the implementation provides the Realtime Threads Feature Group.

The prototypical example of priority inversion is the following scenario:

1. A low priority thread locks a mutex *m*.
2. A high priority thread preempts the low priority thread and attempts to lock the mutex *m*, but blocks because the mutex is already locked by the low priority thread.
3. The low priority thread resumes execution but is immediately preempted by a medium priority thread. This causes priority inversion: the high priority thread is being delayed by lower priority threads. The priority inversion can be unbounded if, for example, medium priority threads continue to arrive.

A proven mechanism for bounding priority inversion is priority inheritance, which causes a thread blocking higher priority threads to execute at the priority of the highest-priority blocked thread. In the above example, priority inheritance would cause the low priority thread to inherit the high priority of the thread being blocked on the mutex lock operation, and would consequently reduce the period of priority inversion caused by the low priority thread to the duration of the critical section that the low priority thread is executing under the protection of the mutex. However, other low priority threads could be holding other mutexes required by the high priority thread, leading to an extended period of priority inversion, namely, a chain of blocking of duration equal to the sum of the lengths of all the critical sections in the chain. Basic priority inheritance can be extended, through priority ceiling protocols, to address this problem (Sha and Goodenough 90; Sha et al. 90).

POSIX.1c specifies the basic priority inheritance protocol under the option _POSIX_THREAD_PRIO_INHERIT. It specifies the *priority ceiling protocol emulation*, an efficiently implementable variant of the original priority ceiling protocol, under the option _POSIX_THREAD_PRIO_PROTECT. The facilities use the mutex attributes object, adding the following attributes:

- Mutex protocol (*protocol*). The protocol indicates whether the mutex should be used with:
  1. the basic priority inheritance protocol
  2. the priority ceiling protocol emulation

29. Priority inversion is a problem associated with realtime systems. It is not generally regarded as a serious problem in non-realtime systems for two main reasons. First, non-realtime systems have fairness, throughput, and average response time as measures of merit. The lengthening of a single response time is not considered to be a disaster in non-realtime systems, whereas in realtime systems it can lead to a missed deadline and ultimately failure of the mission. Second, fairness-based schedulers typically employ various mechanisms to ensure the forward progress of all processes and threads, albeit slowly, so the inversion eventually resolves itself.

3. no priority inheritance protocol.

- Mutex priority ceiling (*prioceiling*). If the priority ceiling protocol emulation is specified, then a priority ceiling needs to be specified. The priority ceiling of a mutex is the priority of the highest-priority thread that ever locks it. (The application developer knows which thread, because the developer assigns priorities to threads and also determines which threads use which mutexes for synchronization). Under the priority ceiling protocol emulation, a thread executes a critical section at a priority equal to the highest priority ceiling of all the mutexes it owns at the time of entry to the critical section. The use of the priority ceiling protocol emulation eliminates chained blocking, reducing the period of priority inversion to the length of at most one critical section.

For each of these attributes, POSIX.1c defines functions for setting and getting the value of the attribute in a specified mutex attributes object (*pthread_mutexattr_setprotocol*( ), *pthread_mutexattr_getprotocol*( ), *pthread_mutexattr_setprioceiling*( ), *pthread_mutexattr_getprioceiling*( )). The mutex attributes object can be used at mutex initialization time to initialize the attributes of a mutex to specified values. Furthermore, the standard defines functions for dynamically changing and examining the priority ceiling of a specified mutex (*pthread_mutex_setprioceiling*( ) and *pthread_mutex_getprioceiling*( )). These functions can be used to alter the priority ceilings of mutexes when the priorities of the threads that use them are changed (for example, when a realtime system changes mode, to move from one phase of a mission to another).

10.8 Process Creation

POSIX.1c amends the process creation facilities of POSIX.1. In particular, it specifies how the process creation functions behave in the case of multi-threaded processes.

It should be recalled that in POSIX.1, process creation is achieved through the *fork*( ) and *exec*( ) functions. The *fork*( ) function is used to create a child process, whose process image is identical to the parent process image, with the exception of a few attributes, such as process ID, parent process ID, and accumulated user and system CPU times. Upon successful completion of the *fork*( ) function, both the parent process and the child process resume execution at the point following the return from *fork*( ). Typically, a conditional statement follows the call to *fork*( ); the conditional statement specifies one action for the parent and another for the child. If the child process is intended to run a different program, its action is to call one of the *exec*( ) functions to replace its current process image with a new process image from a specified executable file. On the other hand, if the child process is intended to serve as a new thread of control within the same program, then it simply continues executing its original process image.

POSIX.1c amends the *fork*( ) and *exec*( ) functions as follows:

- The *fork*( ) function is required to create a single-threaded process; when called from within a multi-threaded process, only one thread — the calling thread — is replicated in the child process.
- When called from within a multi-threaded process, the *exec*( ) functions cause all threads of the calling process to be terminated, and the specified executable file to be loaded and made ready for execution.

In addition, POSIX.1c introduces the following function:

- Registration of fork handlers (*pthread_atfork*( )). The fork handlers are routines that are to be executed in association with calls to the *fork*( ) function. There are three classes of fork handlers: *prepare*, *parent*, and *child*. Prepare fork handlers are executed prior to *fork*( )

processing, in the context of the calling thread. Parent fork handlers are executed upon completion of *fork*( ) processing in the parent, again in the context of the calling thread. Child fork handlers are executed upon completion of fork() processing in the child, in the context of the single thread initially existing in the child process.

Fork handlers are envisioned as a mechanism for dealing with the problem of *orphaned mutexes* that can occur when a multi-threaded process calls *fork*( ). The problem arises when threads other than the calling thread own mutexes at the time of the call to *fork*( ). Since the non-calling threads are not replicated in the child process, the child process is created with mutexes locked by non-existent threads. These mutexes can therefore never be unlocked.

Fork handlers are intended to resolve the problem of orphaned mutexes in the following way. Prepare fork handlers can be written to lock all mutexes. In this way, orphaned mutexes are avoided, and the resources protected by the mutexes are not left in inconsistent states. This is due to the fact that the calling thread itself, which is replicated in the child process, has locked all mutexes. Thus, both the parent and child processes have all mutexes locked upon completion of *fork*( ) processing, at which time the parent and child fork handlers execute. The parent and child fork handlers unlock mutexes locked by the prepare fork handler.

Fork handlers are especially useful in enabling independently-developed libraries and application programs to protect themselves from one another. A multi-threaded library can protect itself from application programs that issue *fork*( ) operations, possibly without even knowing that the library is multi-threaded, by providing fork handlers. Similarly, an application program can protect itself from *fork*( ) operations issued by library functions.

10.9 Signal Interfaces

Signals are the mechanism for notifying processes of POSIX.1 events such as keyboard interrupts, timer expirations, floating point overflows, invalid hardware instructions and invalid memory references, as well as POSIX.1b events such as asynchronous I/O completion, timer expiration, and message arrival. Signals are also used for limited interprocess communication; a process can send a specified signal (for example, terminate, stop, continue, or application-defined in the case of POSIX.1b realtime signals) to a specified process.

POSIX.1c specifies how signals behave in a multi-threaded process. In particular, it amends the POSIX.1 signal facilities, as amended by POSIX.1b, as follows:

- At generation, a signal is associated with either:

  1. the process, or

  2. a specific thread within the process.

  As stated in ISO/IEC 9945-1: 1996 (POSIX-1), §3.3.1.2:

  > "Signals that are generated by some action attributable to a particular thread, such as a hardware fault, shall be generated for the thread that caused the signal to be generated. Signals that are generated in association with a process ID or process group ID or an asynchronous event such as terminal activity shall be generated for the process."

  Timer expirations represent another class of asynchronous events.[30] In keeping with the

POSIX.1c signal model quoted above, in which signals denoting asynchronous events are generated for the process, the signals stemming from POSIX.1b timer expirations are left intact by POSIX.1c. In other words, the signals are generated for the process, and not for the thread that created the timer. Moreover, POSIX.1c clarifies the POSIX.1 *alarm*( ) function by specifying that the SIGALRM signal is generated for the process, and not for the thread that called *alarm*( ).[31]

- Signal masks are maintained on a per-thread basis. Thus, each thread of a multi-threaded process can independently specify which signals are to be blocked from delivery to it. A new function (*pthread_sigmask*( )) is defined for examining and changing the signal mask of a thread within a multi-threaded process. The interface is modeled on the POSIX.1 interface *sigprocmask*( ), whose behavior is declared by POSIX.1c to be unspecified in a multi-threaded process.
- However, in the interest of minimality and efficiency, the action to be taken upon delivery of a signal is specified on a process-wide basis as being one of the following: take the default action associated with the signal, ignore the signal, or execute a specified signal-catching function.
- Also in the interest of minimality and efficiency, signals are not delivered to multiple threads. POSIX.1 signals are delivered to at most one thread; POSIX.1b signals are delivered to exactly one thread.[32] If a signal was generated for a specific thread, then it is sent to that thread. If a signal was generated for the process, then it is sent to one thread of the process. The choice of thread is unspecified in POSIX.1c; implementations are free to deliver the signal to any eligible thread. An application can reduce the set of eligible threads to one specific thread through signal masks. The thread that receives the signal can then distribute the signal to the pertinent thread(s); for example, via condition variables or the *pthread_kill*( ) function (described below in the list of new functions).
- Whenever a signal with a specified signal action of terminate, stop, or continue is delivered to a thread, the signal action applies not just to the target thread, but to the entire process in which the thread is embedded. That is, all the threads of the process are terminated, stopped, or continued, in accordance with the specified signal action. This means that single-threaded programs may be rewritten as multi-threaded programs without their externally visible signal behavior changing.
- The POSIX.1 function *sigpending*( ) is amended to apply to signals pending for either the process or the calling thread.
- The POSIX.1 function *sigsuspend*( ) is amended to suspend only the calling thread.
- The POSIX.1b functions *sigwaitinfo*( ) and *sigtimedwait*( ) are amended to suspend only the calling thread. POSIX.1c also introduces the following functions:

---

30. An asynchronous event is simply an event whose time of occurrence is not tied to a specific point in the instruction sequence of a program.

31. Signals resulting from multiple invocations of the *alarm*( ) function are indistinguishable. Thus, the *alarm*( ) function cannot easily be used in a multi-threaded process, unless only one of the threads uses the *alarm*( ) function. On the other hand, signals indicating the expirations of POSIX.1b timers can be distinguished — when used in conjunction with POSIX.1b realtime signals — through the assignment of unique signal numbers or unique signal values to the realtime signals associated with the timers.

32. Recall that in the case of a single-threaded process, POSIX.1 signals are delivered *at most once* (some may be lost), whereas POSIX.1b realtime signals are delivered *exactly once* (they are queued, rather than overwritten).

— Examining and changing the signal mask of a thread within a multi-threaded process (*pthread_sigmask*( ), which was mentioned above in the discussion on signal masks).

— Waiting for a signal from a specified set of signals to become pending (*sigwait*( )). The idea is that a thread would use its signal mask to block asynchronous delivery of signals and then use this function to poll for occurrences of the events represented by the signals.

When more than one thread is using *sigwait*( ) to wait for the same signal, only one thread returns from *sigwait*( ) when the signal becomes pending. The choice of thread is unspecified in POSIX.1c.

— Sending a specified signal to a specified thread (*pthread_kill*( )).[33]

10.10 Thread Creation

POSIX.1c introduces a new event notification mechanism, based on thread creation. It does so by extending the POSIX.1b realtime signal facilities to enable a process to designate thread creation (in particular, execution of a specified notification function within a newly created thread) as a notification mechanism for a specified event (designated by a realtime signal number). The notification function is invoked with the signal value generated at the time of the event as an input parameter.

10.11 Blocking Functions

POSIX.1c amends POSIX.1 and POSIX.1b to ensure that all blocking functions suspend only the calling thread, and not the entire process in which the thread is embedded. The functions that are explicitly amended include the following:

- POSIX.1 functions *wait*( ) and *waitpid*( ) (ISO/IEC 9945-1: 1996 (POSIX-1), §3.2)
- POSIX.1 function *sigsuspend*( ) and POSIX.1b functions *sigwaitinfo*( ) and *sigtimedwait*( ) (ISO/IEC 9945-1: 1996 (POSIX-1), §3.3)[34]
- POSIX.1 functions *pause*( ) and *sleep*( ) (ISO/IEC 9945-1: 1996 (POSIX-1), §3.4)
- POSIX.1 function *open*( ) (ISO/IEC 9945-1: 1996 (POSIX-1), §5)
- POSIX.1 functions *read*( ), *write*( ), *fcntl*( ) (when the command argument F_SETLKW is used), and POSIX.1b functions *lio_listio*( ) (when the synchronization option LIO_WAIT is used) and *aio_suspend*( ) (ISO/IEC 9945-1: 1996 (POSIX-1), §6)
- POSIX.1b function *sem_wait*( ) (ISO/IEC 9945-1: 1996 (POSIX-1), §11)
- POSIX.1b function *nanosleep*( ) (ISO/IEC 9945-1: 1996 (POSIX-1), §14).

The IEEE PASC Realtime Working Group[35] did not find it necessary to explicitly amend all

33. The name *pthread_kill*( ) is used to denote the similarity of this function to the POSIX.1 *kill*( ) function, which is the general interface used to send a signal to a process. Both are misnamed, because only certain signals, sent under certain conditions, cause the termination of the thread or process.

34. Previously noted in Section 10.9 on page 96. Repeated here for completeness.

35. This working group was originally designated the IEEE P1003.4 Working Group, and is now a subgroup of the larger IEEE PASC System Services Working Group (SSWG). It is sometimes referred to as SSWG-RT.

POSIX.1 and POSIX.1b blocking functions, due to the wording used in the descriptions of some of the functions. That is, some of the descriptions do not state that the calling process blocks; instead, they state that the function call blocks. For example, the *mqsend*( ) function specification states the following (POSIX.1b, §5.2.4.2):

> "If the specified message queue is full ... *mq_send*( ) shall block until space becomes available to enqueue the message ..."

POSIX.1c amends selected POSIX.1b functions to use thread priorities, if applicable, in the resolution of resource contention. The selected functions are those that were defined in POSIX.1b to use process priorities for resolving resource contention:

- *sem_wait*( ) and *sem_post*( ) (ISO/IEC 9945-1: 1996 (POSIX-1), §11.2.6-11.2.7)
- *mq_send*( ) and *mq_receive*( ) (ISO/IEC 9945-1: 1996 (POSIX-1), §15.2.4-15.2.5).

As in POSIX.1b, the focus of POSIX.1c is on processor scheduling, in part to minimize the impact on existing standards (that is, POSIX.1), as well as existing implementations, which typically do not depend on priorities for resolving all resource contention. This is why only selected functions are mandated to use process and/or thread priorities in resolving resource contention.

10.12 Thread-safe POSIX.1 and C-language Functions

POSIX.1 and C-language functions were written to work in an environment of single-threaded processes. Reentrancy was not an issue in their design: the possibility of a process attempting to *re-enter* a function through concurrent invocations was not considered, because threads — the enabler of concurrency within a process — were not anticipated.

So, as it turns out, some POSIX.1 and C-language functions are inherently non-reentrant with respect to threads; that is, their interface specifications preclude reentrancy.[36] For example, some functions (such as *asctime*( )) return a pointer to a result stored in memory space allocated by the function on a per-process basis. Such a function is non-reentrant, because its result can be overwritten by successive invocations. Other POSIX.1 and C-language functions, while not inherently non-reentrant, may be implemented in ways that lead to non-reentrancy. For example, some functions (such as *rand*( )) store state information (such as a seed value, which survives multiple function invocations) in memory space allocated by the function on a per-process basis. The implementation of such a function is non-reentrant if the implementation fails to synchronize invocations of the function and thus fails to protect the state information. The problem is that when the state information is not protected, concurrent invocations can interfere with one another (for example, see the same seed value).

Functions must be reentrant in an environment of multi-threaded processes, in order to ensure that they can be safely invoked by concurrently executing threads. POSIX.1c takes three actions in the pursuit of reentrancy. First, POSIX.1c imposes reentrancy as a general rule: all functions, unless explicitly singled out as exceptions to the rule, must be implemented in a way that preserves reentrancy. Second, POSIX.1c redefines *errno*, as described below in Section 10.13 on page 102. Third, for those functions whose interface specifications preclude

36. In POSIX.1c, a *reentrant function* is defined as a "function whose effect, when called by two or more threads, is guaranteed to be as if the threads each executed the function one after another in an undefined order, even if the actual execution is interleaved" (ISO/IEC 9945-1: 1996 (POSIX-1), §2.2.2).

reentrancy, POSIX.1c defines alternative reentrant versions as follows:

- As previously noted, some functions are non-reentrant because they return results in per-process library-allocated structures that may be static and thus subject to overwriting by successive calls. These include:

  — The POSIX.1 process environment functions *getlogin*( ) and *ttyname*( ) (see ISO/IEC 9945-1: 1996 (POSIX-1), §4.2.4 and 4.7.2)

  — The C-language functions *asctime*( ), *ctime*( ), *gmtime*( ), and *localtime*( ) (see ISO/IEC 9945-1: 1996 (POSIX-1), §8.3.4 to 8.3.7)

  — The POSIX.1 system database functions *getgrgid*( ), *getgrnam*( ), *getpwuid*( ), and *getpwnam*( ) (see ISO/IEC 9945-1: 1996 (POSIX-1), §9.2.1 and 9.2.2).

  POSIX.1c defines reentrant versions of these functions; the new functions have _r appended to the function names (for example, *asctime_r*( )). To achieve reentrancy, the new _r functions replace library-allocated structures with application-allocated structures that are passed as arguments to the functions at invocation.

- Some functions can be reentrant or non-reentrant, depending on their arguments. These include the C-language function *tmpnam*( ) and the POSIX.1 process environment function *ctermid*( ). These functions have pointers to character strings as arguments. If the pointers are not NULL, the functions store their results in the character string; however, if the pointers are NULL, the functions store their results in an area that may be static and thus subject to overwriting by successive calls.

  To ensure reentrancy of these functions, POSIX.1c simply restricts their arguments to non-NULL (ISO/IEC 9945-1: 1996 (POSIX-1), §4.7.1 and 8.2.5).

- As previously noted, some functions are non-reentrant because they communicate across multiple function invocations by maintaining state information in static library-allocated storage, which is shared by all the threads of a process, possibly without the benefit of synchronization. These include the C-language function *rand*( ), which is used to generate a process-wide pseudorandom number sequence. The function *rand*( ), which is called with no arguments, returns the next pseudorandom number in a sequence determined by an initial seed value (set via the function *srand*( )). As a side effect, the function *rand*( ) updates the seed value, enabling the sequence to progress. The seed value is held in a library-allocated static memory location. In a multi-threaded process, two or more threads might concurrently invoke *rand*( ), read the same seed value, and thus acquire the same pseudorandom number.

  POSIX.1c defines a reentrant version, *rand_r*( ), of this function (ISO/IEC 9945-1: 1996 (POSIX-1), §8.3.3). To ensure reentrancy, the *rand_r*( ) function is required to synchronize (that is, serialize) calls to itself, so that a thread is forced to finish acquiring one pseudorandom number in a sequence before another thread can begin to acquire the next number in the sequence.

  In addition to reentrancy, the *rand_r*( ) function offers applications flexibility in generating pseudorandom number sequences. It does so through the introduction of an argument: a pointer to an application-supplied memory location that is used to hold the seed value. As indicated above, an application can use *rand_r*( ) to generate a reliable process-wide pseudorandom number sequence (that is, a sequence without replicates). Alternatively, an application can use *rand_r*( ) to generate per-thread pseudorandom number sequences, by having each thread use a distinct seed as its *rand_r*( ) argument. In fact, an application can use *rand_r*( ) to generate an arbitrary number of uncorrelated sequences of pseudorandom numbers (each sequence governed by a distinct seed), which could prove to be useful in

Monte Carlo simulations and other similar applications.

Other functions in this class include:

— The C-language function *strtok*( ) (see ISO/IEC 9945-1: 1996 (POSIX-1), §8.3.3), which is used to find the next token in a string.

— The POSIX.1 file and directory function *readdir*( ), which is used to read the next entry in a directory stream. Note that this function also suffers from the problem of returning its result in a library-allocated structure. Both deficiencies are resolved in the reentrant version *readdir_r*( ) (ISO/IEC 9945-1: 1996 (POSIX-1), §5.1.2).

- The POSIX.1 and C-language functions that operate on character streams (represented by pointers to objects of type FILE) are required by POSIX.1c to be implemented in such a way that reentrancy is achieved (see ISO/IEC 9945-1: 1996 (POSIX-1), §8.2). This requirement has a drawback; it imposes substantial performance penalties because of the synchronization that must be built into the implementations of the functions for the sake of reentrancy. POSIX.1c addresses this tradeoff between reentrancy (safety) and performance by introducing high-performance, but non-reentrant (potentially unsafe), versions of the following C-language standard I/O functions: *getc*( ), *getchar*( ), *putc*( ), and *putchar*( ). The non-reentrant versions are named *getc_unlocked*( ), and so on, to stress their unsafeness.

  To make it possible for multi-threaded applications to use the non-reentrant versions of the standard I/O functions safely, POSIX.1c introduces the following character stream locking functions: *flockfile*( ), *ftrylockfile*( ), and *funlockfile*( ). An application thread can use these functions to ensure that a sequence of I/O operations on a given character stream is executed as a unit (without interference from other threads).[37]

  As stated in the description of the character stream locking functions, all standard I/O functions that reference character streams shall behave as if they use *flockfile*( ) and *funlockfile*( ) internally to obtain ownership of the character streams. Thus, when an application thread locks a character stream, the standard I/O functions cannot be used by other threads to operate on the character stream until the thread holding the lock releases it.

The specifications introduced by POSIX.1c for the purpose of ensuring reentrancy of POSIX.1 and C-language functions are mandatory for operating system implementations that support threads. They are optional for implementations that do not support threads. This is accomplished in the standard by associating the reentrancy specifications with a separate option, _POSIX_THREAD_SAFE_FUNCTIONS, which is declared to be mandatory for implementations supporting the threads option. Accordingly, this option is mandatory for conformance to the Single UNIX Specification, Version 2.

37. It should be noted that the *flockfile*( ) function, like the *pthread_mutex_lock*( ) function, can lead to priority inversion. The application developer should take this into account when designing an application and analyzing its performance.

10.13 Redefinition of errno

In POSIX.1, *errno* is defined as an external global variable. But this definition is unacceptable in a multi-threaded environment, because its use can result in non-deterministic results. The problem is that two or more threads can encounter errors, all causing the same *errno* to be set. Under these circumstances, a thread might end up checking *errno* after it has already been updated by another thread.

To circumvent the resulting non-determinism, POSIX.1c redefines *errno* as a service that can access the per-thread error number as follows (ISO/IEC 9945-1: 1996 (POSIX-1), §2.4):

> "Some functions may provide the error number in a variable accessed through the symbol *errno*. The symbol *errno* is defined by including the header **<errno.h>**, as specified by the ISO C standard ... For each thread of a process, the value of *errno* shall not be affected by function calls or assignments to *errno* by other threads."

In addition, all POSIX.1c functions avoid using *errno* and, instead, return the error number directly as the function return value, with a return value of zero indicating that no error was detected. This strategy is, in fact, being followed on a POSIX-wide basis for all new functions.

Chapter 11

X/Open Threads

System Interfaces and Headers, Issue 5 (XSH) includes the threads model and interfaces defined in IEEE Std 1003.1c-1995 together with a number of extensions. These extensions, based on widely accepted existing industry practice, were developed by the Aspen Group and submitted to X/Open. This chapter is a brief introduction to these extensions. It assumes a working knowledge of the threads model specified in POSIX.1c and threads programming concepts in general.

11.1 Introduction

The X/Open Threads Extension is built upon the threads model and interfaces defined in IEEE Std 1003.1c-1995, commonly known as POSIX.1c or Pthreads. POSIX.1c contains much optional functionality. When POSIX.1c was incorporated into XSH, Issue 5, the majority of the POSIX.1c optional functionality was made mandatory and additional functionality, known as the Aspen threads extensions, was incorporated at the request of the Aspen Group.

11.2 The Aspen Group

Over the past few years almost all UNIX system vendors implemented some flavor of a threads package based on the POSIX.1c interfaces. Each vendor found that the POSIX.1c interfaces were not complete in solving all their threads requirements. Consequently, each vendor implemented extensions to their thread packages to meet those requirements.

Unfortunately for application developers, not all vendors implemented the same exact set of extensions. To make things worse, the same functionality was added, but used different interface names or parameter sets. In short, this resulted in proprietary threads interfaces that are not portable across implementations, yet certain applications, such as database engines, were making heavy use of these proprietary interfaces.

Fortunately, many of the threads extensions developed were general enough that they are easily supported on any UNIX system threads implementation. In late 1995, the Aspen Group formed a subgroup to standardize the interfaces and functionality of the common thread extensions that various UNIX system vendors had implemented. The threads extensions that came out of this work by the Aspen Group comprise extensions that were made for OSF DCE 1.0 as well as others by Sun, HP, and Digital. The Aspen Group handed the completed work over to X/Open in 1996 as input to the next issue of XSH.

The following extensions to POSIX.1c were agreed by the Aspen Group:

- extended mutex attribute types
- read-write locks and attributes
- thread concurrency level

- thread stack guard size
- parallel I/O.

A total of 19 new functions were specified.

The Aspen Group carefully followed the threads programming model specified in POSIX.1c when developing these extensions. As with POSIX.1c all the new functions return zero if successful, otherwise an error number is returned to indicate the error.

The concept of attribute objects was introduced in POSIX.1c to allow implementations to extend the standard without changing the existing interfaces. Attribute objects were defined for threads, mutexes, and condition variables. Attributes objects are defined as implementation-dependent opaque types to aid extensibility, and functions are defined to allow attributes to be set or retrieved. The Aspen Group followed this model when adding the new type attribute of **pthread_mutexattr_t** or the new read-write lock attributes object **pthread_rwlockattr_t**.

11.3 Extended Mutex Attributes

POSIX.1c defines a mutex attributes object as an implementation-dependent opaque object of type **pthread_mutexattr_t**, and specifies a number of attributes which this object must have and a number of functions which manipulate these attributes. These attributes include *detachstate*, *inheritsched*, *schedparm*, *schedpolicy*, *contentionscope*, *stackaddr*, and *stacksize*.

XSH, Issue 5 specifies another mutex attribute called *type*. The *type* attribute allows applications to specify the behavior of mutex locking operations in situations where the POSIX.1c behavior is undefined. The OSF DCE threads implementation, based on Draft 4 of POSIX.1c, specified a similar attribute. Note that the names of the attributes have changed somewhat from the OSF DCE threads implementation.

XSH, Issue 5 also extends the specification of the following POSIX.1c functions which manipulate mutexes:

pthread_mutex_lock( )
pthread_mutex_trylock( )
pthread_mutex_unlock( )

to take account of the new mutex attribute type and to specify behavior which was declared as undefined in POSIX.1c. How a calling thread acquires or releases a mutex now depends upon the mutex *type* attribute.

The *type* attribute can have the following values:

Value	Definition
PTHREAD_MUTEX_NORMAL	Basic mutex with no specific error checking built in. Does not report a deadlock error.
PTHREAD_MUTEX_RECURSIVE	Allows any thread to recursively lock a mutex. The mutex must be unlocked an equal number of times to release the mutex.
PTHREAD_MUTEX_ERRORCHECK	Detects and reports simple usage errors; that is, an attempt to unlock a mutex that is not locked by the calling thread or that is not locked at all, or an attempt to relock a mutex the thread

Value	Definition
	already owns.
PTHREAD_MUTEX_DEFAULT	The default mutex type. May be mapped to any of the above mutex types or may be an implementation-dependent type.

Normal mutexes do not detect deadlock conditions; for example, a thread will hang if it tries to relock a normal mutex that it already owns. Attempting to unlock a mutex locked by another thread, or unlocking an unlocked mutex, results in undefined behavior. Normal mutexes will usually be the fastest type of mutex available on a platform but provide the least error checking.

Recursive mutexes are useful for converting old code where it is difficult to establish clear boundaries of synchronization. A thread can relock a recursive mutex without first unlocking it. The relocking deadlock which can occur with normal mutexes cannot occur with this type of mutex. However, multiple locks of a recursive mutex require the same number of unlocks to release the mutex before another thread can acquire the mutex. Furthermore, this type of mutex maintains the concept of an owner. Thus, a thread attempting to unlock a recursive mutex which another thread has locked returns with an error. A thread attempting to unlock a recursive mutex that is not locked shall return with an error. Never use a recursive mutex with condition variables because the implicit unlock performed by *pthread_cond_wait*( ) or *pthread_cond_timedwait*( ) will not actually release the mutex if it had been locked multiple times.

Errorcheck mutexes provide error checking and are useful primarily as a debugging aid. A thread attempting to relock an errorcheck mutex without first unlocking it returns with an error. Again, this type of mutex maintains the concept of an owner. Thus, a thread attempting to unlock an errorcheck mutex which another thread has locked returns with an error. A thread attempting to unlock an errorcheck mutex that is not locked also returns with an error. It should be noted that errorcheck mutexes will almost always be much slower than normal mutexes due to the extra state checks performed.

The *default* mutex type provides implementation-dependent error checking. The default mutex may be mapped to one of the other defined types or may be something entirely different. This enables each vendor to provide the mutex semantics which the vendor feels will be most useful to their target users. Most vendors will probably choose to make normal mutexes the default so as to give applications the benefit of the fastest type of mutexes available on their platform. Check your implementation's documentation.

An application developer can use any of the mutex types almost interchangeably as long as the application does not depend upon the implementation detecting (or failing to detect) any particular errors. Note that a recursive mutex can be used with condition variable waits as long as the application never recursively locks the mutex.

Two functions are provided in XSH, Issue 5 for manipulating the *type* attribute of a mutex attributes object. This attribute is set or returned in the *type* parameter of these functions. The *pthread_mutexattr_settype*( ) function is used to set a specific type value while *pthread_mutexattr_gettype*( ) is used to return the type of the mutex. Setting the *type* attribute of a mutex attributes object affects only mutexes initialized using that mutex attributes object. Changing the *type* attribute does not affect mutexes previously initialized using that mutex attributes object.

11.4 Read-Write Locks and Attributes

Read-write locks (also known as readers-writer locks) allow a thread to exclusively lock some shared data while updating that data, or allow any number of threads to have simultaneous read-only access to the data.

Unlike a mutex, a read-write lock distinguishes between reading data and writing data. A mutex excludes all other threads. A read-write lock allows other threads access to the data, providing no thread is modifying the data. Thus, a read-write lock is less primitive than either a mutex-condition variable pair or a semaphore.

Application developers should consider using a read-write lock rather than a mutex to protect data that is frequently referenced but seldom modified. Most threads (readers) will be able to read the data without waiting and will only have to block when some other thread (a writer) is in the process of modifying the data. Conversely a thread that wants to change the data is forced to wait until there are no readers. This type of lock is often used to facilitate parallel access to data on multiprocessor platforms or to avoid context switches on single processor platforms where multiple threads access the same data.

If a read-write lock becomes unlocked and there are multiple threads waiting to acquire the write lock, the implementation's scheduling policy determines which thread shall acquire the read-write lock for writing. If there are multiple threads blocked on a read-write lock for both read locks and write locks, it is unspecified whether the readers or a writer acquire the lock first. However, for performance reasons, implementations often favor writers over readers to avoid potential writer starvation.

A read-write lock object is an implementation-dependent opaque object of type **pthread_rwlock_t** as defined in **<pthread.h>**. There are two different sorts of locks associated with a read-write lock — a *read lock* and a *write lock*.

The *pthread_rwlockattr_init*( ) function initializes a read-write lock attributes object with the default value for all the attributes defined in the implementation. After a read-write lock attributes object has been used to initialize one or more read-write locks, changes to the read-write lock attributes object, including destruction, do not affect previously initialized read-write locks.

Implementations must provide at least the read-write lock attribute process-shared. This attribute can have the following values:

Value	Definition
PTHREAD_PROCESS_SHARED	Any thread of any process that has access to the memory where the read-write lock resides can manipulate the read-write lock.
PTHREAD_PROCESS_PRIVATE	Only threads created within the same process as the thread that initialized the read-write lock can manipulate the read-write lock. This is the default value.

The *pthread_rwlockattr_setpshared*( ) function is used to set the process-shared attribute of an initialized read-write lock attributes object while the function *pthread_rwlockattr_getpshared*( ) obtains the current value of the process-shared attribute.

A read-write lock attributes object is destroyed using the *pthread_rwlockattr_destroy*( ) function. The effect of subsequent use of the read-write lock attributes object is undefined.

A thread creates a read-write lock using the *pthread_rwlock_init*( ) function. The attributes of the read-write lock can be specified by the application developer, otherwise the default implementation-dependent read-write lock attributes are used if the pointer to the read-write lock attributes object is NULL. In cases where the default attributes are appropriate, the PTHREAD_RWLOCK_INITIALIZER macro can be used to initialize statically allocated read-write locks.

A thread which wants to apply a read lock to the read-write lock can use either *pthread_rwlock_rdlock*( ) or *pthread_rwlock_tryrdlock*( ). If *pthread_rwlock_rdlock*( ) is used, the thread acquires a read lock if a writer does not hold the write lock and there are no writers blocked on the write lock. If a read lock is not acquired, the calling thread blocks until it can acquire a lock. However, if *pthread_rwlock_tryrdlock*( ) is used, the function returns immediately with the error EBUSY if any thread holds a write lock or there are blocked writers waiting for the write lock.

A thread which wants to apply a write lock to the read-write lock can use either of two functions: *pthread_rwlock_wrlock*( ) or *pthread_rwlock_trywrlock*( ). If *pthread_rwlock_wrlock*( ) is used, the thread acquires the write lock if no other reader or writer threads hold the read-write lock. If the write lock is not acquired, the thread blocks until it can acquire the write lock. However, if *pthread_rwlock_trywrlock*( ) is used, the function returns immediately with the error EBUSY if any thread is holding either a read or a write lock.

The *pthread_rwlock_unlock*( ) function is used to unlock a read-write lock object held by the calling thread. Results are undefined if the read-write lock is not held by the calling thread. If there are other read locks currently held on the read-write lock object, the read-write lock object shall remain in the read locked state but without the current thread as one of its owners. If this function releases the last read lock for this read-write lock object, the read-write lock object shall be put in the unlocked read state. If this function is called to release a write lock for this read-write lock object, the read-write lock object shall be put in the unlocked state.

The same POSIX working group which developed POSIX.1b and POSIX.1c is currently developing IEEE PASC P1003.1j draft standard, which specifies a set of extensions for realtime and threaded programming. This includes readers-writer locks which are nearly identical to the XSH, Issue 5 read-write locks. The Aspen Group was aware of this draft standard, but felt that there was an immediate and urgent need for standardization in the area of read-write locks.

The following table maps the XSH, Issue 5 read-write lock functions to their equivalent IEEE PASC P1003.1j draft 5 functions:

XSH, Issue 5	IEEE PASC P1003.1j
pthread_rwlock_init( )	*rwlock_init*( )
pthread_rwlock_destroy( )	*rwlock_destroy*( )
pthread_rwlock_rdlock( )	*rwlock_rlock*( )
pthread_rwlock_tryrdlock( )	*rwlock_tryrlock*( )
pthread_rwlock_wrlock( )	*rwlock_wlock*( )
pthread_rwlock_trywrlock( )	*rwlock_trywlock*( )
pthread_rwlock_unlock( )	*rwlock_unlock*( )
pthread_rwlockattr_init( )	*rwlock_attr_init*( )
pthread_rwlockattr_destroy( )	*rwlock_attr_destroy*( )
pthread_rwlockattr_setpshared( )	*rwlock_attr_setpshared*( )
pthread_rwlockattr_getpshared( )	*rwlock_attr_getpshared*( )

The Aspen Group chose function names which are different from those used in the IEEE PASC P1003.1j draft standard to avoid name space conflicts with those interfaces. Note that draft 5 requires the header **<semaphore.h>** while XSH, Issue 5 requires the **<pthread.h>** header. However, it is hoped that the final POSIX.1j standard will adopt the Aspen functions names and headers instead of the current ones.

11.5 Thread Concurrency Level

On threads implementations that multiplex user threads onto a smaller set of kernel execution entities, the system attempts to create a reasonable number of kernel execution entities for the application upon application startup.

On some implementations, these kernel entities are retained by user threads that block in the kernel. Other implementations do not *timeslice* user threads so that multiple compute-bound user threads can share a kernel thread. On such implementations, some applications may use up all the available kernel execution entities before its user-space threads are used up. The process may be left with user threads capable of doing work for the application but with no way to schedule them.

The *pthread_setconcurrency*( ) function enables an application to request more kernel entities; that is, specify a desired concurrency level. However, this function merely provides a hint to the implementation. The implementation is free to ignore this request or to provide some other number of kernel entities. If an implementation does not multiplex user threads onto a smaller number of kernel execution entities, the *pthread_setconcurrency*( ) function has no effect.

The *pthread_setconcurrency*( ) function may also have an effect on implementations where the kernel mode and user mode schedulers cooperate to ensure that ready user threads are not prevented from running by other threads blocked in the kernel.

The *pthread_getconcurrency*( ) function always returns the value set by a previous call to *pthread_setconcurrency*( ). However, if *pthread_setconcurrency*( ) was not previously called, this function shall return zero to indicate that the threads implementation is maintaining the concurrency level.

11.6 Thread Stack Guard Size

DCE threads introduced the concept of a *thread stack guard size*. Most thread implementations add a region of protected memory to a thread's stack, commonly known as a *guard region*, as a safety measure to prevent stack pointer overflow in one thread from corrupting the contents of another thread's stack. The default size of the guard regions attribute is PAGESIZE bytes and is implementation-dependent.

Some application developers may wish to change the stack guard size. When an application creates a large number of threads, the extra page allocated for each stack may strain system resources. In addition to the extra page of memory, the kernel's memory manager has to keep track of the different protections on adjoining pages. When this is a problem, the application developer may request a guard size of 0 bytes to conserve system resources by eliminating stack overflow protection.

Conversely an application that allocates large data structures such as arrays on the stack may wish to increase the default guard size in order to detect stack overflow. If a thread allocates two pages for a data array, a single guard page provides little protection against thread stack overflows since the thread can corrupt adjoining memory beyond the guard page.

XSH, Issue 5 defines a new attribute of a thread attributes object; that is, the *guardsize* attribute which allows applications to specify the size of the guard region of a thread's stack.

Two functions are provided for manipulating a thread's stack guard size. The *pthread_attr_setguardsize*( ) function sets the thread *guardsize* attribute, and the *pthread_attr_getguardsize*( ) function retrieves the current value.

An implementation may round up the requested guard size to a multiple of the configurable system variable PAGESIZE. In this case, *pthread_attr_getguardsize*( ) returns the guard size specified by the previous *pthread_attr_setguardsize*( ) function call and not the rounded up value.

If an application is managing its own thread stacks using the *stackaddr* attribute, the *guardsize* attribute is ignored and no stack overflow protection is provided. In this case, it is the responsibility of the application to manage stack overflow along with stack allocation.

11.7 Parallel I/O

Many I/O intensive applications, such as database engines, attempt to improve performance through the use of parallel I/O. However, POSIX.1 does not support parallel I/O very well because the current offset of a file is an attribute of the file descriptor.

Suppose two or more threads independently issue read requests on the same file. To read specific data from a file, a thread must first call *lseek*( ) to seek to the proper offset in the file, and then call *read*( ) to retrieve the required data. If more than one thread does this at the same time, the first thread may complete its seek call, but before it gets a chance to issue its read call a second thread may complete its seek call, resulting in the first thread accessing incorrect data when it issues its read call. One workaround is to lock the file descriptor while seeking and reading or writing, but this reduces parallelism and adds overhead.

Instead, XSH, Issue 5 provides two functions to make seek/read and seek/write operations atomic. The file descriptor's current offset is unchanged, thus allowing multiple read and write operations to proceed in parallel. This improves the I/O performance of threaded applications. The *pread*( ) function is used to do an atomic read of data from a file into a buffer. Conversely, the *pwrite*( ) function does an atomic write of data from a buffer to a file.

11.8 Functional Overview

The **<pthread.h>** header defines the following new types:

- **pthread_rwlock_t**

  Read-write lock object.

- **pthread_rwlockattr_t**

  Read-write lock attributes object.

The **<pthread.h>** header defines the following new macros:

- PTHREAD_RWLOCK_INITIALIZER

  Statically initialize a read-write lock object.

All of the following functions have their prototypes defined in **<pthread.h>**:

- *pthread_mutexattr_gettype*( )

  Get the value of the *type* attribute of the specified mutex attribute object *attr*.

```
int pthread_mutexattr_gettype(const pthread_mutexattr_t *attr,
    int *type);
```

- *pthread_mutexattr_settype*( )

  Set the value of the *type* attribute of the specified mutex attribute object *attr*.

  ```
  int pthread_mutexattr_settype(pthread_mutexattr_t *attr,
      int *type);
  ```

- *pthread_rwlock_init*( )

  Initialize the read-write lock object *rwlock*.

  ```
  int pthread_rwlock_init(pthread_rwlock_t *rwlock,
      const pthread_rwlockattr_t *attr);
  ```

- *pthread_rwlock_rdlock*( )

  Lock the read-write lock object *rwlock* for reading.

  ```
  int pthread_rwlock_rdlock(pthread_rwlock_t *rwlock);
  ```

- *pthread_rwlock_tryrdlock*( )

  Lock the read-write lock object *rwlock* for reading unless there is an existing write lock or blocked writers.

  ```
  int pthread_rwlock_tryrdlock(pthread_rwlock_t *rwlock);
  ```

- *pthread_rwlock_wrlock*( )

  Lock the read-write lock object *rwlock* for writing. Block, if necessary, until the write lock becomes available.

  ```
  int pthread_rwlock_wrlock(pthread_rwlock_t *rwlock);
  ```

- *pthread_rwlock_trywrlock*( )

  Lock the read-write lock object *rwlock* for writing unless there are any existing read or write locks.

  ```
  int pthread_rwlock_trywrlock(pthread_rwlock_t *rwlock);
  ```

- *pthread_rwlock_unlock*( )

  Unlock the read-write lock object *rwlock*.

  ```
  int pthread_rwlock_unlock(pthread_rwlock_t *rwlock);
  ```

- *pthread_rwlock_destroy*( )

  Destroy the read-write lock object *rwlock*.

  ```
  int pthread_rwlock_destroy(pthread_rwlock_t *rwlock);
  ```

- *pthread_rwlockattr_init*( )

  Initialize the read-write lock attributes object *rwlockattr*.

  ```
  int pthread_rwlockattr_init(pthread_rwlock_t *rwlockattr);
  ```

- *pthread_rwlockattr_getpshared*( )

  Get the value of the process-shared attribute of the read-write lock attributes object *rwlockattr*.

  ```
  int pthread_rwlockattr_getpshared(const pthread_rwlockattr_t
      *rwlockattr, int *pshared);
  ```

- *pthread_rwlockattr_setpshared*( )

  Set the value of the process-shared attribute of the read-write lock attributes object *rwlockattr*.

  ```
  int pthread_rwlockattr_setpshared(pthread_rwlockattr_t *rwlockattr,
      int *pshared);
  ```

- *thread_rwlockattr_destroy*( )

  Destroy the read-write lock attributes object *rwlockattr*.

  ```
  int pthread_rwlockattr_destroy(pthread_rwlock_t *rwlockattr);
  ```

- *pthread_getconcurrency*( )

  Get the level of thread concurrency.

  ```
  int pthread_getconcurrency(void);
  ```

- *pthread_setconcurrency*( )

  Set the level of thread concurrency.

  ```
  int pthread_setconcurrency(int new_level);
  ```

- *pthread_attr_getguardsize*( )

  Get the value of the *guardsize* attribute of the thread attributes object *attr*.

  ```
  int pthread_attr_getguardsize(const pthread_attr_t *attr,
      size_t *guardsize);
  ```

- *pthread_attr_setguardsize*( )

  Set the value of the *guardsize* attribute of the thread attributes object *attr*.

  ```
  int pthread_attr_setguardsize(pthread_attr_t *attr, size_t guardsize);
  ```

- *pread*( )

  Read *nbyte* bytes from offset *offset* in the file opened on file descriptor *filedes*.

  ```
  size_t pread(int filedes, void *buf, size_t nbyte, off_t offset);
  ```

- *pwrite*( )

  Write *nbyte* bytes from offset *offset* in the file opened on file descriptor *filedes*.

  ```
  size_t pwrite(int filedes, void *buf, size_t nbyte, off_t offset);
  ```

Chapter 12

Dynamic Linking

This chapter gives a brief outline of the Dynamic Linking Extension included in Single UNIX Specification, Version 2. These changes were put forward by the Aspen Group.

12.1 Introduction

The Dynamic Linking Extension that came out of the Aspen Group comprises a set of four interfaces and a header file to provide a portable API for manipulation of an implementation-dependent class of files, which typically could be shared libraries. These interfaces are based on those introduced in UNIX System V Release 4.

Use of dynamic linking allows several benefits for application developers:

- the ability to share commonly used code across many applications, leading to disk and memory savings
- the implementation of services to be hidden from applications
- the reimplementation of services — for example, to permit bug and performance fixes — or to allow multiple implementations selectable at run time.

12.2 Functional Overview

- *dlopen*( )

  Gain access to an executable object file.

  This interface can be used to attach a shared object during a process lifetime; for example:

  ```
  #include <dlfcn.h>
  void *mylib;

  mylib = dlopen ("mylib.so.1", RTLD_LAZY);
  ```

  A successful *dlopen*( ) returns a handle which the caller may use on subsequent calls to *dlsym*( ) and *dlclose*( ). The value of this handle should not be interpreted in any way by the caller.

- *dlsym*( )

  Obtain address of a symbol from *dlopen*( ) object.

  This interface can be used to obtain the address of a symbol within an object; for example:

  ```
  int (*myptr) ();

  myptr = (int (*) ()) dlsym (mylib, "mysymname");
  ```

  and then, it is possible to manipulate the data or function by a dereference to the address:

```
int foobar;

foobar = (*myptr) ();
```

- *dlclose*( )

  Close a *dlopen*( ) object.

  This function is used to inform the system that the object attached by a previous call to *dlopen*( ) is no longer needed by the application; for example:

  ```
  int foo;

  foo = dlclose( mylib );
  ```

  The use of *dlclose*( ) reflects a statement of intent on the part of the process, but does not create any requirement upon the implementation, such as removal of the code or symbols referenced by the handle. Once an object has been closed using *dlclose*( ), an application should assume that its symbols are no longer available to *dlsym*( ). All objects loaded automatically as a result of invoking *dlopen*( ) on the referenced object are also closed.

- *dlerror*( )

  Get diagnostic information.

  This function is used to find out diagnostic information if any of the other dynamic linking interfaces returned an error. A call to *dlerror*( ) will then return a string describing the error; for example:

  ```
  char    *errstr;

  errstr = dlerror();
  ```

  Note that this interface is not thread safe, since the string may reside in a static area which is overwritten whenever an error occurs. Application code should not write to this buffer. Programs wishing to preserve an error message should make their own copies of that message. Depending on the application environment with respect to asynchronous execution events, such as signals or other asynchronous computation sharing the address space, portable applications should use a critical section to retrieve the error pointer and buffer.

Chapter 13

ISO C Amendment 1 (MSE)

System Interfaces and Headers, Issue 5 (XSH) includes the ISO/IEC 9899:1990/Amendment 1:1995 (E) to ISO/IEC 9899: 1990, Programming Languages — C (ISO C). This chapter is a brief introduction to this extension. It is assumed that the reader is familiar with the C language, and has some basic understanding of internationalization concepts and character encoding methods.

13.1 Introduction

ISO C Amendment 1 (MSE) was part of the first amendment made to the ISO C standard. The MSE consists of a set of library functions that provide a relatively complete and consistent set of functions for application programming using multibyte and wide-characters.

The other major items included in this amendment are digraphs, alternate spellings for several C tokens, and the header **<iso646.h>**. These items are not discussed here since they are outside the scope of this chapter.

The ISO C standard laid some groundwork for multibyte and wide-character programming by providing a small number of multibyte and wide character functions. The working group decided to wait for the C developer community to acquire more experience with implementing multibyte and wide-character libraries before extending this model further.

A working group (ISO/JTC1/SC22/WG14) was set up to study the various existing implementations and developed the Multibyte Support Extension as part of the first amendment (called *C Integrity*) to the ISO C standard.

XSH, Issue 4, Version 2, which was developed in 1994, incorporated a draft version of the MSE. XSH, Issue 5 incorporates the final version of the MSE. There were a small number of differences between the draft and final versions of the MSE and these are detailed in Section 13.11 on page 130.

13.2 Extended Characters

We traditionally think of characters as one byte entities represented by the **char** data type. For example, in the ISO 8859-1: 1987 codeset,[38] a sequence of ISO 8859-1: 1987 characters is a sequence of consecutive bytes, with each ISO 8859-1: 1987 character represented by one byte. This is simple, but allows for a maximum of 256 distinct characters.

38. The ISO 8859-1: 1987 codeset is used to represent Western European languages. In fact, all ISO 8859-1: 1987-* codesets fit this model of the one byte/one character model, and are typically referred to as single byte codesets.

In the MSE model, the concept of a character has been extended. Extended characters can be represented in three ways:

- multibyte character encodings
- wide-character encodings
- generalized multibyte encodings.

A multibyte character is a sequence of one or more bytes that can be represented as an array of type **char**; in other words a single character may occupy one or more consecutive bytes. An example of such an encoding is EUC (Extended UNIX Code). EUC provides a structure by which any number of codesets may be encoded into a multibyte encoding.

The primary advantage to the one byte/one character model is that it is very easy to process data in fixed-width chunks. For this reason, the concept of the wide character was invented. A wide character is an abstract data type large enough to contain the largest character that is supported on a particular platform. To date, most system implementors have chosen 32 bits, although there are implementations with 16 bit and 8 bit wide characters. It should be noted that although many vendors have chosen a 32-bit wide character, because the wide character is an abstract type it is not guaranteed to be the same across all platforms.

To support the concept of wide-characters, the MSE defines the integral type **wchar_t**. However, it does not define the size of **wchar_t**, but states it shall be as wide as necessary to hold the largest character in the code sets of the locales that an implementation supports.

In addition to the traditional concept of the multibyte character, the MSE has added the concept of the generalized multibyte character — see Section 13.2.1.

13.2.1 Multibyte Characters

There are many different multibyte encoding schemes, but these can be broken down into three basic categories:

- restartable multibyte encodings
- stateful multibyte encodings
- generalized multibyte encodings.

Restartable multibyte encodings are defined such that if you were to process a multibyte data stream it would be possible to determine the correct separation of characters no matter where you were positioned in the data stream. In the case of stateful encodings, you need one extra piece of information to be able to correctly process characters in the data stream. This extra piece of information is commonly referred to as the state of the data stream.

Why must we be able to unambiguously restart a data stream? If any byte sequence can have more than one meaning as a sequence of characters, then the multibyte code is ambiguous; that is, you could have multiple meanings for the same data stream depending upon where you started in the data stream. For example, the following multibyte encoding is not restartable:

```
0x41  0x42  0x61  0x62  0x43
```

In this particular encoding, the combination of 0x61 and 0x62 produces an F. If we start processing this string at the beginning, all the characters would be processed correctly and the result would be the string:

```
A B F C
```

If we start processing the string at 0x62, then the result would be the partial string:

```
b C
```

In a restartable encoding, the conversion interfaces would have recognized the 0x62 as an illegal multibyte character, and our program could choose to ignore that illegal character and move on, or perhaps it might try to back up and see if it could form a complete multibyte character.

In restartable multibyte encodings, each byte sequence in a particular encoding scheme stands for one character; the same character regardless of context. Stateful multibyte encoding schemes have a concept of shift state; certain codes called *shift sequences* effectively change the data stream to a different shift state, and the meaning of byte sequences is changed according to the current shift state.

If we use the same multibyte encoding and make it a stateful encoding, we will introduce two new operators called *shift state operators*, SS0 and SS1. The default shift state for this particular codeset is SS0. In this example, the 0x61 in its shifted state produces an F, and in its default state produces an a:

```
0x41  0x42  SS1  0x61  SS0  0x43  0x61
```

Since the default shift state is SS0, the above sequence of bytes should produce the string:

```
A B F C a
```

The stateful multibyte encodings are not restartable either, because if we started processing the string after a shift state operator, we could potentially get the wrong string.

Normally, if you try to pass a string containing multibyte characters to a function that does not know about them, such a function treats a string as a sequence of bytes, and interprets certain byte values specially; for example, the null byte, the slash character. Since it is illegal for a multibyte character to use any of the special byte values as part of its encoding, the function should pass it through as if it were a single byte string.[39]

This is where the concept of the generalized multibyte encoding arises. Traditionally, we think of multibyte encodings as file code and wide characters as process code, where file code resides on disk and process code is used by an application. This is not to say that multibyte encodings are not used by applications. Indeed many applications today use multibyte encodings routinely, but because they do not require the ability to process characters as discreet chunks they have no need to convert the multibyte encodings to wide characters.

In summary, generalized multibyte encodings can be encoded in any way. The special byte values discussed above have no meaning in generalized multibyte encodings. Functions that have no concept of multibyte encodings would fail if they tried to process generalized multibyte encodings. By defining the concept of generalized multibyte encodings, we provide a method by which we can say a particular file is associated with a particular locale, and can only be processed by specific routines running in this locale. Generalized multibyte encodings are more of a logical grouping than a specific definition. They provide us with a way to associate files with specific locales and codesets, and allow us to safely operate on those files as long as we are in the proper locale. The important restriction is that generalized multibyte characters can never be processed[40] directly, they can exist only on disk.

39. The multibyte encoding may still use the slash or null byte, it just cannot use them as part of another multibyte character.

40. *Processed* refers to the parsing routines available in C. Any file may be processed as binary data.

To take an example of a generalized multibyte encoding, Unicode is a 16-bit codeset that can be found on Windows 95 and Windows NT. One of the problems with Unicode is that it has NULL bytes embedded in its encoding. For example, the string:

```
a b c
```

is actually encoded as follows:

```
0x00  0x61  0x00  0x62  0x00  0x63  0x00 0x00
```

Those who are familiar with any of the string handling routines in C, can see that these routines will have problems with this string. Similarly, if you tried to read this file from a disk as a text file you would have problems. However, with the concept of generalized multibyte encodings we can say this file is associated with a Unicode locale and the *stdio* routines can be smart enough to know that when they are in the Unicode locale they can read the Unicode file properly.

13.3 Headers

The MSE defines two headers to support the new functionality:

- **<wctype.h>**

  Contains the declarations for the functions analogous to those in **<ctype.h>**; that is, the classification and mapping functions.

- **<wchar.h>**

  Contains the remaining declarations.

The header **<wchar.h>** declares the following types:

- **wchar_t**

  An integer type whose range is large enough to represent all distinct values in any extended character set in the supported locales. Known as the *wide character* type.

- **mbstate_t**

  Stores the current parse state of a stream.

- **wint_t**

  An integer type that can hold any wide-character and WEOF.

The following macros are declared:

- WCHAR_MAX

  Maximum value representable by an object of type **wchar_t**.

- WCHAR_MIN

  Minimum value representable by an object of type **wchar_t**.

- WEOF

  Wide-character end-of-file.

and the following error macro was added to the header **<error.h>**:

- EILSEQ

  A invalid wide-character encoding, or a sequence of bytes which do not form a valid multibyte character, was encountered.

Two standard macros can be used to find out the maximum possible number of bytes in a character:

- MB_LEN_MAX

  Returns the maximum length of a multibyte character for any supported locale as a positive integer. It is defined in **<limits.h>**.

- MB_CUR_MAX

  Returns the maximum number of bytes in a multibyte character in the current locale as a positive integer. The value is never greater than MB_LEN_MAX. It is defined in **<stdlib.h>**.

13.4 Character Classification

Character classification determines whether a particular character code refers to an upper-case alphabetic, lower-case alphabetic, alphanumeric, digit, punctuation, control or space character, or any one of a number of other groupings.

In the past macros were often used to classify character codes. This was possible since the assumption was that an application was dealing with ASCII characters. Today, classification functions are used which classify wide-character codes according to the type rules defined by the category LC_CTYPE of the application's current locale.

In the ISO C standard the behavior of character classification functions is affected by the current locale. Some functions have implementation-dependent behavior when not in the POSIX locale. For example, in the POSIX locale, *isupper*( ) returns true (non-zero) only for upper-case letters. The MSE contains no description of how the POSIX locale affects the behavior of the above functions, but states that when a character *c* causes an *isxxx*(*c*) function to return true, the corresponding wide-character *wc* shall cause the corresponding wide-character function to return true. Note, however, that the converse is not true.

The ISO C standard defines 11 classification (also known as *character testing*) functions. The MSE defines an analogous set of wide-character classification functions, returning non-zero for true and zero for false, as follows:

MSE	ISO C	Purpose
iswalnum( )	*isalnum*( )	Test for any wide character for which *isalpha*( ) or *isdigit*( ) is true.
iswalpha( )	*isalpha*( )	Test for any wide-character for which *iswupper*( ) or *iswlower*( ) is true, or any locale-specific wide character for which *iswcntrl*( ), *iswdigit*( ) *iswpunct*( ), or *iswspace*( ) is true.
iswcntrl( )	*iscntrl*( )	Test for any control wide character.
iswdigit( )	*isdigit*( )	Test for any wide character that corresponds to a decimal-digit character.
iswgraph( )	*isgraph*( )	Test for any wide character for which *iswprint*( ) is true and *iswspace*( ) is false.
iswlower( )	*islower*( )	Test for any wide character which is a lower-case letter or any locale-specific wide character for which none of *iswcntrl*( ), *iswdigit*( ), *iswpunct*( ), or *iswspace*( ) are true.

MSE	ISO C	Purpose
iswprint( )	*isprint*( )	Test for any printing wide character.
iswpunct( )	*ispunct*( )	Test for any printing wide character that is one of a locale-specific set of wide characters for which neither *iswspace*( ) or *iswalnum*( ) are true.
iswspace( )	*isspace*( )	Test for any printing wide character that is one of a locale-specific set of wide characters for which none of *iswalnum*( ), *iswgraph*( ), or *iswpunct*( ) are true.
iswupper( )	*isupper*( )	Test for any wide character which is an upper-case letter or any locale-specific wide character for which none of *iswcntrl*( ), *iswdigit*( ), *iswpunct*( ), or *iswspace*( ) are true.
iswxdigit( )	*isxdigit*( )	Test for any wide character that corresponds to a hexadecimal-digit character.

As the number of defined locales increased, the requirement for additional character classes increased. For example, while a classification function such as *isupper*( ) makes perfect sense in the English language, it does not make any sense in a language such as Japanese that has no concept of case. Conversely, a function such as *iskana*( ) makes perfect sense for Japanese, but doesn't make any sense in English. For this reason, the MSE defined two extensible wide-character classification functions — *wctype*( ) and *iswctype*( ) — as general-purpose solutions to this problem.

Name	Purpose	Syntax
wctype( )	Construct a value with type **wctype_t** that describes a class of wide characters identified by *property*.	`wctype_t wctype(const char *property);`
iswctype( )	Determine whether a wide-character has the property identified by *desc*.	`int iswctype(wint_t wc, wctype_t desc);`

These two functions are generally used in combination. However, sometimes the *wctype*( ) function is used on its own by an application to test whether a character classification is available in a specific locale. If the current setting of the LC_CTYPE locale changes between calls, the behavior is undefined.

The MSE specifies that the following code segments are equivalent to each other:

```
iswctype(wc, wctype("alnum"))     iswalnum(wc)
iswctype(wc, wctype("alpha"))     iswalpha(wc)
iswctype(wc, wctype("cntrl"))     iswcntrl(wc)
iswctype(wc, wctype("digit"))     iswdigit(wc)
iswctype(wc, wctype("graph"))     iswgraph(wc)
iswctype(wc, wctype("lower"))     iswlower(wc)
iswctype(wc, wctype("print"))     iswprint(wc)
iswctype(wc, wctype("punct"))     iswpunct(wc)
iswctype(wc, wctype("space"))     iswspace(wc)
iswctype(wc, wctype("upper"))     iswupper(wc)
iswctype(wc, wctype("xdigit"))    iswxdigit(wc)
```

13.5 Mapping Functions

Mapping functions are sometimes called *case conversion functions*, because the original mapping functions simply mapped upper-case to lower-case and *vice versa*.

In the past, case conversion was often handled by means of macros. This was possible since the assumption was that an application was dealing with ASCII characters. Mapping functions are used to provide case conversion according to shift tables defined in the LC_CTYPE category of the application's current locale.

The following wide-character mapping functions are provided:

MSE	ISO C	Purpose
towlower( )	*tolower*( )	Convert an upper-case letter to its corresponding lower-case letter if *iswupper*( ) is true and there is a corresponding wide character for which *iswlower*( ) is true.
towupper( )	*toupper*( )	Convert a lower-case letter to its corresponding upper-case letter if *iswlower*( ) is true and there is a corresponding wide character for which *iswupper*( ) is true.

As the number of defined locales increased, the requirement for additional characters increased. For example, while a function such as *toupper*( ) makes perfect sense in the English language, it doesn't make any sense in a language such as Japanese which has no concept of case. Conversely, the *tokana*( ) function makes no sense in the English language.

For this reason, the MSE defined two extensible wide-character classification functions — *wctrans*( ) and *towctrans*( ) — as general-purpose solutions to this problem. The name of the required character conversion is passed as an argument to the *wctrans*( ) function to avoid name space pollution.

Name	Purpose	Syntax
wctrans( )	Construct a value with type **wctrans_t** that describes the mapping between wide characters identified by *property*.	`wctrans_t wctrans(const char *property);`
towctrans( )	Map the wide character per specified mapping.	`wint_t towctrans(wint_t wc, wctrans_t desc);`

In addition, the MSE specifies that the following code segments are equivalent to each other:

```
towctrans(wc, wctrans("tolower"))    towlower(wc)
towctrans(wc, wctrans("toupper"))    towupper(wc)
```

The *wctype*( ) function also enables an application to test whether a character classification is available in a specific locale.

13.6 Number Conversion Functions

Three new functions are included to facilitate conversion from wide-character strings (also known as *wide strings*) to a variety of numeric formats.

MSE	ISO C	Purpose	Syntax
wcstod( )	*strtod*( )	Convert the initial portion of a wide string to a **double**.	`double wcstod(const wchar_t *n, wchar_t **end);`
wcstol( )	*strtol*( )	Convert the initial portion of a wide string to a **long**.	`long wcstol(const wchar_t *n, wchar_t **end, int base);`
wcstoul( )	*strtoul*( )	Convert the initial portion of a wide string to an **unsigned long**.	`unsigned long wcstoul(const wchar_t *n, wchar_t **end, int base);`

These functions work as follows:

- First, the function decomposes the wide-character string into three parts:
  - — An initial, possibly empty, sequence of white-space wide characters as determined by the *iswspace*( ) function
  - — a subject sequence interpreted as either a floating point constant, **long** or **unsigned long**
  - — a final sequence of one or more unrecognized wide-character codes including the terminating null wide character.
- The function then attempts to convert the subject sequence into the required number format by parsing the subject sequence and returning the result. If the subject sequence is empty or does not have the expected form, no conversion is performed.

In other than the POSIX locale, implementation-dependent forms of a subject sequence may be supported.

The function *wcstod*( ) has a dependency on the value of the RADIXCHAR item in the applications current locale. In locales where the radix character is not defined, it defaults to a period.

13.7 String Handling

Sixteen new wide-character string functions are defined. Most are similar to their char-based counterparts. The data types of some parameters differ, but the purpose of the parameters is the same.

MSE	ISO C	Purpose	Syntax
wcscpy( )	*strcpy*( )	Copy a wide string.	`wchar_t *wcscpy(wchar_t *s1, const wchar_t *s2);`
wcsncpy( )	*strncpy*( )	Copy at most *n* wide characters of a wide string.	`wchar_t *wcsncpy(wchar_t *s1, const wchar_t *s2, size_t n);`

MSE	ISO C	Purpose	Syntax
wcscat( )	*strcat*( )	Append a wide string.	`wchar_t *wcscat(wchar_t *s1, const wchar_t *s2);`
wcsncat( )	*strncat*( )	Append at most *n* wide characters.	`wchar_t *wcsncat(wchar_t *s1, const wchar_t *s2, size_t n);`
wcscmp( )	*strcmp*( )	Compare two wide strings.	`int wcscmp(const wchar_t *s1, const wchar_t *s2);`
wsncmp( )	*strncmp*( )	Compare at most *n* wide characters in two wide strings.	`int wcsncmp(const wchar_t *s1, const wchar_t *s2, size_t n);`
wcscoll( )	*strcoll*( )	Compare two wide strings based on their collation sequence.	`int wcscoll(const wchar_t *s1, const wchar_t *s2);`
wcsxfrm( )		Transform a wide string.	`size_t wcsxfrm(wchar_t *s1, const wchar_t *s2, size_t n);`
wcschr( )	*strchr*( )	Locate first occurrence of a wide character.	`wchar_t *wcschr(const wchar_t *s1, wchar_t wc);`
wcscspn( )	*strscspn*( )	Return length of maximum initial segment of *s1* which consists entirely of wide characters not from *s2*.	`size_t wcscspn(const wchar_t *s1, const wchar_t *s2);`
wcspbrk( )	*strpbrk*( )	Return pointer to first wide character in *s1* which is also in *s2*.	`wchar_t *wcspbrk(const wchar_t *s1, const wchar_t *s2);`
wcsrchr( )	*strrchr*( )	Return pointer to last occurrence of wide character in wide string.	`wchar_t *wcsrchr(const wchar_t *s, wchar_t c);`
wcsspn( )	*strspn*( )	Return length of maximum initial segment of *s1* which consists entirely of wide characters from *s2*.	`size_t wcsspn(const wchar_t *s1, const wchar_t s2);`
wcsstr( )	*strstr*( )	Return pointer to first occurrence of wide string *s2* in wide string *s1*.	`wchar_t *wcsstr(const wchar_t *s1, const wchar_t *s2);`
wcstok( )	*strtok*( )	Split wide string into tokens.	`wchar_t *wcstok(wchar_t *s1, const wchar_t *s2, wchar_t **ptr);`
wcslen( )	*strlen*( )	Get length of wide string.	`size_t wcslen(const wchar_t *s);`

The comparison functions *wcscmp*( ) and *wcsncmp*( ) compare two wide-character strings by comparing the wide characters based on the character's encoded value, while the *wcscoll*( ) function compares each wide character interpreted according to the collating sequence information specified by the LC_COLLATE category of the current locale.

The *wcsxfrm*( ) function transforms a wide-character string and places the result in an array of wide characters. The transformation is such that if the *wcscmp*( ) function is applied to two transformed wide-character strings, the result is the same as if the two wide-character strings were compared using *wcscoll*( ). Both wide-character strings must be transformed using *wcsxfrm*( ). It is invalid to compare a transformed string to a non-transformed string. Note that no function is defined to restore a transformed string to its original layout.

When wide-character strings are likely to be compared more than once, it is more efficient to transform them using *wcsxfrm*( ), compare them using *wcscmp*( ), and retain the transformed strings for subsequent comparisons.

The MSE also defines a number of wide-character array functions. These functions operate on arrays of type **wchar_t** whose size is specified by a separate count argument. These functions are not affected by locale and all **wchar_t** values are treated identically, including the null wide character and wide characters not corresponding to valid multibyte characters. Thus, the *wmemcmp*( ) function compares each wide-character array element using the encoded value of each wide-character.

MSE	ISO C	Purpose	Syntax
wmemchr( )	*memchr*( )	Locate first occurrence of wide character *c* in the initial *n* wide characters of *s*.	`wchar_t *wmemchr(const wchar_t *s, wchar_t c, size_t n);`
wmemcmp( )	*memcmp*( )	Compare first *n* wide characters of *s1* and *s2*.	`int wmemcmp(const wchar_t *s1, const wchar_t *s2, size_t n);`
wmemcpy( )	*memcpy*( )	Copy first *n* wide characters from *s2* to *s1*.	`wchar_t *wmemcpy(wchar_t *s1, const wchar_t *s2, size_t n);`
wmemmove( )	*memmove*( )	Copy first *n* wide characters from *s2* to *s1*.	`wchar_t *wmemmove(wchar_t *s1, const wchar_t *s2, size_t n);`
wmemset( )	*memset*( )	Set first *n* wide characters of *s* to wide character *c*.	`wchar_t *wmemset(wchar_t *s, wchar_t c, size_t n);`

The *wmemmove*( ) function copies the specified number of wide characters from the object pointed to by *s2* into *s1*. However, unlike *wmemcpy*( ), the objects *s1* and *s2* can safely overlap. Copying occurs as if the required elements of the object *s2* are first copied into a temporary area and then copied into the object pointed to by *s1*.

13.8 The Input/Output Model

The MSE input/output model assumes that characters are handled as wide-characters within an application and stored as multibyte characters in files, and that all the wide-character input/output functions begin executing with the stream positioned at the boundary between two multibyte characters.

The definition of a stream was changed to include the concept of an orientation for both text and binary streams. After a stream is associated with a file, but before any operations are performed on the stream, the stream is without orientation. If a wide-character input or output function is applied to a stream without orientation, the stream becomes wide-oriented. Likewise, if a byte input or output operation is applied to a stream with orientation, the stream becomes byte-oriented. Thereafter, only the *fwide*( ) or *freopen*( ) functions can alter the orientation of a stream.

Byte input/output functions shall not be applied to a wide-oriented stream and wide-character input/output functions shall not be applied to a byte-oriented stream.

While wide-oriented streams are sequences of wide characters, the external file associated with a wide-oriented stream may be an implementation-dependent multibyte encoding. Furthermore, it is acceptable that the file associated with this stream is a generalized multibyte encoding such as Unicode.

The following function is specified to enable applications to determine and/or set the orientation of a stream:

Name	Purpose	Syntax
fwide( )	Determine the orientation of a stream.	`int fwide(FILE *stream, int mode);`

If mode is zero, stream orientation is not altered. If mode is >0, the function first attempts to make the stream wide-oriented. If mode <0, the function first attempts to make the stream byte-oriented.

Note that the input/output model does not preclude applications from storing date in external files as wide characters.

13.8.1 Wide-character Input Functions

Wide-character input functions read multibyte characters from a stream and convert them to wide characters. An encoding error occurs if the byte sequence does not form a valid wide character in the current locale.

The following table lists the wide-character input functions specified in the MSE together with their equivalent char-based functions:

MSE	ISO C	Purpose	Syntax
getwc( )	*getc*( )	Get a wide character from a stream.	`wint_t getwc(FILE *stream);`
getwchar( )	*getchar*( )	Get a wide character from *stdin*.	`wint_t getwchar(void);`
fgetwc( )	*fgetc*( )	Get a wide character from a stream.	`wint_t fgetwc(FILE *stream);`

MSE	ISO C	Purpose	Syntax
fgetws( )	*fgetc*( )	Get a wide-character string from a stream.	`wchar_t *fgetws(wchar_t *s, int n, FILE *stream);`
fwscanf( )	*fscanf*( )	Get formatted input from a stream.	`int fwscanf(FILE *stream, const wchar_t *format, ...);`
swscanf( )	*sscanf*( )	Get formatted input from a wide-character string.	`int swscanf(const whar_t *s, const wchar_t *format, ...);`
wscanf( )	*scanf*( )	Get formatted input from *stdin*.	`int wscanf(const wchar_t *format, ....);`
ungetwc( )	*ungetc*( )	Push a wide character back on a stream.	`wint_t ungetwc(wint_t c, FILE *stream);`

All of the above functions work in a similar manner to their corresponding char-based functions, except that format strings must be wide-character strings.

However, the following format specifiers accept an additional *l* (ell) qualifier:

[Matches a non-empty sequence of wide characters from a set of expected characters. If an *l* qualifier is present, the corresponding argument shall be a pointer to a wide-character array; otherwise the corresponding argument is a pointer to a character array.

c Matches a sequence of wide-characters. If an *l* qualifier is present, the corresponding argument is a pointer to a wide-character array large enough to hold the sequence; otherwise the corresponding argument is a pointer to a character array, and characters are converted as if by repeated calls to the *wcrtomb*( ) function.

s Matches a sequence of non-white-space wide characters. If an *l* qualifier is present, the corresponding argument is a pointer to a wide-character array; otherwise it is a pointer to a character array, and characters from the input fields are converted as if by repeated calls to the *wcrtomb*( ) function.

13.8.2 Wide-character Output Functions

Wide-character output functions convert wide characters to multibyte characters and write them to the stream. An encoding error occurs if the wide character does not correspond to a valid multibyte character in the current locale.

The following table lists the wide-character output functions specified in the MSE together with their equivalent char-based functions:

MSE	ISO C	Purpose	Syntax
putwc( )	*putc*( )	Write a wide character to a stream.	`wint_t putwc(wchar_t c, FILE *stream);`
putwchar( )	*putchar*( )	Write a wide character to *stdout*.	`wint_t putwchar(wchar_t c);`
fputwc( )	*fputc*( )	Write a wide character to a stream.	`wint_t fputwc(wchar_t c, FILE *stream);`

MSE	ISO C	Purpose	Syntax
fputws( )	*fputs*( )	Write a wide-character string to a stream.	`int fputws(const wchar_t *s, FILE *stream);`
fwprintf( )	*wprintf*( )	Write to a stream using a wide-character format specification.	`int fwprintf(FILE *stream, const wchar_t *format, ...);`
wprintf( )	*printf*( )	Write to *stdout* using a wide-character format specification.	`int wprintf(const wchar_t *format, ...);`
swprintf( )	*sprintf*( )	Write to a wide-character array using a wide-character format specification.	`int swprintf(wchar_t *s, size_t n, const wchar_t *format, ...);`
vfwprintf( )	*vfprintf*( )	Equivalent to *fwprintf*( ) except using *va_list* syntax.	`int vfwprintf(FILE *stream, const wchar_t *format, va_list arg);`
vwprintf( )	*vprintf*( )	Equivalent to *wprintf*( ) except using *va_list* syntax.	`int vwprintf(const wchar_t *format, va_list arg);`
vswprintf( )	*vsprintf*( )	Equivalent to *swprintf*( ) except using *va_list* syntax.	`int vswprintf(wchar_t *s, size_t n, const wchar_t *format, va_list arg);`

All of the above functions work in a similar manner to their corresponding char-based functions, except that format strings must be wide-character strings.

The following format specifiers accept an additional *l* (ell) qualifier:

c Write a character. If an *l* qualifier is present, the corresponding **wint_t** argument is converted to **wchar_t** and written; otherwise the argument is converted to a wide character as if by calling *btowc*( ), and the resulting wide-character is written.

s Write a string. If an *l* qualifier is present, the corresponding argument is a pointer to a wide-character array; otherwise it is a pointer to a character array, and characters from the array are converted as if by repeated calls to the *mbrtowc*( ) function.

13.9 Conversion Functions

As discussed earlier, multibyte character streams may have state-dependent encodings. To handle state-dependent encodings, the MSE includes the concept of a conversion state that is associated with each FILE object that effects the behavior of a conversion between multibyte and a wide-character encoding.

The conversion state information augments the FILE object's information about the current position of the multibyte character stream with information about the parse state for the next multibyte character to be obtained from the stream. For state-dependent encodings, the remembered shift state is part of this parse state. Every wide-character input or output function makes use of this state information and updates its corresponding FILE object's conversion state accordingly.

The non-array type **mbstate_t** is defined to encode the conversion state under the rules of the current locale and provide a character accumulator. This implies that encoding rule information is part of the conversion state. No initialization function is provided to initialize **mbstate_t**. A zero-valued **mbstate_t** is assumed to describe the initial conversion state. Such a zero-valued **mbstate_t** object is said to be unbound. Once a multibyte or wide-character conversion function is called with the **mbstate_t** object as an argument, the object becomes bound and holds the conversion state information which it obtains from the LC_CTYPE category of the current locale. No comparison function is specified for comparing two **mbstate_t** objects.

The MSE assumes that only wide-character input/output functions can maintain consistency between a stream and its corresponding conversion state. Byte input/output functions do not manipulate or use conversion state information. Wide-character input/output functions are assumed to begin processing a stream at the boundary between two multibyte characters. Seek operations reset the conversion state corresponding to the new file position.

The function *mbsinit*( ) is specified because many conversion functions treat the initial shift state as a special case and need a portable means of determining whether an **mbstate_t** object is at initial conversion state.

Name	Purpose	Syntax
mbsinit( )	Determine whether the referenced **mbstate_t** object describes an initial conversion state.	`int mbsinit(const mbstate_t *ps);`

The MSE provides a method to distinguish between an invalid sequence of bytes in a multibyte stream and a valid prefix to a still incomplete multibyte character. Upon encountering such an incomplete multibyte sequence, the functions *mbrlen*( ) and *mbrtowc*( ) return –2 instead of –1, and the character accumulator in the **mbstate_t** object may store the partial character information. This allows applications to convert streams one byte at a time or even to suspend and resume conversion if required. The conversion functions are thus said to be restartable.

The MSE specifies the following single-byte wide-character conversion functions:

Name	Purpose	Syntax
btowc( )	Determine whether valid multibyte character is in the initial shift state and return corresponding wide character.	`wint_t btowc(int c);`
wctob( )	Determine whether member of the extended character set whose multibyte character representation is a single byte when in the initial shift state, and return corresponding single-byte character.	`int wctob(wint_t c);`

The function *btowc*( ) returns WEOF if the character has a value of EOF or if it is not a valid multibyte character in the initial shift state.

The function *wctob*( ) returns EOF if the character does not correspond to a valid multibyte character of length 1 in the initial shift state.

The MSE specifies the following restartable functions which take as their last argument a pointer to an object of type **mbstate_t**. If the pointer is NULL, each function uses its own internal **mbstate_t** object instead, which is initialized at startup to the initial conversion state. Note that, unlike their corresponding ISO C standard functions, a function's return value does not represent whether the encoding is state-dependent.

MSE	ISO C	Purpose	Syntax
mbrlen( )	*mblen*( )	Determine the length in bytes of a multibyte character.	`size_t mbrlen(const char *mbs, size_t n, mbstate_t *ps);`
mbrtowc( )	*mbtowc*( )	Convert a multibyte character into a wide character.	`size_t mbrtowc(wchar_t *pwc, const char *s, size_t n, mbstate_t *ps);`
wcrtomb( )	*wctomb*( )	Convert a wide character into a multibyte character.	`size_t wcrtomb(char *s, whar_t wc, mbstate_t *ps);`
mbsrtowcs( )	*mbstowcs*( )	Convert a multibyte string into a wide-character string.	`size_t mbsrtowcs(wchar_t *dst, const char **src, size_t len, mbstate_t *ps);`
wcsrtombs( )	*wcstombs*( )	Convert a wide-character string into a multibyte string.	`size_t wcsrtombs(char *dst, const wchar_t **src, size_t len, mbstate_t *ps);`

A more detailed explanation of two of the above functions will help to clarify the concept of restartable functions.

The function *mbrtowc*( ) inspects at most *n* bytes to determine the number of bytes needed to complete the next multibyte character. If a multibyte character can be completed, *mbrtowc*( ) determines the corresponding wide character and returns it in **pwc*. If the corresponding wide character is the null wide character, the conversion state is reset to the initial conversion state. This function returns one of the following:

(size_t)–2 The next *n* bytes contribute to, but do not complete, a valid multibyte character, and all *n* bytes have been processed.

(size_t)–1 An encoding error has occurred. The next *n* or fewer bytes do not contribute to a valid multibyte character. *errno* is set to EILSEQ. The conversion state is undefined.

Note: **(size_t)**–2 and **(size_t)**–1 should be tested before the >0 case.

0 If the next *n* or fewer bytes complete a valid multibyte character that corresponds to the null wide character.

>0 The number of bytes used to complete a valid multibyte character.

The function *mbsrtowcs*( ) is a restartable string conversion routine which converts a sequence of multibyte characters, beginning with the conversion state described by the **mbstate_t** object pointed to by *ps*, from the array indirectly pointed to by *src* into a sequence of corresponding wide characters pointed to by *dst*. Conversion continues up to and including a terminating null character which is also stored in *dst*. Each conversion takes place as if by a call to the *mbrtowc*( ) function. If an error occurs, *errno* is set to the macro EILSEQ and *mbsrtowcs*( ) returns **(size_t)**–1.

Conversion stops when one of the following occurs:

- A null multibyte character is encountered and processed. In this case the conversion state is reset to the initial conversion state and *scr* is assigned a null pointer.

- A sequence of bytes is encountered which do not form a valid multibyte character.
- When *len* multibyte characters have been processed.

13.10 Miscellaneous Functions

MSE	ISO C	Purpose	Syntax
wcsftime( )	*strftime*( )	Convert a date and time to a wide-character string.	`size_t wcsftime(wchar_t *wcs, size_t maxsize, const wchar_t *format, const struct tm *tptr);`

The *wcsftime*( ) function behaves as if the character string generated by the *strftime*( ) function is passed to the *mbstowcs*( ) function as the character string parameter, and the *mbstowcs*( ) function places the result in the *wcs* parameter of *wcsftime*( ), up to the limit of the number of wide characters specified by *maxsize*.

This function uses the local timezone information. The format parameter is a wide-character string consisting of a sequence of wide-character format codes that specify the format of the date and time to be written to *wcs*.

13.11 Compatibility Issues

When XSH, Issue 4, Version 2 was under development, the MSE had not yet been ratified as an amendment to the ISO C standard, but the working draft used (ISO Working Paper SC22/WG14/N204 dated 31st March 1992) was regarded as being stable.

Unfortunately, a number of interfaces changed slightly before the MSE became part of ISO/IEC 9899:1990/Amendment 1:1995 (E), and three functions, *wcswcs*( ), *wcswidth*( ), and *wcwidth*( ), were dropped.

The differences between XSH, Issue 4, Version 2 and XSH, Issue 5 are detailed in the following table:

Name	Purpose	XSH, Issue 4, Version 2	XSH, Issue 5
wcswcs( )	Find a wide-character substring in a wide-character string.	Included per draft MSE.	Included but marked EX. Application developers are strongly encouraged to use *wcsstr*( ) instead.
wcswidth( )	Number of column positions of a wide-character string.	Included per draft MSE.	Included as an extension.
wcwidth( )	Number of column positions of a wide-character code.	Included per draft MSE.	Included as an extension.
fputwc( )	Put a wide character code on a stream.	`wint_t fputwc(wint_t wc, FILE *stream);`	`wint_t fputwc(wchar_t wc, FILE *stream);`

Name	Purpose	XSH, Issue 4, Version 2	XSH, Issue 5
putwc( )	Put a wide character on a stream.	`wint_t putwc(wint_t wc, FILE *stream);`	`wint_t putwc(wchar_t wc, FILE *stream);`
putwchar( )	Put a wide character on a stream.	`wint_t putwchar(wint_t wc);`	`wint_t putwchar(wchar_t wc);`
wcsftime( )	Convert date and time to wide-character string.	`size_t wcsftime(wchar_t *wcs, size_t maxsize, const char *format, const struct tm *timptr);`	`size_t wcsftime(wchar_t *wcs, size_t maxsize, const wchar_t *format, const struct tm *timptr);`
wcstok( )	Split wide-character string into tokens.	`wchar_t *wcstok(wchar_t *ws1, const wchar_t *ws2);`	`wchar_t *wcstok(wchar_t *ws1, const wchar_t *ws2, wchar_t **ptr);`

Chapter 14

Data Size Neutrality and 64-bit Support

The Single UNIX Specification, Version 2 provides enhanced support for 64-bit programming models by being n-bit clean and data size neutral. This chapter is a brief introduction to 64-bit programming models, data size neutrality, and application porting issues.

14.1 Introduction

When the UNIX operating system was first created in 1969 it was developed to run on a 16-bit computer architecture. The C language of the time supported 16-bit integer and pointer data types and also supported a 32-bit integer data type that could be emulated on hardware which did not support 32-bit arithmetic operations.

When 32-bit computer architectures, which supported 32-bit integer arithmetic operators and 32-bit pointers, were introduced in the late 1970s, the UNIX operating system was quickly ported to this new class of hardware platforms. The C language data model developed to support these 32-bit architectures quickly evolved to consist of a 16-bit short-integer type, a 32-bit integer type, and a 32-bit pointer. During the 1980s, this was the predominant C data model available for 32-bit UNIX platforms.

To describe these two data models in modern terms, the 16-bit UNIX platforms used an IP16 data model, while 32-bit UNIX platforms use the ILP32 programming model. The notation describes the width assigned to the basic data types; for example, ILP32 denotes that **int** (I), **long** (L), and **pointer** (P) types are all 32-bit entities. This notation is used extensively throughout this chapter.

The first UNIX standardization effort was begun in 1983 by a /usr/group committee. This work was merged into the work program of the IEEE POSIX committee in 1985. By 1988, both POSIX and X/Open committees had developed detailed standards and specifications that were based upon the predominant UNIX implementations of the time. These committees endeavored to develop architecture-neutral definitions that could be implemented on any hardware architecture.

The transition from 16-bit to 32-bit processor architectures happened quite rapidly just before the UNIX standardization work was begun. Since the specifications were based on existing practice and the predominant data model did not change during this gestation period, some dependencies upon the ILP32 data model were inadvertently incorporated into the final specifications.

Most of today's 32-bit UNIX platforms use the ILP32 data model. However another data model, the LP32 model, is also very popular for other operating systems. The majority of C-language programs written for Microsoft Windows 3.1 are written for the Win-16 API which uses the LP32 data model. The Apple Macintosh also uses the LP32 data model.

32-bit platforms have a number of limitations which are increasingly a source of frustration to developers of large applications, such as databases, who wish to take advantage of advances in computer hardware. There is much discussion today in the computer industry about the barrier presented by 32-bit addresses. 32-bit pointers can only address 4GB of virtual address space.

There are ways of overcoming this limitation, but application development is more complicated and performance is significantly reduced. Until recently the size of a data file could not exceed 4GB. However, the 4GB file size limitation was overcome by the Large File Summit extensions which are included in XSH, Issue 5.

Disk storage has been improving in real density at the rate of 70% compounded annually, and drives of 4GB and larger are readily available. Memory prices have not dropped as sharply, but 16MB chips are readily available, with 64MB chips in active development. CPU processing power continues to increase by about 50% every 18 months, providing the power to process ever larger quantities of data. This conjunction of technological forces, along with the continued demand for systems capable of supporting ever larger databases and simulation models and full-motion video, have generated requirements for support of larger addressing structures.

A number of 64-bit processors are now available, and the transition from 32-bit to 64-bit architectures is rapidly occurring amongst all the major hardware vendors. 64-bit UNIX platforms do not suffer from the file size or flat address space limitations of 32-bit platforms. Applications can access files that occupy terabytes of disk space because 64-bit file offsets are possible. Similarly, applications can now theoretically access terabytes of memory because pointers can be 64 bits. More physical memory results in faster operations. The performance of memory-mapped file access, caching, and swapping, is greatly improved. 64-bit virtual addresses simplify the design of large applications. All the major database vendors now support 64-bit platforms because of dramatically improved performance for very large database applications available on very large memory (VLM) systems.

The world is currently dominated by 32-bit computers, a situation that is likely to continue to exist for the near future. These computers run 16 or 32-bit applications or some mixture of the two. Meanwhile, 64-bit computers will run 32-bit code, 64-bit code, or mixtures of the two (and perhaps even some 16-bit code). New 64-bit applications and operating systems must integrate smoothly into this environment. Key issues facing the computing industry are the interchange of data between 64 and 32-bit systems (in some cases on the same system) and the cost of maintaining software in both environments. Such interchange is especially needed for large application suites such as database systems, where one may want to distribute most of the applications as 32-bit binaries that run across a large installed base, but be able to choose 64-bits for a few crucial applications.

14.2 64-bit Data Models

Prior to the introduction of 64-bit platforms, it was generally believed that the introduction of 64-bit UNIX operating systems would naturally use the ILP64 data model. However, this view was too simplistic and overlooked optimizations that could be obtained by choosing a different data model.

Unfortunately, the C programming language does not provide a mechanism for adding new fundamental data types. Thus, providing 64-bit addressing and integer arithmetic capabilities involves changing the bindings or mappings of the existing data types or adding new data types to the language.

ISO/IEC 9899: 1990, Programming Languages — C (ISO C) left the definition of the **short int**, the **int**, the **long int**, and the **pointer** deliberately vague to avoid artificially constraining hardware architectures that might benefit from defining these data types independent from the other. The only constraints were that **int**s must be no smaller than **short**s, and **long**s must be no smaller than **int**s, and **size_t** must represent the largest unsigned type supported by an implementation. It is possible, for instance, to define a **short** as 16 bits, an **int** as 32 bits, a **long** as 64 bits and a **pointer** as 128 bits. The relationship between the fundamental data types can be expressed as:

```
sizeof(char) <= sizeof(short) <= sizeof(int) <= sizeof(long)
    = sizeof(size_t)
```

Ignoring non-standard types, all three of the following 64-bit pointer data models satisfy the above relationship:

- LP64 (also known as 4/8/8)
- ILP64 (also known as 8/8/8)
- LLP64 (also known as 4/4/8).

The differences between the three models lies in the non-pointer data types. The table below details the data types for the above three data models and includes LP32 and ILP32 for comparison purposes.

Data Type	LP32	ILP32	ILP64	LLP64	LP64
char	8	8	8	8	8
short	16	16	16	16	16
int32			32		
int	16	32	64	32	32
long	32	32	64	32	64
long long (int64)				64	
pointer	32	32	64	64	64

When the width of one or more of the C data types is changed, applications may be affected in various ways. These effects fall into two main categories:

- Data objects, such as a structure, defined with one of the 64-bit data types will be different in size from those declared in an identical way on a 16 or 32-bit system.
- Common assumptions about the relationships between the fundamental data types may no longer be valid in a 64-bit data model. Applications which depend on those relationships often cease to work properly when compiled on a 64-bit platform. A typical assumption made by many application developers is that:

  ```
  sizeof(int) = sizeof(long) = sizeof(pointer)
  ```

  This relationship is not codified in any C programming standard, but it is valid for the ILP32 data model. However, it is not valid for two of the three 64-bit data models described above, nor is it valid for the LP32 data model.

The ILP64 data model attempts to maintain the relationship between **int**, **long**, and **pointer** which exists in the ILP32 model by making all three types the same size. Assignment of a pointer to an **int** or a **long** will not result in data loss.

The downside of this model is that it depends on the addition of a new 32-bit data type such as **int32** to handle true 32-bit quantities. There is thus a potential for conflict with existing **typedef**s in applications. An application which was developed on an ILP32 platform, and subsequently ported to an ILP64 platform, may be forced to make frequent use of the **int32** data type to preserve the size and alignment of data because of interoperability requirements or binary compatibility with existing data files.

The LLP64 data model preserves the relationship between **int** and **long** by leaving both as 32-bit types. Data objects, such as structures, which do not contain pointers will be the same size as on a 32-bit system. This model is sometimes described as a 32-bit model with 64-bit addresses. Most of the run-time problems associated with the assumptions between the sizes of the data types are related to the assumption that a pointer will fit in an **int**. To solve this class of problems, **int** or **long** variables which should be 64-bits in length are changed to **long long** (or **int64**), a non-standard data type. This data model is thus again dependent on the introduction of a new data type. Again there is potential for conflict with existing **typedef**s in applications.

The LP64 data model takes the middle road. 8, 16, and 32-bit scalar types (**char**, **short**, and **int**) are provided to support objects that must maintain size and alignment with 32-bit systems. A 64-bit type, **long**, is provided to support the full arithmetic capabilities, and is available to use in conjunction with pointer arithmetic. Applications that assign addresses to scalar objects need to specify the object as **long** instead of **int**.

In the LP64 data model, data types are natural. Each scalar type is larger than the preceding type. No new data types are required. As a language design issue, the purpose of having **long** in the language anticipates cases where there is an integral type longer than **int**. The fact that **int** and **long** represent different width data types is a natural and common sense approach, and is the standard in the PC world where **int** is 16-bits and **long** is 32-bits.

A major test for any C data model is its ability to support the very large existing UNIX applications code base. The investment in code, experience, and data surrounding these applications is the largest determiner of the rate at which new technology is adopted and spread. In addition, it must be easy for an application developer to build code which can be used in both existing and new environments.

The UNIX development community is driven technically by a set of API agreements embodied in standards and specifications documents from groups such as X/Open, IEEE, ANSI, and ISO. These documents were developed over many years to codify existing practice and define agreement on new capabilities. As a result these specifications are of major value to the system developers, application developers, and end-users. There are numerous test suites which verify that implementations correctly embody the details of a specification and certify that fact to interested parties. Any 64-bit data model cannot invalidate large portions of these specifications and expect to achieve wide adoption.

A number of vendors have extensive experience with the LP64 data model. By far, the largest body of existing 32-bit code already modified for 64-bit environments runs on LP64 platforms. Experience has shown that it is relatively easy to modify existing code so that it can be compiled on either an 32-bit or 64-bit platform. Interoperability with existing ILP32 platforms is well proven and is not an issue. At least one LP64-based operating system (Digital UNIX V4.0) has met and passed the majority of existing verification suites and has obtained the UNIX 95 brand.

A small number of ILP64-based platforms have also shipped. These have demonstrated that it is feasible to complete the implementation of an ILP64 environment. However, as of early 1997, no LLP64 or ILP64-based systems have achieved the same level of standards conformance or met the requirements of the UNIX 95 brand.

Although the number of applications written in C requiring a large virtual address space is growing rapidly, there has not been a requirement to date for a 64-bit **int** data type. The majority of existing 64-bit applications previously ran only on 32-bit platforms, and had no expectation of a greater range for the **int** data type. The extra 32 bits of data space in a 64-bit **int** would appear to be wasted. Any future applications which require a larger scalar data type can use the **long** type.

Nearly all applications moving from a 32-bit platform require some minor modifications to handle 64-bit pointers, especially where erroneous assumptions about the relative size of **int** and **pointer** data types were made. Common assumptions about the relative sizes of **int**, **char**, **short**, and **float** data types generally do not cause problems on LP64 platforms (since the sizes of those data types are identical to those on an ILP32 platform), but do so on an ILP64 platform.

Other language implementations will continue to support a 32-bit **int** type. For example, the FORTRAN-77 standard requires that the type INTEGER be the same size as REAL, which is half the size of DOUBLE PRECISION. This, together with customer expectations, means that FORTRAN-77 implementations will generally leave INTEGER as a 32-bit type, even on 64-bit platforms. A significant number of applications use C and FORTRAN together, either calling each other or sharing data files. Such applications have been amongst the first to move to 64-bit environments. Experience has shown that it is usually easier to modify the data sizes and types on the C side than the FORTRAN side of such applications. These applications will continue to require a 32-bit **int** data type in C regardless of the size of the **int** data type.

In 1995, a number of major UNIX vendors agreed to standardize on the LP64 data model for a number of reasons:

- Experience suggests that neither the LP64 nor the ILP64 data models provide a painless porting path from a 32-bit platform, but that all other things being equal, the smaller data types in the LP64 data model enable better application performance.
- A crucial investment for end-users is the existing data built up over decades in their computer systems. Any proposed solution must make it easy to utilize such data on a continuing basis. Unfortunately, the ILP64 data model does not provide a natural way to describe 32-bit data types, and must resort to non-portable constructs such as **int32** to describe such types. This is likely to cause practical problems in producing code which can run on both 32 and 64-bit platforms without numerous **#ifdef** constructions. It has been possible to port large quantities of code to LP64 platforms without the need to make such changes, while maintaining the investment made in data sets, even in cases where the typing information was not made externally visible by the application.
- Most **ints** in existing applications can remain as 32 bits in a 64-bit environment; only a small number are expected to be the same size as **pointer** or **long**. Under the ILP64 data model, most **ints** will need to change to **int32**. However, **int32** does not behave like a 32-bit **int**. Instead, **int32** is like **short** in that all operations have to be converted to **int** (64-bits, sign extended) and performed in 64-bit arithmetic. Thus, **int32** in the ILP64 data model is not exactly the same as **int** in the ILP32 data model. These differences may cause subtle and hard-to-find bugs.
- Instruction cycle penalties are incurred whenever additional cycles are required to properly implement the semantics of the intended data model. For example, in the LP64 data model it is only necessary to perform sign extension on **int** when you have a mixed expression including **long**s. However, most integral expressions do not include **long**s and compilers can be made smart enough to only sign extend when necessary.
- **int** is by far the most frequent data type to be found (statically and sometimes dynamically) within C and C++ programs. 64-bit integers require twice as much space as 32-bit integers. Applications using 64-bit integers consume additional memory and CPU cycles transporting that memory throughout the system. Furthermore, the latency penalty of 64-bit integers can be enormous, especially to disk, where it can exceed 1,000,000 CPU cycles (3 nsec to 3 msec). The memory size penalty for unneeded 64-bit integers could therefore be very high for some applications.
- Portability, especially for combined FORTRAN and C applications, is enhanced by the LP64 data model, and the most common types of problems that can occur are susceptible to automatic detection.
- Interoperability is improved by the ability to use a standard data type to declare data structures that can be used in both 32-bit and 64-bit environments.

- Standards conformance has been demonstrated both in the practical sense by the porting of many programs and in the formal sense of compliance with industry standards through verification test suites.
- Transition from the current industry practice is smooth and direct following a path grooved with experience and demonstrated success.
- No new non-portable data types are required. The data model makes natural use of the C fundamental data types.

14.3 Data Size Neutrality

When it was understood that the Single UNIX Specification was constraining system implementations that were other than ILP32, the relevant specifications were reviewed and recommendations drafted to make these specifications data size- and architecture-neutral. These recommendations were incorporated into the Single UNIX Specification, Version 2 published in 1997.

The following is a summary of the changes that were made. Changes are identified with respect to the CAE Specifications which made up the previous version of the Single UNIX Specification.

14.3.1 System Interface Definitions, Issue 5 (XBD)

The following text was added to System Interface Definitions, Issue 4, Version 2 (XBD), Chapter 10, page 130, point 6, as a fourth bullet item:

> "Ranges greater than those listed here are allowed."

This section describes the argument syntax of the standard utilities and introduces terminology used throughout the Single UNIX Specification for describing the arguments processed by the utilities. It was updated so that the maximum value of a numerical argument is allowed to be greater than a 32-bit value, thus permitting support of 64-bit values.

14.3.2 System Interfaces and Headers, Issue 5 (XSH)

Two general changes were made to System Interfaces and Headers, Issue 4, Version 2 (XSH):

- Use of the type **int** for return values, arguments, and structure members.

  Several functions using the type **int** for return values, arguments, or structure members are not able to represent 64-bit values correctly on architectures implementing an LP64 data model. Where alternate functions were available which do not have this limitation, the functions were marked LEGACY and the alternate functions noted in the Application Usage section. Where no alternative function was available, the types were changed in a data model-neutral manner to overcome this limitation.

- **size_t** *versus* **ssize_t**.

  Several functions have a parameter declared to be **size_t** where the parameter specifies the length of an object to manipulate, and returns the portion of the length of the object processed in a type **ssize_t**. The type **ssize_t** is required so that a negative return value can be used to indicate an error. However, in these functions it is possible for the return value to exceed the range of the type **ssize_t** (since **size_t** has a larger range of positive values than **ssize_t**). Some functions, such as *mq_receive*( ), *msgrcv*( ), *read*( ), *strfmon*( ), and *write*( ), resolve this conflict by restricting the object size in the description section. For example, the description section for the *read*( ) function states: "If the value of *nbyte* is greater than {SSIZE_MAX}, the result is implementation-dependent."

The following were the detailed changes:

- *getdtablesize*( )

  The *getdtablesize*( ) function returns the size of the file descriptor table. This is equivalent to *getrlimit*( ) with the RLIMIT_NOFILE option. Whereas the *getrlimit*( ) function returns a value of type **rlim_t**. This function, returning an **int**, may have problems representing appropriate values in the future. A note about this was added to the Application Usage section, and the function marked LEGACY, with the recommendation that applications should use the *getrlimit*( ) function instead.

- *getpagesize*( )

  The *getpagesize*( ) function returns the current page size. It is equivalent to *sysconf*(_SC_PAGE_SIZE) and *sysconf*(_SC_PAGESIZE). This function, returning an **int**, may have problems representing appropriate values on non-32-bit platforms. Also, the behavior is not specified for this function on systems that support variable size pages. On variable page size systems, a page can be extremely large (theoretically, up to the size of memory). This allows very efficient address translations for large segments of memory that have common page attributes. A note about this has been added to the Application Usage section, and the function marked LEGACY, with the recommendation that applications should use the *sysconf*( ) function instead.

- *readlink*( )

  The *readlink*( ) function returns the size of the information that it reads as a type **int**, but the size of the buffer area is specified by a **size_t**. This function is specified in the IEEE PASC P1003.1a draft standard, and the return value may change in a future version of the Single UNIX Specification to reflect the final POSIX.1a standard.

- *sbrk*( )

  The parameter to the *sbrk*( ) function is a type **int** defining the number of bytes by which to change the break value. This function may not be able to address the full memory range in the future for certain data models. A new type has been introduced to be used in place of the type **int**. This is the **intptr_t** type which is an abstract data type equating to a signed integral type large enough to hold any pointer. This new type is one of a new set of types introduced in a new header **<inttypes.h>** to address the issues of data sizes for specific types.

- **<inttypes.h>**

  The **<inttypes.h>** header is a new header in the Single UNIX Specification, Version 2 and includes definitions for at least the following types:

int16_t	16-bit signed integral type.
int32_t	32-bit signed integral type.
int64_t	64-bit signed integral type.
uint16_t	16-bit unsigned integral type.
uint32_t	32-bit unsigned integral type.
uint64_t	64-bit unsigned integral type.
intptr_t	Signed integral type large enough to hold any pointer.
uintptr_t	Unsigned integral type large enough to hold any pointer.

- **<sys/shm.h>**

  The element *shm_segsz* of structure **shmid_ds**, specifying the size of a memory segment was of type **int**. This has been changed to type **size_t**.

- **<sys/stat.h>** and **<sys/statvfs.h>**

  The element *st_blocks* of the structure **stat** was changed to the new abstract **blkcnt_t** type.

  The elements *f_blocks*, *f_bfree*, and *f_bavail* of the structure **statvfs** were changed to the new abstract **fsblkcnt_t** type.

  The elements *f_files*, *f_ffree*, and *f_favail* of the structure **statvfs** were changed to the new abstract **fsfilcnt_t** type.

  To support the above changes, the following definitions were added to **<sys/types.h>**:

  blkcnt_t A signed arithmetic type, used for file block counts.

  fsblkcnt_t An arithmetic type, used for filesystem block counts.

  fsfilcnt_t An arithmetic type, used for file serial numbers.

- **<sys/time.h>**

  The *tv_usec* element of the **timeval** structure was of type **long**. This has been changed to use a new abstract data type for signed integral time values, known as **suseconds_t**. **suseconds_t** was added to **<sys/types.h>**.

- *msgrcv*( )

  In XSH, Issue 4, Version 2, *msgrcv*( ) returns the size of the message received as an integer value, but the size of the message area is specified by a **size_t**. On 64-bit systems where **size_t** may be a different data type to **int**, this will cause problems. XSH, Issue 5 addresses this problem by changing the type of the return value from **int** to **ssize_t**, and adding a warning to the Description about values of *msgsz* larger the {SSIZE_MAX}.

- *sysconf*( ) and **<unistd.h>**

  There is now a way to find out the data model supported by the platform. This can be queried at compile time, using the constants defined in **<unistd.h>**, or at run time using the *sysconf*( ) function.

  The following symbolic constants are defined to have the value −1 if the implementation never provides the feature, and to have a value other than −1 if the implementation always provides the feature. If these are undefined, the *sysconf*( ) function can be used to determine whether the feature is provided for a particular invocation of the application.

  _XBS5_ILP32_OFF32 Implementation provides a C-language compilation environment with 32-bit **int**, **long**, **pointer**, and **off_t** types.

  _XBS5_ILP32_OFFBIG Implementation provides a C-language compilation environment with 32-bit **int**, **long**, and **pointer** types, and an **off_t** type using at least 64 bits.

  _XBS5_LP64_OFF64 Implementation provides a C-language compilation environment with 32-bit **int** and 64-bit **long**, **pointer**, and **off_t** types.

  _XBS5_LPBIG_OFFBIG Implementation provides a C-language compilation environment with an **int** type using at least 32 bits and **long**, **pointer**, and **off_t** types, using at least 64 bits.

14.3.3 Commands and Utilities, Issue 5 (XCU)

A new section of text was added to the end of the first paragraph of Section 1.9, Utility Description Defaults, to align with requirements in POSIX.2, and restates that integer variables and constants used by utilities are permitted to be 64-bit values.

Programming Environments

The *c89* reference page has some new text describing programming environments. All conforming implementations must support one of the following programming environments by default. Applications can use the *sysconf*( ) function or the *getconf* utility to determine which programming environments the implementation supports.

The following table describes the supported programming environments.

Programming Environment	int	long	pointer	off_t
XBS5_ILP32_OFF32	32	32	32	32
XBS5_ILP32_OFFBIG	32	32	32	>=64
XBS5_LP64_OFF64	32	64	64	64
XBS5_LPBIG_OFFBIG	>= 32	>= 64	>= 64	>= 64

The *c89* reference page also has text describing new support in *getconf* and *sysconf*( ) to determine configuration strings for C compiler flags, linker/loader flags, and libraries for each supported environment.

When an application wishes to use a specific programming environment rather than an implementation's default programming environment while compiling, the application must first verify that the implementation supports the desired environment. If the desired programming environment is supported, the application can then invoke *c89* with the appropriate C compiler flags as the first options for the compile, the appropriate linker/loader flags after any other options but before any operands, and the appropriate libraries at the end of the operands.

The following table shows the various options available:

Programming Environment	Use	Compiler Flags
XBS5_ILP32_OFF32	C Compiler Flags Linker/Loader Flags Libraries Flags	XBS5_ILP32_OFF32_CFLAGS XBS5_ILP32_OFF32_LDFLAGS XBS5_ILP32_OFF32_LIBS
XBS5_ILP32_OFFBIG	C Compiler Flags Linker/Loader Flags Libraries Flags	XBS5_ILP32_OFFBIG_CFLAGS XBS5_ILP32_OFFBIG_LDFLAGS XBS5_ILP32_OFFBIG_LIBS
XBS5_LP64_OFF64	C Compiler Flags Linker/Loader Flags Libraries Flags	XBS5_LP64_OFF64_CFLAG XBS5_LP64_OFF64_LDFLAGS XBS5_LP64_OFF64_LIBS
XBS5_LPBIG_OFFBIG	C Compiler Flags Linker/Loader Flags Libraries Flags	XBS5_LPBIG_OFFBIG_CFLAGS XBS5_LPBIG_OFFBIG_LDFLAGS XBS5_LPBIG_OFFBIG_LIBS

14.4 Porting Issues

Porting an application to a 64-bit UNIX system can be accomplished with a minimal amount of effort if the application was developed using good modern software engineering practices such as:

- ISO C function prototypes
- consistent and careful use of data types
- all declarations are in headers.

First of all, determine which data model is available on the platform you are porting to. The data model you are porting to will have a major impact on the amount of work required to achieve a successful port.

Then take the time to create and use ISO C function prototypes if they are absent from the source code. Unfortunately large quantities of perfectly good legacy code developed in the days before portability was a major issue may not have function prototypes. Fortunately many compilers have an option to generate ISO C function prototypes.

The remainder of this article assumes that you are porting to an LP64 platform since this is the data model of choice amongst major vendors, but the issues raised are equally valid on some or all of the other 64-bit data models.

14.4.1 General

Use utilities such as *grep* to locate and check all instances of the following:

- Shift and complement operators; that is, “<<”, “>>”, “~”. If used with **long**, add “L” to value shifted to avoid an incorrect result.
- Addresses of “&”. Make sure they are not being stored in an **int**.
- Declarations of type **long**. Many of these can be converted to type **int** to save space. This is particularly true for network code.
- The functions *lseek*( ), *fseek*( ), *ftell*( ), *fgetpos*( ), and so on. Use either **off_t** or **fpos_t** as appropriate for offset arguments. Do not use **int** or **long** to store file offsets.
- All (**int** *) and (**long** *) casts.
- Use of (**char** *) 0 for zero or (**char** *) comparisons. Use NULL instead.
- Hard-coded byte counts or memory sizes. These will be wrong if they assume **long**s or **pointer**s are 32 bits. Applications should use the *sizeof*( ) operator to avoid such problems.

14.4.2 Declarations

To enable application code to work on both 32-bit and 64-bit platforms, check all **int** and **long** declarations. Declare integer constants using “L” or “U” as appropriate. Ensure an **unsigned int** is used where appropriate to prevent sign extension. If you have specific variables that need to be 32 bits on both platforms, define the type to be **int**. If the variable should be 32 bits on an ILP32 platform and 64 bits on an LP64 platform, define the variables to be **long**.

Declare numeric variables as **int** or **long** for alignment and performance. Don’t worry about trying to save bytes by using **char** or **short**. Remember that if the type specifier is missing from a declaration, it defaults to an **int**. Declare character pointers and character bytes as **unsigned** to avoid sign extension problems with 8-bit characters.

14.4.3 Assignments and Function Parameters

All assignments require checking. Since **pointer**, **int**, and **long** are no longer the same size on LP64 platforms, problems may arise depending on how the variables are assigned and used within an application.

Do not use **int** and **long** interchangeably because of the possible truncation of significant digits, as shown in the following example:

```
int iv;
long lv;
iv = lv;
```

Do not use **int** to store a pointer. The following example works on an ILP32 platform but fails on an LP64 platform because a 32-bit integer cannot hold a 64-bit pointer:

```
unsigned int i, *p;

i = (unsigned) p;
```

The converse of the above example is sign extension:

```
int *p;
int i;

p = (int *)i;
```

Do not pass **long** arguments to functions expecting **int** arguments. Avoid assignments similar to the following:

```
int foo(int);

int iv;
long lv;
iv = foo( lv );
```

Do not freely exchange **pointer**s and **int**s. Assigning a pointer to an **int**, assigning back to a **pointer**, and dereferencing the pointer may result in a segmentation fault. Avoid assignments similar to the following example:

```
int iv;
char *buffer;

buffer = (char *) malloc((size_t)MAX_LINE);

iv = (int) buffer;

......
buffer = (char *) iv;
```

Do not pass a pointer to a function expecting an **int** as this will result in lost information. For example, avoid assignments similar to the following:

```
void f();
char *cp;

f(cp);
```

Use of ISO C function prototypes should avoid this problem. Use the **void*** type if you need to use a generic pointer type. This is preferable to converting a **pointer** to type **long**.

Examine all assignments of a **long** to a **double** as this can result in a loss of accuracy. On an ILP32 platform, an application can assume that a **double** contains an exact representation of any value stored in a **long** (or a **pointer**). On LP64 platforms this is no longer a valid assumption.

14.4.4 External Interfaces

An external interface mismatch occurs when an external interface requires data in a particular size or layout, but the data is not supplied in the correct format.

For example, an external interface may expect a 64-bit quantity, but receive instead a 32-bit quantity. Another example is an external structure which expects a pointer to a structure with 2 **ints** (8 bytes) but instead receives a pointer to a structure with an **int** and a **long** (16 bytes, 12 of data, 4 of alignment padding). External interface mismatching is a major cause of porting problems.

14.4.5 Format Strings

The function *printf*( ) and related functions can be a major source of problems. For example, on 32-bit platforms, using "%d" to print either an **int** or **long** will usually work, but on LP64 platforms "%ld" must be used to print a **long**. Use the modifier "l" with the d, u, o, and x conversion characters to specify assignment of type **long** or **unsigned long**. When printing a pointer, use "%p". If you wish to print the pointer as a specific representation, the pointer should be cast to an appropriate integer type before using the desired format specifier. For example, to print a pointer as a **unsigned long** decimal number, use %lu:

```
char *p;

printf( "%p %lu\n", (void *)p, (unsigned long)p );
```

As a rule, to print an integer of arbitrary size, cast the integer to **long** or **unsigned long** and use the "%ld" conversion character.

14.4.6 Constants

The results of arithmetic operations on a 64-bit platform can differ from those obtained using the same code on a 32-bit platform. Differing results are often caused by sign extension problems. These are generally the result of mixing **signed** and **unsigned** types and the use of hexadecimal constants. Consider the following code example:

```
long lv = 0xFFFFFFFF;

if ( lv < 0 ) {
```

On an ILP32 platform, *lv* is interpreted as –1 and the *if* condition succeeds. On an LP64 platform *lv* is interpreted as 4294967295 and the if condition fails.

14.4.7 Pointers

On ILP32 platforms, an **int** and a **pointer** are the same size (32 bits) and application code can generally use them interchangeably. For example, a structure could contain a field declared as an **int**, and most of the time contain an **integer**, but occasionally be used to store a **pointer**.

Another example, which most 32-bit **int** utilities will not catch, is the following:

```
int iv, *pv;

iv = (int) pv;
pv = (int *) iv;
```

This code fails on an LP64 platform. Not only do you lose the high 4 bytes of "p", but by default these high bytes are significant.

14.4.8 Sizeof( )

On ILP32 platforms **sizeof(int)** = **sizeof(long)** = **sizeof(ptr *)**. Using the wrong *sizeof*( ) operand does not cause a problem. On LP64 platforms, however, using the wrong *sizeof*( ) will almost certainly cause a problem. For example, the following 32-bit code which copies an array of **pointer**s to **int**s:

```
memcpy((char *)dest, (char *)src, number * sizeof(int))
```

must be changed to use **sizeof(int *)**:

```
memcpy((char *)dest, (char *)src, number * sizeof(int *))
```

on an LP64 platform.

Note that the result of the *sizeof*( ) operation is type **size_t** which is an **unsigned long** on LP64 platforms.

14.4.9 Structures and Unions

The size of structures and unions on 64-bit platforms can be different from those on 32-bit platforms. For example, on ILP32 platforms the size of the following structure is 8 bytes:

```
struct Node {
    struct Node *left;
    struct Node *right;
}
```

but on an LP64 platform its size is 16 bytes.

If you are sharing data defined in structures between 32-bit and 64-bit platforms, be careful about using **long**s and **pointer**s as members of shared structures. These data types introduce sizes that are not generally available on 32-bit platforms. Avoid storing structures with pointers in data files. This code then becomes non-portable between 32-bit and 64-bit platforms.

To increase the portability of your code, use **typedef**'d types for the fields in structures to set up the types as appropriate for the platform, and use the *sizeof*( ) operator to determine the size of a structure. If necessary, use the **#pragma** pack[41] statement to avoid compiler structure padding. This is important if data alignment cannot change (network packets, and so on).

Structures are aligned according to the strictest aligned member. Padding may be added to ensure proper alignment. This padding may be added within the structure, or at the end of the structure to terminate the structure on the same alignment boundary which it started.

Problems can occur when the use of a union is based on an implicit assumption, such as the size of member types.

Consider the following code fragment which works on ILP32 platforms. The code assumes that an array of two **unsigned long** overlays a double.

```
union double_union {
    double d;
    unsigned long ul[2];
};
```

41. This is not portable and is not a general solution.

To work on an LP64 platform, *ul* must be changed to an **unsigned int** type:

```
union double_union {
     double d;
     unsigned int ul[2]
};
```

This problem also occurs when building unions between **int**s and **pointer**s since they are not the same size on LP64 platforms.

Beware of all aliasing which is different multiple definitions of the same data. For example, assume the following two structures refer to the same data in different ways:

```
struct node {
     int src_addr, dst_addr;
     char *name;
}

struct node {
     struct node *src, *dst;
     char *name;
}
```

This works on an ILP32 platform, but fails on an LP64 platform. The two structure definitions should be replaced with a union declaration to ensure portability.

Chapter 15

Large File Support

This chapter is an abridged version of the submission received by X/Open from the Large File Summit, an industry initiative to produce a common specification for support of files that are bigger than the current limit of 2GB on existing 32-bit systems. It details the modifications to the Single UNIX Specification to support large files with unlimited file offsets. These changes have been incorporated into the Single UNIX Specification, Version 2.

The full text of the submission is included on the CD-ROM that accompanies this document.

15.1 Introduction

As UNIX systems have become increasingly powerful, a number of system vendors and UNIX independent software vendors have developed a requirement to access files that contain more information than can be addressed using a **signed long** integer. One possible solution could be to convert every program using files to a larger size for **long** integers, including the operating system. However, the work to do this is undesirable for many vendors.

A number of major system vendors and users met at the Large File Summit for over a year to develop a set of changes to the existing Single UNIX Specification that allow both new and converted programs to address files of arbitrary sizes. This set of changes was provided to X/Open for inclusion into the Single UNIX Specification, Version 2.

15.2 Changes to XBD, Issue 4, Version 2

The following definitions have been added to System Interface Definitions, Issue 4, Version 2 (XBD), Chapter 2, Glossary:

extended signed integral type
: A **signed** integral type or an implementation-dependent type with similar properties.

extended unsigned integral type
: An **unsigned** integral type or an implementation-dependent type with similar properties.

offset maximum
: An attribute of an open file description representing the largest value that can be used as a file offset.

saved resource limits
: An attribute of a process that provides some flexibility in the handling of unrepresentable resource limits,[42] as described in the *exec* family of functions and *setrlimit*( ).

42. The attribute *resource limits* as used in the Single UNIX Specification is not defined.

15.3 Changes to XSH, Issue 4, Version 2

The following changes have been made to System Interfaces and Headers, Issue 4, Version 2 (XSH), Chapters 3 and 4 to incorporate support for large files:

- *aio_read*( )

  Description For regular files, no data transfer will occur past the offset maximum established in the open file description associated with *aiocbp->aio_fildes*.

  Errors The following is a new error condition which may be detected synchronously or asynchronously:

  [EOVERFLOW] The file is a regular file, *aiocbp->aio_nbytes* is greater than 0, and the starting offset in *aiocbp->aio_offset* is before the end-of-file and is at or beyond the offset maximum in the open file description associated with *aiocbp->aio_fildes*.

- *aio_write()*( )

  Description For regular files, no data transfer will occur past the offset maximum established in the open file description associated with *aiocbp->aio_fildes*.

  Errors The following is an additional condition which may be detected synchronously or asynchronously:

  [EFBIG] The file is a regular file, *aiocbp->aio_nbytes* is greater than 0, and the starting offset in *aiocbp->aio_offset* is at or beyond the offset maximum in the open file description associated with *aiocbp->aio_fildes*.

- *exec*( )

  Description The saved resource limits in the new process image are set to be a copy of the process' corresponding hard and soft resource limits.

- *fclose*( ), *fflush*( ), *fputwc*( ), *fputws*( ), *fseek*( ), *putwc*( ), and *putwchar*( )

  Errors These functions will fail if:

  [EFBIG] The file is a regular file and an attempt was made to write at or beyond the offset maximum associated with the corresponding stream.

  Note: This is an additional [EFBIG] error condition.

- *fcntl*( )

  Description An unlock (F_UNLCK) request in which **l_len** is non-zero and the offset of the last byte of the requested segment is the maximum value for an object of type **off_t**, when the process has an existing lock in which **l_len** is 0 and which includes the last byte of the requested segment, will be treated as a request to unlock from the start of the requested segment with an **l_len** equal to 0. Otherwise an unlock (F_UNLCK) request will attempt to unlock only the requested segment.

  Errors The *fcntl*( ) function will fail if:

  [EOVERFLOW] One of the values to be returned cannot be represented correctly.

[EOVERFLOW] The *cmd* argument is F_GETLK, F_SETLK, or F_SETLKW and the smallest or, if **l_len** is non-zero, the largest, offset of any byte in the requested segment cannot be represented correctly in an object of type **off_t**.

Note: These are new error conditions.

- *fdopen*( )

  Description The *fdopen*( ) function will preserve the offset maximum previously set for the open file description corresponding to *fildes*.

- *fgetc*( ), *fgets*( ), *fgetwc*( ), *fgetws*( ), *fread*( ), *fscanf*( ), *getc*( ), *getchar*( ), *gets*( ), *getw*( ), *getwc*( ), *getwchar*( ), *scanf*( )

  Errors These functions will fail if data needs to be read and:

  [EOVERFLOW] The file is a regular file and an attempt was made to read at or beyond the offset maximum associated with the corresponding stream.

  Note: This is a new error condition.

- *fgetpos*( )

  Errors The *fgetpos*( ) function will fail if:

  [EOVERFLOW] The current value of the file position cannot be represented correctly in an object of type **fpos_t**.

  Note: This is a new error condition.

- *fopen*( ), *freopen*( ), *tmpfile*( )

  Description The largest value that can be represented correctly in an object of type **off_t** will be established as the offset maximum in the open file description.

  Errors The *fopen*( ) and *freopen*( ) functions will fail if:

  [EOVERFLOW] The named file is a regular file and the size of the file cannot be represented correctly in an object of type **off_t**.

  Note: This is a new error condition.

- *fpathconf*( ), *pathconf*( )

  Description

Variable	**Value of *name***	**Notes**
FILESIZEBITS	_PC_FILESIZEBITS	3, 4

- *fprintf*( ), *fputc*( ), *fputs*( ), *fwrite*( ), *printf*( ), *putc*( ), *putchar*( ), *puts*( ), *putw*( ), *vfprintf*( ), *vprintf*( )

  Errors These functions will fail if either the stream is unbuffered or the stream's buffer needed to be flushed and:

  [EFBIG] The file is a regular file and an attempt was made to write at or beyond the offset maximum.

  Note: This is an additional [EFBIG] error condition.

- *fseek*( )

Errors — The *fseek*( ) function will fail if:

[EOVERFLOW] The resulting file offset would be a value which cannot be represented correctly in an object of type **long**.

Note: This is a new error condition.

- *fseeko*( )

Description — The *fseeko*( ) function is identical to the modified *fseek*( ) except that the *offset* argument is of type **off_t** and the [EOVERFLOW] error is changed.

Errors — The [EOVERFLOW] error is changed as follows:

[EOVERFLOW] The resulting file offset would be a value which cannot be represented correctly in an object of type **off_t**.

Note: This is a new function.

- *fstat*( ), *lstat*( ), *stat*( )

Errors — These functions will fail if:

[EOVERFLOW] The file size in bytes or the number of blocks allocated to the file or the file serial number cannot be represented correctly in the structure pointed to by *buf*.

Note: This is an additional [EOVERFLOW] error condition.

- *fstatvfs*( ), *statvfs*( )

Errors — These functions will fail if:

[EOVERFLOW] One of the values to be returned cannot be represented correctly in the structure pointed to by *buf*.

Note: This is a new error condition.

- *ftell*( )

Errors — The *ftell*( ) function will fail if:

[EOVERFLOW] The current file offset cannot be represented correctly in an object of type **long**.

Note: This is a new error condition.

- *ftello*( )

Description — The *ftello*( ) function is identical to the modified *ftell*( ) except that the return value is of type **off_t** and the [EOVERFLOW] error is changed.

Errors — The [EOVERFLOW] error is changed as follows:

[EOVERFLOW] The current file offset cannot be represented correctly in an object of type **off_t**.

Note: This is a new function.

- *ftruncate*( )

Errors — The *ftruncate*( ) function will fail if:

[EFBIG] The file is a regular file and *length* is greater than the offset maximum established in the open file description associated with *fildes*.

Note: This is an additional [EFBIG] error condition.

- *getrlimit*( ), *setrlimit*( )

Description When using the *getrlimit*( ) function, if a resource limit can be represented correctly in an object of type **rlim_t**, then its representation is returned; otherwise if the value of the resource limit is equal to that of the corresponding saved hard limit the value returned is RLIM_SAVED_MAX; otherwise the value returned is RLIM_SAVED_CUR.

When using the *setrlimit*( ) function, if the requested new limit is RLIM_INFINITY the new limit will be "no limit"; otherwise if the requested new limit is RLIM_SAVED_MAX the new limit will be the corresponding saved hard limit; otherwise if the requested new limit is RLIM_SAVED_CUR the new limit will be the corresponding saved soft limit; otherwise the new limit will be the requested value. In addition, if the corresponding saved limit can be represented correctly in an object of type **rlim_t**, then it will be overwritten with the new limit.

The result of setting a limit to RLIM_SAVED_MAX or RLIM_SAVED_CUR is unspecified unless a previous call to *getrlimit*( ) returned that value as the soft or hard limit for the corresponding resource limit.

The determination of whether a limit can be correctly represented in an object of type **rlim_t** is implementation-dependent. For example, some implementations permit a limit whose value is greater than RLIM_INFINITY and others do not.

The *exec* family of functions also cause resource limits to be saved (see Section 15.3.0 on page 148).

- *lio_listio*( )

Description For regular files, no data transfer will occur past the offset maximum established in the open file description associated with *aiocbp->aio_fildes*.

Errors The following are additional error codes which may be set for each *aiocb* control block:

[EOVERFLOW] The *aiocbp->aio_lio_opcode* is LIO_READ, the file is a regular file, *aiocbp->aio_nbytes* is greater than 0, and the *aiocbp->aio_offset* is before the end-of-file and is greater than or equal to the offset maximum in the open file description associated with *aiocbp->aio_fildes*.

[EFBIG] The *aiocbp->aio_lio_opcode* is LIO_WRITE, the file is a regular file, *aiocbp->aio_nbytes* is greater than 0, and the *aiocbp->aio_offset* is greater than or equal to the offset maximum in the open file description associated with *aiocbp->aio_fildes*.

Note: These are additional [EFBIG] and [EOVERFLOW] error conditions.

- *lockf*( )

Description An F_ULOCK request in which size is non-zero and the offset of the last byte of the requested section is the maximum value for an object of type **off_t**, when the process has an existing lock in which size is 0 and which includes the last byte of the requested section, will be treated as a request to unlock from the start of the requested section with a size equal to 0. Otherwise an F_ULOCK request will attempt to unlock only the requested section.

Errors The *lockf*( ) function will fail if:

[EINVAL] The *function* argument is not one of F_LOCK, F_TLOCK, F_TEST, or F_ULOCK; or *size* plus the current file offset is less than 0.

[EOVERFLOW] The offset of the first, or if *size* is not 0 then the last, byte in the requested section cannot be represented correctly in an object of type **off_t**.

Notes:

1. This is a clarification of the [EINVAL] error condition.
2. [EOVERFLOW] is a new error condition.

- *lseek*( )

Errors The *lseek*( ) function will fail if:

[EOVERFLOW] The resulting file offset would be a value which cannot be represented correctly in an object of type **off_t**.

Note: This is a new error condition.

- *mmap*( )

Errors The *mmap*( ) function will fail if:

[EOVERFLOW] The file is a regular file and the value of *off* plus *len* exceeds the offset maximum established in the open file description associated with *fildes*.

Note: This is a new error condition.

- *open*( )

Description The largest value that can be represented correctly in an object of type **off_t** will be established as the offset maximum in the open file description.

Errors The *open*( ) function will fail if:

[EOVERFLOW] The named file is a regular file and the size of the file cannot be represented correctly in an object of type **off_t**.

Note: This is a new error condition.

- *read*( ), *readv*( )

Description For regular files, no data transfer will occur past the offset maximum established in the open file description associated with *fildes*.

Errors The *read*( ) and *readv*( ) functions will fail if:

[EOVERFLOW] The file is a regular file, *nbyte* is greater than 0, the starting position is before the end-of-file, and the starting position is greater than or equal to the offset maximum established in the open file description associated with *fildes*.

Note: This is a new error condition.

- *readdir*( )

  Errors The *readdir*( ) function will fail if:

  [EOVERFLOW] One of the values in the structure to be returned cannot be represented correctly.

  Note: This is a new error condition.

- *write*( ), *writev*( )

  Description For regular files, no data transfer will occur past the offset maximum established in the open file description associated with *fildes*.

  Errors These functions will fail if:

  [EFBIG] The file is a regular file, *nbyte* is greater than 0, and the starting position is greater than or equal to the offset maximum established in the open file description associated with *fildes*.

  Note: This is an additional [EFBIG] error condition.

- **<limits.h>**

  The following symbolic constant is defined as a Pathname Variable Value:

  FILESIZEBITS Minimum number of bits needed to represent, as a **signed** integer value, the maximum size of a regular file allowed in the specified directory.
  Minimum Acceptable Value: 32

- **<stdio.h>**

  The following are declared as functions and may also be defined as macros:

```
int    fseeko(FILE *stream, off_t offset, int whence);
off_t  ftello(FILE *stream);
```

  The type **off_t** is defined through **typedef** as described in **<sys/types.h>**.

- **<sys/resource.h>**

  The following symbolic constants are defined:

  RLIM_SAVED_MAX A value of type **rlim_t** indicating an unrepresentable saved hard limit.

  RLIM_SAVED_CUR A value of type **rlim_t** indicating an unrepresentable saved soft limit.

  On implementations where all resource limits are representable in an object of type **rlim_t**, RLIM_SAVED_MAX and RLIM_SAVED_CUR need not be distinct from RLIM_INFINITY.

- **<sys/stat.h>**

  The type of *st_blocks* in the **stat** structure will be changed to:

  `blkcnt_t` `st_blocks` Number of blocks allocated for this object.

- **<sys/statvfs.h>**

  The types of the fields below in the **statvfs** structure will be changed to:

`fsblkcnt_t`	`f_blocks`	Total number of blocks on filesystem in units of *f_frsize*
`fsblkcnt_t`	`f_bfree`	Total number of free blocks.
`fsblkcnt_t`	`f_bavail`	Number of free blocks available to non-privileged process.
`fsfilcnt_t`	`f_files`	Total number of file serial numbers.
`fsfilcnt_t`	`f_ffree`	Total number of free file serial numbers.
`fsfilcnt_t`	`f_favail`	Number of file serial numbers available to non-privileged process.

- **<sys/types.h>**

  The following data types will be defined:

`blkcnt_t`	A signed arithmetic type, used for file block counts.
`fsblkcnt_t`	An arithmetic type, used for filesystem block counts.
`fsfilcnt_t`	An arithmetic type, used for file serial numbers.

- **<unistd.h>**

  The following symbolic constant is defined for *pathconf*( ): _PC_FILESIZEBITS.

15.4 Changes to XCU, Issue 4, Version 2

The following changes have been made to Commands and Utilities, Issue 4, Version 2 (XCU), Chapter 3, Utilities.

Considerations for Utilities in Support of Files of Arbitrary Size

(This is a new section added to XCU, Issue 4, Version 2, Chapter 3 after Section 1.2.1, Symbolic Links.)

The following utilities will support files of any size up to the maximum that can be created by the implementation. This support includes correct writing of file size-related values (such as file sizes and offsets, line numbers, and block counts) and correct interpretation of command line arguments that contain such values:

basename	Return non-directory portion of pathname.
cat	Concatenate and print files.
cd	Change working directory.
chgrp	Change file group ownership.
chmod	Change file modes.
chown	Change file ownership.
cksum	Write file checksums and sizes.
cmp	Compare two files.
cp	Copy files.
dd	Convert and copy a file.
df	Report free disk space.
dirname	Return directory portion of pathname.

du	Estimate file space usage.
find	Find files.
ln	Link files.
ls	List directory contents.
mkdir	Make directories.
mv	Move files.
pathchk	Check pathnames.
pwd	Return working directory name.
rm	Remove directory entries.
rmdir	Remove directories.
sh	Shell, the standard command language interpreter.
sum	Print checksum and block or byte count of a file.
test	Evaluate expression.
touch	Change file access and modification times.
ulimit	Set or report file size limit.

Exceptions to the requirement that utilities support files of any size up to the maximum are:

1. Utilities such as *tar* and *cpio* cannot support arbitrary file sizes due to limitations imposed by fixed file formats.
2. Use of files as command scripts, or for configuration or control, are exempt. For example, it is not required that *sh* be able to read an arbitrarily large "**.profile**".
3. Shell input and output redirection are exempt. For example, it is not required that the redirections *sum < file* or *echo foo > file* succeed for an arbitrarily large existing file.

- *sh*

  Description — Pathname expansion will not fail due to the size of a file.

  Shell input and output redirections will have an implementation-dependent offset maximum that will be established in the open file description.

- *pax*

  Application Usage

  The *pax* utility is not able to handle arbitrary file sizes. There is currently a proposal in ballot in IEEE PASC P1003.2b to address this issue.

15.5 Rationale for Changes

The reader is referred to the unabridged Large File Summit Submission included on the accompanying CD-ROM for the full rationale for this section. Only the rationale relevant to the Single UNIX Specification is included in this abridged chapter.

15.5.1 Functions not Modified

The following functions do not require modification:

- *aio_error*( ), *aio_cancel*( ), *aio_return*( ), *aio_suspend*( )

  No large file implications were identified for these functions.

- *aio_fsync*( )

  It is possible that an *aio_fsync*( ) could try to write out file blocks that are beyond the offset maximum, just as *fsync*( ) could. There is no compelling reason for either to fail. Clearly, the original write request had to be within the offset maximum for the file description used. The *aio_fsync*( ) function will not enforce the offset maximum on the blocks which it writes out.

- *glob*( ), *wordexp*( )

  The subroutines that expand filename wild cards need to be large file capable.

15.5.2 Functions Modified

- *aio_read*( )

  The *aio_read*( ) function enforces the offset maximum rules for consistency with *read*( ) and *readv*( ).

- *aio_write*( )

  The *aio_write*( ) function enforces the offset maximum rules for consistency with *write*( ) and *writev*( ).

- *creat*( )

  The *creat*( ) function will fail if the named file is a regular file and the size of the file cannot be represented correctly in an object of type **off_t** (see Section 15.3 on page 148, *open*( )). This offers protection from the following coding style:

```
if (stat(path, ...) < 0) {
    /* assume file does not exist, so create it */
    if ((fd = creat(path, ...)) < 0) {
       /* print out error text */
    }
}
```

  In this example, the *stat*( ) function is being used to determine the existence of a file. But if the file size cannot be represented correctly in an object of type **off_t** then *stat*( ) will fail (see Section 15.3 on page 148, *fstat*( )), and if *creat*( ) did not then fail it would have the unintended effect of truncating the file to 0 length. Many applications and standard utilities have code similar to this example, including typical implementations of the *touch* utility.

- *fcntl*( ), *lockf*( )

  Unlock requests are sometimes rounded to infinity so that a process can create a whole-file lock and then successfully issue a request to clip off the beginning of the lock without leaving behind an unrepresentable lock. This is to avoid breaking any existing 32-bit applications which may do this.

  Several existing implementations of *fcntl*( ) permit locking the byte whose offset is the maximum value that can be represented correctly in an object of type **off_t**, even though *write*( ) cannot write to that offset. This specification permits that behavior.

  The *fcntl*( ) function will fail if the *cmd* argument is F_GETLK and the first lock which blocks the lock description has a starting offset or length which cannot be represented correctly in an object of type **off_t**. Information about such a lock cannot be correctly returned.

  Discussion of the semantics of *fcntl*( ) locks that cross the **off_t** boundary resulted in six competing proposals:

  1. An unlock request fails if it would create an unrepresentable lock.
  2. If any lock request includes the byte whose offset is the maximum value that fits in an **off_t**, then the request is equivalent to a request where **l_len** is 0 and **l_start** refers to the first byte of the affected area.
  3. (Proposal dropped.)
  4. If **l_len** is 0, then the lock is through and includes the maximum value of **off_t** (and not beyond).
  5. Just no lies.
  6. If an unlock request includes the byte whose offset is the maximum value that fits in an **off_t**, and there is an existing lock with **l_len** equal to 0 which also includes that byte, then the request is equivalent to a request where **l_len** is 0 and **l_start** refers to the first byte of the affected area.

  An advantage of 2., 4., and 6. is that they do not change the existing behavior of a 32-bit application.

  Proposals 1. and 5. can result in a new type of failure in the case where the program creates a lock with **l_len** equal to 0 and then clips off the beginning, leaving behind an unrepresentable lock.

  Proposal 4. precludes truly whole-file locking.

  Proposal 6. was adopted because it preserves existing 32-bit behavior and is less disruptive than proposal 2. (which extends lock requests in addition to unlock requests).

  The *fcntl*( ) and *lockf*( ) functions will fail if the offset of the first byte in the region exceeds the largest possible value in an object of type **off_t**, or if **l_len** is non-zero then the offset of the last byte in the region exceeds the largest possible value in an object of type **off_t**. Otherwise, the process could create a lock which would be *beyond* the ability of the program to represent.

- *fgetpos*( ), *fseek*( ), *ftell*( ), *lseek*( )

  These functions will fail if the resulting file offset would exceed the largest value that can be represented correctly in the related type which is in use for the call, and will set *errno* to [EOVERFLOW] (permitted by PASC Interpretation 1003.1-90 #75).

Programs typically, but incorrectly, fail to check the return value of these functions, which renders the error return less useful. On the other hand, returning an incorrect offset can also result in serious malfunction.

An *lseek*( ) to the end of a file using:

```
lseek(fd, 0, SEEK_END);
```

is quite common. It is unfortunate that these fail on a too-large file since the return value is usually ignored. One alternative considered was for *lseek*( ) to move the file offset for all valid requests and then return an error if the resulting offset is too large. That is, the call would succeed for applications that do not check the return code, but also fail for applications that do. This option was deemed unsuitable to adopt. For example, it might be difficult to implement using a remote procedure call system that was constructed to return either results or an error, but not both. In addition, POSIX.1 requires the file offset to remain unchanged if an error is returned by *lseek*( ). It was felt that the open protection and the read/write limit rules (see the unabridged version of the Large File Summit Submission on the accompanying CD-ROM) are more effective defenses against this problem.

Another potentially serious consequence of ignoring the return value of *lseek*( ) is that programs which extend data files by attempting to seek beyond the end-of-file and then writing may instead overwrite existing data.

For example, typical implementations of the *dbm* and *ndbm* libraries contain code such as:

```
(void) lseek(db->dbm_pagf, blkno*PBLKSIZ, L_SET);
if (write(db->dbm_pagf, pagebuf, PBLKSIZ) != PBLKSIZ)
            ... error handling ...
```

The problem is that the return code of *lseek*( ) is not checked and so if *blkno*PBLKSIZ* overflows, the *lseek*( ) will fail (or will seek to an unintended offset) and the data will be written to an unintended offset.

- *fpathconf*( ), *pathconf*( )

  The reference "See Note 3,4" refers to notes in the XSH specification for *fpathconf*( ) and *pathconf*( ). These notes indicate that the option _PC_FILESIZEBITS is valid only for a directory, and the results are for files that exist or may be created in that directory.

  The _PC_FILESIZEBITS option makes it possible for a process to determine how large a file can be created in a given directory. It takes into account implementation limitations in the filesystem (for example, due to the size of file size and block count variables), and it takes into account long-term policy limitations (for example, due to the mount utility's *-o nolargefiles* option). It does not take into account dynamic restrictions such as the RLIM_FSIZE resource limit or the number of available file blocks, so the process must perform appropriate checks.

  When the current directory is on a typical large file capable filesystem and is mounted with the *-o nolargefiles* option:

  ```
  pathconf(".", _PC_FILESIZEBITS);
  ```

  will return 32. In general, if the maximum size file that could ever exist on the mounted filesystem is *maxsize* then the returned value is 2 plus the floor of the base 2 logarithm of *maxsize*.

- *fseeko*( ), *ftello*( )

  These functions are needed because *fseek*( ) and *ftell*( ) are limited by the **long** offset type required by the ISO C standard. The *fsetpos*( ) and *fgetpos*( ) functions, although they do use an abstract offset type, are not complete replacements for *fseek*( ) and *ftell*( ) because they do not allow relative seeks or arithmetic on **fpos_t** values.

- *fsetpos*( )

  Since *fsetpos*( ) sets an absolute file position, which is always legal regardless of the implementation-dependent sizes of **off_t**, there are no new error returns or other new semantics.

- *fstatvfs*( ), *statvfs*( )

  These functions will fail if the total, free, or available number of blocks or files cannot be represented correctly in the structure to be returned (*f_blocks*, *f_bfree*, *f_bavail*, *f_files*, *f_ffree*, *f_favail*).

- *ftruncate*( ), *truncate*( ), *unlink*( )

  These functions are used only on pre-existing files and so do not have the potential programming hazards as *creat*( ).

  When *ftruncate*( ) is used to increase the size of a file, the semantics are similar to a *write*( ) of zeros to the file. For consistency with *write*( ), the *ftruncate*( ) function will fail when the request is beyond the offset maximum (even if the effect of the request would be to shorten the file).

- *ftw*( ), *nftw*( )

  The *ftw*( ) and *nftw*( ) functions may fail if a *stat*( ) in the underlying implementation fails with [EOVERFLOW]. This is unfortunate because "small" binaries using these functions cannot reasonably be used on file trees containing "large" files. Some systems have a non-standard extension to *nftw*( ) which permits it to continue when *stat*( ) fails (typical failures also include [ESTALE] and [ELOOP]).

- *getrlimit*( ) *setrlimit*( )

  These functions map limits that they cannot represent correctly to and from RLIM_SAVED_MAX and RLIM_SAVED_CUR. These values do not require any special handling by programs. They may be thought of as tokens that the kernel hands out to programs that cannot handle the real answer, and that remind the kernel, when the tokens come back from the user, of what value is really meant.

  If *setrlimit*( ) fails for any reason (for example, [EPERM]), the resource limits and saved resource limits remain unchanged.

  This proposal does not specify any particular value for RLIM_INFINITY, RLIM_SAVED_MAX, or RLIM_SAVED_CUR. Typical current implementations use the value 0x7FFFFFFF for RLIM_INFINITY, and it is recommended that RLIM_SAVED_MAX and RLIM_SAVED_CUR have similar large values.

  Few, if any, programs need to refer explicitly to RLIM_SAVED_MAX or RLIM_SAVED_CUR. Those that do should not use them in C-language switch cases since they may have the same value in some implementations (see Section 15.3 on page 148, **<sys/resource.h>**).

  A limit that can be represented correctly in an object of type **rlim_t** is either "no limit", which is represented with RLIM_INFINITY, or has a value not equal to RLIM_INFINITY, RLIM_SAVED_MAX, or RLIM_SAVED_CUR and which can be represented correctly in an object of type **rlim_t**, and which meets any additional implementation-dependent criteria for correct representation.

A rejected alternative proposal was to map limits that could not be represented to and from RLIM_INFINITY. This would avoid the need for the new symbols RLIM_SAVED_MAX and RLIM_SAVED_CUR. But such mapping would arguably be untrue, and the resulting information loss would cause unintuitive program behavior, especially in programs running with appropriate privileges needed to raise hard limits.

A rejected alternative proposal was that if *getrlimit*( ) could not correctly return a current limit, then it should instead return −1 and set *errno* to [EOVERFLOW]. But that would result in unnecessary breakage of programs. (Note that this breakage occurs even when no large files are present.) It would also result in malfunction of programs that assume that they are calling *getrlimit*( ) properly and so failure "cannot happen". For example, in the 4.4BSD-Lite distribution, there are at least 15 unchecked calls to *getrlimit*( ). When the 4.4BSD *csh* limit function is used to report the current limits, there is no check of the return code and so the reported results can be entirely incorrect. Also, non-superuser programs typically unlimit themselves with:

```
getrlimit(RLIMIT_STACK, &rl);
rl.rlim_cur = rl.rlim_max;
setrlimit(RLIMIT_STACK, &rl);
```

If the *getrlimit*( ) fails, then garbage is passed to *setrlimit*( ) which may result in an unwanted and extremely restricted limit. Several utilities that are part of the GNU C compiler have this problem.

- *lio_listio*( )

  The *lio_listio*( ) function enforces the offset maximum rules since they are logically equivalent to *aio_read*( ) and *aio_write*( ) which enforce it.

- *mmap*( )

  For consistency with *read*( ) and *write*( ), the *mmap*( ) function will fail when the request extends beyond the offset maximum.

- *open*( )

  The *open*( ) function called with O_TRUNC set will fail without truncation if the named file is a regular file and the size of the file cannot be represented correctly in an object of type **off_t**. (See *creat*( ) above .)

- *read*( ), *readv*( ), *write*( ), *writev*( )

  These functions may do a partial read or write due to the offset maximum. That is, the value returned may be less than *nbyte* if the number of bytes remaining which may be transferred is less than *nbyte*.

- *ulimit*( )

  The *ulimit*( ) function will return an unspecified result if the result cannot be represented correctly in an object of type **long**. As this function is already obsolescent, the use of *getrlimit*( ) and *setrlimit*( ) is recommended for getting and setting process limits.

15.5.3 General Porting Suggestions

When porting a program to be large file capable, general areas of concern include:

- command line arguments
- API conversion
- output formatting
- fixed format media issues
- other languages.

Command Line Arguments

Numeric arguments which are file size-related, such as a file offset or block count, need to be handled as an appropriately large type. Converting arguments to an **off_t** that is larger than a **long** may need to be accomplished with non-standard *scanf*( ) formats, if available, or with portable user-written functions that convert ASCII to a large **off_t** analogous to the *strtol*( ) function.

API Conversion

The program should be recompiled in a large **off_t** environment or, alternatively, should be converted to use the transitional API[43] .

Output Formatting

Output of types that have been converted will probably involve using a different *printf*( ) format or using a revised user-written conversion routine. Since there is a larger range of values which take up more space, revision of the output layout may be required.

Fixed Format Media Issues

Current implementations of the *tar* and *cpio* utilities are defective in their support of arbitrarily large files. The *pax* utility is also equally defective, but is the subject of a proposal in ballot. (See Section 15.4 on page 154, *pax*.)

Vendor and third-party backup software is also unable to support large files and will require modification in order to do so.

Other Languages

This specification is for the C language only. Other languages have different support requirements; for example, the Fortran I/O API has a limit on the number of records, not bytes.

---

43. The transitional API is not part of the Single UNIX Specification and is included in the unabridged version of this document, included on the accompanying CD-ROM.

15.5.4 Considerations for Utilities in Support of Files of Arbitrary Size

The utilities listed in *Considerations for Utilities in Support of Files of Arbitrary Size* are utilities which are used to perform administrative tasks such as to create, move, copy, remove, change the permissions, or measure the resources of a file. They are useful both as end-user tools and as utilities invoked by applications during software installation and operation.

Typical core utilities must be compiled in a "large" **off_t** compilation environment or must use the transitional APIs. Using the compilation environment reduces the number of editing changes required to port a program, but it does not reduce the effort required to ensure the correctness of the port.

The *chgrp*, *chmod*, *chown*, *ln*, and *rm* utilities probably require use of large file capable versions of *stat*( ), *lstat*( ), *ftw*( ), and the **stat** structure.

The *cat*, *cksum*, *cmp*, *cp*, *dd*, *mv*, *sum*, and *touch* utilities probably require use of large file capable versions of *creat*( ), *open*( ), and *fopen*( ).

The *cat*, *cksum*, *cmp*, *dd*, *df*, *du*, *ls*, and *sum* utilities may require writing large integer values. For example:

- The *cat* utility might have a **–n** option which counts newlines.
- The *cksum* and *ls* utilities report file sizes.
- The *cmp* utility reports the line number at which the first difference occurs, and also has a **–l** option which reports file offsets.
- The *dd*, *df*, *du*, *ls*, and *sum* utilities report block counts.

The *dd*, *find*, and *test* utilities may need to interpret command arguments that contain 64-bit values. For *dd*, the arguments include *skip=n*, *seek=n*, and *count=n*. For *find*, the arguments include *–size n*. For *test*, the arguments are those associated with algebraic comparisons.

The *df* utility might need to access large filesystems with *statvfs*( ).

The *ulimit* utility will need to use large file capable versions of *getrlimit*( ) and *setrlimit*( ) and be able to read and write large integer values.

Conversion between **off_t** (or other derived types) and ASCII is unspecified, which is a significant practical deficiency. This is being considered by the ISO WG14 working group.

Additional Requirements for the sh Utility — Porting Recommendations

Pathname expansion (for example, expanding ***/foo.c** to **a/foo.c b/foo.c c/foo.c**) and pathname completion might in some cases use the *stat*( ) function which would need to be large file capable.

The offset maximum used for shell input and output redirections is implementation-dependent. Some vendors prefer to use the smallest supported **off_t**, others prefer the largest.

15.6 Further Information

The CD-ROM that accompanies this document contains the following information resources:

- the unabridged Large File Summit Submission
- a white paper from SunSoft entitled *Large Files in Solaris: A White Paper*.

Chapter 16

Year 2000: The Millennium Rollover

Many existing computer programs use dates represented by only two digits for the year value rather than the full four digits (for example, 84 rather than 1984). This works for years in the range 1900-1999 (on some systems this range may be limited to 1970-1999) but will yield unpredictable results when used with years outside of this range. We will all experience the results of this software problem in less than 1000 working days time; that is, in January 2000.

This chapter outlines the problem, gives some general advice on how to prepare, and gives practical advice on how to use interfaces within the Single UNIX Specification to cope with the millennium rollover.

16.1 Introduction

In its simplest terms, this is a programming error in that data has been processed and stored in log files and databases using a two-digit format for the year value; that is, 99 rather than 1999. This has occurred mainly since programmers have attempted to minimize the amount of expensive disk storage and memory used. Calculations based on the year value in its two-digit format are likely to yield unspecified results once the value rolls over to 00 in the year 2000.

Many COBOL programmers have tended to mix data and control information, usually to save space in databases. In particular, for example, the year field would be a date if numerically larger than say 20, and a command or EOF flag if from 0 to 19. So, the rollover will potentially cause great excitement for some database users; much more so than wrong dates.

Some operating systems have taken a different approach to handling two-digit dates by adopting a sliding window. Depending on the size of the sliding window, this can cause other problems, and is generally not suitable for applications considering large date ranges, such as pension funds.

The solution proposed in this chapter takes an alternative approach, and is a workaround to maintain backwards compatibility for existing users. The proper solution is to specify all years in four digits.

16.2 Preparation

Examine your source code and look for date usage within the code. Update your source code so that it can handle data in the range 1900-2099. If the system you are using has a 32-bit **signed time_t**, be aware that problems may occur as soon as the year 2038. If this matters, you should consider upgrading to a platform supporting 64-bit **signed time_t** values.

Look for any log files that store dates in two-digit format, and examine how the data is processed. Consider converting such log files to use a four-digit format. Alternately, adopt an approach for interpreting two-digit date formats. (See the Advice to Implementors section in *getdate*( ).)

Test your source code by looking for usage for the Single UNIX Specification interfaces noted below, setting the date on your system to the year 2000, and executing the code.[44]

There are some interfaces within the Single UNIX Specification that can use two-digit notation for year values; these are highlighted below together with recommendations on how the two-digit dates should be interpreted.

Note: The *Future Directions* identified in this chapter have been applied in the Single UNIX Specification, Version 2.

16.3 API Usage

- *getdate*( )

```
struct tm *getdate(const char *string);
```

XSH, Issue 4, Version 2, Page 231 states the following with respect to the format code %y:

`%y` Year within century (00-99).

Suppose there is a line of the form %m/%d/%y in the template file, and a call is made:

```
struct tm * p_tm;
p_tm = getdate( "11/22/02" );
```

It is not specified what would be represented in the **struct tm** for the century. This could be interpreted as either 11/22/1902 or 11/22/2002, since the implementation does not know which century this is to refer to.

— Advice to Programmers:

Use the %Y field descriptor which defines year as a four-digit field (ccyy).

— Advice to Implementors:

Define %y such that when a century is not otherwise specified, values in the range 69-99 refer to the twentieth century, and values in the range 00-68 refer to the twenty-first century. This is consistent with the *touch* command in XCU.

— Future Directions:

XSH, Issue 5 adds the %C specifier to the interface to denote the century, and interprets the %y specifier in the absence of a century as per Advice to Implementors above. An

44. Warning: It is recommended that such tests are run on a testbed system and not a live production system.

Application Usage note is added recommending use of %Y over %y.

- *strptime*( )

```
char *strptime(const char *buf, const char *format, struct tm *tm);
```

XSH, Issue 4, Version 2, Page 615 states the following with respect to the format code %y:

`%y` is the year within century [00,99]; leading zeros are permitted but not required.

Suppose that the following call is made:

```
struct tm thetime;
strptime( "11/22/02", "%m/%d/%y", &thetime );
```

It is not specified what would be represented in the **struct tm** for the century. This could be interpreted as either 11/22/1902 or 11/22/2002, since the implementation does not know which century this is to refer to.

— Advice to Programmers:

Use the %Y field descriptor which defines year as a four-digit field (ccyy).

— Advice to Implementors:

Define %y such that when a century is not otherwise specified, values in the range 69-99 refer to the twentieth century and values in the range 00-68 refer to the twenty-first century. This is consistent with the *touch* command in XCU.

— Future Directions:

XSH, Issue 5 denotes the interpretation of the ranges in the Advice to Implementors above.

16.4 Command Usage

- *date*

The following excerpt from the Operands section of the *date* command in XCU, Issue 4, Version 2, Page 247 states:

EX `mmddhhmm[yy]`

Attempt to set the system date and time from the value given in the operand. This is only possible if the user has appropriate privileges and the system permits the setting of the system date and time. The first mm is the month (number); dd is the day (number); hh is the hour (number, 24-hour system); the second mm is the minute (number), and yy is the last two digits of the year and is optional.

The yy specifier is a two-digit specifier to the year and thus does not denote the century.

— Advice to Programmers:

Consult each of your target platform suppliers for their handling of the yy specifier.

— Advice to Implementors:

Define yy such that if century is not specified, then values in the range [69-99] refer to years in the twentieth century (1969 to 1999 inclusive), and values in the range [00-68] refer to years in the twenty-first century (2000 to 2068 inclusive). This is consistent with the *touch* command in XCU.

— Future Directions:

XCU, Issue 5 denotes the interpretation of the ranges in the Advice to Implementors above, and also adjusts the Synopsis for this command such that century handling is added as follows:

EX `mmddhhmm[[cc]yy]`

Attempt to set the system date and time from the value given in the operand. This is only possible if the user has appropriate privileges and the system permits the setting of the system date and time. The first mm is the month (number); dd is the day (number); hh is the hour (number, 24-hour system); the second mm is the minute (number); cc is the century and is the first two digits of the year (this is optional), yy is the last two digits of the year and is optional. If century is not specified, then values in the range [69-99] refer to years in the twentieth century (1969 to 1999 inclusive), and values in the range [00-68] refer to years in the twenty-first century (2000 to 2068 inclusive).

- *prs*, *get*

The following excerpt from the Options section of the *prs* and *get* commands in XCU, Issue 4, Version 2,Pages 588 and 361 respectively, states:

```
-c cutoff
```

and indicates the cutoff date-time, in the form:

```
YY[MM[DD[HH[MM[SS]]]]]
```

The YY specifier is a two-digit specifier to the year and thus does not denote the century.

— Advice to Programmers:

Consult each of your target platform suppliers for their handling of the YY specifier.

— Advice to Implementors:

Define YY such that values in the range 69-99 refer to the twentieth century and values in the range 00-68 refer to the twenty-first century. This is consistent with the *touch* command in XCU.

— Future Directions:

XCU, Issue 5, denotes the interpretation of the ranges in the Advice to Implementors above. The *prs* and *get* commands are the only commands where users will not be able to specify a full four-digit date, and this is due to the existing file format limitations.

Chapter 17

POSIX Software Administration

The UNIX 98 brand, introduced with the Single UNIX Specification, Version 2, includes a new Component Definition defined by IEEE Std. 1387.2-1995, Software Administration (POSIX-7.2). This standard provides a comprehensive set of software packaging and administration utilities and a standard format for software packages that simplify all of the major functions of distributing and managing software in stand-alone or distributed heterogeneous environments.

The UNIX 98 Software Administration Component enables software packagers to package software into a single distribution for multiple platforms, and to define relationships between software components which can range from simple to complex. For example, software packages can be a simple set of files, an application, or a bundle of related applications. This also provides the administrator with a consistent way to distribute, install, and control software (including listing, verifying, reconfiguring, and removing). Software providers and administrators will no longer have to write their own tools and repackage software for use with these tools.

17.1 Introduction

The packaging, distribution, and control of software is an important and time-consuming task for software developers and administrators. In order to manage software in a distributed, heterogeneous environment, both software developers and administrators have often been required to develop their own management tools.

Software developers are currently faced with one of two choices. They can develop their own installation procedure and port it to each of their target platforms, or they can design different installation procedures for each target platform using the formats and procedures supported by that platform.

Administrators in heterogeneous environments often resort to defining their own tools so that they have a common way to manage software across all of their systems. Even though comprehensive software management solutions are becoming more prevalent in the market, many of these solutions require repackaging the software into a supported format.

This chapter describes the capabilities provided by POSIX-7.2 that can help address the complexities of distributed software administration. It starts by summarizing the history, scope, and components of POSIX-7.2. Next, it presents the software structures and packaging layout available to software developers to create and distribute portable software packages. Finally, it describes the standard utilities available for the administrator to install and manage software in a distributed environment.

17.2 History

This section covers the way in which the POSIX-7.2 standard evolved. This is useful in understanding why the standard contains what it does, and why the facilities are defined the way they are.

One of the conditions of starting out on the process of producing a POSIX standard is that there should be sufficient commitment to enable the work to be done. The working group was fortunate that there was a high level of commitment by several companies and individuals. Most major vendors were represented, as were users in the form of living/breathing system administrators.

Another condition for a POSIX standard is that it should be based on existing practice and not be an invention of the group. One of the first actions taken by the working group, therefore, was to examine the existing practice. This was done by inviting submissions via specifications or presentations of existing technologies. The companies and organizations that made such submissions are given below:

Digital Equipment Corporation (setld suite)
Fermi Labs
Hewlett Packard (SD utilities)
IBM
ICL
Open Software Foundation (DME/SDS)
SNI (SAX/LSM)
SCO (custom/distmaster+)
UNIX System Laboratories (SV pkg* tools)

The working group found that all the submissions had many features in common (including both utilities and supported software structures) and that there was a good deal of agreement in the facilities that should be provided. Obviously some features were only found in some submissions and there were some misalignments. Therefore, while there was no one existing practice that provided all the facilities identified as necessary for the standard, nearly all of the resulting standard was based on the existing practices.

The working group was established in 1991 and worked to develop and refine the standard for several years. During that time, the standard went though one preliminary and three formal ballots. The balloting process involved many other contributions that provided hundreds of comments and issues, nearly all of which were eventually resolved. The standard was finally approved in June, 1995. As is customary for POSIX standards, it was then registered as an ISO/IEC Draft International Standard that same year.

17.3 Scope of POSIX

Another important consideration in defining a standard is to limit its scope to something that can be achieved in a reasonable time. There is a trade-off here between what one would like to do, and what is necessary for a reasonable standard. Additionally, there had been a constraint that POSIX standards cannot rely on non-standard facilities. Because of this last point, the protocols by which the distributed aspects of this standard could interoperate between implementations were not included in the standard. Note that efforts to address areas not covered by this standard have been taking place in The Open Group Systems Management Technical Working Group. These efforts are summarized at the end of the chapter.

The original work going into POSIX-7.2 focused on UNIX systems. Over the course of development, the standard was broadened to permit implementation by other operating systems, including those for personal computers.

The scope of POSIX Software Administration can be viewed in two ways: the components of the standard from a functionality point of view, and the various roles that operate on software from the time it is developed to its execution by end users. These are presented next.

17.3.1 Components

There are three main components that the standard addresses:

1. Standard Software Structures and Software Packaging Layout

   The standard defines a hierarchical set of structures that the software developer can use to organize software files into manageable components. These structures can be built to reflect both purchasing options and installation options ranging from the simple to the complex.

   The standard also defines the layout of the distribution media containing packaged software. This provides portability of installation media, as the media can be processed by any conforming system. Both serial and directory access formats are defined so that a wide range of media can be supported using the same layout.

2. Standard Utilities and Software Catalog Information

   By providing an interface for software administration that is consistent for all conforming implementations, administrators are able to use any such systems without retraining. Additionally, this greatly simplifies the installation documentation that software developers need to provide, as they can point to standard interfaces.

   The standard provides utilities to package software files into *distributions* using the software packaging layout. There are utilities to install the software from the distribution onto target systems, and then manage that software once it is on the system. There are also utilities to manage the distributions themselves, including distributing software between systems.

   Inventory information about the distributions is maintained both within the distribution as well as on the system after the software is installed. This information is stored in a software *catalog*, and is used to drive the management utilities. These management utilities include listing, verifying, or removing software. Thus, once the software package is defined, there are utilities to manage it throughout the software lifecycle.

3. Distributed Software Administration

   The standard defines the concepts and the utility syntax for managing software in a distributed environment. An implementation of the standard can either provide the fully distributed utilities as defined in the standard, or provide *limited* conformance, meaning only local, or stand-alone, operations are supported. In order to understand the distributed aspects of the standard, it helps to present the distributed roles provided in the POSIX-7.2 rationale.

17.3.2 Distributed Roles

POSIX-7.2 roles can be viewed as processes that take software from one state to another; for example, from the form it has when it is in a distribution, to the form it has after installation. The software administration roles are shown in Figure 17-1.

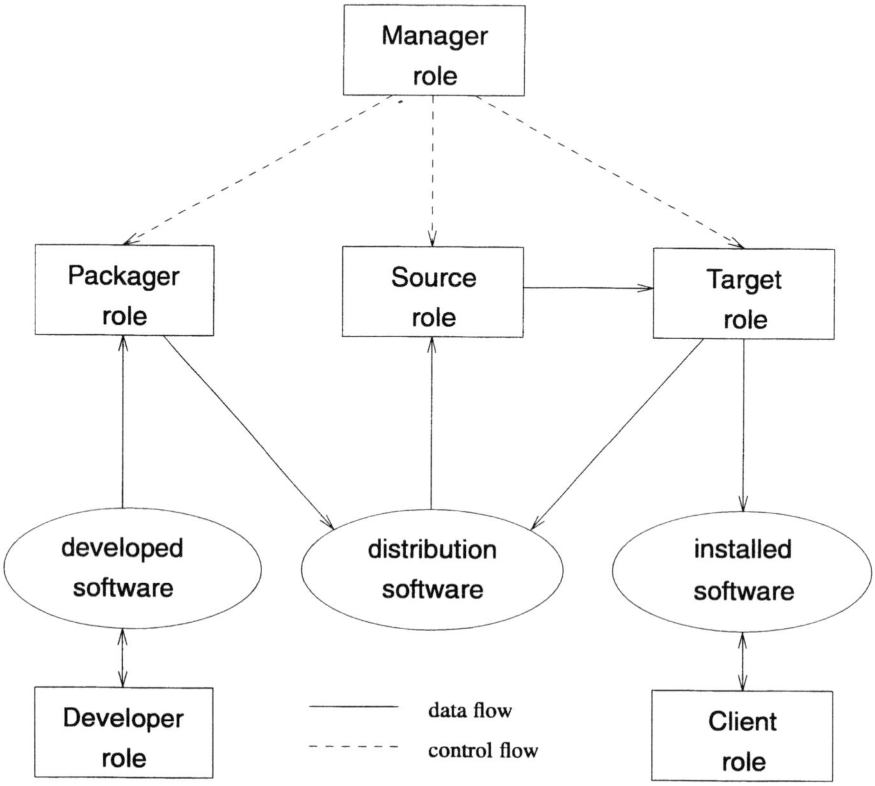

Figure 17-1 Software Administration Roles

In a distributed environment, each of these roles can be on a separate system, although for local operations they would obviously all be on the same system.

- Developer Role

  The developer role is specifically outside the scope of the standard. In the developer role, software is constructed into the form known as *developed software* which is the form in which it can be accepted by the packager role. Typically, the developer role involves activities such as compilation, source control, and so on.

- Manager Role

  The manager role provides for the distributed control of the software administration process. The manager role is where the POSIX tasks are initiated, and is the role with which the administrator directly interacts, either through the command line interface provided in the standard or through a management application. The manager role directs the other roles to actually package, install, or manage software.

- Packager Role

  The packager role transforms software from the locations where it exists after being developed into the standard packaging layout suitable for distribution. The packager role can package directly to media, or can package to file system-based distributions that can later be copied to media, or from where installation can be directly performed.

- Source Role

  The source role serves the files in the software distribution source to the target role for actual installation onto a target system, or for copying to a second distribution. The source role also makes the logical software structures available to the manager role for user selection of software to be operated on.

- Target Role

  It is the target role that actually installs the software and places it into a form from which it will eventually be used. Normally, the software is installed on the system where the software is run, in which case, the software is also configured. Note that, while this may be the usual case, the target role is not necessarily on the system that will run the software, but instead may be on a file server that serves the installed software to other client systems.

- Client Role

  The client role is where the software is configured so that it is in a state where it can be executed. Configuration usually needs to take place on the system and architecture on which the software is to run, so the standard supports configuration independent of installation. Installed software may be subject to being configured several times. How the installed software is made available to the client role (for example, via a remote filesystem) is also outside the scope of the POSIX standard. In addition to making the installed software files available to the client, an implementation must also make the installed software catalog information available so that the clients can be configured by running configure scripts (described below).

17.4 Defining and Creating Software Packages

Once the software has been created, it is the task of the software packager to define the logical organization of the software, and then package the software into a distribution.

17.4.1 Defining Software Structures

The standard provides a hierarchical set of software structures that the software packager can use to structure the software in a way that matches the product and installation options of the software. Shown in Figure 17-2, these various structures define a range of attributes such as the component name, description, contents, dependencies, and so on. Thus, the administrator can easily identify and install the products, and also easily install supported subsets of those products.

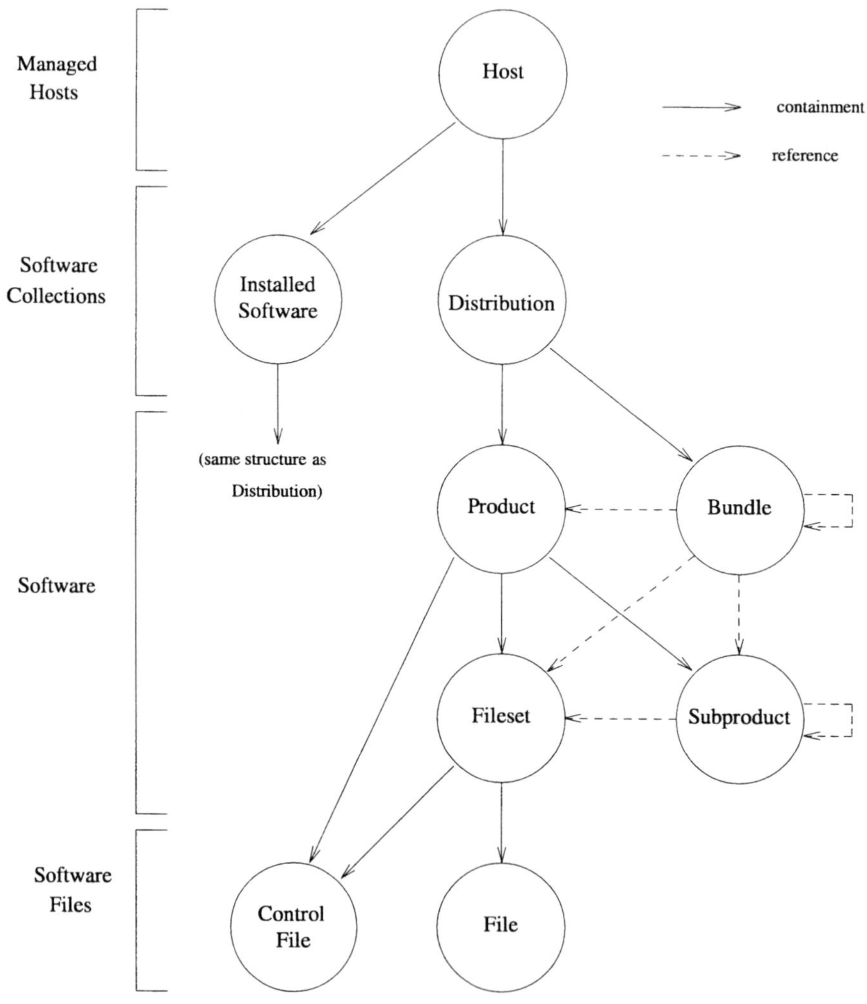

Figure 17-2 Software Structures

All of the software information is defined by the packager in a standard format called the *Product Specification File,* or PSF. This includes the logical structures, file lists, and detailed information (attributes) of these structures and files. The PSF is the input to the packaging utility that parses the file and uses the information in it to build the distribution.

Files, Control Files and Filesets

A *fileset* is a collection of *files* that are logically related. The important point about a fileset is that it is the smallest unit that can be specified for the utilities defined in this standard. The packager can provide information about the fileset such as a tag (short, identifying name), title (a more descriptive name), description, and revision, as well as dependencies on other software objects.

The packager can also provide scripts to control actions beyond those provided automatically by the utilities. These *control files* (also referred to as *control scripts*) can be defined to provide additional checks on the target system before the software is installed, configuration steps after the product is installed, and additional steps to be executed when removing the product.

Products, Subproducts and Bundles

One common aspect of most submissions was that there were two levels of software structure: products that had optional components, or filesets. In the standard, all filesets are contained within *products* even in the case where the product only has one fileset. In addition to having tags, titles, descriptions, and revisions like filesets, products also define attributes such as copyright, supported architectures for the product, the default location where the product is installed, and information about the vendor providing the product.

Any combination of unique product tag, revision, architecture, installation location, and vendor defines a unique *version* of a product. In this way, multiple versions of the same product (different releases or supported architectures for the same release) can be managed by the utilities, and collisions between vendors using the same tag for a product are avoided.

While filesets provide a physical subsetting of the files in a product, *subproducts* provide a logical grouping of supported subsets of a product. Subproducts do not physically contain filesets, but instead reference filesets within the same product. Hence, a fileset (or another subproduct) may be referred to from more than one subproduct. This allows core filesets to be members of multiple subproducts.

A common practice of software developers is to bundle sets of products into product suites. The standard supports *bundles*, which enable several products to be grouped and managed together. Hence, like subproducts, bundles only reference their contents. Products, or parts of products, can be referenced by multiple bundles. Bundles can also be used to define configurations of products for a particular user or type of system.

Distributions and Installed Software

The top level of the POSIX software hierarchy is a *software collection.* A particular software collection is identified by the *host* from which the software collection is available and the path to that software collection. If no host is specified, then the local host is assumed.

There are two types of software collection. A *distribution* is a collection of products and bundles that are organized in the software packaging layout, and are available for installation or copying to another distribution. An *installed software* collection is the set of products and bundles that have been installed onto a system. When a software item is installed, the corresponding catalog information from the distribution is recorded in the installed software catalog.

A host can contain multiple software collections. For example, a host can act as the source role for multiple distributions. Also, there can be multiple installed software collections. These can serve two purposes:

1. Alternate Roots

   First, there is a concept of an *alternate root* where software is installed onto a particular filesystem for the purpose of serving files to other, client systems. This means that absolute references in the installation of the files are instead taken to be relative to the alternate root. This is particularly useful for installing operating system software for a diskless client or on a disk unit that will be installed as the primary root of another system (for example, when preloading software).

2. Multiple Catalogs

   Second, there is the concept of *multiple catalogs* which provides a way to segregate the catalog information for different groups of installed software, although it is all installed and being used on the same system. This is useful for software used by individuals or groups. For example, different projects can maintain catalogs of project-specific software, and users can have private catalogs of software installed into their private working directories.

17.4.2 Compatibility Matching

The software developer or packager can specify a set of patterns that help the utilities automatically select and install the version of software appropriate for that architecture. These patterns are based on the POSIX *uname*( ) attributes of a system. The utilities compare the patterns to the values returned by each target system.

17.4.3 Dependencies

Filesets can define dependencies on other filesets. Dependencies can also be defined on subproducts, products, or bundles, meaning that all filesets in those objects are needed to meet the dependency.

Dependencies provide an important way to ensure that the software is correctly installed, configured, copied, or removed. The utilities provide a means to automatically include needed dependencies. If these dependencies cannot be met, then the task will fail.

The three types of dependencies defined by the standard are described below:

- Prerequisites

  A prerequisite must already have been installed before the software that depends on it is installed. Thus, prerequisites are used to determine the order of operations within a task if the dependencies have not already been met before the task begins.

- Corequisites

  In the case of a corequisite, the software that is depended on must be installed and configured before the dependent software is used. This type of dependency does not imply any particular order of operations.

- Exrequisites

  In this case, installation cannot take place if the exrequisite has already been installed, or if it has previously been selected within the same task. Exrequisites are useful for products that cannot coexist on a system.

17.4.4 Control Scripts

A common feature of all submissions was the use of scripts to allow installation and configuration to be customized. These scripts are defined by the software packager to perform any additional operations not performed by the utilities during a particular task.

The utilities provide information to the scripts in the form of environment variables, and the scripts return codes to affect the outcome of the task. A return code of zero (0) means the script was successful, one (1) means the operation failed, and two (2) means the script encountered a problem, but the operation should continue. Additionally, a return code of three (3) directs the utility to exclude the software from further operation without generating an error. This can be used to automatically exclude parts of a selected product based on target information. Output from the scripts is logged by the utilities, along with the other utility logging defined by the standard.

Scripts may be associated with both filesets and products. In principle, each fileset in a product could have a different set of scripts. Any operation that needs to be run when any part of the product is operated on can be defined in a product control script.

Scripts are executed at various phases of the install, configure, verify, and remove processes. (Each task may have *selection*, *analysis*, and *execution* phases, described in more detail below). The main types of scripts are described next. Note that the standard allows for either individual control scripts for each phase, or a single control script that is executed at each phase. Parameters are passed to help the scripts determine the current context. In the development of the standard this was a particular example of combining the best practices from multiple submissions.

- Request Scripts

  Although it is highly desirable for software to be installed non-interactively, especially for unattended installation in a distributed environment, many software components still require some interaction with the user during the installation of that component. The standard provides a means to execute a request script during the selection phase of an install task. This script can query information from the user and store the responses in a response file that the utilities then transfer to the target for use by the other scripts, particularly the configure script. The request script is run by the manager role.

  The request script can be run independently from the installation or configuration task to which it applies, generating response files used to eliminate interaction during execution of those tasks at a later time.

- Check Scripts

  The *checkinstall* script is run during the analysis phase of an install task to supplement the checks done automatically. The check script is run by the target role (on each target if there are multiple targets). For example, the check script could check for additional hardware requirements. Likewise, a *checkremove* script is run during the analysis phase of a remove task. Since the scripts are run during the analysis phase, they are not allowed to make any modifications to the system. Finally, a *verify* script can provide additional checks by verifying that installed software is still installed properly. Errors found by the *verify* script may also be corrected by a fix script.

- Execution Scripts

  There are two installation scripts, *preinstall* and *postinstall*, that are run just before and after the files are copied from the distribution. These scripts are executed on the target, which, as described above, may not be the client system on which the software is run. For that reason, they are only allowed to provide steps that manage the files on the target (that is, the files just installed), and not the system itself (or its configuration files). Similarly, there are two remove scripts, *preremove* and *postremove,* that are run just before and after removing files from the target.

- Configuration Scripts

  The *configure* scripts perform steps that must take place on the architecture on which the software will run, or which are associated with a particular instance of the software (that is, a particular client). Since the only substantive action defined in the standard for the configuration task is the running of the configuration script, a product can only effectively be configured if such a script is provided. Information can be provided to the configuration script via the request script and response file. Examples of configuration steps are compilations on the target architecture or the definition of particular services. Likewise, the remove task will run an unconfigure script.

  There is a utility to configure or unconfigure software independently of installing or removing it. In addition to the obvious case where the client system is a different machine than the target system, this is useful for managing multiple versions of software on the same client.

17.4.5 Packaging Software

Once the software structures, files, and control files have been defined in the Product Specification File (PSF), the packager runs the *swpackage* utility to create the distribution. This utility gathers up the files and organizes them into a distribution conforming to the software packaging layout. The developer can package directly in serial or directory form onto media types supported by the implementation (such as tapes or floppies).

The output of *swpackage* can also be a distribution located on a filesystem. Distributions can be used to master a CD-ROM, although actual CD-ROM mastering is outside the scope of the standard. Distributions can be the source of installation tasks for testing or validating the software, or can be copied into other distributions as part of a larger system integration process. Once the software in a distribution has been validated, the packager can then use that distribution as a source for copying software onto media for shipping in the same way as if done directly.

Software Packaging Layout

The software packaging layout is the standard organization of files in a distribution that provides the portability of the media. It is defined in such a way as to utilize both serial and directory media. The distribution is organized into a software catalog containing the software structure description and the control files, followed by the actual software files.

The catalog **INDEX** file describes the software structures for all products and filesets in the distribution. This is the file that is made available to the manager role for software selection. Next, the catalog includes the **INFO** files that list the detailed file information for each fileset, and the control files for the filesets and products that help control the installation and other tasks on the target. Finally, the actual fileset files are included. Example 17-1 on page 179 shows an example set of catalog and actual files.

```
catalog/
catalog/INDEX

catalog/productA/
catalog/productA/pfiles/
catalog/productA/pfiles/<product control scripts>
catalog/productA/filesetA/INFO
catalog/productA/filesetA/<fileset control scripts>
catalog/productA/filesetB/INFO
catalog/productA/filesetB/<fileset control scripts>
catalog/productB/
 . . .

productA/
productA/filesetA/
productA/filesetA/<actual fileset files>
productA/filesetB/
productA/filesetB/<actual fileset files>
productB/
 . . .
```

Example 17-1 Example Software Packaging Layout

File Compression

The developer can specify that the *swpackage* command compress the files when creating the package, or when copying software from a distribution to a media. The standard does not define the compression mechanism, but instead allows different compression types to be supplied to the utilities. Although the compression type is stored as an attribute of the compressed files, cooperation between implementors and users of the standard is necessary in order to have portable, compressed distributions.

17.5 Distributing, Installing and Managing Software

The previous section described how software packages are defined in the Product Specification File and packaged into a distribution using the *swpackage* command. This section addresses the second component of the POSIX standard, the utilities available to the administrator to distribute, install, and manage software.

17.5.1 Command Overview

The standard provides a comprehensive set of software administration utilities shown in Table 17-1 on page 180.

Command	Purpose
swpackage	Create software distributions.
swcopy	Copy software from one distribution to another.
swinstall	Install software from a distribution.
swask	Ask for user responses independent of the install task.
swconfig	Configure software independent of the install task.
swlist	List catalog information about distribution or installed software.
swverify	Verify correctness of distribution or installed software.
swmodify	Modify catalog information in distribution or installed software.
swremove	Remove software in a distribution or installed software.

Table 17-1 Software Administration Utilities

As Table 17-1 shows, the management utilities operate on software in a distribution in addition to installed software. This gives the administrator the ability to control the distributions to be used for installation sources in their environment.

Task Phases

POSIX tasks are implemented in three phases: the selection phase, the analysis phase, and the execution phase. This breakdown of phases was defined for two purposes. First, it supports the distributed model of software administration where the manager role may be on a different system than the source or target roles. Second, it allows for consistent *preview* of tasks by running the task through the analysis phase on all targets in order to help predict success without actually modifying the target.

- Selection Phase

  In the selection phase, the filesets that are to be the subject of the task are determined. A fileset may be included because it has been specified explicitly, or because it is part of a higher level component (for example, a product or bundle) that was specified. In addition, a fileset may be automatically included because it is needed to satisfy a dependency.

- Analysis Phase

  The analysis phase determines whether the task is likely to succeed. This involves evaluating whether there are enough resources, whether the dependencies are satisfied, and so on. Success in this phase does not guarantee that the task will succeed, but failure of the phase should only occur if the task would certainly fail.

- Execution Phase

  In the execution phase, the actual work of the task takes place in the target software collection, operating on the selections gathered from the selection phase and successfully passing the analysis phase.

Interfaces to the Utilities

One of the objectives of the standard is administrator portability, meaning that on any system that complies with the standard, an administrator would find a well-known set of command line interfaces with which to perform software administration tasks. Nevertheless, it is recognized that the interface to software administration, particularly distributed software administration, would increasingly be the province of an integrated interface, particularly one based on a graphical user interface (GUI). However, this was deemed to be outside the scope of the standard, although the interfaces defined by the standard could be used to implement such an interface.

The basic form of a command is shown in Example 17-2. The command performs the task by applying the selections specified onto the target software collections. If no targets are specified, then the default local distribution or installed software collection is assumed. Additionally, the default behaviors of the command and the assumed policies can be controlled by a rich set of options to the command.

```
command   [ options ]   selections   [ @ targets ]
```

Example 17-2 Command Line Format

- Selections

  A selection defines the software items that are the subject of an operation. A selection can specify bundles, products, subproducts, or filesets. There can be multiple versions of products available on a distribution, or installed on a system. For this reason, the standard defines how particular revisions, architectures, or installed instances can be individually specified. Additionally, the install task is able to automatically choose the correct architecture of a product for a particular target system based on its compatibility attributes described previously.

- Targets

  Target software collections are optionally specified as operands to the command after the selections, and separated from the selections by the "at" symbol (@). Despite some initial controversy, this syntax was found to be both consistent with POSIX.2 guidelines and relatively intuitive ("Apply this task to these selections *at* these targets"). The software collections are identified both by the host on which the collection can be found, and the path on that host to the collection. The default path for installed software is /, while the default path for distributions is implementation-dependent.

- Options

  Particular care was taken when defining the standard not to interfere with administrator policies for managing software. Therefore, while nearly every behavior or policy has a default behavior, most can be overridden or modified by the administrator. This approach leads to a very large number of possible options to each command. The standard addresses this issue by defining the concept of *extended options* that are defined by setting the extended option keyword to a particular value (for example, *autoselect_dependencies=true).* The values for these options can be controlled in a series of definitions of increasing precedence:

  1. System-wide Defaults

     Each system can contain a defaults file to define default values for particular extended options for that system.

  2. User Defaults

     Each administrator can override the built-in or system defaults by defining values for extended options in a user-level defaults file.

  3. Options File

     A command can be supplied an options file using the **–X** option that points to a file of extended option definitions.

4. Command Line Options

   A command can be supplied with individual extended options using the **–x** option followed by the option keyword and value.

A few common options can be specified either by extended options or by normal command line options (for example, the source distribution for an install task can be specified via **–s** *<source>* on the command line or **–x** *source=<source>* on the command line or in a defaults file.

17.5.2 Copying Software

Copying involves taking all or part of a source distribution and copying it to a target distribution using the *swcopy* utility. Where the target distribution already exists, copying involves adding to the distribution. Copying can also take place to and from different storage media; for example, from a tape onto a filesystem distribution, or from a filesystem distribution onto a tape or other removable medium.

Software in a distribution can also be managed using other utilities defined below. This includes being able to list information in the distribution, verify information and file contents, modify information, and remove software from the distribution.

Like most utilities in the standard, copying involves selection, analysis, and execution phases. In the analysis phase, dependencies are checked, so that subsequent installations can be assured that the needed dependencies exist, and disk space analysis is performed. In the execution phase, software can be compressed if that has not already been done during packaging.

Copying software can serve many purposes. As mentioned previously, it can be used to manufacture media from all or part of an integrated distribution previously used as the source for installation into test environments. It can be used by administrators receiving software distributions from independent software vendors (ISVs) to copy these distributions from a media into a centrally available source distribution. Copying can also be used to stage software distribution. Fanout capability can be built by pushing multiple copies of software through a hierarchy of staging servers. Also, software can be copied to a target system and then installed from that local copy to increase reliability.

Note, however, that copying is not a required step. Using the *swinstall* utility, software can be installed into its final location on a target directly from a media or an available network source, negating the need for space for an intermediate copy.

17.5.3 Installing Software

Installation is performed using the *swinstall* utility. Installation takes place on the target system and involves transforming software from the distribution format to the installed form from which the software can be configured to be run. This involves operations such as creating directories, installing files, setting permissions, and running the control scripts provided by the software developer. The install utility, *swinstall,* is the most comprehensive, and therefore complex, utility defined by the standard.

- Install Selection Phase

  Unless an explicit version of the software is specified, the *swinstall* utility compares the available versions in the distribution to the target architectures and automatically selects the *highest compatible version* (the version with the highest revision compatible with the target or targets). Next, by default, it adds any needed dependencies to the list of selections. The final step in the selection phase is to run any necessary *request* scripts, unless previously generated responses have been provided using the *swask* utility described below.

- Install Analysis Phase

  The selections, along with any response files, are distributed to each target which then performs the analysis. Each target rechecks the software selections, including dependencies, against the revisions of software already installed. Filesets that are already up-to-date are, by default, skipped. Software *checkinstall* scripts are executed, and disk space analysis is performed.

- Install Execute Phase

  Once analysis is completed on a target, the install task proceeds to the execution phase. In this phase, the files in each fileset are installed onto the target system, running any *preinstall* and *postinstall* scripts just before or after each fileset and product. If the files are compressed in the distribution, the installation process will uncompress them. Another default behavior designed to minimize network traffic ensures that only needed files are reinstalled. If the file already exists with the right *checksum* and other attributes, it is not reinstalled. By default, the final step in the install process is to configure the software, assuming the target system is also the system where the software is to be run.

  During the installation process, the utility builds the catalog information for the software items and files contained within those items. The state of the fileset is recorded at various points in the installation process, and this state controls what operations are applicable to the installed software. For example, software that is already in an installed state is not reinstalled by default, and software already in a configured state is not reconfigured by default. The state transitions for installed software are shown in Figure 17-3 on page 184.

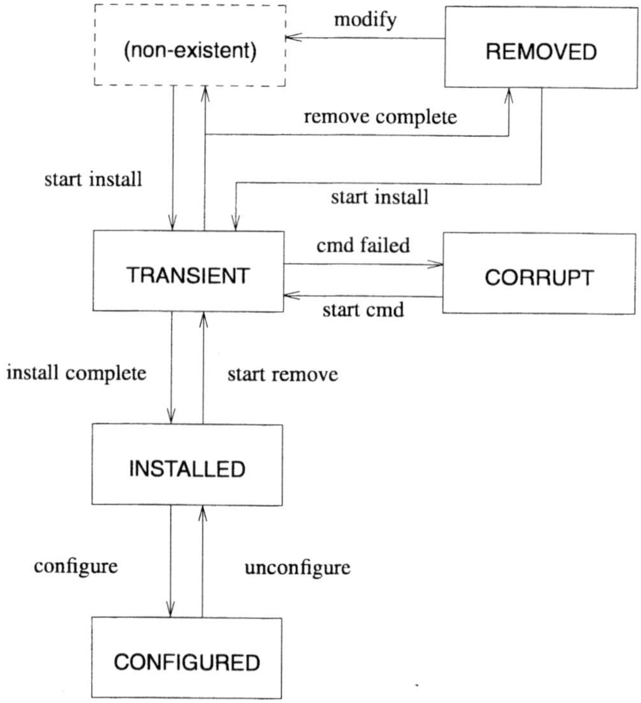

Figure 17-3 Installed Software State Transitions

Updating Software

The default location below which all files in a product are installed is defined as part of the software definition and packaging process. Most software should be *locatable,* allowing this location to be changed when installing the software. This leads to two possible strategies for updating (or upgrading) software to a new version: overlaying and multiple versions.

Partial updates of existing software (software fixes or patches) have different requirements than full updates or upgrades. For example, patches may not receive the same level of system integration testing as full releases, and therefore more frequently need to be removed if they cause unforeseen side effects. Also patches are usually applied directly to installed files, replacing those files or parts of them. The standard does not currently address many of the features required to optimally support patches. This area is currently being investigated as an extension to the current standard (see Section 17.6 on page 187).

- Overlaying

  By default (that is, unless the administrator specifies a different location), the *swinstall* utility will overlay older versions of products and filesets over the newer version. Only one fileset from different versions of the same product can exist at any one location at a time. When overlaying a fileset, the *swinstall* utility will delete the catalog information for the existing filesets as they are successfully updated (for failed installations, see *Recovery* below). In this case, the software configure scripts need to take care of the steps needed to migrate the previous configuration to the new one (for example, stopping a previous version of a service, and then starting the new version).

For software that cannot be overlaid, a *checkinstall* script can check for existing versions and reject this type of update.

- Multiple Versions

  It is possible to install different versions of a product on the same system, provided the product is locatable. The version of the product is defined by its revision, the architecture it is run on, the vendor providing the product, and the location of the product. Thus, multiple copies of the exact same product installed to different locations are considered by the utilities to be different versions.

  Depending on the product, it may or may not be possible to configure multiple revisions simultaneously. It is up to the product *configure* script to check for other configured versions by examining the state of the filesets in that product. In the general case, the administrator can install the new version, unconfigure the old version, then configure the new version. When the older version is no longer needed, the administrator can remove it.

Recovery

Recovery is the process of undoing the effect of a failed task. This is addressed by the standard as part of the install task. Recovery is different from rollback in that the latter is usually defined to be a user-initiated task performed at any time (in particular when dealing with patches). Recovery is only significant when the product is being updated by overlaying it with a new version, and involves removing the partially installed new version and restoring the existing version.

The standard defines a minimum level of support for recovery, this being that when a fileset installation fails, it can be recovered to the point where the existing fileset is restored. Fileset installation involves running the fileset preinstall script, followed by installation of the new files, and then running the fileset postinstall script. If any of these steps fails, then reverse steps are executed, including running any unpostinstall and unpreinstall scripts provided for the fileset.

An implementation can choose to implement additional recovery, such as recovering the entire product if any fileset fails, or recovering products previously installed in the same task when encountering any error.

Operating System Support

While the standard does not address all aspects of operating system update or initial install, it does provide the basic functionality so that it can be used as a fundamental part of these processes. Facilities provided include marking filesets that require rebuilding of the kernel, or indicating that a product or fileset requires a reboot of the system to become effective.

Excluded, however, are the final stages of switching from the old to the new version of the operating system, which takes place after a system reboot as part of the configuration phase. Also, the initial installation of the operating system on an empty system requires special techniques, since services that are normally assumed to be present (for example, the filesystem) are not initially available.

The standard only deals with installation of software when a POSIX-compliant operating system is present, and so is not applicable to the initial installation of the operating system until this is true. This does not, of course, preclude a vendor from providing such facilities, but that would be an extension to the standard.

17.5.4 Requesting Responses from the User

In order to facilitate unattended installation or configuration of software, perhaps scheduled for a later time, the administrator can run a separate *swask* utility that runs the installation or configuration process through the selection phase, including execution of the software request scripts, and stores the responses in a user-specified directory. This directory can then be supplied to later *swinstall* or *swconfig* commands. This process can also be used to save responses and reuse them when installing the same software on subsequent systems.

The standard does not provide any special support when different responses may be necessary for different targets. However, the utilities do provide the request scripts with the list of intended targets, and the scripts can use this to request and store information for multiple targets in the response file and then look up the correct information on each target.

17.5.5 Configuring Software

Configuring software is the final step before the software is actually made operational, and, unlike installation, always takes place on the client architecture. Configuration is, by default, performed as the last step of the *swinstall* utility, and it can be run independently using the *swconfig* utility. In a similar manner, software is usually unconfigured as the first execution step of the *swremove* utility, but can also be unconfigured independently using the *swconfig* utility.

The definition of configuration depends on the software, but it is expected that it will normally be an operation that can be performed in significantly less time than the installation task. An example might be the installation of a new revision of a Message Transfer Agent. Configuring would specialize the software for a particular situation and make it the revision actually in use. Software might be configured more than once, each giving rise to a different configured instance. Taking the example of the MTA again, it may be that the software is configured for several different services. The configuration parameters are specific to the software being configured, and are hence not part of the standard. They can be supplied via a request script, or preferably by querying the system directly and without user interaction.

17.5.6 Listing Software

Listing is performed using the *swlist* utility, which can list the contents of either the source or target software collections. It can list catalog information for both distribution and installed software. The selection process determines the items to be listed. Both the depth of information (from bundles down to individual files) and the attributes listed can be controlled by options. This control allows administrators to get the desired inventory information about the software installed on a system.

17.5.7 Verifying Software

Verification of software is performed using the *swverify* utility in its analysis phase. Verification can be performed on source or target distributions as well as target or client installed software collections. It establishes the integrity of the software by checking the actual file attributes and *checksums* against the stored catalog information. It also checks for existence of necessary dependencies of the software, and runs any verify scripts that can perform additional steps, such as ensuring proper execution of configured components.

The *swverify* utility also contains an optionally-run execution phase that can perform limited repair to the installed software. This step resets proper permissions on the installed files and directories, and can run a fix script (for example, that can restart a service). Otherwise, if the contents of an installed file are corrupt, then only reinstalling the software will repair that file.

17.5.8 Modifying Software

Once files are created or modified by configuration scripts, their catalog information can be updated by the scripts using the *swmodify* utility. This allows *swverify* and *swremove* to subsequently operate on those new files. Files that are modifiable after installation can be marked by the packager as *volatile*, and their attributes will not be checked when verifying the software.

The *swmodify* utility can also be used to add, modify, or delete other software information. Uses can range from cleanup of catalog information beyond that done automatically by the utilities, to creation of new catalog information for software not installed using the standard utilities.

17.5.9 Removing Software

Removing software is the final step in the software lifecycle, and is performed using the *swremove* utility. Removing a software item involves deletion of the files that were created by the packaging, copying, or installation process, as well as removing the catalog information associated with that software. Packager-supplied control scripts are also run during the analysis and execution phases of the remove task.

During the remove phase, the utility checks whether the selected software items will violate the dependencies of software remaining in the software collection. A *checkremove* script can provide additional checks. For example, this script can make a core operating system product *unremovable* by always returning with a return code of 1 or 3.

The first step of the execution phase is to unconfigure the software if it is still configured, followed by the actual removal of the software files. Any supplied *preremove* and *postremove* scripts are run just before and after the file removal for each fileset and product.

17.6 Extensions to the Standard

There are two key aspects that the original POSIX-7.2 working group wanted to address in the standard but were unable to do at the time. The first was the definition of the protocols to allow the distributed components of the standard to interoperate. The second was to address how software servicing, or patching, was to be managed.

17.6.1 Distributed Interoperability

Distributed interoperability means that implementations of the standard can interoperate at the task level. For example, the manager role could manage any of the other roles, irrespective of the systems on which the roles were implemented, provided they conform to a standard.

This would provide not only the capability of heterogeneous management, using the commands defined in the standard, but also a mechanism for enabling management applications to be written which could manage conforming systems.

The Open Group Systems Management Technical Working Group has undertaken the task to define protocols or managed object definitions to support this interoperability. The first of these protocols was based on DCE RPC and is defined by the XDSA-DCE Specification.

17.6.2 Patching

Patching is the term adopted to describe modifications made to the product other than replacement by a different version of the product. This includes replacement of one or more files and *in situ* modification of the data within a file (the classic form of patching).

When this was initially considered by the POSIX working group, many different methods of achieving it were described. However, there was no common core that could be discerned in these methods and the submitters were generally not enthusiastic about their own methods. It was therefore difficult for the group to select an existing practice to standardize, and for this reason it was omitted entirely from the standard.

After POSIX-7.2 was approved, many of The Open Group member companies attempted again to address this issue as a subgroup to The Open Group Systems Management Technical Working Group. This time, existing practice for a patching specification did exist, and was already based on the POSIX standard. A specification based on this practice has undergone several revisions by the subgroup and is at a state to be submitted to The Open Group as an extension to the POSIX standard.

17.6.3 Other Extensions

There are other areas for extending the standard that have been raised during the balloting process, and in POSIX working group meetings subsequent to the standard's adoption. These include:

- the procedures for making installed software collections available to client systems and configuration of those systems
- ways in which to support multiple simultaneous localizations of catalog information in a distribution, in particular the *title* and *description* attributes of software objects
- rules and conventions for the layout and organization of installed software files; this includes how to locate and manage private and shared files so software can more easily be shared
- developing a set of portable interfaces available to control script writers for common management tasks such as adding a user account to the system, configuring services, and so on
- agreement on a default compression format that would ensure that all distributions compressed with this format could be uncompressed by any implementation.

Go Solo 2

Part 3:

Migration

The Open Group

Chapter 18

Program Migration and Portability

This chapter covers the following:

- migrating applications from implementations conforming to earlier issues of the XPG to the Single UNIX Specification, Version 2
- migrating applications originally developed on traditional UNIX systems to systems that conform to X/Open UNIX.

Specific topics covered include:

- feature groups
- the compilation environment
- determining the platform support
- functional duplication in the XSI specification set
- other programming considerations
- interprocess communication (IPC)
- STREAMS
- thread-safety
- makefile portability.

18.1 Feature Groups

The concept of Feature Groups was introduced in XPG4. The majority of functions belong to the BASE capability. These functions are mandatory on XSI-conforming systems; applications can rely on their existence.

In addition to the BASE capability, there are four Feature Groups as follows:

- Encryption, covering the functions *crypt*( ), *encrypt*( ), and *setkey*( ). The reference pages for these functions are marked CRYPT.
- Realtime, covering the functions derived from the POSIX Realtime Extension. The reference pages for these functions are marked REALTIME. Where additional semantics are added to existing pages, the new material is marked by the RT legend.
- Realtime Threads, covering the functions, derived from the POSIX Threads Extension, which are related to realtime functionality. The reference pages for these functions are marked REALTIME THREADS. Where additional semantics are added to existing pages, the new material is marked by the RTT legend.
- Legacy, including the interfaces and headers which were mandatory in previous versions of the specifications but are optional in this version. The reference pages for these functions are marked LEGACY.

Anything that does not fall into the Feature Groups listed above is considered to be base functionality.

To conform to the Single UNIX Specification, only the base interfaces are mandatory.

XSH defines which Feature Groups are mandatory and which are optional for specific profiles or component definitions. Refer to Chapter 2 on page 13 for an overview of the XPG4 profiles. Some interfaces in Feature Groups also define optional behavior. Developers must refer to a product's Conformance Statement to determine what Feature Groups are supported on that particular implementation.

Feature test macros are defined by an implementation and are available for the application source-code to check to determine whether a Feature Group is supported at compile time.

Feature Test Macro	Feature Group
_XOPEN_CRYPT	Encryption
_XOPEN_REALTIME	Realtime
_XOPEN_REALTIME_THREADS	Realtime Threads
_XOPEN_LEGACY	Legacy

Table 18-1 Feature Test Macros and Feature Groups

The implementation shall define the feature test macro to be other than −1 if the Feature Group is provided, and −1 if the Feature Group is not implemented.

18.2 The Compilation Environment

The feature test macro _XOPEN_SOURCE must be defined to be 500 before the inclusion of any header defined in XSH to enable the functionality in the Single UNIX Specification, Version 2. Its definition subsumes the use of _POSIX_SOURCE and _POSIX_C_SOURCE. This macro causes all of the proper symbols to be exposed with respect to base functionality and any of the XSH Feature Groups that are provided on that particular UNIX branded system.

The _XOPEN_SOURCE macro may be defined automatically by the compilation environment, but to ensure maximum portability, the application should define the macro either on the compilation command line, or best at the beginning of each source module prior to the inclusion of any headers.

An extract of code from a conforming application, that appears before any **#include** statements, is given below:

```
#define _POSIX_SOURCE            /* not required */
#define _POSIX_C_SOURCE 199506L /* not required */
#define _XOPEN_SOURCE 500        /* Single UNIX Specification, Version 2 */

#include ....
```

Note that the definition of _XOPEN_SOURCE with the value 500 makes the definitions of _POSIX_SOURCE and _POSIX_C_SOURCE redundant and they can be omitted. See Section 3.9.2 on page 24 for more information.

Application developers are advised to study XSH, **Chapter 2**, **General Information** when migrating or developing programs on X/Open UNIX branded systems.

18.3 Determining the Platform Support

The following code extracts can be used to determine the standards support claimed by a platform.

Example 1 – POSIX Support

This first example determines the version of POSIX claimed.

```
#define _XOPEN_SOURCE 500
#include <unistd.h>         /* If this is a standards-based platform,    */
                            /* the symbol _POSIX_VERSION will be defined */
                            /* by inclusion of <unistd.h>.               */
#include <stdio.h>
#ifdef _POSIX_VERSION
#include <sys/utsname.h>
#endif

int main (void)
{
#ifdef _POSIX_VERSION
    switch (_POSIX_VERSION) {

    case 199009L: /* classic dot1 - ISO version */
        (void) printf("IEEE Std POSIX.1-1990/ISO/IEC 9945-1:1990\n");
        break;
    case 198808L:  /* classic dot 1 - non ISO version */
        (void) printf("IEEE Std POSIX.1-1988\n");
        break;
    case 199309L: /* POSIX realtime */
        (void) printf("IEEE Std POSIX.1b-1993 [Realtime]\n");
        break;
    case 199506L:  /* POSIX threads */
        (void) printf("IEEE Std POSIX.1-1996/ISO/IEC 9945-1:1996\n");
        break;
    default:
        (void) printf("Unknown _POSIX_VERSION=%ldL\n", _POSIX_VERSION);
        break;
    }
#else
        (void) printf("Not a standards based platform\n");
#endif
    exit(0);
}
```

The table below gives the equivalent mapping between _POSIX_VERSION and the X/Open specifications:

_POSIX_VERSION	X/Open Portability Guide
198808L	XPG3
199009L	XPG4, Single UNIX Specification
199506L	Single UNIX Specification, Version 2

Example 2 — Checking the UNIX System Support

This example determines whether the platform claims support for the Single UNIX Specification, Version 2. Note that this simplified example omits any error checking.

```
#define _XOPEN_SOURCE 500
#include <unistd.h>         /* If this is a standards-based platform,   */
                            /* the symbol _POSIX_VERSION will be defined */
                            /* by inclusion of <unistd.h>.               */
#include <stdio.h>
#ifdef _POSIX_VERSION
#include <sys/utsname.h>
#endif

int main (void)
{
    if ( (_XOPEN_XCU_VERSION == 4) &&
         (_XOPEN_VERSION == 500 )  &&
#ifdef _XOPEN_UNIX
       ( 1 ) &&
#else
       ( 0 ) &&
#endif
       (_POSIX_VERSION == 199506L)  {

       (void) printf ("This system claims support to \n");
       (void) printf ("the Single UNIX Specification, Version 2 \n");
           (void) printf ("Please check the branded products catalogue \n");
       exit (0);
       }

    if ( (_XOPEN_XCU_VERSION == 4) &&
       (_XOPEN_VERSION == 4 )  &&
#ifdef _XOPEN_UNIX
       ( 1 ) &&
#else
       ( 0 ) &&
#endif
       (_POSIX_VERSION >= 199009L)  {
       (void) printf ("This system claims support to \n");
       (void) printf ("the Single UNIX Specification (UNIX 95) \n");
           (void) printf ("Please check the branded products catalogue \n");
       exit (0);
       }
    else
       (void) printf ("This system does not claim support\n");

    exit(1);
}
```

18.4 Functional Duplication

Part of the development of the Single UNIX Specification involved merging three industry portability specifications and surveying existing applications. Some functionality is duplicated in some interfaces because of this approach. This functional duplication was carefully managed in the specification, and serves the portability of existing applications originally developed for UNIX environments. A number of things have been done with the format of the Single UNIX Specification to provide direction for new application development work, and to support the migration of applications that need to be portable to earlier versions of the Single UNIX Specification.

- Text shading and portability codes in the reference pages notify programmers of potential functionality that may reduce portability to other platforms.
- Interfaces that duplicate functionality and are not intended to be the preferred future direction:
  - may be marked as LEGACY on the Name line to draw attention to areas that need attention
  - have clearly marked migration paths in favor of current industry standards in the Application Usage section of the reference page.

The following summarizes the areas in the Single UNIX Specification where duplicated functionality exists. References to the recommended interfaces are found in the appropriate sections of Chapter 20 on page 237, and in the appropriate Application Usage sections of XSH.

<strings.h> versus <string.h>

There is direct overlap between the BSD byte-string functions (*bcmp*( ), *bcopy*( ), *bzero*( )) and the ISO C standard memory handling functions (*memcmp*( ), *memmove*( ), *memset*( )). Other string functions traditionally found on BSD systems are also covered by ISO C standard functions: *index*( ) maps to *strchr*( ), and *rindex*( ) maps to *strrchr*( ). The ISO C standard functions are the preferred method of performing these operations.

The ISO C standard functions are all defined in **<string.h>**, while the BSD functions have been moved to **<strings.h>**.

For maximum portability it is recommended to replace function calls to *bcopy*( ), *bzero*( ), *bcmp*( ), *index*( ), and *rindex*( ) as follows:

```
#define bcopy(b1,b2,len) memmove((b2), (b1), (size_t)(len))
#define bzero(b,len) memset((b), 0, (size_t)(len))
#define bcmp(b1,b2,len) memcmp((b1), (b2), (size_t)(len))
#define index(a,b) strchr((a),(b))
#define rindex(a,b) strrchr((a),(b))
```

Temporary File Creation

There are a number of interfaces to create temporary files and temporary filenames. The interfaces *tempnam*( ) and *tmpnam*( ) create filenames suitable for temporary files, and *tmpfile*( ) actually creates a temporary file for use.

The functions *mkstemp*( ) and *mktemp*( ) are present in the Single UNIX Specification, but only exist to support historical usage.

Regular Expression Handling

There are several ways to handle regular expressions and pattern matching:

- the newer more functional POSIX.2-defined functions *regcomp*( ) and *regexec*( ) included through **<regex.h>**
- the historical model covered by *compile*( ), *step*( ), and *advance*( ) included through **<regexp.h>**
- the *regcmp*( ) and *regex*( ) functions as defined in **<libgen.h>**
- the *re_comp*( ) and *re_exec*( ) functions as defined in **<re_comp.h>**.

The POSIX.2 functionality is the preferred method of handling regular expressions, and the other methods are marked LEGACY.

Multiple Signal Models

The development of the Single UNIX Specification brought together three separate signal models from POSIX.1, BSD, and the SVID. While the BSD and SVID signal models are now supported on X/Open UNIX systems supporting ports of historical applications, the reliable POSIX.1 signals model should be used to plan for future portability, and support portability to implementations that conform to an earlier version of XSH. Reference pages point to equivalent calls in the POSIX.1 signal model in the Application Usage sections, for the calls based on the other two models.

If an application depends upon historical BSD signal behavior, it will need to replace all calls to *signal*( ) with calls to *bsd_signal*( ), to avoid the overloading of the *signal*( ) call that occurred when the models came together in the specification.

An implementation of *signal*( ) in terms for *sigaction*( ) to provide reliable signal handling is given below:

```
#include <signal.h>

typedef void Sigfunc(int);

Sigfunc *signal(int signo, Sigfunc *func)
{
    struct sigaction act, oact;

    act.sa_handler = func;
    sigemptyset(&act.sa_mask);
    act.sa_flags = 0;
    if (signo != SIGALRM) {
      act.sa_flags |= SA_ESTART;
    }
    if (sigaction(signo, &act, &oact) < 0)
      return(SIG_ERR);
    return(oact.sa_handler);
}
```

Advisory Record Locking

Advisory record locking is supported with the *lockf*( ) interface, and also with the *fcntl*( ) interface. The latter method is preferred for applications portability.

mknod( ) and mkfifo( )

The *mknod*( ) interface is included in the Single UNIX Specification, but the only portable use of the function is for creating FIFO-special files. Because of this, and the existence of *mkfifo*( ) as the POSIX.1 standard method of creating a FIFO-special file, developers are encouraged to use *mkfifo*( ) for applications portability.

Non-local Goto

The *_longjmp*( ) and *_setjmp*( ) interfaces are identical to the ISO C standard interfaces *longjmp*( ) and *setjmp*( ), with the exception that they do not manipulate the signal mask. Applications that depend on the value of the signal mask should use the POSIX.1-specified *siglongjmp*( ) and *sigsetjmp*( ) interfaces.

Current Working Directory

The *getcwd*( ) interface should be used to determine the current working directory instead of *getwd*( ) for applications portability.

Text String to Number Conversion

Text strings representing numbers should be converted to numbers using the standard *strtod*( ) and *strtol*( ) interfaces, rather than the historical *atof*( ), *atoi*( ), and *atol*( ) functions. While these interfaces have been included in the Single UNIX Specification to support the porting of historical applications, the newer standards-based interfaces have better error checking.

In a similar vein, the floating-point number to string conversion interfaces, *ecvt*( ), *fcvt*( ), and *gcvt*( ), should be replaced with *sprintf*( ) for maximum portability.

utimes( ) versus utime( )

To set file access and modification times, a developer should use the *utime*( ) function, which is aligned with POSIX.1, rather than *utimes*( ).

18.5 Other Programming Considerations

Functional duplication should be of concern to programmers developing new applications, as they want to write the application to be as portable as possible over the long term. Programmers porting existing applications are less likely to be concerned about these issues immediately, but may discover a number of other issues effecting their portability.

18.5.1 Argument Type Changes

Argument type changes tend to be to more exact definitions, such as **int** to **mode_t** or **size_t**. Much of this is as a result of the C-language and POSIX standards efforts, but function prototypes not covered by either standard have been rationalized as well. For example, the second argument to *bzero*( ) changed from an **int** to a **size_t** from 4.3BSD to 4.4BSD, and the Single UNIX Specification reflects the newer more exact definition.

18.5.2 Prototype Changes and Movement

Certain function prototypes may have changed in subtle ways (types), or moved entirely to different header files. Prototypes moved from one header to another due once again to standards efforts. For example, the ISO C standard memory functions have historically appeared in **<memory.h>**, but moved to **<string.h>** with the standard. The BSD byte-string functions such as *bcopy*( ) and *bcmp*( ), have their prototypes defined in **<string.h>** in the 4.4BSD documentation, but **<strings.h>** in the Single UNIX Specification. Again, these moves are not strictly because of standards efforts. For example, the older regular expression handling functions *compile*( ), *step*( ), and *advance*( ), moved from **<regexpr.h>** to **<regexp.h>** as part of the move to the Single UNIX Specification.

18.5.3 Process Environment Access

For C-language processes, the environment is an array of pointers to strings defined as:

```
extern char **environ;
```

C-language programs can use *getenv*( ) to determine the existence and value of environment variables. Environment variables can be placed in a program's environment using *putenv*( ), directly manipulating the *environ* array (not recommended), or using the *envp* arguments when creating a process (using *exec*( )). The *environ* array should not be directly accessed from the application.

System V platforms support a third argument to *main*( ) that is a null-terminated array of character string pointers to the environment. Applications that rely on this behavior will need to be reworked to use the *environ* array, a two argument *main*( ), and possibly *getenv*( ) and *putenv*( ).

18.5.4 Pseudo-terminals

The Single UNIX Specification includes pseudo-terminals. This raises a portability problem for applications source-code that may have been developed on a BSD-based system and is being moved to a System V-based system, or *vice versa*. Pseudo-terminal implementations differ in these two operating environments with respect to initialization.

The following example code (adapted from the module **SRC/userintf.c** in the VSX4 test suite) illustrates opening a pseudo-terminal to handle both environments.

Example 18-1 Pseudo-terminal Initialization

```
/*
 * Openpty() opens the master and slave sides of a pseudo-terminal.
 * Both device names are supplied, but if master ptys are obtained
 * from a clone device, the slave name is a dummy which must be
 * overwritten with the real device name. If cntrl is true,
 * the slave must be opened as a controlling terminal by calling
```

```
 * openctl() instead of plain open(). Both devices must be opened
 * for reading and writing. On many systems, master devices can
 * only be opened once, giving [EBUSY], for example, on subsequent
 * opens. If openpty() encounters a busy master device, it must
 * simply open the slave.
 *
 * The open file descriptors are returned via the pointers mfdp and
 * sfdp. Openpty() returns 0 for success or -1 for failure.
 *
 */

#define CLONE_MPTY  /* delete this define if master ptys are not
                       obtained from a clone device (e.g., /dev/ptmx) */
#define STREAMS_PTY /* delete this define if ptys do not use STREAMS */

#ifdef STREAMS_PTY
#include <sys/stropts.h>
#endif

int
openpty(char *master, char *slave, int *mfdp, int *sfdp, int cntrl) {
    *mfdp = open(master, O_RDWR|O_NOCTTY);
    if (*mfdp < 0 && errno != EBUSY)
        return -1;

#ifdef CLONE_MPTY
    if (*mfdp >= 0)
    {
        char *newslave;
        size_t len;
        static struct { char *ptr; size_t len; } slavelen[2];
        extern char *ptsname();

        (void) grantpt(*mfdp);   /* change permission of slave */
        (void) unlockpt(*mfdp);  /* unlock slave */
        newslave=ptsname(*mfdp); /* get a slave */
        if (slavelen[0].ptr == NULL)
        {
            /* remember length of original dummy name
               to be used if called again */
            slavelen[0].ptr = slave;
            slavelen[0].len = strlen(slave);
        }
        else if (slave != slavelen[0].ptr && slavelen[1].ptr == NULL)
        {
            /* remember length of original dummy name
               to be used if called again */
            slavelen[1].ptr = slave;
            slavelen[1].len = strlen(slave);
        }
        if (slave == slavelen[0].ptr)
            len = slavelen[0].len;
        else
            len = slavelen[1].len;
```

```
            if (strlen(newslave) > len)
            {
                (void) fprintf(stderr, "Error in openpty()\n");
                return -1;
            }
            (void) strcpy(slave, newslave);
        }
#endif

        if (cntrl)
            *sfdp = openctl(slave, O_RDWR);
        else
            *sfdp = open(slave, O_RDWR|O_NOCTTY);

        if (*sfdp < 0)
            return -1;

#ifdef STREAMS_PTY
        if (*mfdp >= 0)
        {
            (void) ioctl(*sfdp, I_PUSH, "ptem");   /* pseudo tty emulator */
            (void) ioctl(*sfdp, I_PUSH, "ldterm"); /* line discipline */
        }
#endif

        return 0;
}

/*
 * Ptygetattr() obtains terminal attributes for the slave pseudo-
 * terminal corresponding to the master device addressed by mfd.
 * It returns 0 for success, -1 for failure.
 *
 */

int
ptygetattr(int mfd, struct termios *termios_p) {
#ifdef STREAMS_PTY
        extern char *ptsname();
        char *slave;
        int ret, sfd = -1;

        /* Obtain slave device name and call tcgetattr() on the slave */
        slave = ptsname(mfd);
        if (slave && (sfd = open(slave, O_RDWR)) >= 0)
            ret = tcgetattr(sfd, termios_p);
        else
            ret = -1;
        if (sfd >= 0)
            (void) close(sfd);
        return ret;
#else
        /* This code assumes tcgetattr() on the master returns the
           settings of the slave (true for BSD-style pseudo-terminals) */
```

```
    return tcgetattr(mfd, termios_p);
#endif
}
```

18.6 Interprocess Communication (IPC)

There are two forms of IPC supported in the Single UNIX Specification, Version 2. The traditional System V IPC routines; that is, the *msg**(), *sem**(), and *shm**() interfaces, are mandatory and part of the base. Thus, all XSI-conforming systems provide the same mechanisms for manipulating messages, shared memory, and semaphores.

In addition, inclusion of the POSIX Realtime Extension in the Single UNIX Specification, Version 2 now provides an alternate set of routines for those systems supporting the Realtime Feature Group.

For maximum portability to UNIX systems, the former are recommended. However, if the target for an application is a realtime system, then application developers are advised to write their code in such a way that modules using IPC interfaces can be modified easily in the future to use either interfaces.

18.7 STREAMS

STREAMS are a method of implementing network services and other character-based input/output mechanisms, with the STREAM being a full-duplex connection between a process and a device. STREAMS provides direct access to protocol modules, and optional protocol modules can be interposed between the process-end of the STREAM and the device-driver at the device-end of the STREAM.

XSH, **Chapter 2**, **General Information** introduces X/Open UNIX STREAMS I/O, the message types used to control them, an overview of the priority mechanism, and the interfaces used to access them.

18.8 Threads-safety

A portable threaded application should only call thread-safe routines or serialize access to non-thread-safe routines.

For example:

```
. . .
/*
 * An example of thread-safety by serializing access
 * to a non-reentrant function.
 */

pthread_mutex_t mtx = PTHREAD_MUTEX_INITIALIZER;

void my_l64a( long value, char *buffer)
{
int i=0;
char *ptr;

    (void) pthread_mutex_lock (&mtx);
    ptr = l64a( value);
    (void) strcpy (buffer, ptr);
    (void) pthread_mutex_unlock (&mtx);
}
. . .
```

When writing thread-safe code using any of the following functions:

asctime( )
ctime( )
getgrgid( )
getgrnam( )
getpwuid( )
gmtime( )
localtime( )
rand( )
readdir( )
strtok( )

the code should be converted to use the equivalent reentrant version of the function:

asctime_r( )
ctime_r( )
getgrgid_r( )
getgrnam_r( )
getpwnam_r( )
getpwuid_r( )
gmtime_r( )
localtime_r( )
rand_r( )
readdir_r( )
strtok_r( )

Application writers are advised to study XSH, **Chapter 2**, **General Information**.

18.9 Makefile Portability

Makefiles are as much a part of the source-code to be ported as the C-language files that implement the application's function. Every implementation of *make* has extended the syntax and added functionality to serve specific groups of users, and satisfy certain perceived shortcomings of the original utility. Some of the disparate features found include:

- syntax to support parallel (multi-processor) execution
- additional special targets
- additional operators
- support for preprocessor-like functionality to "include" other files, and conditionally process sections of the makefile
- changes in internal macro semantics when working with library targets
- support for remote execution.

The Single UNIX Specification defers to the POSIX.2 *make* utility. The POSIX.2 working group chose to describe the most common features found in System V and BSD variants of *make* to define the standard behavior.

The special target *.POSIX* was defined such that if it appears prior to the first non-comment line in a makefile, it ensures that the makefile is processed in the standard manner. This target does not prevent or preclude extended functions and features, but these extensions shall not alter the behavior of the "standard" definition. The only extension to the POSIX.2 standard definition of *make* defined by XCU is to allow for support for *sccs*. To use the extended *sccs*-based default rules, the special target *.SCCS_GET* must appear in the makefile.

An organization may have a considerable amount of history and folklore embedded in their makefiles. Determining how old makefiles work can be a labor-intensive part of porting an application. Investing the effort in the first "port" of the makefiles to the Single UNIX Specification definition of *make* means that they will be portable from that point forward to all platforms that are X/Open UNIX or XPG4 Base branded, or support POSIX.2.

There are a number of issues to be aware of with the standard *make*:

- The default macro for the C-compiler is *CC=c89*, and not *cc*. The *c89* compiler front-end invokes the standard C-language compiler.
- Although the Single UNIX Specification extends its specification of makefile syntax to support *sccs*, no support for RCS was added.
- Implementations support MAKEFLAGS with both the System V letter-string and the BSD command-line syntax, but they need not support both behaviors mixed together.
- The historical MAKESHELL feature is not supported.
- The **–n** option specifies that commands should be written to standard output but not executed. However, it should be noted that commands with a plus sign (+) prefix will still be executed. The System V behavior of still executing command-lines that contain the strings *$(MAKE)* or *${MAKE}* when a **–n** option is present is not supported.
- While there is existing *make* practice that allows the use of blanks to delimit command-lines, as well as the more traditional tab character, the standard *make* does not support this feature.
- New macros defined using other macros evaluate when the new macro is used, not when it was defined.

- The debug option (–**d**) is not specified, although implementations will likely provide it in an implementation-dependent manner. The output format of the –**p** option to see the complete presentation of macro definitions and target descriptions is not described.

Chapter 19

Interface Tables

19.1 System Service Table

This section contains a table of all the interfaces defined in UNIX 98, complete with an indication of their availability in UNIX 95, POSIX.1, POSIX.2, the ISO C standard, SVID 3, and 4.3BSD. The following conventions are used in columns 2 through 7:

m Indicates that the interface is defined as mandatory.

f Indicates that the interface is part of a Feature Group; refer to Section 18.1 on page 191 and Chapter 2 on page 13 for a description of Feature Groups and under what conditions these interfaces are mandatory or optional.

r In POSIX.1 this indicates that the interface is part of the POSIX Realtime Extension.

t In POSIX.1 this indicates that the interface is part of the POSIX Threads Extension.

1 In the ISO C standard this indicates that the interface is part of the ISO/IEC 9899:1990/Amendment 1:1995 (E).

. Indicates that the interface is not specified.

The table is intended as a quick reference guide for programmers migrating to or developing applications for UNIX 98. Products that brand to the UNIX 98 profile may not provide all of the interfaces listed, depending on which Feature Groups are supported.

Interface	UNIX 98	UNIX 95	POSIX.1 and POSIX.2	ISO C Standard	SVID 3	4.3BSD
_exit( )	m	m	m	.	m	m
_longjmp( )	m	m	.	.	.	m
_setjmp( )	m	m	.	.	.	m
_tolower( )	m	m	.	.	m	.
_toupper( )	m	m	.	.	m	.
a64l( )	m	m	.	.	m	.
abort( )	m	m	m	m	m	m
abs( )	m	m	m	m	m	m
accept( )	m	m	.	.	.	m
access( )	m	m	m	.	m	m
acos( )	m	m	m	m	m	m
acosh( )	m	m	.	.	m	m
add_wch( )	m	m	.	.	.	.
add_wchnstr( )	m	m	.	.	.	.
add_wchstr( )	m	m	.	.	.	.
addch( )	m	m	.	.	m	.
addchnstr( )	m	m	.	.	m	.
addchstr( )	m	m	.	.	m	.
addnstr( )	m	m	.	.	m	.
addnwstr( )	m	m	.	.	.	.
addstr( )	m	m	.	.	m	.
addwstr( )	m	m	.	.	.	.
advance( )	f	m	.	.	m	.
aio_cancel( )	f	.	r	.	.	.
aio_error( )	f	.	r	.	.	.
aio_fsync( )	f	.	r	.	.	.
aio_read( )	f	.	r	.	.	.
aio_return( )	f	.	r	.	.	.
aio_suspend( )	f	.	r	.	.	.
aio_write( )	f	.	r	.	.	.
alarm( )	m	m	m	.	m	m
asctime( )	m	m	m	m	m	m
asctime_r( )	m	.	t	.	.	.
asin( )	m	m	m	m	m	m
asinh( )	m	m	.	.	m	m
assert( )	m	m	m	m	m	m
atan2( )	m	m	m	m	m	m
atan( )	m	m	m	m	m	m
atanh( )	m	m	.	.	m	m
atexit( )	m	m	.	m	m	.
atof( )	m	m	m	m	m	m
atoi( )	m	m	m	m	m	m
atol( )	m	m	m	m	m	m
attr_get( )	m	m	.	.	.	.
attr_off( )	m	m	.	.	.	.
attr_on( )	m	m	.	.	.	.

Interface	UNIX 98	UNIX 95	POSIX.1 and POSIX.2	ISO C Standard	SVID 3	4.3BSD
attr_set( )	m	m	.	.	.	.
attroff( )	m	m	.	.	m	.
attron( )	m	m	.	.	m	.
attrset( )	m	m	.	.	m	.
basename( )	m	m	.	.	.	.
baudrate( )	m	m	.	.	m	.
bcmp( )	m	m	.	.	.	m
bcopy( )	m	m	.	.	.	m
beep( )	m	m	.	.	m	.
bind( )	m	m	.	.	.	m
bkgd( )	m	m	.	.	m	.
bkgdset( )	m	m	.	.	m	.
bkgrnd( )	m	m	.	.	.	.
bkgrndset( )	m	m	.	.	.	.
border( )	m	m	.	.	m	.
border_set( )	m	m	.	.	.	.
box( )	m	m	.	.	m	.
box_set( )	m	m	.	.	.	.
brk( )	f	m	.	.	.	m
bsd_signal( )	m	m	.	.	.	.
bsearch( )	m	m	m	m	m	.
btowc( )	m	.	.	1	.	.
bzero( )	m	m	.	.	.	m
calloc( )	m	m	m	m	m	m
can_change_color( )	m	m	.	.	m	.
catclose( )	m	m	.	.	m	.
catgets( )	m	m	.	.	m	.
catopen( )	m	m	.	.	m	.
cbreak( )	m	m	.	.	m	.
cbrt( )	m	m	.	.	m	m
ceil( )	m	m	m	m	m	m
cfgetispeed( )	m	m	m	.	m	.
cfgetospeed( )	m	m	m	.	m	.
cfsetispeed( )	m	m	m	.	m	.
cfsetospeed( )	m	m	m	.	m	.
chdir( )	m	m	m	.	m	m
chgat( )	m	m	.	.	.	.
chmod( )	m	m	m	.	m	m
chown( )	m	m	m	.	m	m
chroot( )	f	m	.	.	m	m
clear( )	m	m	.	.	m	.
clearerr( )	m	m	m	m	m	m
clearok( )	m	m	.	.	m	.
clock( )	m	m	.	m	m	.
clock_getres( )	f	.	r	.	.	.
clock_gettime( )	f	.	r	.	.	.

Interface	UNIX 98	UNIX 95	POSIX.1 and POSIX.2	ISO C Standard	SVID 3	4.3BSD
clock_settime( )	f	.	r	.	.	.
close( )	m	m	m	.	m	m
closedir( )	m	m	m	.	m	m
closelog( )	m	m	.	.	.	m
clrtobot( )	m	m	.	.	m	.
clrtoeol( )	m	m	.	.	m	.
color_content( )	m	m	.	.	.	.
color_set( )	m	m	.	.	.	.
compile( )	f	m	.	.	m	.
confstr( )	m	m	m	.	.	.
connect( )	m	m	.	.	.	m
copywin( )	m	m	.	.	m	.
cos( )	m	m	m	m	m	m
cosh( )	m	m	m	m	m	m
creat( )	m	m	m	.	m	m
crypt( )	f	f	.	.	m	m
ctermid( )	m	m	m	.	m	.
ctime( )	m	m	m	m	m	m
ctime_r( )	m	.	t	.	.	.
curs_set( )	m	m	.	.	m	.
cuserid( )	f	m	.	.	m	.
daylight	m	m	.	.	m	.
dbm_clearerr( )	m	m	.	.	.	.
dbm_close( )	m	m	.	.	.	.
dbm_delete( )	m	m	.	.	.	.
dbm_error( )	m	m	.	.	.	.
dbm_fetch( )	m	m	.	.	.	.
dbm_firstkey( )	m	m	.	.	.	.
dbm_nextkey( )	m	m	.	.	.	.
dbm_open( )	m	m	.	.	.	.
dbm_store( )	m	m	.	.	.	.
def_prog_mode( )	m	m	.	.	m	.
def_shell_mode( )	m	m	.	.	m	.
del_curterm( )	m	m	.	.	m	.
delay_output( )	m	m	.	.	m	.
delch( )	m	m	.	.	m	.
deleteln( )	m	m	.	.	m	.
delscreen( )	m	m	.	.	m	.
delwin( )	m	m	.	.	m	.
derwin( )	m	m	.	.	m	.
difftime( )	m	m	.	m	m	.
dirname( )	m	m	.	.	.	.
div( )	m	m	.	m	m	.
dlclose( )	m	.	.	.	.	.
dlerror( )	m	.	.	.	.	.
dlopen( )	m	.	.	.	.	.

Interface	UNIX 98	UNIX 95	POSIX.1 and POSIX.2	ISO C Standard	SVID 3	4.3BSD
dlsym( )	m	.	.	.	.	.
doupdate( )	m	m	.	.	m	.
drand48( )	m	m	.	.	m	.
dup2( )	m	m	m	.	m	m
dup( )	m	m	m	.	m	m
dupwin( )	m	m	.	.	m	.
echo( )	m	m	.	.	m	.
echo_wchar( )	m	m	.	.	.	.
echochar( )	m	m	.	.	m	.
ecvt( )	m	m	.	.	.	m
encrypt( )	f	f	.	.	m	m
endgrent( )	m	m	.	.	m	m
endhostent( )	m	m	.	.	.	m
endnetent( )	m	m	.	.	.	m
endprotoent( )	m	m	.	.	.	m
endpwent( )	m	m	.	.	m	m
endservent( )	m	m	.	.	.	m
endutxent( )	m	m	.	.	.	.
endwin( )	m	m	.	.	m	.
environ	m	m	m	.	m	m
erand48( )	m	m	.	.	m	.
erase( )	m	m	.	.	m	.
erasechar( )	m	m	.	.	m	.
erasewchar( )	m	m	.	.	.	.
erf( )	m	m	.	.	m	m
erfc( )	m	m	.	.	m	m
errno	m	m	m	m	m	m
execl( )	m	m	m	.	m	m
execle( )	m	m	m	.	m	m
execlp( )	m	m	m	.	m	m
execv( )	m	m	m	.	m	m
execve( )	m	m	m	.	m	m
execvp( )	m	m	m	.	m	m
exit( )	m	m	m	m	m	m
exp( )	m	m	m	m	m	m
expm1( )	m	m	.	.	.	m
fabs( )	m	m	m	m	m	m
fattach( )	m	m	.	.	m	.
fchdir( )	m	m	.	.	m	.
fchmod( )	m	m	.	.	m	m
fchown( )	m	m	.	.	m	m
fclose( )	m	m	m	m	m	m
fcntl( )	m	m	m	.	m	m
fcvt( )	m	m	.	.	.	m
fdatasync( )	f	.	r	.	.	.
fdetach( )	m	m	.	.	m	.

Interface	UNIX 98	UNIX 95	POSIX.1 and POSIX.2	ISO C Standard	SVID 3	4.3BSD
fdopen( )	m	m	m	.	m	m
feof( )	m	m	m	m	m	m
ferror( )	m	m	m	m	m	m
fflush( )	m	m	m	m	m	m
ffs( )	m	m	.	.	.	m
fgetc( )	m	m	m	m	m	m
fgetpos( )	m	m	.	m	m	.
fgets( )	m	m	m	m	m	m
fgetwc( )	m	m	.	1	.	.
fgetws( )	m	m	.	1	.	.
fileno( )	m	m	m	.	m	m
filter( )	m	m	.	.	m	.
flash( )	m	m	.	.	m	.
flockfile( )	m	.	t	.	.	.
floor( )	m	m	m	m	m	m
flushinp( )	m	m	.	.	m	.
fmod( )	m	m	m	m	m	.
fmtmsg( )	m	m	.	.	m	.
fnmatch( )	m	m	m	.	.	.
fopen( )	m	m	m	m	m	m
fork( )	m	m	m	.	m	m
fpathconf( )	m	m	m	.	m	.
fprintf( )	m	m	m	m	m	m
fputc( )	m	m	m	m	m	m
fputs( )	m	m	m	m	m	m
fputwc( )	m	m	.	1	.	.
fputws( )	m	m	.	1	.	.
fread( )	m	m	m	m	m	m
free( )	m	m	m	m	m	m
freopen( )	m	m	m	m	m	m
frexp( )	m	m	m	m	m	m
fscanf( )	m	m	m	m	m	m
fseek( )	m	m	m	m	m	m
fseeko( )	m	.	.	.	.	.
fsetpos( )	m	m	.	m	m	.
fstat( )	m	m	m	.	m	m
fstatvfs( )	m	m	.	.	m	.
fsync( )	m	m	.	.	m	m
ftell( )	m	m	m	m	m	m
ftello( )	m	.	.	.	.	.
ftime( )	m	m	.	.	.	m
ftok( )	m	m	.	.	.	.
ftruncate( )	m	m	.	.	.	.
ftrylockfile( )	m	.	t	.	.	.
ftw( )	m	m	.	.	m	.
funlockfile( )	m	.	t	.	.	.

Interface	UNIX 98	UNIX 95	POSIX.1 and POSIX.2	ISO C Standard	SVID 3	4.3BSD
fwide( )	m	.	.	1	.	.
fwprintf( )	m	.	.	1	.	.
fwrite( )	m	m	m	m	m	m
fwscanf( )	m	.	.	1	.	.
gamma( )	f	m	.	.	m	.
gcvt( )	m	m	.	.	.	m
get_wch( )	m	m	.	.	.	.
get_wstr( )	m	m	.	.	.	.
getbegyx( )	m	m	.	.	m	.
getbkgd( )	m	m	.	.	.	.
getbkgrnd( )	m	m	.	.	.	.
getc( )	m	m	m	m	m	m
getc_unlocked( )	m	.	t	.	.	.
getcchar( )	m	m	.	.	.	.
getch( )	m	m	.	.	m	.
getchar( )	m	m	m	m	m	m
getchar_unlocked( )	m	.	t	.	.	.
getcontext( )	m	m	.	.	m	.
getcwd( )	m	m	m	.	m	.
getdate( )	m	m	.	.	m	.
getdtablesize( )	f	m	.	.	.	m
getegid( )	m	m	m	.	m	m
getenv( )	m	m	m	m	m	m
geteuid( )	m	m	m	.	m	m
getgid( )	m	m	m	.	m	m
getgrent( )	m	m	.	.	m	m
getgrgid( )	m	m	m	.	m	m
getgrgid_r( )	m	.	t	.	.	.
getgrnam( )	m	m	m	.	m	.
getgrnam_r( )	m	.	t	.	.	.
getgroups( )	m	m	m	.	m	m
gethostbyaddr( )	m	m	.	.	.	m
gethostbyname( )	m	m	.	.	.	m
gethostent( )	m	m	.	.	.	m
gethostid( )	m	m	.	.	.	m
gethostname( )	m	m	.	.	.	m
getitimer( )	m	m	.	.	m	m
getlogin( )	m	m	m	.	m	m
getlogin_r( )	m	.	t	.	.	.
getmaxyx( )	m	m	.	.	m	.
getmsg( )	m	m	.	.	m	.
getn_wstr( )	m	m	.	.	.	.
getnetbyaddr( )	m	m	.	.	.	m
getnetbyname( )	m	m	.	.	.	m
getnetent( )	m	m	.	.	.	m
getnstr( )	m	m	.	.	.	.

Interface	UNIX 98	UNIX 95	POSIX.1 and POSIX.2	ISO C Standard	SVID 3	4.3BSD
getopt( )	m	m	m	.	m	m
getpagesize( )	f	m	.	.	.	m
getparyx( )	m	m	.	.	m	.
getpass( )	f	m	.	.	m	m
getpeername( )	m	m	.	.	.	m
getpgid( )	m	m	.	.	m	.
getpgrp( )	m	m	m	.	m	m
getpid( )	m	m	m	.	m	m
getpmsg( )	m	m	.	.	m	.
getppid( )	m	m	m	.	m	m
getpriority( )	m	m	.	.	.	m
getprotobyname( )	m	m	.	.	.	m
getprotobynumber( )	m	m	.	.	.	m
getprotoent( )	m	m	.	.	.	m
getpwent( )	m	m	.	.	m	m
getpwnam( )	m	m	m	.	m	m
getpwnam_r( )	m	.	t	.	.	.
getpwuid( )	m	m	m	.	m	m
getpwuid_r( )	m	.	t	.	.	.
getrlimit( )	m	m	.	.	m	m
getrusage( )	m	m	.	.	.	m
gets( )	m	m	m	m	m	m
getservbyname( )	m	m	.	.	.	m
getservbyport( )	m	m	.	.	.	m
getservent( )	m	m	.	.	.	m
getsid( )	m	m	.	.	m	.
getsockname( )	m	m	.	.	.	m
getsockopt( )	m	m	.	.	.	m
getstr( )	m	m	.	.	m	.
getsubopt( )	m	m	.	.	m	.
gettimeofday( )	m	m	.	.	m	m
getuid( )	m	m	m	.	m	m
getutxent( )	m	m	.	.	.	.
getutxid( )	m	m	.	.	.	.
getutxline( )	m	m	.	.	.	.
getw( )	f	m	.	.	m	m
getwc( )	m	m	.	1	.	.
getwchar( )	m	m	.	1	.	.
getwd( )	m	m	.	.	.	m
getwin( )	m	m	.	.	.	.
getyx( )	m	m	.	.	m	.
glob( )	m	f	m	.	.	.
globfree( )	m	f	m	.	.	.
gmtime( )	m	m	m	m	m	m
gmtime_r( )	m	.	t	.	.	.
grantpt( )	m	m	.	.	m	.

Interface	UNIX 98	UNIX 95	POSIX.1 and POSIX.2	ISO C Standard	SVID 3	4.3BSD
halfdelay( )	m	m	.	.	m	.
has_colors( )	m	m	.	.	m	.
has_ic( )	m	m	.	.	m	.
has_il( )	m	m	.	.	m	.
hcreate( )	m	m	.	.	m	.
hdestroy( )	m	m	.	.	m	.
hline( )	m	m	.	.	.	.
hline_set( )	m	m	.	.	.	.
hsearch( )	m	m	.	.	m	.
htonl( )	m	m	.	.	.	m
htons( )	m	m	.	.	.	m
hypot( )	m	m	.	.	m	m
iconv( )	m	m	.	.	.	.
iconv_close( )	m	m	.	.	.	.
iconv_open( )	m	m	.	.	.	.
idcok( )	m	m	.	.	m	.
idlok( )	m	m	.	.	m	.
ilogb( )	m	m	.	.	.	.
immedok( )	m	m	.	.	m	.
in_wch( )	m	m	.	.	.	.
in_wchnstr( )	m	m	.	.	.	.
in_wchstr( )	m	m	.	.	.	.
inch( )	m	m	.	.	m	.
inchnstr( )	m	m	.	.	m	.
inchstr( )	m	m	.	.	m	.
index( )	m	m	.	.	.	m
inet_addr( )	m	m	.	.	.	m
inet_lnaof( )	m	m	.	.	.	m
inet_makeaddr( )	m	m	.	.	.	m
inet_netof( )	m	m	.	.	.	m
inet_network( )	m	m	.	.	.	m
inet_ntoa( )	m	m	.	.	.	m
init_color( )	m	m	.	.	m	.
init_pair( )	m	m	.	.	m	.
initscr( )	m	m	.	.	m	.
initstate( )	m	m	.	.	.	m
innstr( )	m	m	.	.	m	.
innwstr( )	m	m	.	.	.	.
ins_nwstr( )	m	m	.	.	.	.
ins_wch( )	m	m	.	.	.	.
ins_wstr( )	m	m	.	.	.	.
insch( )	m	m	.	.	m	.
insdelln( )	m	m	.	.	m	.
insertln( )	m	m	.	.	m	.
insnstr( )	m	m	.	.	m	.
insque( )	m	m	.	.	.	m

Interface	UNIX 98	UNIX 95	POSIX.1 and POSIX.2	ISO C Standard	SVID 3	4.3BSD
insstr( )	m	m	.	.	m	.
instr( )	m	m	.	.	m	.
intrflush( )	m	m	.	.	m	.
inwstr( )	m	m	.	.	.	.
ioctl( )	m	m	.	.	m	m
is_linetouched( )	m	m	.	.	m	.
is_wintouched( )	m	m	.	.	m	.
isalnum( )	m	m	m	m	m	m
isalpha( )	m	m	m	m	m	m
isascii( )	m	m	.	.	m	m
isastream( )	m	m	.	.	m	.
isatty( )	m	m	m	.	m	m
iscntrl( )	m	m	m	m	m	m
isdigit( )	m	m	m	m	m	m
isendwin( )	m	m	.	.	m	.
isgraph( )	m	m	m	m	m	m
islower( )	m	m	m	m	m	m
isnan( )	m	m	.	.	m	.
isprint( )	m	m	m	m	m	m
ispunct( )	m	m	m	m	m	m
isspace( )	m	m	m	m	m	m
isupper( )	m	m	m	m	m	m
iswalnum( )	m	m	.	1	.	.
iswalpha( )	m	m	.	1	.	.
iswcntrl( )	m	m	.	1	.	.
iswctype( )	m	m	.	1	.	.
iswdigit( )	m	m	.	1	.	.
iswgraph( )	m	m	.	1	.	.
iswlower( )	m	m	.	1	.	.
iswprint( )	m	m	.	1	.	.
iswpunct( )	m	m	.	1	.	.
iswspace( )	m	m	.	1	.	.
iswupper( )	m	m	.	1	.	.
iswxdigit( )	m	m	.	1	.	.
isxdigit( )	m	m	m	m	m	m
j0( )	m	m	.	.	m	m
j1( )	m	m	.	.	m	m
jn( )	m	m	.	.	m	m
jrand48( )	m	m	.	.	m	.
key_name( )	m	m	.	.	.	.
keyname( )	m	m	.	.	m	.
keypad( )	m	m	.	.	m	.
kill( )	m	m	m	.	m	m
killchar( )	m	m	.	.	m	.
killpg( )	m	m	.	.	.	m
killwchar( )	m	m	.	.	.	.

Interface	UNIX 98	UNIX 95	POSIX.1 and POSIX.2	ISO C Standard	SVID 3	4.3BSD
l64a( )	m	m	.	.	m	.
labs( )	m	m	.	m	m	.
lchown( )	m	m	.	.	m	.
lcong48( )	m	m	.	.	m	.
ldexp( )	m	m	m	m	m	m
ldiv( )	m	m	.	m	m	.
leaveok( )	m	m	.	.	m	.
lfind( )	m	m	.	.	m	.
lgamma( )	m	m	.	.	m	m
link( )	m	m	m	.	m	m
lio_listio( )	f	.	r	.	.	.
listen( )	m	m	.	.	.	m
loc1	m	m	.	.	m	.
localeconv( )	m	m	.	m	m	.
localtime( )	m	m	m	m	m	m
localtime_r( )	m	.	t	.	.	.
lockf( )	m	m	.	.	m	.
locs	m	m	.	.	m	.
log10( )	m	m	m	m	m	m
log1p( )	m	m	.	.	.	m
log( )	m	m	m	m	m	m
logb( )	m	m	.	.	m	m
longjmp( )	m	m	m	m	m	m
longname( )	m	m	.	.	m	.
lrand48( )	m	m	.	.	m	.
lsearch( )	m	m	.	.	m	.
lseek( )	m	m	m	.	m	m
lstat( )	m	m	.	.	m	m
makecontext( )	m	m	.	.	.	.
malloc( )	m	m	m	m	m	m
mblen( )	m	m	.	m	m	.
mbrlen( )	m	.	.	1	.	.
mbrtowc( )	m	.	.	1	.	.
mbsinit( )	m	.	.	1	.	.
mbsrtowcs( )	m	.	.	1	.	.
mbstowcs( )	m	m	.	m	m	.
mbtowc( )	m	m	.	m	m	.
memccpy( )	m	m	.	.	m	.
memchr( )	m	m	.	m	m	.
memcmp( )	m	m	.	m	m	.
memcpy( )	m	m	.	m	m	.
memmove( )	m	m	.	m	m	.
memset( )	m	m	.	m	m	.
meta( )	m	m	.	.	m	.
mkdir( )	m	m	m	.	m	m
mkfifo( )	m	m	m	.	m	.

Interface	UNIX 98	UNIX 95	POSIX.1 and POSIX.2	ISO C Standard	SVID 3	4.3BSD
mknod( )	m	m	.	.	m	m
mkstemp( )	m	m	.	.	.	m
mktemp( )	m	m	.	.	m	m
mktime( )	m	m	m	m	m	.
mlock( )	f	.	r	.	.	.
mlockall( )	f	.	r	.	.	.
mmap( )	m	m	.	.	m	.
modf( )	m	m	m	m	m	m
move( )	m	m	.	.	m	.
mprotect( )	m	m	.	.	m	.
mq_close( )	f	.	r	.	.	.
mq_getattr( )	f	.	r	.	.	.
mq_notify( )	f	.	r	.	.	.
mq_open( )	f	.	r	.	.	.
mq_receive( )	f	.	r	.	.	.
mq_send( )	f	.	r	.	.	.
mq_setattr( )	f	.	r	.	.	.
mq_unlink( )	f	.	r	.	.	.
mrand48( )	m	m	.	.	m	.
msgctl( )	m	m	.	.	m	.
msgget( )	m	m	.	.	m	.
msgrcv( )	m	m	.	.	m	.
msgsnd( )	m	m	.	.	m	.
msync( )	m	m	.	.	m	.
munlock( )	f	.	r	.	.	.
munlockall( )	f	.	r	.	.	.
munmap( )	m	m	.	.	m	.
mvadd_wch( )	m	m	.	.	.	.
mvadd_wchnstr( )	m	m	.	.	.	.
mvadd_wchstr( )	m	m	.	.	.	.
mvaddch( )	m	m	.	.	m	.
mvaddchnstr( )	m	m	.	.	m	.
mvaddchstr( )	m	m	.	.	m	.
mvaddnstr( )	m	m	.	.	m	.
mvaddnwstr( )	m	m	.	.	.	.
mvaddstr( )	m	m	.	.	m	.
mvaddwstr( )	m	m	.	.	.	.
mvchgat( )	m	m	.	.	.	.
mvcur( )	m	m	.	.	m	.
mvdelch( )	m	m	.	.	m	.
mvderwin( )	m	m	.	.	m	.
mvget_wch( )	m	m	.	.	.	.
mvget_wstr( )	m	m	.	.	.	.
mvgetch( )	m	m	.	.	m	.
mvgetn_wstr( )	m	m	.	.	.	.
mvgetnstr( )	m	m	.	.	m	.

Interface	UNIX 98	UNIX 95	POSIX.1 and POSIX.2	ISO C Standard	SVID 3	4.3BSD
mvgetstr( )	m	m	.	.	.	.
mvhline( )	m	m	.	.	.	.
mvhline_set( )	m	m	.	.	.	.
mvin_wch( )	m	m	.	.	.	.
mvin_wchnstr( )	m	m	.	.	.	.
mvin_wchstr( )	m	m	.	.	.	.
mvinch( )	m	m	.	.	m	.
mvinchnstr( )	m	m	.	.	m	.
mvinchstr( )	m	m	.	.	m	.
mvinnstr( )	m	m	.	.	m	.
mvinnwstr( )	m	m	.	.	.	.
mvins_nwstr( )	m	m	.	.	.	.
mvins_wch( )	m	m	.	.	.	.
mvins_wstr( )	m	m	.	.	.	.
mvinsch( )	m	m	.	.	m	.
mvinsnstr( )	m	m	.	.	m	.
mvinsstr( )	m	m	.	.	m	.
mvinstr( )	m	m	.	.	m	.
mvinwstr( )	m	m	.	.	.	.
mvprintw( )	m	m	.	.	m	.
mvscanw( )	m	m	.	.	m	.
mvvline( )	m	m	.	.	.	.
mvvline_set( )	m	m	.	.	.	.
mvwadd_wch( )	m	m	.	.	.	.
mvwadd_wchnstr( )	m	m	.	.	.	.
mvwadd_wchstr( )	m	m	.	.	.	.
mvwaddch( )	m	m	.	.	m	.
mvwaddchnstr( )	m	m	.	.	m	.
mvwaddchstr( )	m	m	.	.	m	.
mvwaddnstr( )	m	m	.	.	m	.
mvwaddnwstr( )	m	m	.	.	.	.
mvwaddstr( )	m	m	.	.	m	.
mvwaddwstr( )	m	m	.	.	.	.
mvwchgat( )	m	m	.	.	.	.
mvwdelch( )	m	m	.	.	m	.
mvwget_wch( )	m	m	.	.	.	.
mvwget_wstr( )	m	m	.	.	.	.
mvwgetch( )	m	m	.	.	m	.
mvwgetn_wstr( )	m	m	.	.	.	.
mvwgetnstr( )	m	m	.	.	.	.
mvwgetstr( )	m	m	.	.	m	.
mvwhline( )	m	m	.	.	.	.
mvwhline_set( )	m	m	.	.	.	.
mvwin( )	m	m	.	.	m	.
mvwin_wch( )	m	m	.	.	.	.
mvwin_wchnstr( )	m	m	.	.	.	.

Interface	UNIX 98	UNIX 95	POSIX.1 and POSIX.2	ISO C Standard	SVID 3	4.3BSD
mvwin_wchstr( )	m	m	.	.	.	.
mvwinch( )	m	m	.	.	m	.
mvwinchnstr( )	m	m	.	.	m	.
mvwinchstr( )	m	m	.	.	m	.
mvwinnstr( )	m	m	.	.	m	.
mvwinnwstr( )	m	m	.	.	.	.
mvwins_nwstr( )	m	m	.	.	.	.
mvwins_wch( )	m	m	.	.	.	.
mvwins_wstr( )	m	m	.	.	.	.
mvwinsch( )	m	m	.	.	m	.
mvwinsnstr( )	m	m	.	.	m	.
mvwinsstr( )	m	m	.	.	m	.
mvwinstr( )	m	m	.	.	m	.
mvwinwstr( )	m	m	.	.	.	.
mvwprintw( )	m	m	.	.	m	.
mvwscanw( )	m	m	.	.	m	.
mvwvline( )	m	m	.	.	.	.
mvwvline_set( )	m	m	.	.	.	.
nanosleep( )	f	.	r	.	.	.
napms( )	m	m	.	.	m	.
newpad( )	m	m	.	.	m	.
newterm( )	m	m	.	.	m	.
newwin( )	m	m	.	.	m	.
nextafter( )	m	m	.	.	m	.
nftw( )	m	m	.	.	m	.
nice( )	m	m	.	.	m	m
nl( )	m	m	.	.	m	.
nl_langinfo( )	m	m	.	.	m	.
nocbreak( )	m	m	.	.	m	.
nodelay( )	m	m	.	.	m	.
noecho( )	m	m	.	.	m	.
nonl( )	m	m	.	.	m	.
noqiflush( )	m	m	.	.	m	.
noraw( )	m	m	.	.	m	.
notimeout( )	m	m	.	.	m	.
nrand48( )	m	m	.	.	m	.
ntohl( )	m	m	.	.	.	m
ntohs( )	m	m	.	.	.	m
open( )	m	m	m	.	m	m
opendir( )	m	m	m	.	m	m
openlog( )	m	m	.	.	.	m
optarg	m	m	m	.	m	m
overlay( )	m	m	.	.	m	.
overwrite( )	m	m	.	.	m	.
pair_content( )	m	m	.	.	m	.
pathconf( )	m	m	m	.	m	.

Interface	UNIX 98	UNIX 95	POSIX.1 and POSIX.2	ISO C Standard	SVID 3	4.3BSD
pause( )	m	m	m	.	m	m
pclose( )	m	m	m	.	m	m
pecho_wchar( )	m	m	.	.	.	.
pechochar( )	m	m	.	.	m	.
perror( )	m	m	m	m	m	m
pipe( )	m	m	m	.	m	m
pnoutrefresh( )	m	m	.	.	m	.
poll( )	m	m	.	.	m	.
popen( )	m	m	m	.	m	m
pow( )	m	m	m	m	m	m
pread( )	m	.	.	.	.	.
prefresh( )	m	m	.	.	m	.
printf( )	m	m	m	m	m	m
printw( )	m	m	.	.	m	.
pthread_atfork( )	m	.	t	.	.	.
pthread_attr_destroy( )	m	.	t	.	.	.
pthread_attr_getdetachstate( )	m	.	t	.	.	.
pthread_attr_getguardsize( )	m	.	.	.	.	.
pthread_attr_getinheritsched( )	f	.	t	.	.	.
pthread_attr_getschedparam( )	m	.	t	.	.	.
pthread_attr_getschedpolicy( )	f	.	t	.	.	.
pthread_attr_getscope( )	f	.	t	.	.	.
pthread_attr_getstackaddr( )	m	.	t	.	.	.
pthread_attr_getstacksize( )	m	.	t	.	.	.
pthread_attr_init( )	m	.	t	.	.	.
pthread_attr_setdetachstate( )	m	.	t	.	.	.
pthread_attr_setguardsize( )	m	.	.	.	.	.
pthread_attr_setinheritsched( )	f	.	t	.	.	.
pthread_attr_setschedparam( )	m	.	t	.	.	.
pthread_attr_setschedpolicy( )	f	.	t	.	.	.
pthread_attr_setscope( )	f	.	t	.	.	.
pthread_attr_setstackaddr( )	m	.	t	.	.	.
pthread_attr_setstacksize( )	m	.	t	.	.	.
pthread_cancel( )	m	.	t	.	.	.
pthread_cleanup_pop( )	m	.	t	.	.	.
pthread_cleanup_push( )	m	.	t	.	.	.
pthread_cond_broadcast( )	m	.	t	.	.	.
pthread_cond_destroy( )	m	.	t	.	.	.
pthread_cond_init( )	m	.	t	.	.	.
pthread_cond_signal( )	m	.	t	.	.	.
pthread_cond_timedwait( )	m	.	t	.	.	.
pthread_cond_wait( )	m	.	t	.	.	.
pthread_condattr_destroy( )	m	.	t	.	.	.
pthread_condattr_getpshared( )	m	.	t	.	.	.
pthread_condattr_init( )	m	.	t	.	.	.
pthread_condattr_setpshared( )	m	.	t	.	.	.

Interface	UNIX 98	UNIX 95	POSIX.1 and POSIX.2	ISO C Standard	SVID 3	4.3BSD
pthread_create( )	m	.	t	.	.	.
pthread_detach( )	m	.	t	.	.	.
pthread_equal( )	m	.	t	.	.	.
pthread_exit( )	m	.	t	.	.	.
pthread_getconcurrency( )	m	.	.	.	.	.
pthread_getschedparam( )	f	.	t	.	.	.
pthread_getspecific( )	m	.	t	.	.	.
pthread_join( )	m	.	t	.	.	.
pthread_key_create( )	m	.	t	.	.	.
pthread_key_delete( )	m	.	t	.	.	.
pthread_kill( )	m	.	t	.	.	.
pthread_mutex_destroy( )	m	.	t	.	.	.
pthread_mutex_getprioceiling( )	f	.	t	.	.	.
pthread_mutex_init( )	m	.	t	.	.	.
pthread_mutex_lock( )	m	.	t	.	.	.
pthread_mutex_setprioceiling( )	f	.	t	.	.	.
pthread_mutex_trylock( )	m	.	t	.	.	.
pthread_mutex_unlock( )	m	.	t	.	.	.
pthread_mutexattr_destroy( )	m	.	t	.	.	.
pthread_mutexattr_getprioceiling( )	f	.	t	.	.	.
pthread_mutexattr_getprotocol( )	f	.	t	.	.	.
pthread_mutexattr_getpshared( )	m	.	t	.	.	.
pthread_mutexattr_gettype( )	m	.	.	.	.	.
pthread_mutexattr_init( )	m	.	t	.	.	.
pthread_mutexattr_setprioceiling( )	f	.	t	.	.	.
pthread_mutexattr_setprotocol( )	f	.	t	.	.	.
pthread_mutexattr_setpshared( )	m	.	t	.	.	.
pthread_mutexattr_settype( )	m	.	.	.	.	.
pthread_once( )	m	.	t	.	.	.
pthread_rwlock_destroy( )	m	.	.	.	.	.
pthread_rwlock_init( )	m	.	.	.	.	.
pthread_rwlock_rdlock( )	m	.	.	.	.	.
pthread_rwlock_tryrdlock( )	m	.	.	.	.	.
pthread_rwlock_trywrlock( )	m	.	.	.	.	.
pthread_rwlock_unlock( )	m	.	.	.	.	.
pthread_rwlock_wrlock( )	m	.	.	.	.	.
pthread_rwlockattr_destroy( )	m	.	.	.	.	.
pthread_rwlockattr_getpshared( )	m	.	.	.	.	.
pthread_rwlockattr_init( )	m	.	.	.	.	.
pthread_rwlockattr_setpshared( )	m	.	.	.	.	.
pthread_self( )	m	.	t	.	.	.
pthread_setcancelstate( )	m	.	t	.	.	.
pthread_setcanceltype( )	m	.	t	.	.	.
pthread_setconcurrency( )	m	.	.	.	.	.
pthread_setschedparam( )	f	.	t	.	.	.
pthread_setspecific( )	m	.	t	.	.	.

Interface	UNIX 98	UNIX 95	POSIX.1 and POSIX.2	ISO C Standard	SVID 3	4.3BSD
pthread_sigmask( )	m	.	t	.	.	.
pthread_testcancel( )	m	.	t	.	.	.
ptsname( )	m	m	.	.	m	.
putc( )	m	m	m	m	m	m
putc_unlocked( )	m	.	t	.	.	.
putchar( )	m	m	m	m	m	m
putchar_unlocked( )	m	.	t	.	.	.
putenv( )	m	m	.	.	m	.
putmsg( )	m	m	.	.	m	.
putp( )	m	m	.	.	m	.
putpmsg( )	m	m	.	.	m	.
puts( )	m	m	m	m	m	m
pututxline( )	m	m	.	.	.	.
putw( )	f	m	.	.	m	m
putwc( )	m	m	.	1	.	.
putwchar( )	m	m	.	1	.	.
putwin( )	m	m	.	.	m	.
pwrite( )	m	.	.	.	.	.
qiflush( )	m	m	.	.	m	.
qsort( )	m	m	m	m	m	m
raise( )	m	m	.	m	m	.
rand( )	m	m	m	m	m	m
rand_r( )	m	.	t	.	.	.
random( )	m	m	.	.	.	m
raw( )	m	m	.	.	m	.
re_comp( )	f	m	.	.	.	m
re_exec( )	f	m	.	.	.	m
read( )	m	m	m	.	m	m
readdir( )	m	m	m	.	m	m
readdir_r( )	m	.	t	.	.	.
readlink( )	m	m	.	.	m	m
readv( )	m	m	.	.	m	m
realloc( )	m	m	m	m	m	m
realpath( )	m	m	.	.	.	.
recv( )	m	m	.	.	.	m
recvfrom( )	m	m	.	.	.	m
recvmsg( )	m	m	.	.	.	m
redrawwin( )	m	m	.	.	m	.
refresh( )	m	m	.	.	m	.
regcmp( )	f	m	.	.	.	.
regcomp( )	m	f	m	.	.	.
regerror( )	m	f	m	.	.	.
regex( )	f	m	.	.	.	m
regexec( )	m	f	m	.	.	.
regfree( )	m	f	m	.	.	.
remainder( )	m	m	.	.	m	.

Interface	UNIX 98	UNIX 95	POSIX.1 and POSIX.2	ISO C Standard	SVID 3	4.3BSD
remove( )	m	m	m	m	m	.
remque( )	m	m	.	.	.	m
rename( )	m	m	m	m	m	m
reset_prog_mode( )	m	m	.	.	m	.
reset_shell_mode( )	m	m	.	.	m	.
resetty( )	m	m	.	.	m	.
restartterm( )	m	m	.	.	m	.
rewind( )	m	m	m	m	m	m
rewinddir( )	m	m	m	.	m	m
rindex( )	m	m	.	.	.	m
rint( )	m	m	.	.	.	m
ripoffline( )	m	m	.	.	m	.
rmdir( )	m	m	m	.	m	m
savetty( )	m	m	.	.	m	.
sbrk( )	f	m	.	.	.	m
scalb( )	m	m	.	.	m	m
scanf( )	m	m	m	m	m	m
scanw( )	m	m	.	.	m	.
sched_get_priority_max( )	f	.	r	.	.	.
sched_get_priority_min( )	f	.	r	.	.	.
sched_getparam( )	f	.	r	.	.	.
sched_getscheduler( )	f	.	r	.	.	.
sched_rr_get_interval( )	f	.	r	.	.	.
sched_setparam( )	f	.	r	.	.	.
sched_setscheduler( )	f	.	r	.	.	.
sched_yield( )	m	.	r	.	.	.
scr_dump( )	m	m	.	.	m	.
scr_init( )	m	m	.	.	m	.
scr_restore( )	m	m	.	.	m	.
scr_set( )	m	m	.	.	m	.
scrl( )	m	m	.	.	m	.
scroll( )	m	m	.	.	m	.
scrollok( )	m	m	.	.	m	.
seed48( )	m	m	.	.	m	.
seekdir( )	m	m	.	.	m	m
select( )	m	m	.	.	.	m
sem_close( )	f	.	r	.	.	.
sem_destroy( )	f	.	r	.	.	.
sem_getvalue( )	f	.	r	.	.	.
sem_init( )	f	.	r	.	.	.
sem_open( )	f	.	r	.	.	.
sem_post( )	f	.	r	.	.	.
sem_trywait( )	f	.	r	.	.	.
sem_unlink( )	f	.	r	.	.	.
sem_wait( )	f	.	r	.	.	.
semctl( )	m	m	.	.	m	.

Interface	UNIX 98	UNIX 95	POSIX.1 and POSIX.2	ISO C Standard	SVID 3	4.3BSD
semget( )	m	m	.	.	m	.
semop( )	m	m	.	.	m	.
send( )	m	m	.	.	.	m
sendmsg( )	m	m	.	.	.	m
sendto( )	m	m	.	.	.	m
set_curterm( )	m	m	.	.	m	.
set_term( )	m	m	.	.	m	.
setbuf( )	m	m	m	m	m	m
setcchar( )	m	m	.	.	.	.
setcontext( )	m	m	.	.	m	.
setgid( )	m	m	m	.	m	m
setgrent( )	m	m	.	.	m	m
sethostent( )	m	m	.	.	.	m
setitimer( )	m	m	.	.	m	m
setjmp( )	m	m	m	m	m	m
setkey( )	f	f	.	.	m	m
setlocale( )	m	m	m	m	m	.
setlogmask( )	m	m	.	.	.	m
setnetent( )	m	m	.	.	.	m
setpgid( )	m	m	m	.	m	.
setpgrp( )	m	m	.	.	m	m
setpriority( )	m	m	.	.	.	m
setprotoent( )	m	m	.	.	.	m
setpwent( )	m	m	.	.	m	m
setregid( )	m	m	.	.	.	m
setreuid( )	m	m	.	.	.	m
setrlimit( )	m	m	.	.	m	m
setscrreg( )	m	m	.	.	m	.
setservent( )	m	m	.	.	.	m
setsid( )	m	m	m	.	m	.
setsockopt( )	m	m	.	.	.	m
setstate( )	m	m	.	.	.	m
setuid( )	m	m	m	.	m	m
setupterm( )	m	m	.	.	m	.
setutxent( )	m	m	.	.	.	.
setvbuf( )	m	m	.	m	m	.
shm_open( )	f	.	r	.	.	.
shm_unlink( )	f	.	r	.	.	.
shmat( )	m	f	.	.	m	.
shmctl( )	m	f	.	.	m	.
shmdt( )	m	f	.	.	m	.
shmget( )	m	f	.	.	m	.
shutdown( )	m	m	.	.	.	m
sigaction( )	m	m	m	.	m	.
sigaddset( )	m	m	m	.	m	.
sigaltstack( )	m	m	.	.	m	.

Interface	UNIX 98	UNIX 95	POSIX.1 and POSIX.2	ISO C Standard	SVID 3	4.3BSD
sigdelset( )	m	m	m	.	m	.
sigemptyset( )	m	m	m	.	m	.
sigfillset( )	m	m	m	.	m	.
sighold( )	m	m	.	.	m	.
sigignore( )	m	m	.	.	m	.
siginterrupt( )	m	m	.	.	.	m
sigismember( )	m	m	m	.	m	.
siglongjmp( )	m	m	m	.	m	.
signal( )	m	m	.	m	m	m
signgam	m	m	.	.	m	.
sigpause( )	m	m	.	.	m	m
sigpending( )	m	m	m	.	m	.
sigprocmask( )	m	m	m	.	m	.
sigqueue( )	f	.	r	.	.	.
sigrelse( )	m	m	.	.	m	.
sigset( )	m	m	.	.	m	.
sigsetjmp( )	m	m	m	.	m	.
sigstack( )	f	m	.	.	.	m
sigsuspend( )	m	m	m	.	m	.
sigtimedwait( )	f	.	r	.	.	.
sigwait( )	m	.	t	.	.	.
sigwaitinfo( )	f	.	r	.	.	.
sin( )	m	m	m	m	m	m
sinh( )	m	m	m	m	m	m
sleep( )	m	m	m	.	m	m
slk_attr_off( )	m	m	.	.	.	.
slk_attr_on( )	m	m	.	.	.	.
slk_attr_set( )	m	m	.	.	.	.
slk_attroff( )	m	m	.	.	m	.
slk_attron( )	m	m	.	.	m	.
slk_attrset( )	m	m	.	.	m	.
slk_clear( )	m	m	.	.	m	.
slk_color( )	m	m	.	.	.	.
slk_init( )	m	m	.	.	m	.
slk_label( )	m	m	.	.	m	.
slk_noutrefresh( )	m	m	.	.	m	.
slk_refresh( )	m	m	.	.	m	.
slk_restore( )	m	m	.	.	m	.
slk_set( )	m	m	.	.	m	.
slk_touch( )	m	m	.	.	m	.
slk_wset( )	m	m	.	.	.	.
snprintf( )	m	.	.	.	.	.
socket( )	m	m	.	.	.	m
socketpair( )	m	m	.	.	.	m
sprintf( )	m	m	m	m	m	m
sqrt( )	m	m	m	m	m	m

Interface	UNIX 98	UNIX 95	POSIX.1 and POSIX.2	ISO C Standard	SVID 3	4.3BSD
srand48( )	m	m	.	.	m	.
srand( )	m	m	m	m	m	m
srandom( )	m	m	.	.	.	m
sscanf( )	m	m	m	m	m	m
standend( )	m	m	.	.	m	.
standout( )	m	m	.	.	m	.
start_color( )	m	m	.	.	m	.
stat( )	m	m	m	.	m	m
statvfs( )	m	m	.	.	m	.
stderr	m	m	m	m	m	m
stdin	m	m	m	m	m	m
stdout	m	m	m	m	m	m
step( )	f	m	.	.	m	.
strcasecmp( )	m	m	.	.	.	.
strcat( )	m	m	m	m	m	m
strchr( )	m	m	m	m	m	.
strcmp( )	m	m	m	m	m	m
strcoll( )	m	m	.	m	m	.
strcpy( )	m	m	m	m	m	m
strcspn( )	m	m	m	m	m	.
strdup( )	m	m	.	.	m	.
strerror( )	m	m	.	m	m	.
strfmon( )	m	f	.	.	.	.
strftime( )	m	m	m	m	m	.
strlen( )	m	m	m	m	m	m
strncasecmp( )	m	m	.	.	.	.
strncat( )	m	m	m	m	m	m
strncmp( )	m	m	m	m	m	m
strncpy( )	m	m	m	m	m	m
strpbrk( )	m	m	m	m	m	.
strptime( )	m	f	.	.	.	.
strrchr( )	m	m	m	m	m	.
strspn( )	m	m	m	m	m	.
strstr( )	m	m	m	m	m	.
strtod( )	m	m	.	m	m	.
strtok( )	m	m	m	m	m	.
strtok_r( )	m	.	t	.	.	.
strtol( )	m	m	.	m	m	.
strtoul( )	m	m	.	m	m	.
strxfrm( )	m	m	.	m	m	.
subpad( )	m	m	.	.	m	.
subwin( )	m	m	.	.	m	.
swab( )	m	m	.	.	m	m
swapcontext( )	m	m	.	.	.	.
swprintf( )	m	.	.	1	.	.
swscanf( )	m	.	.	1	.	.

Interface	UNIX 98	UNIX 95	POSIX.1 and POSIX.2	ISO C Standard	SVID 3	4.3BSD
symlink( )	m	m	.	.	m	m
sync( )	m	m	.	.	m	m
syncok( )	m	m	.	.	m	.
sysconf( )	m	m	m	.	m	.
syslog( )	m	m	.	.	.	m
system( )	m	m	.	m	m	m
t_accept( )	m	m	.	.	m	.
t_alloc( )	m	m	.	.	m	.
t_bind( )	m	m	.	.	m	.
t_close( )	m	m	.	.	m	.
t_connect( )	m	m	.	.	m	.
t_error( )	m	m	.	.	m	.
t_free( )	m	m	.	.	m	.
t_getinfo( )	m	m	.	.	m	.
t_getprotaddr( )	m	m	.	.	.	.
t_getstate( )	m	m	.	.	m	.
t_listen( )	m	m	.	.	m	.
t_look( )	m	m	.	.	m	.
t_open( )	m	m	.	.	m	.
t_optmgmt( )	m	m	.	.	m	.
t_rcv( )	m	m	.	.	m	.
t_rcvconnect( )	m	m	.	.	m	.
t_rcvdis( )	m	m	.	.	m	.
t_rcvrel( )	m	m	.	.	m	.
t_rcvreldata( )	m	.	.	.	.	.
t_rcvudata( )	m	m	.	.	m	.
t_rcvuderr( )	m	m	.	.	m	.
t_rcvv( )	m	.	.	.	.	.
t_rcvvudata( )	m	.	.	.	.	.
t_snd( )	m	m	.	.	m	.
t_snddis( )	m	m	.	.	m	.
t_sndrel( )	m	m	.	.	m	.
t_sndreldata( )	m	.	.	.	.	.
t_sndudata( )	m	m	.	.	m	.
t_sndv( )	m	.	.	.	.	.
t_sndvudata( )	m	.	.	.	.	.
t_strerror( )	m	m	.	.	.	.
t_sync( )	m	m	.	.	m	.
t_sysconf( )	m	.	.	.	.	.
t_unbind( )	m	m	.	.	m	.
tan( )	m	m	m	m	m	m
tanh( )	m	m	m	m	m	m
tcdrain( )	m	m	m	.	m	.
tcflow( )	m	m	m	.	m	.
tcflush( )	m	m	m	.	m	.
tcgetattr( )	m	m	m	.	m	.

Interface	UNIX 98	UNIX 95	POSIX.1 and POSIX.2	ISO C Standard	SVID 3	4.3BSD
tcgetpgrp( )	m	m	m	.	m	.
tcgetsid( )	m	m	.	.	m	.
tcsendbreak( )	m	m	m	.	m	.
tcsetattr( )	m	m	m	.	m	.
tcsetpgrp( )	m	m	m	.	m	.
tdelete( )	m	m	.	.	m	.
telldir( )	m	m	.	.	m	m
tempnam( )	m	m	.	.	m	.
term_attrs( )	m	m	.	.	.	.
termattrs( )	m	m	.	.	m	.
termname( )	m	m	.	.	m	.
tfind( )	m	m	.	.	m	.
tgetent( )	m	m	.	.	m	.
tgetflag( )	m	m	.	.	m	.
tgetnum( )	m	m	.	.	m	.
tgetstr( )	m	m	.	.	m	.
tgoto( )	m	m	.	.	m	.
tigetflag( )	m	m	.	.	m	.
tigetnum( )	m	m	.	.	m	.
tigetstr( )	m	m	.	.	m	.
time( )	m	m	m	m	m	m
timeout( )	m	m	.	.	m	.
timer_create( )	f	.	r	.	.	.
timer_delete( )	f	.	r	.	.	.
timer_getoverrun( )	f	.	r	.	.	.
timer_gettime( )	f	.	r	.	.	.
timer_settime( )	f	.	r	.	.	.
times( )	m	m	m	.	m	m
timezone	m	m	.	.	m	.
tmpfile( )	m	m	m	m	m	.
tmpnam( )	m	m	m	m	m	.
toascii( )	m	m	.	.	m	m
tolower( )	m	m	m	m	m	m
touchline( )	m	m	.	.	m	.
touchwin( )	m	m	.	.	m	.
toupper( )	m	m	m	m	m	m
towctrans( )	m	.	.	1	.	.
towlower( )	m	m	.	1	.	.
towupper( )	m	m	.	1	.	.
tparm( )	m	m	.	.	m	.
tputs( )	m	m	.	.	m	.
truncate( )	m	m	.	.	.	m
tsearch( )	m	m	.	.	m	.
ttyname( )	m	m	m	.	m	m
ttyname_r( )	m	.	t	.	.	.
ttyslot( )	f	m	.	.	.	m

Interface	UNIX 98	UNIX 95	POSIX.1 and POSIX.2	ISO C Standard	SVID 3	4.3BSD
twalk( )	m	m	.	.	m	.
typeahead( )	m	m	.	.	m	.
tzname	m	m	m	.	m	.
tzset( )	m	m	m	.	m	.
ualarm( )	m	m	.	.	.	m
ulimit( )	m	m	.	.	m	.
umask( )	m	m	m	.	m	m
uname( )	m	m	m	.	m	.
unctrl( )	m	m	.	.	m	.
unget_wch( )	m	m	.	.	.	.
ungetc( )	m	m	m	m	m	m
ungetch( )	m	m	.	.	m	.
ungetwc( )	m	m	.	1	.	.
unlink( )	m	m	m	.	m	m
unlockpt( )	m	m	.	.	m	.
untouchwin( )	m	m	.	.	m	.
use_env( )	m	m	.	.	m	.
usleep( )	m	m	.	.	.	m
utime( )	m	m	m	.	m	m
utimes( )	m	m	.	.	.	m
valloc( )	f	m	.	.	.	m
vfork( )	m	m	.	.	.	m
vfprintf( )	m	m	.	.	m	.
vfwprintf( )	m	.	.	1	.	.
vid_attr( )	m	m	.	.	.	.
vid_puts( )	m	m	.	.	.	.
vidattr( )	m	m	.	.	m	.
vidputs( )	m	m	.	.	m	.
vline( )	m	m	.	.	.	.
vline_set( )	m	m	.	.	.	.
vprintf( )	m	m	.	m	m	.
vsnprintf( )	m	.	.	.	.	.
vsprintf( )	m	m	.	m	m	.
vswprintf( )	m	.	.	1	.	.
vw_printw( )	m	m	.	.	.	.
vw_scanw( )	m	m	.	.	.	.
vwprintf( )	m	.	.	1	.	.
vwprintw( )	m	m	.	.	m	.
vwscanw( )	m	m	.	.	m	.
wadd_wch( )	m	m	.	.	.	.
wadd_wchnstr( )	m	m	.	.	.	.
wadd_wchstr( )	m	m	.	.	.	.
waddch( )	m	m	.	.	m	.
waddchnstr( )	m	m	.	.	m	.
waddchstr( )	m	m	.	.	m	.
waddnstr( )	m	m	.	.	m	.

Interface	UNIX 98	UNIX 95	POSIX.1 and POSIX.2	ISO C Standard	SVID 3	4.3BSD
waddnwstr( )	m	m	.	.	.	.
waddstr( )	m	m	.	.	m	.
waddwstr( )	m	m	.	.	.	.
wait3( )	f	m	.	.	.	m
wait( )	m	m	m	.	m	m
waitid( )	m	m	.	.	m	.
waitpid( )	m	m	m	.	m	m
wattr_get( )	m	m	.	.	.	.
wattr_off( )	m	m	.	.	.	.
wattr_on( )	m	m	.	.	.	.
wattr_set( )	m	m	.	.	.	.
wattroff( )	m	m	.	.	m	.
wattron( )	m	m	.	.	m	.
wattrset( )	m	m	.	.	m	.
wbkgd( )	m	m	.	.	m	.
wbkgdset( )	m	m	.	.	m	.
wbkgrnd( )	m	m	.	.	.	.
wbkgrndset( )	m	m	.	.	.	.
wborder( )	m	m	.	.	m	.
wborder_set( )	m	m	.	.	.	.
wchgat( )	m	m	.	.	.	.
wclear( )	m	m	.	.	m	.
wclrtobot( )	m	m	.	.	m	.
wclrtoeol( )	m	m	.	.	m	.
wcolor_set( )	m	m	.	.	.	.
wcrtomb( )	m	.	.	1	.	.
wcscat( )	m	m	.	1	.	.
wcschr( )	m	m	.	1	.	.
wcscmp( )	m	m	.	1	.	.
wcscoll( )	m	f	.	1	.	.
wcscpy( )	m	m	.	1	.	.
wcscspn( )	m	m	.	1	.	.
wcsftime( )	m	f	.	1	.	.
wcslen( )	m	m	.	1	.	.
wcsncat( )	m	m	.	1	.	.
wcsncmp( )	m	m	.	1	.	.
wcsncpy( )	m	m	.	1	.	.
wcspbrk( )	m	m	.	1	.	.
wcsrchr( )	m	m	.	1	.	.
wcsrtombs( )	m	.	.	1	.	.
wcsspn( )	m	m	.	1	.	.
wcsstr( )	m	.	.	1	.	.
wcstod( )	m	m	.	1	.	.
wcstok( )	m	m	.	1	.	.
wcstol( )	m	m	.	1	.	.
wcstombs( )	m	m	.	m	m	.

Interface	UNIX 98	UNIX 95	POSIX.1 and POSIX.2	ISO C Standard	SVID 3	4.3BSD
wcstoul( )	m	m	.	1	.	.
wcswcs( )	m	m	.	.	.	.
wcswidth( )	m	m	.	.	.	.
wcsxfrm( )	m	f	.	1	.	.
wctob( )	m	.	.	1	.	.
wctomb( )	m	m	.	m	m	.
wctrans( )	m	.	.	1	.	.
wctype( )	m	m	.	1	.	.
wcursyncup( )	m	m	.	.	m	.
wcwidth( )	m	m	.	.	.	.
wdelch( )	m	m	.	.	m	.
wdeleteln( )	m	m	.	.	m	.
wecho_wchar( )	m	m	.	.	.	.
wechochar( )	m	m	.	.	m	.
werase( )	m	m	.	.	m	.
wget_wch( )	m	m	.	.	.	.
wget_wstr( )	m	m	.	.	.	.
wgetbkgrnd( )	m	m	.	.	.	.
wgetch( )	m	m	.	.	m	.
wgetn_wstr( )	m	m	.	.	.	.
wgetnstr( )	m	m	.	.	m	.
wgetstr( )	m	m	.	.	m	.
whline( )	m	m	.	.	m	.
whline_set( )	m	m	.	.	.	.
win_wch( )	m	m	.	.	.	.
win_wchnstr( )	m	m	.	.	.	.
win_wchstr( )	m	m	.	.	.	.
winch( )	m	m	.	.	m	.
winchnstr( )	m	m	.	.	m	.
winchstr( )	m	m	.	.	m	.
winnstr( )	m	m	.	.	m	.
winnwstr( )	m	m	.	.	.	.
wins_nwstr( )	m	m	.	.	.	.
wins_wch( )	m	m	.	.	.	.
wins_wstr( )	m	m	.	.	.	.
winsch( )	m	m	.	.	m	.
winsdelln( )	m	m	.	.	m	.
winsertln( )	m	m	.	.	m	.
winsnstr( )	m	m	.	.	m	.
winsstr( )	m	m	.	.	m	.
winstr( )	m	m	.	.	m	.
winwstr( )	m	m	.	.	.	.
wmemchr( )	m	.	.	1	.	.
wmemcmp( )	m	.	.	1	.	.
wmemcpy( )	m	.	.	1	.	.
wmemmove( )	m	.	.	1	.	.

Interface	UNIX 98	UNIX 95	POSIX.1 and POSIX.2	ISO C Standard	SVID 3	4.3BSD
wmemset( )	m	.	.	1	.	.
wmove( )	m	m	.	.	m	.
wnoutrefresh( )	m	m	.	.	m	.
wordexp( )	m	f	m	.	.	.
wordfree( )	m	f	m	.	.	.
wprintf( )	m	.	.	1	.	.
wprintw( )	m	m	.	.	m	.
wredrawln( )	m	m	.	.	m	.
wrefresh( )	m	m	.	.	m	.
write( )	m	m	m	.	m	m
writev( )	m	m	.	.	m	m
wscanf( )	m	.	.	1	.	.
wscanw( )	m	m	.	.	m	.
wscrl( )	m	m	.	.	m	.
wsetscrreg( )	m	m	.	.	m	.
wstandend( )	m	m	.	.	m	.
wstandout( )	m	m	.	.	m	.
wsyncdown( )	m	m	.	.	m	.
wsyncup( )	m	m	.	.	m	.
wtimeout( )	m	m	.	.	m	.
wtouchln( )	m	m	.	.	m	.
wunctrl( )	m	m	.	.	.	.
wvline( )	m	m	.	.	m	.
wvline_set( )	m	m	.	.	.	.
y0( )	m	m	.	.	m	m
y1( )	m	m	.	.	m	m
yn( )	m	m	.	.	m	m

19.2 Commands and Utilities Table

The following section lists all the commands and utilities described in the Single UNIX Specification, and indicates what other specifications support the interfaces.

The following conventions are used in columns 2 through 6:

m Indicates that the interface is defined as mandatory.

d Indicates that the interface is part of the DEVELOPMENT option.

f Indicates that the interface is part of the FORTRAN option.

l Indicates that the interface is part of the LEGACY option.

o Indicates that the interface is optional in POSIX.2.

. Indicates that the interface is not specified.

It should be noted that while another specification may support the interface, some of the interface semantics may have changed with evolution and standardization. A developer should not assume that because the interface appears in other specifications, it will behave exactly as described in the Single UNIX Specification.

Interface	UNIX 98	UNIX 95	POSIX.2	SVID 3	4.3BSD
admin	d	d	.	m	.
alias	m	m	m	.	m
ar	m	m	o	m	m
asa	m	m	o	.	.
at	m	m	m	m	m
awk	m	m	m	m	m
banner	m	m	.	m	.
basename	m	m	m	m	m
batch	m	m	m	m	.
bc	m	m	m	.	m
bg	m	m	m	.	m
c89	m	m	o	.	.
cal	m	m	.	m	m
calendar	l	m	.	m	m
cancel	l	m	.	m	.
cat	m	m	m	m	m
cc	l	m	.	m	m
cd	m	m	m	m	m
cflow	d	d	.	m	.
chgrp	m	m	m	m	m
chmod	m	m	m	m	m
chown	m	m	m	m	m
chroot	m	m	.	m	.
cksum	m	m	m	.	.
cmp	m	m	m	m	m
col	l	m	.	m	m
comm	m	m	m	m	m
command	m	m	m	.	.

Interface	UNIX 98	UNIX 95	POSIX.2	SVID 3	4.3BSD
compress	m	m	.	m	m
cp	m	m	m	m	m
cpio	l	m	.	m	.
crontab	m	m	m	m	.
csplit	m	m	m	m	.
ctags	d	d	m	m	m
cu	l	m	.	m	.
cut	m	m	m	m	.
cxref	d	d	.	m	.
date	m	m	m	m	m
dd	m	m	m	m	m
delta	d	d	.	m	.
df	m	m	m	m	m
diff	m	m	m	m	m
dircmp	l	m	.	m	.
dirname	m	m	m	m	.
dis	o	o	.	m	.
du	l	m	m	m	m
echo	m	m	m	m	m
ed	m	m	m	m	m
egrep	l	m	m	m	.
env	m	m	m	m	.
ex	m	m	m	m	m
expand	m	m	m	.	m
expr	m	m	m	m	m
false	m	m	m	m	m
fc	m	m	m	.	m
fg	m	m	m	.	m
fgrep	l	m	m	m	.
file	m	m	m	m	m
find	m	m	m	m	m
fold	m	m	m	.	m
fort77	f	f	o	.	.
fuser	m	.	.	.	.
gencat	m	m	.	.	.
get	d	d	.	m	.
getconf	m	m	.	.	.
getopts	m	m	.	.	.
grep	m	m	m	m	m
hash	m	m	.	.	m
head	m	m	m	m	m
iconv	m	m	.	.	.
id	m	m	m	m	.
ipcrm	m	.	.	.	.
ipcs	m	.	.	.	.
jobs	m	m	m	.	m
join	m	m	m	m	m

Interface	UNIX 98	UNIX 95	POSIX.2	SVID 3	4.3BSD
kill	m	m	m	m	m
lex	d	d	o	m	m
line	l	m	.	m	.
link	m	.	.	.	m
lint	ld	d	.	m	m
ln	m	m	m	m	m
locale	m	m	m	.	.
localedef	m	m	m	.	.
logger	m	m	m	.	m
logname	m	m	m	m	.
lp	m	m	m	m	.
lpstat	l	m	.	m	.
ls	m	m	m	m	m
m4	d	d	.	m	m
mail	l	m	.	m	m
mailx	m	m	m	m	.
make	d	d	m	m	m
man	m	m	m	.	m
mesg	m	m	m	m	m
mkdir	m	m	m	m	m
mkfifo	m	m	m	.	.
more	m	m	m	m	m
mv	m	m	m	m	m
newgrp	m	m	m	m	.
nice	m	m	m	m	m
nl	m	m	.	m	.
nm	d	d	m	m	m
nohup	m	m	m	m	.
od	m	m	m	m	m
pack	l	m	.	m	.
paste	m	m	m	m	.
patch	m	m	m	.	m
pathchk	m	m	m	.	.
pax	m	m	m	.	.
pcat	l	m	.	m	.
pg	l	m	.	m	.
pr	m	m	m	m	m
printf	m	m	m	m	.
prs	d	d	.	m	.
ps	m	m	m	m	m
pwd	m	m	m	m	m
read	m	m	m	.	m
red	m	m	.	m	.
renice	m	m	m	.	m
rm	m	m	m	m	m
rmdel	d	d	.	m	.
rmdir	m	m	m	m	m

Interface	UNIX 98	UNIX 95	POSIX.2	SVID 3	4.3BSD
sact	d	d	.	m	.
sccs	d	d	.		m
sdb	m	m	.	m	.
sed	m	m	m	m	m
sh	m	m	m	m	m
sleep	m	m	m	m	m
sort	m	m	m	m	m
spell	l	m	.	m	m
split	m	m	m	m	m
strings	m	m	m	.	m
strip	d	d	o	m	m
stty	m	m	m	m	m
sum	l	m	.	m	m
tabs	m	m	m	m	m
tail	m	m	m	m	m
talk	m	m	m	.	m
tar	l	m	m	m	m
tee	m	m	.	m	m
test	m	m	m	m	m
time	m	m	m	m	m
touch	m	m	m	m	m
tput	m	m	m	.	m
tr	m	m	m	m	m
true	m	m	m	m	m
tsort	m	m	.	m	m
tty	m	m	m	m	m
type	m	m	.	.	m
ulimit	m	m	.	.	m
umask	m	m	m	m	.
unalias	m	m	m	.	m
uname	m	m	m	m	.
uncompress	m	m	.	m	.
unexpand	m	m	m	.	.
unget	d	d	.	m	.
uniq	m	m	m	m	m
unlink	m	.	.	.	m
unpack	l	m	.	m	.
uucp	m	m	.	m	m
uudecode	m	m	m	m	m
uuencode	m	m	m	m	m
uulog	l	m	.	m	m
uuname	l	m	.	m	m
uupick	l	m	.	m	.
uustat	m	m	.	m	.
uuto	l	m	.	m	.
uux	m	m	.	m	m
val	d	d	.	m	.

Interface	UNIX 98	UNIX 95	POSIX.2	SVID 3	4.3BSD
vi	m	m	m	m	m
wait	m	m	m	m	m
wall	m	m	.	m	m
wc	m	m	m	m	m
what	d	d	.	m	m
who	m	m	m	m	m
write	m	m	m	m	m
xargs	m	m	m	m	.
yacc	d	d	o	m	m
zcat	m	m	.	m	.

Chapter 20

System Interfaces

This chapter contains a section for each system interface defined in XSH, Issue 5. Each section lists the synopsis and identifies syntax and semantic changes made to the interface in Issue 5 (if any), complete with examples where appropriate. Only changes that might affect an application programmer are identified.

a64l( ), l64a( )

Convert between a 32-bit integer and a radix-64 ASCII string.

```
#include <stdlib.h>

long a64l(const char *s);
char *l64a(long value);
```

Issue 5: A note indicating that these interfaces need not be reentrant is added to the Description. A portable multi-threaded application may only safely call these functions when access to the function is serialized. For example:

```
...
/*
 * An example of thread-safety by serializing access
 * to a non-reentrant function.
 */

pthread_mutex_t mtx = PTHREAD_MUTEX_INITIALIZER;

void my_l64a( long value, char *buffer)
{
int i=0;
char *ptr;

(void) pthread_mutex_lock (&mtx);
ptr = l64a( value);
(void) strcpy (buffer, ptr);
(void) pthread_mutex_unlock (&mtx);
}
...
```

abort()

Generate an abnormal process abort.

```
#include <stdlib.h>

void abort(void);
```

Issue 5: No functional changes in this issue.

abs( )

Return an integer absolute value.

```
#include <stdlib.h>
```

```
int abs(int i);
```

Issue 5: No functional changes in this issue.

access( )

Determine accessibility of a file.

```
#include <unistd.h>
```

```
int access(const char *path, int amode);
```

Issue 5: No functional changes in this issue.

acos( )

Arc cosine function.

```
#include <math.h>
```

```
double acos(double x);
```

Issue 5: No functional changes in this issue.

acosh( ), asinh( ), atanh( )

Inverse hyperbolic functions.

```
#include <math.h>
```

```
double acosh(double x);
double asinh(double x);
double atanh(double x);
```

Issue 5: No functional changes in this issue.

advance( )

Pattern match given a compiled regular expression. **(LEGACY)**

```
#include <regexp.h>
```

```
int advance(const char *string, const char *expbuf);
```

Issue 5: This function is marked LEGACY and may not be available on all implementations. New applications should use the *regcomp*( ), *regexec*( ), *regerror*( ), and *regfree*( ) functions, and the **<regex.h>** header, which provide full internationalized regular expression functionality compatible with POSIX.2 and XBD, **Chapter 7**, **Regular Expressions**.

aio_cancel()

Cancel an asynchronous I/O request. (**REALTIME**)

```
#include <aio.h>
```

```
int aio_cancel(int fildes, struct aiocb *aiocbp);
```

Issue 5: This is a new function included for alignment with the POSIX Realtime Extension. This is part of the Realtime Feature Group and may not be available on all implementations.

The *aio_cancel*( ) function attempts to cancel one or more asynchronous I/O requests currently outstanding against file descriptor *fildes*. The *aiocbp* argument points to the asynchronous I/O control block for a particular request to be canceled.

aio_error()

Retrieve errors status for an asynchronous I/O operation. (**REALTIME**)

```
#include <aio.h>
```

```
int aio_error(const struct aiocb *aiocbp);
```

Issue 5: This is a new function included for alignment with the POSIX Realtime Extension. This is part of the Realtime Feature Group and may not be available on all implementations.

The *aio_error*( ) function returns the error status associated with the **aiocb** structure referenced by the *aiocbp* argument. The error status for an asynchronous I/O operation is the *errno* value that would be set by the corresponding *read*( ), *write*( ), or *fsync*( ) operation.

aio_fsync()

Asynchronous file synchronization. (**REALTIME**)

```
#include <aio.h>
```

```
int aio_fsync(int op, struct aiocb *aiocbp);
```

Issue 5: This is a new function included for alignment with the POSIX Realtime Extension. This is part of the Realtime Feature Group and may not be available on all implementations.

The *aio_fsync*( ) function asynchronously forces all I/O operations associated with the file indicated by the file descriptor *aio_fildes* member of the **aiocb** structure referenced by the *aiocbp* argument and queued at the time of the call to *aio_fsync*( ) to the synchronized I/O completion state. The function call returns when the synchronization request has been initiated or queued to the file or device (even when the data cannot be synchronized immediately).

aio_read()

Asynchronous read from a file. (**REALTIME**)

```
#include <aio.h>

int aio_read(struct aiocb *aiocbp);
```

Issue 5: This is a new function included for alignment with the POSIX Realtime Extension. This is part of the Realtime Feature Group and may not be available on all implementations.

The *aio_read*() function allows the calling process to read *aiocbp->aio_nbytes* from the file associated with *aiocbp->aio_fildes* into the buffer pointed to by *aiocbp->aio_buf*. The function call returns when the read request has been initiated or queued to the file or device (even when the data cannot be delivered immediately).

Large File Support extensions are added, see Chapter 15 on page 147.

aio_return()

Retrieve return status of an asynchronous I/O operation. (**REALTIME**)

```
#include <aio.h>

ssize_t aio_return(struct aiocb *aiocbp);
```

Issue 5: This is a new function included for alignment with the POSIX Realtime Extension. This is part of the Realtime Feature Group and may not be available on all implementations.

The *aio_return*() function returns the return status associated with the **aiocb** structure referenced by the *aiocbp* argument. The return status for an asynchronous I/O operation is the value that would be returned by the corresponding *read*(), *write*(), or *fsync*() function call.

aio_suspend()

Wait for an asynchronous I/O request. (**REALTIME**)

```
#include <aio.h>

int aio_suspend(const struct aiocb * const list[], int nent,
    const struct timespec *timeout);
```

Issue 5: This is a new function included for alignment with the POSIX Realtime Extension. This is part of the Realtime Feature Group and may not be available on all implementations.

The *aio_suspend*() function suspends the calling thread until at least one of the asynchronous I/O operations referenced by the *list* argument has completed, until a signal interrupts the function, or, if *timeout* is not NULL, until the time interval specified by *timeout* has passed.

aio_write( )

Asynchronous write to a file. (**REALTIME**)

```
#include <aio.h>
```

```
int aio_write(struct aiocb *aiocbp);
```

Issue 5: This is a new function included for alignment with the POSIX Realtime Extension. This is part of the Realtime Feature Group and may not be available on all implementations.

The *aio_write*( ) function allows the calling process to write *aiocbp->aio_nbytes* to the file associated with *aiocbp->aio_fildes* from the buffer pointed to by *aiocbp->aio_buf*. The function call returns when the write request has been initiated or, at a minimum, queued to the file or device.

Large File Support extensions are added, see Chapter 15 on page 147.

alarm( )

Schedule an alarm signal.

```
#include <unistd.h>
```

```
unsigned int alarm(unsigned int seconds);
```

Issue 5: No functional changes in this issue.

asctime, asctime_r( )

Convert date and time to a string.

```
#include <time.h>
```

```
char *asctime(const struct tm *timeptr);
char *asctime_r(const struct tm *tm, char *buf);
```

Issue 5: No functional changes in this issue.

The *asctime_r*( ) function is a new function included for alignment with the POSIX Threads Extension. It is the thread-safe equivalent of the *asctime*( ) function.

A note indicating that the *asctime*( ) interface need not be reentrant is added to the Description. A portable multi-threaded application should call *asctime_r*( ) instead of *asctime*( ).

asin( )

Arc sine function.

```
#include <math.h>
```

```
double asin(double x);
```

Issue 5: No functional changes in this issue.

asinh()

Hyperbolic arc sine.

```
#include <math.h>
```

```
double asinh(double x);
```

Issue 5: No functional changes in this issue.

assert()

Insert program diagnostics.

```
#include <assert.h>
```

```
void assert(int expression);
```

Issue 5: No functional changes in this issue.

atan()

Arc tangent function.

```
#include <math.h>
```

```
double atan(double x);
```

Issue 5: No functional changes in this issue.

atan2()

Arc tangent function.

```
#include <math.h>
```

```
double atan2(double y, double x);
```

Issue 5: No functional changes in this issue.

atanh()

Hyperbolic arc tangent.

```
#include <math.h>
```

```
double atanh(double x);
```

Issue 5: No functional changes in this issue.

atexit()

Register a function to run at process termination.

```
#include <stdlib.h>
```

```
int atexit(void (*func)(void));
```

Issue 5: No functional changes in this issue.

atof()

Convert a string to a double-precision number.

```
#include <stdlib.h>
double atof(const char *str);
```

Issue 5: No functional changes in this issue.

atoi()

Convert a string to an integer.

```
#include <stdlib.h>
int atoi(const char *str);
```

Issue 5: No functional changes in this issue.

atol()

Convert a string to a long integer.

```
#include <stdlib.h>
long int atol(const char *str);
```

Issue 5: No functional changes in this issue.

basename()

Return the last component of a pathname.

```
#include <libgen.h>
char *basename(char *path);
```

Issue 5: A note indicating that this interface need not be reentrant is added to the Description. A portable multi-threaded application may only safely call *basename*( ) when access to the function is serialized.

bcmp()

Memory operations.

```
#include <strings.h>
int bcmp(const void *s1, const void *s2, size_t n);
```

Issue 5: No functional changes in this issue.

bcopy()

Memory operations.

```
#include <strings.h>
void bcopy(const void *s1, void *s2, size_t n);
```

Issue 5: No functional changes in this issue.

brk, sbrk( )

Change space allocation. **(LEGACY)**

```
#include <unistd.h>
```

```
int brk(void *addr);
void *sbrk(intptr_t incr);
```

Issue 5: This function is marked LEGACY and may not be available on all implementations. Applications are recommended to use *malloc*( ).

The type of the argument to *sbrk*( ) is changed from **int** to **intptr_t**. This change is for data size neutrality whereby systems supporting large address spaces may have problems representing appropriate values in a type **int**.

A note indicating that these interfaces need not be reentrant is added to the Description. A portable multi-threaded application may only safely call these functions when access to the function is serialized.

bsd_signal( )

Simplified signal facilities.

```
#include <signal.h>
```

```
void (*bsd_signal(int sig, void (*func)(int)))(int);
```

Issue 5: No functional changes in this issue.

bsearch( )

Binary search a sorted table.

```
#include <stdlib.h>
```

```
void *bsearch(const void *key, const void *base, size_t nel,
    size_t width, int (*compar)(const void *, const void *));
```

Issue 5: No functional changes in this issue.

btowc( )

Single-byte to wide-character conversion.

```
#include <stdio.h>
#include <wchar.h>
```

```
wint_t btowc(int c);
```

Issue 5: This is a new function included for alignment with the ISO/IEC 9899:1990/Amendment 1:1995 (E). The *btowc*( ) function determines whether *c* constitutes a valid (one-byte) character in the initial shift state.

bzero( )

Memory operations.

```
#include <strings.h>
void bzero(void *s, size_t n);
```

Issue 5: No functional changes in this issue.

calloc( )

A memory allocator.

```
#include <stdlib.h>
void *calloc(size_t nelem, size_t elsize);
```

Issue 5: No functional changes in this issue.

catclose( )

Close a message catalogue descriptor.

```
#include <nl_types.h>
int catclose(nl_catd catd);
```

Issue 5: No functional changes in this issue.

catgets( )

Read a program message.

```
#include <nl_types.h>
char *catgets(nl_catd catd, int set_id, int msg_id, const char *s);
```

Issue 5: A note indicating that this interface need not be reentrant is added to the Description. A portable multi-threaded application may only safely call *catgets*( ) when access to the function is serialized.

catopen( )

Open a message catalogue.

```
#include <nl_types.h>
nl_catd catopen(const char *name, int oflag);
```

Issue 5: No functional changes in this issue.

cbrt( )

Cube root function.

```
#include <math.h>
double cbrt(double x);
```

Issue 5: No functional changes in this issue.

ceil()

Ceiling value function.

```
#include <math.h>
```

```
double ceil(double x);
```

Issue 5: No functional changes in this issue.

cfgetispeed()

Get input baud rate.

```
#include <termios.h>
```

```
speed_t cfgetispeed(const struct termios *termios_p);
```

Issue 5: No functional changes in this issue.

cfgetospeed()

Get output baud rate.

```
#include <termios.h>
```

```
speed_t cfgetospeed(const struct termios *termios_p);
```

Issue 5: No functional changes in this issue.

cfsetispeed()

Set input baud rate.

```
#include <termios.h>
```

```
int cfsetispeed(struct termios *termios_p, speed_t speed);
```

Issue 5: No functional changes in this issue.

cfsetospeed()

Set output baud rate.

```
#include <termios.h>
```

```
int cfsetospeed(struct termios *termios_p, speed_t speed);
```

Issue 5: No functional changes in this issue.

chdir()

Change working directory.

```
#include <unistd.h>
```

```
int chdir(const char *path);
```

Issue 5: No functional changes in this issue.

chmod()

Change mode of a file.

```
#include <sys/types.h>
#include <sys/stat.h>
```

```
int chmod(const char *path, mode_t mode);
```

Issue 5: No functional changes in this issue.

chown()

Change owner and group of a file.

```
#include <sys/types.h>
#include <unistd.h>
```

```
int chown(const char *path, uid_t owner, gid_t group);
```

Issue 5: No functional changes in this issue.

chroot()

Change root directory. **(LEGACY)**

```
#include <unistd.h>
```

```
int chroot(const char *path);
```

Issue 5: This function is marked LEGACY and may not be available on all implementations. Portable applications should not use this function.

A note indicating that this interface need not be reentrant is added to the Description. A portable multi-threaded application may only safely call *chroot*() when access to the function is serialized.

clearerr()

Clear indicators on a stream.

```
#include <stdio.h>
```

```
void clearerr(FILE *stream);
```

Issue 5: No functional changes in this issue.

clock()

Report CPU time used.

```
#include <time.h>
```

```
clock_t clock(void);
```

Issue 5: No functional changes in this issue.

clock_settime( ), clock_gettime( ), clock_getres( )

Clock and timer functions. (**REALTIME**)

```
#include <time.h>
```

```
int clock_settime(clockid_t clock_id, const struct timespec *tp);
int clock_gettime(clockid_t clock_id, struct timespec *tp);
int clock_getres(clockid_t clock_id, struct timespec *res);
```

Issue 5: These are new functions included for alignment with the POSIX Realtime Extension. These are part of the Realtime Feature Group and may not be available on all implementations.

The *clock_settime*( ) function sets the specified clock, *clock_id*, to the value specified by *tp*.

The *clock_gettime*( ) function returns the current value *tp* for the specified clock, *clock_id*.

The *clock_getres*( ) function returns the resolution of the specified clock, *clock_id*.

close( )

Close a file descriptor.

```
#include <unistd.h>
```

```
int close(int fildes);
```

Issue 5: The Description is updated for alignment with the POSIX Realtime Extension. Specifically, the semantics of *close*( ) are described for asynchronous or synchronous input/output, and also for memory mapped or shared memory objects.

The semantics of a *close*( ) function call when *fildes* is the master side of a pseudo-terminal are better described in this issue to match existing practice.

closedir( )

Close a directory stream.

```
#include <sys/types.h>
#include <dirent.h>
```

```
int closedir(DIR *dirp);
```

Issue 5: No functional changes in this issue.

closelog( ), openlog( ), setlogmask( ), syslog( )

Control system log.

```
#include <syslog.h>
```

```
void closelog(void);
void openlog(const char *ident, int logopt, int facility);
int setlogmask(int maskpri);
void syslog(int priority, const char *message, ... /* arguments */);
```

Issue 5: No functional changes in this issue.

compile( )

Produce a compiled regular expression. (**LEGACY**)

```
#include <regexp.h>
```

```
char *compile(char *instring, char *expbuf,
    const char *endbuf, int eof);
```

Issue 5: This function is marked LEGACY and may not be available on all implementations. New applications should use the *regcomp*( ), *regexec*( ), *regerror*( ), and *regfree*( ) functions, and the **<regex.h>** header, which provide full internationalized regular expression functionality compatible with POSIX.2 and XBD, **Chapter 7**, **Regular Expressions**.

confstr( )

Get configurable variables.

```
#include <unistd.h>
```

```
size_t confstr(int name, char *buf, size_t len);
```

Issue 5: This function is changed to support new arguments which can be used to determine configuration strings for C compiler flags, linker/loader flags, and libraries for each different supported programming environment. This is related to the changes for data size neutrality.

The new arguments supported are:

_CS_XBS5_ILP32_OFF32_CFLAGS
_CS_XBS5_ILP32_OFF32_LDFLAGS
_CS_XBS5_ILP32_OFF32_LIBS
_CS_XBS5_ILP32_OFF32_LINTFLAGS
_CS_XBS5_ILP32_OFFBIG_CFLAGS
_CS_XBS5_ILP32_OFFBIG_LDFLAGS
_CS_XBS5_ILP32_OFFBIG_LIBS
_CS_XBS5_ILP32_OFFBIG_LINTFLAGS
_CS_XBS5_LP64_OFF64_CFLAGS
_CS_XBS5_LP64_OFF64_LDFLAGS
_CS_XBS5_LP64_OFF64_LIBS
_CS_XBS5_LP64_OFF64_LINTFLAGS
_CS_XBS5_LPBIG_OFFBIG_CFLAGS
_CS_XBS5_LPBIG_OFFBIG_LDFLAGS
_CS_XBS5_LPBIG_OFFBIG_LIBS
_CS_XBS5_LPBIG_OFFBIG_LINTFLAGS

cos( )

Cosine function.

```
#include <math.h>
```

```
double cos(double x);
```

Issue 5: No functional changes in this issue.

cosh( )

Hyperbolic cosine function.

```
#include <math.h>
```

```
double cosh(double x);
```

Issue 5: No functional changes in this issue.

creat( )

Create a new file or rewrite an existing one.

```
#include <sys/types.h>
#include <sys/stat.h>
#include <fcntl.h>
```

```
int creat(const char *path, mode_t mode);
```

Issue 5: No functional changes in this issue.

crypt( )

String encoding function. **(CRYPT)**

```
#include <unistd.h>
```

```
char *crypt (const char *key, const char *salt);
```

Issue 5: A note indicating that this interface need not be reentrant is added to the Description. A portable multi-threaded application may only safely call this function when access to the function is serialized.

ctermid( )

Generate a pathname for controlling terminal.

```
#include <stdio.h>
```

```
char *ctermid(char *s);
```

Issue 5: The Description is updated for alignment with the POSIX Threads Extension. Specifically, if an application calling *ctermid*( ) uses any of the _POSIX_THREAD_SAFE_FUNCTIONS or _POSIX_THREADS interfaces, the *ctermid*( ) function must be called with a non-NULL parameter, else this function is not thread-safe.

ctime, ctime_r( )

Convert a time value to a date and time string.

```
#include <time.h>
```

```
char *ctime(const time_t *clock);
char *ctime_r(const time_t *clock, char *buf);
```

Issue 5: The *ctime_r*( ) function is a new function included for alignment with the POSIX Threads Extension. It is the thread-safe equivalent of the *ctime*( ) function.

A note indicating that the *ctime*( ) interface need not be reentrant is added to the Description. A portable multi-threaded application should call *ctime_r*( ) instead of *ctime*( ).

cuserid( )

Character login name of the user. (**LEGACY**)

```
#include <stdio.h>
```

```
char *cuserid(char *s);
```

Issue 5: This function is marked LEGACY and may not be available on all implementations. This is due to differences between the functionality of *cuserid*( ) defined in IEEE Std 1003.1-1990 (POSIX.1), and that of historical implementations. In POSIX.1, *cuserid*( ) is removed completely.

Applications can obtain the XCU behavior by using:

```
getpwuid(getuid( ))
```

The historical behavior can be obtained by using:

```
getpwuid(geteuid( ))
```

The Description of this function is also updated for alignment with the POSIX Threads Extension. Specifically, if an application calling *cuserid*( ) uses any of the _POSIX_THREAD_SAFE_FUNCTIONS or _POSIX_THREADS interfaces, the *cuserid*( ) function must be called with a non-NULL parameter, otherwise this function is not thread-safe.

A note indicating that this interface need not be reentrant is added to the Description. A portable multi-threaded application may only safely call *cuserid*( ) with a NULL parameter, when access to the function is serialized.

daylight( )

Daylight savings time flag.

```
#include <time.h>
```

```
extern int daylight;
```

Issue 5: No functional changes in this issue.

dbm_clearerr( ), dbm_close( ), dbm_delete( ), dbm_error( ), dbm_fetch( ), dbm_firstkey( ), dbm_nextkey( ), dbm_open( ), dbm_store( )

Database functions.

```
#include <ndbm.h>
```

```
int dbm_clearerr(DBM *db);
void dbm_close(DBM *db);
int dbm_delete(DBM *db, datum key);
int dbm_error(DBM *db);
datum dbm_fetch(DBM *db, datum key);
datum dbm_firstkey(DBM *db);
datum dbm_nextkey(DBM *db);
DBM *dbm_open(const char *file, int open_flags, mode_t file_mode);
int dbm_store(DBM *db, datum key, datum content, int store_mode);
```

Issue 5: A note indicating that these interfaces need not be reentrant is added to the Description. A portable multi-threaded application may only safely call these functions when access to the function is serialized.

The minimum key/content pair is changed from 1024 to 1023 bytes.

The semantics of the *open_flags* argument when the O_APPEND flag is set are now explicitly described as unspecified.

A new paragraph is added:

> "The sum of the sizes of a key/content pair must not exceed the internal block size. Moreover, all key/content pairs that hash together must fit on a single block. The *dbm_store*( ) function returns an error in the event that a disk block fills with inseparable data."

difftime( )

Compute the difference between two calendar time values.

```
#include <time.h>
```

```
double difftime(time_t time1, time_t time0);
```

Issue 5: No functional changes in this issue.

dirname( )

Report the parent directory name of a file pathname.

```
#include <libgen.h>
```

```
char *dirname(char *path);
```

Issue 5: A note indicating that this interface need not be reentrant is added to the Description. A portable multi-threaded application may only safely call *dirname*( ) when access to the function is serialized.

div( )

Compute the quotient and remainder of an integer division.

```
#include <stdlib.h>
```

```
div_t div(int numer, int denom);
```

Issue 5: No functional changes in this issue.

dlclose( )

Close a dlopen( ) object.

```
#include <dlfcn.h>
```

```
int dlclose(void *handle);
```

Issue 5: This is a new function added to support dynamic linking.

dlclose( ) is used to inform the system that the object referenced by a *handle* returned from a previous *dlopen*( ) invocation is no longer needed by the application.

The use of *dlclose*( ) reflects a statement of intent on the part of the process, but does not create any requirement upon the implementation, such as removal of the code or symbols referenced by *handle*.

For example:

```
. . .
/* open a shared object then close it.... */

#include <dlfcn.h>
void *mylib;
int foo;

mylib = dlopen ("mylib.so.1", RTLD_LAZY);

foo = dlcose( mylib );

. . .
```

dlerror()

Get diagnostic information.

```
#include <dlfcn.h>

char *dlerror(void);
```

Issue 5: This is a new function added to support dynamic linking. This function is used to find out diagnostic information if any of the other dynamic linking functions (*dlopen*( ), *dlclose*( ), and *dlsym*( )) returned an error. A call to *dlerror*( ) returns a null-terminated character string (with no trailing newline) that describes the last error that occurred during dynamic linking processing. If no dynamic linking errors have occurred since the last invocation of *dlerror*( ), *dlerror*( ) returns NULL.

For example:

```
. . .
#include <dlfcn.h>

char *errstr

errstr = dlerror();
if (errstr != NULL )
    printf ("A dynamic linking error occurred: (%s)\n", errstr);
. . .
```

dlopen()

Gain access to an executable object file.

```
#include <dlfcn.h>

void *dlopen(const char *file, int mode);
```

Issue 5: This is a new function added to support dynamic linking.

dlopen( ) makes an executable object file specified by *file* available to the calling program. The class of files eligible for this operation and the manner of their construction are specified by the implementation, although typically such files are executable objects, such as shared libraries, relocatable files, or programs. For example:

```
. . .
/* open the shared object mylib.so.1 for Lazy binding */

#include <dlfcn.h>
void *mylib;

mylib = dlopen ("mylib.so.1", RTLD_LAZY);
```

dlsym( )

Obtain the address of a symbol from a dlopen( ) object.

```
#include <dlfcn.h>

void *dlsym(void *handle, const char *name);
```

Issue 5: This is a new function added to support dynamic linking.

dlsym( ) allows a process to obtain the address of a symbol defined within an object made accessible through a *dlopen*( ) call. *handle* is the value returned from a call to *dlopen*( ) (and which has not since been released via a call to *dlclose*( )). *name* is the symbol's name as a character string.

For example:

```
. . .
#include <dlfcn.h>
void *mylib;
int (*myptr) ();

mylib = dlopen ("mylib.so.1", RTLD_LAZY);

myptr = (int (*) ()) dlsym (mylib, "mysymname");
. . .
```

drand48(), erand48(), jrand48(), lcong48(), lrand48(), mrand48(), nrand48(), seed48(), srand48()

Generate uniformly distributed pseudo-random numbers.

```
#include <stdlib.h>

double drand48(void);
double erand48(unsigned short int xsubi[3]);
long int jrand48(unsigned short int xsubi[3]);
void lcong48(unsigned short int param[7]);
long int lrand48(void);
long int mrand48(void);
long int nrand48(unsigned short int xsubi[3]);
unsigned short int *seed48(unsigned short int seed16v[3]);
void srand48(long int seedval);
```

Issue 5: A note indicating that these interfaces need not be reentrant is added to the Description. A portable multi-threaded application may only safely call these functions when access to the function is serialized.

dup( ), dup2( )

Duplicate an open file descriptor.

```
#include <unistd.h>

int dup(int fildes);
int dup2(int fildes, int fildes2);
```

Issue 5: No functional changes in this issue.

ecvt( ), fcvt( ), gcvt( )

Convert a floating-point number to a string.

```
#include <stdlib.h>

char *ecvt(double value, int ndigit, int *decpt, int *sign);
char *fcvt(double value, int ndigit, int *decpt, int *sign);
char *gcvt(double value, int ndigit, char *buf);
```

Issue 5: A note indicating that these interfaces need not be reentrant is added to the Description. A portable multi-threaded application may only safely call these functions when access to the function is serialized.

encrypt( )

Encoding function. (**CRYPT**)

```
#include <unistd.h>

void encrypt(char block[64], int edflag);
```

Issue 5: A note indicating that this interface need not be reentrant is added to the Description. A portable multi-threaded application may only safely call *encrypt*( ) when access to the function is serialized.

endgrent( ), getgrent( ), setgrent( )

Group database entry functions.

```
#include <grp.h>

void endgrent(void);
struct group *getgrent(void);
void setgrent(void);
```

Issue 5: A note indicating that these interfaces need not be reentrant is added to the Description. A portable multi-threaded application may only safely call these functions when access to the function is serialized.

endpwent( ), getpwent( ), setpwent( )

User database functions.

```
#include <pwd.h>

void endpwent(void);
struct passwd *getpwent(void);
void setpwent(void);
```

Issue 5: A note indicating that these interfaces need not be reentrant is added to the Description. A portable multi-threaded application may only safely call these functions when access to the function is serialized.

endutxent(), getutxent(), getutxid(), getutxline(), pututxline(), setutxent()

User accounting database functions.

```
#include <utmpx.h>
```

```
void endutxent(void);
struct utmpx *getutxent(void);
struct utmpx *getutxid(const struct utmpx *id);
struct utmpx *getutxline(const struct utmpx *line);
struct utmpx *pututxline(const struct utmpx *utmpx);
void setutxent(void);
```

Issue 5: A note indicating that these interfaces need not be reentrant is added to the Description. A portable multi-threaded application may only safely call these functions when access to the function is serialized.

environ()

Array of character pointers to the environment strings.

```
extern char **environ;
```

Issue 5: No functional changes in this issue.

erand48()

Generate uniformly distributed pseudo-random numbers.

```
#include <stdlib.h>
```

```
double erand48(unsigned short int xsubi[3]);
```

Issue 5: No functional changes in this issue.

erf(), erfc()

Error and complementary error functions.

```
#include <math.h>
```

```
double erf(double x);
double erfc(double x);
```

Issue 5: No functional changes in this issue.

errno()

XSI error return value.

```
#include <errno.h>
```

Issue 5: The following sentence is deleted from the Description: "The value of *errno* is 0 at program startup, but is never set to 0 by any XSI function." The Description also no longer states that conforming implementations may support the declaration:

```
extern int errno;
```

Both these historical behaviors are obsolete and may not be supported by some implementations. Applications should include the **<errno.h>** header to receive the appropriate definition of *errno*.

environ( ), execl( ), execv( ), execle( ), execve( ), execlp( ), execvp( )

Execute a file.

```
#include <unistd.h>

extern char **environ;
int execl(const char *path, const char *arg0, ... /*, (char *)0 */);
int execv(const char *path, char *const argv[]);
int execle(const char *path,
    const char *arg0, ... /*, (char *)0, char *const envp[]*/);
int execve(const char *path, char *const argv[], char *const envp[]);
int execlp(const char *file, const char *arg0, ... /*, (char *)0 */);
int execvp(const char *file, char *const argv[]);
```

Issue 5: The Description is updated for alignment with the POSIX Realtime Extension and the POSIX Threads Extension. Specifically, the following changes are made:

- Conforming multi-threaded applications will not use the *environ* variable to access or modify any environment variable while any other thread is concurrently modifying any environment variable.
- A call to any *exec* function from a process with more than one thread results in all threads being terminated and the new executable image being loaded and executed.
- Semantics for named semaphores, memory locking, process scheduling, memory mappings, timers, message passing, and asynchronous input/output are described.
- Large File Support extensions are added, see Chapter 15 on page 147.

exit( ), _exit( )

Terminate a process.

```
#include <stdlib.h>

void exit(int status);

#include <unistd.h>

void _exit(int status);
```

Issue 5: The Description is updated for alignment with the POSIX Realtime Extension and the POSIX Threads Extension. Specifically, semantics are described for named semaphores, memory locking, process scheduling, memory mappings, message passing, and asynchronous input/output.

Threads terminated by a call to *_exit*( ) will not invoke their cancellation cleanup handlers or per-thread data destructors.

Interactions with the SA_NOCLDWAIT flag and SIGCHLD signal are further clarified.

The values of *status* from *exit*( ) are better described.

exp( )

Exponential function.

```
#include <math.h>
double exp(double x);
```

Issue 5: No functional changes in this issue.

expm1( )

Compute exponential functions.

```
#include <math.h>
double expm1 (double x);
```

Issue 5: No functional changes in this issue.

fabs( )

Absolute value function.

```
#include <math.h>
double fabs(double x);
```

Issue 5: No functional changes in this issue.

fattach( )

Attach a STREAMS-based file descriptor to a file in the filesystem name space.

```
#include <stropts.h>
int fattach(int fildes, const char *path);
```

Issue 5: The [EXDEV] error is added to the list of optional errors for the case when a link to a file on another filesystem was attempted. This reflects historical practice of many systems that implement *fattach*( ) in a similar manner to the traditional *mount*( ) function.

fchdir( )

Change working directory.

```
#include <unistd.h>
int fchdir(int fildes);
```

Issue 5: No functional changes in this issue.

fchmod( )

Change mode of a file.

```
#include <sys/stat.h>
int fchmod(int fildes, mode_t mode);
```

Issue 5: Aligned with *fchmod*( ) in the POSIX Realtime Extension. Specifically, the second paragraph of the Description is added, describing the semantics for operations on Shared Memory Objects, and a second instance of [EINVAL] is defined in the list of optional errors. The Realtime semantics may only be supported on implementations supporting the Realtime Feature Group.

fchown( )

Change owner and group of a file.

```
#include <unistd.h>
```

```
int fchown(int fildes, uid_t owner, gid_t group);
```

Issue 5: No functional changes in this issue.

fclose( )

Close a stream.

```
#include <stdio.h>
```

```
int fclose(FILE *stream);
```

Issue 5: Large File Support extensions are added, see Chapter 15 on page 147.

fcntl( )

File control.

```
#include <fcntl.h>
```

```
int fcntl(int fildes, int cmd, ...);
```

Issue 5: The Description is updated for alignment with the POSIX Realtime Extension and the POSIX Threads Extension, specifically the semantics for shared memory objects are described.

Large File Support extensions are added, see Chapter 15 on page 147.

fcvt( )

Convert a floating-point number to a string.

```
#include <stdlib.h>
```

```
char *fcvt(double value, int ndigit, int *decpt, int *sign);
```

Issue 5: No functional changes in this issue.

FD_CLR( )

Macros for synchronous I/O multiplexing.

```
#include <sys/time.h>
```

```
FD_CLR(int fd, fd_set *fdset);
FD_ISSET(int fd, fd_set *fdset);
FD_SET(int fd, fd_set *fdset);
FD_ZERO(fd_set *fdset);
```

Issue 5: No functional changes in this issue.

fdatasync()

Synchronize the data of a file. (**REALTIME**)

```
#include <unistd.h>
```

```
int fdatasync(int fildes);
```

Issue 5: This is a new function included for alignment with the POSIX Realtime Extension. This is part of the Realtime Feature Group and may not be available on all implementations.

The *fdatasync*( ) function forces all currently queued I/O operations associated with the file indicated by file descriptor *fildes* to the synchronized I/O completion state.

The functionality is as per *fsync*( ) (with the symbol _XOPEN_REALTIME defined), with the exception that all I/O operations are completed as defined for synchronized I/O data integrity completion.

fdetach()

Detach a name from a STREAMS-based file descriptor.

```
#include <stropts.h>
```

```
int fdetach(const char *path);
```

Issue 5: No functional changes in this issue.

fdopen()

Associate a stream with a file descriptor.

```
#include <stdio.h>
```

```
FILE *fdopen(int fildes, const char *mode);
```

Issue 5: The Description is updated for alignment with the POSIX Realtime Extension. Specifically, the results of the *fdopen*( ) function on a shared memory object is unspecified.

Large File Support extensions are added, see Chapter 15 on page 147.

feof()

Test end-of-file indicator on a stream.

```
#include <stdio.h>
```

```
int feof(FILE *stream);
```

Issue 5: No functional changes in this issue.

ferror()

Test error indicator on a stream.

```
#include <stdio.h>
```

```
int ferror(FILE *stream);
```

Issue 5: No functional changes in this issue.

fflush()

Flush a stream.

```
#include <stdio.h>
```

```
int fflush(FILE *stream);
```

Issue 5: Large File Support extensions are added, see Chapter 15 on page 147.

ffs()

Find first set bit.

```
#include <strings.h>
```

```
int ffs(int i);
```

Issue 5: No functional changes in this issue.

fgetc()

Get a byte from a stream.

```
#include <stdio.h>
```

```
int fgetc(FILE *stream);
```

Issue 5: Large File Support extensions are added, see Chapter 15 on page 147.

fgetpos()

Get current file position information.

```
#include <stdio.h>
```

```
int fgetpos(FILE *stream, fpos_t *pos);
```

Issue 5: Large File Support extensions are added, see Chapter 15 on page 147.

fgets()

Get a string from a stream.

```
#include <stdio.h>
```

```
char *fgets(char *s, int n, FILE *stream);
```

Issue 5: No functional changes in this issue.

fgetwc( )

Get a wide-character code from a stream.

```
#include <stdio.h>
#include <wchar.h>
```

```
wint_t fgetwc(FILE *stream);
```

Issue 5: The Optional Header (OH) marking is removed from **<stdio.h>**.

Large File Support extensions are added, see Chapter 15 on page 147.

fgetws( )

Get a wide-character string from a stream.

```
#include <stdio.h>
#include <wchar.h>
```

```
wchar_t *fgetws(wchar_t *ws, int n, FILE *stream);
```

Issue 5: The Optional Header (OH) marking is removed from **<stdio.h>**.

fileno( )

Map a stream pointer to a file descriptor.

```
#include <stdio.h>
```

```
int fileno(FILE *stream);
```

Issue 5: No functional changes in this issue.

flockfile( ), ftrylockfile( ), funlockfile( )

Stdio locking functions.

```
#include <stdio.h>
```

```
void flockfile(FILE *file);
int ftrylockfile(FILE *file);
void funlockfile(FILE *file);
```

Issue 5: These are new functions included for alignment with the POSIX Threads Extension.

The *flockfile*( ), *ftrylockfile*( ), and *funlockfile*( ) functions provide for explicit application-level locking of *stdio*(**FILE***) objects.

floor( )

Floor function.

```
#include <math.h>
```

```
double floor(double x);
```

Issue 5: No functional changes in this issue.

fmod()

Floating-point remainder value function.

```
#include <math.h>
```

```
double fmod(double x, double y);
```

Issue 5: No functional changes in this issue.

fmtmsg()

Display a message in the specified format on standard error and/or a system console.

```
#include <fmtmsg.h>
```

```
int fmtmsg(long classification, const char *label, int severity,
    const char *text, const char *action, const char *tag);
```

Issue 5: No functional changes in this issue.

fnmatch()

Match a filename or a pathname.

```
#include <fnmatch.h>
```

```
int fnmatch(const char *pattern, const char *string, int flags);
```

Issue 5: No functional changes in this issue.

fopen()

Open a stream.

```
#include <stdio.h>
```

```
FILE *fopen(const char *filename, const char *mode);
```

Issue 5: Large File Support extensions are added, see Chapter 15 on page 147.

fork()

Create a new process.

```
#include <sys/types.h>
#include <unistd.h>
```

```
pid_t fork(void);
```

Issue 5: The Description is changed for alignment with the POSIX Realtime Extension and the POSIX Threads Extension.

Semantics for named semaphores, memory locking, process scheduling, memory mappings, timers, message passing, and asynchronous input/output are described.

A process is created with a single thread. If a multi-threaded process calls *fork*( ), the new process contains a replica of the calling thread and its entire address space, possibly including the states of mutexes and other resources.

fpathconf( ), pathconf( )

Get configurable pathname variables.

```
#include <unistd.h>
```

```
long int fpathconf(int fildes, int name);
long int pathconf(const char *path, int name);
```

Issue 5: The Description is updated for alignment with the POSIX Realtime Extension. Specifically, the variables _POSIX_ASYNC_IO, _POSIX_PRIO_IO, and _POSIX_SYNC_IO, and the *name* values _PC_ASYNC_IO, _PC_PRIO_IO, and _PC_SYNC_IO are added.

Large File Support extensions are added, see Chapter 15 on page 147.

fprintf( ), printf( ), snprintf( ), sprintf( )

Print formatted output.

```
#include <stdio.h>
```

```
int fprintf(FILE *stream, const char *format, ...);
int printf(const char *format, ...);
int snprintf(char *s, size_t n, const char *format, ...);
int sprintf(char *s, const char *format, ...);
```

Issue 5: These functions are aligned with the ISO/IEC 9899:1990/Amendment 1:1995 (E). Specifically, the l (ell) qualifier can now be used with c and s conversion characters.

The *snprintf*( ) function is new. *snprintf*( ) is identical to *sprintf*( ) with the addition of the *n* argument, which states the size of the buffer referred to by *s*.

fputc( )

Put a byte on a stream.

```
#include <stdio.h>
```

```
int fputc(int c, FILE *stream);
```

Issue 5: Large File Support extensions are added, see Chapter 15 on page 147.

fputs( )

Put a string on a stream.

```
#include <stdio.h>
```

```
int fputs(const char *s, FILE *stream);
```

Issue 5: No functional changes in this issue.

fputwc()

Put a wide-character code on a stream.

```
#include <stdio.h>
#include <wchar.h>
```

```
wint_t fputwc(wchar_t wc, FILE *stream);
```

Issue 5: Aligned with the ISO/IEC 9899:1990/Amendment 1:1995 (E). Specifically, the type of argument *wc* is changed from **wint_t** to **wchar_t**.

The Optional Header (OH) marking is removed from **<stdio.h>**.

Large File Support extensions are added, see Chapter 15 on page 147.

fputws()

Put a wide-character string on a stream.

```
#include <stdio.h>
#include <wchar.h>
```

```
int fputws(const wchar_t *ws, FILE *stream);
```

Issue 5: The Optional Header (OH) marking is removed from **<stdio.h>**.

fread()

Binary input.

```
#include <stdio.h>
```

```
size_t fread(void *ptr, size_t size, size_t nitems, FILE *stream);
```

Issue 5: No functional changes in this issue.

free()

Free allocated memory.

```
#include <stdlib.h>
```

```
void free(void *ptr);
```

Issue 5: No functional changes in this issue.

freopen()

Open a stream.

```
#include <stdio.h>
```

```
FILE *freopen(const char *filename, const char *mode, FILE *stream);
```

Issue 5: The Description is updated to indicate that the orientation of the stream is cleared and the conversion state of the stream is set to an initial conversion state by a successful call to the *freopen*( ) function.

Large File Support extensions are added, see Chapter 15 on page 147.

frexp( )

Extract mantissa and exponent from a double precision number.

```
#include <math.h>

double frexp(double num, int *exp);
```

Issue 5: No functional changes in this issue.

fscanf( ), scanf( ), sscanf( )

Convert formatted input.

```
#include <stdio.h>

int fscanf(FILE *stream, const char *format, ... );
int scanf(const char *format, ... );
int sscanf(const char *s, const char *format, ... );
```

Issue 5: Aligned with the ISO/IEC 9899:1990/Amendment 1:1995 (E). Specifically, the l (ell) qualifier is now defined for c, s, and [conversion characters.

The Description is updated to indicate that if infinity and NaN can be generated by the *fprintf*( ) family of functions, then they will be recognized by the *fscanf*( ) family.

fseek( ), fseeko( )

Reposition a file-position indicator in a stream.

```
#include <stdio.h>

int fseek(FILE *stream, long int offset, int whence);
int fseeko(FILE *stream, off_t offset, int whence);
```

Issue 5: Large File Support extensions are added, see Chapter 15 on page 147. Specifically, the *fseeko*( ) function is new.

fsetpos( )

Set current file position.

```
#include <stdio.h>

int fsetpos(FILE *stream, const fpos_t *pos);
```

Issue 5: No functional changes in this issue.

fstat( )

Get file status.

```
#include <sys/types.h>
#include <sys/stat.h>

int fstat(int fildes, struct stat *buf);
```

Issue 5: The Description is updated for alignment with the POSIX Realtime Extension. Specifically, the semantics for a shared memory object are described.

Large File Support extensions are added, see Chapter 15 on page 147.

fstatvfs( ), statvfs( )

Get filesystem information.

```
#include <sys/statvfs.h>
```

```
int fstatvfs(int fildes, struct statvfs *buf);
int statvfs(const char *path, struct statvfs *buf);
```

Issue 5: Large File Support extensions are added, see Chapter 15 on page 147.

fsync( )

Synchronize changes to a file.

```
#include <unistd.h>
```

```
int fsync(int fildes);
```

Issue 5: Aligned with *fsync*( ) in the POSIX Realtime Extension. Specifically, the Description and Return Value sections are much expanded, and the Errors section is updated to indicate that *fsync*( ) can return the error conditions defined for *read*( ) and *write*( ).

ftell( ), ftello( )

Return a file offset in a stream.

```
#include <stdio.h>
```

```
long int ftell(FILE *stream);
off_t ftello(FILE *stream);
```

Issue 5: Large File Support extensions are added, see Chapter 15 on page 147.

ftime( )

Get date and time.

```
#include <sys/timeb.h>
```

```
int ftime(struct timeb *tp);
```

Issue 5: No functional changes in this issue.

ftok( )

Generate an IPC key.

```
#include <sys/ipc.h>
```

```
key_t ftok(const char *path, int id);
```

Issue 5: No functional changes in this issue.

ftruncate( ), truncate( )

Truncate a file to a specified length.

```
#include <unistd.h>
```

```
int ftruncate(int fildes, off_t length);
int truncate(const char *path, off_t length);
```

Issue 5: Aligned with *ftruncate*( ) in the POSIX Realtime Extension. Specifically, the Description is extensively reworded and [EROFS] is added to the list of mandatory errors that can be returned by *ftruncate*( ).

Large File Support extensions are added, see Chapter 15 on page 147.

ftrylockfile( )

Stdio locking functions.

```
#include <stdio.h>
```

```
int ftrylockfile(FILE *file);
```

Issue 5: This is a new function included for alignment with the POSIX Threads Extension.

ftw( )

Traverse (walk) a file tree.

```
#include <ftw.h>
```

```
int ftw(const char *path, int (*fn)(const char *,
    const struct stat *ptr, int flag), int ndirs);
```

Issue 5: No functional changes in this issue.

funlockfile( )

Stdio locking functions.

```
#include <stdio.h>
```

```
void funlockfile(FILE *file);
```

Issue 5: This is a new function included for alignment with the POSIX Threads Extension.

fwide( )

Set stream orientation.

```
#include <stdio.h>
#include <wchar.h>
```

```
int fwide(FILE *stream, int mode);
```

Issue 5: This is a new function included for alignment with the ISO/IEC 9899:1990/Amendment 1:1995 (E).

The *fwide*( ) function determines the orientation, byte-oriented or wide-oriented, of the stream pointed to by *stream*.

fwprintf( ), wprintf( ), swprintf( )

Print formatted wide-character output.

```
#include <stdio.h>
#include <wchar.h>

int fwprintf(FILE *stream, const wchar_t *format, ...);
int wprintf(const wchar_t *format, ...);
int swprintf(wchar_t *s, size_t n, const wchar_t *format, ...);
```

Issue 5: Included for alignment with the ISO/IEC 9899:1990/Amendment 1:1995 (E). These are wide-character versions of the *fprintf*( ), *printf*( ), and *sprintf*( ) functions.

fwrite( )

Binary output.

```
#include <stdio.h>

size_t fwrite(const void *ptr, size_t size, size_t nitems,
    FILE *stream);
```

Issue 5: No functional changes in this issue.

fwscanf( ), wscanf( ), swscanf( )

Convert formatted wide-character input.

```
#include <stdio.h>
#include <wchar.h>

int fwscanf(FILE *stream, const wchar_t *format, ... );
int wscanf(const wchar_t *format, ... );
int swscanf(const wchar_t *s, const wchar_t *format, ... );
```

Issue 5: These are new functions included for alignment with the the ISO/IEC 9899:1990/Amendment 1:1995 (E). These are wide-character versions of the *fscanf*( ), *scanf*( ), and *sscanf*( ) functions.

gamma( ), signgam( )

Log gamma function. **(LEGACY)**

```
#include <math.h>

double gamma(double x);
extern int signgam;
```

Issue 5: A note indicating that this interface need not be reentrant is added to the Description. A portable multi-threaded application may only safely call *gamma*( ) when access to the function is serialized.

This function is marked LEGACY and may not be available on all implementations.

gcvt()

Convert a floating-point number to a string.

```
#include <stdlib.h>

char *gcvt(double value, int ndigit, char *buf);
```

Issue 5: No functional changes in this issue.

getc()

Get a byte from a stream.

```
#include <stdio.h>

int getc(FILE *stream);
```

Issue 5: No functional changes in this issue.

getchar()

Get a byte from a stdin stream.

```
#include <stdio.h>

int getchar(void);
```

Issue 5: No functional changes in this issue.

getc_unlocked(), getchar_unlocked(), putc_unlocked(), putchar_unlocked()

Stdio with explicit client locking.

```
#include <stdio.h>

int getc_unlocked(FILE *stream);
int getchar_unlocked(void);
int putc_unlocked(int c, FILE *stream);
int putchar_unlocked(int c);
```

Issue 5: These are new functions included for alignment with the POSIX Threads Extension.

These are functionally identical to *getc*( ), *getchar*( ), *putc*( ), and *putchar*( ) with the exception that they are not required to be implemented in a thread-safe manner. They may only safely be used within a scope protected by *flockfile*( ) (or *ftrylockfile*( )) and *funlockfile*( ).

These functions may safely be used in a multi-threaded program if and only if they are called while the invoking thread owns the (**FILE***) object.

getcontext(), setcontext()

Get and set current user context.

```
#include <ucontext.h>

int getcontext(ucontext_t *ucp);
int setcontext(const ucontext_t *ucp);
```

Issue 5: The following sentence was removed from the Description:

"If the *ucp* argument was passed to a signal handler, program execution continues with the program instruction following the instruction interrupted by the signal."

getcwd()

Get the pathname of the current working directory.

```
#include <unistd.h>
```

```
char *getcwd(char *buf, size_t size);
```

Issue 5: No functional changes in this issue.

getdate()

Convert user format date and time.

```
#include <time.h>
```

```
struct tm *getdate(const char *string);
```

Issue 5: The last paragraph of the Description is added, encouraging applications to remove declarations of *getdate_err* and instead incorporate the declaration by including **<time.h>**.

The %C specifier is added, and the exact meaning of the %y specifier is clarified in the Description.

%C century number (00-99; leading zeros are permitted but not required)

%y year within century. When a century is not otherwise specified, values in the range 69-99 refer to years in the twentieth century (1969 to 1999 inclusive); values in the range 00-68 refer to years in the twenty-first century (2000 to 2068 inclusive).

Portable applications are recommended to use the %Y specifier (4-digit years) rather than %y (2-digit years), to avoid problems with the millennium rollover.

A note indicating that this interface need not be reentrant is added to the Description. A portable multi-threaded application may only safely call *getdate*() when access to the function is serialized.

The %R specifier is changed to follow historical practice.

getdtablesize()

Get the file descriptor table size. **(LEGACY)**

```
#include <unistd.h>
```

```
int getdtablesize(void);
```

Issue 5: This function is marked LEGACY and may not be available on all implementations. Applications should use the *getrlimit*() function instead.

A new paragraph is added to the Application Usage section giving reasons why the interface may be withdrawn in a future issue. Specifically, the change is made for data size neutrality. The *getdtablesize*() function returns the size of the file descriptor table. This is equivalent to *getrlimit*() with the RLIMIT_NOFILE option. Whereas the *getrlimit*() function returns a value of type **rlim_t**. This function, returning an **int**, may have problems representing appropriate values in the future.

A note indicating that this interface need not be reentrant is added to the Description. A portable multi-threaded application may only safely call *getdtablesize*( ) when access to the function is serialized.

getegid( )

Get the effective group ID.

```
#include <sys/types.h>
#include <unistd.h>
```

```
gid_t getegid(void);
```

Issue 5: No functional changes in this issue.

getenv( )

Get value of an environment variable.

```
#include <stdlib.h>
```

```
char *getenv(const char *name);
```

Issue 5: A note indicating that this interface need not be reentrant is added to the Description. A portable multi-threaded application may only safely call *getenv*( ) when access to the function is serialized.

geteuid( )

Get the effective user ID.

```
#include <sys/types.h>
#include <unistd.h>
```

```
uid_t geteuid(void);
```

Issue 5: No functional changes in this issue.

getgid( )

Get the real group ID.

```
#include <sys/types.h>
#include <unistd.h>
```

```
gid_t getgid(void);
```

Issue 5: No functional changes in this issue.

getgrent( )

Get the group database entry.

```
#include <grp.h>
```

```
struct group *getgrent(void);
```

Issue 5: No functional changes in this issue.

getgrgid(), getgrgid_r()

Get group database entry for a group ID.

```
#include <grp.h>

struct group *getgrgid(gid_t gid);
int getgrgid_r(gid_t gid, struct group *grp, char *buffer,
    size_t bufsize, struct group **result);
```

Issue 5: The *getgrgid_r*( ) function is included for alignment with the POSIX Threads Extension, and is the thread-safe equivalent of *getgrgid*( ).

A note indicating that the *getgrgid*( ) interface need not be reentrant is added to the Description. A portable multi-threaded application should call *getgrid_r*( ) instead of *getgrid*( ).

getgrnam(), getgrnam_r()

Search group database for a name.

```
#include <sys/types.h>
#include <grp.h>

struct group *getgrnam(const char *name);
int getgrnam_r(const char *name, struct group *grp, char *buffer,
    size_t bufsize, struct group **result);
```

Issue 5: The *getgrnam_r*( ) function is included for alignment with the POSIX Threads Extension, and is the thread-safe equivalent of *getgrnam*( ).

A note indicating that the *getgrnam*( ) interface need not be reentrant is added to the Description. A portable multi-threaded application should call *getgrnam_r*( ) instead of *getgrnam*( ).

getgroups()

Get supplementary group IDs.

```
#include <sys/types.h>
#include <unistd.h>

int getgroups(int gidsetsize, gid_t grouplist[ ]);
```

Issue 5: No functional changes in this issue.

gethostid()

Get an identifier for the current host.

```
#include <unistd.h>

long gethostid(void);
```

Issue 5: No functional changes in this issue.

getitimer( ), setitimer( )

Get or set value of interval timer.

```
#include <sys/time.h>
```

```
int getitimer(int which, struct itimerval *value);
int setitimer(int which, const struct itimerval *value,
    struct itimerval *ovalue);
```

Issue 5: No functional changes in this issue.

getlogin( ), getlogin_r( )

Get login name.

```
#include <unistd.h>
```

```
char *getlogin(void);
int getlogin_r(char *name, size_t namesize);
```

Issue 5: The *getlogin_r*( ) function is included for alignment with the POSIX Threads Extension, and is the thread-safe equivalent of *getlogin*( ).

A note indicating that the *getlogin*( ) interface need not be reentrant is added to the Description. A portable multi-threaded application should call *getlogin_r*( ) instead of *getlogin*( ).

getmsg( ), getpmsg( )

Receive next message from a STREAMS file.

```
#include <stropts.h>
```

```
int getmsg(int fildes, struct strbuf *ctlptr, struct strbuf *dataptr,
    int *flagsp);
int getpmsg(int fildes, struct strbuf *ctlptr, struct strbuf *dataptr,
    int *bandp, int *flagsp);
```

Issue 5: A paragraph regarding "high-priority control parts of messages" is added to the Return Value section.

getopt( ), optarg( ), optind( ), opterr( ), optopt( )

Command option parsing.

```
#include <unistd.h>
```

```
int getopt(int argc, char * const argv[ ], const char *optstring);
extern char *optarg;
extern int optind, opterr, optopt;
```

Issue 5: A note indicating that the *getopt*( ) interface need not be reentrant is added to the Description. A portable multi-threaded application may only safely call *getopt*( ) when access to the function is serialized.

getpagesize()

Get the current page size. (**LEGACY**)

```
#include <unistd.h>
```

```
int getpagesize(void);
```

Issue 5: This function is marked LEGACY and may not be available on all implementations. Portable applications should call *sysconf*(). The *getpagesize*() function is equivalent to *sysconf*(_SC_PAGE_SIZE) and *sysconf*(_SC_PAGESIZE).

A new paragraph is added to the Application Usage section indicating why the interface may be withdrawn in a future issue. This is a change made for data size neutrality. This function, returning an **int**, may have problems representing appropriate values in the future. Also, the behavior is not specified for this function on systems that support variable size pages. On variable page size systems, a page can be extremely large (theoretically, up to the size of memory). This allows very efficient address translations for large segments of memory that have common page attributes.

A note indicating that this interface need not be reentrant is added to the Description. A portable multi-threaded application may only safely call *getpagesize*() when access to the function is serialized.

getpass()

Read a string of characters without echo. (**LEGACY**)

```
#include <unistd.h>
```

```
char *getpass(const char *prompt);
```

Issue 5: This function is marked LEGACY and may not be available on all implementations.

A note indicating that this interface need not be reentrant is added to the Description. A portable multi-threaded application may only safely call *getpass*() when access to the function is serialized.

getpgid()

Get the process group ID for a process.

```
#include <unistd.h>
```

```
pid_t getpgid(pid_t pid);
```

Issue 5: No functional changes in this issue.

getpgrp()

Get the process group ID of the calling process.

```
#include <sys/types.h>
#include <unistd.h>
```

```
pid_t getpgrp(void);
```

Issue 5: No functional changes in this issue.

getpid()

Get the process ID.

```
#include <sys/types.h>
#include <unistd.h>
```

```
pid_t getpid(void);
```

Issue 5: No functional changes in this issue.

getpmsg()

Get the user database entry.

```
#include <pwd.h>
```

```
int getpmsg(int fildes, struct strbuf *ctlptr, struct strbuf *dataptr,
    int *bandp, int *flagsp);
```

Issue 5: No functional changes in this issue.

getppid()

Get the parent process ID.

```
#include <sys/types.h>
#include <unistd.h>
```

```
pid_t getppid(void);
```

Issue 5: No functional changes in this issue.

getpriority(), setpriority()

Get or set the nice value.

```
#include <sys/resource.h>
```

```
int getpriority(int which, id_t who);
int setpriority(int which, id_t who, int value);
```

Issue 5: The Description is reworded in terms of the *nice* value rather than *priority* to avoid confusion with functionality in the POSIX Realtime Extension.

getpwent()

Get user database entry.

```
#include <pwd.h>
```

```
struct passwd *getpwent(void);
```

Issue 5: No functional changes in this issue.

getpwnam( ), getpwnam_r( )

Search user database for a name.

```
#include <sys/types.h>
#include <pwd.h>

struct passwd *getpwnam(const char *name);
int getpwnam_r(const char *nam, struct passwd *pwd, char *buffer,
    size_t bufsize, struct passwd **result);
```

Issue 5: This describes the return value as possibly being a pointer to static data, and how an application should check for an error.

The *getpwnam_r*( ) function is included for alignment with the POSIX Threads Extension, and is the thread-safe equivalent of *getpwnam*( ).

A note indicating that the *getpwnam*( ) interface need not be reentrant is added to the Description. A portable multi-threaded application should call *getpwnam_r*( ) instead of *getpwnam*( ).

getpwuid( ), getpwuid_r( )

Search user database for a user ID.

```
#include <sys/types.h>
#include <pwd.h>

struct passwd *getpwuid(uid_t uid);
int getpwuid_r(uid_t uid, struct passwd *pwd, char *buffer,
    size_t bufsize, struct passwd **result);
```

Issue 5: The *getpwuid_r*( ) function is included for alignment with the POSIX Threads Extension, and is the thread-safe equivalent of *getpwuid*( ).

A note indicating that the *getpwuid*( ) interface need not be reentrant is added to the Description. A portable multi-threaded application should call *getpwuid_r*( ) instead of *getpwuid*( ).

getrlimit( ), setrlimit( )

Control maximum resource consumption.

```
#include <sys/resource.h>

int getrlimit(int resource, struct rlimit *rlp);
int setrlimit(int resource, const struct rlimit *rlp);
```

Issue 5: An Application Usage section is added.

Large File Support extensions are added, see Chapter 15 on page 147.

getrusage()

Get information about resource utilization.

```
#include <sys/resource.h>
```

```
int getrusage(int who, struct rusage *r_usage);
```

Issue 5: No functional changes in this issue.

gets()

Get a string from a stdin stream.

```
#include <stdio.h>
```

```
char *gets(char *s);
```

Issue 5: No functional changes in this issue.

getsid()

Get the process group ID of the session leader.

```
#include <unistd.h>
```

```
pid_t getsid(pid_t pid);
```

Issue 5: No functional changes in this issue.

getsubopt()

Parse suboption arguments from a string.

```
#include <stdlib.h>
```

```
int getsubopt(char **optionp, char * const *tokens, char **valuep);
```

Issue 5: No functional changes in this issue.

gettimeofday()

Get the date and time.

```
#include <sys/time.h>
```

```
int gettimeofday(struct timeval *tp, void *tzp);
```

Issue 5: No functional changes in this issue.

getuid()

Get a real user ID.

```
#include <sys/types.h>
#include <unistd.h>
```

```
uid_t getuid (void);
```

Issue 5: No functional changes in this issue.

getutxent( ), getutxid, getutxline( )

Get user accounting database entries.

```
#include <utmpx.h>
```

```
struct utmpx *getutxent(void);
struct utmpx *getutxid(const struct utmpx *id);
struct utmpx *getutxline(const struct utmpx *line);
```

Issue 5: No functional changes in this issue.

getw( )

Get a word from a stream. (**LEGACY**)

```
#include <stdio.h>
```

```
int getw(FILE *stream);
```

Issue 5: This function is marked LEGACY and may not be available on all implementations.

A note indicating that this interface need not be reentrant is added to the Description. A portable multi-threaded application may only safely call *getw*( ) when access to the function is serialized.

getwc( )

Get a wide character from a stream.

```
#include <stdio.h>
#include <wchar.h>
```

```
wint_t getwc(FILE *stream);
```

Issue 5: The Optional Header (OH) marking is removed from **<stdio.h>**.

getwchar( )

Get a wide character from a stdin stream.

```
#include <wchar.h>
```

```
wint_t getwchar(void);
```

Issue 5: No functional changes in this issue.

getwd( )

Get the current working directory pathname.

```
#include <unistd.h>
```

```
char *getwd(char *path_name);
```

Issue 5: No functional changes in this issue.

glob, globfree()

Generate pathnames matching a pattern.

```
#include <glob.h>

int glob(const char *pattern, int flags,
    int(*errfunc)(const char *epath, int errno), glob_t *pglob);
void globfree(glob_t *pglob);
```

Issue 5: No functional changes in this issue.

gmtime(), gmtime_r()

Convert a time value to a broken-down UTC time.

```
#include <time.h>

struct tm *gmtime(const time_t *timer);
struct tm *gmtime_r(const time_t *clock, struct tm *result);
```

Issue 5: The *gmtime_r*() function is included for alignment with the POSIX Threads Extension, and is the thread-safe equivalent of *gmtime*().

A note indicating that the *gmtime*() interface need not be reentrant is added to the Description. A portable multi-threaded application should call *gmtime_r*() instead of *gmtime*().

grantpt()

Grant access to the slave pseudo-terminal device.

```
#include <stdlib.h>

int grantpt(int fildes);
```

Issue 5: The last paragraph of the Description is moved from the Application Usage section. This notes that the behavior of the *grantpt*() function is unspecified if the application has installed a signal handler to catch SIGCHLD signals.

hcreate(), hdestroy(), hsearch()

Manage hash search table.

```
#include <search.h>

int hcreate(size_t nel);
void hdestroy(void);
ENTRY *hsearch (ENTRY item, ACTION action);
```

Issue 5: No functional changes in this issue.

hypot()

Euclidean distance function.

```
#include <math.h>

double hypot(double x, double y);
```

Issue 5: No functional changes in this issue.

iconv()

Codeset conversion function.

```
#include <iconv.h>

size_t iconv(iconv_t cd, const char **inbuf, size_t *inbytesleft,
    char **outbuf, size_t *outbytesleft);
```

Issue 5: No functional changes in this issue.

iconv_close()

Codeset conversion deallocation function.

```
#include <iconv.h>

int iconv_close(iconv_t cd);
```

Issue 5: No functional changes in this issue.

iconv_open()

Codeset conversion allocation function.

```
#include <iconv.h>

iconv_t iconv_open(const char *tocode, const char *fromcode);
```

Issue 5: No functional changes in this issue.

ilogb()

Return an unbiased exponent.

```
#include <math.h>

int ilogb (double x)
```

Issue 5: No functional changes in this issue.

index()

Character string operations.

```
#include <strings.h>

char *index(const char *s, int c);
```

Issue 5: No functional changes in this issue.

initstate(), random(), setstate(), srandom()

Pseudo-random number functions.

```
#include <stdlib.h>

char *initstate(unsigned int seed, char *state, size_t size);
long random(void);
char *setstate(const char *state);
void srandom(unsigned int seed);
```

Issue 5: For *initstate*() in the Description section, the phrase "values smaller than 8" is replaced with "values greater than or equal to 8, or less than 32"; "size<8" is replaced with "size>=8 and <32"; and a new first paragraph is added to the Return Value section. A note is added to the Application Usage section indicating that these changes restore the historical behavior of the function.

insque(), remque()

Insert or remove an element in a queue.

```
#include <search.h>
```

```
void insque(void *element, void *pred);
void remque(void *element);
```

Issue 5: No functional changes in this issue.

ioctl()

Control a STREAMS device.

```
#include <stropts.h>
```

```
int ioctl(int fildes, int request, ... /* arg */);
```

Issue 5: No functional changes in this issue.

isalnum()

Test for an alphanumeric character.

```
#include <ctype.h>
```

```
int isalnum(int c);
```

Issue 5: No functional changes in this issue.

isalpha()

Test for an alphabetic character.

```
#include <ctype.h>
```

```
int isalpha(int c);
```

Issue 5: No functional changes in this issue.

isascii()

Test for a 7-bit US-ASCII character.

```
#include <ctype.h>
```

```
int isascii(int c);
```

Issue 5: No functional changes in this issue.

isastream( )

Test a file descriptor.

```
#include <stropts.h>
int isastream(int fildes);
```

Issue 5: No functional changes in this issue.

isatty( )

Test for a terminal device.

```
#include <unistd.h>
int isatty(int fildes);
```

Issue 5: No functional changes in this issue.

iscntrl( )

Test for a control character.

```
#include <ctype.h>
int iscntrl(int c);
```

Issue 5: No functional changes in this issue.

isdigit( )

Test for a decimal digit.

```
#include <ctype.h>
int isdigit(int c);
```

Issue 5: No functional changes in this issue.

isgraph( )

Test for a visible character.

```
#include <ctype.h>
int isgraph(int c);
```

Issue 5: No functional changes in this issue.

islower( )

Test for a lower-case letter.

```
#include <ctype.h>
int islower(int c);
```

Issue 5: No functional changes in this issue.

isnan( )

Test for a NaN.

```
#include <math.h>
int isnan(double x);
```

Issue 5: No functional changes in this issue.

isprint( )

Test for a printing character.

```
#include <ctype.h>
int isprint(int c);
```

Issue 5: No functional changes in this issue.

ispunct( )

Test for a punctuation character.

```
#include <ctype.h>
int ispunct(int c);
```

Issue 5: No functional changes in this issue.

isspace( )

Test for a white-space character.

```
#include <ctype.h>
int isspace(int c);
```

Issue 5: No functional changes in this issue.

isupper( )

Test for an upper-case letter.

```
#include <ctype.h>
int isupper(int c);
```

Issue 5: No functional changes in this issue.

iswalnum( )

Test for an alphanumeric wide-character code.

```
#include <wctype.h>
int iswalnum(wint_t wc);
```

Issue 5: The following change has been made in this issue for alignment with the ISO/IEC 9899:1990/Amendment 1:1995 (E).

- The Synopsis has been changed to indicate that this function and associated data types are now made visible by inclusion of the header **<wctype.h>** rather than **<wchar.h>**.

iswalpha( )

Test for an alphabetic wide-character code.

```
#include <wctype.h>
int iswalpha(wint_t wc);
```

Issue 5: The following change has been made in this issue for alignment with the ISO/IEC 9899:1990/Amendment 1:1995 (E).

- The Synopsis has been changed to indicate that this function and associated data types are now made visible by inclusion of the header **<wctype.h>** rather than **<wchar.h>**.

iswcntrl( )

Test for a control wide-character code.

```
#include <wctype.h>
int iswcntrl(wint_t wc);
```

Issue 5: The following change has been made in this issue for alignment with the ISO/IEC 9899:1990/Amendment 1:1995 (E).

- The Synopsis has been changed to indicate that this function and associated data types are now made visible by inclusion of the header **<wctype.h>** rather than **<wchar.h>**.

iswctype( )

Test character for a specified class.

```
#include <wctype.h>
int iswctype(wint_t wc, wctype_t charclass);
```

Issue 5: The following change has been made in this issue for alignment with the ISO/IEC 9899:1990/Amendment 1:1995 (E).

- The Synopsis has been changed to indicate that this function and associated data types are now made visible by inclusion of the header **<wctype.h>** rather than **<wchar.h>**.

iswdigit( )

Test for a decimal digit wide-character code.

```
#include <wctype.h>
int iswdigit(wint_t wc);
```

Issue 5: The following change has been made in this issue for alignment with the ISO/IEC 9899:1990/Amendment 1:1995 (E).

- The Synopsis has been changed to indicate that this function and associated data types are now made visible by inclusion of the header **<wctype.h>** rather than **<wchar.h>**.

iswgraph( )

Test for a visible wide-character code.

```
#include <wctype.h>
int iswgraph(wint_t wc);
```

Issue 5: The following change has been made in this issue for alignment with the ISO/IEC 9899:1990/Amendment 1:1995 (E).

- The Synopsis has been changed to indicate that this function and associated data types are now made visible by inclusion of the header **<wctype.h>** rather than **<wchar.h>**.

iswlower( )

Test for a lower-case letter wide-character code.

```
#include <wctype.h>
int iswlower(wint_t wc);
```

Issue 5: The following change has been made in this issue for alignment with the ISO/IEC 9899:1990/Amendment 1:1995 (E).

- The Synopsis has been changed to indicate that this function and associated data types are now made visible by inclusion of the header **<wctype.h>** rather than **<wchar.h>**.

iswprint( )

Test for a printing wide-character code.

```
#include <wctype.h>
int iswprint(wint_t wc);
```

Issue 5: The following change has been made in this issue for alignment with the ISO/IEC 9899:1990/Amendment 1:1995 (E).

- The Synopsis has been changed to indicate that this function and associated data types are now made visible by inclusion of the header **<wctype.h>** rather than **<wchar.h>**.

iswpunct( )

Test for a punctuation wide-character code.

```
#include <wctype.h>
int iswpunct(wint_t wc);
```

Issue 5: The following change has been made in this issue for alignment with the ISO/IEC 9899:1990/Amendment 1:1995 (E).

- The Synopsis has been changed to indicate that this function and associated data types are now made visible by inclusion of the header **<wctype.h>** rather than **<wchar.h>**.

iswspace()

Test for a white-space wide-character code.

```
#include <wctype.h>
```

```
int iswspace(wint_t wc);
```

Issue 5: The following change has been made in this issue for alignment with the ISO/IEC 9899:1990/Amendment 1:1995 (E).

- The Synopsis has been changed to indicate that this function and associated data types are now made visible by inclusion of the header **<wctype.h>** rather than **<wchar.h>**.

iswupper()

Test for an upper-case letter wide-character code.

```
#include <wctype.h>
```

```
int iswupper(wint_t wc);
```

Issue 5: The following change has been made in this issue for alignment with the ISO/IEC 9899:1990/Amendment 1:1995 (E).

- The Synopsis has been changed to indicate that this function and associated data types are now made visible by inclusion of the header **<wctype.h>** rather than **<wchar.h>**.

iswxdigit()

Test for a hexadecimal digit wide-character code.

```
#include <wctype.h>
```

```
int iswxdigit(wint_t wc);
```

Issue 5: The following change has been made in this issue for alignment with the ISO/IEC 9899:1990/Amendment 1:1995 (E).

- The Synopsis has been changed to indicate that this function and associated data types are now made visible by inclusion of the header **<wctype.h>** rather than **<wchar.h>**.

isxdigit()

Test for a hexadecimal digit.

```
#include <ctype.h>
```

```
int isxdigit(int c);
```

Issue 5: No functional changes in this issue.

j0( ), j1( ), jn( )

Bessel functions of the first kind.

```
#include <math.h>

double j0(double x);
double j1(double x);
double jn(int n, double x);
```

Issue 5: No functional changes in this issue.

jrand48( )

Generate a uniformly distributed pseudo-random long signed integer.

```
#include <stdlib.h>

long int jrand48(unsigned short int xsubi[3]);
```

Issue 5: No functional changes in this issue.

kill( )

Send a signal to a process or a group of processes.

```
#include <sys/types.h>
#include <signal.h>

int kill(pid_t pid, int sig);
```

Issue 5: The Description is updated for alignment with the POSIX Threads Extension. Specifically, the following paragraph is added:

"If the value of *pid* causes *sig* to be generated for the sending process, and if *sig* is not blocked for the calling thread and if no other thread has *sig* unblocked or is waiting in a *sigwait*( ) function for *sig*, either *sig* or at least one pending unblocked signal will be delivered to the sending thread before *kill*( ) returns."

killpg( )

Send a signal to a process group.

```
#include <signal.h>

int killpg(pid_t pgrp, int sig);
```

Issue 5: No functional changes in this issue.

l64a( )

Convert a 32-bit integer to a radix-64 ASCII string.

```
#include <stdlib.h>

char *l64a(long value);
```

Issue 5: No functional changes in this issue.

labs()

Return a long integer absolute value.

```
#include <stdlib.h>
long int labs(long int i);
```

Issue 5: No functional changes in this issue.

lchown()

Change the owner and group of a symbolic link.

```
#include <unistd.h>
int lchown(const char *path, uid_t owner, gid_t group);
```

Issue 5: No functional changes in this issue.

lcong48()

Seed a uniformly distributed pseudo-random signed long integer generator.

```
#include <stdlib.h>
void lcong48(unsigned short int param[7]);
```

Issue 5: No functional changes in this issue.

ldexp()

Load exponent of a floating point number.

```
#include <math.h>
double ldexp(double x, int exp);
```

Issue 5: No functional changes in this issue.

ldiv()

Compute quotient and remainder of a long division.

```
#include <stdlib.h>
ldiv_t ldiv(long int numer, long int denom);
```

Issue 5: No functional changes in this issue.

lfind()

Find entry in a linear search table.

```
#include <search.h>
void *lfind(const void *key, const void *base, size_t *nelp,
    size_t width, int (*compar)(const void *, const void *));
```

Issue 5: No functional changes in this issue.

lgamma( )

Log gamma function.

```
#include <math.h>
```

```
double lgamma(double x);
extern int signgam;
```

Issue 5: A note indicating that this interface need not be reentrant is added to the Description. A portable multi-threaded application may only safely call *lgamma*( ) when access to the function is serialized.

link( )

Link to a file.

```
#include <unistd.h>
```

```
int link(const char *path1, const char *path2);
```

Issue 5: No functional changes in this issue.

lio_listio( )

List directed I/O. (**REALTIME**)

```
#include <aio.h>
```

```
int lio_listio(int mode, struct aiocb * const list[], int nent,
    struct sigevent *sig);
```

Issue 5: This is a new function included for alignment with the POSIX Realtime Extension. This is part of the Realtime Feature Group and may not be available on all implementations.

The *lio_listio*( ) function allows the calling process to initiate a list of I/O requests with a single function call.

The *mode* argument takes one of the values LIO_WAIT or LIO_NOWAIT declared in **<aio.h>**, and determines whether the function returns when the I/O operations have been completed, or as soon as the operations have been queued.

Large File Support extensions are added, see Chapter 15 on page 147.

loc1( ), loc2( )

Pointers to characters matched by regular expressions. (**LEGACY**)

```
#include <regexp.h>
```

```
extern char *loc1;
extern char *loc2;
```

Issue 5: This symbols are marked LEGACY and may not be available on all implementations.

localeconv( )

Determine the program locale.

```
#include <locale.h>

struct lconv *localeconv(void);
```

Issue 5: No functional changes in this issue.

localtime( ), localtime_r( )

Convert a time value to a broken-down local time.

```
#include <time.h>

struct tm *localtime(const time_t *timer);
struct tm *localtime_r(const time_t *clock, struct tm *result);
```

Issue 5: The *localtime_r*( ) function is included for alignment with the POSIX Threads Extension, and is the thread-safe equivalent of *localtime*( ).

A note indicating that the *localtime*( ) interface need not be reentrant is added to the Description. A portable multi-threaded application should call *localtime_r*( ) instead of *localtime*( ).

lockf( )

Record locking on files.

```
#include <unistd.h>

int lockf(int fildes, int function, off_t size);
```

Issue 5: Large File Support extensions are added, see Chapter 15 on page 147. Specifically, the description of [EINVAL] is clarified and moved from optional to mandatory status.

A note is added to the Description indicating the effects of attempting to lock a section of a file that is associated with a buffered stream.

locs( )

Stop regular expression matching in a string. (**LEGACY**)

```
#include <regexp.h>

extern char *locs;
```

Issue 5: This symbol is marked LEGACY and may not be available on all implementations.

log( )

Natural logarithm function.

```
#include <math.h>

double log(double x);
```

Issue 5: No functional changes in this issue.

log10()

Base 10 logarithm function.

```
#include <math.h>

double log10(double x);
```

Issue 5: No functional changes in this issue.

log1p()

Compute a natural logarithm.

```
#include <math.h>

double log1p (double x);
```

Issue 5: No functional changes in this issue.

logb()

Radix-independent exponent.

```
#include <math.h>

double logb(double x);
```

Issue 5: No functional changes in this issue.

_longjmp(), _setjmp()

Non-local goto.

```
#include <setjmp.h>

void _longjmp(jmp_buf env, int val);
int _setjmp(jmp_buf env);
```

Issue 5: No functional changes in this issue.

longjmp()

Non-local goto.

```
#include <setjmp.h>

void longjmp(jmp_buf env, int val);
```

Issue 5: The Description is updated for alignment with the POSIX Threads Extension. Specifically, the effect of a call to *longjmp*() where initialization of the **jmp_buf** structure was not performed in the calling thread is undefined.

lrand48()

Generate uniformly distributed pseudo-random non-negative long integers.

```
#include <stdlib.h>

long int lrand48(void);
```

Issue 5: No functional changes in this issue.

lsearch( ), lfind( )

Linear search and update.

```
#include <search.h>

void *lsearch(const void *key, void *base, size_t *nelp, size_t width,
    int (*compar)(const void *, const void *));
void *lfind(const void *key, const void *base, size_t *nelp,
    size_t width, int (*compar)(const void *, const void *));
```

Issue 5: No functional changes in this issue.

lseek( )

Move the read/write file offset.

```
#include <unistd.h>

off_t lseek(int fildes, off_t offset, int whence);
```

Issue 5: The Description is updated for alignment with the POSIX Realtime Extension. Specifically, if *fildes* refers to a shared memory object, the behavior is unspecified.

Large File Support extensions are added, see Chapter 15 on page 147.

lstat( )

Get symbolic link status.

```
#include <sys/stat.h>

int lstat(const char *path, struct stat *buf);
```

Issue 5: Large File Support extensions are added, see Chapter 15 on page 147.

makecontext( ), swapcontext( )

Manipulate user contexts.

```
#include <ucontext.h>

void makecontext(ucontext_t *ucp, (void *func)(), int argc, ...);
int swapcontext(ucontext_t *oucp, const ucontext_t *ucp);
```

Issue 5: In the Errors section, the description of [ENOMEM] is changed to apply to *swapcontext*( ) only.

malloc( )

A memory allocator.

```
#include <stdlib.h>

void *malloc(size_t size);
```

Issue 5: No functional changes in this issue.

mblen()

Get number of bytes in a character.

```
#include <stdlib.h>
```

```
int mblen(const char *s, size_t n);
```

Issue 5: No functional changes in this issue.

mbrlen()

Get number of bytes in a character (restartable).

```
#include <wchar.h>
```

```
size_t mbrlen(const char *s, size_t n, mbstate_t *ps);
```

Issue 5: This is a new function included for alignment with the ISO/IEC 9899:1990/Amendment 1:1995 (E).

The *mbrlen*() function determines the number of bytes constituting the character pointed to by *s*. It is equivalent to:

```
mbstate_t internal;
mbrtowc(NULL, s, n, ps != NULL ? ps : &internal);
```

mbrtowc()

Convert a character to a wide-character code (restartable).

```
#include <wchar.h>
```

```
size_t mbrtowc(wchar_t *pwc, const char *s, size_t n, mbstate_t *ps);
```

Issue 5: This is a new function included for alignment with the ISO/IEC 9899:1990/Amendment 1:1995 (E).

The *mbrtowc*() function is equivalent to the call:

```
mbrtowc(NULL, ``'', 1, ps)
```

mbsinit()

Determine conversion object status.

```
#include <wchar.h>
```

```
int mbsinit(const mbstate_t *ps);
```

Issue 5: This is a new function included for alignment with the ISO/IEC 9899:1990/Amendment 1:1995 (E).

The *mbsinit*() function determines whether the object pointed to by *ps* describes an initial conversion state.

mbsrtowcs()

Convert a character string to a wide-character string (restartable).

```
#include <wchar.h>
```

```
size_t mbsrtowcs(wchar_t *dst, const char **src, size_t len,
    mbstate_t *ps);
```

Issue 5: This is a new function included for alignment with the ISO/IEC 9899:1990/Amendment 1:1995 (E).

The *mbsrtowcs*( ) function converts a sequence of characters, beginning in the conversion state described by the object pointed to by *ps*, from the array indirectly pointed to by *src* into a sequence of corresponding wide-characters.

mbstowcs()

Convert a character string to a wide-character string.

```
#include <stdlib.h>
```

```
size_t mbstowcs(wchar_t *pwcs, const char *s, size_t n);
```

Issue 5: No functional changes in this issue.

mbtowc()

Convert a character to a wide-character code.

```
#include <stdlib.h>
```

```
int mbtowc(wchar_t *pwc, const char *s, size_t n);
```

Issue 5: No functional changes in this issue.

memccpy()

Copy bytes in memory.

```
#include <string.h>
```

```
void *memccpy(void *s1, const void *s2, int c, size_t n);
```

Issue 5: No functional changes in this issue.

memchr()

Find byte in memory.

```
#include <string.h>
```

```
void *memchr(const void *s, int c, size_t n);
```

Issue 5: No functional changes in this issue.

memcmp( )

Compare bytes in memory.

```
#include <string.h>
```

```
int memcmp(const void *s1, const void *s2, size_t n);
```

Issue 5: No functional changes in this issue.

memcpy( )

Copy bytes in memory.

```
#include <string.h>
```

```
void *memcpy(void *s1, const void *s2, size_t n);
```

Issue 5: No functional changes in this issue.

memmove( )

Copy bytes in memory with overlapping areas.

```
#include <string.h>
```

```
void *memmove(void *s1, const void *s2, size_t n);
```

Issue 5: No functional changes in this issue.

memset( )

Set bytes in memory.

```
#include <string.h>
```

```
void *memset(void *s, int c, size_t n);
```

Issue 5: No functional changes in this issue.

mkdir( )

Make a directory.

```
#include <sys/types.h>
#include <sys/stat.h>
```

```
int mkdir(const char *path, mode_t mode);
```

Issue 5: No functional changes in this issue.

mkfifo( )

Make a FIFO special file.

```
#include <sys/types.h>
#include <sys/stat.h>
```

```
int mkfifo(const char *path, mode_t mode);
```

Issue 5: No functional changes in this issue.

mknod()

Make a directory, a special, or regular file.

```
#include <sys/stat.h>

int mknod(const char *path, mode_t mode, dev_t dev);
```

Issue 5: No functional changes in this issue.

mkstemp()

Make a unique filename.

```
#include <stdlib.h>

int mkstemp(char *template);
```

Issue 5: No functional changes in this issue.

mktemp()

Make a unique filename.

```
#include <stdlib.h>

char *mktemp(char *template);
```

Issue 5: No functional changes in this issue.

mktime()

Convert broken-down time into time since the Epoch.

```
#include <time.h>

time_t mktime(struct tm *timeptr);
```

Issue 5: No functional changes in this issue.

mlock(), munlock()

Lock or unlock a range of process address space. (**REALTIME**)

```
#include <sys/mman.h>

int mlock(const void * addr, size_t len);
int munlock(const void * addr, size_t len);
```

Issue 5: These are new functions included for alignment with the POSIX Realtime Extension. These are part of the Realtime Feature Group and may not be available on all implementations.

The function *mlock*() causes those whole pages containing any part of the address space of the process starting at address *addr* and continuing for *len* bytes to be memory resident until unlocked or until the process exits or *exec*s another process image. The implementation may require that *addr* be a multiple of PAGESIZE.

The function *munlock*() unlocks those whole pages containing any part of the address space of the process starting at address *addr* and continuing for *len* bytes, regardless of how many times *mlock*() has been called by the process for any of the pages in the specified range. The implementation may require that *addr* be a multiple of the {PAGESIZE}.

mlockall( ), munlockall( )

Lock/unlock the address space of a process. (**REALTIME**)

```
#include <sys/mman.h>

int mlockall(int flags);
int munlockall(void);
```

Issue 5: These are new functions included for alignment with the POSIX Realtime Extension. These are part of the Realtime Feature Group and may not be available on all implementations.

The function *mlockall*( ) causes all of the pages mapped by the address space of a process to be memory resident until unlocked or until the process exits or *exec*s another process image.

The *flags* argument is constructed from the inclusive OR of one or more of the following symbolic constants, defined in **<sys/mman.h>**:

MCL_CURRENT
: Lock all of the pages currently mapped into the address space of the process.

MCL_FUTURE
: Lock all of the pages that become mapped into the address space of the process in the future, when those mappings are established.

The *munlockall*( ) function unlocks all currently mapped pages of the address space of the process. Any pages that become mapped into the address space of the process after a call to *munlockall*( ) will not be locked, unless there is an intervening call to *mlockall*( ) specifying MCL_FUTURE or a subsequent call to *mlockall*( ) specifying MCL_CURRENT.

mmap( )

Map pages of memory.

```
#include <sys/mman.h>

void *mmap(void *addr, size_t len, int prot, int flags,
    int fildes, off_t off);
```

Issue 5: Aligned with *mmap*( ) in the POSIX Realtime Extension. Specifically, the Description is extensively reworded; [EAGAIN] and [ENOTSUP] are added to the mandatory errors; and new cases of [ENOMEM] and [ENXIO] are added to the mandatory errors. Also, the value returned on failure is the value of the constant MAP_FAILED; this was previously defined as –1.

Large File Support extensions are added, see Chapter 15 on page 147.

modf( )

Decompose a floating-point number.

```
#include <math.h>
```

```
double modf(double x, double *iptr);
```

Issue 5: No functional changes in this issue.

mprotect( )

Set protection of memory mapping.

```
#include <sys/mman.h>
```

```
int mprotect(void *addr, size_t len, int prot);
```

Issue 5: Aligned with *mprotect*( ) in the POSIX Realtime Extension. Specifically, the Description is largely reworded; [ENOTSUP] and a second form of [ENOMEM] are added to the mandatory errors; and [EAGAIN] is moved from the optional to the mandatory errors.

mq_close( )

Close a message queue. **(REALTIME)**

```
#include <mqueue.h>
```

```
int mq_close(mqd_t mqdes);
```

Issue 5: This is a new function included for alignment with the POSIX Realtime Extension. This is part of the Realtime Feature Group and may not be available on all implementations.

The *mq_close*( ) function removes the association between the message queue descriptor, *mqdes*, and its message queue.

mq_getattr( )

Get message queue attributes. **(REALTIME)**

```
#include <mqueue.h>
```

```
int mq_getattr(mqd_t mqdes, struct mq_attr *mqstat);
```

Issue 5: This is a new function included for alignment with the POSIX Realtime Extension. This is part of the Realtime Feature Group and may not be available on all implementations.

The *mq_getattr*( ) function is used to get status information and attributes of the message queue and the open message queue description associated with the message queue descriptor.

mq_notify()

Notify process that a message is available. (**REALTIME**)

```
#include <mqueue.h>

int mq_notify(mqd_t mqdes, const struct sigevent *notification);
```

Issue 5: This is a new function included for alignment with the POSIX Realtime Extension. This is part of the Realtime Feature Group and may not be available on all implementations.

If the argument *notification* is not NULL, this function registers the calling process to be notified of message arrival at an empty message queue associated with the specified message queue descriptor, *mqdes*.

mq_open()

Open a message queue. (**REALTIME**)

```
#include <mqueue.h>

mqd_t mq_open(const char *name, int oflag, ...);
```

Issue 5: This is a new function included for alignment with the POSIX Realtime Extension. This is part of the Realtime Feature Group and may not be available on all implementations.

The *mq_open*( ) function establishes the connection between a process and a message queue with a message queue descriptor.

mq_receive()

Receive a message from a message queue. (**REALTIME**)

```
#include <mqueue.h>

ssize_t mq_receive(mqd_t mqdes, char *msg_ptr, size_t msg_len,
    unsigned int *msg_prio);
```

Issue 5: This is a new function included for alignment with the POSIX Realtime Extension. This is part of the Realtime Feature Group and may not be available on all implementations.

The *mq_receive*( ) function is used to receive the oldest of the highest priority message(s) from the message queue specified by *mqdes*.

mq_send()

Send a message to a message queue. (**REALTIME**)

```
#include <mqueue.h>

int mq_send(mqd_t mqdes, const char *msg_ptr, size_t msg_len,
    unsigned int msg_prio);
```

Issue 5: This is a new function included for alignment with the POSIX Realtime Extension. This is part of the Realtime Feature Group and may not be available on all implementations.

The *mq_send*( ) function adds the message pointed to by the argument *msg_ptr* to the message queue specified by *mqdes*.

mq_setattr()

Set message queue attributes. (**REALTIME**)

```
#include <mqueue.h>
```

```
int mq_setattr(mqd_t mqdes, const struct mq_attr *mqstat,
    struct mq_attr *omqstat);
```

Issue 5: This is a new function included for alignment with the POSIX Realtime Extension. This is part of the Realtime Feature Group and may not be available on all implementations.

The *mq_setattr*() function is used to set attributes associated with the open message queue description referenced by the message queue descriptor specified by *mqdes*.

mq_unlink()

Remove a message queue. (**REALTIME**)

```
#include <mqueue.h>
```

```
int mq_unlink(const char *name);
```

Issue 5: This is a new function included for alignment with the POSIX Realtime Extension. This is part of the Realtime Feature Group and may not be available on all implementations.

The *mq_unlink*() function removes the message queue named by the pathname *name*.

mrand48()

Generate uniformly distributed pseudo-random signed long integers.

```
#include <stdlib.h>
```

```
long int mrand48(void);
```

Issue 5: No functional changes in this issue.

msgctl()

Message control operations.

```
#include <sys/msg.h>
```

```
int msgctl(int msqid, int cmd, struct msqid_ds *buf);
```

Issue 5: The note about use of POSIX Realtime Extension IPC routines has been moved from Future Directions to a new Application Usage section, and reworded as follows:

"The POSIX Realtime Extension defines alternative interfaces for interprocess communication. Application developers who need to use IPC should design their applications so that modules using the IPC routines can be easily modified to use the alternative interfaces."

msgget( )

Get the message queue identifier.

```
#include <sys/msg.h>

int msgget(key_t key, int msgflg);
```

Issue 5: The note about use of POSIX Realtime Extension IPC routines has been moved from Future Directions to a new Application Usage section, and been reworded as follows:

"The POSIX Realtime Extension defines alternative interfaces for interprocess communication. Application developers who need to use IPC should design their applications so that modules using the IPC routines can be easily modified to use the alternative interfaces."

msgrcv( )

Message receive operation.

```
#include <sys/msg.h>

ssize_t msgrcv(int msqid, void *msgp, size_t msgsz, long int msgtyp,
     int msgflg);
```

Issue 5: The type of the return value is changed from **int** to **ssize_t**, and a warning is added to the Description about values of *msgsz* larger the {SSIZE_MAX}.

The note about use of POSIX Realtime Extension IPC routines has been moved from Future Directions to the Application Usage section, and reworded as follows:

"The POSIX Realtime Extension defines alternative interfaces for interprocess communication. Application developers who need to use IPC should design their applications so that modules using the IPC routines can be easily modified to use the alternative interfaces."

msgsnd( )

Message send operation.

```
#include <sys/msg.h>

int msgsnd(int msqid, const void *msgp, size_t msgsz, int msgflg);
```

Issue 5: The note about use of POSIX Realtime Extension IPC routines has been moved from Future Directions to a new Application Usage section, and reworded as follows:

"The POSIX Realtime Extension defines alternative interfaces for interprocess communication. Application developers who need to use IPC should design their applications so that modules using the IPC routines can be easily modified to use the alternative interfaces."

msync( )

Synchronize memory with physical storage.

```
#include <sys/mman.h>

int msync(void *addr, size_t len, int flags);
```

Issue 5: Aligned with *msync*( ) in the POSIX Realtime Extension. Specifically, the Description is extensively reworded and [EBUSY] and a new form of [EINVAL] are added to the mandatory errors.

munlock( )

Unlock a range of process address space.

```
#include <sys/mman.h>

int munlock(const void * addr, size_t len);
```

Issue 5: This is a new function included for alignment with the POSIX Realtime Extension. This is part of the Realtime Feature Group and may not be available on all implementations.

See *mlock*( ).

munlockall( )

Unlock the address space of a process.

```
#include <sys/mman.h>

int munlockall(void);
```

Issue 5: This is a new function included for alignment with the POSIX Realtime Extension. This is part of the Realtime Feature Group and may not be available on all implementations.

See *mlockall*( ).

munmap( )

Unmap pages of memory.

```
#include <sys/mman.h>

int munmap(void *addr, size_t len);
```

Issue 5: Aligned with *munmap*( ) in the POSIX Realtime Extension. Specifically, the Description is extensively reworded and the SIGBUS error is no longer permitted to be generated.

nanosleep( )

High resolution sleep. (**REALTIME**)

```
#include <time.h>

int nanosleep(const struct timespec *rqtp, struct timespec *rmtp);
```

Issue 5: This is a new function included for alignment with the POSIX Realtime Extension. This is part of the Realtime Feature Group and may not be available on all implementations.

The *nanosleep*( ) function causes the current thread to be suspended from execution until either the time interval specified by the *rqtp* argument has elapsed or a signal is delivered to the calling thread and its action is to invoke a signal-catching function or to terminate the process.

nextafter( )

Next representable double-precision floating-point number.

```
#include <math.h>
```

```
double nextafter(double x, double y);
```

Issue 5: No functional changes in this issue.

nftw( )

Walk a file tree.

```
#include <ftw.h>
```

```
int nftw(const char *path, int (*fn)(const char *,
    const struct stat *, int, struct FTW *), int depth, int flags);
```

Issue 5: In the Description, the definition of the *depth* argument is clarified:

The argument *depth* sets the maximum number of file descriptors that will be used by *nftw*( ) while traversing the file tree. At most one file descriptor will be used for each directory level.

nice( )

Change nice value of a process.

```
#include <unistd.h>
```

```
int nice(int incr);
```

Issue 5: A statement is added to the description indicating the effects of this function on the different scheduling policies and multi-threaded processes.

The effect on processes or threads with other scheduling policies is implementation-dependent.

The nice value set with *nice*( ) is applied to the process. If the process is multi-threaded, the nice value affects all system scope threads in the process.

nl_langinfo( )

Language information.

```
#include <langinfo.h>
```

```
char *nl_langinfo(nl_item item);
```

Issue 5: The last paragraph of the Description, describing that the return value may overwrite an array, is moved from the Application Usage section.

A note indicating that this interface need not be reentrant is added to the Description. A portable multi-threaded application may only safely call *nl_langinfo*( ) when access to the function is serialized.

nrand48()

Generate uniformly distributed pseudo-random non-negative long integers.

```
#include <stdlib.h>
```

```
long int nrand48(unsigned short int xsubi[3]);
```

Issue 5: No functional changes in this issue.

open()

Open a file.

```
#include <fcntl.h>
```

```
int open(const char *path, int oflag, ... );
```

Issue 5: The Description is updated for alignment with the POSIX Realtime Extension and the POSIX Threads Extension. Specifically, the O_DSYNC and O_RSYNC flags are added and the semantics of the *open*() function on the master side of a pseudo-terminal device are better described.

Large File Support extensions are added, see Chapter 15 on page 147.

opendir()

Open a directory.

```
#include <sys/types.h>
#include <dirent.h>
```

```
DIR *opendir(const char *dirname);
```

Issue 5: No functional changes in this issue.

openlog()

Open a connection to the logging facility.

```
#include <syslog.h>
```

```
void openlog(const char *ident, int logopt, int facility);
```

Issue 5: No functional changes in this issue.

optarg(), opterr(), optind(), optopt()

Options parsing variables.

```
#include <stdio.h>
```

```
extern char *optarg;
extern int opterr, optind, optopt;
```

Issue 5: No functional changes in this issue.

pathconf()

Get configurable pathname variables.

```
#include <unistd.h>

long int pathconf(const char *path, int name);
```

Issue 5: The Description is updated for alignment with the POSIX Realtime Extension. See *fpathconf*().

Large File Support extensions are added, see Chapter 15 on page 147.

pause()

Suspend the thread until a signal is received.

```
#include <unistd.h>

int pause(void);
```

Issue 5: The Description is updated for alignment with the POSIX Threads Extension. Specifically, this is now described in terms of the thread rather than the process.

pclose()

Close a pipe stream to or from a process.

```
#include <stdio.h>

int pclose(FILE *stream);
```

Issue 5: No functional changes in this issue.

perror()

Write error messages to standard error.

```
#include <stdio.h>

void perror(const char *s);
```

Issue 5: A paragraph is added to the Description indicating that *perror*() does not change the orientation of the standard error stream.

pipe()

Create an interprocess channel.

```
#include <unistd.h>

int pipe(int fildes[2]);
```

Issue 5: No functional changes in this issue.

poll( )

Input/output multiplexing.

```
#include <poll.h>
```

```
int poll(struct pollfd fds[], nfds_t nfds, int timeout);
```

Issue 5: The description of POLLWRBAND is updated.

popen( )

Initiate pipe streams to or from a process.

```
#include <stdio.h>
```

```
FILE *popen(const char *command, const char *mode);
```

Issue 5: A statement is added to the Description indicating that pipe streams are byte-oriented.

pow( )

Power function.

```
#include <math.h>
```

```
double pow(double x, double y);
```

Issue 5: No functional changes in this issue.

pread( )

Read from a file.

```
#include <unistd.h>
```

```
ssize_t pread(int fildes, void *buf, size_t nbyte, off_t offset);
```

Issue 5: New in Issue 5; see *read*( ).

printf( )

Print formatted output.

```
#include <stdio.h>
```

```
int printf(const char *format, ...);
```

Issue 5: No functional changes in this issue.

pthread_atfork( )

Register fork handlers.

```
#include <sys/types.h>
#include <unistd.h>
```

```
int pthread_atfork(void (*prepare)(void), void (*parent)(void),
    void (*child)(void));
```

Issue 5: This is a new function derived from the POSIX Threads Extension, including PASC 1003.1c-95 #4.

The *pthread_atfork*( ) function declares fork handlers to be called before and after *fork*( ), in the context of the thread that called *fork*( ).

pthread_attr_getguardsize(), pthread_attr_setguardsize()

Get or set the thread guardsize attribute.

```
#include <pthread.h>

int pthread_attr_getguardsize(const pthread_attr_t *attr,
    size_t *guardsize);
int pthread_attr_setguardsize(pthread_attr_t *attr,
    size_t guardsize);
```

Issue 5: These are included as part of the X/Open Threads Extension, see Chapter 11 on page 103.

The *pthread_attr_getguardsize*( ) function gets the *guardsize* attribute in the *attr* object. This attribute is returned in the *guardsize* parameter.

The *pthread_attr_setguardsize*( ) function sets the *guardsize* attribute in the *attr* object. The new value of this attribute is obtained from the *guardsize* parameter.

pthread_attr_init( ), pthread_attr_destroy()

Initialize and destroy threads attribute object.

```
#include <pthread.h>

int pthread_attr_init(pthread_attr_t *attr);
int pthread_attr_destroy(pthread_attr_t *attr);
```

Issue 5: These are new functions included for alignment with the POSIX Threads Extension.

The function *pthread_attr_init*( ) initializes a thread attributes object *attr* with the default value for all of the individual attributes used by a given implementation.

The *pthread_attr_destroy*( ) function is used to destroy a thread attributes object.

pthread_attr_setdetachstate(), pthread_attr_getdetachstate()

Set and get the detachstate attribute.

```
#include <pthread.h>

int pthread_attr_setdetachstate(pthread_attr_t *attr, int detachstate);
int pthread_attr_getdetachstate(const pthread_attr_t *attr,
    int *detachstate);
```

Issue 5: These are new functions included for alignment with the POSIX Threads Extension.

The functions *pthread_attr_setdetachstate*( ) and *pthread_attr_getdetachstate*( ), respectively, set and get the *detachstate* attribute in the *attr* object.

pthread_attr_setinheritsched(), pthread_attr_getinheritsched()

Set and get the inheritsched attribute. (**REALTIME THREADS**)

```
#include <pthread.h>

int pthread_attr_setinheritsched(pthread_attr_t *attr,
    int inheritsched);
int pthread_attr_getinheritsched(const pthread_attr_t *attr,
    int *inheritsched);
```

Issue 5: These are new functions included for alignment with the POSIX Threads Extension.

These are included as part of the Realtime Threads Feature Group, and may not be available on all implementations.

The functions *pthread_attr_setinheritsched*( ) and *pthread_attr_getinheritsched*( ), respectively, set and get the *inheritsched* attribute in the *attr* argument.

pthread_attr_setschedparam(), pthread_attr_getschedparam()

Set and get the schedparam attribute. (**REALTIME THREADS**)

```
#include <pthread.h>

int pthread_attr_setschedparam(pthread_attr_t *attr,
    const struct sched_param *param);
int pthread_attr_getschedparam(const pthread_attr_t *attr,
    struct sched_param *param);
```

Issue 5: These are new functions included for alignment with the POSIX Threads Extension.

The functions *pthread_attr_setschedparam*( ) and *pthread_attr_getschedparam*( ), respectively, set and get the scheduling parameter attributes in the *attr* argument.

pthread_attr_setschedpolicy(), pthread_attr_getschedpolicy()

Set and get the schedpolicy attribute. (**REALTIME THREADS**)

```
#include <pthread.h>

int pthread_attr_setschedpolicy(pthread_attr_t *attr, int policy);
int pthread_attr_getschedpolicy(const pthread_attr_t *attr,
    int *policy);
```

Issue 5: These are new functions included for alignment with the POSIX Threads Extension.

These are included as part of the Realtime Threads Feature Group, and may not be available on all implementations.

The functions *pthread_attr_setschedpolicy*( ) and *pthread_attr_getschedpolicy*( ), respectively, set and get the *schedpolicy* attribute in the *attr* argument.

pthread_attr_setscope(), pthread_attr_getscope()

Set and get the contentionscope attribute. (**REALTIME THREADS**)

```
#include <pthread.h>
```

```
int pthread_attr_setscope(pthread_attr_t *attr, int contentionscope);
int pthread_attr_getscope(const pthread_attr_t *attr,
    int *contentionscope);
```

Issue 5: These are new functions included for alignment with the POSIX Threads Extension.

These are included as part of the Realtime Threads Feature Group, and may not be available on all implementations.

The *pthread_attr_setscope*( ) and *pthread_attr_getscope*( ) functions are used to set and get the *contentionscope* attribute in the *attr* object.

pthread_attr_setstackaddr(), pthread_attr_getstackaddr()

Set and get the stackaddr attribute.

```
#include <pthread.h>
```

```
int pthread_attr_setstackaddr(pthread_attr_t *attr, void *stackaddr);
int pthread_attr_getstackaddr(const pthread_attr_t *attr,
    void **stackaddr);
```

Issue 5: These are new functions included for alignment with the POSIX Threads Extension.

The functions *pthread_attr_setstackaddr*( ) and *pthread_attr_getstackaddr*( ), respectively, set and get the thread creation *stackaddr* attribute in the *attr* object.

pthread_attr_setstacksize(), pthread_attr_getstacksize()

Set and get the stacksize attribute.

```
#include <pthread.h>
```

```
int pthread_attr_setstacksize(pthread_attr_t *attr, size_t stacksize);
int pthread_attr_getstacksize(const pthread_attr_t *attr,
    size_t *stacksize);
```

Issue 5: These are new functions included for alignment with the POSIX Threads Extension.

The functions *pthread_attr_setstacksize*( ) and *pthread_attr_getstacksize*( ), respectively, set and get the thread creation *stacksize* attribute in the *attr* object.

pthread_cancel()

Cancel execution of a thread.

```
#include <pthread.h>
```

```
int pthread_cancel(pthread_t thread);
```

Issue 5: This is a new function included for alignment with the POSIX Threads Extension.

The *pthread_cancel*( ) function requests that *thread* be canceled.

pthread_cleanup_push(), pthread_cleanup_pop()

Establish cancellation handlers.

```
#include <pthread.h>

void pthread_cleanup_push(void (*routine)(void*), void *arg);
void pthread_cleanup_pop(int execute);
```

Issue 5: These are new functions included for alignment with the POSIX Threads Extension.

The *pthread_cleanup_push*( ) function pushes the specified cancellation cleanup handler routine onto the calling thread's cancellation cleanup stack.

The *pthread_cleanup_pop*( ) function removes the routine at the top of the calling thread's cancellation cleanup stack and optionally invokes it (if *execute* is non-zero).

pthread_cond_init(), pthread_cond_destroy()

Initialize and destroy condition variables.

```
#include <pthread.h>

int pthread_cond_init(pthread_cond_t *cond,
    const pthread_condattr_t *attr);
int pthread_cond_destroy(pthread_cond_t *cond);
pthread_cond_t cond = PTHREAD_COND_INITIALIZER;
```

Issue 5: These are new functions included for alignment with the POSIX Threads Extension.

The function *pthread_cond_init*( ) initializes the condition variable referenced by *cond* with attributes referenced by *attr*.

The function *pthread_cond_destroy*( ) destroys the given condition variable specified by *cond*; the object becomes, in effect, uninitialized. An implementation may cause *pthread_cond_destroy*( ) to set the object referenced by *cond* to an invalid value.

pthread_cond_signal(), pthread_cond_broadcast()

Signal or broadcast a condition.

```
#include <pthread.h>

int pthread_cond_signal(pthread_cond_t *cond);
int pthread_cond_broadcast(pthread_cond_t *cond);
```

Issue 5: These are new functions included for alignment with the POSIX Threads Extension.

The *pthread_cond_signal*( ) function unblocks at least one of the threads that are blocked on the specified condition variable *cond* (if any threads are blocked on *cond*).

The *pthread_cond_broadcast*( ) function unblocks all threads currently blocked on the specified condition variable *cond*.

pthread_cond_wait(), pthread_cond_timedwait()

Wait on a condition.

```
#include <pthread.h>

int pthread_cond_wait(pthread_cond_t *cond, pthread_mutex_t *mutex);
int pthread_cond_timedwait(pthread_cond_t *cond,
    pthread_mutex_t *mutex, const struct timespec *abstime);
```

Issue 5: These are new functions included for alignment with the POSIX Threads Extension.

The *pthread_cond_wait*( ) and *pthread_cond_timedwait*( ) functions are used to block on a condition variable.

pthread_condattr_getpshared(), pthread_condattr_setpshared()

Get and set the process-shared condition variable attributes.

```
#include <pthread.h>

int pthread_condattr_getpshared(const pthread_condattr_t *attr,
    int *pshared);
int pthread_condattr_setpshared(pthread_condattr_t *attr,
    int pshared);
```

Issue 5: These are new functions included for alignment with the POSIX Threads Extension.

The *pthread_condattr_getpshared*( ) function obtains the value of the *process-shared* attribute from the attributes object referenced by *attr*.

The *pthread_condattr_setpshared*( ) function is used to set the *process-shared* attribute in an initialized attributes object referenced by *attr*.

pthread_condattr_init(), pthread_condattr_destroy()

Initialize and destroy the condition variable attributes object.

```
#include <pthread.h>

int pthread_condattr_init(pthread_condattr_t *attr);
int pthread_condattr_destroy(pthread_condattr_t *attr);
```

Issue 5: These are new functions included for alignment with the POSIX Threads Extension.

The function *pthread_condattr_init*( ) initializes a condition variable attributes object *attr* with the default value for all of the attributes defined by the implementation.

The *pthread_condattr_destroy*( ) function destroys a condition variable attributes object; the object becomes, in effect, uninitialized.

pthread_create()

Thread creation.

```
#include <pthread.h>

int pthread_create(pthread_t *thread, const pthread_attr_t *attr,
    void *(*start_routine)(void*), void *arg);
```

Issue 5: This is a new function included for alignment with the POSIX Threads Extension.

The *pthread_create*() function is used to create a new thread, with attributes specified by *attr*, within a process.

pthread_detach()

Detach a thread.

```
#include <pthread.h>

int pthread_detach(pthread_t thread);
```

Issue 5: This is a new function included for alignment with the POSIX Threads Extension.

The *pthread_detach*() function is used to indicate to the implementation that storage for the thread *thread* can be reclaimed when that thread terminates.

pthread_equal()

Compare thread IDs.

```
#include <pthread.h>

int pthread_equal(pthread_t t1, pthread_t t2);
```

Issue 5: This is a new function included for alignment with the POSIX Threads Extension.

This function compares the thread IDs *t1* and *t2*.

pthread_exit()

Thread termination.

```
#include <pthread.h>

void pthread_exit(void *value_ptr);
```

Issue 5: This is a new function included for alignment with the POSIX Threads Extension.

The *pthread_exit*() function terminates the calling thread and makes the value *value_ptr* available to any successful join with the terminating thread. Any cancellation cleanup handlers that have been pushed and not yet popped are popped in the reverse order that they were pushed and then executed.

pthread_getconcurrency(), pthread_setconcurrency()

Get or set level of concurrency.

```
#include <pthread.h>
```

```
int pthread_getconcurrency(void);
int pthread_setconcurrency(int new_level);
```

Issue 5: These are included as part of the X/Open Threads Extension, see Chapter 11 on page 103.

The *pthread_setconcurrency*( ) function allows an application to inform the threads implementation of its desired concurrency level, *new_level*.

The *pthread_getconcurrency*( ) function returns the value set by a previous call to the *pthread_setconcurrency*( ) function.

pthread_getschedparam(), pthread_setschedparam()

Dynamic thread scheduling parameters access. **(REALTIME THREADS)**

```
#include <pthread.h>
```

```
int pthread_getschedparam(pthread_t thread, int *policy,
    struct sched_param *param);
int pthread_setschedparam(pthread_t thread, int *policy,
    const struct sched_param *param);
```

Issue 5: These are new functions included for alignment with the POSIX Threads Extension.

These are included as part of the Realtime Threads Feature Group, and may not be available on all implementations.

The *pthread_getschedparam*( ) and *pthread_setschedparam*( ) functions allow the scheduling policy and scheduling parameters of individual threads within a multi-threaded process to be retrieved and set.

pthread_join()

Wait for thread termination.

```
#include <pthread.h>
```

```
int pthread_join(pthread_t thread, void **value_ptr);
```

Issue 5: This is a new function included for alignment with the POSIX Threads Extension.

The *pthread_join*( ) function suspends execution of the calling thread until the target *thread* terminates, unless the target *thread* has already terminated.

pthread_key_create()

Thread-specific data key creation.

```
#include <pthread.h>
```

```
int pthread_key_create(pthread_key_t *key, void (*destructor)(void*));
```

Issue 5: This is a new function included for alignment with the POSIX Threads Extension.

This function creates a thread-specific data key visible to all threads in the process.

pthread_key_delete()

Thread-specific data key deletion.

```
#include <pthread.h>
```

```
int pthread_key_delete(pthread_key_t key);
```

Issue 5: This is a new function included for alignment with the POSIX Threads Extension.

This function deletes a thread-specific data key previously returned by *pthread_key_create*( ).

pthread_kill()

Send a signal to a thread.

```
#include <signal.h>
```

```
int pthread_kill(pthread_t thread, int sig);
```

Issue 5: This is a new function included for alignment with the POSIX Threads Extension.

The *pthread_kill*( ) function is used to request that a signal be delivered to the specified thread.

pthread_mutex_init(), pthread_mutex_destroy()

Initialize or destroy a mutex.

```
#include <pthread.h>
```

```
int pthread_mutex_init(pthread_mutex_t *mutex,
    const pthread_mutexattr_t *attr);
int pthread_mutex_destroy(pthread_mutex_t *mutex);
pthread_mutex_t mutex = PTHREAD_MUTEX_INITIALIZER;
```

Issue 5: These are new functions included for alignment with the POSIX Threads Extension.

The *pthread_mutex_init*( ) function initializes the mutex referenced by *mutex* with attributes specified by *attr*.

The *pthread_mutex_destroy*( ) function destroys the mutex object referenced by *mutex*; the mutex object becomes, in effect, uninitialized. An implementation may cause *pthread_mutex_destroy*( ) to set the object referenced by *mutex* to an invalid value.

pthread_mutex_lock(), pthread_mutex_trylock(), pthread_mutex_unlock()

Lock and unlock a mutex.

```
#include <pthread.h>
```

```
int pthread_mutex_lock(pthread_mutex_t *mutex);
int pthread_mutex_trylock(pthread_mutex_t *mutex);
int pthread_mutex_unlock(pthread_mutex_t *mutex);
```

Issue 5: These are new functions included for alignment with the POSIX Threads Extension.

The function *pthread_mutex_lock*( ) locks a mutex object referenced by *mutex*.

The function *pthread_mutex_trylock*( ) is identical to *pthread_mutex_lock*( ), except that if the mutex object referenced by *mutex* is currently locked (by any thread, including the current thread), the call returns immediately.

The *pthread_mutex_unlock*( ) function releases the mutex object referenced by *mutex*.

pthread_mutex_setprioceiling(), pthread_mutex_getprioceiling()

Change the priority ceiling of a mutex. (**REALTIME THREADS**)

```
#include <pthread.h>

int pthread_mutex_setprioceiling(pthread_mutex_t *mutex,
    int prioceiling, int *old_ceiling);
int pthread_mutex_getprioceiling(const pthread_mutex_t *mutex,
    int *prioceiling);
```

Issue 5: These are new functions included for alignment with the POSIX Threads Extension.

These are included as part of the Realtime Threads Feature Group, and may not be available on all implementations.

The *pthread_mutex_getprioceiling*( ) function returns the current priority ceiling of the mutex.

The *pthread_mutex_setprioceiling*( ) function either locks the mutex if it is unlocked, or blocks until it can successfully lock the mutex, then it changes the mutex' priority ceiling and releases the mutex. When the change is successful, the previous value of the priority ceiling is returned in *old_ceiling*.

pthread_mutexattr_getpshared(), pthread_mutexattr_setpshared()

Set and get the process-shared attribute.

```
#include <pthread.h>

int pthread_mutexattr_getpshared(const pthread_mutexattr_t *attr,
    int *pshared);
int pthread_mutexattr_setpshared(pthread_mutexattr_t *attr,
    int pshared);
```

Issue 5: These are new functions included for alignment with the POSIX Threads Extension.

The *pthread_mutexattr_getpshared*( ) function obtains the value of the *process-shared* attribute from the attributes object referenced by *attr*. The *pthread_mutexattr_setpshared*( ) function is used to set the *process-shared* attribute in an initialized attributes object referenced by *attr*.

pthread_mutexattr_init(), pthread_mutexattr_destroy()

Initialize and destroy mutex attributes object.

```
#include <pthread.h>

int pthread_mutexattr_init(pthread_mutexattr_t *attr);
int pthread_mutexattr_destroy(pthread_mutexattr_t *attr);
```

Issue 5: These are new functions included for alignment with the POSIX Threads Extension.

The function *pthread_mutexattr_init*( ) initializes a mutex attributes object *attr* with the default value for all of the attributes defined by the implementation.

The *pthread_mutexattr_destroy*( ) function destroys a mutex attributes object; the object becomes, in effect, uninitialized.

pthread_mutexattr_setprioceiling(), pthread_mutexattr_getprioceiling()

Set and get the prioceiling attribute of a mutex attribute object. (**REALTIME THREADS**)

```
#include <pthread.h>

int pthread_mutexattr_setprioceiling(pthread_mutexattr_t *attr,
    int prioceiling);
int pthread_mutexattr_getprioceiling(const pthread_mutexattr_t *attr,
    int *prioceiling);
```

Issue 5: These are new functions included for alignment with the POSIX Threads Extension.

These are included as part of the Realtime Threads Feature Group, and may not be available on all implementations.

The *pthread_mutexattr_setprioceiling*( ) and *pthread_mutexattr_getprioceiling*( ) functions, respectively, set and get the priority ceiling attribute of a mutex attribute object pointed to by *attr* which was previously created by the function *pthread_mutexattr_init*( ).

pthread_mutexattr_setprotocol(), pthread_mutexattr_getprotocol()

Set and get the protocol attribute of a mutex attribute object. (**REALTIME THREADS**)

```
#include <pthread.h>

int pthread_mutexattr_setprotocol(pthread_mutexattr_t *attr,
    int protocol);
int pthread_mutexattr_getprotocol(const pthread_mutexattr_t *attr,
    int *protocol);
```

Issue 5: These are new functions included for alignment with the POSIX Threads Extension.

These are included as part of the Realtime Threads Feature Group, and may not be available on all implementations.

The *pthread_mutexattr_setprotocol*( ) and *pthread_mutexattr_getprotocol*( ) functions, respectively, set and get the protocol attribute of a mutex attribute object pointed to by *attr* which was previously created by the function *pthread_mutexattr_init*( ).

pthread_mutexattr_gettype(), pthread_mutexattr_settype()

Get or set a mutex type.

```
#include <pthread.h>

int pthread_mutexattr_gettype(pthread_mutexattr_t *attr, int *type);
int pthread_mutexattr_settype(pthread_mutexattr_t *attr, int type);
```

Issue 5: These are included as part of the X/Open Threads Extension; see Chapter 11 on page 103.

The *pthread_mutexattr_gettype*( ) and *pthread_mutexattr_settype*( ) functions, respectively, get and set the mutex *type* attribute.

pthread_once()

Dynamic package initialization.

```
#include <pthread.h>

int pthread_once(pthread_once_t *once_control,
    void (*init_routine)(void));
pthread_once_t once_control = PTHREAD_ONCE_INIT;
```

Issue 5: This is a new function included for alignment with the POSIX Threads Extension.

The first call to *pthread_once*( ) by any thread in a process, with a given *once_control*, will call the *init_routine*( ) with no arguments.

pthread_rwlock_init(), pthread_rwlock_destroy()

Initialize or destroy a read-write lock object.

```
#include <pthread.h>

int pthread_rwlock_init(pthread_rwlock_t *rwlock,
    const pthread_rwlockattr_t *attr);
int pthread_rwlock_destroy(pthread_rwlock_t *rwlock);
pthread_rwlock_t rwlock=PTHREAD_RWLOCK_INITIALIZER;
```

Issue 5: These are included as part of the X/Open Threads Extension; see Chapter 11 on page 103.

The *pthread_rwlock_init*( ) function initializes the read-write lock referenced by *rwlock* with the attributes referenced by *attr*.

The *pthread_rwlock_destroy*( ) function destroys the read-write lock object referenced by *rwlock* and releases any resources used by the lock.

pthread_rwlock_rdlock(), pthread_rwlock_tryrdlock()

Lock a read-write lock object for reading.

```
#include <pthread.h>

int pthread_rwlock_rdlock(pthread_rwlock_t *rwlock);
int pthread_rwlock_tryrdlock(pthread_rwlock_t *rwlock);
```

Issue 5: These are included as part of X/Open Threads Extension; see Chapter 11 on page 103.

The *pthread_rwlock_rdlock*( ) function applies a read lock to the read-write lock referenced by *rwlock*.

The function *pthread_rwlock_tryrdlock*( ) applies a read lock as in the *pthread_rwlock_rdlock*( ) function, with the exception that the function fails if any thread holds a write lock on *rwlock* or there are writers blocked on *rwlock*.

pthread_rwlock_unlock()

Unlock a read-write lock object.

```
#include <pthread.h>
```

```
int pthread_rwlock_unlock(pthread_rwlock_t *rwlock);
```

Issue 5: This is included as part of X/Open Threads Extension; see Chapter 11 on page 103.

The *pthread_rwlock_unlock*( ) function is called to release a lock held on the read-write lock object referenced by *rwlock*.

pthread_rwlock_wrlock(), pthread_rwlock_trywrlock()

Lock a read-write lock object for writing.

```
#include <pthread.h>
```

```
int pthread_rwlock_wrlock(pthread_rwlock_t *rwlock);
int pthread_rwlock_trywrlock(pthread_rwlock_t *rwlock);
```

Issue 5: These are included as part of the X/Open Threads Extension; see Chapter 11 on page 103.

The *pthread_rwlock_wrlock*( ) function applies a write lock to the read-write lock referenced by *rwlock*.

The function *pthread_rwlock_trywrlock*( ) applies a write lock like the *pthread_rwlock_wrlock*( ) function, with the exception that the function fails if any thread currently holds *rwlock* (for reading or writing).

pthread_rwlockattr_getpshared(), pthread_rwlockattr_setpshared()

Get and set the process-shared attribute of a read-write lock attributes object.

```
#include <pthread.h>
```

```
int pthread_rwlockattr_getpshared(const pthread_rwlockattr_t *attr,
    int *pshared);
int pthread_rwlockattr_setpshared(pthread_rwlockattr_t *attr,
    int pshared);
```

Issue 5: These are included as part of the X/Open Threads Extension; see Chapter 11 on page 103.

The *pthread_rwlockattr_getpshared*( ) function obtains the value of the *process-shared* attribute from the initialized attributes object referenced by *attr*.

The *pthread_rwlockattr_setpshared*( ) function is used to set the *process-shared* attribute in an initialized attributes object referenced by attr.

pthread_rwlockattr_init(), pthread_rwlockattr_destroy()

Initialize and destroy a read-write lock attributes object.

```
#include <pthread.h>
```

```
int pthread_rwlockattr_init(pthread_rwlockattr_t *attr);
int pthread_rwlockattr_destroy(pthread_rwlockattr_t *attr);
```

Issue 5: These are included as part of X/Open Threads Extension; see Chapter 11 on page 103.

The function *pthread_rwlockattr_init*( ) initializes a read-write lock attributes object *attr* with the default value for all of the attributes defined by the implementation.

The *pthread_rwlockattr_destroy*( ) function destroys a read-write lock attributes object. The effect of subsequent use of the object is undefined until the object is re-initialized by another call to *pthread_rwlockattr_init*( ).

pthread_self( )

Get calling thread's ID.

```
#include <pthread.h>
```

```
pthread_t pthread_self(void);
```

Issue 5: This is a new function included for alignment with the POSIX Threads Extension.

The *pthread_self*( ) function returns the thread ID of the calling thread.

pthread_setcancelstate(), pthread_setcanceltype(), pthread_testcancel( )

Set cancelability state.

```
#include <pthread.h>
```

```
int pthread_setcancelstate(int state, int *oldstate);
int pthread_setcanceltype(int type, int *oldtype);
void pthread_testcancel(void);
```

Issue 5: These are new functions included for alignment with the POSIX Threads Extension.

The *pthread_setcancelstate*( ) function atomically both sets the calling thread's cancelability state to the indicated *state* and returns the previous cancelability state at the location referenced by *oldstate*.

The *pthread_setcanceltype*( ) function atomically both sets the calling thread's cancelability type to the indicated *type* and returns the previous cancelability type at the location referenced by *oldtype*.

pthread_setconcurrency()

Get or set the level of concurrency.

```
#include <pthread.h>
```

```
int pthread_setconcurrency(int new_level);
```

Issue 5: This is included as part of the X/Open Threads Extension; see Chapter 11 on page 103.

See *pthread_getconcurrency*( ).

pthread_setspecific( ), pthread_getspecific( )

Thread-specific data management.

```
#include <pthread.h>
```

```
int pthread_setspecific(pthread_key_t key, const void *value);
void *pthread_getspecific(pthread_key_t key);
```

Issue 5: These are new functions included for alignment with the POSIX Threads Extension.

The *pthread_setspecific*( ) function associates a thread-specific *value* with a *key* obtained via a previous call to *pthread_key_create*( ).

The *pthread_getspecific*( ) function returns the value currently bound to the specified *key* on behalf of the calling thread.

pthread_sigmask( )

Examine and change blocked signals.

```
#include <signal.h>
```

```
int pthread_sigmask(int how, const sigset_t *set, sigset_t *oset);
```

Issue 5: This is a new function included for alignment with the POSIX Threads Extension.

The *pthread_sigmask*( ) function is used to examine or change (or both) the calling thread's signal mask, regardless of the number of threads in the process.

ptsname( )

Get name of the slave pseudo-terminal device.

```
#include <stdlib.h>
```

```
char *ptsname(int fildes);
```

Issue 5: A note indicating that this interface need not be reentrant is added to the Description. A portable multi-threaded application may only safely call *ptsname*( ) when access to the function is serialized.

putc( )

Put byte on a stream.

```
#include <stdio.h>
```

```
int putc(int c, FILE *stream);
```

Issue 5: No functional changes in this issue.

putchar( )

Put byte on stdout stream.

```
#include <stdio.h>

int putchar(int c);
```

Issue 5: No functional changes in this issue.

putc_unlocked( )

Stdio with explicit client locking.

```
#include <stdio.h>

int putc_unlocked(int c, FILE *stream);
```

Issue 5: This is a new function included for alignment with the POSIX Threads Extension.

putchar_unlocked( )

Stdio with explicit client locking.

```
#include <stdio.h>

int putchar_unlocked(int c);
```

Issue 5: This is a new function included for alignment with the POSIX Threads Extension.

putenv( )

Change or add a value to the environment.

```
#include <stdlib.h>

int putenv(char *string);
```

Issue 5: The type of the argument to this function is changed from **const char*** to **char***. This was indicated as a Future Direction in previous issues.

A note indicating that this interface need not be reentrant is added to the Description. A portable multi-threaded application may only safely call *putenv*( ) when access to the function is serialized.

putmsg( ), putpmsg( )

Send a message on a STREAM.

```
#include <stropts.h>

int putmsg(int fildes, const struct strbuf *ctlptr,
    const struct strbuf *dataptr, int flags);
int putpmsg(int fildes, const struct strbuf *ctlptr,
    const struct strbuf *dataptr, int band, int flags);
```

Issue 5: The following line of text is removed from the Description: "The STREAM head guarantees that the control part of a message generated by *putmsg*( ) is at least 64 bytes in length."

puts()

Put a string on standard output.

```
#include <stdio.h>
```

```
int puts(const char *s);
```

Issue 5: No functional changes in this issue.

pututxline()

Put an entry into user accounting database.

```
#include <utmpx.h>
```

```
struct utmpx *pututxline(const struct utmpx *utmpx);
```

Issue 5: No functional changes in this issue.

putw()

Put a word on a stream. **(LEGACY)**

```
#include <stdio.h>
```

```
int putw(int w, FILE *stream);
```

Issue 5: This function is marked LEGACY and may not be available on all implementations.

A note indicating that this interface need not be reentrant is added to the Description. A portable multi-threaded application may only safely call *putw*() when access to the function is serialized.

putwc()

Put a wide character on a stream.

```
#include <stdio.h>
#include <wchar.h>
```

```
wint_t putwc(wchar_t wc, FILE *stream);
```

Issue 5: Aligned with the ISO/IEC 9899:1990/Amendment 1:1995 (E). Specifically, the type of argument *wc* is changed from **wint_t** to **wchar_t**.

The Optional Header (OH) marking is removed from **<stdio.h>**.

putwchar()

Put a wide character on a stdout stream.

```
#include <wchar.h>
```

```
wint_t putwchar(wchar_t wc);
```

Issue 5: Aligned with the ISO/IEC 9899:1990/Amendment 1:1995 (E). Specifically, the type of argument *wc* is changed from **wint_t** to **wchar_t**.

pwrite( )

Write on a file.

```
#include <unistd.h>

ssize_t pwrite(int fildes, const void *buf, size_t nbyte,
    off_t offset);
```

Issue 5: New in Issue 5; see *write*( ).

qsort( )

Sort a table of data.

```
#include <stdlib.h>

void qsort(void *base, size_t nel, size_t width
    int (*compar)(const void *, const void *));
```

Issue 5: No functional changes in this issue.

raise( )

Send a signal to the executing process.

```
#include <signal.h>

int raise(int sig);
```

Issue 5: The Description is updated for alignment with the POSIX Threads Extension. Specifically, it now describes the signal *sig* being sent to the executing thread.

The effect of the *raise*( ) function is equivalent to calling:

```
pthread_kill(pthread_self(), sig);
```

rand( ), rand_r( )

Pseudo-random number generator.

```
#include <stdlib.h>

int rand (void);
void srand(unsigned int seed);
int rand_r(unsigned int *seed);
```

Issue 5: The *rand_r*( ) function is included for alignment with the POSIX Threads Extension, and is the thread-safe equivalent of *rand*( ).

A note indicating that the *rand*( ) interface need not be reentrant is added to the Description. A portable multi-threaded application should call *rand_r*( ) instead of *rand*( ).

random( )

Generate a pseudo-random number.

```
#include <stdlib.h>
```

```
long random(void);
```

Issue 5: No functional changes in this issue.

read( ), readv( ), pread( )

Read from a file.

```
#include <unistd.h>
```

```
ssize_t read(int fildes, void *buf, size_t nbyte);
ssize_t pread(int fildes, void *buf, size_t nbyte, off_t offset);
```

```
#include <sys/uio.h>
```

```
ssize_t readv(int fildes, const struct iovec *iov, int iovcnt);
```

Issue 5: The Description is updated for alignment with the POSIX Realtime Extension and the POSIX Threads Extension. Specifically, parts of the description are worded in terms of a thread rather than a process. Also, semantics are described for synchronized input/output and shared memory objects.

Large File Support extensions are added, see Chapter 15 on page 147.

The *pread*( ) function is added.

The *pread*( ) function performs the same action as *read*( ), except that it reads from a given position in the file without changing the file pointer.

readdir( ), readdir_r( )

Read directory.

```
#include <sys/types.h>
#include <dirent.h>
```

```
struct dirent *readdir(DIR *dirp);
int readdir_r(DIR *dirp, struct direct *entry, struct dirent **result);
```

Issue 5: Large File Support extensions are added, see Chapter 15 on page 147.

The *readdir_r*( ) function is included for alignment with the POSIX Threads Extension, and is the thread-safe equivalent of *readdir*( ).

A note indicating that the *readdir*( ) interface need not be reentrant is added to the Description. A portable multi-threaded application should call *readdir_r*( ) instead of *readdir*( ).

readlink( )

Read the contents of a symbolic link.

```
#include <unistd.h>

int readlink(const char *path, char *buf, size_t bufsize);
```

Issue 5: The *readlink*( ) function returns the size of the information that it reads as a type **int**, but the size of the buffer area is specified by a type **size_t**. This function is being specified in the IEEE PASC P1003.1a draft standard, which currently has type **ssize_t** for the return type. A future issue will likely change for alignment.

readv( )

Vectored read from file.

```
#include <sys/uio.h>

ssize_t readv(int fildes, const struct iovec *iov, int iovcnt);
```

Issue 5: No functional changes in this issue.

realloc( )

Memory reallocator.

```
#include <stdlib.h>

void *realloc(void *ptr, size_t size);
```

Issue 5: No functional changes in this issue.

realpath( )

Resolve a pathname.

```
#include <stdlib.h>

char *realpath(const char *file_name, char *resolved_name);
```

Issue 5: No functional changes in this issue.

re_comp( ), re_exec( )

Compile and execute regular expressions. **(LEGACY)**

```
#include <re_comp.h>

char *re_comp(const char *string);
int re_exec(const char *string);
```

Issue 5: This function is marked LEGACY and may not be available on all implementations.

A note indicating that these interfaces need not be reentrant is added to the Description. A portable multi-threaded application may only safely call these functions when access to the function is serialized.

regcmp( ), regex( )

Compile and execute a regular expression. (**LEGACY**)

```
#include <libgen.h>

char *regcmp (const char *string1 , ... /*, (char *)0 */);
char *regex (const char *re, const char *subject , ... );
extern char *__loc1;
```

Issue 5: This function is marked LEGACY and may not be available on all implementations.

A note indicating that these interfaces need not be reentrant is added to the Description. A portable multi-threaded application may only safely call these functions when access to the function is serialized.

regcomp( ), regexec( ), regerror( ), regfree( )

Regular expression matching.

```
#include <sys/types.h>
#include <regex.h>

int regcomp(regex_t *preg, const char *pattern, int cflags);
int regexec(const regex_t *preg, const char *string,
    size_t nmatch, regmatch_t pmatch[ ], int eflags);
size_t regerror(int errcode, const regex_t *preg,
    char *errbuf, size_t errbuf_size);
void regfree(regex_t *preg);
```

Issue 5: No functional changes in this issue.

regex( )

Execute a regular expression. (**LEGACY**)

```
#include <libgen.h>

char *regex (const char *re, const char *subject , ... );
```

Issue 5: This function is marked LEGACY and may not be available on all implementations.

advance( ), compile( ), step( ), loc1( ), loc2( ), locs( )

Compile and match regular expressions. (**LEGACY**)

```
#define INIT declarations
#define GETC( ) getc code
#define PEEK( ) peek code
#define UNGETC( ) ungetc code
#define RETURN(ptr) return code
#define ERROR(val) error code

#include <regexp.h>

char *compile(char *instring, char *expbuf,
    const char *endbuf, int eof);

int step(const char *string, const char *expbuf);

int advance(const char *string, const char *expbuf);
```

```
extern char *loc1, *loc2, *locs;
```

Issue 5: This function is marked LEGACY and may not be available on all implementations.

A note indicating that these interfaces need not be reentrant is added to the Description. A portable multi-threaded application may only safely call these functions when access to the function is serialized.

remainder()

Remainder function.

```
#include <math.h>
```

```
double remainder(double x, double y);
```

Issue 5: No functional changes in this issue.

remove()

Remove files.

```
#include <stdio.h>
```

```
int remove(const char *path);
```

Issue 5: No functional changes in this issue.

remque()

Remove an element from a queue.

```
#include <search.h>
```

```
void remque(void *element);
```

Issue 5: No functional changes in this issue.

rename()

Rename a file.

```
#include <stdio.h>
```

```
int rename(const char *old, const char *new);
```

Issue 5: The [EBUSY] error is added to the "may fail" part of the Errors section.

rewind()

Reset the file position indicator in a stream.

```
#include <stdio.h>
```

```
void rewind(FILE *stream);
```

Issue 5: No functional changes in this issue.

rewinddir()

Reset the position of a directory stream to the beginning of a directory.

```
#include <sys/types.h>
#include <dirent.h>
```

```
void rewinddir(DIR *dirp);
```

Issue 5: No functional changes in this issue.

rindex()

Character string operations.

```
#include <strings.h>
```

```
char *rindex(const char *s, int c);
```

Issue 5: No functional changes in this issue.

rint()

Round-to-nearest integral value.

```
#include <math.h>
```

```
double rint(double x);
```

Issue 5: No functional changes in this issue.

rmdir()

Remove a directory.

```
#include <unistd.h>
```

```
int rmdir(const char *path);
```

Issue 5: No functional changes in this issue.

sbrk()

Change space allocation. **(LEGACY)**

```
#include <unistd.h>
```

```
void *sbrk(intptr_t incr);
```

Issue 5: This function is marked LEGACY and may not be available on all implementations.

The type of the argument to *sbrk*() is changed from **int** to **intptr_t**.

scalb()

Load an exponent of a radix-independent floating-point number.

```
#include <math.h>
```

```
double scalb(double x, double n);
```

Issue 5: No functional changes in this issue.

scanf()

Convert formatted input.

```
#include <stdio.h>
```

```
int scanf(const char *format, ... );
```

Issue 5: No functional changes in this issue.

sched_get_priority_max(), sched_get_priority_min()

Get priority limits. (**REALTIME**)

```
#include <sched.h>
```

```
int sched_get_priority_max(int policy);
int sched_get_priority_min(int policy);
```

Issue 5: This is a new function included for alignment with the POSIX Realtime Extension. This is part of the Realtime Feature Group and may not be available on all implementations.

The *sched_get_priority_max*() and *sched_get_priority_min*() functions return the appropriate maximum or minimum, respectfully, for the scheduling policy specified by *policy*.

sched_getparam()

Get scheduling parameters. (**REALTIME**)

```
#include <sched.h>
```

```
int sched_getparam(pid_t pid, struct sched_param *param);
```

Issue 5: This is a new function included for alignment with the POSIX Realtime Extension. This is part of the Realtime Feature Group and may not be available on all implementations.

The *sched_getparam*() function returns the scheduling parameters of a process specified by *pid* in the **sched_param** structure pointed to by *param*.

sched_getscheduler()

Get scheduling policy. (**REALTIME**)

```
#include <sched.h>
```

```
int sched_getscheduler(pid_t pid);
```

Issue 5: This is a new function included for alignment with the POSIX Realtime Extension. This is part of the Realtime Feature Group and may not be available on all implementations.

The *sched_getscheduler*() function returns the scheduling policy of the process specified by *pid*.

sched_rr_get_interval()

Get execution time limits. (**REALTIME**)

```
#include <sched.h>
```

```
int sched_rr_get_interval(pid_t pid, struct timespec *interval);
```

Issue 5: This is a new function included for alignment with the POSIX Realtime Extension. This is part of the Realtime Feature Group and may not be available on all implementations.

The *sched_rr_get_interval*( ) function updates the **timespec** structure referenced by the *interval* argument to contain the current execution time limit (that is, time quantum) for the process specified by *pid*.

sched_setparam()

Set scheduling parameters. (**REALTIME**)

```
#include <sched.h>
```

```
int sched_setparam(pid_t pid, const struct sched_param *param);
```

Issue 5: This is a new function included for alignment with the POSIX Realtime Extension. This is part of the Realtime Feature Group and may not be available on all implementations.

The *sched_setparam*( ) function sets the scheduling parameters of the process specified by *pid* to the values specified by the **sched_param** structure pointed to by *param*.

sched_setscheduler()

Set scheduling policy and parameters. (**REALTIME**)

```
#include <sched.h>
```

```
int sched_setscheduler(pid_t pid, int policy,
    const struct sched_param *param);
```

Issue 5: This is a new function included for alignment with the POSIX Realtime Extension. This is part of the Realtime Feature Group and may not be available on all implementations.

The *sched_setscheduler*( ) function sets the scheduling policy and scheduling parameters of the process specified by *pid* to *policy* and the parameters specified in the **sched_param** structure pointed to by *param*, respectively.

sched_yield()

Yield processor.

```
#include <sched.h>
```

```
int sched_yield(void);
```

Issue 5: This is a new function included for alignment with the POSIX Realtime Extension and the POSIX Threads Extension.

The *sched_yield*( ) function forces the running thread to relinquish the processor until it again becomes the head of its thread list.

seed48()

Seed uniformly distributed pseudo-random non-negative long integer generator.

```
#include <stdlib.h>

unsigned short int *seed48(unsigned short int seed16v[3]);
```

Issue 5: No functional changes in this issue.

seekdir()

Set position of directory stream.

```
#include <sys/types.h>
#include <dirent.h>

void seekdir(DIR *dirp, long int loc);
```

Issue 5: No functional changes in this issue.

select()

Synchronous I/O multiplexing.

```
#include <sys/time.h>

int select(int nfds, fd_set *readfds, fd_set *writefds,
    fd_set *errorfds, struct timeval *timeout);
void FD_CLR(int fd, fd_set *fdset);
int FD_ISSET(int fd, fd_set *fdset);
void FD_SET(int fd, fd_set *fdset);
void FD_ZERO(fd_set *fdset);
```

Issue 5: In the Errors section, the text has been changed to indicate that [EINVAL] will be returned when *nfds* is less than 0 or greater than FD_SETSIZE. It previously stated less than 0, or greater than or equal to FD_SETSIZE.

Text about **timeout** is moved from the Application Usage section to the Description.

sem_close()

Close a named semaphore. (**REALTIME**)

```
#include <semaphore.h>

int sem_close(sem_t *sem);
```

Issue 5: This is a new function included for alignment with the POSIX Realtime Extension. This is part of the Realtime Feature Group and may not be available on all implementations.

The *sem_close*() function is used to indicate that the calling process is finished using the named semaphore indicated by *sem*.

sem_destroy()

Destroy an unnamed semaphore. (**REALTIME**)

```
#include <semaphore.h>

int sem_destroy(sem_t *sem);
```

Issue 5: This is a new function included for alignment with the POSIX Realtime Extension. This is part of the Realtime Feature Group and may not be available on all implementations.

The *sem_destroy*( ) function is used to destroy the unnamed semaphore indicated by *sem*.

sem_getvalue()

Get the value of a semaphore. (**REALTIME**)

```
#include <semaphore.h>

int sem_getvalue(sem_t *sem, int *sval);
```

Issue 5: This is a new function included for alignment with the POSIX Realtime Extension. This is part of the Realtime Feature Group and may not be available on all implementations.

The *sem_getvalue*( ) function updates the location referenced by the *sval* argument to have the value of the semaphore referenced by *sem* without affecting the state of the semaphore.

sem_init()

Initialize an unnamed semaphore. (**REALTIME**)

```
#include <semaphore.h>

int sem_init(sem_t *sem, int pshared, unsigned int value);
```

Issue 5: This is a new function included for alignment with the POSIX Realtime Extension. This is part of the Realtime Feature Group and may not be available on all implementations.

The *sem_init*( ) function is used to initialize the unnamed semaphore referred to by *sem*.

sem_open()

Initialize and open a named semaphore. (**REALTIME**)

```
#include <semaphore.h>

sem_t *sem_open(const char *name, int oflag, ...);
```

Issue 5: This is a new function included for alignment with the POSIX Realtime Extension. This is part of the Realtime Feature Group and may not be available on all implementations.

The *sem_open*( ) function establishes a connection between a named semaphore and a process. Following a call to *sem_open*( ) with semaphore name *name*, the process may reference the semaphore associated with *name* using the address returned from the call.

sem_post()

Unlock a semaphore. (**REALTIME**)

```
#include <semaphore.h>

int sem_post(sem_t *sem);
```

Issue 5: This is a new function included for alignment with the POSIX Realtime Extension. This is part of the Realtime Feature Group and may not be available on all implementations.

The *sem_post*( ) function unlocks the semaphore referenced by *sem* by performing a semaphore unlock operation on that semaphore.

sem_unlink()

Remove a named semaphore. (**REALTIME**)

```
#include <semaphore.h>

int sem_unlink(const char *name);
```

Issue 5: This is a new function included for alignment with the POSIX Realtime Extension. This is part of the Realtime Feature Group and may not be available on all implementations.

The *sem_unlink*( ) function removes the semaphore named by the string *name*.

sem_wait( ), sem_trywait( )

Lock a semaphore. (**REALTIME**)

```
#include <semaphore.h>

int sem_wait(sem_t *sem);
int sem_trywait(sem_t *sem);
```

Issue 5: These are new functions included for alignment with the POSIX Realtime Extension. These are part of the Realtime Feature Group and may not be available on all implementations.

The *sem_wait*( ) function locks the semaphore referenced by *sem* by performing a semaphore lock operation on that semaphore.

The *sem_trywait*( ) function locks the semaphore referenced by *sem* only if the semaphore is currently not locked; that is, if the semaphore value is currently positive.

semctl( )

Semaphore control operations.

```
#include <sys/sem.h>

int semctl(int semid, int semnum, int cmd, ...);
```

Issue 5: The note about use of POSIX Realtime Extension IPC routines has been moved from Future Directions to the Application Usage section, and reworded as follows:

"The POSIX Realtime Extension defines alternative interfaces for interprocess communication. Application developers who need to use IPC should design their applications so that modules using the IPC routines can be easily modified to use the alternative interfaces."

semget()

Get set of semaphores.

```
#include <sys/sem.h>
```

```
int semget(key_t key, int nsems, int semflg);
```

Issue 5: The note about use of POSIX Realtime Extension IPC routines has been moved from Future Directions to a new Application Usage section, and reworded as follows:

"The POSIX Realtime Extension defines alternative interfaces for interprocess communication. Application developers who need to use IPC should design their applications so that modules using the IPC routines can be easily modified to use the alternative interfaces."

semop()

Semaphore operations.

```
#include <sys/sem.h>
```

```
int semop(int semid, struct sembuf *sops, size_t nsops);
```

Issue 5: The note about use of POSIX Realtime Extension IPC routines has been moved from Future Directions to a new Application Usage section, and reworded as follows:

"The POSIX Realtime Extension defines alternative interfaces for interprocess communication. Application developers who need to use IPC should design their applications so that modules using the IPC routines can be easily modified to use the alternative interfaces."

setbuf()

Assign buffering to a stream.

```
#include <stdio.h>
```

```
void setbuf(FILE *stream, char *buf);
```

Issue 5: No functional changes in this issue.

setcontext()

Set current user context.

```
#include <ucontext.h>
```

```
int setcontext(const ucontext_t *ucp);
```

Issue 5: No functional changes in this issue.

setgid( )

Set-group-ID.

```
#include <sys/types.h>
#include <unistd.h>
```

```
int setgid(gid_t gid);
```

Issue 5: No functional changes in this issue.

setgrent( )

Reset group database to the first entry.

```
#include <grp.h>
```

```
void setgrent(void);
```

Issue 5: No functional changes in this issue.

setitimer( )

Set the value of the interval timer.

```
#include <sys/time.h>
```

```
int setitimer(int which, const struct itimerval *value,
    struct itimerval *ovalue);
```

Issue 5: No functional changes in this issue.

_setjmp( )

Set the jump point for a non-local goto.

```
#include <setjmp.h>
```

```
int _setjmp(jmp_buf env);
```

Issue 5: No functional changes in this issue.

setjmp( )

Set the jump point for a non-local goto.

```
#include <setjmp.h>
```

```
int setjmp(jmp_buf env);
```

Issue 5: No functional changes in this issue.

setkey( )

Set the encoding key. (**CRYPT**)

```
#include <stdlib.h>
```

```
void setkey(const char *key);
```

Issue 5: The Description is updated to indicate that *errno* will not be changed if the function is successful.

setlocale()

Set the program locale.

```
#include <locale.h>
```

```
char *setlocale(int category, const char *locale);
```

Issue 5: The Description is updated for alignment with the POSIX Threads Extension. Specifically, the locale state is now described as common to all threads within a process.

setlogmask()

Set the log priority mask.

```
#include <syslog.h>
```

```
int setlogmask(int maskpri);
```

Issue 5: No functional changes in this issue.

setpgid()

Set the process group ID for job control.

```
#include <sys/types.h>
#include <unistd.h>
```

```
int setpgid(pid_t pid, pid_t pgid);
```

Issue 5: No functional changes in this issue.

setpgrp()

Set the process group ID.

```
#include <unistd.h>
```

```
pid_t setpgrp(void);
```

Issue 5: No functional changes in this issue.

setpriority()

Set the nice value.

```
#include <sys/resource.h>
```

```
int setpriority(int which, id_t who, int nice);
```

Issue 5: The *nice* value is added.

setpwent()

User database function.

```
#include <pwd.h>
```

```
void setpwent(void);
```

Issue 5: No functional changes in this issue.

setregid()

Set real and effective group IDs.

```
#include <unistd.h>

int setregid(gid_t rgid, gid_t egid);
```

Issue 5: The Description is updated to indicate that the saved set-group-ID can be set by any of the *exec*() functions, not just *execv*().

setreuid()

Set real and effective user IDs.

```
#include <unistd.h>

int setreuid(uid_t ruid, uid_t euid);
```

Issue 5: No functional changes in this issue.

setrlimit()

Control maximum resource consumption.

```
#include <sys/resource.h>

int setrlimit(int resource, const struct rlimit *rlp);
```

Issue 5: No functional changes in this issue.

setsid()

Create session and set process group ID.

```
#include <sys/types.h>
#include <unistd.h>

pid_t setsid(void);
```

Issue 5: No functional changes in this issue.

setstate()

Switch pseudo-random number generator state arrays.

```
#include <stdlib.h>

char *setstate(const char *state);
```

Issue 5: No functional changes in this issue.

setuid()

Set-user-ID.

```
#include <sys/types.h>
#include <unistd.h>

int setuid(uid_t uid);
```

Issue 5: No functional changes in this issue.

setutxent()

Reset user accounting database to first entry.

```
#include <utmpx.h>
void setutxent(void);
```

Issue 5: No functional changes in this issue.

setvbuf()

Assign buffering to a stream.

```
#include <stdio.h>
int setvbuf(FILE *stream, char *buf, int type, size_t size);
```

Issue 5: No functional changes in this issue.

shm_open()

Open a shared memory object. (**REALTIME**)

```
#include <sys/mman.h>
int shm_open(const char *name, int oflag, mode_t mode);
```

Issue 5: This is a new function included for alignment with the POSIX Realtime Extension. This is part of the Realtime Feature Group and may not be available on all implementations.

The *shm_open*() function establishes a connection between a shared memory object and a file descriptor.

shm_unlink()

Remove a shared memory object. (**REALTIME**)

```
#include <sys/mman.h>
int shm_unlink(const char * name);
```

Issue 5: This is a new function included for alignment with the POSIX Realtime Extension. This is part of the Realtime Feature Group and may not be available on all implementations.

The *shm_unlink*() function removes the name of the shared memory object named by the string pointed to by *name*.

shmat()

Shared memory attach operation.

```
#include <sys/shm.h>
void *shmat(int shmid, const void *shmaddr, int shmflg);
```

Issue 5: The note about use of POSIX Realtime Extension IPC routines has been moved from Future Directions to a new Application Usage section, and reworded as follows:

"The POSIX Realtime Extension defines alternative interfaces for interprocess communication. Application developers who need to use IPC should design their applications so that modules using the IPC routines can be easily modified to use the alternative interfaces."

shmctl( )

Shared memory control operations.

```
#include <sys/shm.h>
```

```
int shmctl(int shmid, int cmd, struct shmid_ds *buf);
```

Issue 5: The note about use of POSIX Realtime Extension IPC routines has been moved from Future Directions to a new Application Usage section, and reworded as follows:

"The POSIX Realtime Extension defines alternative interfaces for interprocess communication. Application developers who need to use IPC should design their applications so that modules using the IPC routines can be easily modified to use the alternative interfaces."

shmdt( )

Shared memory detach operation.

```
#include <sys/shm.h>
```

```
int shmdt(const void *shmaddr);
```

Issue 5: The note about use of POSIX Realtime Extension IPC routines has been moved from Future Directions to a new Application Usage section, and reworded as follows:

"The POSIX Realtime Extension defines alternative interfaces for interprocess communication. Application developers who need to use IPC should design their applications so that modules using the IPC routines can be easily modified to use the alternative interfaces."

shmget( )

Get shared memory segment.

```
#include <sys/shm.h>
```

```
int shmget(key_t key, size_t size, int shmflg);
```

Issue 5: The note about use of POSIX Realtime Extension IPC routines has been moved from Future Directions to a new Application Usage section, and reworded as follows:

"The POSIX Realtime Extension defines alternative interfaces for interprocess communication. Application developers who need to use IPC should design their applications so that modules using the IPC routines can be easily modified to use the alternative interfaces."

sigaction( )

Examine and change signal action.

```
#include <signal.h>
```

```
int sigaction(int sig, const struct sigaction *act,
    struct sigaction *oact);
```

Issue 5: The Description is updated for alignment with the POSIX Realtime Extension and the POSIX Threads Extension.

In the Description, the second argument to *func*( ) when SA_SIGINFO is set is no longer permitted to be NULL, and the description of permitted **siginfo_t** contents is expanded by reference to **<signal.h>**.

Because the X/Open UNIX Extension functionality is now folded into the BASE, the [ENOTSUP] error is deleted.

sigaddset( )

Add a signal to a signal set.

```
#include <signal.h>
```

```
int sigaddset(sigset_t *set, int signo);
```

Issue 5: The last paragraph of the Description was included as an Application Usage note in previous issues. This states:

"Applications must call either *sigemptyset*( ) or *sigfillset*( ) at least once for each object of type **sigset_t** prior to any other use of that object. If such an object is not initialized in this way, but is nonetheless supplied as an argument to any of *sigaction*( ), *sigaddset*( ), *sigdelset*( ), *sigismember*( ), *sigpending*( ), or *sigprocmask*( ), the results are undefined.

sigaltstack( )

Set and/or get signal alternate stack context.

```
#include <signal.h>
```

```
int sigaltstack(const stack_t *ss, stack_t *oss);
```

Issue 5: The last sentence of the Description was included as an Application Usage note in previous issues. This states:

"In some implementations, a signal (whether or not indicated to execute on the alternate stack) will always execute on the alternate stack if it is delivered while another signal is being caught using the alternate stack."

The following is also added:

"Use of this function by library threads that are not bound to kernel-scheduled entities results in undefined behavior."

sigdelset( )

Delete a signal from a signal set.

```
#include <signal.h>

int sigdelset(sigset_t *set, int signo);
```

Issue 5: The last paragraph of the Description was included as an Application Usage note in previous issues. This states:

"Applications should call either *sigemptyset*( ) or *sigfillset*( ) at least once for each object of type **sigset_t** prior to any other use of that object. If such an object is not initialized in this way, but is nonetheless supplied as an argument to any of *sigaction*( ), *sigaddset*( ), *sigdelset*( ), *sigismember*( ), *sigpending*( ), or *sigprocmask*( ), the results are undefined.

sigemptyset( )

Initialize and empty a signal set.

```
#include <signal.h>

int sigemptyset(sigset_t *set);
```

Issue 5: No functional changes in this issue.

sigfillset( )

Initialize and fill a signal set.

```
#include <signal.h>

int sigfillset(sigset_t *set);
```

Issue 5: No functional changes in this issue.

sighold( ), sigignore( )

Add a signal to the signal mask or set a signal disposition to be ignored.

```
#include <signal.h>

int sighold(int sig);
int sigignore(int sig);
```

Issue 5: No functional changes in this issue.

siginterrupt( )

Allow signals to interrupt functions.

```
#include <signal.h>

int siginterrupt(int sig, int flag);
```

Issue 5: No functional changes in this issue.

sigismember()

Test for a signal in a signal set.

```
#include <signal.h>

int sigismember(const sigset_t *set, int signo);
```

Issue 5: The last paragraph of the Description was included as an Application Usage note in previous issues. This states:

"Applications should call either *sigemptyset*( ) or *sigfillset*( ) at least once for each object of type **sigset_t** prior to any other use of that object. If such an object is not initialized in this way, but is nonetheless supplied as an argument to any of *sigaction*( ), *sigaddset*( ), *sigdelset*( ), *sigismember*( ), *sigpending*( ), or *sigprocmask*( ), the results are undefined.

siglongjmp()

Non-local goto with signal handling.

```
#include <setjmp.h>

void siglongjmp(sigjmp_buf env, int val);
```

Issue 5: The Description is updated for alignment with the POSIX Threads Extension. Specifically, this is now described in terms of a thread rather than a process, and the following statement added:

"The effect of a call to *siglongjmp*( ), where initialization of the **jmp_buf** structure was not performed in the calling thread, is undefined."

signal( ), sigset( ), sighold( ), sigrelse( ), sigignore( ), sigpause( )

Signal management.

```
#include <signal.h>

void (*signal(int sig, void (*func)(int)))(int);
int sighold(int sig);
int sigignore(int sig);
int sigpause(int sig);
int sigrelse(int sig);
void (*sigset(int sig, void (*disp)(int)))(int);
```

Issue 5: The Description is updated to indicate that the *sigpause*( ) function restores the process' signal mask to its original state before returning.

The Return Value section is updated to indicate that the *sigpause*( ) function suspends execution of the process until a signal is received, whereupon it returns −1 and sets *errno* to [EINTR].

signgam()

Storage for sign of lgamma( ).

```
#include <math.h>
```

```
extern int signgam;
```

Issue 5: No functional changes in this issue.

sigpause()

Remove a signal from the signal mask and suspend the thread.

```
#include <signal.h>
```

```
int sigpause(int sig);
```

Issue 5: No functional changes in this issue.

sigpending()

Examine pending signals.

```
#include <signal.h>
```

```
int sigpending(sigset_t *set);
```

Issue 5: The Description is updated for alignment with the POSIX Threads Extension, specifically this now states:

"The *sigpending*( ) function stores, in the location referenced by the *set* argument, the set of signals that are blocked from delivery to the calling thread and that are pending on the process or the calling thread."

sigprocmask(), pthread_sigmask()

Examine and change blocked signals.

```
#include <signal.h>
```

```
int sigprocmask(int how, const sigset_t *set, sigset_t *oset);
int pthread_sigmask(int how, const sigset_t *set, sigset_t *oset);
```

Issue 5: The Description is updated for alignment with the POSIX Threads Extension. Specifically, the following changes are made:

The description is updated to include threads as well as processes.

The use of the *sigprocmask*( ) function is unspecified in a multi-threaded process.

If *sigprocmask*( ) fails, the thread's signal mask is not changed.

The *pthread_sigmask*( ) function is new and is used to examine or change (or both) the calling thread's signal mask, regardless of the number of threads in the process. The effect is the same as described for *sigprocmask*( ), without the restriction that the call be made in a single-threaded process.

sigqueue( )

Queue a signal to a process. (**REALTIME**)

```
#include <sys/types.h>
#include <signal.h>

int sigqueue(pid_t pid, int signo, const union sigval value);
```

Issue 5: This is a new function included for alignment with the POSIX Realtime Extension. This is part of the Realtime Feature Group and may not be available on all implementations and the POSIX Threads Extension.

The *sigqueue*( ) function causes the signal specified by *signo* to be sent with the value specified by *value* to the process specified by *pid.*

sigrelse( ), sigset( )

Remove a signal from the signal mask or modify the signal disposition.

```
#include <signal.h>

int sigrelse(int sig);
void (*sigset(int sig, void (*disp)(int)))(int);
```

Issue 5: No functional changes in this issue.

sigsetjmp( )

Set the jump point for a non-local goto.

```
#include <setjmp.h>

int sigsetjmp(sigjmp_buf env, int savemask);
```

Issue 5: The Description is updated for alignment with the POSIX Threads Extension. Specifically, this now describes the signal mask for the calling thread rather than the process.

sigstack( )

Set and/or get an alternate signal stack context. (**LEGACY**)

```
#include <signal.h>

int sigstack(struct sigstack *ss, struct sigstack *oss);
```

Issue 5: This function is marked LEGACY and may not be available on all implementations.

A note indicating that this interface need not be reentrant is added to the Description. A portable multi-threaded application may only safely call *sigstack*( ) when access to the function is serialized.

A portable application, when being written or rewritten, should use *sigaltstack*( ) instead of *sigstack*( ).

sigsuspend()

Wait for a signal.

```
#include <signal.h>

int sigsuspend(const sigset_t *sigmask);
```

Issue 5: The Description is updated for alignment with the POSIX Threads Extension. The first paragraph is reworded as follows:

"The *sigsuspend*( ) function replaces the current signal mask of the calling thread with the set of signals pointed to by *sigmask* and then suspends the thread until delivery of a signal whose action is either to execute a signal-catching function or to terminate the process. This will not cause any other signals that may have been pending on the process to become pending on the thread."

sigwait( )

Wait for queued signals.

```
#include <signal.h>

int sigwait(const sigset_t *set, int *sig);
```

Issue 5: This is a new function included for alignment with the POSIX Realtime Extension and the POSIX Threads Extension.

The *sigwait*( ) function selects a pending signal from *set*, atomically clears it from the system's set of pending signals, and returns that signal number in the location referenced by *sig*.

sigwaitinfo( ), sigtimedwait( )

Wait for queued signals. (**REALTIME**)

```
#include <signal.h>

int sigwaitinfo(const sigset_t *set, siginfo *info);
int sigtimedwait(const sigset_t *set, siginfo_t *info,
    const struct timespec *timeout);
```

Issue 5: These are new functions included for alignment with the POSIX Realtime Extension. These are part of the Realtime Feature Group and may not be available on all implementations.

The function *sigwaitinfo*( ) selects the pending signal from the set specified by *set*.

The function *sigwaitinfo*( ) behaves the same as the *sigwait*( ) function if the *info* argument is NULL.

sin( )

Sine function.

```
#include <math.h>

double sin(double x);
```

Issue 5: The last two paragraphs of the Description were included as Application Usage notes in previous issues. This describes how applications should check for an error. Note how *sin*( ) may lose accuracy when its argument is far from 0.0 .

sinh()

Hyperbolic sine function.

```
#include <math.h>
```

```
double sinh(double x);
```

Issue 5: No functional changes are made in this issue, although the Description is updated to indicate how an application should check for an error. This text was previously published in the Application Usage section.

sleep()

Suspend execution for an interval of time.

```
#include <unistd.h>
```

```
unsigned int sleep(unsigned int seconds);
```

Issue 5: The Description is updated for alignment with the POSIX Threads Extension. Specifically, this describes the calling thread being suspended, rather than the process. Interactions between *sleep*( ) and any of *setitimer*( ), *ualarm*( ), or *usleep*( ) are unspecified.

sprintf( ), snprintf( )

Print formatted output.

```
#include <stdio.h>
```

```
int snprintf(char *s, size_t n, const char *format, /* args */ ...);
int sprintf(char *s, const char *format, ...);
```

Issue 5: The *snprintf*( ) function is new in Issue 5. See *fprintf*( ).

sqrt()

Square root function.

```
#include <math.h>
```

```
double sqrt(double x);
```

Issue 5: No functional changes in this issue.

srand()

Seed simple pseudo-random number generator.

```
#include <stdlib.h>
```

```
void srand(unsigned int seed);
```

Issue 5: No functional changes in this issue.

srand48()

Seed uniformly distributed double-precision pseudo-random number generator.

```
#include <stdlib.h>
```

```
void srand48(long int seedval);
```

Issue 5: No functional changes in this issue.

srandom()

Seed pseudo-random number generator.

```
#include <stdlib.h>
```

```
void srandom(unsigned int seed);
```

Issue 5: No functional changes in this issue.

sscanf()

Convert formatted input.

```
#include <stdio.h>
```

```
int sscanf(const char *s, const char *format, ...);
```

Issue 5: No functional changes in this issue.

stat()

Get file status.

```
#include <sys/types.h>
#include <sys/stat.h>
```

```
int stat(const char *path, struct stat *buf);
```

Issue 5: Large File Support extensions are added, see Chapter 15 on page 147.

statvfs()

Get filesystem information.

```
#include <sys/statvfs.h>
```

```
int statvfs(const char *path, struct statvfs *buf);
```

Issue 5: No functional changes in this issue.

stderr, stdin, stdout

Standard I/O streams.

```
#include <stdio.h>
```

```
extern FILE *stderr, *stdin, *stdout;
```

Issue 5: No functional changes in this issue.

step( )

Pattern match with regular expressions. (**LEGACY**)

```
#include <regexp.h>
```

```
int step(const char *string, const char *expbuf);
```

Issue 5: This function is marked LEGACY and may not be available on all implementations.

strcasecmp( ), strncasecmp( )

Case-insensitive string comparisons.

```
#include <strings.h>
```

```
int strcasecmp(const char *s1, const char *s2);
int strncasecmp(const char *s1, const char *s2, size_t n);
```

Issue 5: No functional changes in this issue.

strcat( )

Concatenate two strings.

```
#include <string.h>
```

```
char *strcat(char *s1, const char *s2);
```

Issue 5: No functional changes in this issue.

strchr( )

String scanning operation.

```
#include <string.h>
```

```
char *strchr(const char *s, int c);
```

Issue 5: No functional changes in this issue.

strcmp( )

Compare two strings.

```
#include <string.h>
```

```
int strcmp(const char *s1, const char *s2);
```

Issue 5: No functional changes in this issue.

strcoll( )

String comparison using collating information.

```
#include <string.h>
```

```
int strcoll(const char *s1, const char *s2);
```

Issue 5: The Description is updated to indicate that *errno* will not be changed if the function is successful.

strcpy()

Copy a string.

```
#include <string.h>
```

```
char *strcpy(char *s1, const char *s2);
```

Issue 5: No functional changes in this issue.

strcspn()

Get the length of a complementary substring.

```
#include <string.h>
```

```
size_t strcspn(const char *s1, const char *s2);
```

Issue 5: The Return Value section is updated to indicated that *strcspn*() returns the length of *s1*, and not *s1* itself as was previously stated.

strdup()

Duplicate a string.

```
#include <string.h>
```

```
char *strdup(const char *s1);
```

Issue 5: No functional changes in this issue.

strerror()

Get an error message string.

```
#include <string.h>
```

```
char *strerror(int errnum);
```

Issue 5: The Description is updated to indicate that *errno* will not be changed if the function is successful.

A note indicating that this interface need not be reentrant is added to the Description. A portable multi-threaded application may only safely call *strerror*() when access to the function is serialized.

strfmon()

Convert a monetary value to a string.

```
#include <monetary.h>
```

```
ssize_t strfmon(char *s, size_t maxsize, const char *format, ...);
```

Issue 5: A sentence is added to the Description warning about values of *maxsize* that are greater than {SSIZE_MAX}.

strftime( )

Convert date and time to a string.

```
#include <time.h>

size_t strftime(char *s, size_t maxsize, const char *format,
    const struct tm *timptr);
```

Issue 5: The description of %OV is changed to be consistent with %V and defines Monday as the first day of the week.

The description of %Oy is clarified.

%Oy is replaced by the year (offset from %C) using the locale's alternative numeric symbols.

strlen( )

Get string length.

```
#include <string.h>

size_t strlen(const char *s);
```

Issue 5: The Return Value section is updated to indicate that *strlen*( ) returns the length of *s*, and not *s* itself as was previously stated.

strncasecmp( )

Case-insensitive string comparison.

```
#include <strings.h>

int strncasecmp(const char *s1, const char *s2, size_t n);
```

Issue 5: No functional changes in this issue.

strncat( )

Concatenate part of two strings.

```
#include <string.h>

char *strncat(char *s1, const char *s2, size_t n);
```

Issue 5: No functional changes in this issue.

strncmp( )

Compare part of two strings.

```
#include <string.h>

int strncmp(const char *s1, const char *s2, size_t n);
```

Issue 5: No functional changes in this issue.

strncpy()

Copy part of a string.

```
#include <string.h>

char *strncpy(char *s1, const char *s2, size_t n);
```

Issue 5: No functional changes in this issue.

strpbrk()

Scan a string for a byte.

```
#include <string.h>

char *strpbrk(const char *s1, const char *s2);
```

Issue 5: No functional changes in this issue.

strptime()

Date and time conversion.

```
#include <time.h>

char *strptime(const char *buf, const char *format, struct tm *tm);
```

Issue 5: The exact meaning of the %y and %Oy specifiers is clarified in the Description.

%y is the year within century. When a century is not otherwise specified, values in the range 69-99 refer to years in the twentieth century (1969 to 1999 inclusive); values in the range 00-68 refer to years in the twenty-first century (2000 to 2068 inclusive). Leading zeros are permitted but not required.

%Oy is the year (offset from %C) using the locale's alternative numeric symbols.

strrchr()

String scanning operation.

```
#include <string.h>

char *strrchr(const char *s, int c);
```

Issue 5: No functional changes in this issue.

strspn()

Get length of a substring.

```
#include <string.h>

size_t strspn(const char *s1, const char *s2);
```

Issue 5: The Return Value section is updated to indicate that *strspn*() returns the length of *s*, and not *s* itself as was previously stated.

strstr()

Find a substring.

```
#include <string.h>
```

```
char *strstr(const char *s1, const char *s2);
```

Issue 5: No functional changes in this issue.

strtod()

Convert a string to a double-precision number.

```
#include <stdlib.h>
```

```
double strtod(const char *str, char **endptr);
```

Issue 5: The Description is updated to indicate that *errno* will not be changed if the function is successful.

strtok(), strtok_r()

Split a string into tokens.

```
#include <string.h>
```

```
char *strtok(char *s1, const char *s2);
char *strtok_r(char *s, const char *sep, char **lasts);
```

Issue 5: The *strtok_r*() function is included for alignment with the POSIX Threads Extension, and is the thread-safe equivalent of *strtok*().

A note indicating that the *strtok*() interface need not be reentrant is added to the Description. A portable multi-threaded application should call *strtok_r*() instead of *strtok*().

strtol()

Convert a string to a long integer.

```
#include <stdlib.h>
```

```
long int strtol(const char *str, char **endptr, int base);
```

Issue 5: The Description is updated to indicate that *errno* will not be changed if the function is successful.

strtoul()

Convert a string to an unsigned long.

```
#include <stdlib.h>
```

```
unsigned long int strtoul(const char *str, char **endptr, int base);
```

Issue 5: The Description is updated to indicate that *errno* will not be changed if the function is successful.

strxfrm()

String transformation.

```
#include <string.h>
```

```
size_t strxfrm(char *s1, const char *s2, size_t n);
```

Issue 5: The Description is updated to indicate that *errno* will not be changed if the function is successful.

swab()

Swap bytes.

```
#include <unistd.h>
```

```
void swab(const void *src, void *dest, ssize_t nbytes);
```

Issue 5: No functional changes in this issue.

swapcontext()

Swap user context.

```
#include <ucontext.h>
```

```
int swapcontext(ucontext_t *oucp, const ucontext_t *ucp);
```

Issue 5: No functional changes in this issue.

swprintf()

Print formatted wide-character output.

```
#include <stdio.h>
#include <wchar.h>
```

```
int swprintf(wchar_t *s, size_t n, const wchar_t *format, ...);
```

Issue 5: Included for alignment with the ISO/IEC 9899:1990/Amendment 1:1995 (E).

The is the wide character equivalent of *sprintf*( ).

swscanf()

Convert formatted wide-character input.

```
#include <stdio.h>
#include <wchar.h>
```

```
int swscanf(const wchar_t *s, const wchar_t *format, ... );
```

Issue 5: This is a new function included for alignment with the ISO/IEC 9899:1990/Amendment 1:1995 (E).

The is the wide character equivalent of *sscanf*( ).

symlink()

Make a symbolic link to a file.

```
#include <unistd.h>

int symlink(const char *path1, const char *path2);
```

Issue 5: No functional changes in this issue.

sync()

Schedule filesystem updates.

```
#include <unistd.h>

void sync(void);
```

Issue 5: No functional changes in this issue.

sysconf()

Get configurable system variables.

```
#include <unistd.h>

long int sysconf(int name);
```

Issue 5: The Description is updated for alignment with the POSIX Realtime Extension and the POSIX Threads Extension. Specifically, the following variables and name values are added:

Variable	Value of Name
AIO_LISTIO_MAX	_SC_AIO_LISTIO_MAX
AIO_MAX	_SC_AIO_MAX
AIO_PRIO_DELTA_MAX	_SC_AIO_PRIO_DELTA_MAX
DELAYTIMER_MAX	_SC_DELAYTIMER_MAX
MQ_OPEN_MAX	_SC_MQ_OPEN_MAX
MQ_PRIO_MAX	_SC_MQ_PRIO_MAX
RTSIG_MAX	_SC_RTSIG_MAX
SEM_NSEMS_MAX	_SC_SEM_NSEMS_MAX
SEM_VALUE_MAX	_SC_SEM_VALUE_MAX
SIGQUEUE_MAX	_SC_SIGQUEUE_MAX
TIMER_MAX	_SC_TIMER_MAX
_POSIX_ASYNCHRONOUS_IO	_SC_ASYNCHRONOUS_IO
_POSIX_FSYNC	_SC_FSYNC
_POSIX_MAPPED_FILES	_SC_MAPPED_FILES
_POSIX_MEMLOCK	_SC_MEMLOCK
_POSIX_MEMLOCK_RANGE	_SC_MEMLOCK_RANGE
_POSIX_MEMORY_PROTECTION	_SC_MEMORY_PROTECTION
_POSIX_MESSAGE_PASSING	_SC_MESSAGE_PASSING
_POSIX_PRIORITIZED_IO	_SC_PRIORITIZED_IO
_POSIX_PRIORITY_SCHEDULING	_SC_PRIORITY_SCHEDULING
_POSIX_REALTIME_SIGNALS	_SC_REALTIME_SIGNALS
_POSIX_SEMAPHORES	_SC_SEMAPHORES
_POSIX_SHARED_MEMORY_OBJECTS	_SC_SHARED_MEMORY_OBJECTS
_POSIX_SYNCHRONIZED_IO	_SC_SYNCHRONIZED_IO

Variable	Value of Name
_POSIX_TIMERS	_SC_TIMERS
Maximum size of *getgrgid_r*( ) and *getgrnam_r*( ) data buffers	_SC_GETGR_R_SIZE_MAX
Maximum size of *getpwuid_r*( ) and *getpwnam_r*( ) data buffers	_SC_GETPW_R_SIZE_MAX
LOGIN_NAME_MAX	_SC_LOGIN_NAME_MAX
PTHREAD_DESTRUCTOR_ITERATIONS	_SC_THREAD_DESTRUCTOR_ ITERATIONS
PTHREAD_KEYS_MAX	_SC_THREAD_KEYS_MAX
PTHREAD_STACK_MIN	_SC_THREAD_STACK_MIN
PTHREAD_THREADS_MAX	_SC_THREAD_THREADS_MAX
TTY_NAME_MAX	_SC_TTY_NAME_MAX
_POSIX_THREADS	_SC_THREADS
_POSIX_THREAD_ATTR_STACKADDR	_SC_THREAD_ATTR_STACKADDR
_POSIX_THREAD_ATTR_STACKSIZE	_SC_THREAD_ATTR_STACKSIZE
_POSIX_THREAD_PRIORITY_ SCHEDULING	_SC_THREAD_PRIORITY_SCHEDULING
_POSIX_THREAD_PRIO_INHERIT	_SC_THREAD_PRIO_INHERIT
_POSIX_THREAD_PRIO_PROTECT	_SC_THREAD_PRIO_PROTECT
_POSIX_THREAD_PROCESS_SHARED	_SC_THREAD_PROCESS_SHARED
_POSIX_THREAD_SAFE_FUNCTIONS	_SC_THREAD_SAFE_FUNCTIONS

and the new Feature Groups and data size neutrality values are added to the table of system variables:

Variable	Value of Name
_XBS5_ILP32_OFF32	_SC_XBS5_ILP32_OFF32
_XBS5_ILP32_OFFBIG	_SC_XBS5_ILP32_OFFBIG
_XBS5_LP64_OFF64	_SC_XBS5_LP64_OFF64
_XBS5_LPBIG_OFFBIG	_SC_XBS5_LPBIG_OFFBIG
_XOPEN_REALTIME	_SC_XOPEN_REALTIME
_XOPEN_REALTIME_THREADS	_SC_XOPEN_REALTIME_THREADS
_XOPEN_LEGACY	_XOPEN_LEGACY

syslog( )

Log a message.

```
#include <syslog.h>

void syslog(int priority, const char *message, ... /* argument */);
```

Issue 5: No functional changes in this issue.

system( )

Issue a command.

```
#include <stdlib.h>

int system(const char *command);
```

Issue 5: No functional changes in this issue.

tan()

Tangent function.

```
#include <math.h>
```

```
double tan(double x);
```

Issue 5: The last two paragraphs of the Description were included as Application Usage notes in previous issues.

tanh()

Hyperbolic tangent function.

```
#include <math.h>
```

```
double tanh(double x);
```

Issue 5: No functional changes in this issue.

tcdrain()

Wait for transmission of output.

```
#include <termios.h>
```

```
int tcdrain(int fildes);
```

Issue 5: No functional changes in this issue.

tcflow()

Suspend or restart the transmission or reception of data.

```
#include <termios.h>
```

```
int tcflow(int fildes, int action);
```

Issue 5: No functional changes in this issue.

tcflush()

Flush non-transmitted output data, non-read input data, or both.

```
#include <termios.h>
```

```
int tcflush(int fildes, int queue_selector);
```

Issue 5: No functional changes in this issue.

tcgetattr()

Get the parameters associated with the terminal.

```
#include <termios.h>
```

```
int tcgetattr(int fildes, struct termios *termios_p);
```

Issue 5: No functional changes in this issue.

tcgetpgrp( )

Get the foreground process group ID.

```
#include <sys/types.h>
#include <unistd.h>
```

```
pid_t tcgetpgrp(int fildes);
```

Issue 5: No functional changes in this issue.

tcgetsid( )

Get the process group ID for the session leader for the controlling terminal.

```
#include <termios.h>
```

```
pid_t tcgetsid(int fildes);
```

Issue 5: The [EACCES] error has been removed from the list of mandatory errors, and the description of [ENOTTY] has been reworded.

tcsendbreak( )

Send a break for a specific duration.

```
#include <termios.h>
```

```
int tcsendbreak(int fildes, int duration);
```

Issue 5: No functional changes in this issue.

tcsetattr( )

Set the parameters associated with the terminal.

```
#include <termios.h>
```

```
int tcsetattr(int fildes, int optional_actions,
    const struct termios *termios_p);
```

Issue 5: No functional changes in this issue.

tcsetpgrp( )

Set the foreground process group ID.

```
#include <sys/types.h>
#include <unistd.h>
```

```
int tcsetpgrp(int fildes, pid_t pgid_id);
```

Issue 5: No functional changes in this issue.

tdelete()

Delete a node from the binary search tree.

```
#include <search.h>
```

```
void *tdelete(const void *key, void **rootp,
    int (*compar)(const void *, const void *));
```

Issue 5: No functional changes in this issue.

telldir()

Current location of a named directory stream.

```
#include <dirent.h>
```

```
long int telldir(DIR *dirp);
```

Issue 5: No functional changes in this issue.

tempnam()

Create a name for a temporary file.

```
#include <stdio.h>
```

```
char *tempnam(const char *dir, const char *pfx);
```

Issue 5: The last paragraph of the Description was included as an Application Usage note in previous issues. This states:

> "Some implementations of *tempnam*() may use *tmpnam*() internally. On such implementations, if called more than {TMP_MAX} times in a single process, the behavior is implementation-dependent."

tfind()

Search a binary search tree.

```
#include <search.h>
```

```
void *tfind(const void *key, void *const *rootp,
    int (*compar)(const void *, const void *));
```

Issue 5: No functional changes in this issue.

time()

Get time.

```
#include <time.h>
```

```
time_t time(time_t *tloc);
```

Issue 5: No functional changes in this issue.

timer_create( )

Create a per-process timer. (**REALTIME**)

```
#include <time.h>
#include <signal.h>

int timer_create(clockid_t clockid, struct sigevent *evp,
    timer_t *timerid);
```

Issue 5: This is a new function included for alignment with the POSIX Realtime Extension. This is part of the Realtime Feature Group and may not be available on all implementations.

The *timer_create*( ) function creates a per-process timer using the specified clock, *clock_id*, as the timing base.

timer_delete( )

Delete a per-process timer. (**REALTIME**)

```
#include <time.h>

int timer_delete(timer_t timerid);
```

Issue 5: This is a new function included for alignment with the POSIX Realtime Extension. This is part of the Realtime Feature Group and may not be available on all implementations.

The *timer_delete*( ) function deletes the specified timer, *timerid*, previously created by the *timer_create*( ) function.

timer_settime( ), timer_gettime( ), timer_getoverrun( )

Per-process timers. (**REALTIME**)

```
#include <time.h>

int timer_settime(timer_t timerid, int flags,
    const struct itimerspec *value, struct itimerspec *ovalue);
int timer_gettime(timer_t timerid, struct itimerspec *value);
int timer_getoverrun(timer_t timerid);
```

Issue 5: These are new functions included for alignment with the POSIX Realtime Extension. These are part of the Realtime Feature Group and may not be available on all implementations.

The *timer_settime*( ) function sets the time until the next expiration of the timer specified by *timerid* from the *it_value* member of the *value* argument and arms the timer if the *it_value* member of *value* is non-zero.

The *timer_gettime*( ) function stores the amount of time until the specified timer, *timerid*, expires and the reload value of the timer into the space pointed to by the *value* argument.

The *timer_getoverrun*( ) function returns the timer expiration overrun count for the specified timer, when a timer expiration signal occurs for the process.

times( )

Get a process and waited-for child process times.

```
#include <sys/times.h>
```

```
clock_t times(struct tms *buffer);
```

Issue 5: No functional changes in this issue.

timezone( )

Difference from UTC and local standard time.

```
#include <time.h>
```

```
extern long int timezone;
```

Issue 5: No functional changes in this issue.

tmpfile( )

Create a temporary file.

```
#include <stdio.h>
```

```
FILE *tmpfile(void);
```

Issue 5: Large File Support extensions are added, see Chapter 15 on page 147.

The last two paragraphs of the Description were included as Application Usage notes in previous issues.

tmpnam( )

Create a name for a temporary file.

```
#include <stdio.h>
```

```
char *tmpnam(char *s);
```

Issue 5: The Description is updated for alignment with the POSIX Threads Extension. Specifically, this adds the following statements:

The implementation will behave as if no function defined in XSH, Issue 5 calls *tmpnam*( ).

If the application uses any of the interfaces guaranteed to be available if either _POSIX_THREAD_SAFE_FUNCTIONS or _POSIX_THREADS is defined, the *tmpnam*( ) function must be called with a non-NULL parameter.

toascii( )

Translate an integer to a 7-bit ASCII character.

```
#include <ctype.h>
```

```
int toascii(int c);
```

Issue 5: No functional changes in this issue.

_tolower()

Transliterate upper-case characters to lower-case.

```
#include <ctype.h>
```

```
int _tolower(int c);
```

Issue 5: No functional changes in this issue.

tolower()

Transliterate upper-case characters to lower-case.

```
#include <ctype.h>
```

```
int tolower(int c);
```

Issue 5: No functional changes in this issue.

_toupper()

Transliterate lower-case characters to upper-case.

```
#include <ctype.h>
```

```
int _toupper(int c);
```

Issue 5: No functional changes in this issue.

toupper()

Transliterate lower-case characters to upper-case.

```
#include <ctype.h>
```

```
int toupper(int c);
```

Issue 5: No functional changes in this issue.

towctrans()

Character transliteration.

```
#include <wctype.h>
```

```
wint_t towctrans(wint_t wc, wctrans_t desc);
```

Issue 5: This is a new function derived from the ISO/IEC 9899:1990/Amendment 1:1995 (E).

The *towctrans*() function transliterates the wide-character code *wc* using the mapping described by *desc*.

towlower()

Transliterate upper-case wide-character code to lower-case.

```
#include <wctype.h>
```

```
wint_t towlower(wint_t wc);
```

Issue 5: The following change has been made in this issue for alignment with the ISO/IEC 9899:1990/Amendment 1:1995 (E):

The Synopsis has been changed to indicate that this function and associated data types are now made visible by inclusion of the header **<wctype.h>** rather than **<wchar.h>**.

towupper( )

Transliterate lower-case wide-character code to upper-case.

```
#include <wctype.h>
```

```
wint_t towupper(wint_t wc);
```

Issue 5: The following change has been made in this issue for alignment with the ISO/IEC 9899:1990/Amendment 1:1995 (E):

The Synopsis has been changed to indicate that this function and associated data types are now made visible by inclusion of the header **<wctype.h>** rather than **<wchar.h>**.

truncate( )

Truncate a file to a specified length.

```
#include <unistd.h>
```

```
int truncate(const char *path, off_t length);
```

Issue 5:

No functional changes in this issue.

tdelete( ), tfind( ), tsearch( ), twalk( )

Manage a binary search tree.

```
#include <search.h>
```

```
void *tsearch(const void *key, void **rootp,
     int (*compar)(const void *, const void *));
void *tfind(const void *key, void *const *rootp,
     int(*compar)(const void *, const void *));
void *tdelete(const void *key, void **rootp,
     int(*compar)(const void *, const void *));
void twalk(const void *root,
     void (*action)(const void *, VISIT, int));
```

Issue 5: The last paragraph of the Description was included as an Application Usage note in previous issues. This states:

"If the calling function alters the pointer to the root, the result is undefined."

ttyname( ), ttyname_r( )

Find the pathname of a terminal.

```
#include <unistd.h>
```

```
char *ttyname(int fildes);
int ttyname_r(int fildes, char *name, size_t namesize);
```

Issue 5: The *ttyname_r*( ) function is included for alignment with the POSIX Threads Extension, and is the thread-safe equivalent of *ttyname*( ).

A note indicating that the *ttyname*( ) interface need not be reentrant is added to the Description. A portable multi-threaded application should call *ttyname_r*( ) instead of *ttyname*( ).

ttyslot( )

Find the slot of the current user in the user accounting database. **(LEGACY)**

```
#include <stdlib.h>
```

```
int ttyslot(void);
```

Issue 5: This function is marked LEGACY and may not be available on all implementations.

A note indicating that this interface need not be reentrant is added to the Description. A portable multi-threaded application may only safely call *ttyslot*( ) when access to the function is serialized.

twalk( )

Traverse a binary search tree.

```
#include <search.h>
```

```
void twalk(const void *root,
    void (*action)(const void *, VISIT, int ));
```

Issue 5: No functional changes in this issue.

tzname( )

Timezone strings.

```
#include <time.h>
```

```
extern char *tzname[ ];
```

Issue 5: No functional changes in this issue.

tzset( )

Set timezone conversion information.

```
#include <time.h>
```

```
void tzset (void);
extern char *tzname[ ];
extern long int timezone;
extern int daylight;
```

Issue 5: No functional changes in this issue.

ualarm( )

Set the interval timer.

```
#include <unistd.h>
```

```
useconds_t ualarm(useconds_t useconds, useconds_t interval);
```

Issue 5: No functional changes in this issue.

ulimit( )

Get and set process limits.

```
#include <ulimit.h>
```

```
long int ulimit(int cmd, ...);
```

Issue 5: In the description of UL_SETFSIZE, the text is corrected to refer to **rlim_t** rather than the spurious **rlimit_t**.

The Description is updated to indicate that *errno* will not be changed if the function is successful.

umask( )

Set and get the file mode creation mask.

```
#include <sys/types.h>
#include <sys/stat.h>
```

```
mode_t umask(mode_t cmask);
```

Issue 5: No functional changes in this issue.

uname( )

Get the name of the current system.

```
#include <sys/utsname.h>
```

```
int uname(struct utsname *name);
```

Issue 5: No functional changes in this issue.

ungetc( )

Push a byte back into the input stream.

```
#include <stdio.h>
```

```
int ungetc(int c, FILE *stream);
```

Issue 5: No functional changes in this issue.

ungetwc( )

Push a wide-character code back into the input stream.

```
#include <stdio.h>
#include <wchar.h>
```

```
wint_t ungetwc(wint_t wc, FILE *stream);
```

Issue 5: The Optional Header (OH) marking is removed from **<stdio.h>**.

unlink( )

Remove a directory entry.

```
#include <unistd.h>
```

```
int unlink(const char *path);
```

Issue 5: The [EBUSY] error is added to the "may fail" part of the Errors section.

unlockpt( )

Unlock a pseudo-terminal master/slave pair.

```
#include <stdlib.h>
```

```
int unlockpt(int fildes);
```

Issue 5: No functional changes in this issue.

usleep( )

Suspend execution for an interval.

```
#include <unistd.h>
```

```
int usleep(useconds_t useconds);
```

Issue 5: The Description is changed to indicate that timers are now thread-based rather than process-based.

utime( )

Set the file access and modification times.

```
#include <sys/types.h>
#include <utime.h>
```

```
int utime(const char *path, const struct utimbuf *times);
```

Issue 5: No functional changes in this issue.

utimes( )

Set the file access and modification times.

```
#include <sys/time.h>
```

```
int utimes(const char *path, const struct timeval times[2]);
```

Issue 5: No functional changes in this issue.

valloc( )

Page-aligned memory allocator. **(LEGACY)**

```
#include <stdlib.h>
```

```
void *valloc(size_t size);
```

Issue 5: This function is marked LEGACY and may not be available on all implementations.

A note indicating that this interface need not be reentrant is added to the Description. A portable multi-threaded application may only safely call *valloc*( ) when access to the function is serialized.

va_arg( ), va_end( ), va_start( )

Handle a variable argument list.

```
#include <stdarg.h>

type va_arg(va_list ap, type);
void va_end(va_list ap);
void va_start(va_list ap, argN);
```

Issue 5: No functional changes in this issue.

vfork( )

Create a new process; share virtual memory.

```
#include <unistd.h>

pid_t vfork(void);
```

Issue 5: No functional changes in this issue.

vfprintf( ), vprintf( ), vsnprintf( ), vsprintf( )

Format the output of a stdarg argument list.

```
#include <stdarg.h>
#include <stdio.h>

int vfprintf(FILE *stream, const char *format, va_list ap);
int vprintf(const char *format, va_list ap);
int vsnprintf(char *s, size_t n, const char *format, va_list ap);
int vsprintf(char *s, const char *format, va_list ap);
```

Issue 5: The *vsnprintf*( ) function is added.

The *vsnprintf*( ) function is the same as *snprintf*( ) except that instead of being called with a variable number of arguments, it is called with an argument list as defined by **<stdarg.h>**.

vfwprintf( ), vwprintf( ), vswprintf( )

Wide-character formatted output of a stdarg argument list.

```
#include <stdarg.h>
#include <stdio.h>
#include <wchar.h>

int vwprintf(const wchar_t *format, va_list arg);
int vfwprintf(FILE *stream, const wchar_t *format, va_list arg);
int vswprintf(wchar_t *s, size_t n, const wchar_t *format,
    va_list arg);
```

Issue 5: These are new functions included for alignment with the ISO/IEC 9899:1990/Amendment 1:1995 (E). These are the wide-character equivalents of *vprintf*( ), *vfprintf*( ), and *vsprintf*( ).

vsprintf( ), vsnprintf( )

Print formatted output.

```
#include <stdarg.h>
#include <stdio.h>

int vsprintf(char *s, const char *format, va_list ap);
int vsnprintf(char *s, size_t n, const char *format, va_list ap);
```

Issue 5: The *vsnprintf*( ) is new. See *vfprintf*( ).

wait( ), waitpid( )

Wait for a child process to stop or terminate.

```
#include <sys/types.h>
#include <sys/wait.h>

pid_t wait(int *stat_loc);
pid_t waitpid(pid_t pid, int *stat_loc, int options);
```

Issue 5: The Description is updated for alignment with the POSIX Threads Extension. Specifically, the semantics are now described for threads.

wait3( )

Wait for a child process to change state. (**LEGACY**)

```
#include <sys/wait.h>

pid_t wait3 (int *stat_loc, int options, struct rusage *resource_usage);
```

Issue 5: This function is marked LEGACY and may not be available on all implementations. New applications should use *waitpid*( ).

A note indicating that this interface need not be reentrant is added to the Description. A portable multi-threaded application may only safely call *wait3*( ) when access to the function is serialized.

waitid( )

Wait for a child process to change state.

```
#include <sys/wait.h>

int waitid(idtype_t idtype, id_t id, siginfo_t *infop, int options);
```

Issue 5: The Description is updated for alignment with the POSIX Threads Extension.

waitpid( )

Wait for a child process to stop or terminate.

```
#include <sys/types.h>
#include <sys/wait.h>

pid_t waitpid(pid_t pid, int *stat_loc, int options);
```

Issue 5: No functional changes in this issue.

wcrtomb()

Convert a wide-character code to a character (restartable).

```
#include <stdio.h>

size_t wcrtomb(char *s, wchar_t wc, mbstate_t *ps);
```

Issue 5: This is a new function included for alignment with the ISO/IEC 9899:1990/Amendment 1:1995 (E).

wcscat()

Concatenate two wide-character strings.

```
#include <wchar.h>

wchar_t *wcscat(wchar_t *ws1, const wchar_t *ws2);
```

Issue 5: No functional changes in this issue.

wcschr()

Wide-character string scanning operation.

```
#include <wchar.h>

wchar_t *wcschr(const wchar_t *ws, wchar_t wc);
```

Issue 5: No functional changes in this issue.

wcscmp()

Compare two wide-character strings.

```
#include <wchar.h>

int wcscmp(const wchar_t *ws1, const wchar_t *ws2);
```

Issue 5: No functional changes in this issue.

wcscoll()

Wide-character string comparison using collating information.

```
#include <wchar.h>

int wcscoll(const wchar_t *ws1, const wchar_t *ws2);
```

Issue 5: The Description is updated to indicate that *errno* will not be changed if the function is successful.

wcscpy()

Copy a wide-character string.

```
#include <wchar.h>

wchar_t *wcscpy(wchar_t *ws1, const wchar_t *ws2);
```

Issue 5: No functional changes in this issue.

wcscspn()

Get the length of a complementary wide substring.

```
#include <wchar.h>

size_t wcscspn(const wchar_t *ws1, const wchar_t *ws2);
```

Issue 5: The Return Value section is updated to indicate that *wcscspn*() returns the length of *ws1*, rather than *ws1* itself.

wcsftime()

Convert date and time to a wide-character string.

```
#include <wchar.h>

size_t wcsftime(wchar_t *wcs, size_t maxsize, const wchar_t *format,
     const struct tm *timptr);
```

Issue 5: Aligned with the ISO/IEC 9899:1990/Amendment 1:1995 (E). Specifically, the type of the format argument is changed from **const char*** to **const wchar_t***.

wcslen()

Get a wide-character string length.

```
#include <wchar.h>

size_t wcslen(const wchar_t *ws);
```

Issue 5: No functional changes in this issue.

wcsncat()

Concatenate part of two wide-character strings.

```
#include <wchar.h>

wchar_t *wcsncat(wchar_t *ws1, const wchar_t *ws2, size_t n);
```

Issue 5: No functional changes in this issue.

wcsncmp()

Compare part of two wide-character strings.

```
#include <wchar.h>

int wcsncmp(const wchar_t *ws1, const wchar_t *ws2, size_t n);
```

Issue 5: No functional changes in this issue.

wcsncpy()

Copy part of a wide-character string.

```
#include <wchar.h>

wchar_t *wcsncpy(wchar_t *ws1, const wchar_t *ws2, size_t n);
```

Issue 5: No functional changes in this issue.

wcspbrk( )

Scan a wide-character string for a wide-character code.

```
#include <wchar.h>
wchar_t *wcspbrk(const wchar_t *ws1, const wchar_t *ws2);
```

Issue 5: No functional changes in this issue.

wcsrchr( )

Wide-character string scanning operation.

```
#include <wchar.h>
wchar_t *wcsrchr(const wchar_t *ws, wchar_t wc);
```

Issue 5: No functional changes in this issue.

wcsrtombs( )

Convert a wide-character string to a character string (restartable).

```
#include <wchar.h>
size_t wcsrtombs(char *dst, const wchar_t **src, size_t len,
    mbstate_t *ps);
```

Issue 5: This is a new function included for alignment with the ISO/IEC 9899:1990/Amendment 1:1995 (E).

The *wcsrtombs*( ) function converts a sequence of wide-characters from the array indirectly pointed to by *src* into a sequence of corresponding characters, beginning in the conversion state described by the object pointed to by *ps*.

wcsspn( )

Get the length of a wide substring.

```
#include <wchar.h>
size_t wcsspn(const wchar_t *ws1, const wchar_t *ws2);
```

Issue 5: The Return Value section is updated to indicate that *wcsspn*( ) returns the length of *ws1* rather that *ws1* itself.

wcsstr( )

Find a wide-character substring.

```
#include <wchar.h>
wchar_t *wcsstr(const wchar_t *ws1, const wchar_t *ws2);
```

Issue 5: This is a new function included for alignment with the ISO/IEC 9899:1990/Amendment 1:1995 (E).

The *wcsstr*( ) function locates the first occurrence in the wide-character string pointed to by *ws1* of the sequence of wide-characters (excluding the terminating null wide-character) in the wide-character string pointed to by *ws2*.

In an earlier draft of the ISO/IEC 9899:1990/Amendment 1:1995 (E) the *wcsstr*( ) function was named *wcswcs*( ). Applications using *wcswcs*( ) should be rewritten to use *wcsstr*( ).

wcstod( )

Convert a wide-character string to a double-precision number.

```
#include <wchar.h>

double wcstod(const wchar_t *nptr, wchar_t **endptr);
```

Issue 5: The Description is updated to indicate that *errno* will not be changed if the function is successful.

wcstok( )

Split a wide-character string into tokens.

```
#include <wchar.h>

wchar_t *wcstok(wchar_t *ws1, const wchar_t *ws2, wchar_t **ptr);
```

Issue 5: Aligned with the ISO/IEC 9899:1990/Amendment 1:1995 (E). Specifically, a third argument is added to the definition of this function in the Synopsis.

wcstol( )

Convert a wide-character string to a long integer.

```
#include <wchar.h>

long int wcstol(const wchar_t *nptr, wchar_t **endptr, int base);
```

Issue 5: The Description is updated to indicate that *errno* will not be changed if the function is successful.

wcstombs( )

Convert a wide-character string to a character string.

```
#include <stdlib.h>

size_t wcstombs(char *s, const wchar_t *pwcs, size_t n);
```

Issue 5: No functional changes in this issue.

wcstoul( )

Convert a wide-character string to an unsigned long.

```
#include <wchar.h>

unsigned long int wcstoul(const wchar_t *nptr, wchar_t **endptr,
      int base);
```

Issue 5: The Description is updated to indicate that *errno* will not be changed if the function is successful.

wcswcs( )

Find a wide substring.

```
#include <wchar.h>
```

```
wchar_t *wcswcs(const wchar_t *ws1, const wchar_t *ws2);
```

Issue 5: Marked as EX.

wcswidth( )

Number of column positions of a wide-character string.

```
#include <wchar.h>
```

```
int wcswidth(const wchar_t *pwcs, size_t n);
```

Issue 5: No functional changes in this issue.

wcsxfrm( )

Wide-character string transformation.

```
#include <wchar.h>
```

```
size_t wcsxfrm(wchar_t *ws1, const wchar_t *ws2, size_t n);
```

Issue 5: The Description is updated to indicate that *errno* will not be changed if the function is successful.

wctob( )

Wide-character to single-byte conversion.

```
#include <stdio.h>
#include <wchar.h>
```

```
int wctob(wint_t c);
```

Issue 5: This is a new function included for alignment with the ISO/IEC 9899:1990/Amendment 1:1995 (E).

The *wctob*( ) function determines whether *c* corresponds to a member of the extended character set whose character representation is a single byte when in the initial shift state.

wctomb( )

Convert a wide-character code to a character.

```
#include <stdlib.h>
```

```
int wctomb(char *s, wchar_t wchar);
```

Issue 5: No functional changes in this issue.

wctrans()

Define character mapping.

```
#include <wctype.h>

wctrans_t wctrans(const char *charclass);
```

Issue 5: This is a new function derived from the ISO/IEC 9899:1990/Amendment 1:1995 (E).

The *wctrans*() function is defined for valid character mapping names identified in the current locale.

wctype()

Define character class.

```
#include <wctype.h>

wctype_t wctype(const char *property);
```

Issue 5: The following change has been made in this issue for alignment with ISO/IEC 9899:1990/Amendment 1:1995 (E):

The Synopsis has been changed to indicate that this function and associated data types are now made visible by inclusion of the header **<wctype.h>** rather than **<wchar.h>**.

wcwidth()

Number of column positions of a wide-character code.

```
#include <wchar.h>

int wcwidth(wchar_t wc);
```

Issue 5: No functional changes in this issue.

wmemchr()

Find a wide character in memory.

```
#include <wchar.h>

wchar_t *wmemchr(const wchar_t *ws, wchar_t wc, size_t n);
```

Issue 5: This is a new function included for alignment with the ISO/IEC 9899:1990/Amendment 1:1995 (E).

The *wmemchr*() function locates the first occurrence of *wc* in the initial *n* wide characters of the object pointed to be *ws*.

wmemcmp()

Compare wide characters in memory.

```
#include <wchar.h>

int wmemcmp(const wchar_t *ws1, const wchar_t *ws2, size_t n);
```

Issue 5: This is a new function included for alignment with the ISO/IEC 9899:1990/Amendment 1:1995 (E).

The *wmemcmp*( ) function compares the first *n* wide-characters of the object pointed to by *ws1* to the first *n* wide-characters of the object pointed to by *ws2*.

wmemcpy( )

Copy wide characters in memory.

```
#include <wchar.h>
```

```
wchar_t *wmemcpy(wchar_t *ws1, const wchar_t *ws2, size_t n);
```

Issue 5: This is a new function included for alignment with the ISO/IEC 9899:1990/Amendment 1:1995 (E).

The *wmemcpy*( ) function copies *n* wide characters from the object pointed to by *ws2* to the object pointed to by *ws1*.

wmemmove( )

Copy wide-characters in memory with overlapping areas.

```
#include <wchar.h>
```

```
wchar_t *wmemmove(wchar_t *ws1, const wchar_t *ws2, size_t n);
```

Issue 5: This is a new function included for alignment with the ISO/IEC 9899:1990/Amendment 1:1995 (E).

The *wmemmove*( ) function copies *n* wide characters from the object pointed to by *ws2* to the object pointed to by *ws1*.

wmemset( )

Set wide characters in memory.

```
#include <wchar.h>
```

```
wchar_t *wmemset(wchar_t *ws, wchar_t wc, size_t n);
```

Issue 5: This is a new function included for alignment with the ISO/IEC 9899:1990/Amendment 1:1995 (E).

The *wmemset*( ) function copies the value of *wc* into each of the first *n* wide characters of the object pointed to by *ws*.

wordexp( ), wordfree( )

Perform word expansions.

```
#include <wordexp.h>
```

```
int wordexp(const char *words, wordexp_t *pwordexp, int flags);
void wordfree(wordexp_t *pwordexp);
```

Issue 5: No functional changes in this issue.

wprintf( )

Print formatted wide-character output.

```
#include <stdio.h>
#include <wchar.h>

int wprintf(const wchar_t *format, ...);
```

Issue 5: Included for alignment with the ISO/IEC 9899:1990/Amendment 1:1995 (E).

This is the wide character equivalent of *printf*( ).

write( ), writev( ), pwrite( )

Write on a file.

```
#include <unistd.h>

ssize_t write(int fildes, const void *buf, size_t nbyte);
ssize_t pwrite(int fildes, const void *buf, size_t nbyte,
    off_t offset);

#include <sys/uio.h>

ssize_t writev(int fildes, const struct iovec *iov, int iovcnt);
```

Issue 5: The Description is updated for alignment with the POSIX Realtime Extension and the POSIX Threads Extension.

Large File Support extensions are added, see Chapter 15 on page 147.

The *pwrite*( ) function is added.

wscanf( )

Convert formatted wide-character input.

```
#include <stdio.h>
#include <wchar.h>

int wscanf(const wchar_t *format, ... );
```

Issue 5: This is a new function included for alignment with the ISO/IEC 9899:1990/Amendment 1:1995 (E).

This is the wide character equivalent of *scanf*( ).

y0( ), y1( ), yn( )

Bessel functions of the second kind.

```
#include <math.h>

double y0(double x);
double y1 (double x);
double yn (int n, double x);
```

Issue 5: No functional changes in this issue.

Chapter 21

Headers

21.1 Header and Name Space Rules

XSH, Issue 5 specifies headers from a number of formal standards and specifications, and must handle the name space issues carefully. Each specification builds on its predecessors. The Single UNIX Specification, Version 2 includes everything from POSIX.1 (including, the POSIX Realtime Extension and the POSIX Threads Extension), POSIX.2, the ISO C standard (including ISO/IEC 9899:1990/Amendment 1:1995 (E)), and additionally the X/Open UNIX Extensions.

21.1.1 ISO C Headers

The ISO C standard describes general rules for implementations *versus* applications with respect to headers and name space.

Headers:

1. Headers need not be regular text files and the characters between the < and > need not name a source file.
2. Headers should be self-sufficient such that any standard header does not need any other standard header to be included using **#include** before or after it (and thus headers can be included in any order).
3. Headers should be idempotent, such that any standard header can be included any number of times without causing problems.
4. Headers can provide macro versions of functions which should behave in a semantically identical fashion. By undefining such a macro, a regular declaration of the function is made visible.
5. Headers can assume that they are included outside of any file scope declaration or definition.
6. Headers can assume that they are included prior to the first use of its functions, objects, or macros.

With the exception of **<assert.h>**, the ISO C standard headers are both self-sufficient and idempotent.

The ISO C standard specifies the rules for its 15 standard headers. Items 2. through 6. listed above for headers are requirements for these.

<assert.h>	**<float.h>**	**<math.h>**	**<stdarg.h>**	**<stdlib.h>**
<ctype.h>	**<limits.h>**	**<setjmp.h>**	**<stddef.h>**	**<string.h>**
<errno.h>	**<locale.h>**	**<signal.h>**	**<stdio.h>**	**<time.h>**

The ISO/IEC 9899:1990/Amendment 1:1995 (E) adds 3 additional headers:

<iso646.h>
<wchar.h>
<wctype.h>

A compilation system can provide more headers, but a strictly conforming ISO C standard program can only use these.

Name space:

1. _[_A-Z][0-9a-z_A-Z]* are reserved for implementation use anywhere.
2. _[0-9a-z_A-Z]* are reserved for implementation use as identifiers with external linkage and in any header as a tag or an ordinary identifier with file scope.

21.1.2 POSIX.1 and POSIX.2 Headers

Other standards disagree slightly regarding the contents of some of these headers. For example, POSIX.1 specifies that *fdopen*() is declared in **<stdio.h>**. To allow these two standards to coexist, POSIX.1 requires that the macro _POSIX_SOURCE or _POSIX_C_SOURCE be defined using **#define** before a standard header is included. The POSIX-specific names are then declared and no others are permitted by POSIX.

POSIX.1 specifies general rules for name space control through *feature test macros.*

1. Feature test macros have names that match _[_A-Z][0-9a-z_A-Z]*. (Thus, the use of such names takes advantage of the loophole left in the ISO C standard.) They almost always match _[A-Z]+_SOURCE. The original feature test macro for the 1990 revision of POSIX.1 is _POSIX_SOURCE. The 1996 revision of POSIX.1 introduces a more powerful feature test macro called _POSIX_C_SOURCE, which allows you to specify the revision of POSIX to which your application conforms. The value of _POSIX_C_SOURCE which corresponds to the functionality contained in the Single UNIX Specification, Version 2 is 199506L.
2. If the feature test macro associated with a particular header is defined prior to its inclusion, the header must obey the name space rules of the matching specification.
3. If such a header is included without the feature test macro being defined, it has no restrictions (at least with respect to the associated specification).

POSIX.1 specifies general rules for its headers:

1. [a-z_A-Z][0-9a-z_A-Z]*_t are reserved for all POSIX.1 headers. It is unclear whether this reservation is intended to be in effect for those headers that are covered by the ISO C standard. This makes the assumption that it does apply.
2. Each function must be declared with a prototype in at least one header (ISO C standard implementations).
3. The default location for this declaration is **<unistd.h>**.

POSIX.1 specifies the rules for its 18 standard headers and subsumes the 15 headers from the ISO C standard, giving additional rules to 6 of them.

<aio.h>	**<pthread.h>**	**<sys/stat.h>**	**<termios.h>**
<dirent.h>	**<pwd.h>**	**<sys/times.h>**	**<unistd.h>**
<fcntl.h>	**<sched.h>**	**<sys/types.h>**	**<utime.h>**
<grp.h>	**<semaphore.h>**	**<sys/utsname.h>**	
<mqueue.h>	**<sys/mman.h>**	**<sys/wait.h>**	

The 6 modified ISO C standard headers are:

<errno.h>
<limits.h>
<setjmp.h>
<signal.h>
<stdio.h>
<time.h>

The POSIX.2 C language binding adds 2 headers:

<glob.h>
<wordexp.h>

21.1.3 X/Open UNIX Headers

The Single UNIX Specification subsumes the formal standards and adds the following headers:

<cpio.h>	**<ndbm.h>**	**<sys/ipc.h>**	**<sys/un.h>**
<fmtmsg.h>	**<nl_types.h>**	**<sys/msg.h>**	**<syslog.h>**
<fnmatch.h>	**<poll.h>**	**<sys/resource.h>**	**<tar.h>**
<ftw.h>	**<re_comp.h>**	**<sys/sem.h>**	**<ucontext.h>**
<iconv.h>	**<regex.h>**	**<sys/shm.h>**	**<ulimit.h>**
<inttypes.h>	**<regexp.h>**	**<sys/statvfs.h>**	**<utmpx.h>**
<langinfo.h>	**<search.h>**	**<sys/time.h>**	**<varargs.h>**
<libgen.h>	**<strings.h>**	**<sys/timeb.h>**	
<monetary.h>	**<stropts.h>**	**<sys/uio.h>**	

A feature test macro named _XOPEN_SOURCE provides for all the X/Open extensions to the ISO C standard, in a similar way to the _POSIX_SOURCE macro. For conformance to the Single UNIX Specification, Version 2, _XOPEN_SOURCE should be set to the value 500. The definition of _XOPEN_SOURCE subsumes the use of _POSIX_SOURCE and _POSIX_C_SOURCE, ensuring that the appropriate POSIX name space is also exposed.

21.2 Names Safe to Use

Reserved name rules are complicated and set out below in the following sections. There are, however, four fairly simple rules which, if followed, avoid collisions with any reserved names:

1. Use **#include** to include all system headers at the top of source files.
2. Do not define or declare any names that begin with an underscore.
3. Use an underscore or a capital letter somewhere within the first few characters of all file scope tags and regular names.

   Note: Beware of the **va_** prefix found in **stdarg.h**.
4. Use a digit or a non-capital letter somewhere within the first few characters of all macro names.

Note: Almost all names beginning with an E are reserved if **<errno.h>** is included.

Most implementations continue to add names to the standard headers. The _POSIX_SOURCE, _POSIX_C_SOURCE, and _XOPEN_SOURCE macros can be used to remove the added declarations, so that a predictable standard name space is visible.

21.2.1 ISO C Reserved Names

The ISO C standard reserves all names that match the following patterns. These are reserved for implementations and future standards:

<errno.h> `E[0-9A-Z].*`
<ctype.h> `(to|is)[a-z].*`
<locale.h> `LC_[A-Z].*`
<math.h> Existing function names suffixed with *f* or *l*.
<signal.h> `(SIG|SIG_)[A-Z].*`
<stdlib.h> `str[a-z].*`
<string.h> `(str|mem|wcs)[a-z].*`

Names that begin with a capital letter are macros and are thus reserved only when the associated header is included. The rest of the names designate functions and therefore cannot be used to name global objects or functions.

21.2.2 X/Open Reserved Names

When _XOPEN_SOURCE is defined, each header defines or declares some identifiers, potentially conflicting with identifiers used by the application. The set of identifiers visible to the application consists of precisely those identifiers from the header pages of the included headers, as well as additional identifiers reserved for the implementation. In addition, some headers may make visible identifiers from other headers as indicated on the relevant header pages.

If any header in the following table is included, identifiers with the prefixes, suffixes, or complete names shown are reserved for any use by the implementation.

Header	Prefix	Suffix	Complete Name
<aio.h>	aio_, lio_, AIO_, LIO_		
<dirent.h>	d_		
<errno.h>	E		
<fcntl.h>	l_		
<glob.h>	gl_		
<grp.h>	gr_		
<limits.h>		_MAX	
<locale.h>	LC_[A-Z]		
<mqueue.h>	mq_, MQ_		
<ndbm.h>	dbm_		
<poll.h>	pd_, ph_, ps_		
<pthread.h>	pthread_, PTHREAD_		
<pwd.h>	pw_		
<regex.h>	re_, rm_		
<sched.h>	sched_, SCHED_		

Header	Prefix	Suffix	Complete Name
<semaphore.h>	sem_, SEM_		
<signal.h>	sa_, SIG[A-Z], SIG_[A-Z] ss_, sv_ si_, SI_, sigev_, SIGEV_, sival_		
<stropts.h>	bi_, ic_, l_, sl_, str_		
<sys/ipc.h>	ipc_		key, pad, seq
<sys/mman.h>	shm_, MAP_, MCL_, MS_, PROT_		
<sys/msg.h>	msg		msg
<sys/resource.h>	rlim_, ru_		
<sys/sem.h>	sem		sem
<sys/shm.h>	shm		
<sys/stat.h>	st_		
<sys/statvfs.h>	f_		
<sys/time.h>	fds_, it_, tv_, FD_		
<sys/times.h>	tms_		
<sys/uio.h>	iov_		
<sys/utsname.h>	uts_		
<sys/wait.h>	si_, W[A-Z], P_		
<termios.h>	c_		
<time.h>	tm_ clock_, timer_, it_, tv_, CLOCK_, TIMER_		
<ucontext.h>	uc_		
<ulimit.h>	UL_		
<utime.h>	utim_		
<utmpx.h>	ut_	_LVL, _TIME, _PROCESS	
<wordexp.h>	we_		
ANY header		_t	

Note: The notation [A-Z] indicates any upper-case letter in the portable character set. The notation [a-z] indicates any lower-case letter in the portable character set. Commas and spaces in the lists of prefixes and complete names in the above table are not part of any prefix or complete name.

If any header in the following table is included, macros with the prefixes shown may be defined. After the last inclusion of a given header, an application may use identifiers with the corresponding prefixes for its own purpose, provided their use is preceded by an **#undef** of the corresponding macro.

Header	Prefix				
<fcntl.h>	F_	O_	S_		
<fmtmsg.h>	MM_				
<fnmatch.h>	FNM_				
<ftw.h>	FTW				
<glob.h>	GLOB_				
<ndbm.h>	DBM_				
<nl_types.h>	NL_				
<poll.h>	POLL				
<regex.h>	REG_				
<signal.h>	SA_	SIG_[0-9a-z_]			
	BUS_	CLD_	FPE_	ILL_	POLL_
	SEGV_	SI_	SS_	SV_	TRAP_
<stropts.h>	FLUSH[A-Z]	I_	M_	MUXID_R[A-Z]	
	S_	SND[A-Z]	STR		
<syslog.h>	LOG_				
<sys/ipc.h>	IPC_				
<sys/mman.h>	PROT_	MAP_	MS_		
<sys/msg.h>	MSG[A-Z]	MSG_[A-Z]			
<sys/resource.h>	PRIO_	RLIM_	RLIMIT_	RUSAGE_	
<sys/sem.h>	SEM_				
<sys/shm.h>	SHM[A-Z]	SHM_[A-Z]			
<sys/socket.h>	AF_	MSG_	PF_	SO	
<sys/stat.h>	S_				
<sys/statvfs.h>	ST_				
<sys/time.h>	FD_	ITIMER_			
<sys/uio.h>	IOV_				
<sys/wait.h>	BUS_	CLD_	FPE_	ILL_	POLL_
	SEGV_	SI_	TRAP_		
<termios.h>	V	I	O	TC	B[0-9]
<wordexp.h>	WRDE_				

Note: The notation [0-9] indicates any digit. The notation [A-Z] indicates any upper-case letter in the portable character set. The notation [0-9a-z_] indicates any digit, any lower-case letter in the portable character set, or underscore.

21.3 Header Migration Information

This section contains information for each header defined in XSH, Issue 5. Each section identifies changes made to the interface in Issue 5 (if any), complete with examples where appropriate. Only changes that might affect an application programmer are identified.

<aio.h>

Asynchronous input and output. (**REALTIME**)

```
#include <aio.h>
```

Issue 5: This is a new header included for alignment with the POSIX Realtime Extension.

The **<aio.h>** header defines the **aiocb** structure.

This header also includes the following constants:

AIO_CANCELED
AIO_NOTCANCELED
AIO_ALLDONE
LIO_WAIT
LIO_NOWAIT
LIO_READ
LIO_WRITE
LIO_NOP

This header includes declarations for the following functions: *aio_cancel*( ), *aio_error*( ), *aio_fsync*( ), *aio_read*( ), *aio_return*( ), *aio_suspend*( ), *aio_write*( ), and *lio_listio*( ).

<assert.h>

Verify program assertion.

```
#include <assert.h>
```

Issue 5: No functional changes in this issue.

<cpio.h>

Cpio archive values.

```
#include <cpio.h>
```

Issue 5: No functional changes in this issue.

<ctype.h>

Character types.

```
#include <ctype.h>
```

Issue 5: No functional changes in this issue.

<dirent.h>

Format of directory entries.

```
#include <dirent.h>
```

Issue 5: The Description is updated for alignment with the POSIX Threads Extension. Specifically, the thread-safe function *readdir_r*( ) is added.

<dlfcn.h>

Dynamic linking.

```
#include <dlfcn.h>
```

Issue 5: The **<dlfcn.h>** header defines the following macros for use in the *dlopen*( ) mode argument:

RTLD_LAZY Relocations are performed at an implementation-dependent time.
RTLD_NOW Relocations are performed when the object is loaded.
RTLD_GLOBAL All symbols are available for relocation processing of other modules.
RTLD_LOCAL All symbols are not made available for relocation processing by other modules.

This header includes declarations for the following functions: *dlopen*( ), *dlsym*( ), *dlclose*( ), and *dlerror*( ).

<errno.h>

System error numbers.

```
#include <errno.h>
```

Issue 5: Updated for alignment with the POSIX Realtime Extension. Specifically, the following error number is added:

[ECANCELED] Operation canceled.

<fcntl.h>

File control options.

```
#include <fcntl.h>
```

Issue 5: The Description is updated for alignment with the POSIX Realtime Extension. Specifically, the following changes are made:

File status flags used for *open*( ) and *fcntl*( ) are added:

O_DSYNC Write according to synchronized I/O data integrity completion.
O_RSYNC Synchronized read I/O operations.

<float.h>

Floating types.

```
#include <float.h>
```

Issue 5: No functional changes in this issue.

<fmtmsg.h>

Message display structures.

```
#include <fmtmsg.h>
```

Issue 5: No functional changes in this issue.

<fnmatch.h>

Filename-matching types.

```
#include <fnmatch.h>
```

Issue 5: No functional changes in this issue.

<ftw.h>

File tree traversal.

```
#include <ftw.h>
```

Issue 5: A description of FTW_DP is added:

FTW_DP Directory with subdirectories visited.

<glob.h>

Pathname pattern-matching types.

```
#include <glob.h>
```

Issue 5: No functional changes in this issue.

<grp.h>

Group structure.

```
#include <grp.h>
```

Issue 5: The Description is updated for alignment with the POSIX Threads Extension. Specifically, the thread-safe functions *getgrid_r*( ) and *getgrnam_r*( ) are added.

<iconv.h>

Codeset conversion facility.

```
#include <iconv.h>
```

Issue 5: No functional changes in this issue.

<inttypes.h>

Fixed size integral types.

```
#include <inttypes.h>
```

Issue 5: The **<inttypes.h>** header is a new header in the Single UNIX Specification, Version 2, included for data size neutrality.

This header includes definitions of at least the following types:

int16_t	16-bit signed integral type.
int32_t	32-bit signed integral type.
int64_t	64-bit signed integral type.
uint16_t	16-bit unsigned integral type.
uint32_t	32-bit unsigned integral type.
uint64_t	64-bit unsigned integral type.
intptr_t	Signed integral type large enough to hold any pointer.
uintptr_t	Unsigned integral type large enough to hold any pointer.

<iso646.h>

Alternative spellings.

```
#include <iso646.h>
```

Issue 5: This is a new header derived from the ISO/IEC 9899:1990/Amendment 1:1995 (E).

The **<iso646.h>** header defines the following eleven macros (on the left) that expand to the corresponding tokens (on the right):

<table>
<tr><td>and</td><td>&&</td></tr>
<tr><td>and_eq</td><td>&=</td></tr>
<tr><td>bitand</td><td>&</td></tr>
<tr><td>bitor</td><td>|</td></tr>
<tr><td>compl</td><td>~</td></tr>
<tr><td>not</td><td>!</td></tr>
<tr><td>not_eq</td><td>!=</td></tr>
<tr><td>or</td><td>||</td></tr>
<tr><td>or_eq</td><td>|=</td></tr>
<tr><td>xor</td><td>^</td></tr>
<tr><td>xor_eq</td><td>^=</td></tr>
</table>

<langinfo.h>

Language information constants.

```
#include <langinfo.h>
```

Issue 5: The constants YESSTR and NOSTR are marked LEGACY.

<libgen.h>

Definitions for pattern matching functions.

```
#include <libgen.h>
```

Issue 5: The function prototypes for *basename*( ) and *dirname*( ) are changed to indicate that the first argument is of type **char*** rather than **const char***.

<limits.h>

Implementation-dependent constants.

```
#include <limits.h>
```

Issue 5: The Description is updated for alignment with the POSIX Realtime Extension and the POSIX Threads Extension. Specifically, the following changes are made:

New **Run-time Invariant Values** are added.

AIO_LISTIO_MAX
AIO_MAX
AIO_PRIO_DELTA_MAX
DELAYTIMER_MAX
LOGIN_NAME_MAX
MQ_OPEN_MAX
MQ_PRIO_MAX
PTHREAD_DESTRUCTOR_ITERATIONS
PTHREAD_KEYS_MAX
PTHREAD_STACK_MIN
PTHREAD_THREADS_MAX
RTSIG_MAX
SEM_NSEMS_MAX
SEM_VALUE_MAX
SIGQUEUE_MAX
TIMER_MAX
TTY_NAME_MAX

New **Pathname Variable Values** are added:

FILESIZEBITS

FILESIZEBITS is a Large File Support extension.

A new **Maximum Value** is added:

_POSIX_CLOCKRES_MIN

New **Minimum Values** are added:

_POSIX_AIO_LISTIO_MAX
_POSIX_AIO_MAX
_POSIX_DELAYTIMER_MAX
_POSIX_MQ_OPEN_MAX
_POSIX_MQ_PRIO_MAX
_POSIX_RTSIG_MAX
_POSIX_SEM_NSEMS_MAX
_POSIX_SEM_VALUE_MAX
_POSIX_SIGQUEUE_MAX
_POSIX_THREAD_DESTRUCTOR_ITERATIONS
_POSIX_THREAD_KEYS_MAX
_POSIX_THREAD_THREADS_MAX
_POSIX_TIMER_MAX
_POSIX_TTY_NAME_MAX

The minimum acceptable values for INT_MAX, INT_MIN, and UINT_MAX are changed to make 32-bit values the minimum requirement.

<locale.h>

Category macros.

```
#include <locale.h>
```

Issue 5: No functional changes in this issue.

<math.h>

Mathematical declarations.

```
#include <math.h>
```

Issue 5: No functional changes in this issue.

<monetary.h>

Monetary types.

```
#include <monetary.h>
```

Issue 5: No functional changes in this issue.

<mqueue.h>

Message queues. (**REALTIME**)

```
#include <mqueue.h>
```

Issue 5: This is a new header included for alignment with the POSIX Realtime Extension.

The **<mqueue.h>** header defines the **mqd_t** type.

The **<mqueue.h>** header defines the **sigevent** structure (as described in **<signal.h>**) and the **mq_attr** structure.

This header includes declarations for the following functions: *mq_close*( ), *mq_getattr*( ), *mq_notify*( ), *mq_open*( ), *mq_receive*( ), *mq_send*( ), *mq_setattr*( ), and *mq_unlink*( ).

<ndbm.h>

Definitions for ndbm database operations.

```
#include <ndbm.h>
```

Issue 5: No functional changes are made, although explicit references to the definitions of **size_t** and **mode_t** are added to the Description.

<nl_types.h>

Data types.

```
#include <nl_types.h>
```

Issue 5: No functional changes in this issue.

<poll.h>

Definitions for the poll( ) function.

```
#include <poll.h>
```

Issue 5: No functional changes are made, although the definition of POLLIN is reworded:

POLLIN Same effect as POLLRDNORM | POLLRDBAND.

<pthread.h>

Threads.

```
#include <pthread.h>
```

Issue 5: This is a new header included for alignment with the POSIX Threads Extension.

The **<pthread.h>** header defines the following symbols:

PTHREAD_CANCEL_ASYNCHRONOUS
PTHREAD_CANCEL_ENABLE
PTHREAD_CANCEL_DEFERRED
PTHREAD_CANCEL_DISABLE
PTHREAD_CANCELED
PTHREAD_COND_INITIALIZER
PTHREAD_CREATE_DETACHED
PTHREAD_CREATE_JOINABLE
PTHREAD_EXPLICIT_SCHED
PTHREAD_INHERIT_SCHED
PTHREAD_MUTEX_DEFAULT
PTHREAD_MUTEX_ERRORCHECK
PTHREAD_MUTEX_NORMAL
PTHREAD_MUTEX_INITIALIZER
PTHREAD_MUTEX_RECURSIVE
PTHREAD_ONCE_INIT
PTHREAD_PRIO_INHERIT
PTHREAD_PRIO_NONE
PTHREAD_PRIO_PROTECT
PTHREAD_PROCESS_SHARED
PTHREAD_PROCESS_PRIVATE
PTHREAD_RWLOCK_INITIALIZER
PTHREAD_SCOPE_PROCESS

PTHREAD_SCOPE_SYSTEM

The **pthread_attr_t**, **pthread_cond_t**, **pthread_condattr_t**, **pthread_key_t**, **pthread_mutex_t**, **pthread_mutexattr_t**, **pthread_once_t**, **pthread_rwlock_t**, **pthread_rwlockattr_t**, and **pthread_t** types are defined as described in **<sys/types.h>**.

This header includes declarations for the following functions:

pthread_attr_destroy( )
pthread_attr_getdetachstate( )
pthread_attr_getguardsize( )
pthread_attr_getinheritsched( )
pthread_attr_getschedparam( )
pthread_attr_getschedpolicy( )
pthread_attr_getscope( )
pthread_attr_getstackaddr( )
pthread_attr_getstacksize( )
pthread_attr_init( )
pthread_attr_setdetachstate( )
pthread_attr_setguardsize( )
pthread_attr_setinheritsched( )
pthread_attr_setschedparam( )
pthread_attr_setschedpolicy( )
pthread_attr_setscope( )
pthread_attr_setstackaddr( )
pthread_attr_setstacksize( )
pthread_cancel( )
pthread_cleanup_push( )
pthread_cleanup_pop( )
pthread_cond_broadcast( )
pthread_cond_destroy( )
pthread_cond_init( )
pthread_cond_signal( )
pthread_cond_timedwait( )
pthread_cond_wait( )
pthread_condattr_destroy( )
pthread_condattr_getpshared( )
pthread_condattr_init( )
pthread_condattr_setpshared( )
pthread_create( )
pthread_detach( )
pthread_equal( )
pthread_exit( )
pthread_getconcurrency( )
pthread_getschedparam( )
pthread_getspecific( )
pthread_join( )
pthread_key_create( )
pthread_key_delete( )
pthread_mutex_destroy( )
pthread_mutex_getprioceiling( )
pthread_mutex_init( )
pthread_mutex_lock( )

pthread_mutex_setprioceiling( )
pthread_mutex_trylock( )
pthread_mutex_unlock( )
pthread_mutexattr_destroy( )
pthread_mutexattr_getprioceiling( )
pthread_mutexattr_getprotocol( )
pthread_mutexattr_getpshared( )
pthread_mutexattr_gettype( )
pthread_mutexattr_init( )
pthread_mutexattr_setprioceiling( )
pthread_mutexattr_setprotocol( )
pthread_mutexattr_setpshared( )
pthread_mutexattr_settype( )
pthread_once( )
pthread_rwlock_destroy( )
pthread_rwlock_init( )
pthread_rwlock_rdlock( )
pthread_rwlock_tryrdlock( )
pthread_rwlock_trywrlock( )
pthread_rwlock_unlock( )
pthread_rwlock_wrlock( )
pthread_rwlockattr_destroy( )
pthread_rwlockattr_getpshared( )
pthread_rwlockattr_init( )
pthread_rwlockattr_setpshared( )
pthread_self( )
pthread_setcancelstate( )
pthread_setcanceltype( )
pthread_setconcurrency( )
pthread_setschedparam( )
pthread_setspecific( )
pthread_testcancel( )

<pwd.h>

Password structure.

```
#include <pwd.h>
```

Issue 5: The Description is updated for alignment with the POSIX Threads Extension. Specifically, the thread-safe functions *getpwnam_r*( ) and *getpwuid_r*( ) are added.

<regex.h>

Regular-expression-matching types.

```
#include <regex.h>
```

Issue 5: No functional changes in this issue.

<re_comp.h>

Regular-expression-matching functions for re_comp( ). **(LEGACY)**

```
#include <re_comp.h>
```

Issue 5: This header is marked LEGACY. New applications should use the *regcomp*( ), *regexec*( ), *regerror*( ), and *regfree*( ) functions, and the **<regex.h>** header, which provide full internationalized regular expression functionality compatible with the POSIX.2 and XBD, **Chapter 7**, **Regular Expressions**.

<regexp.h>

Regular-expression declarations. **(LEGACY)**

```
#include <regexp.h>
```

Issue 5: This header is marked LEGACY. New applications should use the *regcomp*( ), *regexec*( ), *regerror*( ), and *regfree*( ) functions, and the **<regex.h>** header, which provide full internationalized regular expression functionality compatible with the POSIX.2 and XBD, **Chapter 7**, **Regular Expressions**.

<sched.h>

Execution scheduling. **(REALTIME)**

```
#include <sched.h>
```

Issue 5: This is a new header included for alignment with the POSIX Realtime Extension.

The **<sched.h>** header defines the **sched_param** structure.

This header defines three standard scheduling policies indicated by the values of the following symbolic constants:

SCHED_FIFO	First in-first out (FIFO) scheduling policy.
SCHED_RR	Round robin scheduling policy.
SCHED_OTHER	Another scheduling policy.

This header includes declarations for the following functions: *sched_get_priority_max*( ), *sched_get_priority_min*( ), *sched_getparam*( ), *sched_getscheduler*( ), *sched_rr_get_interval*( ), *sched_setparam*( ), *sched_setscheduler*( ), and *sched_yield*.( )

<search.h>

Search tables.

```
#include <search.h>
```

Issue 5: No functional changes in this issue.

<semaphore.h>

Semaphores. (**REALTIME**)

```
#include <semaphore.h>
```

Issue 5: This is a new header included for alignment with the POSIX Realtime Extension.

The **<semaphore.h>** header defines the **sem_t** type.

This header includes declarations for the following functions: *sem_close*( ), *sem_destroy*( ), *sem_getvalue*( ), *sem_init*( ), *sem_open*( ), *sem_post*( ), *sem_trywait*( ), *sem_unlink*( ), and *sem_wait*( ).

<setjmp.h>

Stack environment declarations.

```
#include <setjmp.h>
```

Issue 5: No functional changes in this issue.

<signal.h>

Signals.

```
#include <signal.h>
```

Issue 5: The Description is updated for alignment with the POSIX Realtime Extension and the POSIX Threads Extension. Specifically:

The **<signal.h>** header defines the **sigevent** structure.

The **sigval** union is defined.

This header also declares the macros SIGRTMIN and SIGRTMAX.

This header includes the following new function declarations: *pthread_kill*( ), *pthread_sigmask*( ), *sigqueue*( ), *sigtimedwait*( ), *sigwaitinfo*( ), and *sigwait*( ).

The default action for SIGURG is changed from i to iii. The function prototype for *sigmask*( ) is removed.

<stdarg.h>

Handle variable argument list.

```
#include <stdarg.h>
```

```
void va_start(va_list ap, argN);
type va_arg(va_list ap, type);
void va_end(va_list ap);
```

Issue 5: No functional changes in this issue.

<stddef.h>

Standard type definitions.

```
#include <stddef.h>
```

Issue 5: No functional changes in this issue.

<stdio.h>

Standard buffered input/output.

```
#include <stdio.h>
```

Issue 5: The Description is updated for alignment with the POSIX Threads Extension. Specifically, the *flockfile*( ), *ftrylockfile*( ), *funlockfile*( ), *getc_unlocked*( ), *getchar_unlocked*( ), *putc_unlocked*( ), and *putchar_unlocked*( ) functions are added.

Large File Support extensions are added; specifically, the declarations of the *fseeko*( ) and *ftello*( ) functions.

The constant *L_cuserid* and the external variables *optarg*, *opterr*, *optind*, and *optopt* are marked as extensions and LEGACY.

The *cuserid*( ) and *getopt*( ) functions are marked LEGACY.

<stdlib.h>

Standard library definitions.

```
#include <stdlib.h>
```

Issue 5: The Description is updated for alignment with the POSIX Threads Extension. Specifically, the *rand_r*( ) function is added.

The *ttyslot*( ) and *valloc*( ) functions are marked LEGACY.

The type of the third argument to *initstate*( ) is changed from **int** to **size_t**. The type of the return value from *setstate*( ) is changed from **char** to **char***, and the type of the first argument is changed from **char*** to **const char***.

<string.h>

String operations.

```
#include <string.h>
```

Issue 5: The Description is updated for alignment with the POSIX Threads Extension. Specifically, the *strtok_r*( ) function is added.

<strings.h>

String operations.

```
#include <strings.h>
```

Issue 5: No functional changes in this issue.

<stropts.h>

STREAMS interface.

```
#include <stropts.h>
```

Issue 5: The *flags* member of the **strpeek** and **strfdinsert** structures is changed from type **long** to type **t_uscalar_t**.

<syslog.h>

Definitions for system error logging.

```
#include <syslog.h>
```

Issue 5: No functional changes in this issue.

<sys/ipc.h>

Interprocess communication access structure.

```
#include <sys/ipc.h>
```

Issue 5: No functional changes in this issue.

<sys/mman.h>

Memory management declarations.

```
#include <sys/mman.h>
```

Issue 5: Updated for alignment with the POSIX Realtime Extension; specifically:

The following symbolic constants are defined for the *mlockall*( ) function:

MCL_CURRENT	Lock currently mapped pages.
MCL_FUTURE	Lock pages that become mapped.

The symbolic constant MAP_FAILED is defined to indicate a failure from the *mmap*( ) function.

This header includes new declarations for the following functions: *mlock*( ), *mlockall*( ), *munlock*( ), *munlockall*( ), *shm_open*( ), and *shm_unlink*( ).

<sys/msg.h>

Message queue structures.

```
#include <sys/msg.h>
```

Issue 5: No functional changes in this issue.

<sys/resource.h>

Definitions for XSI resource operations.

```
#include <sys/resource.h>
```

Issue 5: Large File Support extensions are added. Specifically, the following changes are made:

New symbolic constants are defined:

RLIM_SAVED_MAX A value of type **rlim_t** indicating an unrepresentable saved

	hard limit.
RLIM_SAVED_CUR	A value of type **rlim_t** indicating an unrepresentable saved soft limit.

On implementations where all resource limits are representable in an object of type **rlim_t**, RLIM_SAVED_MAX and RLIM_SAVED_CUR need not be distinct from RLIM_INFINITY.

<sys/sem.h>

Semaphore facility.

```
#include <sys/sem.h>
```

Issue 5: No functional changes in this issue.

<sys/shm.h>

Shared memory facility.

```
#include <sys/shm.h>
```

Issue 5: The element of *shm_segsz* specifies the size of a memory segment. This has been changed for data size neutrality. The type of *shm_segsz* is changed from **int** to **size_t**.

<sys/stat.h>

Data returned by the stat( ) function.

```
#include <sys/stat.h>
```

Issue 5: The Description is updated for alignment with the POSIX Realtime Extension. Specifically, the following macros are added:

S_TYPEISMQ (*buf*)	Test for a message queue.
S_TYPEISSEM (*buf*)	Test for a semaphore.
S_TYPEISSHM (*buf*)	Test for a shared memory object.

The following Large File Support extension is made:

The type of *st_blksize* is changed from **long** to **blksize_t**; the type of *st_blocks* is changed from **long** to **blkcnt_t**.

<sys/statvfs.h>

VFS Filesystem information structure.

```
#include <sys/statvfs.h>
```

Issue 5: The following Large File Support extension is made:

The type of *f_blocks*, *f_bfree*, and *f_bavail* is changed from **unsigned long** to **fsblkcnt_t;** the type of *f_files*, *f_ffree*, and *f_favail* is changed from **unsigned long** to **fsfilcnt_t**.

<sys/time.h>

Time types.

```
#include <sys/time.h>
```

Issue 5: The type of *tv_usec* is changed from **long** to **suseconds_t**, which is a signed arithmetic type used for time in microseconds.

<sys/timeb.h>

Additional definitions for date and time.

```
#include <sys/timeb.h>
```

Issue 5: No functional changes in this issue.

<sys/times.h>

File access and modification times structure.

```
#include <sys/times.h>
```

Issue 5: No functional changes in this issue.

<sys/types.h>

Data types.

```
#include <sys/types.h>
```

Issue 5: The **clockid_t** and **timer_t** types are defined for alignment with the POSIX Realtime Extension.

Large File Support extensions are added; specifically, the types **blkcnt_t**, **blksize_t**, **fsblkcnt_t**, **fsfilcnt_t**, and **suseconds_t** are added.

Updated for alignment with the POSIX Threads Extension and the X/Open Threads Extension. Specifically, the **pthread_attr_t**, **pthread_cond_t**, **pthread_condattr_t**, **pthread_key_t**, **pthread_mutex_t**, **pthread_mutexattr_t**, **pthread_once_t**, **pthread_rwlock_t**, **pthread_rwlockattr_t** , and **pthread_t** types are added.

<sys/uio.h>

Definitions for vector I/O operations.

```
#include <sys/uio.h>
```

Issue 5: No functional changes in this issue.

<sys/utsname.h>

System name structure.

```
#include <sys/utsname.h>
```

Issue 5: No functional changes in this issue.

<sys/wait.h>

Declarations for waiting.

```
#include <sys/wait.h>
```

Issue 5: No functional changes in this issue.

<tar.h>

Extended tar definitions.

```
#include <tar.h>
```

Issue 5: No functional changes in this issue.

<termios.h>

Define values for termios.

```
#include <termios.h>
```

Issue 5: No functional changes in this issue.

<time.h>

Time types.

```
#include <time.h>
```

Issue 5: The Description is updated for alignment with the POSIX Realtime Extension and the POSIX Threads Extension. Specifically, the following changes are made:

The **<time.h>** header declares the structure **timespec**.

This header also declares the **itimerspec** structure.

The following constants are defined:

CLOCK_REALTIME	The identifier of the system-wide realtime clock.
TIMER_ABSTIME	Flag indicating time is absolute with respect to the clock associated with a timer.

The following new function declarations are added: *asctime_r*( ), *clock_getres*( ), *clock_gettime*( ), *clock_settime*( ), *ctime_r*( ), *gmtime_r*( ), *localtime_r*( ), *nanosleep*( ), *timer_create*( ), *timer_delete*( ), *timer_gettime*( ), *timer_getoverrun*( ), and *timer_settime*( ).

<ucontext.h>

User context.

```
#include <ucontext.h>
```

Issue 5: No functional changes in this issue.

<ulimit.h>

Ulimit commands.

```
#include <ulimit.h>
```

Issue 5: No functional changes in this issue.

<unistd.h>

Standard symbolic constants and types.

```
#include <unistd.h>
```

Issue 5: The Description is updated for alignment with the POSIX Realtime Extension and the POSIX Threads Extension.

The following symbolic constants are always defined to unspecified values to indicate that this functionality from the POSIX Threads Extension is always present on XSI-conformant systems:

_POSIX_THREADS
_POSIX_THREAD_ATTR_STACKADDR
_POSIX_THREAD_ATTR_STACKSIZE
_POSIX_THREAD_PROCESS_SHARED
_POSIX_THREAD_SAFE_FUNCTIONS

The symbolic constants _XOPEN_REALTIME and _XOPEN_REALTIME_THREADS are added. _POSIX2_C_BIND, _XOPEN_ENH_I18N and _XOPEN_SHM must now be set to a value other than −1 by a conforming implementation.

If _XOPEN_REALTIME is defined to have a value other than −1, then the following symbolic constants will be defined to an unspecified value to indicate that the features are supported:

_POSIX_ASYNCHRONOUS_IO
_POSIX_MEMLOCK
_POSIX_MEMLOCK_RANGE
_POSIX_MESSAGE_PASSING
_POSIX_PRIORITY_SCHEDULING
_POSIX_REALTIME_SIGNALS
_POSIX_SEMAPHORES
_POSIX_SHARED_MEMORY_OBJECTS
_POSIX_SYNCHRONIZED_IO
_POSIX_TIMERS

The following symbolic constants are always defined to unspecified values to indicate that the functionality is always present on XSI-conformant systems:

_POSIX_FSYNC
_POSIX_MAPPED_FILES
_POSIX_MEMORY_PROTECTION

The following symbolic constant will be defined if the option is supported; otherwise, it will be undefined:

_POSIX_PRIORITIZED_IO

If _XOPEN_REALTIME_THREADS is defined to have a value other than −1, then the following symbolic constants will be defined to an unspecified value to indicate that the features are supported:

_POSIX_THREAD_PRIORITY_SCHEDULING
_POSIX_THREAD_PRIO_INHERIT
_POSIX_THREAD_PRIO_PROTECT

Large File Support extensions added.

The type of the argument to *sbrk*( ) is changed from **int** to **intptr_t**.

XBS constants are added to the list of Constants for Options and Feature Groups, to the list of constants for the *confstr*( ) function, and to the list of constants to the *sysconf*( ) function. These are to support the different programming models:

_XBS5_ILP32_OFF32
_XBS5_ILP32_OFFBIG
_XBS5_LP64_OFF64
_XBS5_LPBIG_OFFBIG

The following new symbolic constants are defined for the *confstr*( ) function:

_CS_XBS5_ILP32_OFF32_CFLAGS
_CS_XBS5_ILP32_OFF32_LDFLAGS
_CS_XBS5_ILP32_OFF32_LIBS
_CS_XBS5_ILP32_OFF32_LINTFLAGS
_CS_XBS5_ILP32_OFFBIG_CFLAGS
_CS_XBS5_ILP32_OFFBIG_LDFLAGS
_CS_XBS5_ILP32_OFFBIG_LIBS
_CS_XBS5_ILP32_OFFBIG_LINTFLAGS
_CS_XBS5_LP64_OFF64_CFLAGS
_CS_XBS5_LP64_OFF64_LDFLAGS
_CS_XBS5_LP64_OFF64_LIBS
_CS_XBS5_LP64_OFF64_LINTFLAGS
_CS_XBS5_LPBIG_OFFBIG_CFLAGS
_CS_XBS5_LPBIG_OFFBIG_LDFLAGS
_CS_XBS5_LPBIG_OFFBIG_LIBS
_CS_XBS5_LPBIG_OFFBIG_LINTFLAGS

The following new symbolic constants are defined for the *sysconf*( ) function:

_SC_AIO_LISTIO_MAX
_SC_AIO_MAX
_SC_AIO_PRIO_DELTA_MAX
_SC_ASYNCHRONOUS_IO
_SC_DELAYTIMER_MAX
_SC_FSYNC
_SC_GETGR_R_SIZE_MAX
_SC_GETPW_R_SIZE_MAX
_SC_MAPPED_FILES
_SC_MEMLOCK
_SC_MEMLOCK_RANGE
_SC_MEMORY_PROTECTION
_SC_MESSAGE_PASSING
_SC_MQ_OPEN_MAX

_SC_MQ_PRIO_MAX
_SC_PRIORITIZED_IO
_SC_PRIORITY_SCHEDULING
_SC_REALTIME_SIGNALS
_SC_RTSIG_MAX
_SC_SEMAPHORES
_SC_SEM_NSEMS_MAX
_SC_SEM_VALUE_MAX
_SC_SHARED_MEMORY_OBJECTS
_SC_SIGQUEUE_MAX
_SC_SYNCHRONIZED_IO
_SC_THREADS
_SC_THREAD_ATTR_STACKADDR
_SC_THREAD_ATTR_STACKSIZE
_SC_THREAD_DESTRUCTOR_ITERATIONS
_SC_THREAD_KEYS_MAX
_SC_THREAD_PRIORITY_SCHEDULING
_SC_THREAD_PRIO_INHERIT
_SC_THREAD_PRIO_PROTECT
_SC_THREAD_PROCESS_SHARED
_SC_THREAD_SAFE_FUNCTIONS
_SC_THREAD_STACK_MIN
_SC_THREAD_THREADS_MAX
_SC_TIMERS
_SC_TIMER_MAX
_SC_XBS5_ILP32_OFF32
_SC_XBS5_ILP32_OFFBIG
_SC_XBS5_LP64_OFF64
_SC_XBS5_LPBIG_OFFBIG

The following new symbolic constants are defined for the *pathconf*( ) and *fpathconf*( ) functions:

_PC_ASYNCH_IO
_PC_SYNC_IO
_PC_PRIO_IO

The following new function declarations are added to this header: *getlogin_r*( ) *pread*( ), *pthread_atfork*( ), *pwrite*( ), and *ttyname_r*( ).

<utime.h>

Access and modification times structure.

```
#include <utime.h>
```

Issue 5: No functional changes in this issue.

<utmpx.h>

User accounting database definitions.

```
#include <utmpx.h>
```

Issue 5: No functional changes in this issue.

<varargs.h>

Handle variable argument list. (**LEGACY**)

```
#include <varargs.h>
```

```
va_alist
va_dcl
void va_start(pvar)
va_list pvar;
type va_arg(pvar, type)
va_list pvar;
void va_end(pvar)
va_list pvar;
```

Issue 5: This header is marked LEGACY. New applications should use **<stdarg.h>**.

<wchar.h>

Wide-character types.

```
#include <wchar.h>
```

Issue 5: Aligned with the ISO/IEC 9899:1990/Amendment 1:1995 (E). Specifically, the prototypes for *putwc*( ), *wcsftime*( ), and *wcstok*( ) have been changed in this issue.

The *wcswcs*( ) function has been marked as an Extension. New applications should use the *wcsstr*( ) function instead.

<wctype.h>

Wide-character classification and mapping utilities.

```
#include <wctype.h>
```

Issue 5: This header is a new header derived from the ISO/IEC 9899:1990/Amendment 1:1995 (E).

The **<wctype.h>** header defines the following data types through **typedef**:

wint_t As described in **<wchar.h>**.

wctrans_t A scalar type that can hold values which represent locale-specific character mappings.

wctype_t As described in **<wchar.h>**.

This header includes declarations for the following functions: *iswalnum*( ), *iswalpha*( ), *iswcntrl*( ), *iswdigit*( ), *iswgraph*( ), *iswlower*( ), *iswprint*( ), *iswpunct*( ), *iswspace*( ), *iswupper*( ), *iswxdigit*( ), *iswctype*( ), *towctrans*( ), *towlower*( ), *towupper*( ), *wctrans*( ), and *wctype*( ).

<wordexp.h>

Word-expansion types.

```
#include <wordexp.h>
```

Issue 5: No functional changes in this issue.

Chapter 22

Utilities

22.1 Introduction

This chapter contains migration information for the XSI utilities in XCU, Issue 5. Each section lists the synopsis and identifies syntax and semantic changes made to the interface in Issue 5 (if any).

22.2 Utility Migration Information

admin

Create and administer SCCS files. (**DEVELOPMENT**)

```
admin -i[name][-n][-a login][-d flag][-f flag][-m mrlist]
[-r rel][-t[name][-y[comment]] newfile
admin -n[-a login][-d flag][-f flag][-m mrlist][-t[name]][-y[comment]]
newfile ...
admin [-a login][-d flag][-m mrlist][-r rel][-t[name]]
file ...
admin -h file ...
admin -z file ...
```

Issue 5: No functional changes in this issue.

alias

Define or display aliases.

```
alias [alias-name[=string] ...]
```

Issue 5: No functional changes in this issue.

ar

Create and maintain library archives.

```
ar -d[-v][-l] archive file ...

ar -m[-abilv][posname] archive file ...

ar -p[-v][-s]archive [file ...]

ar -q[-clv] archive file ...

ar -r[-cuv][-abil][posname]archive file ...

ar -t[-v][-s]archive [file ...]
```

`ar -x[-v][-sCT]`*archive* `[`*file* `...]`

Issue 5: A Future Directions section has been added documenting that this utility will change to align with POSIX.2b when finalized.

asa

Interpret carriage-control characters.

`asa [`*file* `...]`

Issue 5: No functional changes in this issue.

at

Execute commands at a later time.

`at [-m][-f` *file*`][-q` *queuename*`] -t` *time*

`at [-m][-f` *file*`][-q` *queuename*`]` *timespec* `...`

`at -r` *at_job_id* `...`

`at -l -q` *queuename*

`at -l [`*at_job_id* `...]`

Issue 5: No functional changes in this issue.

awk

Pattern scanning and processing language.

`awk [-F` *ERE*`][-v` *assignment*`] ...` *program* `[`*argument* `...]`

`awk [-F` *ERE*`] -v` *progfile*`] ... [-v` *assignment*`] ...[`*argument* `...]`

Issue 5: A Future Directions section has been added documenting that this utility will change to align with POSIX.2b when finalized.

basename

Return non-directory portion of a pathname.

`basename` *string* `[`*suffix*`]`

Issue 5: No functional changes in this issue.

batch

Execute commands when the system load permits.

`batch`

Issue 5: No functional changes in this issue.

bc

Arbitrary-precision arithmetic language.

`bc [-l] [file ...]`

Issue 5: A Future Directions section has been added documenting that this utility will change to align with POSIX.2b when finalized.

bg

Run jobs in the background.

`bg [job_id ...]`

Issue 5: No functional changes in this issue.

c89

Compile standard C programs.

`c89 [-c][-D name[=value]]...[-E][-g][-I directory] ... [-L directory] ... [-o outfile][-O][-s][-U name]... operand ...`

Issue 5: In the **Standard Libraries** subsection, the **–l pthread** and **–l rt** operands are added. Specifically, the changed parts of this section are:

–l pthread This operand makes visible all functions referenced in **<pthread.h>** and *pthread_atfork*( ) referenced in **<unistd.h>**.

–l rt This operand makes visible all functions referenced in **<aio.h>**, **<mqueue.h>**, **<sched.h>**, and **<semaphore.h>**, and those functions marked as POSIX Realtime Extensions in **<sys/mman.h>** and **<time.h>**.

A new section on supported programming environments is added. This is for data size neutrality and support for 64-bit environments.

All implementations will support one or more of the following programming environments. Applications should use *sysconf*( ) or *getconf* to determine which programming environments are supported.

Programming Environment *getconf* Name	Bits in int	Bits in long	Bits in pointer	Bits in off_t
XBS5_ILP32_OFF32	32	32	32	32
XBS5_ILP32_OFFBIG	32	32	32	≥64
XBS5_LP64_OFF64	32	64	64	64
XBS5_LPBIG_OFFBIG	≥32	≥64	≥64	≥64

Table 22-1 Programming Environments — Type Sizes

Implementations provide configuration strings for C compiler flags, linker/loader flags, and libraries for each supported environment. When an application needs to use a specific programming environment rather than the implementation default programming environment while compiling, the application must first verify that the implementation supports the desired environment. If the desired programming environment is supported, the application must then invoke *c89* with the appropriate C compiler flags as the first options for the compile, the appropriate linker/loader flags after any other options but before any operands, and the appropriate libraries at the end of the operands.

Portable applications must not attempt to link together object files compiled for different programming models. Applications must also be aware that binary data placed in shared memory or in files might not be recognized by applications built for other programming models.

Programming Environment *getconf* **Name**	**Use**	*c89* **and** *cc* **Arguments** *getconf* **Name**
XBS5_ILP32_OFF32	C Compiler Flags Linker/Loader Flags Libraries	XBS5_ILP32_OFF32_CFLAGS XBS5_ILP32_OFF32_LDFLAGS XBS5_ILP32_OFF32_LIBS
XBS5_ILP32_OFFBIG	C Compiler Flags Linker/Loader Flags Libraries	XBS5_ILP32_OFFBIG_CFLAGS XBS5_ILP32_OFFBIG_LDFLAGS XBS5_ILP32_OFFBIG_LIBS
XBS5_LP64_OFF64	C Compiler Flags Linker/Loader Flags Libraries	XBS5_LP64_OFF64_CFLAGS XBS5_LP64_OFF64_LDFLAGS XBS5_LP64_OFF64_LIBS
XBS5_LPBIG_OFFBIG	C Compiler Flags Linker/Loader Flags	XBS5_LPBIG_OFFBIG_CFLAGS XBS5_LPBIG_OFFBIG_LDFLAGS

Table 22-2 Programming Environments — *c89* and *cc* Arguments

cal

Print a calendar.

`cal [[`*`month`*`]`*` year `*`]`

Issue 5: No functional changes in this issue.

calendar

Reminder service. (**LEGACY**)

`calendar`

Issue 5: This utility is marked LEGACY and may not be available on all implementations. A portable application should not use the *calendar* utility.

cancel

Cancel printer requests. (**LEGACY**)

`cancel [`*`ID`*` ...] `*`printer`*` ...`

`cancel `*`ID`*` ...[`*`printer`*` ...]`

Issue 5: This utility is marked LEGACY and may not be available on all implementations. A portable application should not use the *cancel* utility.

cat

Concatenate and print files.

`cat [-u][file ...]`

Issue 5: No functional changes in this issue.

cc

A C-language compilation system. (**LEGACY**)

`cc [-c][-C][-e epsym] [-D name[=value]]... [-E][-f][-F][-g] [-I directory]... [-L directory]... [-o outfile][-O][-p][-P] [-q][-r][-s][-S][-u symname]... [-U name]... [-W options]... operand...`

Issue 5: The EXTENDED DESCRIPTION is changed to reference *c89* for standard libraries.

This utility is marked LEGACY and may not be available on all implementations. The intent of marking *cc* LEGACY is to highlight the fact that portable shell scripts should use *c89* to ensure they are using a Standard C compiler.

cd

Change the working directory.

`cd [directory]`

`cd -`

Issue 5: No functional changes in this issue.

cflow

Generate a C-language flowgraph. (**DEVELOPMENT**)

`cflow [r][-d num][-D name[=def]] ... [-i incl][-I dir] ... [-U dir] ... file ...`

Issue 5: No functional changes in this issue.

chgrp

Change the file group ownership.

`chgrp [-R] group file ...`

Issue 5: No functional changes in this issue.

chmod

Change the file modes.

`chmod [-R] mode file...`

Issue 5: No functional changes in this issue.

chown

Change the file ownership.

`chown [-R] owner[:group] file ...`

Issue 5: No functional changes in this issue.

cksum

Write file checksums and sizes.

`cksum [file ...]`

Issue 5: No functional changes in this issue.

cmp

Compare two files.

`cmp [ -l | -s ] file1 file2`

Issue 5: No functional changes in this issue.

col

Filter reverse line-feeds. **(LEGACY)**

`col [-bfpx]`

Issue 5: This utility is marked LEGACY and may not be available on all implementations. A portable application should not use the *col* utility.

comm

Select or reject lines common to two files.

`comm [-123] file1 file2`

Issue 5: No functional changes in this issue.

command

Execute a simple command.

`command [-p] command_name [argument ...]`

`command [ -v | -V ] command_name`

Issue 5: No functional changes in this issue.

compress

Compress data.

`compress [-fv][-b bits][file ...]`

`compress [-cfv][-b bits][file]`

Issue 5: No functional changes in this issue.

cp

Copy files.

```
cp [-fip] source_file target_file
cp [-fip] source_file ... target
cp -R[-fip] source_file ... target
cp -r[-fip] source_file ... target
```

Issue 5: No functional changes in this issue.

cpio

Copy file archives in and out. (**LEGACY**)

```
cpio -o[aBcv]
cpio -i[Bcdmrtuvf] [pattern ...]
cpio -p[adlmuv] directory
```

Issue 5: A note is added to the Application Usage section indicating that *cpio* will only archive files up to 8 gigabytes in size.

This utility is marked LEGACY and may not be available on all implementations. A portable application should not use the *cpio* utility, and should instead use *pax*.

crontab

Schedule periodic background work.

```
crontab [file]
crontab [ -e | -l | -r ]
```

Issue 5: No functional changes in this issue.

csplit

Split files based on context.

```
csplit [-ks][-f prefix][-n number] file arg1 ...argn
```

Issue 5: A Future Directions section has been added documenting that this utility will change to align with POSIX.2b when finalized.

ctags

Create a tags file. (**DEVELOPMENT**, **FORTRAN**)

```
ctags [-a][-f tagsfile] pathname ...
ctags -x pathname ...
```

Issue 5: A Future Directions section has been added documenting that this utility will change to align with POSIX.2b when finalized.

cu

Call another system. (**LEGACY**)

```
cu -n[-dht] [-o | -e ][-l line][-s speed]
cu [-dht] [-o | -e ][-l line][-s speed] telno
cu [-dht] [-o | -e ][-s speed] -l line
cu [-dht] [-o | -e ] systemname
```

Issue 5: This utility is marked LEGACY and may not be available on all implementations. A portable application should not use the *cu* utility.

cut

Cut out selected fields of each line of a file.

```
cut -b list [-n] [file ...]
cut -c list [file ...]
cut -f list [-d delim][-s][file ...]
```

Issue 5: No functional changes in this issue.

cxref

Generate a C-language program cross-reference table. (**DEVELOPMENT**)

```
cxref [-cs][-o file][-w num] [-D name[=def]]...[-I dir]...[-U name]...
file ...
```

Issue 5: In the Synopsis, [–**U** *dir*] is changed to [–**U** *name*]. This is a minor editorial correction.

date

Write the date and time.

```
date [-u] [+format]
date [-u] mmddhhmm[[cc]yy]
```

Issue 5: Changes are made for Year 2000 alignment. Specifically, century handling is now added and, if a century is not specified, the interpretation of year ranges is added:

mmddhhmm[[*cc*]*yy*]
: Attempt to set the system date and time from the value given in the operand. This is only possible if the user has appropriate privileges and the system permits the setting of the system date and time. The first *mm* is the month (number); *dd* is the day (number); *hh* is the hour (number, 24-hour system); the second *mm* is the minute (number); *cc* is the century and is the first two digits of the year (this is optional); *yy* is the last two digits of the year and is optional. If century is not specified, then values in the range [69-99] refer to years in the twentieth century (1969 to 1999 inclusive), and values in the range [00-68] refer to years in the twenty-first century (2000 to 2068 inclusive).

dd

Convert and copy a file.

`dd [operand ...]`

Issue 5: The second paragraph of the **cbs=** description is reworded and marked EX. This is the application of Corrigendum 1170/47 which replaced the paragraph as follows:

> "This operand must also be specified if the *conv=* operand is specified with a value of *ascii*, *ebcdic*, or *ibm*. For a *conv=* operand with an *ascii* value, the input is handled as described for the *unblock* value, except that characters are converted to ASCII before any trailing space characters are deleted. For *conv=* operands with *ebcdic* or *ibm* values, the input is handled as described for the *block* value, except that the characters are converted to EBCDIC or IBM EBCDIC, respectively, after any trailing space characters are added."

A Future Directions section has been added documenting that this utility will change to align with POSIX.2b when finalized.

delta

Make a delta (change) to an SCCS file. **(DEVELOPMENT)**

`delta [-nps][-g list][-m mrlist][-r SID][-y[comment]] file...`

Issue 5: The output format description in the stdout section is corrected. This is a minor editorial correction.

df

Report free disk space.

`df [-k][ -P|-t][file...]`

Issue 5: No functional changes in this issue.

diff

Compare two files.

`diff [-c| -e| -f| -C n][-br] file1 file2`

Issue 5: A Future Directions section has been added documenting that this utility will change to align with POSIX.2b when finalized.

dircmp

Directory comparison. **(LEGACY)**

`dircmp [-ds] dir1 dir2`

Issue 5: This utility is marked LEGACY and may not be available on all implementations. A portable application should not use the *dircmp* utility.

dirname

Return the directory portion of pathname.

`dirname string`

Issue 5: No functional changes in this issue.

dis

Disassembler. (**DEVELOPMENT**, **LEGACY**)

`dis [-olV] [-F function] ... [-l string] file...`

Issue 5: This utility is marked LEGACY and may not be available on all implementations. A portable application should not use the *dis* utility.

du

Estimate file space usage. (**LEGACY**)

`du [-a| -s] [-kx] [-r] [file ...]`

Issue 5: This utility is marked LEGACY and may not be available on all implementations. A portable application should not use the *du* utility.

echo

Write arguments to standard output.

`echo [string ...]`

Issue 5: In the Options section, the last sentence is changed to indicate that implementations "will not" support any options; in the previous issue this said "need not". This is the application of Corrigendum 1170/65 which mandates that "Implementations will not support any options" to *echo*. Thus:

```
echo -n
```

will output:

```
-n
```

New applications should use *printf* instead of *echo*.

ed

Edit text.

`ed [-p string] [-s] [file]`

`ed [-p string] [-] [file]`

Issue 5: In the Options section, the meaning of **–s** and – is clarified. Specifically, – is the same as the –s option.

A second Future Direction is added documenting that this utility will change to align with POSIX.2b when finalized.

egrep

Search a file with an ERE pattern. (**LEGACY**)

`egrep [ -c| -l][-inv] -e pattern_list [file...]`

`egrep [ -c| -l][-inv] -f pattern_list [file...]`

`egrep [ -c| -l][-inv] pattern_list [file...]`

Issue 5: This utility is marked LEGACY and may not be available on all implementations. Portable applications should use *grep* instead of *egrep*.

A command invoking the *egrep* utility with the **–e** option specified is equivalent to the command:

`grep -E [ -c| -l][-inv] -e pattern_list [file...`
`7]`

A command invoking the *egrep* utility with the **–f** option specified is equivalent to the command:

`grep -E [ -c| -l][-inv] -f pattern_list [file...`
`7]`

A command invoking the *egrep* utility with neither the **–e** nor the **–f** option specified is equivalent to the command:

`grep -E [ -c| -l][-inv] pattern_list [file...]`

env

Set the environment for command invocation.

`env [-i][name=value]... [utility [argument...]]`

`env [-][name=value]... [utility [argument...]]`

Issue 5: No functional changes in this issue.

ex

Text editor.

`ex [-rR][-l][-s | -v ][-c command]-t tagstring][-w size][file...]`

`ex [-rR][-l][- | -v ][+command][-t tagstring][-w size][file...]`

Issue 5: A Future Directions section has been added documenting that this utility will change to align with POSIX.2b when finalized.

expand

Convert tabs to spaces.

`expand [-t tablist][file ...]`

`expand [-tabstop][-tab1,tab2,...,tabn][file...]`

Issue 5: No functional changes in this issue.

expr

Evaluate arguments as an expression.

```
expr operand
```

Issue 5: A Future Directions section has been added documenting that this utility will change to align with POSIX.2b when finalized.

false

Return false value.

```
false
```

Issue 5: No functional changes in this issue.

fc

Process the command history list.

```
fc [-r][-e editor] [first[last]]
fc -l[-nr] [first[last]]
fc -s[old=new][first]
```

Issue 5: A Future Directions section has been added documenting that this utility will change to align with POSIX.2b when finalized.

fg

Run jobs in the foreground.

```
fg [job_id]
```

Issue 5: No functional changes in this issue.

fgrep

Search a file for a fixed-string pattern. **(LEGACY)**

```
fgrep [ -c| -l][-invx] -e pattern_list [file...]
fgrep [ -c| -l][-invx] -f pattern_list [file...]
fgrep [ -c| -l][-invx] pattern_list [file...]
```

Issue 5: This utility is marked LEGACY and may not be available on all implementations. Portable applications should use *grep* instead of *fgrep*.

A command invoking the *fgrep* utility with the **-e** option specified is equivalent to the command:

```
grep -F [ -c| -l][-invx] -e pattern_list [file...f7]
```

A command invoking the *fgrep* utility with the **-f** option specified is equivalent to the command:

```
grep -F [ -c| -l][-invx] -f pattern_list [file...f7]
```

A command invoking the *fgrep* utility with neither the **-e** nor the **-f** option operand specified is equivalent to the command:

```
grep -F [ -c| -l][-invx] pattern_list [file...]
```

file

Determine file type.

```
file file ...
```

Issue 5: No functional changes in this issue.

find

Find files.

```
find path... [operand_expression]
```

Issue 5: A Future Directions section has been added documenting that this utility will change to align with POSIX.2b when finalized.

fold

Filter for folding lines.

```
fold [-bs][-w width][file...]
```

Issue 5: No functional changes in this issue.

fort77

FORTRAN compiler. (**FORTRAN**)

```
fort77 [-c][-g][-L directory]... [-O optlevel][-o outfile][-s][-w]
operand...
```

Issue 5: No functional changes in this issue.

fuser

List process IDs of all processes that have one or more files open.

```
fuser [ -cfu ] file ...
```

Issue 5: This is a new utility in Issue 5.

The *fuser* utility writes to standard output the process IDs of processes running on the local system that have one or more named files open. For block special devices, all processes using any file on that device are listed.

gencat

Generate a formatted message catalogue.

```
gencat catfile msgfile...
```

Issue 5: No functional changes in this issue.

get

Get a version of an SCCS file. (**DEVELOPMENT**)

```
get [-begkmlLpst][-c cutoff][-i list][-r SID][-x list] file...
get [-begkmpst][-c cutoff][-i list][ -l[p]][-r SID][-x list] file...
```

Issue 5: The first format string in the stdout section is corrected. This is a minor editorial correction.

The interpretation of the *YY* component of the **–c** *cutoff* argument is noted as follows:

"Indicate the **cutoff** date-time, in the form:

YY[*MM*[*DD*[*HH*[*MM*[*SS*]]]]]

For the *YY* component, values in the range [69-99] refer to years in the twentieth century (1969 to 1999 inclusive); values in the range [00-68] refer to years in the twenty-first century (2000 to 2068 inclusive)."

getconf

Get configuration values.

```
getconf [ -v specification ] system_var
getconf [ -v specification ] path_var pathname
```

Issue 5: In the Operands section:

- NL_MAX is changed to NL_NMAX. This is a minor editorial correction.
- Entries beginning NL_ are deleted from the list of standard configuration variables.
- The list of variables previously marked UX is merged with the list marked EX.
- Operands are added to support new Feature Groups: _XOPEN_REALTIME, _XOPEN_REALTIME_THREADS, and _XOPEN_LEGACY.
- Operands are added so that *getconf* can determine supported programming environments:

system_var	*confstr*( ) **Name Value**
PATH	_CS_PATH
XBS5_ILP32_OFF32_CFLAGS	_CS_XBS5_ILP32_OFF32_CFLAGS
XBS5_ILP32_OFF32_LDFLAGS	_CS_XBS5_ILP32_OFF32_LDFLAGS
XBS5_ILP32_OFF32_LIBS	_CS_XBS5_ILP32_OFF32_LIBS
XBS5_ILP32_OFF32_LINTFLAGS	_CS_XBS5_ILP32_OFF32_LINTFLAGS
XBS5_ILP32_OFFBIG_CFLAGS	_CS_XBS5_ILP32_OFFBIG_CFLAGS
XBS5_ILP32_OFFBIG_LDFLAGS	_CS_XBS5_ILP32_OFFBIG_LDFLAGS
XBS5_ILP32_OFFBIG_LIBS	_CS_XBS5_ILP32_OFFBIG_LIBS
XBS5_ILP32_OFFBIG_LINTFLAGS	_CS_XBS5_ILPBIG_OFF32_LINTFLAGS
XBS5_LP64_OFF64_CFLAGS	_CS_XBS5_LP64_OFF64_CFLAGS
XBS5_LP64_OFF64_LDFLAGS	_CS_XBS5_LP64_OFF64_LDFLAGS

system_var	*confstr*( ) **Name Value**
XBS5_LP64_OFF64_LIBS	_CS_XBS5_LP64_OFF64_LIBS
XBS5_LP64_OFF64_LINTFLAGS	_CS_XBS5_LP64_OFF64_LINTFLAGS
XBS5_LPBIG_OFFBIG_CFLAGS	_CS_XBS5_LPBIG_OFFBIG_CFLAGS
XBS5_LPBIG_OFFBIG_LDFLAGS	_CS_XBS5_LPBIG_OFFBIG_LDFLAGS
XBS5_LPBIG_OFFBIG_LIBS	_CS_XBS5_LPBIG_OFFBIG_LIBS
XBS5_LPBIG_OFFBIG_LINTFLAGS	_CS_XBS5_LPBIG_OFFBIG_LINTFLAGS

getopts

Parse utility options.

```
getopts optstring name [arg...]
```

Issue 5: No functional changes in this issue.

grep

Search a file for a pattern.

```
grep [ -E| -F][ -c| -l| -q ][-insvx] -e pattern_list
[-f pattern_file]...[file...]
```

```
grep [ -E| -F][ -c| -l| -q ][-insvx][-e pattern_list
-f pattern_file...[file...]
```

```
grep [ -E| -F][ -c| -l| -q ][-insvx] pattern_list[file...]
```

Issue 5: No functional changes in this issue.

hash

Remember or report utility locations.

```
hash [utility...]
```

```
hash -r
```

Issue 5: No functional changes in this issue.

head

Copy the first part of files.

```
head [-n number][file...]
```

```
head [number][file...]
```

Issue 5: No functional changes in this issue.

iconv

Codeset conversion.

```
iconv -f fromcode -t tocode [file...]
```

Issue 5: No functional changes in this issue.

id

Return user identity.

```
id [user]
id -G[-n] [user]
id -g[-nr] [user]
id -u[-nr] [user]
```

Issue 5: No functional changes in this issue.

ipcrm

Remove a message queue, semaphore set, or shared memory segment identifier.

```
ipcrm [ -q msgid | -Q msgkey | -s semid | -S semkey |
    -m shmid | -M shmkey ] ...
```

Issue 5: This is a new utility added in Issue 5.

The *ipcrm* utility removes zero or more message queues, semaphore sets, or shared memory segments. The interprocess communication facilities to be removed are specified by the options.

Only a user with appropriate privilege is allowed to remove an interprocess communication facility that was not created by or owned by the user invoking *ipcrm*.

ipcs

Report interprocess communication facilities status.

```
ipcs [ -qms ] [ -abcopt ]
```

Issue 5: This is a new utility in Issue 5.

The *ipcs* utility writes information about active interprocess communication facilities.

Without options, information is written in short format for message queues, shared memory segments, and semaphore sets that are currently active in the system.

jobs

Display status of jobs in the current session.

```
jobs [ -l| -p][job_id...]
```

Issue 5: No functional changes in this issue.

join

Relational database operator.

```
join [ -a file_number | -v file_number ][-e string][-o list][-t char]
[-1 field][-2 field] file1 file2

join [-a file_number][-e string][-j field][-j1 field][-j2 field]
[-o list...][-t char][-t char] file1 file2
```

Issue 5: No functional changes in this issue.

kill

Terminate or signal processes.

`kill -s` *signal_name pid*...

`kill -l` [*exit_status*]

`kill` [-*signal_name*] *pid*...

`kill` [-*signal_number*] *pid*...

Issue 5: No functional changes in this issue.

lex

Generate programs for lexical tasks. (**DEVELOPMENT**)

`lex -c`[-t][-n| -v][*file*...]

Issue 5: No functional changes in this issue.

line

Read one line. (**LEGACY**)

`line`

Issue 5: This utility is marked LEGACY and may not be available on all implementations. Portable applications should use the *read* utility instead of *line*.

link

Call *link*( ) function.

`link` *file1 file2*

Issue 5: This is a new utility in Issue 5.

lint

Check C-language programs. (**DEVELOPMENT**, **LEGACY**)

`lint` [-abcnpuxv] [-D *name=value*]][-I *directory*][-L *directory*]
[-o *x*][-U *name*] *operand*...

Issue 5: This utility is marked LEGACY and may not be available on all implementations. A portable application should not use the *lint* utility.

ln

Link files.

`ln` [-f] *source_file target_file*

`ln` [-f] *source_file... target_dir*

Issue 5: No functional changes in this issue.

locale

Get locale-specific information.

`locale [ -a| -m]`

`locale [-ck] name...`

Issue 5: A Future Directions section has been added documenting that this utility will change to align with POSIX.2b when finalized.

localedef

Define locale environment.

`localedef [-c][-f charmap][-i sourcefile] name`

Issue 5: No functional changes in this issue.

logger

Log messages.

`logger string ...`

Issue 5: No functional changes in this issue.

logname

Return the user's login name.

`logname`

Issue 5: No functional changes in this issue.

lp

Send files to a printer.

`lp [-c][-d dest][-n copies][-msw][-o option]... [-t title] [file...]`

Issue 5: No functional changes in this issue.

lpstat

Report printer status information. (**LEGACY**)

`lpstat [-drst] [-a[list]] [-c[list]] [-o[list]] [-p[list]] [-u[list]] [-v[list]] [ID...]`

Issue 5: This utility is marked LEGACY and may not be available on all implementations. A portable application should not use the *lpstat* utility.

ls

List directory contents.

`ls [-CFRacdilqrtu1] [-fgmnopsx] [file...]`

Issue 5: A second Future Direction is added documenting that this utility will change to align with POSIX.2b when finalized.

m4

Macro processor. **(DEVELOPMENT)**

`m4 [-s] [ -D name[=val]]...[-U name]... file...`

Issue 5: The phrase "the defined text for macros written by the dumpdef macro" is added to the Description of stderr, and the description of **dumpdef** is updated to indicate that output is written to standard error. The description of **eval** is updated to indicate that the list of excluded C operators includes unary "&" and ".". In the description of **ifdef**, the phrase "and it is not defined to be zero" is deleted.

mail

Send or read mail. **(LEGACY)**

`mail [-e] [-f file]`

`mail [-e| -p] [-qr] [-f file]`

`mail [-t] name ...`

Issue 5: This utility is marked LEGACY and may not be available on all implementations. Portable applications should use the *mailx* utility.

mailx

Process messages.

Send mode:

`mailx [-s subject] address...`

Receive mode:

`mailx -e`

`mailx [-HiNn] [-F] [-u user]`

`mailx -f [-HiNn] [-F] [file]`

Issue 5: The description of the EDITOR environment variable is changed to indicate that *ed* is the default editor if this variable is not set. In previous issues, this default was not stated explicitly at this point, but was implied later in the text.

A Future Directions section has been added documenting that this utility will change to align with POSIX.2b when finalized.

make

Maintain, update, and regenerate groups of programs. (**DEVELOPMENT**)

`make [-einpqrst][-f` *`makefile`*`]...[ -k| -S][`*`macros=name`*`]...`
`[`*`target_name...`*`]`

Issue 5: A Future Directions section has been added documenting that this utility will change to align with POSIX.2b when finalized.

man

Display system documentation.

`man [-k]` *`name...`*

Issue 5: A Future Directions section has been added documenting that this utility will change to align with POSIX.2b when finalized.

mesg

Permit or deny messages.

`mesg [y|n]`

Issue 5: No functional changes in this issue.

mkdir

Make directories.

`mkdir [-p][-m` *`mode`*`]` *`dir...`*

Issue 5: A Future Directions section has been added documenting that this utility will change to align with POSIX.2b when finalized.

mkfifo

Make FIFO special files.

`mkfifo [-m` *`mode`*`]` *`file...`*

Issue 5: No functional changes in this issue.

more

Display files on a page-by-page basis.

`more [-ceisu][-n` *`number`*`][-p` *`command`*`][-t` *`tagstring`*`][`*`file...`*`]`

`more [-ceisu][-n` *`number`*`][+`*`command`*`][-t` *`tagstring`*`][`*`file...`*`]`

Issue 5: A Future Directions section has been added documenting that this utility will change to align with POSIX.2b when finalized.

mv

Move files.

`mv [-fi] source_file target_file`

`mv [-fi] source_file... target_file`

Issue 5: No functional changes in this issue.

newgrp

Change to a new group.

`newgrp [-l][group`

`newgrp [-][group]`

Issue 5: No functional changes in this issue.

nice

Invoke a utility with an altered system scheduling priority.

`nice [-n increment] utility [argument...]`

`nice [-increment] utility [argument...]`

Issue 5: No functional changes in this issue.

nl

Line numbering filter.

`nl [-p][-b type][-d delim][-f type][-h type][-i incr][-l num][-n format] [-s sep][-v startnum][-w width][file]`

Issue 5: The option [**–f** *type*] is added to the Synopsis. The option descriptions are presented in alphabetic order. The description of **–bt** is changed to "Number only non-empty lines".

nm

Write the name list of an object file. (**DEVELOPMENT**)

`nm [-APv][-efox][ -g| -u][-t format] file...`

Issue 5: No functional changes in this issue.

nohup

Invoke a utility immune to hangups.

`nohup utility [argument...]`

Issue 5: No functional changes in this issue.

od

Dump files in various formats.

od [-v][-A *address_base*][-j *skip*][-N *count*][-t *type_string*]...
[*file*...]

od [-bcdosx][*file*] [[+]*offset*[.][b]]

Issue 5: In the description of the **-c** option, the phrase "This is equivalent to **-t c**." is deleted.

A Future Directions section has been added documenting that this utility will change to align with POSIX.2b when finalized.

pack

Compress files. (**LEGACY**)

pack [-f][-] *file*...

Issue 5: This utility is marked LEGACY and may not be available on all implementations. Portable applications should use the *compress* utility.

paste

Merge corresponding or subsequent lines of files.

paste [-s][-d *list*] *file*...

Issue 5: No functional changes in this issue.

patch

Apply changes to files.

patch [-blNR][-c| -e| -n][-d *dir*][-D *define*][-i *patchfile*]
[-o *outfile*][-p *num*][-r *rejectfile*][*file*]

Issue 5: A Future Directions section has been added documenting that this utility will change to align with POSIX.2b when finalized.

pathchk

Check pathnames.

pathchk [-p] *pathname*...

Issue 5: No functional changes in this issue.

pax

Portable archive interchange.

pax [-cdnv][-f *archive*][-s *replstr*]...[*pattern*...]

pax -r[-cdiknuv][-f *archive*][-o *options*]...[-p *string*]...
[-s *replstr*]...[*pattern*...]

pax -w[-dituvX][-b *blocksize*][[-a][-f *archive*][-o *options*]...
[-s *replstr*]...[-x *format*][*file*...]

```
pax -r -w[-diklntuvX][-p string]...[-s replstr]...[file...]
directory
```

Issue 5: A note is added to the Application Usage section indicating that the *cpio* and *tar* formats can only support files up to 8 gigabytes in size.

pcat

Expand and concatenate files. (**LEGACY**)

```
pcat file...
```

Issue 5: This utility is marked LEGACY and may not be available on all implementations. A portable application should not use the *pcat* utility, but use *compress*, *uncompress*, and *zcat*.

pg

File perusal filter for soft-copy terminals. (**LEGACY**)

```
pg[-number][-cefns][-p string][+linenumber][+/re/][file...]
```

Issue 5: This utility is marked LEGACY and may not be available on all implementations. Portable applications should not use the *pg* utility, but use the *more* utility instead.

pr

Print files.

```
pr [+page][-column][-adFmrt][-e[char][gap]][-h header][-i[char][gap]]
[-l lines][-n[char][width]][-o offset][-s[char]][-w width][-fp]
[file...]
```

Issue 5: No functional changes in this issue.

printf

Write formatted output.

```
printf format[argument...]
```

Issue 5: No functional changes in this issue.

prs

Print an SCCS file. (**DEVELOPMENT**)

```
prs [-a][-d dataspec][-r[SID]] file...
```

```
prs [ -e| -l] -c cutoff [-d dataspec] file...
```

```
prs [ -e| -l] -r[SID][-d dataspec]file...
```

Issue 5: The phrase "in which keyword substitution is followed by a newline" is deleted from the end of the second paragraph of **Data Keywords** in the stdout section.

The interpretation of the *YY* component of the **–c** *cutoff* argument is noted.

ps

Report process status.

`ps [-aA][-defl][-G grouplit][-o format]...[-p proclist][-t termlist] [-U userlist][-g grouplist][-n namelist][-u userlist]`

Issue 5: No functional changes in this issue.

pwd

Return working directory name.

`pwd`

Issue 5: No functional changes in this issue.

read

Read a line from standard input.

`read [-r] var...`

Issue 5: No functional changes in this issue.

renice

Set system scheduling priorities of running processes.

`renice [-n increment][ -g| -p| -u] ID...`

`renice nice_value[-p] pid...[-g gid...][-p pid...][-u user...]`

`renice nice_value -g gid...[-g gid...][-p pid...][-u user...]`

`renice nice_value -u user...[-g gid...][-p pid...][-u user...]`

Issue 5: In the Synopsis, an ellipsis is added to the –**u** option in all three obsolescent forms.

rm

Remove directory entries.

`rm [-fiRr] file...`

Issue 5: A Future Directions section has been added documenting that this utility will change to align with POSIX.2b when finalized.

rmdel

Remove a delta from an SCCS file. **(DEVELOPMENT)**

`rmdel -r SID file...`

Issue 5: No functional changes in this issue.

rmdir

Remove directories.

`rmdir [-p] dir...`

Issue 5: No functional changes in this issue.

sact

Print current SCCS file-editing activity. (**DEVELOPMENT**)

`sact file...`

Issue 5: No functional changes in this issue.

sccs

Front end for the SCCS subsystem. (**DEVELOPMENT**)

`sccs [-r][-d path][-p path] command [options...][operands...]`

Issue 5: No functional changes in this issue.

sed

Stream editor.

`sed [-n] script[file...]`

`sed [-n][-e script]...[-f script_file]...[file...]`

Issue 5: A Future Directions section has been added documenting that this utility will change to align with POSIX.2b when finalized.

sh

Shell, the standard command language interpreter.

`sh [-abCefimnuvx][-o option][+abCefmnuvx][+o option] [command_file [argument...]]`

`sh [-abCefimnuvx][-o option][+abCefmnuvx][+o option]command_string [command_name [argument...]]`

`sh -s[-abCefimnuvx][-o option][+abCefmnuvx][+o option][argument...]]`

Issue 5: A Future Directions section has been added documenting that this utility will change to align with POSIX.2b when finalized.

Text is added to the DESCRIPTION for the Large File Summit Submission, specifically:

- Pathname expansion will not fail due to the size of a file.
- Shell input and output redirections will have an implementation-dependent offset maximum that will be established in the open file description.

sleep

Suspend execution for an interval.

`sleep` *time*

Issue 5: No functional changes in this issue.

sort

Sort, merge, or sequence check text files.

`sort [-m][-o` *output*`][-bdfinru][-t` *char*`][-k` *keydef*`]...[-z` *recsz*`]`
`[`*file*`...]`

`sort -c [-bdfinru][-t` *char*`][-k` *keydef*`]...[-z` *recsz*`][`*file*`...]`

`sort [-mu][-o` *output*`][-bdfir][-t` *char*`][+`*pos1*`[-`*pos2*`]]...[-z` *recsz*`]`
`[`*file*`...]`

`sort -c[-u][-bdfinr][-t` *char*`][+`*pos1*`[-`*pos2*`]]...[-z` *recsz*`][`*file*`]`

Issue 5: No functional changes in this issue.

spell

Find spelling errors. **(LEGACY)**

`spell [-bvx][+`*local_file*`][`*file*`...]`

Issue 5: This utility is marked LEGACY and may not be available on all implementations. Portable applications should not use the *spell* utility.

split

Split files into pieces.

`split [-l` *line_count*`][-a` *suffix_length*`][`*file*`[`*name*`]]`

`split -b` *n*`[k|m][-a` *suffix_length*`][`*file*`[`*name*`]]`

`split [-`*line_count*`][-a` *suffix_length*`][`*file*`[`*name*`]]`

Issue 5: No functional changes in this issue.

strings

Find printable strings in files.

`strings [-a][-t` *format*`][-n` *number*`][`*file*`...]`

`strings [-][-t` *format*`][-`*number*`][`*file*`...]`

Issue 5: No functional changes in this issue.

strip

Remove unnecessary information from executable files. **(DEVELOPMENT)**

`strip` *file*...

Issue 5: No functional changes in this issue.

stty

Set the options for a terminal.

`stty [ -a| -g]`

`stty` *operands*

Issue 5: The description of **tabs** is clarified.

A Future Directions section has been added documenting that this utility will change to align with POSIX.2b when finalized.

sum

Print checksum and block count of a file. **(LEGACY)**

`sum [-r][file...]`

Issue 5: This utility is marked LEGACY and may not be available on all implementations. Portable applications should use the *cksum* utility.

tabs

Set terminal tabs.

`tabs [ -n| -a| -a2| -c| -c2| -c3| -f| -p| -s| -u][+m[n]]`
`[-T type]`

`tabs [-T type][ +[n]] n1[,n2,...]`

Issue 5: No functional changes in this issue.

tail

Copy the last part of a file.

`tail [-f][ -c number| -n number] [file]`

`tail -[number][b|c|l][f] [file]`

`tail +[number][b|c|l][f] [file]`

Issue 5: No functional changes in this issue.

talk

Talk to another user.

`talk address [terminal]`

Issue 5: No functional changes in this issue.

tar

File archiver. (**LEGACY**)

`tar key [file...]`

Issue 5: A note is added to the Application Usage section indicating that the *tar* format can only support files up to 8 gigabytes in size.

This utility is marked LEGACY and may not be available on all implementations. Portable applications should use the *pax* utility instead of *tar*.

tee

Duplicate standard input.

`tee [-ai][file...]`

Issue 5: No functional changes in this issue.

test

Evaluate expression.

`test [expression]`

`[ [expression] ]`

Issue 5: A Future Directions section has been added documenting that this utility will change to align with POSIX.2b when finalized.

time

Time a simple command.

`time [-p] utility [argument...]`

Issue 5: No functional changes in this issue.

touch

Change file access and modification times.

`touch [-acm][ -r ref_file| -t time] file...`

`touch [-acm][date_time] file...`

Issue 5: No functional changes in this issue.

tput

Change terminal characteristics.

`tput [-T type] operand...`

Issue 5: No functional changes in this issue.

tr

Translate characters.

`tr [-cs] string1 string2`

`tr -s[-c] string1`

`tr -d[-c] string1`

`tr -ds[-c] string1 string2`

Issue 5: No functional changes in this issue.

true

Return true value.

`true`

Issue 5: No functional changes in this issue.

tsort

Topological sort.

`tsort [file]`

Issue 5: No functional changes in this issue.

tty

Return user's terminal name.

```
tty
tty -s
```

Issue 5: The Synopsis is changed to indicate two forms of the command, with the second form marked as obsolete. This is a clarification and does not change the functionality published in previous issues.

type

Write a description of command type.

`type name...`

Issue 5: No functional changes in this issue.

ulimit

Set or report file size limit.

`ulimit [-f][blocks]`

Issue 5: No functional changes in this issue.

umask

Get or set the file mode creation mask.

`umask [-S] [mask]`

Issue 5: No functional changes in this issue.

unalias

Remove alias definitions.

`unalias alias-name...`

`unalias -a`

Issue 5: No functional changes in this issue.

uname

Return system name.

`uname [snrvma]`

Issue 5: No functional changes in this issue.

uncompress

Expand compressed data.

`uncompress [-cfv] [file...]`

Issue 5: No functional changes in this issue.

unexpand

Convert spaces to tabs.

`unexpand [ -a| -t tablist] [file...]`

Issue 5: No functional changes in this issue.

unget

Undo a previous get of an SCCS file. (**DEVELOPMENT**)

`unget [-ns] [-r SID] file...`

Issue 5: No functional changes in this issue.

uniq

Report or filter out repeated lines in a file.

`uniq [-c|-d|-u] [-f fields] [-s char] [input_file [output_file]]`

`uniq [-c|-d|-u] [-n] [+m] [input_file [output_file]]`

Issue 5: No functional changes in this issue.

unlink

Call the *unlink*( ) function

`unlink` *`file`*

Issue 5: This is a new utility in Issue 5.

The *unlink* utility performs the function call:

```
unlink(file);
```

unpack

Expand files. (**LEGACY**)

`unpack` *`file...`*

Issue 5: This utility is marked LEGACY and may not be available on all implementations. Portable applications should use the *compress* and *uncompress* utilities.

uucp

System-to-system copy.

`uucp [-cCdfjmr][-n` *`user`*`]` *`source-file... destination-file`*

Issue 5: No functional changes in this issue.

uudecode

Decode a binary file.

`uudecode [`*`file`*`]`

Issue 5: No functional changes in this issue.

uuencode

Encode a binary file.

`uuencode [`*`file`*`]` *`decode_pathname`*

Issue 5: No functional changes in this issue.

uulog

Query system-to-system transaction log. (**LEGACY**)

`uulog [-s` *`system`*`]`

Issue 5: This utility is marked LEGACY and may not be available on all implementations. Portable applications should not use this utility.

uuname

List names of other known uucp systems. (**LEGACY**)

`uuname [-l]`

Issue 5: This utility is marked LEGACY and may not be available on all implementations. Portable applications should not use this utility.

uupick

Receive public system-to-system file copies. (**LEGACY**)

`uupick [-s system]`

Issue 5: This utility is marked LEGACY and may not be available on all implementations. Portable applications should not use this utility.

uustat

uucp status inquiry and job control.

`uustat [ -q| -k jobid| -r jobid]`

`uustat [-s system][-u user]`

Issue 5: No functional changes in this issue.

uuto

Send public system-to-system file copies. (**LEGACY**)

`uuto [-mp] source-file... destination`

Issue 5: This utility is marked LEGACY and may not be available on all implementations. Portable applications should not use this utility.

uux

Remote command execution.

`uux [-np] command-string`

`uux [-jnp] command-string`

`uux [-][-jn] command-string`

Issue 5: No functional changes in this issue.

val

Validate SCCS files. (**DEVELOPMENT**)

`val -`

`val [-s][-m name][-r SID][-y type] file...`

Issue 5: No functional changes in this issue.

vi

Screen-oriented (visual) display editor.

`vi [-rR] [-l] [-c` *`command`*`] [-t` *`tagstring`*`] [-w` *`size`*`] [`*`file...`*`]`

`vi [-rR] [-l] [+`*`command`*`] [-t` *`tagstring`*`] [-w` *`size`*`] [`*`file...`*`]`

Issue 5: A Future Directions section has been added documenting that this utility will change to align with POSIX.2b when finalized.

wait

Await process completion.

`wait [`*`pid...`*`]`

Issue 5: No functional changes in this issue.

wc

Word, line, and byte or character count.

`wc [-c|-m] [-lw] [`*`file...`*`]`

Issue 5: No functional changes in this issue.

what

Identify SCCS files. (**DEVELOPMENT**)

`what [-s]` *`file...`*

Issue 5: No functional changes in this issue.

who

Display who is on the system.

`who [-mu] -s [-bHlprt] [`*`file`*`]`

`who [-mTu] [-abdHlprt] [`*`file`*`]`

`who -q [`*`file`*`]`

`who am i`

`who am I`

Issue 5: No functional changes in this issue.

write

Write to another user.

`write` *`user_name`* `[`*`terminal`*`]`

Issue 5: A Future Directions section has been added documenting that this utility will change to align with POSIX.2b when finalized.

xargs

Construct argument lists and invoke utility.

```
xargs [-t][-p][-e[eofstr]][-E eofstr][-I replstr][-i[replstr]]
[-L number][-l[number]][-n number [-x]][-s size][utility [argument...]]
```

Issue 5: A second Future Direction is added documenting that this utility will change to align with POSIX.2b when finalized.

yacc

Yet another compiler compiler. (**DEVELOPMENT**)

```
yacc [-dltv][-b file_prefix][-p sym_prefix] grammar
```

Issue 5: A Future Directions section has been added documenting that this utility will change to align with POSIX.2b when finalized.

zcat

Expand and concatenate data.

```
zcat [file...]
```

Issue 5: No functional changes in this issue.

Chapter 23

C-language Migration

23.1 Introduction

This chapter describes techniques for writing C-language code that conforms to the ISO C standard.

ISO C is the term used to refer to the language specified in the ISO C standard. The ISO C standard is based on ANSI C, which is defined in ANSI standard X3.159-1989, Programming Language C (ANSI C). Recent changes to the ISO C standard include adoption of Amendment 1 and technical corrigendum to form ISO/IEC 9899:1990/Amendment 1:1995 (E). This document assumes the reader is already familiar with the C Language in use before standardization; this is frequently termed *Common Usage C* or *K&R C*. Throughout the remainder of this document, the term Common Usage C is used to describe the C Language used before standardization.

This chapter is useful for programmers who are:

- upgrading existing C-language code written for a Common Usage C compiler
- writing new code which is to be compiled with an ISO C standard compiler.

XCU describes the interface to the ISO C standard compiler.

23.2 Compiler

The command *c89* provides access to the language defined in the ISO C standard, whereas *cc* is the command used to access Common Usage C. In XCU, Issue 5 , *cc* is marked LEGACY. The intent of marking *cc* LEGACY is to highlight the fact that *c89* should be used in preference for developing new applications.

A program written to Common Usage C can be compiled using the *c89* command, provided that migration guidelines given in this part of the document are followed. In this case, Common Usage C function definitions are handled as functions with empty argument lists. Thus, compile-time argument checking is bypassed, but the code should still compile and run correctly.

23.3 Function Prototypes

This section explains the implications of function prototypes, which are the most visible ISO C standard addition to the syntax of the C Language.

23.3.1 Function Declarations

A *function declaration* defines the return type of the function, the name of the function, and an optional list of arguments. The type of each argument is defined within the argument list, along with an optional argument name. For example:

```
int f(int, char);
```

This declares a function that returns a type **int**. The name of the function is *f*( ) and it takes two arguments. The first is a type **int** and the second is a type **char**.

The two arguments could also be named as in the following example:

```
int f(int i, char c);
```

The keyword **void** is used for two purposes in function prototypes. The first is for stating that a function does not return a result. For example:

```
void f(int);
```

Here, the function *f*( ) has one argument but does not return a result.

Another use of **void** is to indicate that a function does not have any arguments, for example:

```
int f(void);
```

This states that the function *f*( ) does not take any arguments, but it does return a type **int**.

Note the difference between this second use of **void** and the following example:

```
int f();
```

This indicates that nothing is specified about the arguments, not necessarily that there are no arguments.

There are two further details worth noting about function prototypes; the use of **const** and the use of ellipsis (. . .). They are both used in the following example:

```
int fprintf(FILE *, const char *, ...);
```

Using type **const** for the second argument indicates that it is a pointer to a type **char** string that is not changed by this function. The ellipsis indicates that there are an unknown number of additional arguments to this function (see Section 23.3.5 on page 444).

Argument Checking

The introduction of function prototypes means that the compiler can perform argument checks for each function call, in a similar fashion to the *lint* command. The compiler produces a diagnostic indicating an improper pointer or integer combination; for example, if a function is declared as:

```
int f(int);
```

and invoked by:

```
f("Hello");
```

Type Conversion

The introduction of function prototypes also means that arguments to functions are automatically converted, if possible, to the type expected by the function. This conversion is the same conversion that is performed during assignment. In the following example:

```
int f(float);
    . . .
int i = 32;
    . . .
f(i);
```

the call to the function converts the type **int** to a type **float**.

23.3.2 Writing New Code

The ISO C standard includes rules that govern the mixing of old-style and new-style function declarations. These rules recognize that there are many lines of existing C code that will not be converted to use prototypes.

When writing an entirely new program, new-style function declarations should be used in headers, and new-style function declarations and definitions should be used in C source files. However, if the code is to be compiled on an Common Usage C compiler, the __STDC__ macro should be used. This macro should be used with **#ifdef** or **#if** to decide which declarations to use dependent on the type of compilation system as shown in Example 23-1.

Example 23-1 Use of the __STDC__ Macro

```
#ifdef __STDC__
#if __STDC__ - 0 == 1
    void errmsg(int, ...);
    struct s *f(const char *);
    int g(void);
#else
    void errmsg();
    struct s *f();
    int g();
#endif
#else
    void errmsg();
    struct s *f();
    int g();
#endif
```

If an ISO C compiler is being used, the first three declarations are used; otherwise, the last three declarations are used. Note that the first three declarations say more about the functions than the last three declarations.

It is good programming practice to declare and define all functions with prototypes. An ISO C standard compiler issues a diagnostic message when two incompatible declarations exist for the same function. This ensures that all calls agree with the definition of the functions, eliminating some of the most common C programming mistakes.

Example 23-1 demonstrates the most robust way of handling this situation, which even works for old transitionary compilers which define __STDC__ to expand to nothing. The ISO C standard says that a conforming implementation will define __STDC__ to have the value 1.

However, non-conforming implementations may still define __STDC__. For editorial purposes, the rest of the examples in this section use a simpler preprocessor test, but recognize it is also less robust.

23.3.3 Updating Existing Code

There are four approaches possible when updating existing code to use function prototypes:

- Recompile without making any changes.

  The compiler may provide warnings about mismatches in argument type and number.

- Add function prototypes to the headers.

  This covers all calls to global functions. Example 23-1 on page 441, which shows the use of __STDC__, is a good example of this change.

- Add function prototypes to the headers and start each source file with function prototypes for its local functions.

  This covers all calls to functions. However, this requires duplicating the interface for each local function in the source file as shown in Example 23-2.

  Example 23-2 Duplicating an Interface

```
#ifdef __STDC__
    static void del(struct s *);
#endif
  ...
static void del(p)
struct s *p;
{
  ...
}
```

  Here the **#ifdef** ... **#endif** lines are added to declare the function *del*( ), but the function itself is unchanged.

- Change all function declarations and definitions to use function prototypes.

  This is the most extensive change. For Example 23-2, it involves changing *del*( ) to be:

```
static void del(struct s *p)
{
  ...
}
```

23.3.4 Mixing Old and New Styles

If a function prototype declaration is to work with an old-style function definition, they must both specify functionally identical interfaces. In ISO terminology, they must have *compatible types*.

For functions with a variable number of arguments, the ISO C standard ellipsis notation cannot be mixed with the old-style function definitions as specified in **<varargs.h>**. However, the situation is straightforward for functions with a fixed number of arguments. The types of the arguments need to be specified *as they are passed* in Common Usage C. For example, if the original definition of the function is:

```
int f(i, l)
int i;
long l;
{
  . . .
}
```

the function prototype declaration is:

```
int f(int, long);
```

However, it is also necessary to understand how the arguments are converted in Common Usage C when a function is called.

In Common Usage C, each argument is converted just before it is passed to the called function. The conversion is based on the default argument promotions. These specify that all integral types narrower than type **int** are promoted to type **int** size, and any type **float** argument is promoted to type **double**. These promotions are used to simplify both the compiler and the libraries.

Function prototypes are more expressive, and hence the conversion can be exact. The specified argument type is the actual type of the object that is passed to the function. This means that if a function prototype is written to match an old-style function definition, the function prototype cannot include arguments of the following types:

char
float
short
signed char
signed short
unsigned char
unsigned short

There still remain two complications with writing prototypes: **typedef** names and the promotion rules for narrow unsigned types.

If arguments in old-style functions are declared using **typedef** names, such as **off_t** and **ino_t**, it is important to know whether or not the **typedef** name designates a type that is affected by the default argument promotions. For these two, **off_t** will not be shorter than **int**, so it is appropriate to use in a function prototype. However, **ino_t** usually is a type **unsigned short**, so if it is used in a prototype, the compiler issues a diagnostic message (possibly fatal), because the old-style definition and the prototype specify different and incompatible interfaces.

The main incompatibility between Common Usage C and the ISO C standard is the promotion rule for the widening of type **unsigned char** and type **unsigned short** to a value the size of type **int**. (See Section 23.4 on page 446.) The ISO C standard converts them to type **int** if type **int** can represent all values of the original type. Otherwise, they are converted to type **unsigned int**.

The best approach is to change the old-style definition to specify either type **int** or type **unsigned int**, and to use the matching type in the function prototype. If the narrower object is required, the value can be assigned to a local variable with the narrower type inside the function.

23.3.5 Variable Number of Arguments

The ISO C standard encourages the use of function prototypes to specify the types of a function's arguments. In order to support functions which have a variable number of arguments, such as *printf*( ), a special ellipsis terminator (...) is added to the language syntax. The ISO C standard requires that all declarations and the definition of such a function include the ellipsis terminator. This is because an implementation might be required to do unusual things to handle a variable number of arguments.

Since there are no names for the ... part of the arguments, a special set of macros contained in the **<stdarg.h>** header gives the function access to these arguments. Pre-ISO C standard used similar macros contained in the **<varargs.h>** header. In XSH, Issue 5, the **<varargs.h>** header is now marked LEGACY to highlight the fact that new applications should use **<stdarg.h>** instead.

Example

This example is an error-handling function *errmsg*( ). This function returns **void** and has only one fixed argument, of type **int**, that specifies details about the error message. This argument may be followed by a filename, or a line number, or both, and these are followed by a format similar to *printf*( ) and arguments that specify the text of the error message.

To allow earlier compilers to compile the example correctly, it makes extensive use of the __STDC__ macro, which is only defined for the ISO C standard compilation systems.

To declare the function in an appropriate header file:

```
#ifdef __STDC__
    void errmsg(int code, ...);
#else
    void errmsg();
#endif
```

Note that the ISO C standard permits the fixed arguments to be named.

In order to define *errmsg*( ), old and new styles must be mixed, as described in Section 23.3.4 on page 442.

First, include different headers, dependent on the compilation system:

```
#ifdef __STDC__
#include <stdarg.h>
#else
#include <varargs.h>
#endif

#include <stdio.h>
```

Include **<stdio.h>** because the program calls the functions *fprintf*( ) and *vfprintf*( ).

For the ISO C standard, the function's declaration is the same as the one in the header file. For Common Usage C, use the identifiers **va_alist** and **va_dcl**:

```
void
#ifdef __STDC__
errmsg(int code, ...)
#else
errmsg(va_alist) va_dcl    /* note: no semicolon */
#endif
  {
    va_list ap;
    char *fmt;
    /* continued below */
```

The old-style variable argument mechanism does not allow fixed arguments to be specified. To permit access to the fixed arguments before the variable arguments, the ellipsis must have a handle. This is done by using the *va_start*() macro. The first argument to this macro is the handle for Issue 5; the second is the name of the argument immediately before the ellipsis:

```
#ifdef __STDC__
    va_start(ap, code);
#else
    int code;
    va_start(ap);
    code = va_arg(ap, int);  /* extract the fixed argument */
#endif
```

The rest of the code is the same for both compilation systems:

```
    if (code & FILENAME)
        (void)fprintf(stderr, "\"%s\": ", va_arg(ap, char *));
    if (code & LINENUMBER)
        (void)fprintf(stderr, "%d: ", va_arg(ap, int));
    if (code & WARNING)
        (void)fputs("warning: ", stderr);
    fmt = va_arg(ap, char *);
    (void)vfprintf(stderr, fmt, ap);
    va_end(ap);
}
```

Both the *va_arg*() and *va_end*() macros work the same for the old-style and ISO C standard versions. Note that *va_arg*() changes the value of *ap*, so the call to *vfprintf*() cannot be:

```
(void)vfprintf(stderr, va_arg(ap, char *), ap);
```

The macros FILENAME, LINENUMBER, and WARNING must be defined in the same header in which *errmsg*() is declared.

A sample call to *errmsg*() could be:

```
errmsg(FILENAME, file, "cannot open: %s\n", argv[i]);
```

23.4 Promotion

This section considers the implications of the change in the type of *promotion* used by ISO C standard compilers. Promotion means changing the type of an object so that it is compatible with other objects in an arithmetic expression. The difference between the promotion used in Common Usage C compilers and ISO C standard compilers is such that a program behaves differently, but without complaint.

23.4.1 Converting Types

The following expression is valid only when both objects have the same numerical type:

```
i + c
```

If *i* is a type **int** and *c* is a type **char**, *c* must be converted to an integer before the addition can be performed. This process is called *promotion*.

23.4.2 Background

Most Common Usage C compilers use the rule called *unsigned preserving*. This rule states that when an **unsigned** type needs to be promoted, it is promoted to an **unsigned** type. It also states that when an **unsigned** type is mixed with a **signed** type, the result is an **unsigned** type.

The other rule is called *value preserving*. This is the rule used by the ISO C standard. It states that promotion depends on the relative sizes of the types involved. For example, when a type **unsigned char** or **unsigned short** is promoted, the resulting type is **int** if an **int** is large enough to represent all the values of the smaller type. Otherwise, the resulting type is **unsigned int**. This value preserving rule produces the least surprises for most expressions.

The ISO C standard comments as follows:

QUIET CHANGE

> A program that depends on unsigned preserving arithmetic conversions behaves differently, probably without complaint. This is considered to be the most serious change made by the Committee to a widespread current practice.

23.4.3 Using a Cast

In the following code, a promotion is needed if a type **unsigned char** is smaller than a type **int**:

```
int f()
{
    int i = -2;
    unsigned char uc = 1;

    return (i + uc) < 17;
}
```

This is an example where the result differs dependent on the promotion rule used. An ISO C standard compiler may issue a warning for the (i + uc) operation to indicate that the result depends on the promotion rule being used.

The result of the addition has type **int** when using value preserving promotion and **unsigned int** for unsigned preserving promotion. However, the bit pattern is the same in both cases; for example, on a two's-complement machine:

```
    i: 111...110  (-2)
+ uc: 000...001  ( 1)
  ______________________
       111...111  (-1 or UINT_MAX)
```

This bit representation corresponds to −1 for type **int** and {UINT_MAX} for type **unsigned int**. For objects of type **int**, a signed comparison is used and the less-than test is true. For objects of type **unsigned int**, an unsigned comparison is used and the less-than test is false.

A cast should be used explicitly to define the behavior that is required. This removes the ambiguity from the expression.

The value preserving cast is:

```
(i + (int)uc) < 17
```

The unsigned preserving cast is:

```
(i + (unsigned int)uc) < 17
```

23.4.4 Same Result

In the following code, two promotions are performed if types **unsigned short** and **unsigned char** are both smaller than type **int**:

```
int f()
{
    unsigned short us;
    unsigned char uc;

    return uc < us;
}
```

Both variables are promoted to either **int** or **unsigned int**, dependent on which promotion rule is in force. Therefore, the comparison is sometimes **signed** and sometimes **unsigned**. However, the result is the same in either case, because both values are always non-negative and therefore the sense of the comparison does not matter.

23.4.5 Integral Constants

As with expressions, the rules for the types of certain integral constants have changed. In Common Usage C, an unsuffixed decimal constant has type **int** if its value fits in a type **int**; otherwise, it has type **long**. Similarly, an unsuffixed octal or hexadecimal constant has type **int** if its value fits in an **unsigned int**; otherwise, it has type **long**.

In the ISO C standard, the type of the constant is the first from one of the following lists:

```
unsuffixed decimal:
    int, long, unsigned long
unsuffixed octal or hexadecimal:
    int, unsigned int, long, unsigned long
u-suffixed or U-suffixed:
    unsigned int, unsigned long
l-suffixed or L-suffixed:
    long, unsigned long
ul-suffixed or UL-suffixed:
    unsigned long
```

In the following code, the objects of type **int** have 16 bits:

```
int f()
{
    int i = 0;

    return i > 0xffff;
}
```

For a Common Usage C compiler, the constant's type is **int**, with a value of –1 on a two's-complement machine. Therefore, the result of the comparison is true.

For an ISO C standard compiler, the constant's type is **unsigned int**, with a value of 65535. Therefore, the result of the comparison is false.

Again, an appropriate cast clarifies the code and silences an ISO C standard compiler.

For Common Usage C behavior use:

```
i > (int)0xffff
```

For ISO C standard behavior use:

```
i > (unsigned int)0xffff
```
or
```
i > 0xffffU
```

Note: The U suffix is a new feature of the ISO C standard and probably produces an error message with older C compilers.

23.5 Tokenization and Preprocessing

This section discusses the operations that transform each source file from a sequence of characters into a sequence of tokens ready for parsing. These operations include recognition of white spaces and comments, bundling consecutive characters into tokens, handling preprocessing directive lines, and replacement of macros. These operations are probably the least specified part of Common Usage C; their ordering was never guaranteed.

This section also describes some new macros and the changes to the **#define** directive.

23.5.1 ISO C Translation Phases

The ISO C standard specifies eight conceptual steps, called *translation phases*. Although an implementation can merge adjacent phases together, the result must be the same as if they were distinct phases, each performed in sequence.

1. Every *trigraph sequence* in the source file is replaced by a corresponding single character.
2. Every backslash and new-line character pair is deleted.
3. The source file is converted into preprocessing tokens and sequences of white spaces. Each comment is effectively replaced by a space character.
4. Each preprocessing directive is handled and all macro invocations are replaced. Each **#include** source file is run through phases 1 to 4, recursively, before its contents replace the directive line.
5. All escape sequences in character constants and string literals are converted to their character equivalents.

6. Adjacent string literals are concatenated and wide-character string literals are concatenated.
7. Every preprocessing token is converted into a token. These tokens are then analyzed for correct syntax and semantics. The compiler then uses these tokens to generate the code.
8. All external object and function references are resolved, resulting in the final program.

23.5.2 Digraph Sequences

The ISO C standard has 6 digraph sequences that were invented as a concession to the 7-bit ISO/IEC 646: 1991 character set (which does not contain the characters [ ] { } #). These are the following character sequences:

```
<:    :>    <%    %>    %:    %:%:
```

These digraphs are equivalent to the following tokens:

```
[     ]     {     }     #     ##
```

Be careful of their use, since it is possible to construct source files that change behavior due to the introduction of %: and %:%:.

23.5.3 Trigraph Sequences

The ISO C standard has nine trigraph sequences that were invented solely as a concession to character sets that are deficient as far as the ISO C standard is concerned. They are three-character sequences that name a character that is not in the ISO/IEC 646: 1991 character set:

```
??<   {        ??(   [        ??'   ^
??>   }        ??)   ]        ??!   |
??=   #        ??-   ~        ??/   \
```

Be careful of their use; in the following example:

```
/* comment *??/
/* still a comment? */
```

the ??/ becomes a backslash. This backslash and the following newline are removed (during the second translation phase) and the resulting characters are:

```
/* comment */* still a comment? */
```

The first forward slash from the second line is the end of the comment. The next token is *.

23.5.4 Common Usage C Translation Phases

The Common Usage C compilers do not follow such a simple sequence of phases, nor do they guarantee when these steps are applied. A separate preprocessor recognizes tokens and white spaces at the same time that it replaces macros and handles directive lines. The output is then completely retokenized by the compiler before it parses the language and generates the code.

The tokenization process within the preprocessor is performed on a moment-by-moment basis, and macro replacement is done as a character-based operation and not as a token-based operation. This means that tokens and white spaces could have a great deal of variation during preprocessing.

There are a number of differences that arise between these two approaches. The following sections discuss differences in code behavior due to line-splicing, macro replacement, string literal production, and token pasting.

23.5.5 Logical Source Lines

In Common Usage C, backslash and new-line pairs are allowed only as a means to continue a directive, a string literal, or a character constant to the next line. The ISO C standard extended the notion so that a backslash and new-line pair can continue anything to the next line. The result is called a *logical source line*. Therefore, any code that relies on the separate recognition of tokens on either side of a backslash and new-line pair does not behave as expected with an ISO C standard compiler.

23.5.6 Macro Replacement

Prior to the ISO C standard, the macro replacement process was never described in any significant detail. This vagueness spawned many divergent implementations. Any Common Usage C code that relies on anything fancier than constant replacement and simple macros is probably not truly portable. There are a number of differences between the Common Usage C macro replacement implementation and the ISO C standard version. However, nearly all uses of macro replacement, with the exception of token pasting and string literal production, produce exactly the same series of tokens as before.

The major change to macro replacement is to require macro arguments (other than those that are operands of the macro substitution operators # and ##) to be expanded recursively prior to their substitution in the replacement token list. However, this change seldom produces an actual difference in the resulting tokens.

23.5.7 String Literal Production

In Common Usage C, the following code:

```
#define str(a) "a!"
str(x y)
```

produced the string literal:

```
"x y!"
```

To do this, the preprocessor searched inside string literals (and character constants) for characters that looked like the macro's arguments.

The ISO C standard recognized the importance of this feature, but could not condone operations on parts of tokens. In the ISO C standard, all invocations of the above macro produce the string literal:

```
"a!"
```

To achieve the desired effect in the ISO C standard, make use of the # macro substitution operator and the concatenation of string literals. A macro argument preceded by # has its corresponding unexpanded argument tokens converted into a string literal:

```
#define str(a) #a "!"
str(x y)
```

The above produces the two string literals:

```
"x y" "!"
```

which, after concatenation, produces:

```
"x y!"
```

Unfortunately, there is no direct replacement for the analogous operation for character constants. For example, in Common Usage C:

```
#define CNTL(ch) (037 & 'ch')
CNTL(L)
```

would produce:

```
(037 & 'L')
```

which, in turn, evaluates to the ASCII <control>-L character.

The best solution for the ISO C standard is to change all uses of this macro to:

```
#define CNTL(ch) (037 & (ch))
CNTL('L')
```

which is arguably more readable and more useful, as it can also be applied to expressions.

23.5.8 Token Pasting

In Common Usage C, there are at least two ways to combine two tokens. Both invocations in the following code produce a single identifier **x1** out of the two tokens **x** and **1**:

```
#define self(a) a
#define glue(a,b) a/**/b
self(x)1
glue(x,1)
```

In the ISO C standard, both the above invocations produce the two separate tokens **x** and **1**.

The second of the above two methods can be rewritten for the ISO C standard by using the ## macro substitution operator. This operator removes any white space around it and concatenates the adjacent tokens to create a new token:

```
#define glue(a,b) a ## b
glue(x, 1)
```

Since ## is an actual operator, the invocation can be much freer with white space both in the definition and invocation.

There is no direct approach to produce the first of the old-style pasting schemes. However, since that scheme put the burden of the pasting at the invocation, it was used less frequently than the second form.

Remember that # and ## operators should only be used when __STDC__ is defined.

23.5.9 New Macros

The ISO C standard has five predefinition macros. They are:

__LINE__ The current line number in decimal.

__FILE__ The name of the file being compiled, as a string literal.

__DATE__ The date of compilation, as a string literal.

__TIME__ The time of compilation, as a string literal.

__STDC__ The decimal constant 1. This indicates a conforming implementation.

These macros should not be defined using **#define** or undefined using **#undef**.

23.5.10 Changes to #define

The operation of the **#define** directive has some additional features and some additional constraints on how the directive can be used.

From the viewpoint of existing code, only the following constraints are relevant:

- Macros are no longer recursive. The name of the macro currently being expanded is not itself expanded if it occurs in the replacement string.
- Preprocessing directives are not allowed within a list of arguments to a macro.
- A macro name should not be redefined without an intervening **#undef** directive, unless the new definition is identical to the old one. If in doubt, the **#undef** directive should be used. This is ignored if the specified identifier is not currently defined as a macro name.

23.6 Types

This section explains the use of the ISO C standard *type qualifiers* category, which contains the keywords **const** and **volatile**. It also describes the new types: **incomplete**, **compatible**, and **composite**. This section explains where new types are permitted, and why they are useful.

23.6.1 Using Type Qualifiers

If an object is declared as a type qualifier **const**, the compiler may place that object in read-only memory. The program is not allowed to change its value, and cannot make a further assignment to it.

Declaring an object as a type qualifier **volatile** warns the compiler that unexpected, asynchronous events may affect that object. Knowing this, the compiler does not make any assumptions about that object. For example, the compiler does not try to optimize that object.

Type Qualifiers in Derived Types

The type qualifiers are unique in that they may modify names declared with **typedef**, such as **size_t**, and derived types, such as pointers. Derived types are those parts of the C-language declarations that construct more complex types from the basic types. Pointers, arrays, functions, structures, and unions are derived types. Except for functions, one or both type qualifiers can be used to change the behavior of a derived type.

An example use of the type qualifier **const** is:

```
const int five = 5;
```

This declares and initializes an object with type **const int**, whose value is not changed by a correct program.

In fact, the order of the keywords is not significant to an ISO C standard compiler. For example, the declarations:

```
int const five = 5;
```

and:

```
const five = 5;
```

are identical to the above declaration in their effects.

The next example shows a type qualifier **const** applied to a pointer to an integer; that is, to a derived type:

```
const int *pci = &five;
```

Here an object with type pointer to **const int** is declared, which initially points to the previously declared object. Note that the pointer itself does not have a qualified type, but it points to a qualified type. This means that the pointer can be changed to point to another integer, but it cannot be used directly to modify the object that it points to.

The object that *pci* points to can be modified by using a cast, for example:

```
*(int *)pci = 17;
```

Note that the behavior of this code is undefined if *pci* actually points to a type **const** object.

The next example declares a type **const** pointer to a type **int** that is defined elsewhere in the program:

```
extern int *const cpi;
```

Here, the value of *cpi* is not changed by a correct program, but it can be used to modify the object to which it points. Note that **const** comes after the ***** in the above declaration.

The following pair of declarations produces the same effect as the previous example:

```
typedef int *INT_PTR;
extern const INT_PTR cpi;
```

The next example results in a type qualifier **const** pointer to a **const int**:

```
extern const int *const cpci;
```

The const Keyword

With hindsight, **readonly** would have been a better choice for this keyword than **const**. If **const** is read as **readonly**, declarations such as:

```
char *strcpy(char *, const char *);
```

are more easily understood. Here, the second argument is only used to read type **char** values, while the first argument overwrites the type **char** values to which it points.

Furthermore, a pointer to a **const int** (as in a previous example), can still change the value of the object to which it points by use of a cast.

The two main uses for **const** are:

- to declare, possibly large, compile-time initialized tables of information as unchanging
- to specify that pointer arguments do not modify the objects to which they point.

The first use allows a program's data to be shared by other concurrent invocations of the same program. Any attempt to modify this invariant data can be detected immediately by some sort of memory protection fault.

The second use probably helps locate potential errors in programs. For example, functions that temporarily place a null character into the middle of a string are detected at compile time, if passed a pointer to a string that cannot be modified.

The volatile Keyword

For the programmer, **volatile** has several implications. For a compiler writer, it has one implication: no code generation shortcuts can be taken when accessing such an object.

It is a programmer's responsibility to declare every object that has the appropriate special properties, with a type qualifier **volatile**.

Four example uses of **volatile** objects are:

- an object that is a memory-mapped I/O port
- an object that is shared between multiple concurrent processes or threads
- an object that is modified by an asynchronous signal handler
- an automatic storage duration object declared in a function that calls *setjmp*( ) and whose value is changed between the call to *setjmp*( ) and a corresponding call to *longjmp*( ).

The first three examples are all instances of an object whose value can be modified at any point during the execution of the program. For example, the seemingly infinite loop:

```
flag = 1;
while (flag)
    ;
```

is reasonable as long as *flag* has a type qualifier **volatile**, for example:

```
volatile int flag;
```

If the program is not going to loop forever, some asynchronous event needs to set *flag* to zero.

If *flag* does not have a type qualifier **volatile**, for example:

```
int flag;
```

the compilation system is free to change the above loop into a truly infinite loop that completely ignores the value of *flag*.

The fourth example, involving variables local to functions that call *setjmp*( ), is more involved. There are no guarantees about the values for objects matching the fourth case. To provide the most desirable behavior, the *longjmp*( ) function would be required to examine every stack frame between the function calling *setjmp*( ) and the function calling *longjmp*( ) for saved register values. The possibility of asynchronously created stack frames makes this task even more complex. Therefore most implementors only document the undesirable side effect.

When an automatic object is declared with a type qualifier **volatile**, the compilation system knows that it has to produce code that exactly matches what the programmer wrote. Therefore, the most recent value for such an object is always in memory, and as such is guaranteed to be up-to-date when *longjmp*( ) is called.

23.6.2 Incomplete Types

The ISO C standard uses the term *incomplete type* to formalize a fundamental aspect of the language that is often misunderstood.

The ISO C standard separates types into three distinct sets:

- function types
- object types

- incomplete types.

Function types are well known. Object types cover everything else, except when the size of the object is not known. Incomplete types refer to objects whose size is not known.

There are only three variations of incomplete types:

- void
- arrays of unspecified length
- structures and unions with unspecified content.

The type **void** differs from the other two in that it is an incomplete type that cannot be completed; it serves as a special function return and argument type.

Examples of incomplete types, include:

```
char s[];
struct a { struct b *bp; };
```

where the content of **struct** *b* is not yet listed.

Completing Incomplete Types

An array type is completed by specifying the array size in a following declaration which is in the same scope as the object.

An incomplete structure or union type is completed by specifying the content in a following declaration which is in the same scope.

Declarations

Certain declarations can use incomplete types, but others require complete object types. Those declarations that require object types are:

- array elements
- members of structures or unions
- objects local to a function.

All other declarations permit incomplete types. For example, the following are permitted:

- pointers to incomplete types
- functions returning incomplete types
- incomplete function argument types
- **typedef** names for incomplete types.

The return and argument types for functions are special. Except for **void**, an incomplete type used in such a manner must be completed by the time the function is defined or called.

Note that since array and function argument types are rewritten to be pointer types, a seemingly incomplete array argument type is not actually incomplete. The typical declaration of *argv* in *main*( ):

```
char *argv[];
```

as an unspecified length array of type **char** pointers, is rewritten to be a pointer to **char** pointers, and is therefore a complete type.

Expressions

Most expression operators require (complete) object types. The only three exceptions are:

- the unary **&** operator
- the first operand of the comma operator
- the second and third operands of the **?:** operator.

Most operators that accept pointer operands also permit pointers to incomplete types, unless pointer arithmetic is required.

Rationale

The ISO C standard would be simpler without incomplete types, but incomplete types allow forward references in structures and unions, which cannot be done any other way in C.

The only way to get two structures that have pointers to each other (without resorting to potentially invalid casts) is with incomplete types, for example:

```
struct a { struct b *bp; };
struct b { struct a *ap; };
```

Examples

Defining **typedef** names for incomplete structure and union types is quite useful. Complex data structures that contain pointers to each other can be simplified by declaring a list of **typedef** statements as follows:

```
typedef struct item_tag Item;
typedef union  note_tag Note;
typedef struct list_tag List;
   . . .
struct item_tag { . . . };
   . . .
struct list_tag {
    List  *next;
    . . .
};
```

If structures and unions exist whose contents should not be available to the rest of the program, the tag can be declared, without the contents, in a header. Other parts of the program can use pointers to the incomplete structure or union without any problems, provided they do not attempt to use any of its members.

Another useful incomplete type is an external array of unspecified length. It is not always necessary to know the exact size of an array to make use of its contents, for example:

```
extern char *tzname[];
...
printf("Alternative time zone: %s\n", tzname[1]);
```

23.6.3 Compatible and Composite Types

With the ISO C standard it is possible to make two declarations for the same entity that are not identical. the ISO C standard uses the term *compatible type* to denote those types that are close enough to be considered the same.

Composite types are types that are the result of combining two compatible types.

Multiple Declarations

If a C program were only allowed one declaration for each object or function, compatible types would not be needed. However, function prototypes, separate compilation, and linkage all require such a capability.

Separate translation units (that is, source files) have different rules for type compatibility from the rules for type compatibility within a single translation unit.

Separate Compilation

Since each compilation probably looks at different source files, most of the rules for compatible types across separate compilations are structural in nature.

- Matching scalar (that is, integral, floating, and pointer) types must be compatible, as if they were in the same source file.
- Matching structures, unions, and enumeration types must have the same number of members, and each matching member must have a compatible type. This includes bit-field widths.
- Matching structures and unions must have the members in the same order. The order of enumeration type members does not matter.
- Matching enumeration type members must have the same value.

An additional requirement is that the names of members, including the lack of names for unnamed members, must match for structures, unions, and enumeration types. However, their respective tags need not necessarily match.

Single Compilation

When two declarations in the same scope describe the same object or function, the two declarations must specify compatible types. These two types are then combined into a single composite type that is compatible with the first two.

Compatible types are defined recursively. At the bottom are the type specifier keywords, along with the rules that say that type **unsigned short** is the same as type **unsigned short int**, and that a type without type specifiers is the same as one with type **int**.

All other types are compatible only if the types from which they are derived are compatible. For example, two qualified types are compatible if the qualifiers, **const** and **volatile**, are identical and the unqualified base types are compatible.

Compatible Pointer Types

Two pointer types are compatible if the types they point to are compatible and the two pointers are identically qualified. The qualifiers for a pointer are specified after the *, so that these two declarations:

```
int *const cpi;
int *volatile vpi;
```

declare two differently qualified pointers to the same type: **int**.

Compatible Array Types

Two array types are compatible if their element types are compatible and, if both array types have a specified size, they match. This last part means that an incomplete array type is compatible both with another incomplete array type and an array type with a specified size.

Compatible Function Types

Two function types are compatible if their return types are compatible. If either or both function types have prototypes, the rules get more complicated.

For two function types with prototypes to be compatible, they must also have the same number of arguments, including use of the ellipsis notation, and the corresponding arguments must be argument-compatible.

For an old-style function definition to be compatible with a function type with a prototype, the prototype arguments must not end with an ellipsis and each of the prototype arguments must be argument-compatible with the corresponding old-style argument, after application of the default argument promotions.

For an old-style function declaration (not a definition) to be compatible with a function type with a prototype, the prototype arguments must not end with an ellipsis (...) and all of the prototype arguments must have types that are unaffected by the default argument promotions.

For two types to be argument-compatible, the types must be compatible after the top-level qualifiers, if any, are removed, and after a function or array type is converted to the appropriate pointer type.

Note: There are a few surprises in this area. For example, type **signed int** behaves the same as type **int**.

Also, each enumeration type must be compatible with some integral type. For portable programs, this means that enumeration types are effectively separate types; for the most part, the ISO C standard views them in that manner.

Composite Type

The construction of a composite type from two compatible types is also defined recursively. The ways compatible types can differ from each other are due either to incomplete arrays or to old-style function types. As such, the simplest description of the composite type is that it is the type compatible with both of the original types, including every available array size and every available argument list from the original types.

For example, the following two function declarations are compatible:

```
int f(int (*)(),       double (*)[3]);
int f(int (*)(char *), double (*)[]);
```

The resultant composite type, which is compatible with both declarations, is:

```
int f(int (*)(char *), double (*)[3]);
```

23.7 Expressions

This section discusses the differences between Common Usage C and the ISO C standard in the rules for grouping and evaluating expressions. It also describes some other changes to expressions.

23.7.1 Common Usage C Rearrangement

Common Usage C compilers are allowed to rearrange expressions involving adjacent operators that are mathematically associative and commutative, even in the presence of parentheses.

An operator, *op*, is commutative if:

```
a op b = b op a
```

For example, + is commutative, but – is not.

An operator, *op*, is associative if:

```
(a op b) op c = a op (b op c)
```

+ is associative, but – is not.

The following example is used to compare Common Usage C and the ISO C standard features:

```
int i, *p, f(), g();
i = *++p + f() + g();
```

For Common Usage C, the following three possible groupings are valid for the example. The groupings are shown using left and right braces:

```
i = { {*++p + f()} + g() };
i = { *++p + {f() + g()} };
i = { {*++p + g()} + f() };
```

Moreover, all of these groupings are valid for either of the following:

```
i = *++p + (f() + g());
i = (g() + *++p) + f();
```

If this expression is evaluated on an architecture for which either overflows cause an exception, or when the sign of the value can be inverted across an overflow, these three groupings behave differently if one of the additions overflows.

For such expressions on these architectures, the only recourse available in Common Usage C is to split the expression to force a particular grouping. The following are possible rewrites that enforce the above three groupings respectively:

```
i = *++p;    i += f();    i += g();
i = f();     i += g();    i += *++p;
i = *++p;    i += g();    i += f();
```

23.7.2 ISO C Rules

The ISO C standard does not allow the rearrangement of operations that are mathematically associative and commutative, also but are not actually so on the target architecture. Thus, the precedence and associativity of the ISO C standard grammar completely describes the grouping for all expressions. All expressions must be grouped as they are parsed. This means that the example is grouped in the following way:

```
i = { {*++p + f()} + g() };
```

However, note that this still does not mean that *f*( ) must be called before *g*( ), nor that *p* must be incremented before *g*( ) is called.

It does mean, however, that in the ISO C standard, expressions need not be split to guard against unintended overflows.

Parentheses

The ISO C standard is often erroneously described as honoring parentheses or evaluating according to parentheses; this is not true.

In the ISO C standard, expressions are grouped according to the way they are parsed. This means that parentheses still only serve as a way of controlling how an expression is parsed. The natural precedence and associativity of expressions carry exactly the same weight as parentheses.

If the example is:

```
i = (((*(++p)) + f()) + g());
```

it makes no difference to its grouping, and thus to its evaluation.

23.7.3 Advantages of Rearrangement

The reasons for the Common Usage C rearrangement rules are:

- The rearrangements provide many more opportunities for optimizations, such as compile-time constant folding.
- The rearrangements do not change the result of integral-typed expressions on most machines.
- Some of the operations are both mathematically and computationally commutative and associative on all machines.

In general, an implementation is permitted to deviate from the abstract machine description, provided that deviations do not change the behavior of a valid C program. Therefore, any rearrangement that has no effect on the application is permissible. The result is that this change in C does not have a significant impact on most C programs.

23.7.4 Other Changes to Expressions

Type Float

A type **float** might not be lengthened to a type **double** when it appears in an expression. This means that expressions with operands of type **float** might be computed at a lower precision than double precision. Casts can be used to force double precision computations.

Pointer Subtraction

The resulting type of pointer subtraction no longer needs to be type **int**. It is a **signed** integral type given the name **ptrdiff_t** in **<stddef.h>**.

Empty Structure Declarations

A special meaning is given to the form:

```
struct x;
```

This hides any previous declarations of **x** (as a tag) from an outer scope. This is useful when declaring two mutually referencing structures. For example, the following code does not behave as the programmer probably intended:

```
struct x {int i;};
{
    struct y { struct x *xp; };
    struct x { struct y *yp; };
}
```

The **x** of **struct y** refers to the outer declaration of **x**. But by adding the empty structure declaration as follows:

```
struct x {int i;};
{
    struct x;
    struct y { struct x *xp; };
    struct x { struct y *yp; };
}
```

the outer declaration of **x** is not associated with the inner declaration of **y**.

23.7.5 Scope of Identifiers

Many Common Usage C compilers promote the scope of identifiers with external linkage to file scope. However, in the ISO C standard, identifiers declared in a nested scope are forgotten once the scope ends, for example:

```
f1()
{
    float ffun();
}

f2()
{
    int i = ffun();
}
```

Here, the declaration of *ffun*( ) is not visible in *f2*( ). This means that no conversion is performed because it is assumed that *ffun*( ) returns a type **int**.

String Literals

In Common Usage C, each string literal is required to be distinct and modifiable. (This is why they are called literals instead of constants.) The ISO C standard allows these to be constant, permitting string literals to be placed into read-only memory, as well as encouraging the elimination of duplicate identical storage.

Code that modifies a string literal should replace the string with the name of a static array initialized to contain the string, as follows:

```
p = make_temp("tempXXX");
```

should be replaced with:

```
static char template[] = "tempXXX";
   . . .
p = make_temp(template);
```

if *make_temp*( ) overwrites the string's characters, even if only temporarily.

23.8 Internationalization

This section describes the internationalization features of the ISO C standard:

- multi-byte characters
- wide-character codes.

It also explains how they are used.

23.8.1 Multi-byte Characters

A basic difficulty in an Asian environment is that a large number of ideograms are needed for input and output. To work within the constraints of typical computer architectures, these ideograms are encoded as sequences of bytes. The associated operating systems, application programs, and terminals understand these sequences as individual ideograms. These encodings also allow single-byte characters to be intermixed with ideogram byte sequences. The difficulty associated with recognizing distinct ideograms depends on the encoding scheme used.

The term *multi-byte character* denotes a byte sequence that encodes a character, no matter what encoding scheme is employed. All multi-byte characters are members of the *extended character set*. A single-byte character is a special case of a multi-byte character. Essentially, the only requirement placed on a multi-byte character's encoding is that it cannot use a null character as part of its encoding.

The ISO C standard specifies that program comments, string literals, character constants, and header names are sequences of multi-byte characters.

23.8.2 Encoding Variations

An encoding scheme can be described as being *stateless* or *stateful*. In the first type, each multi-byte character is self-identifying. This means that any multi-byte character can simply be inserted between any pair of multi-byte characters. For example, one possible encoding choice is that each byte of a character that is not a single byte has the high-order bit set; the number of bytes in the character is determined by the value of the initial byte. The coded representation of each character is determined by applying the codeset encoding rules that associate a numeric value to each character.

In the second scheme, special *shift bytes* change the interpretation of subsequent bytes. An example is the method by which most character terminals get in and out of line-drawing mode. For this case, the ISO C standard has the additional requirement that each comment, string literal, character constant, and header name must both begin and end in the unshifted state.

23.8.3 Wide-character Codes

Some of the inconvenience of handling multi-byte characters would be eliminated if all characters were of a uniform number of bytes or bits. There can be thousands of ideograms in a character set, so a 16-bit or 32-bit sized integral value should be used to hold all its members. The full Chinese alphabet includes more than 65,000 ideograms.

The ISO C standard includes the **typedef** name **wchar_t** as the implementation-dependent integral type large enough to hold all members of the extended character set, for example:

```
wchar_t c;
```

declares a wide-character code **c** which can hold any member of the extended character set.

For each wide-character code there is a corresponding multi-byte character and *vice versa*. The wide-character code that corresponds to a character of the portable character set is required to have the same value as the character of the portable character set. This requirement includes the null character. However, there is no guarantee that the value of the macro EOF can be stored in a **wchar_t**. (Just as EOF might not be representable as a **char**.)

23.8.4 Conversion Functions

Text recorded or generated externally to a program is normally encoded as a series of multi-byte characters. To process these characters internally, it is often convenient first to convert them to wide-character codes, process them, and convert them back to byte sequences for output. The ISO C standard provides five library functions for this purpose:

mblen( ) Length of next multi-byte character.

mbtowc( ) Convert multi-byte character to wide-character code.

wctomb( ) Convert wide-character code to multi-byte character.

mbstowcs( ) Convert multi-byte character string to wide-character string.

wcstombs( ) Convert wide-character string to multi-byte character string.

ISO C Amendment 1 (MSE) provides a further seven new functions:

btowc( ) Convert single-byte to wide-character.

mbrlen( ) Length of next multi-byte character (restartable).

mbrtowc( ) Convert multi-byte character to wide-character code (restartable).

mbsrtowcs( ) Convert multi-byte character string to wide-character string (restartable).

wcrtomb( ) Convert wide-character code to multi-byte character (restartable).

wcsrtombs( ) Convert wide-character string to multi-byte character string (restartable).

wctob( ) Convert wide-character to single byte.

The following is an example use of *mbtowc*( ):

```
char *mb;
wchar_t wchar;
   . . .
mbtowc(&wchar, mb, strlen(mb));
```

The argument *mb* points to a multi-byte character. After the call to *mbtowc*( ), *wchar* holds the equivalent wide-character code.

For most application programs, there is no need to convert any multi-byte characters to or from wide-character codes. Utilities such as *diff*, for example, read in and write out multi-byte characters, only needing to check for an exact byte-for-byte match. More complicated programs that use regular expression pattern matching, such as *grep*, may need to understand multi-byte characters. However, this knowledge can be localized to the functions that manage the regular expressions. The utility *grep* requires no other special knowledge about how to handle multi-byte characters.

23.8.5 Features of the C Language

The ISO C standard provides wide-character constants and wide string literals. These have the same form as their non-wide versions except that they are immediately prefixed by the letter L:

```
'x'             regular character constant
'¥'             regular character constant
"abc¥xyz"       regular string literal
L'x'            wide-character constant
L'¥'            wide-character constant
L"abc¥xyz"      wide string literal
```

Note that multi-byte characters are valid in both the regular and wide versions. The sequence of bytes necessary to produce the ideogram ¥ is encoding-specific, but if it consists of more than one byte, the value of the character constant '¥' is implementation-dependent.

When the compilation system encounters a wide-character constant or wide-string literal, each multi-byte character is converted, as if by calling the *mbtowc*( ) function, into a wide-character code. Thus:

```
L'¥'            /* has type wchar_t */
L"abc¥xyz"      /* has type wchar_t[8] */
```

Note the length of the string is eight because it is terminated by a zero-valued **wchar_t**.

Just as regular string literals can be used as a shorthand method for character array initialization, wide-string literals can be used to initialize **wchar_t** arrays:

```
wchar_t *wp = L"a¥z";
wchar_t x[] = L"a¥z";
wchar_t y[] = {L'a', L'¥', L'z', 0};
wchar_t z[] = {'a', L'¥', 'z', '\0'};
```

In the above example, the three arrays **x**, **y**, and **z**, and the sequence pointed to by *wp*, have the same length and all are initialized with identical values.

Finally, adjacent wide-string literals are concatenated, just as with regular string literals. However, adjacent regular and wide-string literals cannot be concatenated. In fact, a compiler is not even required to complain if it does not accept such concatenations.

Go Solo 2

Part 4:

Case Studies

The Open Group

Chapter 24

The Creation of OpenEdition MVS

In the late 1980s, IBM was faced with an urgent problem: how to accommodate customers' desire for open interfaces while making it possible for them to preserve a 30-year investment in MVS applications and continue to rely on MVS services for reliability and availability. IBM addressed this issue with OS/390 Release 2, known as OpenEdition, which met the requirements for the UNIX 95 brand in 1996.

This chapter provides an in-depth description of the creation of OpenEdition MVS; in particular, the implementation of the key UNIX functionality for process creation and management, signal handling, and interprocess communication.

24.1 Introduction

In November 1990, the OpenEdition MVS group was formed with the mission of implementing the POSIX.1 and POSIX.2 standards on MVS. At this point in time, the group had no knowledge of POSIX or UNIX system functions. In a remarkable show of democracy, developers were polled to determine which areas they wanted to work on. Groups were then formed to work on the kernel, filesystem, communications, and the shell. This chapter focuses on the implementation of the kernel.

The kernel group then proceeded to identify the major areas of work as *fork*, *exec*, signals, and security. In subsequent releases, the kernel also needed to tackle threading and interprocess communication.

Before any work could be started, the fundamental question had to be addressed of how the POSIX functionality would fit in with existing MVS functions and address spaces. The initial reaction was to build an isolated environment in which the POSIX services would behave according to the standards.

After several days of discussion, the conclusion was reached that POSIX C programs could not be isolated from the rest of MVS. From that point on, the design assumption was that kernel services would be available to any program running on an MVS task. This design philosophy has been the source of much debate, but has allowed the kernel services to be exploited from most existing MVS environments, as well as the POSIX environments they were created to serve.

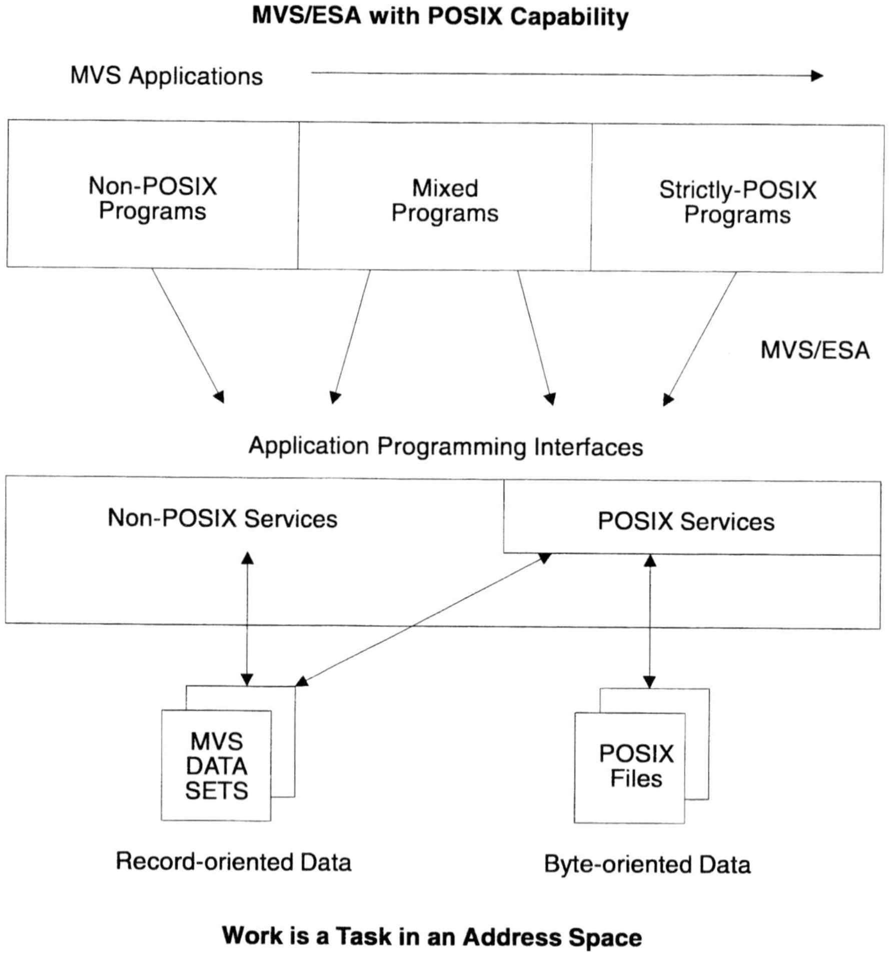

Figure 24-1 Mixing POSIX and MVS

Figure 24-1 shows the range of programming options available with OpenEdition MVS. Existing MVS applications can continue to be run without any disruption. POSIX or XPG4 Base-compliant applications from other platforms can be ported and run on MVS. In between, is a world of options. Existing MVS applications can be taken and converted to use services typically found on UNIX systems. For example, an MVS application could be updated to access data from a filesystem on a remote system using *Network File System* (NFS). Conversely, a UNIX system application could be changed so that it exploits MVS services.

The following sections look at the design assumptions and considerations for some of the major components of POSIX services.

24.2 Fork and the Process Model

The one factor which makes *fork*( ) a difficult function to implement is that the parent and child must end up with identical virtual storage. The parent and child can then modify their copy of the storage independently. Figure 24-2 shows a high-level flow of the *fork*( ) design.

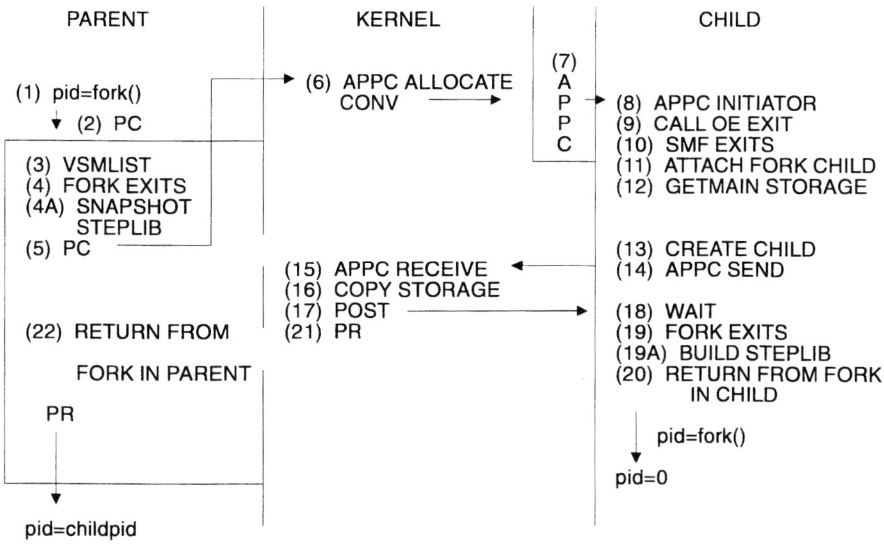

Figure 24-2 Fork Design

The following steps occur in a *fork*( ) flow. This is a greatly simplified explanation with many underlying steps eliminated.

A process issues *fork*( ) This caller of *fork*( ) is defined as the parent process (STEP 1). *fork*( ) switches to some kernel code using a *Program Call* (PC) instruction (STEP 2).

The kernel needs to determine which storage to propagate from the parent to the child. One possible approach was to put all storage in a data space. *fork*( ) would then simply replicate the data space and create a new task for the child. The program would remain shared between parent and child. The main drawbacks to this approach are that there are many MVS services which do not tolerate data spaces, the C run-time library has major problems when putting the stack and heap in data spaces, and this also causes problems for the debugger.

Propagation of virtual storage provides some interesting challenges. It was quickly realized that system storage could not be blindly copied. A simple example is the *Task Control Block* (TCB). When the child is created, a TCB is already provided and is frequently not at the same address as the TCB in the parent. Virtual storage was divided into user storage and system storage. User storage was restricted to key 8. The *Virtual Storage Manager List* (VSMLIST) service (STEP 3) is used to determine what is allocated, and a *Real Storage Manager* (RSM) service (IARVSERV) (STEP 16) is used to propagate storage from parent to child. The storage could not simply be copied. For example, if the child obtained a large area of storage, it could be in the first referenced state, which means the virtual storage is not yet backed by real storage. A direct copy of this area would cause the virtual storage to be backed by real storage in both the parent and child. This would slow down *fork*( ) processing, as well as consume excessive storage. So, the RSM service is designed to propagate the state of virtual pages from the parent to the child in an optimal way. Prior to propagating the storage, it first had to be allocated in the child. To do this, GETMAIN (MVS equivalent of *malloc*()) was enhanced to support GETMAIN by address (STEP 12). This allowed the output to be taken from VSMLIST and to simply GETMAIN the storage at the appropriate addresses.

It was soon realized that *fork*() would need to create a new address space for the child process. In the interest of saving time and code, APPC (a transaction scheduler) was chosen to manage the address space pool. APPC allocate conversation (STEP 6) provides the mechanism to obtain an address space to run in. We simply needed to define a transaction to APPC which we call *fork child*.

Now that an address space existed, there was still a long list of problems to solve. The parent space could have MVS *Data Definitions* (DDs) — DDs define a file and are needed prior to open. Should they be ignored or propagated? How should address space limits of region and time be handled? How should accounting be managed? Should *fork*() be allowed from *Time Sharing Option* (TSO) (MVS equivalent of a shell), batch, *Information Management System* (IMS) (transaction processor), or other specialized environments? The following answers to these questions were sometimes painfully discovered after several false starts.

The initial design point relating to DDs was that no DDs would be propagated from parent to child. In addition to being a lot of code, there was no way to propagate a DISP=OLD DD (UNIX system equivalent of a byte range lock on an entire file). The reason is due to the exclusive lock obtained by allocation. Both the parent and child cannot own an exclusive lock. After making this decision, it was learned that many customers run programs using STEPLIB (the MVS equivalent of PATH= and LIBPATH=). These programs access the run-time libraries from STEPLIB and would fail in the child process if the STEPLIB was not present. So, the design was changed to propagate STEPLIB and provide the ability to change or remove the STEPLIB when executing a new program (STEPS 4A and 19A).

Propagating system storage had to be handled in a totally different manner. To accomplish this, it was determined which system components would need to propagate data from the parent to the child and an exit mechanism was created. The exits are given control in the parent (STEP 4) with a mechanism that allows them to save data. The same exit is given control in the child (STEP 19) with access to the data that was saved in the parent. Executable programs were propagated as part of normal storage, but a contents supervisor exit is used to replicate the system control blocks used to describe those loaded programs. A security product exit is given control to propagate the user identity from the parent to the child. A *Recovery Termination Manager* (RTM) exit is used to propagate the recovery environment which is typically managed by the run-time libraries.

The address space provided by APPC comes with a time limit, region size, and accounting data, as defined for the transaction and user. Standards compliance required the child to inherit the time limit as well as the region size, although standards do not call it a region size. Although standards do not define any behavior for accounting, we felt it was required to propagate the accounting data. Propagating these limits and accounting data (STEP 9) is additionally complicated by installation exits (STEP 10) which are allowed to screen and modify these values at program start time. The child process inherits these values from the parent or the values that are set by the installation exits. Note that an installation exit change to the time or region limit could cause a program to cease to be compliant to the behavior defined in the standards.

In addition to the MVS issues cited above, there were all the process attributes, such as file descriptors, which needed to be propagated (STEP 13). This was a simple matter of programming, with little interference from existing MVS constructs.

24.3 Exec and Contents Supervision

The *exec* services defined in POSIX provide the contents supervisor services necessary to load an executable program into storage and transfer control to it. When *exec* was first designed for MVS, the closest contents supervision function that could be modeled was *Transfer Control* (XCTL). The XCTL function provides the transfer of control mechanism that *exec* requires, but does not provide the necessary cleanup of the resources of the calling program that *exec* requires. So, to properly implement *exec* on MVS required some invention to enable the target executable program to gain control in an environment clean of the resources of the calling program. This was accomplished by creating a new interface with the MVS initiator to allow for the insertion of a new jobstep to be executed in the current job. This mechanism allowed for a design where the *exec* caller's jobstep environment could be terminated and cleaned up and then the creation of a new jobstep could be done to run the target executable program in a clean environment. Figure 24-3 shows a high level flow of the *exec* design.

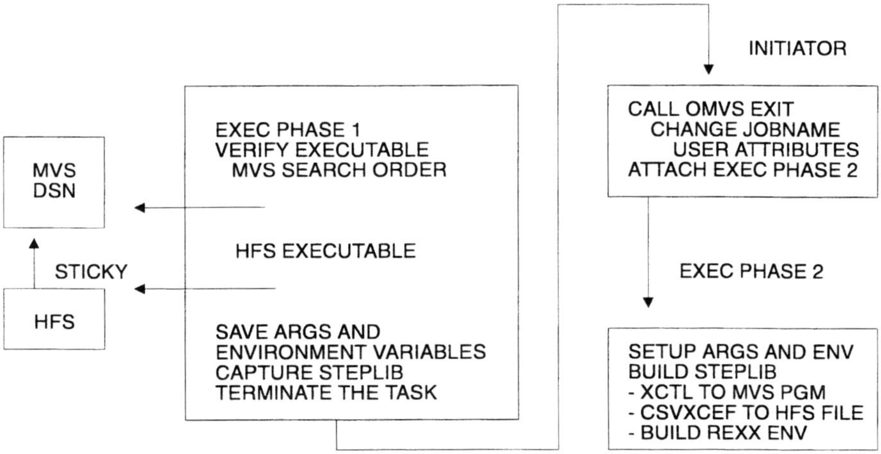

Figure 24-3 Exec Design

Before the flow of control of *exec* is described, the following terminology is introduced describing the different sorts of *exec*:

exec — The basic *exec* supports the execution of a file in the *Hierarchical File System* (HFS); for example, **/bin/sh**.

execmvs — Allows the execution of an executable program which can be located in the normal MVS program search order of STEPLIB, LPALIB, and then linklist.

attach_exec — ATTACH a new task which is treated as a new process and invoke an executable retrieved from the filesystem. This creates the *multiproc* environment which was described under Section 24.2 on page 471.

attach_execmvs — ATTACH a new task which is treated as a new process and invoke an executable retrieved from the MVS program search order (also *multiproc*).

spawn — Create a new process and invoke an executable retrieved from the filesystem. A *spawn* is essentially a *fork*( ) and *exec* combination, where *exec* phase 1 occurs in the parent to validate the request prior to creating the child process, and *exec* phase 2 occurs in the newly created child process where the target program is run.

The following additional twists can occur on the above requests:

- A mode flag called the STICKY-BIT can be turned on for an HFS file. The STICKY-BIT causes *exec* to bypass the HFS and use the regular MVS search order to look for a program. The main reason for the STICKY-BIT is to allow frequently accessed HFS executables to reside in a *Link Pack Area* (LPA) which is common storage shared by all processes. This allows hundreds of users to share the same copy of the shell (**/bin/sh**). Another major use of the STICKY bit is to allow an unauthorized C application to execute an *Authorized Program Facility* (APF) authorized program. An APF authorized program in MVS is analogous to running as superuser in UNIX. A variant of the STICKY-BIT, that provides the equivalent function, is the invocation of an HFS file that is an external link to an MVS program.
- The executable in the HFS can be a REXX *exec*, in which case, the proper TSO environment is established prior to passing control to the REXX processor to run the *exec*.
- An *exec* which is preceded by a change of user identity (*setuid*), will trigger some special OpenEdition MVS processing. Similar special processing is done for a requested jobname change or account information change.
- A *spawn*( ) request that targets the invocation of an HFS program that is found to be neither an executable nor a REXX *exec*, can optionally be turned into the invocation of the OpenEdition interactive shell to run the target HFS program as a shell script.
- An *exec* issued from a local process (see Section 24.2 on page 471) will terminate the current task and cause a new task to be reATTACHed. In this case, the Initiator task does not get involved.

When one of the *exec* functions is called, *exec* phase 1 processing occurs under the caller's unit of work. *exec* phase 1 copies the caller's arguments and environment variables to storage, which will persist across the task termination. It then attempts to locate the executable which has been requested. If it is an HFS executable, the STICKY-BIT is checked to determine whether the request needs to be rerouted to the MVS search order. If the caller of *exec* is running with a STEPLIB active, normal *exec* processing will capture the list of data sets in the STEPLIB for later allocation in *exec* phase 2.

Once all the necessary data has been captured, *exec* phase 1 will terminate the current task. If the application has changed its user ID (*setuid*) or requested a jobname or account data change, then the termination is done in such a way that the initiator thinks it is processing a new job request. This new job processing causes the initiator to pass control to an OpenEdition MVS exit which will do the following:

- Modify the jobname. A typical use of this would be for the *rlogin* daemon. Once it determines the user attempting to *rlogin*, it performs a *setuid* followed by *exec*. The net result is that *exec* will change the jobname of the address space to the USERID. This makes *rlogin* behave in a similar manner to a TSO LOGON.
- Modify the account number for the job. By setting an environment variable for the account number, a user can run programs and have the resource consumption billed to specific accounts. By virtue of being treated as a new job, the resources consumed up to the *exec* will be recorded via a *Systems Measurement Facility* (SMF) type 30 record and a new type 30 record will be written for the start of the new job.

The next step is for the initiator to attach the *exec* phase 2 routine as a new job step. *exec* phase 2 will retrieve and set up the arguments and environment variables which need to be passed to the executable. If the target program is a traditional MVS program in a PDS (MVS equivalent to a directory), then XCTL will be used to invoke the program. If the target program is an executable in the HFS, then a contents supervisor service called CSVXCEF is used to perform the same function as XCTL, but for HFS executables. If the target program is a REXX *exec*, then *exec* phase 2 sets up the TSO environment necessary to run the REXX processor. Once *exec* phase 2 passes control, it never receives control back again.

In addition to the steps listed above, *exec* does other things under the covers like making sure we maintain the integrity of the MVS operation system. This is done by enforcing the basic contents supervisor rules about who can load which programs into authorized environments, and by only propagating steplibs that are sanctioned when invoking a Set-User-Id or Set-Group-Id HFS executable program.

24.4 Signals

This section describes the OpenEdition implementation of Signals in the MVS environment.

The term *Signal* has a fairly generic meaning of any event used to interrupt execution of a program. Here, we will use the term to denote a particular class of event. Typically, a signal is generated by the kernel or user application to perform a specific action in a target process. The possible actions taken upon delivery are:

- Catch
- Terminate
- Stop
- Continue
- Ignore.

The challenge to OpenEdition MVS signal processing was to handle each of the above actions in an MVS address space where a mix of traditional MVS and OpenEdition programs can exist together.

The first problem to solve was how to generate a signal to a particular *Program Request Block* (PRB) (MVS dispatcher control block), of a particular task, of a particular address space, especially when all three of the above can be in a state of flux. To solve this, a signal model was developed around the POSIX signal threading model that included how to choose a PRB of a multiple *Request Block* (RB) task. RBs are tracked by the kernel via RB sequence numbers, which are unique within the scope of the task. The kernel remembers which RB bound itself to signals either because it did a signal registration call or was the first RB to call the kernel from that task. The task interest model, however, has more to do with POSIX semantics, and signal generation will choose the most interested task based upon a history of certain signal functions and signal blocking masks. The target address space is tied to the process ID which is maintained within the kernel and serialized with process latches. All work together, such that, when a signal is generated, the process latch is obtained for the target process which also latches the task. The latch will prevent both process and tasks from terminating. Generation will set the specified signal pending for the chosen task. Once pending, any kernel call will trigger the signal to be delivered. But since the chosen task cannot be counted on to call the kernel (that is, infinite loop), generation must trigger an interrupt mechanism. This mechanism includes scheduling a *Service Request Block* (SRB) to the target address space passing along the target task and target PRB information. SRBs have no equivalent counterpart in UNIX. They provide a way to get into a user process, in this case to interrupt the user work. Once the signal is on its way, control is returned to the invoker of signal generation.

The next hurdle was to effect delivery of the generated signal in the address space of the target process. There are two general types of signal delivery: synchronous and asynchronous.

24.5 Synchronous Signal Delivery

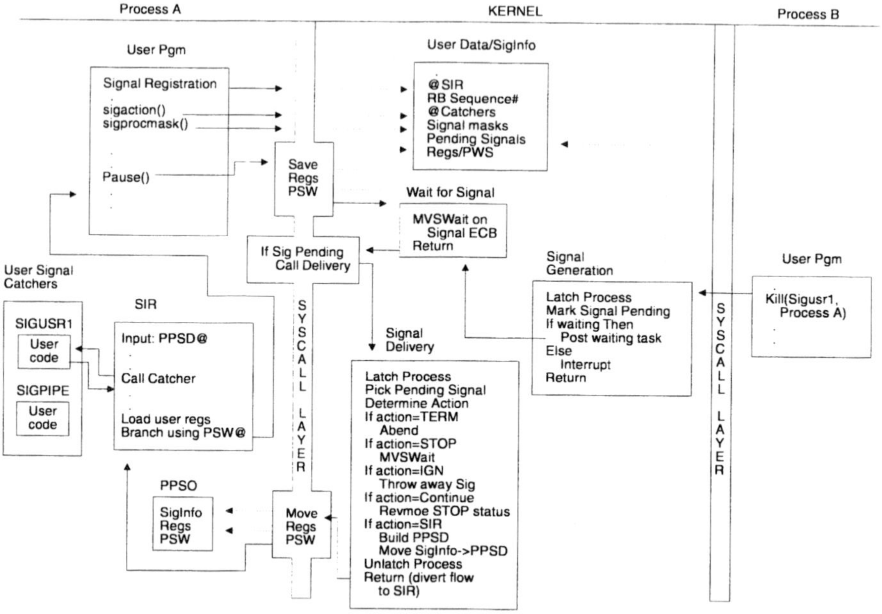

Figure 24-4 Synchronous Signal Delivery

Figure 24-4 shows the signal delivery flow of a signal that is delivered synchronously to an OpenEdition process. This type of delivery occurs when signal processing detects that the target of the signal is in a kernel system service. In this flow, the kernel delivers the signal on the backend of the kernel call. Once the signal processor gains control, it will determine what action to take based on the signal that was generated.

Catch — The signal is packaged into a data structure — *POSIX Process Signal Delivery* (PPSD) block — which describes the many attributes of the signal, including type of signal, signal action, source of signal, and much more. The registers and *Program Status Word* (PSW) — contains instruction counter — of the invoker of the kernel are saved in the PPSD for later use and, instead of returning to the invoker, control is diverted to a preregistered *Signal Interface Routine* (SIR). This routine will typically be owned by a *Run-time Library* (RTL), which will then process the signal based on the information in the PPSD.

Terminate — Two flows can occur for a terminating signal:

1. A process can specify on a registration service if it wants to perform the default actions for terminating signals. This is called *signal default interception*. In this case, the signal is treated as if it's action is Catch. The PPSD is built and control is given to the SIR for handling.

2. If signal default interception is not in effect for the pending signal, then the kernel will abend the process, which in turn will trigger process termination.

Stop When an action of stop is detected, the process is placed in an MVS wait within the OpenEdition kernel.

Continue An action of continue will cause any stopped process to be posted. Execution will continue without any other behavioral side effects.

Ignore No action is taken and execution continues.

Implementing this type of signal delivery was straightforward since the possible states of the invoking process have been greatly reduced by the very nature of the kernel function layer.

24.6 Asynchronous Signal Delivery

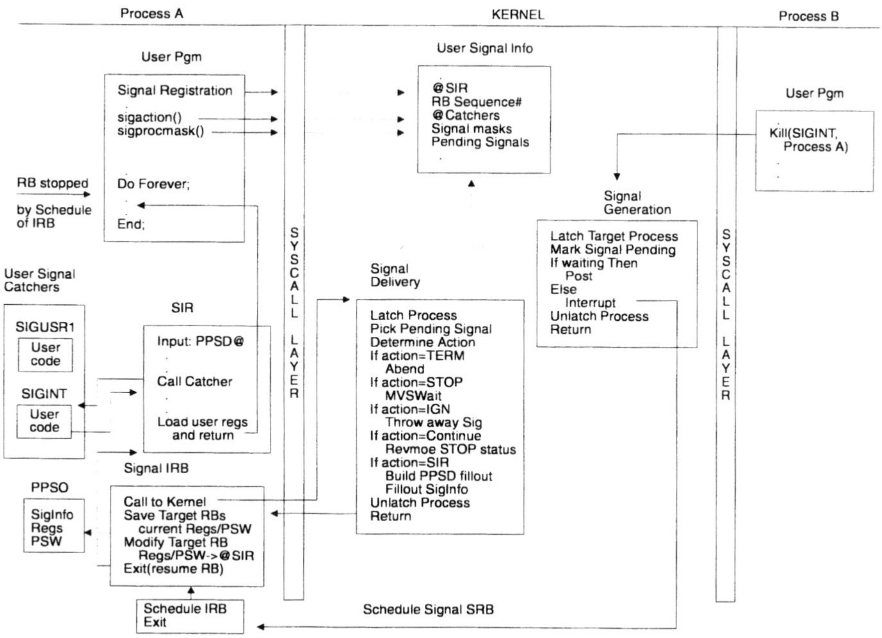

Figure 24-5 Asynchronous Signal Delivery

Figure 24-5 shows the flow of a signal being delivered asynchronously. In this flow, generation of the signal causes an SRB routine to be scheduled to the address space of the target process. The SRB routine then must schedule an *Interrupt Request Block* (IRB) routine to the appropriate task. When the IRB routine is scheduled, it is placed on top of the RB chain, thereby interrupting execution of the previous running RB. In order for the IRB to modify the correct PRB to accept delivery of the signal, the IRB must run directly before the PRB that is doing the OpenEdition work.

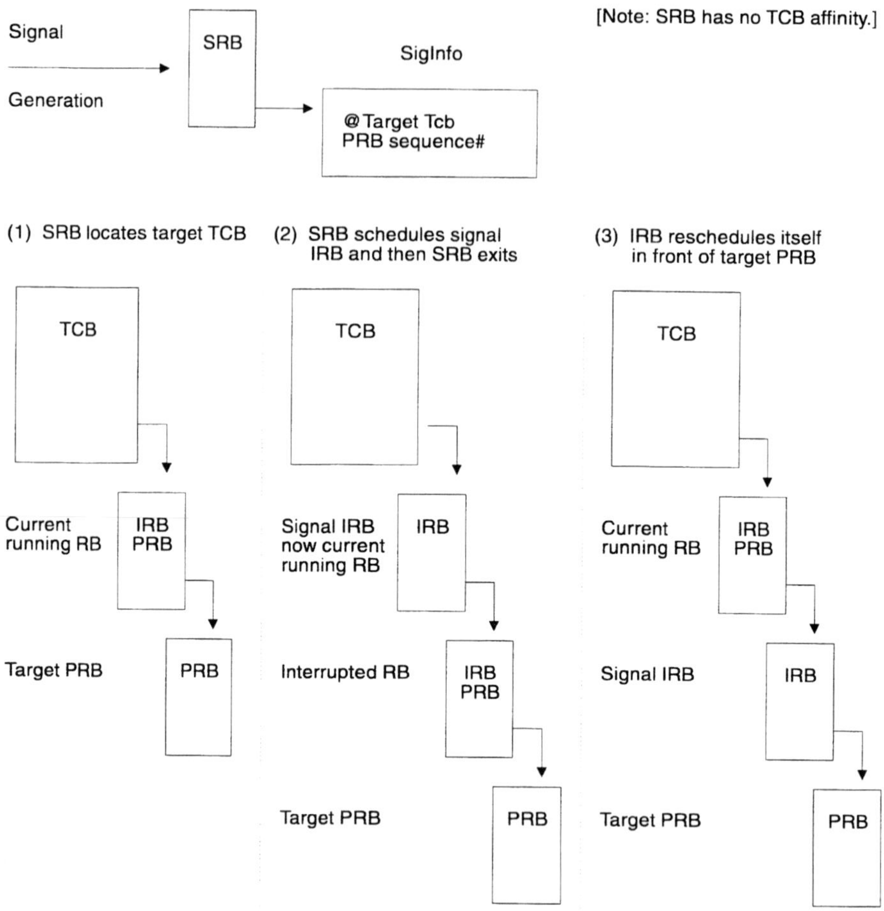

Figure 24-6 Signal IRB Scheduling and Rescheduling

Figure 24-6 shows how the IRB gets scheduled directly in front of the OpenEdition PRB.

Once the IRB is positioned correctly, it will enter the kernel via a special system service whose sole purpose is to drive signal delivery. Once in the kernel, asynchronous delivery processing will perform the same logic as synchronous delivery processing with regard to signal actions. If a PPSD is built, it will be passed back to the IRB when control is returned from the system service. The IRB will then save the interrupted PRB's state (Registers, PSW, and so on) into the PPSD, and then modify the PRB's state such that after the IRB exits and the PRB is rescheduled, control will be given to the SIR.

Another issue to be resolved was to develop an interface between the kernel and the RTL for handling signals. As discussed before, the SIR is an integral part of this interface and, being owned by the RTL, was written to run in user key. The problem here was that even though the RTL was part of OpenEdition, it appears to the kernel as part of the application and is subject to interruption by asynchronous signals. To avoid the recursion scenario of being interrupted by a signal while handling a signal, the kernel defers all other signals whenever handing off a signal to the RTL. This is done by an internal blocking mechanism that will temporarily leave signals pending in the kernel until the RTL asks for them. There are also other places in the RTL where handling signals is a real problem. For instance, take the obvious problem that exists if the RTL were in the middle of expanding the heap and a signal interrupts. If the RTL allowed that signal to be handled by the application signal catcher, it would lose control of the heap. To avoid this, the kernel provides a *signal putback* function which provides the RTL with the ability to re-queue a signal back to the kernel which will then be delivered later when the RTL asks for it.

24.7 Security

UID versus Userid

UNIX system security and MVS security have some basic differences. On UNIX systems, most security decisions are based on a numeric UID value. On MVS systems, most security decisions are based on an 8-character user ID. UNIX systems also have user IDs, but these are generally used to determine the UID. Similarly, UNIX systems support group IDs which are called GIDs. GIDs are numerical values just like UIDs.

In the first release of OpenEdition MVS, there was not a strong correlation between UID and user ID. That is, it supported the *setuid*( ) function, but did not change the MVS user ID when the UID was changed. In the second release of OpenEdition MVS, support was added for sockets and several daemons were introduced. A typical sequence of C functions used by a daemon to create a new process for a user goes like this:

- prompt a user for a user ID
- *getpwnam*( ) to get the uid and gid for the user
- *initgroups*( ) to set the supplemental groups for the user
- *setgid*( ) to set the real and effective GID for the user
- *setuid*( ) to set the real and effective UID for the user
- *exec*( ) typically to put the user into a shell program.

On a UNIX system, the above sequence is sufficient to establish the user identity in a process. But on OpenEdition MVS, this will only establish a UNIX system identity, not an MVS identity. To solve this problem, the behavior of setuid and seteuid (set effective UID) was modified so that it would also change the MVS identity. Now when a daemon executes the above steps, the new process has the correct UNIX system identity as well as the correct MVS identity.

Superuser

Another issue which needed to be addressed was the concept of superuser. On many (but not all) UNIX systems, a superuser is identified by having a UID of 0. Superuser authority allows the user to perform any of the following functions:

- access or delete any file or directory
- send a signal to any process for any user
- change UID to any value, thus becoming any other user.

The first two capabilities did not cause any problems for OpenEdition MVS. The ability to become any user is a function which is typically reserved for system code. On MVS, this problem does not occur, because individual users are given permission to different resources through *Resource Access Control Facility* (RACF) profiles. On MVS, a user must be running *Authorization Protection Facility* (APF) — MVS equivalent of superuser — authorized in order to change the user identity. Our problem was not to have UID zero equivalent to APF authorized.

In order to solve this problem, an additional RACF — plug-compatible security product — profile was created called the BPX.DAEMON (just a name — could have been FOO) facility class. In order for a program to be able to call *setuid*( ), the caller must be permitted to BPX.DAEMON. This allowed for having daemon programs (like *rlogin*) which could do *setuid*( ) to logon a user. It also allows a user to have superuser authority so they can manage the filesystem, without having the ability to change their user ID. Along with defining the BPX.DAEMON class comes an extra layer of security that scrutinizes the DAEMON's address space. Any program loads from an uncontrolled library will cause functions like *setuid*( ) and *seteuid*( ) to fail. This prevents the Trojan horse syndrome.

Most UNIX systems have a user ID called ROOT which is assigned a UID of 0. This is where the term *ROOT authority* comes from. On UNIX systems, any system administrator that requires ROOT authority, needs to know the password for the ROOT user ID. If multiple users require this authority, then they share this password. On MVS, sharing passwords is unacceptable. To get around this problem, MVS allows the installation to assign UID zero to multiple user IDs. There is also a RACF profile called BPX.SUPERUSER which allows an installation to define which users are allowed to switch to superuser in order to maintain the system. This way, there is no need to share passwords.

24.8 Thread Support

MVS has supported multitasking for many years. When OpenEdition MVS was required to support POSIX threads, the following alternatives were considered:

Light Weight Thread (LWT)
: An LWT was defined as a unit of work that was not permanently bound to an MVS task (*Task Control Block* (TCB)). You could create more LWTs than there were tasks ro run them on, and a mini-dispatcher would switch LWTs on and off a task to run.

Medium Weight Thread (MWT)
: An MWT was defined as a unit of work which would be bound to an MVS task until it completed its work. At that point, the same task would pick up another MWT to run.

Heavy Weight Thread (HWT)
: An HWT was defined as a unit of work which would be bound to an MVS task until it completed its work. At that point, the task would be terminated.

The final decision was to implement MWTs and HWTs. Some of the reasons why LWTs were not implemented were:

- Many of the POSIX functions were blocking. These functions would have needed to be redesigned to support a redispatch of another LWT. In other words, asynchronous I/O.
- It would have been very difficult to make the LWTs POSIX compliant.
- In order to support the calling of traditional MVS services from LWTs, it would have been necessary to create an affinity between some LWTs and MVS TCBs.

The final conclusion on LWTs was that any application that required a very fast switching of LWTs could implement their own. Since any LWT design will impose many restrictions on the services that can be called, it was far easier for a local implementation to define those restrictions for a particular application.

The current implementation provides 1 task per active thread. The POSIX model of threads is different than MVS, in that MVS threads are hierarchical (mother/daughter tasks) and POSIX threads are all considered equals. A POSIX thread can *pthread_create*( ) another thread and then terminate without causing the created thread to terminate. In order to implement this TCB structure in MVS, an IRB is scheduled (as shown in Figure 24-7) to the main task, which then performs the ATTACH.

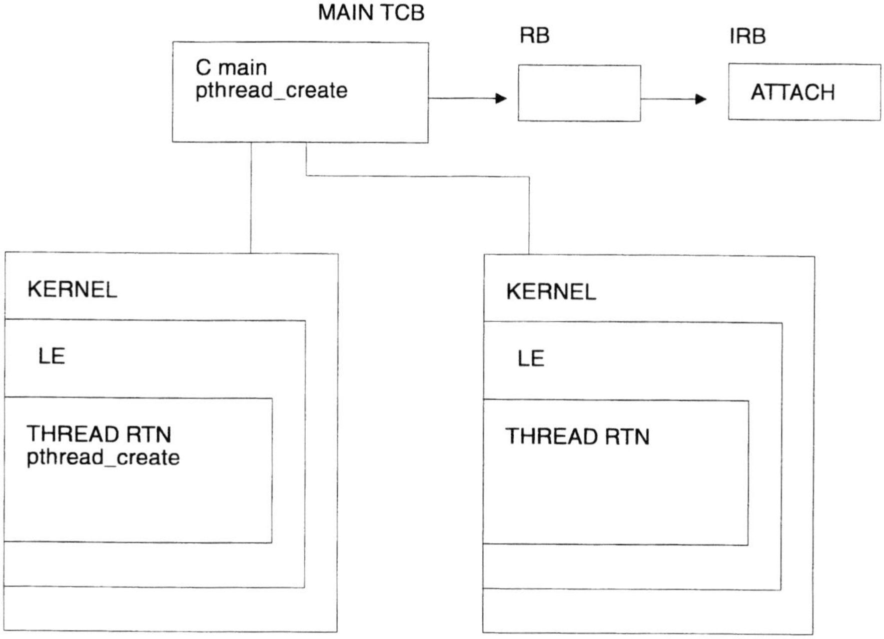

Figure 24-7 TCB Hierarchy for Threads

One of the more perplexing requirements of the thread support was the desire to have hundreds to thousands of threads. Until then, any attempt to create more than 20 tasks in an address space resulted in significant performance degradation, due to the dispatcher design of running the TCB chain looking for a dispatchable task. To solve this problem, the MVS dispatcher was rewritten to implement a true ready queue which contained ready tasks, not just ready address spaces. The dispatcher change also provided fairness of thread dispatching, by no longer giving preference to the TCB highest on the TCB chain.

The next major concern that was addressed is storage below the 16M line. Each new task that is attached consumes about 700 bytes of *Local System Queue Area* (LSQA) — private storage below 16M. In addition to the system overhead, *Language Environment* (LE) and the C RTL consume 12K below the 16M line. The current storage usage sets the maximum number of threads that can be supported at about 500 tasks per address space. This number will vary depending on the REGION size and the activity of the threads. The *pthread_create*( ) service monitors storage below the 16M line and will prevent the creation of additional threads if the storage becomes constrained.

The implementation of HWTs was relatively straightforward. A *pthread_create*( ) request triggers an IRB to the main task. The IRB attaches a kernel stub which sets up the threading environment and passes control to LE which initializes its environment. Then LE passes control to the user program identified on the *pthread_create*( ). When the program completes, it can either call *pthread_exit*( ) or return to LE which will exit the thread. LE returns to the kernel which terminates the task. Task termination will drive the MVS *End Of Task* (EOT) resource managers. All of this processing is fairly costly if the thread is being created to perform some trivial work. If the thread is being created to run for a long time, then this overhead is acceptable. The main reason for using HWTs is that the thread may be allocating MVS resources which need the EOT resource managers to clean up.

The implementation of MWTs builds on the HWT base. The initial creation of a task and passing control to the environment is the same. The difference occurs when the task terminates. At this point, a kernel service is invoked to request another MWT to process. If there are no other MWTs ready to run, the task is put into a wait. When another *pthread_create*( ) request is received, the kernel passes the request to the environment to activate.

Significant effort was spent on dealing with errors in the threading environment. The POSIX standard states that an unhandled error on a thread will cause the process to terminate. This philosophy is at odds with normal MVS task behavior. In general, MVS treats tasks as independent units of work, and if one task fails, it is up to the application to decide how it wants to react to the failure. The exception to this is what MVS would do if the initial thread terminates normally via a *pthread_exit*( ) or *pthread_cancel*( ). The created thread subtasks could not tolerate the mother task terminating even though the POSIX standard treats the initial thread the same as any other thread in the process. To deal with this, the kernel places the initial thread in a wait if it terminates while other threads exist. To deal with abnormal thread termination (the entire process must be terminated), OpenEdition MVS has implemented *pthread_quiesce*( ) services which are used by the kernel and by LE to control the thread behavior in certain environments. The *pthread_quiesce*( ) service allows termination of all threads without generating asynchronous ABENDs (ABnormal ENDs — MVS equivalent of SIGKILL) at each task. The *pthread_quiesce*( ) service also supports a freeze and unfreeze function which allows the threads to be stopped and restarted. This capability is exploited when debugging a multi-threaded environment.

24.9 Interprocess Communication

The Single UNIX Specification defines InterProcess Communication (IPC) as the functions provided by shared memory, message queues, and semaphores. This section provides a brief description of message queues and semaphores and will go into more detail on the shared memory implementation.

The semaphore services provide for counting semaphores as opposed to binary semaphores. This allows programs to create complicated serialization mechanisms to control access to shared resources. A frequent use of semaphores is to control access and updates to a piece of shared memory. Semaphores provide atomic operations that will either grant access to a caller or suspend the caller until the resource is available. The net result is the ability to serialize work across multiple processes. Semaphores cannot be used to serialize work across multiple systems.

Message queues provide the ability to place a variable amount of data on specific message queues. The data placed into a message queue is permanent, in that it will not be deleted until a program receives the message or the system terminates. It is possible to place messages on the message queue from one job and then minutes or days later, have another job retrieve the messages. There can be hundreds of message queues on the system where access to each message queue is based on UID (user ID) and GID (group ID) of the process creating the message queue. OpenEdition MVS backs the data in the message queue in one or more kernel data spaces. Message queues support many concurrent users adding and retrieving messages from a message queue, making it an ideal way for clients to request functions from a server.

Shared memory provided the greatest challenge to implement in OpenEdition MVS. MVS has had the concept of common storage since its beginnings. The *Common System Area* (CSA) is the closest analogy MVS has to shared memory. During the design phase, the naive question was often asked: Why don't you just allocate key 8 CSA? The answer to this is two-fold. The primary detractor of using key 8 CSA is that it provides no integrity for the data. Any program in the system could access and modify key 8 CSA storage. The second reason is that CSA does not provide the ability for multiple users to have different views of the same piece of virtual storage. The shared memory implementation must allow for:

- controlled access by UID and GID
- different views of the same virtual storage; that is, one user has read access and the other has write access
- the access permissions must be dynamically changeable between read, write, and access none.

Figure 24-8 on page 484 shows a high-level view of the shared memory design.

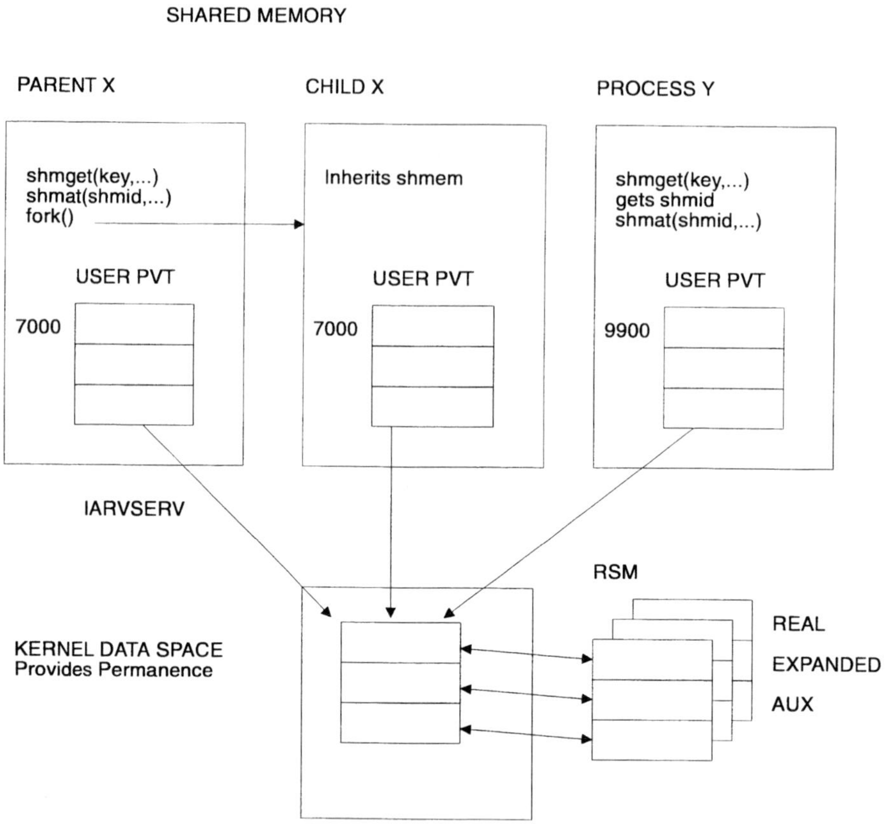

Figure 24-8 Shared Memory Design

In order to accomplish the shared memory function, support was provided by the *Real Storage Manager* (RSM) of MVS. The IARVSERV function was created. IARVSERV allows the caller to create relationships between multiple virtual pages and a single real page. OpenEdition MVS allocates the base pages of any shared memory request in a kernel data space. These pages represent the permanent location for the shared pages, should all of the users detach from the page. When a user wants to attach to a shared memory page (the *shmat*( ) function), the kernel support invokes IARVSERV to build the requested relationship between a virtual page in user private storage and the page within the kernel data space. The resulting virtual page in the user address space is byte addressable like any other virtual storage. The only difference is that all address spaces attached to the same shared page will immediately see any updates. It is for this reason that most applications which use shared memory also use semaphores to control who is accessing or modifying a given page at any moment in time.

In addition to providing the shared memory functions to C programs, the callable services are usable from assembler and other languages. This provides the equivalent function to being able to GETMAIN key 8 CSA from an unauthorized address space.

24.10 Further Information

Up-to-date information on OpenEdition MVS can be found at the URL **http://www.s390.ibm.com/products/oe/index.html**.

Chapter 25

The Mainframe Operating System BS2000/OSD

BS2000/OSD is the mainframe operating system of Siemens Nixdorf Informationssysteme AG. In terms of its functionality and scope, it is equivalent to IBM MVS. Within the framework of BS2000's *Open System Direction* (OSD), the operating system has systematically been moving toward the use of *open* interfaces. This has resulted in the implementation of the XPG4 interfaces (1995) and the Single UNIX Specification interfaces in 1996 and 1997.

This chapter describes the implementation of UNIX system interfaces in BS2000, the problems that were encountered, and how they were solved.

The second part describes how and why the standard BS2000 software utilizes the open interfaces, and the experience gained from porting several open software applications.

25.1 Introduction

BS2000 is a uniform operating system for the whole spectrum of mainframes marketed by Siemens Nixdorf, ranging from workstation systems for office use to mainframes with 20,000 attached workstations. In 1997, BS2000/OSD will be the first mainframe operating system to be released on non-390 architecture, namely on RISC hardware. The standard configuration of the operating system has approximately 4.5 million net lines of code, spread between the Assembler, C/C++, and SPL implementation languages (SPL is an SNI-specific implementation language).

The functionality of BS2000 corresponds to that of IBM MVS; both batch and interactive processing are possible. Hardware multiprocessor architectures are supported and virtual address space can be up to 2 Gigabytes in size. Currently, BS2000 has an installed base of 4,000 units, the majority located in Europe.

The market demand has led to the implementation of UNIX system interfaces in BS2000. But this is just one (although not insignificant) reason to offer open interfaces. A further important reason is that open interfaces provide access to a large number of software applications. In the absence of such interfaces, the implementation of applications on proprietary systems would require great effort. Where open interfaces are available, the implementation effort is reduced by orders of magnitude (refer to the sections below on porting experience). There were thus compelling reasons to introduce open interfaces in BS2000. At the end of 1992, implementation of the XPG4 Base began and the XPG4 Base brand was obtained at the end of 1995. In 1994, work commenced on the Single UNIX Specification interfaces and a UNIX brand is planned for 1997.

In principle, there are two ways of implementing open interfaces in BS2000:

1. Based on the interface description, the functionality is implemented in the same way as the native BS2000 interfaces (for example, the *open*() interface of UNIX systems is implemented using the OPEN interface of BS2000).
2. Porting an existing UNIX kernel (in this case, the port provides a hosted environment).

The second option was chosen for good reason:

- It is less expensive; code need not be rewritten as existing code can be reused.
- Updates are simpler; if it is necessary to support new functions, as when moving, for example, from XPG4 Base to the Single UNIX Specification, the existing kernel is exchanged for one with new functionality. Rebasing of this kind requires less effort than writing the additionally needed functionality.

The port undertaken is thus not to a hardware platform, but to a software platform; that is, the low levels of the BS2000 kernel. The code base for the port is SINIX, Siemens Nixdorf's UNIX system derivative.

25.2 The POSIX Subsystem

In BS2000, subsystems are units that can be loaded, started, and terminated independently. BS2000 features powerful tools to manage such subsystems. The BS2000 operating system is divided into a number of subsystems in order to minimize complexity. Their external interfaces are guaranteed. It therefore seemed practical to package the ported SINIX kernel in a BS2000 subsystem. The subsystem was given the name "POSIX", although the choice of name does not do justice to the fact that the subsystem offers greater functionality than the POSIX specifications of IEEE. This subsystem is referred to as POSIX hereinafter.

There are command procedures for starting and terminating the POSIX subsystem. A menu system is available for generating filesystems and installing additional software packages.

BS2000 tasks are automatically attached to the POSIX subsystem when interfaces implemented in POSIX are called (for example, calling *fork*( ) in a program establishes this connection).

25.2.1 Process Concept

UNIX system processes are mapped onto BS2000 tasks. In doing so, it was necessary to introduce some new concepts in BS2000 task management in order to simplify implementation of the POSIX interfaces.

In BS2000 there had always been a one-to-one relationship between task and associated terminal. This had to be changed to a one-to-many relationship in order to allow a terminal to handle several BS2000 tasks (corresponding to UNIX system processes).

In BS2000, program termination does not lead to task termination, as can be the case with forked tasks in UNIX. BS2000 had to be updated to recognize this new situation and to take appropriate measures.

As the generation of new processes in a UNIX system is fairly simple and much used (*fork*( )), an equivalent mechanism had to be found in BS2000 to efficiently implement this interface. On systems where hardware permitted, a "copy on write" mechanism was implemented (the address spaces of parent and child are not split in the event of a *fork*( ) until a write access operation is performed); on other systems a "copy on access" mechanism with lesser functionality was implemented (address spaces are split when the first access operation is performed).

25.2.2 POSIX Filesystem

The BS2000 filesystem has no hierarchical nesting, as is common in UNIX systems. Also, as the attributes of BS2000 files and normal POSIX files differ greatly, it was not possible to implement POSIX files as a special type of BS2000 file. Consequently, POSIX filesystems were incorporated as follows. The carrier of a POSIX filesystem is a (sufficiently large) BS2000 file containing all familiar data of a UNIX filesystem such as *superblock*, *vnodes*, and so on. POSIX addresses data in this file linearly from the top of the file, and accesses data using the familiar file access functions of BS2000. In this case, the hard disk drivers located in a UNIX kernel are replaced by a driver that does not directly access the hardware, but a low layer of the BS2000 I/O system for file management. This fulfills an important requirement for efficient access to POSIX files, and is further supported by implementing a buffer cache, as is usual in UNIX systems.

25.2.3 Coexistence of Interfaces

Prior to the implementation of the POSIX subsystem and for historical reasons, BS2000 already featured a C library with interfaces in accordance with UNIX system semantics, albeit a subset of the interfaces and with access only to BS2000 data (principally to sequential text files of ISAM or SAM type). For reasons of compatibility, it was necessary to retain this library and to add to it the POSIX interfaces. This has the positive effect that access both to BS2000 resources and to POSIX resources (for example, to BS2000 and POSIX files) is possible from a C program. The decision as to which resources are to be accessed can be made by name selection at generation time or at run time by setting appropriate environment variables.

BS2000 programming interfaces are traditionally offered in Assembler; there is a linkage between Assembler and C programs to permit the trouble-free linking of C modules containing POSIX functions to an existing program in Assembler. This is an extremely important aspect in the context of enriching programs of the BS2000 software configuration through the addition of POSIX features.

COBOL or FORTRAN programs can also use the POSIX interfaces (via their run-time systems) and can be combined with Assembler or C programs.

25.2.4 User Access

All registered BS2000 users may use POSIX interfaces. Access to POSIX is via the defined UNIX interfaces. However, for security reasons, the implementation makes use exclusively of the authentication mechanisms provided by BS2000.

BS2000 users have a number of options for using POSIX interfaces:

- In BS2000 they can write a program which utilizes POSIX resources (for example, POSIX files) and start the program in BS2000.
- In BS2000 command mode they can start the shell (/START-POSIX-SHELL) and write and start a program, as above.

In both cases access to BS2000 is handled via "dumb" block-mode terminals. The *character mode* typical of UNIX systems is not available on these terminals. The resultant restrictions are, however, limited to a small number of programs, such as the vi editor.

This restriction is by-passed by using remote login, either from a UNIX system or from a PC via telnet, without the need for any intervening UNIX system. In these circumstances, POSIX provides access to a 100%-compatible UNIX system. This is the configuration that was used to achieve the XPG4 Base brand.

25.2.5 ASCII versus EBCDIC

The code set in which BS2000 runs is EBCDIC, reflecting the fact that the operating system was developed in the mid-sixties. In contrast, UNIX systems make use of ASCII. As the POSIX subsystem is closely coupled to BS2000, it was decided to run it in EBCDIC. Data storage in BS2000 is in EBCDIC so that if (text) data is imported from UNIX systems, using NFS, for example, it can be converted manually (using the *iconv* command, for example) or automatically. Obviously, conversion is only needed for text files. Automatic conversion is performed on the basis of an indicator (for each filesystem) defining the code set of the file system. For reasons of compatibility, this indicator is automatically set to ASCII for filesystems not generated by POSIX (for example, file systems generated on an external UNIX system). To take the example of a large development project, this means that source and include files can be maintained on different systems in different code sets. The code sets are then always correctly converted by the (BS2000) C compiler.

25.2.6 Implementation of Network Interfaces

When implementing the network interfaces, it was necessary to build on the existing BCAM/DCAM network components in BS2000; these already support TCP/IP. The implementation of sockets and XTI (and also TLI) did not make use of STREAMS as is common in UNIX; instead they were implemented as autonomous filesystems in the POSIX subsystem. This measure, which is sometimes used in "pure" UNIX systems, delivers substantial performance benefits, said to be up to a 50% improvement on the STREAMS implementation.

25.3 Shell

When porting shell commands, the corresponding SINIX commands were used as a basis. Due to dependence on terminal type, a small number of commands react differently depending on the terminal from which they are called. For example, the full functionality of the vi editor is available only on character terminals (that is, when access is by means of remote login). If vi is called at a block terminal, only a subset of its functionality is available.

New commands have been added in the shell to support interaction with BS2000. For example, one new command is *bs2cp* (BS2000 Copy) which enables files to be copied from the BS2000 to the POSIX filesystem and *vice versa*. Various file types and library formats of BS2000 are supported and there is optional conversion of file contents from ASCII to EBCDIC. Similarly to the *system*( ) function in UNIX, there is a new shell command *bs2system* which allows BS2000 commands to be executed from the shell.

25.4 Libraries

The programming interfaces are made available in libraries. For compatibility reasons, old C interfaces that existed in BS2000 prior to POSIX continue to be supported. There is also an add-on library including non-XPG4 interfaces which are present in SINIX and which have proved extremely useful when porting from the SINIX world (a large number of these interfaces are included in the Single UNIX Specification).

Programs using these libraries can be linked either statically or dynamically. When linking statically, the required functions are also linked in. When linking dynamically, only a small adapter containing references to the required library interfaces is linked in (in this case the library is preloaded as a subsystem). The references are resolved when the program runs. This approach greatly reduces program size.

25.5 Synergy between BS2000 and POSIX

As already stated, the goal of the POSIX implementation was to achieve the closest possible coupling of the two interface worlds.

The technical platform for the merging of the two worlds is what is known as *mixed mode*. Both the proprietary BS2000 interfaces and the new POSIX interfaces can be used together in the same programs.

The first step was to adapt the existing BS2000 software configuration to the POSIX interfaces. In certain cases (for example, the C compiler), this was a crucial and high-priority requirement in order to be able to implement POSIX at all.

Modifications were made both in the utilities and commands of BS2000 (in contrast to UNIX, programs and commands in BS2000 are not identical; BS2000 programs correspond to UNIX programs/commands but BS2000 commands are an integral part of the operating system and are handled exclusively in privileged operating system mode).

The modifications primarily affect access to POSIX files in order to process data from those files and to store data in them. The following utilities/commands of BS2000 have been enhanced:

- C compiler
- Linker/loader
- EDT (editor)
- SORT
- SPOOL including PRINT command
- (BS2000) FILE TRANSFER
- COBOL compiler
- HSMS (hierarchical storage management system)
- ARCHIVE.

This reflects only the current status. Further modifications will be made during the ongoing development of BS2000.

25.6 Porting of Open Software to BS2000

The provision of the POSIX subsystem, the shell, and individual libraries is of course only the first step on the road to an open system. What is still missing are applications to run on open BS2000, and that's why application software must be ported to BS2000.

25.6.1 The Porting Procedure

To port the POSIX subsystem itself, it was necessary to create a rather complex, heterogeneous development environment. Once the POSIX subsystem existed, this complicated construction was no longer required and could be replaced by a standardized, homogeneous development environment — as common in UNIX — with *make*, *vi*, and other important program-development tools. Both data storage and development can take place exclusively in BS2000.

As a basis for porting, the POSIX subsystem has the following to offer:

- the C library covering all XPG4 interfaces (and also, for reasons of compatibility, the "old" BS2000 C interfaces)
- ADD-ON-LIB with non-XPG4 interfaces (which have been included for reasons of compatibility with SINIX)
- SOCKETS library
- NSL library with interfaces to RPC, XDR and TLI, and XTI
- C-ISAM
- POSIX shell with 170 command interfaces based on XPG4
- NFS
- RCS (revision control system) as a source management system.

Siemens Nixdorf has already ported the following:

- NFS V2.0
- DCE
- SNMP
- ARCIS + MOTIF
- WWW server
- ACRYL (encryption software).

Currently a number of software houses are also working on the following: adaptation of software running on BS2000 to POSIX, porting software running on UNIX systems to BS2000, and investigation of software running on UNIX systems with a view to porting to BS2000.

25.7 Porting Experience

Porting experience gained in projects of different sizes and complexity is described below.

25.7.1 RCS Source Management System

RCS is a system for managing source code on a local UNIX system. It forms the basis for the distributed source management system SMS. RCS is a shareware product of GNU. The code size was 18,000 lines.

The problems encountered were as follows:

- adaptation to the installation
- adaptation of the supplied test scripts
- no changes in the code, only adaptations in the makefiles.

The total porting effort required was 0.5 man-months.

25.7.2 ARCIS Document Server

ARCIS is a system for storing documents. The documents are stored on WORM disks and access to data is supported by a database (SESAM or ORACLE). Administration is undertaken by BS2000 systems; ARCIS is operated from PCs.

The ARCIS product was developed by iXOS and runs on various UNIX platforms. ARCIS comprises 380,000 lines of code, supplemented by MOTIF and the X Window System with approximately 350,000 lines of code .

The problems encountered (and how they were solved) were as follows:

- GNU *make* was used instead of the standard *make* command. The advantage of this was greater functionality. This GNU *make* was ported by the ARCIS development team.

  This is a general problem as GNU components are used in many of the products to be ported. In many cases, however, porting has caused few problems because of the number of platforms on which shareware runs. Adaptation of the makefiles and regeneration was possible in quite a few cases, without the need to modify code.

- Interfaces (both headers and functions) going beyond XPG4 were affected; for example, **<malloc.h>** or *mmap*( ).

  If functions were not XPG4-compatible, they were simply removed. It took one man-week to by-pass the *mmap*( ) function (which is not part of XPG4, but is included in the Single UNIX Specification) used by ARCIS (simulation using shared memory).

- RPCgen is not available in the POSIX subsystem. RPCgen is performed in SINIX until porting of the product is completed.
- ASCII and EBCDIC have a few minor dependencies.
- There is a different byte order for originator and recipient.
- There are missing commands; for example, *su* and validation tools. These were ported by the POSIX developers.
- Adaptation of authentication.
- Adaptation of the installation.

- Stabilization of the RPC functions in the library and kernel, as previously only used implicitly via NFS.

The total number of changed lines of code was 1,000.

The time required, from the first compilation to first run, was 6 man-months.

25.7.3 WWW Server

The original code comes from CERN. The code size was 60,000 lines.

The Problems encountered were as follows:

- ASCII/EBCDIC: Data to be sent over the network must be ASCII; the internal configuration data which is managed in BS2000 must be stored in EBCDIC.

The total porting effort required was 1 man-month.

25.8 Summary of Porting Experience

The examples above show how straightforward it is to port even complex software from UNIX systems to BS2000 using the POSIX subsystem. The experience gained during porting is summarized below:

- The larger the number of ports on which software already runs, the simpler it is to port. (This could be compared to a stone on a beach which is rounded by the action of the waves.)
- Correct adaptation of makefiles (for BS2000 it was never wrong to stay with the SINIX port, if one existed) should prevent many problems from arising (selection of correct preprocessor options). In the simplest case, recompilation is sufficient.

Problems could be caused by:

- ASCII/EBCDIC Dependencies

  These may be well concealed and are only detected when debugging. Often this is a result of the age of the code to be ported. Experience has shown that the more recent the code, the fewer the problems.
- The BS2000 C compiler checks more stringently than the UNIX C compiler (errors instead of warnings).
- Counters: Arithmetic overflow is handled differently on different hardware architectures (390, INTEL).
- Different number formats (little endian, big endian).

Chapter 26

OpenNT

The Windows NT architecture provides a kernel designed to be retargetable to different hardware platforms, with the user interface and programming interfaces provided through subsystems that map to the underlying kernel. Individual subsystems provide different concurrent "environments". Microsoft's primary environment is the Win32 subsystem. Windows NT also ships with POSIX and OS/2 subsystems. The Microsoft POSIX subsystem is a strict implementation of POSIX.1.

Softway Systems, through an agreement with Microsoft, have been developing and extending the original Microsoft POSIX subsystem to provide a complete environment that will lead to a UNIX 95 brand. The implementation strategy has been to use the relevant ISO portability standards and the Single UNIX Specification as technical specifications for the interfaces.

This chapter covers the following topics:

- a brief history of the OPENNT development efforts
- the architecture of OPENNT
- current functionality supported in OPENNT
- interoperability with the Win32 subsystem environment
- early applications porting experiences.

26.1 A Brief History of OPENNT

The Single UNIX Specification is a robust specification that serves as the basis for a model for portable applications source code. It strongly leverages the work of the formal ISO C standard and POSIX standards that account for about 75% of the specifications. By describing an interface for programs, rather than a specific implementation, it allows any computing platform to provide the interfaces. Developing applications source code to such a portability model protects the development investment by allowing the programs to be more easily ported to new platforms supporting the model. Systems obtain the X/Open brand based on the Single UNIX Specification, warranting their conformance to the specification. Applications written carefully to leverage the portability model described in these standards and specifications can have a reasonable expectation of porting to any system that carries the X/Open brand. To date, systems as diverse as Digital UNIX, SCO UnixWare, HP-UX, AIX, and OpenEdition MVS have met the requirements for the X/Open UNIX 95 brand, aligned with the 1995 edition of the Single UNIX Specification. Every major operating system that is based upon the traditional UNIX[45]

45. The adjective phrases "historical UNIX" or "traditional UNIX" will be applied consistently to differentiate a family of operating systems that were historically referred to collectively as "UNIX". Likewise, applications source code developed on such historical systems will be referred to as "traditional UNIX applications code". The term "UNIX 95 branded system" or "XPG4 UNIX system" will be consistently used to describe a system that warrants its conformance through the X/Open brand program.

system has branded to the X/Open XPG4 Base or XPG4 Base 95 brand.

The Microsoft Windows NT operating system has a micro-kernel architecture similar to Mach, and supports multiple concurrent subsystems that present programming and user interfaces to the user. The primary environmental subsystem from Microsoft's point of view is the Win32 subsystem. This provides the services a programmer uses when programming with the Win32 API, and supports the Windows 3.1 and Windows 95 desktops.

Windows NT also ships with POSIX and OS/2 subsystems. (This paper does not discuss the OS/2 subsystem.) The Microsoft POSIX subsystem implements exactly POSIX.1. The Microsoft POSIX subsystem was arguably developed to satisfy U.S. government procurement rules described in FIPS 151-2 on the Federal Register, and was not particularly accessible. It did, however, demonstrate that the subsystem approach was powerful and flexible. Windows NT could transparently host multiple concurrent operating system environments to support applications written to different system interface models.

In September 1995, Softway Systems, Inc. entered into a long-term agreement with Microsoft to extend the Microsoft POSIX subsystem into a complete UNIX subsystem, capable of branding to the X/Open UNIX 95 brand. Work began immediately to wrap the POSIX subsystem in a shell and utilities environment (March 1996) that conformed to the POSIX.2 Execution Environment. An X11R6 server was added (July 1996), along with a telnet service (August 1996). A software development kit (SDK) was added such that developers could begin porting their own applications (September 1996). At that time, the SDK essentially supported the POSIX.1 interfaces, ISO C standard library, and approximately 60 historical Berkeley library routines from the 4.4BSD-Lite distribution that were required while developing the first POSIX.2 implementation. It further provided the additional tools required to develop applications (the *RCS* version control suite, *ar*, *cc*, *c89*) and wrapped the command-line version of the Microsoft Visual C/C++ compiler.

Extending the subsystem to map more of the kernel interface and adding libraries and utilities have been ongoing. As of March 1997, the 2.0 release of OPENNT supports:

- POSIX.1, including the terminal interfaces from Section 7
- ISO C standard libraries
- Berkeley sockets via Winsock
- System V Interprocess Communication facilities (shared memory, semaphores, message queues)
- memory mapped files
- traditional curses
- X11R5 client libraries (Xlib, Xt, Xaw) and nearly all the X11R5 clients
- considerable other library interfaces
- POSIX.2, including the Execution Environment, the User Portability Extension with full job control in the shells, the Software Development Tools, and the C-language Development Option
- numerous other tools ported into the environment, including a *KornShell*, a *csh*, *Perl* version 5.0, the *RCS* revision control suite, a test port of the *Apache* web server, and *xv*, the X11-based image manipulator.

26.2 The OPENNT Extended POSIX Subsystem Architecture

OPENNT is based on the OPENNT Extended POSIX subsystem. The subsystem architecture on Windows NT supports multiple subsystems active at the same time. From an end-user point of view, there is a screen full of applications. Some of them may be Win32 GUI applications; for example, Microsoft Excel, clients of the Win32 subsystem. Others are Win32 command line applications active through a console window and accessed via the DOS command interface. Others can be traditional UNIX system applications running as clients of the OPENNT Extended POSIX subsystem. If an X11 server is present, still other applications may be presenting an X11-based graphic interface and running locally or on another machine in the network.

26.2.1 Architecture

The OPENNT Extended POSIX subsystem is not a Windows NT service, but operates at a lower level as a kernel integrated environment subsystem. The subsystem directly maps operating system service requests from POSIX applications to the underlying Windows NT kernel. Examples of system services mapped and managed by the subsystem include:

- process control and process hierarchies
- signal semantics
- file I/O semantics
- shared memory semantics
- terminal console and session semantics
- Berkeley socket interfaces to Winsock.

The OPENNT Extended POSIX subsystem consists of a dynamic linked library (DLL), the OPENNT subsystem process itself, and a console session manager. Some system services directly map the kernel via the DLL, while others map service requests to the OPENNT subsystem process. A console session manager runs for each process group, managing the terminal I/O to and from a Win32 console window on the user's desktop. The console session manager provides all the traditional tty semantics. Additional features, such as scroll bars and window cut-and-paste, are also provided via the session manager.

The NT filesystem (NTFS) provides proper POSIX-defined file and directory semantics.

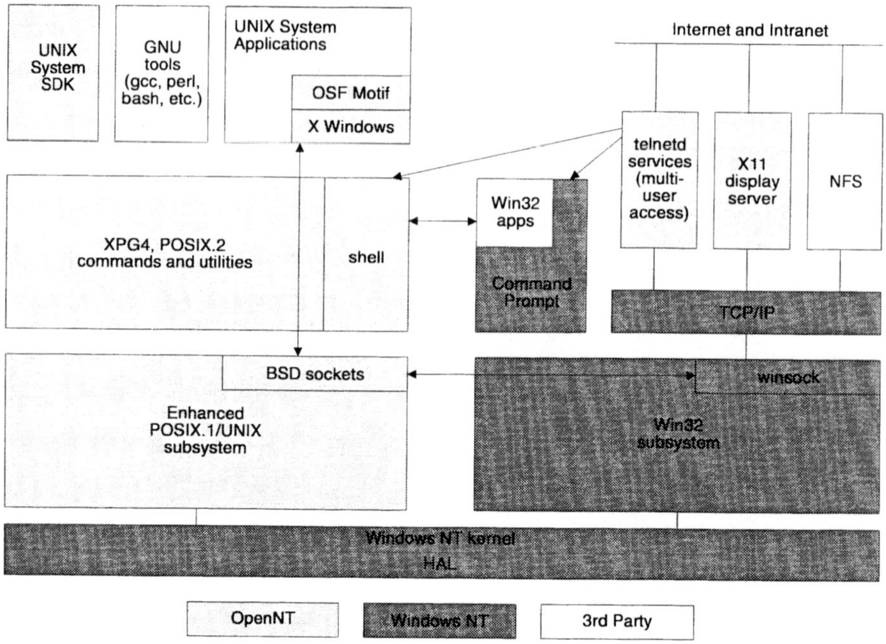

Figure 26-1 Simple Architecture of OPENNT on Windows NT

26.2.2 The Windows NT Filesystem

The Windows NT filesystem was a new filesystem developed for Windows NT to provide a fully functional filesystem and address the shortcomings of the traditional DOS FAT filesystem. It provides:

- recoverability and redundancy of critical disk structures
- enhanced security consistent with the Windows NT object security model
- data redundancy capabilities to support disk mirroring and striping
- support for large files and large volumes
- support for multiple file data streams
- Unicode-based filenames
- bad cluster remapping
- POSIX filesystem semantics for case-sensitive names, hard links, and the file change timestamp.

File access is mapped from process to data on the disk via the I/O manager using a layered driver approach. The NTFS driver is simply another I/O driver under the control of the Windows NT Executive's I/O Manager. The NTFS driver can layer on the fault tolerant drivers, and ultimately layers on the disk driver.

All system service calls with respect to file access vector through the I/O Manager, regardless of whether or not they are made from OPENNT subsystem or Win32 subsystem applications. Files are treated as objects within the Windows NT Executive, and hence are managed by the Object Manager with respect to object (file) sharing and protection. The Object Manager works with the Security Reference Monitor.

While both subsystems share a common view of the files in NTFS, they do not both provide support for the same file functionality. The Win32 subsystem does not support the creation of file links, nor does it support filename case-sensitivity. For example, from an OPENNT shell one can create a hard link, and see another "file" appear in the Win32-based File Manager. Editing the link edits the real file and both "files" will appear to change from the Win32 File Manager's point of view.

Likewise, if a set of filenames differ only in case; for example, *Makefile* and *makefile*, and one tries in the Win32-based File Manager to delete the latter one listed, the first is deleted. This case-sensitivity problem does not exist from the OPENNT Extended POSIX subsystem. The correct file would be deleted.

Because of the common view of NTFS shared by all subsystems, advanced features of the NT filesystem work regardless of the type of process (POSIX or Win32) accessing the file. For example, the NTFS auditing features that track the success and/or failure of read, write, execute, delete, ownership, and permission changes can be turned on for any file on NTFS. All operations from the OPENNT Extended POSIX subsystem will be audited as well as operations from Win32 subsystem processes.

It is the same filesystem, and both Win32 and the OPENNT subsystems can see all the files, but both subsystems interact with the filesystem according to the semantics required by their environments.

26.3 Performance Issues

The OPENNT Extended POSIX subsystem is a peer subsystem to the Win32 subsystem. POSIX processes and the OPENNT subsystem use the same combination of communication mechanisms — message passing, shared memory sections, quick Local Procedure Calls (LPC) — as Win32 processes and the Win32 subsystem under Windows NT 3.51. The subsystems communicate with the relevant parts of the Windows NT executive in the same manner. There is no particular performance penalty running a traditional UNIX application ported into the OPENNT world over running a similar Win32 application with the Win32 subsystem. Both applications are running as native Windows NT applications.

Comprehensive benchmarking has not been done at this time, but early informal benchmarks indicate that:

- CPU bound applications perform virtually the same between the Win32 and OPENNT subsystems.
- CPU bound OPENNT applications performed better (by about 50%) than a mainstream traditional UNIX platform on identical hardware.
- OPENNT and the traditional UNIX platform showed comparable disk performance trends.
- For small block *read*( ) and *write*( ) operations, Win32 outperforms OPENNT.
- For large block *read*( ) and *write*( ) operations, OPENNT outperforms Win32.
- Socket throughput between Windows NT and a traditional Berkeley machine on a local network is virtually the same regardless of whether the performance testing programs are running with the OPENNT subsystem or the Win32 subsystem.

Performance tuning is an ongoing task with a number of new projects in planning to increase the overall performance of the OPENNT Extended POSIX subsystem.

26.4 The Windows NT Security Model and OPENNT

Windows NT has obtained its United States Department of Defense Orange Book C2 security certification, supporting all required discretionary access controls. OPENNT works with the Windows NT security model as it is integrated subsystem technology. It does nothing to contravene the robust security provided by the Windows NT kernel.

In general, objects (such as files) on Windows NT are protected by access control lists (ACLs) made up from access control entries (ACEs). When a user logs onto Windows NT, authentication is provided via username and password, which is confirmed with the Security Administration Monitor. A security ID token is associated with the process if authentication is successful. This security token is used in all actions with objects to determine whether the object's ACL gives access to the process.

There are a number of interesting issues that arise with respect to files on NTFS and the security model. Group ownership and the concept of a primary group were added to the Windows NT design to support POSIX semantics. The user and group name space is shared, however, and there is no concept of separate password and group databases. As well as a shared name space, Windows NT groups can "own" objects. Some Win32-based utilities and applications assign a group as the owner of the file, and a POSIX-based long file listing will show group names in both the owner and group fields. This can be disconcerting the first time it is seen. Files created from a POSIX process through the OPENNT subsystem assign file ownership consistent with the POSIX standards and traditional UNIX behavior.

There are no permission bits in the NTFS file entry. ACLs are used. When a POSIX application creates a file, an ACL is associated with the file that has three ACEs, one for the owner, one for the process' primary group, and one for a group named "Everyone". These ACEs are interpreted correctly through the OPENNT subsystem as mode bits. The ACL can be displayed via the File Manager. With *ls* and *chmod*, the permissions in the mode are interpreted against the file's ACL. Additional levels of security can be added with additional ACEs, providing an extended security administration capability to traditional UNIX applications is ported to the OPENNT environment.

There is no **/etc/passwd** file, and secure user information is kept in a database accessed via the Security Administration Monitor.

There is no appropriate privilege on Windows NT to turn on the *setuid* or *setgid* bits in a file mode. Likewise, there is no appropriate privilege for a process that allows it to take on the different user or group IDs via the *setuid*( ) or *setgid*( ) functions. This is a security feature of the Windows NT operating system.

26.5 Interoperability with the Win32 Subsystem

Most operating systems provide functionality beyond that described in the various standards or the Single UNIX Specification. For example, most systems provide the X11 windowing system to support networked graphic applications. Other systems provide simple extensions to system services that are not described by the relevant standards and specifications, but neither are they prohibited.

Any use of these other interfaces can render an application less portable. Discussion of such portability models can become very grey, very quickly. Using the X11 example, most systems provide support for the X11 client libraries. Use of these calls in applications is relatively portable. Other extensions are clearly out-of-bounds.

Standards-based environments that are considered "hosted"; that is, they map the services described in the standards to underlying native system services, provide a different set of challenges. Digital's VMS, IBM's MVS, and Microsoft's Windows NT all provide their own system service interfaces, as well as the portability standards and specifications-based interfaces. Each system also provides a different approach to integrating the standards-based environment to the original environment.

The Windows NT subsystem architecture prevents applications that are clients of one subsystem making calls to another subsystem's functionality; that is, a traditional UNIX application ported to the OPENNT Extended POSIX subsystem cannot make Win32 GUI calls. Likewise, Win32-based applications cannot make calls to the *link*( ) system call to hard link a file, despite NTFS support for hard links.

This is a strength. When attempting to maintain and protect an application's development investment, a programmer does not want to add code to an application that is platform dependent unless there is a very good reason. This platform-specific code makes the application harder to maintain, harder to deploy on multiple architectures, and harder to port to future platforms that support the portability model described by the POSIX standards and X/Open specifications. Depending on how the system-specific calls are integrated into the application can render the application source code completely unportable, only capable of being built in the hybrid fashion.

Using non-standard tools or functionality on a computer platform is sometimes necessary in solving real business problems. Indeed, this very issue is what often decides a computer platform purchase. Finding the balance between protecting applications source code investments, and using a platform's unique attributes to solve an overall business problem, is a difficult challenge.

The OPENNT Extended POSIX subsystem provides a number of original ways for applications developed on traditional UNIX systems running with the OPENNT subsystem to interact with applications running with the Win32 environment subsystem, while protecting the UNIX application source investment. These interactions involve the filesystem, the user interface, the ability to execute Win32-based applications from the OPENNT subsystem, the use of sockets, and Winsock. These methods all work outside the application source code, thereby protecting the applications source code investment, while providing access to other Windows NT functionality to solve the business problem.

26.5.1 NTFS

One of the most fundamental ways the OPENNT Extended POSIX subsystem and the Win32 subsystem interact is with the filesystem. There is only one filesystem — NTFS — and it provides complete POSIX filesystem semantics. One of the fundamental design goals of Windows NT was to support POSIX, so NTFS supports all the required functionality. A container filesystem, where the POSIX filesystem is emulated inside a "native" file, was not necessary.

Likewise, all the advanced filesystem functionality described elsewhere (for example, file audit and additional security capabilities) are transparently available to the application.

26.5.2 The Desktop and User Interface

The Win32 desktop presents either the traditional Windows 3.1 or Windows 95 graphic user interfaces to the user. This environment easily supports interaction between the Win32 and OPENNT subsystems.

When a POSIX process (the OPENNT shell, for example) is associated with an icon in a program group, clicking on the icon launchs the OPENNT subsystem application in a console window. (Console windows are the traditional tty device of the OPENNT environment.) Icons can be associated with OPENNT subsystem shell scripts as well. Likewise, a Win32 GUI program (for example, **REGEDT32.EXE**, the registry editor) can be run from an OPENNT shell prompt. The Win32 graphic interface appears in a new window on the desktop.

Cut-and-paste between applications running in different subsystems is also supported. It is quite easy to capture text from a Win32-based application (for example, Microsoft Write) into the clipboard, then paste it into an OPENNT shell or a *vi* edit session running in the OPENNT subsystem space.

26.5.3 Win32 Application Execution

After the release of the original OPENNT shell and utilities product, one of the earliest requirements that became apparent was for the OPENNT shell to be able to execute Win32-based programs. Until that point, the *exec*( ) family of interfaces could only execute other OPENNT POSIX executables.

The OPENNT Extended POSIX subsystem was re-engineered to allow it to execute Win32-based binaries. This proved quite challenging. For a command line-based Win32 program, essentially a client of the Win32 subsystem, to be able to write output and read input from a shell process that is a client of the OPENNT subsystem is a non-trivial process. The next version of OPENNT to ship (September 1996) provided this ability, and the ability to redirect the standard input and standard output streams to and from files. Pipe support was added for the March 1997 release.

This ability to provide a *Win32exec* instantly allowed certain other functionality to be added to the OPENNT environment in a manner most natural for the platform. The *lp* utility shipped in release 1.0 was one of the two utilities that were an implementation to the letter of the standard; it did not, unfortunately, include the ability to reach a printer. With the addition of *Win32exec*, the *lp* utility became a shell script that wrapped the Win32 command-line print utility (**PRINT.EXE**) and now provides complete printer functionality to any printer on the network. Likewise, the C compiler environment (*cc* and *c89*) is shell scripted around the Win32 command line compiler interface (**CL.EXE**). The ability to add users from a command-line tool following the semantics of the traditional System V *useradd* tool is a simple shell script wrapping the **NET.EXE** family of Win32 commands.

Using hard links or shell aliases, any Win32-based program can be easily integrated into the OPENNT shell environment with a shorter, lower-case name.

26.5.4 OPENNT Sockets and Win32 Winsock

The OPENNT Extended POSIX subsystem supports the Berkeley sockets interfaces, wrapping them around the Winsock stack provided on the system. This easily allows programs in the OPENNT subsystem space to interact with Win32 subsystem applications with TCP/IP over sockets.

One question often posed is how to use a Win32 GUI API with a POSIX application. Rather than lock the POSIX application into a non-portable set of graphic interface calls, one can architect it in a client/server model, maintaining the server as a sockets-based OPENNT subsystem program, portable to any traditional UNIX system, and maintaining the client in a manner most appropriate to the users' needs. For example, the client could be written as an X11-based client running either locally or remotely on either a traditional UNIX system or Windows NT via an X11 server. Or one can rewrite the client with Microsoft Visual Basic and Winsock to provide a Windows GUI front-end that will run locally or remotely on Windows NT and Windows95 systems. Or provide both.

26.5.5 X11R5 Clients and X11R6 Server

Building on the idea of sockets through the OPENNT Extended POSIX subsystem and Winsock from the Win32 subsystem, we can use an implementation example from the OPENNT world. The X11R6-based server shipped with OPENNT is a Win32 subsystem process. The X11R5 clients and client libraries are wrapped around the Berkeley sockets implementation in the OPENNT Extended POSIX subsystem.

Traditional UNIX-based X11 client applications running against the OPENNT Extended POSIX subsystem communicate with the local Win32-based server.

26.6 Early Applications Porting Experiences

A substantial amount of application source code originally developed on traditional UNIX-based systems has been ported to OPENNT. Much of the original utility code was built from the 4.4BSD-Lite distribution, with most of the work effort being to make the utility conform to the POSIX.2 and X/Open XCU specifications. Application source code developed on traditional UNIX systems ports as directly to the OPENNT Extended POSIX subsystem as it does to other traditional UNIX systems. A number of examples follow.

26.6.1 4.4BSD-Lite Source Code

As pointed out, much of the initial utility source base was 4.4BSD-Lite code. The typical process of getting the utility to compile involved removing **<sys/params.h>**, replacing it with **<sys/types.h>** and **<limits.h>**, and stepping around any symbolic link or memory mapped file code. This typically meant the utility would compile and was functional, and the real work of making the utility conform to the specifications could begin. (Since then, the code based on *mmap*( ) has all been turned back on in the utilities. Symbolic links are still not implemented at this time.)

26.6.2 GNU Code

Most GNU utilities come with a configure script that probes the system to determine what kind of system it is, building a makefile and configuration header as it goes. The configure scripts do not typically work well with the OPENNT compiler environment wrapped around the Microsoft command line compiler. The simple answer is typically to create a simple makefile, and hand configure the configuration header to turn on all POSIX.1 and ANSI C-related macro definitions.

One of the example programs shipped with OPENNT is GNU's *awk* utility, *gawk*. Aside from the simple hand tuning of the configure header and makefile, the only changes that needed to be made to the 17,000 lines of code was to change a couple of instances of **<varargs.h>** code to use the ISO C standard **<stdarg.h>** methods.

26.6.3 Perl 5.0

The popular Perl distribution has been built and is available from the Tool Warehouse on the OPENNT web site at the URL **http://www.OpenNT.com**. The Perl distribution is 78,796 lines of code. It has many options and permutations, and running the configure script was the only reasonable way to determine what options needed to be turned on.

The configure script needed to be modified in the following ways:

1. The OPENNT compiler driver expected compilation order to be correct according to the POSIX.2 standard; that is, **-o output-name** comes before the command line arguments — the *configure* utility makes liberal use of a different ordering.
2. The location of header files needed to be changed to **$OPENNT_ROOT/usr/include**.

The configure script produces another set of scripts that, when run, produce the makefiles and configuration-based headers. While the overall configure script could not be run from start to finish due to other problems with what *configure* expects of its environment, it could be run well enough to produce these individual subscripts, and these all ran correctly, producing a set of makefiles and headers.

There were some minor problems with the assumptions made with *makedepend* that needed to be corrected in these generated makefiles. The only source code changes were to step around some non-portable use of the user database fields *pw_gecos* and *pw_passwd*.

After making these changes, Perl 5.0 passed the test suite included with the distribution.

26.6.4 xv

The *xv* utility is an X11-based tool for browsing and manipulating graphic images (for example, JPEG). A full file browser is part of the utility. The distribution is approximately 83,600 lines of code. Trivial source changes were required to step around non-portable use of *mknod*( ) and a use of *endpwent*( ), and the addition of a *#define* to properly use *strerror*( ). *xmkmf* was used on the makefile to build the Makefile, and then *xv* was made.

26.6.5 Apache

Apache is a popular public-domain http daemon. The distribution is 45,726 lines of code. It was ported as an experiment early in the alpha test cycle of the 2.0 release of OPENNT. Some of the functionality that was dealt with in the configuration below has since been supported.

Essentially, symbolic links, *setsid*( ), and *setpgrp*( ) were stepped around. Calls to *mktemp*( ) were changed to use *getenv*("*TMPDIR*") instead of hard coding the path. Uses of *chown*( ) which gave file ownership to other users were also avoided as Windows NT supports the U.S. government FIPS 151-2 functionality associated with the POSIX.1 option POSIX_CHOWN_RESTRICTED. The *crypt*( ) routine was added from the 4.4BSD-Lite distribution. The following OPENNT stanza was added to the configuration header.

```
#elif defined(OPENNT)
#define  S_ISLNK(m) (0)    /* No symlinks in OPENNT yet */
#define  bzero(a,b) memset(a,0,b)
#define  USE_FCNTL_SERIALIZED_ACCEPT
#undef   HAS_GMTOFF
#define  NO_KILLPG
#define  NO_SETSID
#define  JMP_BUF sigjmp_buf
#include <sys/time.h>
#define  getwd(d) getcwd(d,MAX_STRING_LEN)
#define  SIGURG SIGUSR1
```

This was about the same size as other system-specific configuration stanzas.

26.7 In Summary

The Microsoft Windows NT operating system is architected to support multiple concurrent environment sybsystems. Software Systems, Inc. is extending and developing the POSIX subsystem into a complete traditional UNIX environment subsystem, capable of being branded to the X/Open UNIX 95 brand.

Up-to-date information on OPENNT can be found at the URL

http://www.OpenNT.com

Go Solo 2

Part 5:

Appendices

The Open Group

Appendix A

CD-ROM Instructions

This chapter covers the contents and installation of the Go Solo 2 CD-ROM.

The Go Solo 2 CD-ROM conforms to ISO 9660:1988. ISO 9660:1988 has been used as the lowest common denominator, so that the CD-ROM may be used on the widest range of platforms (UNIX, OS/2, Windows, and Macintosh). As such, there are some limitations on the filenames: they are mono-case, and limited to eight characters with a three character extension. Thus, the HTML index files are named **index.htm**.

The Go Solo 2 CD-ROM has a simple HTML interface. The easiest way to read the CD-ROM is by means of a Web browser. The top-level directory contains an HTML document, **index.htm**, that describes the full contents of the disk.

A.1 Contents

The Go Solo 2 CD-ROM contains two versions of each of the five specifications which make up the Single UNIX Specification, Version 2:

- System Interface Definitions, Issue 5 (XBD)
- Commands and Utilities, Issue 5 (XCU)
- System Interfaces and Headers, Issue 5 (XSH)
- Networking Services, Issue 5
- X/Open Curses, Issue 4, Version 2.

The versions supplied are:

- An HTML translation of the specification which can be viewed directly off the CD-ROM using a Web browser, or alternately installed on your local machine, and viewed using a Web browser.
- PDF of the publications which may be viewed directly off the CD-ROM using a PDF viewer. Two PDF viewers are supplied on the CD-ROM.

A.2 Web Browsers

Netscape Navigator is a popular Web browser which is readily available for Windows 3.1, Windows 95, Windows NT, Macintosh, and UNIX. To find out how to obtain the latest version of Netscape, go to URL **http://home.netscape.com**.

MS Explorer is available for Windows 95 and Windows NT, and is also readily available. To find out how to obtain the latest version of MS Explorer, go to URL **http://www.microsoft.com/ie/**.

The **.htm** files on the Go Solo 2 CD-ROM can be viewed using the Netscape Navigator or MS Explorer, or other Web browsers.

A.3 The HTML Version

Start your favorite browser and open the file **INDEX.HTM** (possibly **index.htm**) in the top-level directory. Select the link *HTML Version*, and then select the link *CD-ROM Version*. You can then view the specification directly off the CD-ROM.

The following sections are only applicable if you want to install the html locally on your hard disk.

System Requirements

The system requirements for installing the HTML version of the Single UNIX Specification, Version 2 are:

- 12MB disk space free
- support for long filenames (that is, UNIX, Windows 95, Windows NT, OS/2, Macintosh).

Formats

The HTML version is supplied in the following file formats, which can be installed on your system:

- **susv2.tar** – a tar format archive.
- **susv2.taz** – a compress'd tar format archive.
- **susv2.zip** – a zip format archive.

To download your selection, you should use the *Save Next Link As...* or *Save to Disk* functions of your Web browser. Once on the hard disk, follow the appropriate steps below.

Installing the Tar Format Archive

Extract the file using:

```
$ tar -xvf susv2.tar
```

This will then create a subdirectory **susv2** into which the HTML files will be placed.

Installing the TAZ Format Archive

Decompress the archive file using the *zcat* utility, piping the output to the *tar* utility:

```
$ zcat susv2.taz | tar -xvf -
```

This will then create a subdirectory **susv2** into which the files will be placed.

Installing the ZIP Format Archive

Extract the archive file using the *pkunzip* utility (with the **–d** option to recreate the directory structure), or equivalent.

Viewing the HTML

To view the HTML, direct a Web browser to open the **index.htm** file in the top-level **susv2** directory. On a typical system, this could be by opening the URL **file:/home/ajosey/susv2/index.htm**.

Errors

From time to time, when errors are found in the HTML version, errata will be made available at the URL **http://www.opengroup.org/unix/gosolo2**.

A.4 The PDF Version

The PDF version consists of fifteen files. Each of the five specifications includes front matter, the main text, and the index. The file **docs/pdf/index.htm** contains an index of the available files:

- XBD, Issue 5: [Front | Text | Index]
- XSH, Issue 5: [Front | Text | Index]
- XCU, Issue 5: [Front | Text | Index]
- Networking Services, Issue 5: [Front | Text | Index]
- X/Open Curses, Issue 4, Version 2: [Front | Text | Index]

To view the files you need to use a PDF viewer. Included with the CD-ROM are two PDF viewers: Adobe Acrobat Reader and Xpdf.

Adobe Acrobat 3.0 Reader

The file **readers/acroread/sysreq.htm** contains the system requirements for installing the Acrobat Reader software. The file **readers/acroread/eula.htm** contains the End User License agreement for the Acrobat reader.

Available platform support is as follows:

Version	Platform	File Size
Acrobat Reader 3.0	Windows (32-bit)	3,919,312 bytes
Acrobat Reader 3.0	Windows (16-bit)	3,820,092 bytes
Acrobat Reader 3.0	Macintosh (MacBinary)	4,856,064 bytes
Acrobat Reader 3.0 (beta)	OS/2 Warp	3,902,083 bytes
Acrobat Reader 3.0	IBM-AIX	4,552,164 bytes
Acrobat Reader 3.0	SGI-IRIX	5,672,893 bytes
Acrobat Reader 3.0	Sun Solaris (SPARC)	5,348,455 bytes
Acrobat Reader 3.0	SunOS (SPARC)	5,432,694 bytes
Acrobat Reader 3.0	HP-UX	4,926,807 bytes
Acrobat Reader 3.0	Linux (Intel)	3,672,729 bytes

To download your selection, you may need to use the *Save Next Link As...* or *Save to Disk* functions of your Web browser. The Windows, Macintosh, and OS/2 files are self-extracting executables. The other files are in **.taz** format; that is, compressed tar format, apart from the Linux version which is in **.tgz** format (gzip'd tar format).

Xpdf

Xpdf is a freely available PDF viewer for UNIX systems. It is available in source and binary format on the CD-ROM. See the file **readers/xpdf/README** for more information.

Available platform support is as follows:

Version	Platform	File Size
Xpdf 0.6	IBM-AIX 4.1	235565 bytes
Xpdf 0.6	HP-UX 9.05	190351 bytes
Xpdf 0.6	Linux 2.x ELF	141778 bytes
Xpdf 0.6	OSF/1 3.2 (Alpha)	206235 bytes
Xpdf 0.6	Solaris 2.5 SPARC	144582 bytes
Xpdf 0.6	UnixWare 2.x	141167 bytes
Xpdf 0.6	SCO Open Server	150773 bytes
Xpdf 0.6	Solaris 2.4 SPARC	171165 bytes
Xpdf 0.6	Solaris 2.4 x86	165547 bytes
Xpdf 0.6	SunOS 4.1	275224 bytes
Xpdf 0.6	BSD/OS 2.1	398991 bytes
Xpdf 0.6	VMS 5.5, VMS 6.6	1286099 bytes

To download your selection, you may need to use the *Save Next Link As...* or *Save to Disk* functions of your Web browser. All files are in **.tgz** format; that is, gzip'd tar format.

Appendix B

Go Solo 2 CD-ROM Terms and Conditions

1. Definitions

   In these Terms and Conditions the following words have the meanings given:

CD-ROM	the CD-ROM with the functionality set out in the "Help Text" or user documentation;
Derivative work	any work which incorporates a substantial portion of any published material from any Work, whether or not authorized by this or any other License;
Internet	the world-wide publically-accessible network of inter-linked computers;
Intranet	a company-wide network of computers, accessible by company employees but protected from enquiry from internet users and public dial-in access;
Licensee	the company/organization/individual to whom the CD-ROM is supplied;
Re-publication	the act of re-publishing whether or not the new work is made public;
Re-publish	to reproduce or make available publicly or otherwise the text, design or graphic material from any Work, whether or not in a form or on a medium different from that in or on which it was supplied by The Open Group;
Work	any data on the CD-ROM;
The Open Group	The Open Group, Apex Plaza, Forbury Road, Reading, Berkshire, RG1 1AX, United Kingdom.

2. Right of Use

   The Licensee shall have the right to use the Works contained on the CD-ROM for any purpose, subject to the limitations of these Terms and Conditions on Re-publication. Furthermore, the Licensee shall have the right:

   a. to store and have the CD-ROM stored in electronic form on one computer at a time, subject to the waiver set out in Clause 4;

   b. to display the contents of the CD-ROM on a computer screen; and

   c. for the Licensee's internal use only, to produce paper copies of limited parts of any Work, as provided within the functionality of the software.

   For the avoidance of doubt, nothing in these Terms and Conditions shall entitle the Licensee to use the Work in any way other than for the Licensee's own internal business purposes, nor to disclose the Work to any third party.

   Where any Work is subject to the copyright of any person other than The Open Group ("a joint publication") the rights set out here are subject to any further conditions or limitations prescribed in respect of that Work (as set out therein) in order to protect the rights of that other copyright owner.

Where more than one CD-ROM is supplied under this Agreement, these rights shall apply separately in respect of each CD-ROM.

3. Restrictions in Liability

   THE OPEN GROUP ACCEPTS LIABILITY UP TO A LIMIT EQUAL TO THE PRICE PAID FOR THE CD-ROM. THERE SHALL BE NO LIMIT TO ANY LEGAL LIABILITY FOR ANY DEATH OR PERSONAL INJURY.

4. Use of html files

   Files ending in the extension **.htm** are intended for viewing by intranet browser software. Implicit in this method of browsing is the concept that the files may be viewed simultaneously by users on remote computers or consoles. It is permitted that the **.htm** files on the CD-ROM be simultaneously accessed by two or more computers or consoles at any given time, provided that the users of those computers or consoles are employees of the Licensee.

   The Licensee shall not be permitted to distribute the CD-ROM **.htm** files (or any other files on the CD-ROM) onto the Internet without prior written permission of The Open Group.

5. Re-publication

   Save as set out above or as separately agreed, the Licensee shall have no right to Re-publish or distribute the CD-ROM or its contents in any way or on any medium whatever.

6. Termination

   Either party may by written notice forthwith terminate this Agreement if the other party commits any material breach of these Terms and Conditions and fails to remedy it within a reasonable period after receiving written notice from the other party; the other party suffers distress or execution, commits an act of bankruptcy, goes or is put into liquidation (otherwise than solely for the purpose of solvent amalgamation or reconstruction), or seeks any form of protection against its creditors from any competent Court or Tribunal; or a receiver or administrative receiver is appointed over any substantial part of the other party's business.

   Upon termination under this Clause or otherwise, the Licensee shall within one month deliver up any materials or equipment, including any special computer programs or electronic media supplied by The Open Group and shall certify that all copies (in electronic or other form) derived from the CD-ROM have been destroyed.

   Termination of this Agreement (however occurring) shall not affect any accrued rights or liabilities of either party nor shall it affect the coming into force or the continuance in force of any provision which is expressly or by implication intended to come into or continue in force on or after such termination.

7. Disputes

   These Terms and Conditions shall be construed in accordance with the law of England and Wales. Any dispute arising under or in connection with these Terms and Conditions shall be referred to arbitration before a sole arbitrator to be appointed jointly or, in default of agreement, to be appointed by the President of the British Computer Society.

Terms and Conditions of Supply of the Go Solo 2 CD-ROM, May 1997.

Appendix C

Glossary

absolute pathname
See **pathname resolution** on page 533.

access mode
A particular form of access permitted to a file.

additional file access control mechanism
See **file access permissions** on page 524.

address space
The memory locations that can be referenced by a process or the threads of a process.

affirmative response
An input string that matches one of the responses acceptable to the LC_MESSAGES category keyword **yesexpr**, matching an extended regular expression in the current locale.

alert
To cause the user's terminal to give some audible or visual indication that an error or some other event has occurred. When the standard output is directed to a terminal device, the method for alerting the terminal user is unspecified. When the standard output is not directed to a terminal device, the alert is accomplished by writing the alert character to standard output (unless the utility description indicates that the use of standard output produces undefined results in this case).

alert character
A character that in the output stream should cause a terminal to alert its user via a visual or audible notification. The alert character is the character designated by \a in the C Language. It is unspecified whether this character is the exact sequence transmitted to an output device by the system to accomplish the alert function.

alias name
A word consisting solely of underscores, digits, and alphabetics from the portable character set and any of the following characters:

```
!    %    ,    @
```

Implementations may allow other characters within alias names as an extension.

alternate file access control mechanism
See **file access permissions** on page 524.

alternate signal stack
Memory associated with a thread, established upon request by the implementation for a thread, separate from the thread signal stack, in which signal handlers responding to signals sent to that thread may be executed.

angle brackets
The characters < (left-angle-bracket) and > (right-angle-bracket). When used in the phrase "enclosed in angle brackets", the symbol < immediately precedes the object to be enclosed, and > immediately follows it. When describing these characters in the portable character

set, the names <less-than-sign> and <greater-than-sign> are used.

appropriate privileges
An implementation-dependent means of associating privileges with a process with regard to the function calls and function call options defined in XSH, and the commands in XCU that need special privileges. There may be zero or more such means.

argument
In the shell, a parameter passed to a utility as the equivalent of a single string in the *argv* array created by one of the *exec*( ) functions. See XCU, **Chapter 2**, **Shell Command Language**. An argument is one of the options, option-arguments, or operands following the command name.

In the C Language, an expression in a function call expression or a sequence of preprocessing tokens in a function-like macro invocation.

arm (a timer)
To start a timer measuring the passage of time, enabling notifying a process when the specified time or time interval has passed.

assignment
See **variable assignment** on page 546.

asterisk
The character *.

async-cancel-safe function
A function that may be safely invoked by an application while the asynchronous form of cancellation is enabled. No function is async-cancel-safe unless explicitly described as such.

async-signal-safe function
A function that may be invoked, without restriction, from signal-catching functions. No function is async-signal-safe unless explicitly described as such.

asynchronously generated signal
A signal that is not attributable to a specific thread. Examples are: signals sent via *kill*( ), signals sent from the keyboard, and signals delivered to process groups. Being asynchronous is a property of how the signal was generated and not a property of the signal number. All signals may be generated asynchronously.

asynchronous I/O operation
An I/O operation that does not of itself cause the thread requesting the I/O to be blocked from further use of the processor.

This implies that the process and the I/O operation may be running concurrently.

asynchronous I/O completion
For an asynchronous read or write operation, when a corresponding synchronous read or write would have completed and when any associated status fields have been updated.

background job
See **background process group**.

background process
A process that is a member of a background process group.

background process group
(Or **background job**.) Any process group, other than a foreground process group, that is a member of a session that has established a connection with a controlling terminal.

backquote
The character ‘ also known as a *grave accent*.

backslash
The character \, also known as a *reverse solidus*.

backspace character
A character that, in the output stream, should cause printing (or displaying) to occur one column position previous to the position about to be printed. If the position about to be printed is at the beginning of the current line, the behavior is unspecified. The backspace is the character designated by \b in the C Language. It is unspecified whether this character is the exact sequence transmitted to an output device by the system to accomplish the backspace function. The backspace character defined here is not necessarily the ERASE special character.

base character
One of the set of characters defined in the Latin alphabet. In Western European languages other than English, these characters are commonly used with diacritical marks (accents, cedilla, and so on) to extend the range of characters in an alphabet.

basename
The final, or only, filename in a pathname.

basic regular expression
A pattern constructed according to the rules defined in XBD, **Chapter 7**, **Regular Expressions**.

blank character
One of the characters that belong to the **blank** character class as defined via the LC_CTYPE category in the current locale. In the POSIX locale, a blank character is either a tab or a space character.

blank line
A line consisting solely of zero or more blank characters terminated by a newline character. See also **empty line** on page 523.

blocked process (or thread)
A process (or thread) that is waiting for some condition (other than the availability of a processor) to be satisfied before it can continue execution.

block-mode terminal
A terminal device operating in a mode incapable of the character-at-a-time input and output operations described by some of the standard utilities.

block special file
A file that refers to a device. A block special file is normally distinguished from a character special file by providing access to the device in a manner such that the hardware characteristics of the device are not visible.

braces
The characters { (left brace) and } (right brace), also known as *curly braces*. When used in the phrase "enclosed in (curly) braces" the symbol { immediately precedes the object to be enclosed, and } immediately follows it. When describing these characters in the portable character set, the names <left-brace> and <right-brace> are used.

brackets
The characters [(left-bracket) and] (right-bracket), also known as *square brackets*. When used in the phrase "enclosed in (square) brackets" the symbol [immediately precedes the

object to be enclosed, and] immediately follows it. When describing these characters in the portable character set, the names <left-square-bracket> and <right-square-bracket> are used.

break value
The address at which dynamic memory allocation starts.

built-in utility
(Or **built-in**.) A utility implemented within a shell. The utilities referred to as *special built-ins* have special qualities, described in XCU, **Chapter 2**, **Shell Command Language**. Unless qualified, the term *built-in* includes the special built-in utilities. The utilities referred to as *regular built-ins* are those named in XCU, **Chapter 2**, **Shell Command Language**. There is no requirement that these utilities be actually built into the shell on the implementation, but they do have special command-search qualities.

byte
An individually addressable unit of data storage that is equal to or larger than an octet, used to store a character or a portion of a character; see **character**. A byte is composed of a contiguous sequence of bits, the number of which is implementation-dependent. The least significant bit is called the *low-order* bit; the most significant is called the *high-order* bit. Note that this definition of *byte* deviates intentionally from the usage of *byte* in some international standards, where it is used as a synonym for *octet* (always eight bits). On a system based on POSIX.2, a byte may be larger than eight bits so that it can be an integral portion of larger data objects that are not evenly divisible by eight bits (such as a 36-bit word that contains four 9-bit bytes).

carriage-return character
A character that in the output stream indicates that printing should start at the beginning of the same physical line in which the carriage-return character occurred. The carriage-return is the character designated by \r in the C Language. It is unspecified whether this character is the exact sequence transmitted to an output device by the system to accomplish the movement to the beginning of the line.

character
A sequence of one or more bytes representing a single graphic symbol or control code. This term corresponds to the ISO C standard term *multibyte character*, where a single-byte character is a special case of a multi-byte character. Unlike the usage in the ISO C standard, *character* here has no necessary relationship with storage space, and *byte* is used when storage space is discussed.

See XBD, **Chapter 4**, **Character Set** for a further explanation of the graphical representations of characters, or *glyphs*, as opposed to character encodings.

character array
An array of type **char**.

character class
A named set of characters sharing an attribute associated with the name of the class. The classes and the characters that they contain are dependent on the value of the LC_CTYPE category in the current locale.

character set
A finite set of different characters used for the representation, organization, or control of data.

character special file
A file that refers to a device. One specific type of character special file is a terminal device

file, whose access is defined in XBD, **Chapter 9**, **General Terminal Interface**.

character string
A contiguous sequence of characters terminated by and including the first null byte.

child process
See **process** on page 535.

circumflex
The character ^.

clock
An object that measures the passage of time.

The current value of the time measured by a clock can be queried and, possibly, set to a value within the legal range of the clock.

clock tick
An interval of time; an implementation-dependent number of these occur each second.

coded character set
A set of unambiguous rules that establishes a character set and the one-to-one relationship between each character of the set and its bit representation.

codeset
The result of applying rules that map a numeric code value to each element of a character set. An element of a character set may be related to more than one numeric code value, but the reverse is not true. However, for state-dependent encodings the relationship between numeric code values to elements of a character set may be further controlled by state information. The character set may contain fewer elements than the total number of possible numeric code values; that is, some code values may be unassigned.

collating element
The smallest entity used to determine the logical ordering of character or wide-character strings. See **collation sequence**. A collating element consists of either a single character, or two or more characters collating as a single entity. The value of the LC_COLLATE category in the current locale determines the current set of collating elements.

collation
The logical ordering of character or wide-character strings according to defined precedence rules. These rules identify a collation sequence between the collating elements, and such additional rules that can be used to order strings consisting of multiple collating elements.

collation sequence
The relative order of collating elements as determined by the setting of the LC_COLLATE category in the current locale. The character order, as defined for the LC_COLLATE category in the current locale, defines the relative order of all collating elements, such that each element occupies a unique position in the order. This is the order used in ranges of characters and collating elements in regular expressions and pattern matching. In addition, the definition of the collating weights of characters and collating elements uses collating elements to represent their respective positions within the collation sequence.

Multi-level sorting is accomplished by assigning elements one or more collation weights, up to the limit {COLL_WEIGHTS_MAX}; see **<limits.h>**. On each level, elements may be given the same weight (at the primary level, called an equivalence class; see **equivalence class** on page 523) or be omitted from the sequence. Strings that collate equal using the first assigned weight (primary ordering) are then compared using the next assigned weight (secondary ordering), and so on.

column position

A unit of horizontal measure related to characters in a line.

It is assumed that each character in a character set has an intrinsic column width independent of any output device. Each printable character in the portable character set has a column width of one. The standard utilities, when used as described in the XSI specification set. assume that all characters have integral column widths. The column width of a character is not necessarily related to the internal representation of the character (numbers of bits or bytes).

The column position of a character in a line is defined as one plus the sum of the column widths of the preceding characters in the line. Column positions are numbered starting from 1.

command

A directive to the shell to perform a particular task; see XCU, **Chapter 2**, **Shell Command Language**.

command language interpreter

An interface that interprets sequences of text input as commands. It may operate on an input stream or it may interactively prompt and read commands from a terminal. It is possible for applications to invoke utilities through a number of interfaces, which are collectively considered to act as command interpreters. The most obvious of these are the *sh* utility and the *system*( ) function, although *popen*( ) and the various forms of *exec* may also be considered to behave as interpreters.

composite graphic symbol

A graphic symbol consisting of a combination of two or more other graphic symbols in a single character position, such as a diacritical mark and a basic letter.

condition variable

A synchronization object which allows a thread to suspend execution, repeatedly, until some associated predicate becomes true.

control character

A character, other than a graphic character, that affects the recording, processing, transmission, or interpretation of text.

control operator

In the shell, a token that performs a control function. It is one of the following symbols:

```
&    &&    (    )    ;    ;;    newline    |    ||
```

The end-of-input indicator used internally by the shell is also considered a control operator; see XCU, **Chapter 2, Shell Command Language**.

On some systems, the symbol ((is a control operator; its use produces unspecified results. Applications that wish to have nested subshells, such as:

```
((echo Hello);(echo World))
```

must separate the ((characters into two tokens by including white space between them. Some systems may treat these as invalid arithmetic expressions instead of subshells.

The ((and)) symbols are control operators in the KornShell, used for an alternative syntax of an arithmetic expression command. A portable application cannot use ((as a single token (with the exception of the $((form for shell arithmetic).

controlling process
The session leader that established the connection to the controlling terminal. If the terminal ceases to be a controlling terminal for this session, the session leader ceases to be the controlling process.

controlling terminal
A terminal that is associated with a session. Each session may have at most one controlling terminal associated with it, and a controlling terminal is associated with exactly one session. Certain input sequences from the controlling terminal (see XBD, **Chapter 9**, **General Terminal Interface**) cause signals to be sent to all processes in the process group associated with the controlling terminal.

conversion descriptor
A per-process unique value used to identify an open codeset conversion.

core file
A file of unspecified format that may be generated when a process terminates abnormally.

current working directory
See **working directory** on page 546.

cursor position
The line and column position on the screen denoted by the terminal's cursor.

data segment
Memory associated with a process, that may be used to contain dynamically allocated data.

device
A computer peripheral or an object that appears to the application as such.

device ID
A non-negative integer used to identify a device.

direct I/O
An operation that attempts to circumvent a system performance optimization for the optimization of the individual I/O operation.

directory
A file that contains directory entries. No two directory entries in the same directory have the same name.

directory entry
(Or **link**.) An object that associates a filename with a file. Several directory entries can associate names with the same file.

directory stream
A sequence of all the directory entries in a particular directory. An open directory stream may be implemented using a file descriptor.

disarm (a timer)
To stop a timer from measuring the passage of time, disabling any future process notifications (until the timer is armed again).

display
To output to the user's terminal. If the output is not directed to a terminal, the results are undefined.

XCU assigns precise requirements for the terms *display* and *write*. Some historical systems have chosen to implement certain utilities without using the traditional UNIX system file descriptor model. For example, the *vi* editor might employ direct screen memory updates on a personal computer, rather than a *write*( ) system call. An instance of user prompting might appear in a dialogue box, rather than with standard error. When XCU uses the term *display,* the method of outputting to the terminal is unspecified; many historical implementations use *termcap* or *terminfo*, but this is not a requirement. The term *write* is used when XCU mandates that a file descriptor be used and that the output can be redirected. However, it is assumed that when the writing is directly to the terminal (it has not been redirected elsewhere), there is no practical way for a user or test suite to determine whether a file descriptor is being used or not. Therefore, the use of a file descriptor is mandated only for the redirection case and the implementation is free to use any method when the output is not redirected. The verb *write* is used almost exclusively, with the few exceptions of those utilities where output redirection need not be supported: *tabs*, *talk*, *tput*, and *vi*.

dollar sign
The character $.

dot
The filename consisting of a single dot character (.). See **pathname resolution** on page 533. In the context of shell special built-in utilities, see *dot* in XCU, **Chapter 2**, **Shell Command Language**.

dot-dot
The filename consisting solely of two dot characters (. .). See **pathname resolution** on page 533.

double-quote
The character ", also known as *quotation-mark*.

downshifting
The conversion of an upper-case character to its lower-case representation.

(clock) drift rate
The rate at which the time measured by a clock deviates from the actual passage of real time.

A positive drift rate causes a clock to gain time with respect to real time; a negative drift rate causes a clock to lose time with respect to real time.

driver
A module that controls data transferred to and received from peripheral devices. Drivers are traditionally written to be a part of the system implementation, although they are frequently written separately from the writing of the implementation. A driver may contain processor-specific code, and therefore be non-portable.

effective group ID
An attribute of a process that is used in determining various permissions, including file access permissions, described in **file access permissions** on page 524. See **group ID** on page 527. This value is subject to change during the process lifetime, as described in the *exec* family of functions and *setgid*( ).

effective user ID
An attribute of a process that is used in determining various permissions, including file access permissions. See **user ID** on page 545. This value is subject to change during the process lifetime, as described in *exec* and *setuid*( ).

eight-bit transparency
The ability of a software component to process 8-bit characters without modifying or utilizing any part of the character in a way that is inconsistent with the rules of the current coded

character set.

empty directory
A directory that contains, at most, directory entries for dot and dot-dot.

empty line
A line consisting of only a newline character. See also **blank line** on page 517.

empty string
(Or **null string**.) A string whose first byte is a null byte.

empty wide-character string
A wide-character string whose first element is a null wide-character code.

epoch
The time zero hours, zero minutes, zero seconds, on January 1, 1970 Coordinated Universal Time. See **seconds since the epoch** on page 539.

equivalence class
A set of collating elements with the same primary collation weight.

Elements in an equivalence class are typically elements that naturally group together, such as all accented letters based on the same base letter.

The collation order of elements within an equivalence class is determined by the weights assigned on any subsequent levels after the primary weight.

era
An alternative method for counting and displaying years. See XBD, **Chapter 5**, **Locale**.

executable file
A regular file acceptable as a new process image file by the equivalent of the *exec* family of functions, and thus usable as one form of a utility. The standard utilities described as compilers can produce executable files, but other unspecified methods of producing executable files may also be provided. The internal format of an executable file is unspecified, but a conforming application cannot assume an executable file is a text file.

execute
To perform the actions described in XCU, **Chapter 2**, **Shell Command Language**. See also **invoke** on page 528.

expand
In the shell, when not qualified, the act of applying all the expansions described in XCU, **Chapter 2**, **Shell Command Language**.

extended regular expression
A pattern constructed according to the rules defined in XBD, **Chapter 7**, **Regular Expressions**.

extended signed integral type
A signed integral type or an implementation-dependent type with similar properties.

extended security controls
The access control (see **file access permissions** on page 524) and privilege (see **appropriate privileges** on page 516) mechanisms have been defined to allow implementation-dependent extended security controls. These permit an implementation to provide security mechanisms to support different security policies from those described in the XSI specification set. These mechanisms do not alter or override the defined semantics of any of the functions or utilities in the XSI specification set.

extended unsigned integral type
An unsigned integral type or an implementation-dependent type with similar properties.

feature test macro
A macro used to determine whether a particular set of features will be included from a header. See XSH, **Chapter 2**, **General Information**.

field
In the shell, a unit of text that is the result of parameter expansion, arithmetic expansion, command substitution, or field splitting. During command processing, the resulting fields are used as the command name and its arguments. See XCU, **Chapter 2**, **Shell Command Language**.

FIFO special file
(Or **FIFO**.) A type of file with the property that data written to such a file is read on a first-in-first-out basis. Other characteristics of FIFOs are described in *open*( ), *read*( ), *write*( ), and *lseek*( ).

file
An object that can be written to, or read from, or both. A file has certain attributes, including access permissions and type. File types include regular file, character special file, block special file, FIFO special file, and directory. Other types of files may be supported by the implementation.

file access permissions
The standard file access control mechanism uses the file permission bits, as described below. These bits are set at the time of file creation by functions such as *open*( ), *creat*( ), *mkdir*( ), and *mkfifo*( ), and are changed by *chmod*( ). These bits are read by *stat*( ) or *fstat*( ).

Implementations may provide *additional* or *alternate* file access control mechanisms, or both. An additional access control mechanism will only further restrict the access permissions defined by the file permission bits. An alternate file access control mechanism will:

- specify file permission bits for the file owner class, file group class, and file other class of that file, corresponding to the access permissions, to be returned by *stat*( ) or *fstat*( )
- be enabled only by explicit user action, on a per-file basis by the file owner or a user with the appropriate privilege
- be disabled for a file after the file permission bits are changed for that file with *chmod*( ). The disabling of the alternate mechanism need not disable any additional mechanisms supported by an implementation.

Whenever a process requests file access permission for read, write, or execute/search, if no additional mechanism denies access, access is determined as follows:

- If a process has the appropriate privilege:
  — If read, write, or directory search permission is requested, access is granted.
  — If execute permission is requested, access is granted if execute permission is granted to at least one user by the file permission bits or by an alternate access control mechanism; otherwise, access is denied.
- Otherwise:
  — The file permission bits of a file contain read, write, and execute/search permissions for the file owner class, file group class, and file other class.

— Access is granted if an alternate access control mechanism is not enabled and the requested access permission bit is set for the class (file owner class, file group class, or file other class) to which the process belongs, or if an alternate access control mechanism is enabled and it allows the requested access; otherwise, access is denied.

file description
See **open file description** on page 531.

file descriptor
A per-process unique, non-negative integer used to identify an open file for the purpose of file access. The value of a file descriptor is from zero to {OPEN_MAX} −1. A process can have no more than {OPEN_MAX} file descriptors open simultaneously. File descriptors may also be used to implement message catalogue descriptors and directory streams. See **open file description** on page 531 and {OPEN_MAX} in **<limits.h>**.

file group class
The property of a file indicating access permissions for a process related to the group identification of a process. A process is in the file group class of a file if the process is not in the file owner class and if the effective group ID or one of the supplementary group IDs of the process matches the group ID associated with the file. Other members of the class may be implementation-dependent.

file hierarchy
Files in the system are organized in a hierarchical structure in which all of the non-terminal nodes are directories and all of the terminal nodes are any other type of file. Because multiple directory entries may refer to the same file, the hierarchy is properly described as a *directed graph*.

file mode
An object containing the *file mode bits* and file type of a file, as described in **<sys/stat.h>**.

file mode bits
A file's file permission bits, set-user-ID-on-execution bit (S_ISUID), and set-group-ID-on-execution bit (S_ISGID); see **<sys/stat.h>**.

filename
A name consisting of 1 to {NAME_MAX} bytes used to name a file. The characters composing the name may be selected from the set of all character values excluding the slash character and the null byte. The filenames dot and dot-dot have special meaning; see **pathname resolution** on page 533. A filename is sometimes referred to as a *pathname component*.

Filenames should be constructed from the portable filename character set because the use of other characters can be confusing or ambiguous in certain contexts. (For instance, the use of a colon (:) in a pathname would cause ambiguity if that pathname were included in a *PATH* definition.)

file offset
The byte position in the file where the next I/O operation begins. Each open file description associated with a regular file, block special file, or directory has a file offset. A character special file that does not refer to a terminal device may have a file offset. There is no file offset specified for a pipe or FIFO.

file other class
The property of a file indicating access permissions for a process related to the user and group identification of a process. A process is in the file other class of a file if the process is

not in the file owner class or file group class.

file owner class
The property of a file indicating access permissions for a process related to the user identification of a process. A process is in the file owner class of a file if the effective user ID of the process matches the user ID of the file.

file permission bits
Information about a file that is used, along with other information, to determine whether a process has read, write, or execute/search permission to a file. The bits are divided into three parts: owner, group, and other. Each part is used with the corresponding file class of processes. These bits are contained in the file mode, as described in **<sys/stat.h>**. The detailed usage of the file permission bits in access decisions is described in **file access permissions** on page 524.

file serial number
A per-file-system unique identifier for a file.

filesystem
A collection of files and certain of their attributes. It provides a name space for file serial numbers referring to those files.

file times update
Each file has three associated time values that are updated when file data has been accessed, file data has been modified, or file status has been changed, respectively. These values are returned in the file characteristics structure, as described in **<sys/stat.h>**.

For each function or utility in the XSI specification set that reads or writes file data or changes the file status, the appropriate time-related fields are noted as "marked for update". At an update point in time, any marked fields are set to the current time and the update marks cleared. Two such update points are when the file is no longer open by any process and when *stat*( ) or *fstat*( ) is performed on the file. Additional update points are unspecified. Marks for update, and updates themselves, are not done for files on read-only filesystems.

file type
See **file** on page 524.

filter
A command whose operation consists of reading data from standard input or a list of input files and writing data to standard output. Typically, its function is to perform some transformation on the data stream.

first open (of a file)
When a process opens a file that is not currently an open file within any process.

foreground job
See **foreground process group**.

foreground process
A process that is a member of a foreground process group.

foreground process group
(Or **foreground job**.) A process group whose member processes have certain privileges, denied to processes in background process groups, when accessing their controlling terminal. Each session that has established a connection with a controlling terminal has exactly one process group of the session as the foreground process group of that controlling terminal.

foreground process group ID
The process group ID of the foreground process group.

form-feed character
A character that in the output stream indicates that printing should start on the next page of an output device. The form-feed is the character designated by \f in the C Language. If the form-feed is not the first character of an output line, the result is unspecified. It is unspecified whether this character is the exact sequence transmitted to an output device by the system to accomplish the movement to the next page.

graphic character
A character, other than a control character, that has a visual representation when handwritten, printed, or displayed.

group database
A system database of implementation-dependent format that contains at least the following information for each group ID:

- group name
- numerical group ID
- list of users allowed in the group.

The list of users allowed in the group is used by the *newgrp* utility.

group ID
A non-negative integer that is used to identify a group of system users. Each system user is a member of at least one group. When the identity of a group is associated with a process, a group ID value is referred to as a real group ID, an effective group ID, one of the supplementary group IDs, or a saved set-group-ID.

group name
A string that is used to identify a group, as described in **group database**. To be portable across XSI-conformant systems, the value must be composed of characters from the portable filename character set. The hyphen should not be used as the first character of a portable group name.

hard limit
A system resource limitation that may be reset to a lesser or greater limit by a privileged process. A non-privileged process is restricted to only lowering its hard limit.

hard link
The relationship between two directory entries that represent the same file; see **directory entry** on page 521. This term is contrasted against **symbolic link**; see **symbolic link** on page 542.

home directory
The current directory associated with a user at the time of login.

incomplete line
A sequence of one or more non-newline characters at the end of the file.

Inf
A value representing infinity that can be stored in a floating type. Not all systems support the *Inf* value.

interactive shell
A processing mode of the shell that is suitable for direct user interaction.

internationalization

The provision within a computer program of the capability of making itself adaptable to the requirements of different native languages, local customs, and coded character sets.

invoke

To perform the actions described in XCU, **Chapter 2**, **Shell Command Language**, except that searching for shell functions and special built-in utilities is suppressed. See also **execute** on page 523.

ISO/IEC 646: 1991

ISO 7-bit coded character set for information interchange. The reference version of the standard contains 95 graphic characters, which are identical to the graphic characters defined in the ASCII coded character set.

ISO 6937: 1983

ISO 7-bit or 8-bit coded character set for text communication using public communication networks, private communication networks, or interchange media such as magnetic tapes and discs.

ISO 8859-1: 1987

ISO 8-bit single-byte coded character set Part 1, Latin Alphabet No 1. This standard character set comprises 191 graphic characters covering the requirements of most of Western Europe.

job

A set of processes, comprising a shell pipeline, and any processes descended from it, that are all in the same process group. See the definition of **pipeline** in XCU, **Chapter 2**, **Shell Command Language**.

job control

A facility that allows users selectively to stop (suspend) the execution of processes and continue (resume) their execution at a later point. The user typically employs this facility via the interactive interface jointly supplied by the terminal I/O driver and a command interpreter.

job control job ID

A handle that is used to refer to a job. The job control job ID can be any of the forms shown in the following table:

Job Control Job ID	Meaning
%%	Current job
%+	Current job
%–	Previous job
%*n*	Job number *n*
%*string*	Job whose command begins with *string*
%?*string*	Job whose command contains *string*

Table C-1 Job Control Job ID Formats

last close (of a file)

When a process closes a file, resulting in the file not being an open file within any process.

line

A sequence of zero or more non-newline characters plus a terminating newline character.

link
See **directory entry** on page 521.

link count
The number of directory entries that refer to a particular file.

local customs
The conventions of a geographical area or territory for such things as date, time, and currency formats.

locale
The definition of the subset of a user's environment that depends on language and cultural conventions; see XBD, **Chapter 5**, **Locale**.

localization
The process of establishing information within a computer system specific to the operation of particular native languages, local customs, and coded character sets.

login
The unspecified activity by which a user gains access to the system. Each login is associated with exactly one login name.

login name
A user name that is associated with a login.

map
To create an association between a page-aligned range of the address-space of a process and a range of physical memory or some memory object, such that a reference to an address in that range of the address-space results in a reference to the associated physical memory or memory object. The mapped memory or memory object is not necessarily memory-resident.

marked message
A STREAMS message on which a certain flag is set. Marking a message gives the application protocol-specific information. An application can use *ioctl*( ) to determine whether a given message is marked.

memory object
Either a file or shared memory object.

When used in conjunction with *mmap*( ), a memory object will appear in the address-space of the calling process.

message
Information that can be transferred between processes or threads by being added to and removed from a message queue. A message consists of a fixed-size message buffer.

message catalog
A file or storage area containing program messages, command prompts, and responses to prompts for a particular native language, territory, and codeset.

message catalogue descriptor
A per-process unique value used to identify an open message catalogue. A message catalogue descriptor may be implemented using a file descriptor.

message queue
An object to which messages can be added and removed. Messages may be removed in the order in which they were added or in priority order.

mode

A collection of attributes that specifies a file's type and its access permissions. See **file access permissions** on page 524.

mount point

Either the system root directory or a directory for which the *st_dev* field of structure **stat** (see **<sys/stat.h>**) differs from that of its parent directory.

multi-character collating element

A sequence of two or more characters that collate as an entity. For example, in some coded character sets, an accented character is represented by a non-spacing accent, followed by the letter. Other examples are the Spanish elements ch and ll.

mutex

A synchronization object used to allow multiple threads to serialize their access to shared data. The name derives from the capability it provides; namely, mutual exclusion. The thread that has locked a mutex becomes its owner and remains the owner until that same thread unlocks the mutex.

name

In the shell, a word consisting solely of underscores, digits, and alphabetics from the portable character set (see XBD, **Chapter 4**, **Character Set**). The first character of a name must not be a digit.

There are no explicit limits in the XSI specification set on the sizes of names, words (see **word** on page 546), lines, or other objects. However, other implicit limits do apply: shell script lines produced by many of the standard utilities cannot exceed {LINE_MAX} and the sum of exported variables comes under the {ARG_MAX} limit. Historical shells dynamically allocate memory for names and words and parse incoming lines a byte at a time. Lines cannot have an arbitrary {LINE_MAX} limit because of historical practice such as makefiles, where *make* removes the newline characters associated with the commands for a target and presents the shell with one very long line. The Input Files section in XCU, **Chapter 1**, **Introduction** does allow a shell to run out of memory, but it cannot have arbitrary programming limits.

named STREAM

A STREAMS-based file descriptor that is attached to a name in the file-system name space. All subsequent operations on the named STREAM act on the STREAM that was associated with the file descriptor until the name is disassociated from the STREAM.

NaN (not a number)

A value that can be stored in a floating type but that is not a valid floating point number. Not all systems support the NaN value.

native language

A computer user's spoken or written language, such as American English, British English, Danish, Dutch, French, German, Italian, Japanese, Norwegian, or Swedish.

negative response

An input string that matches one of the responses acceptable to the LC_MESSAGES category keyword **noexpr**, matching an extended regular expression in the current locale.

newline character

A character that in the output stream indicates that printing should start at the beginning of the next line. The newline is the character designated by \n in the C Language. It is unspecified whether this character is the exact sequence transmitted to an output device by the system to accomplish the movement to the next line.

non-spacing characters
A character, such as a character representing a diacritical mark in the ISO 6937:1983 coded character set, which is used in combination with other characters to form composite graphic symbols.

NUL
A character with all bits set to zero.

null byte
A byte with all bits set to zero.

null pointer
The value that is obtained by converting the number 0 into a pointer; for example, (**void** *) 0. The C Language guarantees that this value will not match that of any legitimate pointer, so it is used by many functions that return pointers to indicate an error.

null string
See **empty string** on page 523.

null wide-character code
A wide-character code with all bits set to zero.

number sign
The character #, also known as the *hash sign*.

object file
A regular file containing the output of a compiler, formatted as input to a linkage editor for linking with other object files into an executable form. The methods of linking are unspecified and may involve the dynamic linking of objects at run time. The internal format of an object file is unspecified, but a conforming application cannot assume an object file is a text file.

offset maximum
An attribute of an open file description representing the largest value that can be used as a file offset.

open file
A file that is currently associated with a file descriptor.

open file description
A record of how a process or group of processes is accessing a file. Each file descriptor refers to exactly one open file description, but an open file description can be referred to by more than one file descriptor. File offset, file status, and file access modes are attributes of an open file description.

operand
An argument to a command that is generally used as an object supplying information to a utility necessary to complete its processing. Operands generally follow the options in a command line.

operator
In the shell, either a control operator or a redirection operator.

option
An argument to a command that is generally used to specify changes in the utility's default behavior.

option-argument
A parameter that follows certain options. In some cases an option-argument is included

within the same argument string as the option; in most cases it is the next argument.

orphaned process group

A process group in which the parent of every member is either itself a member of the group or is not a member of the group's session.

page

The granularity of process memory mapping or locking.

Physical memory and memory objects can be mapped into the address-space of a process on page boundaries and in integral multiples of pages. Process address-space can be locked into memory (made memory-resident) on page boundaries and in integral multiples of pages.

page size

The size, in bytes, of the system unit of memory allocation, protection, and mapping. On systems that have segment- rather than page-based memory architectures, the term "page" means a segment.

parameter

In the shell, an entity that stores values. There are three types of parameters: variables (named parameters), positional parameters, and special parameters. Parameter expansion is accomplished by introducing a parameter with the $ character. See XCU, **Chapter 2, Shell Command Language**.

In the C Language, an object declared as part of a function declaration or definition that acquires a value on entry to the function, or an identifier following the macro name in a function-like macro definition.

parent directory

When discussing a given directory, the directory that both contains a directory entry for the given directory and is represented by the pathname dot-dot in the given directory.

When discussing other types of files, a directory containing a directory entry for the file under discussion.

This concept does not apply to dot and dot-dot.

parent process

See **process** on page 535.

parent process ID

An attribute of a new process identifying the parent of the process. The parent process ID of a process is the process ID of its creator, for the lifetime of the creator. After the creator's lifetime has ended, the parent process ID is the process ID of an implementation-dependent system process.

pathname

A character string that is used to identify a file. A pathname consists of, at most, {PATH_MAX} bytes, including the terminating null byte. It has an optional beginning slash, followed by zero or more filenames separated by slashes. If the pathname refers to a directory, it may also have one or more trailing slashes. Multiple successive slashes are considered to be the same as one slash. A pathname that begins with two successive slashes may be interpreted in an implementation-dependent manner, although more than two leading slashes are treated as a single slash. The interpretation of the pathname is described in **pathname resolution** on page 533.

pathname component

See **filename** on page 525.

pathname resolution

Pathname resolution is performed for a process to resolve a pathname to a particular file in a file hierarchy. There may be multiple pathnames that resolve to the same file.

Each filename in the pathname is located in the directory specified by its predecessor (for example, in the pathname fragment **a/b**, file **b** is located in directory **a**). Pathname resolution fails if this cannot be accomplished. If the pathname begins with a slash, the predecessor of the first filename in the pathname is taken to be the root directory of the process (such pathnames are referred to as *absolute pathnames*). If the pathname does not begin with a slash, the predecessor of the first filename of the pathname is taken to be the current working directory of the process (such pathnames are referred to as *relative pathnames*).

The interpretation of a pathname component is dependent on the values of {NAME_MAX} and _POSIX_NO_TRUNC associated with the path prefix of that component. If any pathname component is longer than {NAME_MAX}, because _POSIX_NO_TRUNC is in effect on all XSI-conformant systems for the path prefix of that component (see *pathconf*( )), the implementation will consider this an error condition.

If a symbolic link (see **symbolic link** on page 542) is encountered during pathname resolution, then pathname resolution is complete if all of the following are true:

- This is the last component of the pathname.
- The pathname has no trailing slash.
- The function is required to act on the symbolic link itself, or certain arguments direct that the function act on the symbolic link itself.

In all other cases, the system prefixes the remaining pathname, if any, with the contents of the symbolic link. The function may fail, setting *errno* to [ENAMETOOLONG], if the combined length exceeds {PATH_MAX}. Otherwise, the resolved pathname is the resolution of the pathname just created. The result is either an absolute pathname that is resolved from the root directory of the process, or a relative pathname that is resolved from the directory containing the symbolic link.

The special filename **dot** refers to the directory specified by its predecessor. The special filename **dot-dot** refers to the parent directory of its predecessor directory. As a special case, in the root directory, **dot-dot** may refer to the root directory itself.

A pathname consisting of a single slash resolves to the root directory of the process. A null pathname is invalid.

path prefix

A pathname, with an optional ending slash, that refers to a directory.

pattern

A sequence of characters used either with regular expression notation or for pathname expansion (see XCU, **Chapter 2**, **Shell Command Language**), as a means of selecting various character strings or pathnames, respectively.

The syntaxes of the two patterns are similar, but not identical; the XSI specification set always indicates the type of pattern being referred to in the immediate context of the use of the term.

period

The character ".". The term *period* is contrasted against **dot**, which is used to describe a specific directory entry.

permissions

See **file access permissions** on page 524.

persistence

A mode for semaphores, shared memory, and message queues requiring that the object and its state (including data, if any) are preserved after the object is no longer referenced by any process.

Persistence of an object does not imply that the state of the object is maintained across a system crash or a system reboot.

pipe

An object accessed by one of the pair of file descriptors created by the *pipe*( ) function. Once created, the file descriptors can be used to manipulate it, and it behaves identically to a FIFO special file when accessed in this way. It has no name in the file hierarchy.

positional parameter

In the shell, a parameter denoted by a single digit or one or more digits in curly braces. See XCU, **Chapter 2**, **Shell Command Language**.

portable character set

The collection of characters that is required to be present in all locales supported by XSI-conformant systems:

```
A B C D E F G H I J K L M N O P Q R S T U V W X Y Z
a b c d e f g h i j k l m n o p q r s t u v w x y z
0 1 2 3 4 5 6 7 8 9 ! # % ^ & * ( ) _ + - = { } [ ]
: " ~ ; ' ` < > ? , . | \ / @ $
```

Also included are the alert, backspace, tab, newline, vertical-tab, form-feed, carriage-return, and space characters and the null character, NUL.

This term is contrasted against the smaller portable filename character set.

portable filename character set

The set of characters from which portable filenames are constructed. For a filename to be portable across implementations conforming to XSI specification set and POSIX.1, it must consist only of the following characters:

```
A B C D E F G H I J K L M N O P Q R S T U V W X Y Z
a b c d e f g h i j k l m n o p q r s t u v w x y z
0 1 2 3 4 5 6 7 8 9 . _ -
```

The last three characters are the period, underscore, and hyphen characters, respectively. The hyphen must not be used as the first character of a portable filename. Upper- and lower-case letters retain their unique identities between conforming implementations. In the case of a portable pathname, the slash character may also be used.

preallocation

The reservation of resources in a system for a particular use.

Preallocation does not imply that the resources are immediately allocated to that use, but merely indicates that they are guaranteed to be available in bounded time when needed.

preempted process (or thread)
A running thread whose execution is suspended due to another thread becoming runnable at a higher priority.

printable character
One of the characters included in the **print** character classification of the LC_CTYPE category in the current locale.

printable file
A text file consisting only of the characters included in the **print** and **space** character classifications of the LC_CTYPE category and the backspace character, all in the current locale.

priority
A non-negative integer associated with processes or threads whose value is constrained to a range defined by the applicable scheduling policy. Numerically higher values represent higher priorities.

priority band
The queueing order applied to normal priority STREAMS messages. High priority STREAMS messages are not grouped by priority bands. The only differentiation made by the STREAMS mechanism is between zero and non-zero bands, but specific protocol modules may differentiate between priority bands.

priority-based scheduling
Scheduling in which the selection of a running thread is determined by the priorities of the runnable threads.

privilege
See **appropriate privileges** on page 516.

process
An address space with one or more threads executing within that address space, and the required system resources for those threads.

Many of the system resources defined by this specification are shared among all of the threads within a process. These include: the process ID, the parent process ID, process group ID, session membership, real, effective and saved-set user ID, real, effective and saved-set group ID, supplementary group IDs, current working directory, root directory, file mode creation mask, and file descriptors.

A process is created by another process issuing the *fork*() function. The process that issues *fork*() is known as the parent process, and the new process created by *fork*() is known as the child process.

process group
A collection of processes that permits the signaling of related processes. Each process in the system is a member of a process group that is identified by a process group ID. A newly created process joins the process group of its creator.

process group ID
The unique identifier representing a process group during its lifetime. A process group ID is a positive integer. A process group ID will not be reused by the system until the process group lifetime ends.

process group leader
A process whose process ID is the same as its process group ID.

process group lifetime

A period of time that begins when a process group is created and ends when the last remaining process in the group leaves the group, due either to the end of the last process' lifetime or to the last remaining process calling the *setsid*( ) or *setpgid*( ) functions.

process ID

The unique identifier representing a process. A process ID is a positive integer. A process ID will not be reused by the system until the process lifetime ends. In addition, if there exists a process group whose process group ID is equal to that process ID, the process ID will not be reused by the system until the process group lifetime ends. A process that is not a system process will not have a process ID of 1.

process lifetime

The period of time that begins when a process is created and ends when its process ID is returned to the system. After a process is created with a *fork*( ) function, it is considered active. At least one thread of control and address space exist until it terminates. It then enters an inactive state where certain resources may be returned to the system, although some resources, such as the process ID, are still in use. When another process executes a *wait*( ), *wait3*( ), *waitid*( ), or *waitpid*( ) function for an inactive process, the remaining resources are returned to the system. The last resource to be returned to the system is the process ID. At this time, the lifetime of the process ends.

process list

See **thread list** on page 544.

process virtual time

The measurement of time in units elapsed by the system clock while a process is executing.

program

A prepared sequence of instructions to the system to accomplish a defined task. The term *program* in the XSI specification set encompasses applications written in the XSI Shell Command Language, complex utility input languages (for example, *awk*, *lex*, *sed*, and so on), and high-level languages.

pseudo-terminal

A pseudo-terminal provides the process with an interface that is identical to the terminal subsystem. A pseudo-terminal is composed of 2 devices, the master device and a slave device. The slave device provides processes with an interface that is identical to the terminal interface, although there need not be hardware behind that interface. Anything written on the master device is presented to the slave as an input, and anything written on the slave device is presented as an input on the master side.

This specification requires a STREAMS-based implementation of pseudo-terminals to be available, but does not preclude others also being available.

radix character

The character that separates the integer part of a number from the fractional part.

read-only filesystem

A filesystem that has implementation-dependent characteristics restricting modifications.

read-write lock

Multiple readers, single writer (read-write) locks allow many threads to have simultaneous read-only access to data while allowing only one thread to have write access at any given time. They are typically used to protect data that is read-only more frequently than it is changed.

Read-write locks can be used to synchronize threads in the current process and other processes if they are allocated in memory that is writable and shared among the cooperating processes, and have been initialized for this behavior.

real group ID
The attribute of a process that, at the time of process creation, identifies the group of the user who created the process. See **group ID** on page 527. This value is subject to change during the process lifetime, as described in *setgid*( ).

real time
Time measured as total units elapsed by the system clock without regard to which thread is executing.

real user ID
The attribute of a process that, at the time of process creation, identifies the user who created the process. See **user ID** on page 545. This value is subject to change during the process lifetime, as described in *setuid*( ).

redirection
In the shell, a method of associating files with the input or output of commands. See XCU, **Chapter 2**, **Shell Command Language**.

redirection operator
In the shell, a token that performs a redirection function. It is one of the following symbols:

<   >   >| <<   >>   <&   >&   <<−   <>

reentrant function
A function whose effect, when called by two or more threads, is guaranteed to be as if the threads each executed the function one after another in an undefined order, even if the actual execution is interleaved.

referenced shared memory object
A shared memory object that is open or has one or more mappings defined on it.

refresh
To ensure that the information on the user's terminal screen is up-to-date.

regular expression
A pattern constructed according to the rules defined in XBD, **Chapter 7**, **Regular Expressions**.

region
In the context of the address space of a process, a sequence of addresses.

In the context of a file, a sequence of offsets.

regular file
A file that is a randomly accessible sequence of bytes, with no further structure imposed by the system.

relative pathname
See **pathname resolution** on page 533.

(time) resolution
The minimum time interval that a clock can measure or whose passage a timer can detect.

root directory
A directory, associated with a process, that is used in pathname resolution for pathnames that begin with a slash.

runnable process (or thread)

A thread that is capable of being a running thread, but for which no processor is available.

running process (or thread)

A thread currently executing on a processor. On multi-processor systems there may be more than one such thread in a system at a time.

saved resource limits

An attribute of a process that provides some flexibility in the handling of unrepresentable resource limits, as described in the *exec* family of functions and *setrlimit*( ).

saved set-group-ID

An attribute of a process that allows some flexibility in the assignment of the effective group ID attribute, as described in the *exec* family of functions and *setgid*( ).

saved set-user-ID

An attribute of a process that allows some flexibility in the assignment of the effective user ID attribute, as described in *exec* and *setuid*( ).

scheduling

The application of a policy to select a runnable process or thread to become a running process or thread, or to alter one or more of the thread lists.

scheduling allocation domain

The set of processors on which an individual thread can be scheduled at any given time.

scheduling contention scope

A property of a thread that defines the set of threads against which that thread competes for resources.

For example, in a scheduling decision, threads sharing scheduling contention scope compete for processor resources. In this specification, a thread has scheduling contention scope of either PTHREAD_SCOPE_SYSTEM or PTHREAD_SCOPE_PROCESS.

scheduling policy

A set of rules that is used to determine the order of execution of threads to achieve some goal.

In the context of XSI, a scheduling policy affects thread ordering:

- when a thread is a running thread and it becomes a blocked thread
- when a thread is a running thread and it becomes a preempted thread
- when a thread is a blocked thread and it becomes a runnable thread
- when a running thread calls a function that can change the priority or scheduling policy of a thread
- in other scheduling policy-defined circumstances.

Conforming implementations are required to define the manner in which each of the scheduling policies may modify the priorities or otherwise affect the ordering of threads at each of the occurrences listed above. Additionally, conforming implementations will define at what other circumstances and in what manner each scheduling policy may modify the priorities or affect the ordering of threads.

screen

A rectangular region of columns and lines on a terminal display. A screen may be a portion of a physical display device or may occupy the entire physical area of the display device.

scroll

To move the representation of data vertically or horizontally relative to the terminal screen. There are two types of scrolling:

1. The cursor moves with the data.
2. The cursor remains stationary while the data moves.

seconds since the epoch

A value to be interpreted as the number of seconds between a specified time and the epoch. A Coordinated Universal Time name (specified in terms of seconds (*tm_sec*), minutes (*tm_min*), hours (*tm_hour*), days since January 1 of the year (*tm_yday*), and calendar year minus 1900 (*tm_year*)) is related to a time represented as seconds since the Epoch, according to the expression below.

If the year < 1970 or the value is negative, the relationship is undefined. If the year ≥ 1970 and the value is non-negative, the value is related to a Coordinated Universal Time name according to the expression:

$$tm\_sec + tm\_min*60 + tm\_hour*3\,600 + tm\_yday*86\,400 + (tm\_year-70)*31\,536\,000 + ((tm\_year-69)/4)*86\,400$$

semaphore

A shareable resource that has a non-negative integral value. When the value is zero, there is a (possibly empty) set of threads awaiting the availability of the semaphore.

semaphore lock operation

An operation that is applied to a semaphore. If, prior to the operation, the value of the semaphore is zero, the semaphore lock operation causes the calling thread to be blocked and added to the set of threads awaiting the semaphore. Otherwise, the value is decremented.

semaphore unlock operation

An operation that is applied to a semaphore. If, prior to the operation, there are any threads in the set of threads awaiting the semaphore, then some thread from that set will be removed from the set and become unblocked. Otherwise, the semaphore value is incremented.

session

A collection of process groups established for job control purposes. Each process group is a member of a session. A process is considered to be a member of the session of which its process group is a member. A newly created process joins the session of its creator. A process can alter its session membership; see *setsid*( ). There can be multiple process groups in the same session.

session leader

A process that has created a session; see *setsid*( ).

session lifetime

The period between when a session is created and the end of the lifetime of all the process groups that remain as members of the session.

shared memory object

An object that represents memory that can be mapped concurrently into the address space of more than one process.

shell

A program that interprets sequences of text input as commands. It may operate on an input stream or it may interactively prompt and read commands from a terminal.

shell, the

The XSI Shell Command Language Interpreter (see *sh*), a specific instance of a shell.

shell script

A file containing shell commands. If the file is made executable, it can be executed by specifying its name as a simple command (see XCU, **Chapter 2**, **Shell Command Language**). Execution of a shell script causes a shell to execute the commands within the script. Alternatively, a shell can be requested to execute the commands in a shell script by specifying the name of the shell script as the operand to the *sh* utility.

signal

A mechanism by which a process or thread may be notified of, or affected by, an event occurring in the system. Examples of such events include hardware exceptions and specific actions by processes. The term *signal* is also used to refer to the event itself.

signal stack

Memory established for a thread, in which signal handlers catching signals sent to that thread are executed.

single-quote

The character ', also known as *apostrophe*.

slash

The character /, also known as *solidus*.

socket

A communications endpoint associated with a file descriptor that provides communications services using a specified communications protocol; see Networking Services, Issue 5.

soft limit

A resource limitation established for each process that the process may set to any value less than or equal to the hard limit.

source code

When dealing with the XSI Shell Command Language, input to the command language interpreter. The term *shell script* is synonymous with this meaning.

When dealing with the C Language, input to a C compiler conforming to the ISO C standard.

When dealing with another XSI-compliant language, input to a compiler conforming to that language standard.

Source code also refers to the input statements prepared for the following standard utilities: *awk*, *bc*, *ed*, *lex*, *localedef*, *make*, *sed*, and *yacc*.

Source code can also refer to a collection of sources meeting any or all of these meanings.

special parameter

In the shell, a parameter named by a single character from the following list:

```
*   @   #   ?   !   -   $   0
```

See XCU, **Chapter 2**, **Shell Command Language**.

space character

The character defined in the portable character set as <space>. The space character is a member of the **space** character class of the current locale, but represents the single character, and not all of the possible members of the class. (See **white space** on page 546.)

standard error
An output stream usually intended to be used for diagnostic messages.

standard input
An input stream usually intended to be used for primary data input.

standard output
An output stream usually intended to be used for primary data output.

standard utilities
The utilities described in XCU.

stream
Appearing in lower case, a stream is a file access object that allows access to an ordered sequence of characters, as described by the ISO C standard. Such objects can be created by the *fdopen*( ), *fopen*( ), or *popen*( ) functions, and are associated with a file descriptor. A stream provides the additional services of user-selectable buffering and formatted input and output. See XSH, **Chapter 2**, **General Information**.

STREAM
Appearing in upper case, STREAM refers to a full duplex connection between a process and an open device or pseudo-device. It optionally includes one or more intermediate processing modules that are interposed between the process end of the STREAM and the device driver (or pseudo-device driver) end of the STREAM. See XSH, **Chapter 2**, **General Information**.

STREAM end
The STREAM end is the driver end of the STREAM and is also known as the downstream end of the STREAM.

STREAM head
The STREAM head is the beginning of the STREAM and is at the boundary between the system and the application process. This is also known as the upstream end of the STREAM.

STREAMS multiplexor
A driver with multiple STREAMS connected to it. Multiplexing with STREAMS connected above is referred to as *N-to-1*, or *upper multiplexing*. Multiplexing with STREAMS connected below is referred to as *1-to-N* or *lower multiplexing*.

string
A contiguous sequence of bytes terminated by and including the first null byte.

subshell
A shell execution environment, distinguished from the main or current shell execution environment by the attributes described in XCU, **Chapter 2**, **Shell Command Language**.

successfully transferred
For a write operation to a regular file, when the system ensures that all data written is readable on any subsequent open of the file (even one that follows a system or power failure) in the absence of a failure of the physical storage medium.

For a read operation, when an image of the data on the physical storage medium is available to the requesting process.

supplementary group ID
An attribute of a process used in determining file access permissions. A process has up to {NGROUPS_MAX} supplementary group IDs in addition to the effective group ID. The supplementary group IDs of a process are set to the supplementary group IDs of the parent

process when the process is created. Whether a process' effective group ID is included in or omitted from its list of supplementary group IDs is unspecified.

suspended job
A job that has received a SIGSTOP, SIGTSTP, SIGTTIN, or SIGTTOU signal that caused the process group to stop. A suspended job is a background job, but a background job is not necessarily a suspended job.

symbolic link
A type of file that contains a pathname. The pathname is interpolated into a pathname being resolved, during pathname resolution, to create a new pathname when it is encountered.

synchronized I/O completion
The state of an I/O operation that has either been successfully transferred or diagnosed as unsuccessful.

synchronized I/O data integrity completion

- For read, when the operation has been completed or diagnosed if unsuccessful. The read is complete only when an image of the data has been successfully transferred to the requesting process. If there were any pending write requests affecting the data to be read at the time that the synchronized read operation was requested, these write requests shall be successfully transferred prior to reading the data.
- For write, when the operation has been completed or diagnosed if unsuccessful. The write is complete only when the data specified in the write request is successfully transferred and all filesystem information required to retrieve the data is successfully transferred.

File attributes that are not necessary for data retrieval (access time, modification time, status change time) need not be successfully transferred prior to returning to the calling process.

synchronized I/O file integrity completion
Identical to a synchronized I/O data integrity completion with the addition that all file attributes relative to the I/O operation (including access time, modification time, status change time) will be successfully transferred prior to returning to the calling process.

synchronized I/O operation
An I/O operation performed on a file that provides the application assurance of the integrity of its data and files.

synchronous I/O operation
An I/O operation that causes the thread requesting the I/O to be blocked from further use of the processor until that I/O operation completes.

Note that a synchronous I/O operation does not imply synchronized I/O data integrity completion, or synchronized I/O file integrity completion.

synchronously generated signal
A signal that is attributable to a specific thread.

For example, a thread executing an illegal instruction or touching invalid memory causes a synchronously generated signal. Being synchronous is a property of how the signal was generated and not a property of the signal number.

system
An implementation of the XSI.

system crash
An interval initiated by an unspecified circumstance that causes all processes (possibly other than special system processes) to be terminated in an undefined manner, after which any changes to the state and contents of files created or written to by an application prior to the interval are undefined, except as required elsewhere in the XSI specification set.

system console
An optional file that receives messages sent by *fmtmsg*( ) when the MM_CONSOLE flag is set.

system documentation
All documentation provided with an XSI-conformant implementation except for the Conformance Statement (CS). Electronically distributed documents for an XSI-conformant implementation are considered part of the system documentation.

system process
An implementation-dependent object, other than a process executing an application, that has a process ID.

system scheduling priority
A number used as advice to the system to alter process scheduling priorities. Raising the value should give a process additional preference when scheduling a process to run. Lowering the value should reduce the preference and make a process less likely to run. Typically, a process with higher system scheduling priority will run to completion more quickly than an equivalent process with lower system scheduling priority. A scheduling priority of zero specifies the default policy of the system.

This definition is not intended to suggest that all processes in a system have priorities that are comparable. Scheduling policy extensions, such as adding real-time priorities, make the notion of a single underlying priority for all scheduling policies problematic. Some systems may implement the features related to *nice* to affect all processes on the system, others to affect just the general time-sharing activities implied by the XSI specification set, and others may have no effect at all. Because of the use of "implementation-dependent" in *nice* and *renice*, a wide range of implementation strategies is possible.

system reboot
An implementation-dependent sequence of events that may result in the loss of transitory data; that is, data that is not saved in permanent storage. For example, message queues, shared memory, semaphores, and processes.

tab character
A character that in the output stream indicates that printing or displaying should start at the next horizontal tabulation position on the current line. The tab is the character designated by \t in the C Language. If the current position is at or past the last defined horizontal tabulation position, the behavior is unspecified. It is unspecified whether this character is the exact sequence transmitted to an output device by the system to accomplish the tabulation.

terminal
(Or **terminal device**.) A character special file that obeys the specifications of the general terminal interface.

text column
A roughly rectangular block of characters capable of being laid out side-by-side next to other text columns on an output page or terminal screen. The widths of text columns are measured in column positions.

text file

A file that contains characters organized into one or more lines. The lines must not contain NUL characters and none can exceed {LINE_MAX} bytes in length, including the newline character. Although the XSI does not distinguish between text files and binary files (see the ISO C standard), many utilities only produce predictable or meaningful output when operating on text files. The standard utilities that have such restrictions always specify *text files* in their stdin or Input Files sections.

The term *text file* does not prevent the inclusion of control or other non-printable characters (other than NUL). Therefore, standard utilities that list text files as inputs or outputs are either able to process the special characters gracefully or they explicitly describe their limitations within their individual sections. The only difference between text and binary files is that text files have lines of less than {LINE_MAX} bytes, with no NUL characters, each terminated by a newline character. The definition allows a file with a single newline character, but not a totally empty file, to be called a text file. If a file ends with an incomplete line, it is not strictly a text file by this definition. The newline character referred to in the XSI specification set is not some generic line separator, but a single character; files created on systems where they use multiple characters for ends of lines are not portable to all XSI-conformant systems without some translation process.

thread

A single flow of control within a process. Each thread has its own thread ID, scheduling priority and policy, *errno* value, thread-specific key/value bindings, and the required system resources to support a flow of control. Anything whose address may be determined by a thread, including but not limited to static variables, storage obtained via *malloc*( ), directly addressable storage obtained through implementation-supplied functions, and automatic variables, are accessible to all threads in the same process.

thread ID

Each thread in a process is uniquely identified during its lifetime by a value of type **pthread_t** called a thread ID.

thread list

An ordered set of runnable processes that all have the same ordinal value for their priority.

The ordering of processes on the list is determined by a scheduling policy or policies. The set of thread lists includes all runnable processes in the system.

thread-safe

A function that may be safely invoked concurrently by multiple threads. Examples are any "pure" function, a function which holds a mutex locked while it is accessing static storage, or objects shared among threads.

thread-specific data key

A process global handle of type **pthread_key_t** which is used for naming thread-specific data.

Although the same key value may be used by different threads, the values bound to the key by *pthread_setspecific*( ) and accessed by *pthread_getspecific*( ) are maintained on a per-thread basis and persist for the life of the calling thread.

tilde

The character ˜.

timer

A mechanism that can notify a thread when the time as measured by a particular clock has reached or passed a specified value, or when a specified amount of time has passed.

timer overrun

A condition that occurs each time a timer, for which there is already an expiration signal queued to the process, expires.

token

A sequence of characters that the shell considers as a single unit when reading input, according to the rules in XCU, **Chapter 2**, **Shell Command Language**. A token is either an operator or a word.

upshifting

The conversion of a lower-case character to its upper-case representation.

user database

A system database of implementation-dependent format that contains at least the following information for each user ID:

- user name
- numerical user ID
- initial numerical group ID
- initial working directory
- initial user program.

The initial numerical group ID is used by the *newgrp* utility. Any other circumstances under which the initial values are operative are implementation-dependent.

If the initial user program field is null, an implementation-dependent program is used.

If the initial working directory field is null, the interpretation of that field is implementation-dependent.

user ID

A non-negative integer that is used to identify a system user. When the identity of a user is associated with a process, a user ID value is referred to as a real user ID, an effective user ID, or a saved set-user-ID.

user name

A string that is used to identify a user, as described in **user database**. To be portable across XSI-conformant systems, the value must be composed of characters from the portable filename character set. The hyphen should not be used as the first character of a portable user name.

utility

A program that can be called by name from a shell to perform a specific task, or related set of tasks. This program is either an executable file, such as might be produced by a compiler or linker system from computer source code, or a file of shell source code, directly interpreted by the shell. The program may have been produced by the user, provided by the system implementor, or acquired from an independent distributor. The term *utility* does not apply to the special built-in utilities provided as part of the XSI Shell Command Language; see XCU, **Chapter 2**, **Shell Command Language**. The system may implement certain utilities as shell functions (see XCU, **Chapter 2**, **Shell Command Language**) or built-in utilities, but only an application that is aware of the command search order described in XCU, **Chapter 2**, **Shell Command Language** or of performance characteristics can discern differences between the behavior of such a function or built-in utility and that of a true executable file.

variable
In the shell, a named parameter; see XCU, **Chapter 2**, **Shell Command Language**.

variable assignment
In the shell, a word consisting of the following parts:

```
varname=value
```

When used in a context where assignment is defined to occur (see XCU, **Chapter 2**, **Shell Command Language**) and at no other time, the *value* (representing a word or field) will be assigned as the value of the variable denoted by *varname*. The *varname* and *value* parts meet the requirements for a name and a word, respectively, except that they are delimited by the embedded unquoted equals-sign in addition to the delimiting described in XCU, **Chapter 2**, **Shell Command Language**. In all cases, the variable will be created if it did not already exist. If *value* is not specified, the variable will be given a null value.

An alternative form of variable assignment:

```
symbol=value
```

(where *symbol* is a valid word delimited by an equals-sign, but not a valid name) produces unspecified results. This form is used by the KornShell *name[expression]=value* syntax.

vertical-tab character
A character that in the output stream indicates that printing should start at the next vertical tabulation position. The vertical-tab is the character designated by \v in the C Language. If the current position is at or past the last defined vertical tabulation position, the behavior is unspecified. It is unspecified whether this character is the exact sequence transmitted to an output device by the system to accomplish the tabulation.

white space
A sequence of one or more characters that belong to the **space** character class as defined via the LC_CTYPE category in the current locale.

In the POSIX locale, white space consists of one or more blank characters (space and tab characters), newline characters, carriage-return characters, form-feed characters, and vertical-tab characters.

wide-character code (C Language)
An integer value corresponding to a single graphic symbol or control code.

wide-character string
A contiguous sequence of wide-character codes terminated by and including the first null wide-character code.

word
In the shell, a token other than an operator. In some cases a word is also a portion of a word token: in the various forms of parameter expansion (see XCU, **Chapter 2**, **Shell Command Language**), such as ${*name–word*}, and variable assignment, such as *name=word*, the word is the portion of the token depicted by *word*. The concept of a word is no longer applicable following word expansions — only fields remain; see XCU, **Chapter 2**, **Shell Command Language**.

working directory
(Or **current working directory**.) A directory, associated with a process, that is used in pathname resolution for pathnames that do not begin with a slash.

world-wide portability interface
Functions for handling characters in a codeset-independent manner.

write

To output characters to a file, such as standard output or standard error. Unless otherwise stated, standard output is the default output destination for all uses of the term *write*. See the distinction between *display* and *write* in **display** on page 521.

XSI-conformant

A system which allows an application to be built using a set of services that are consistent across all systems that conform to the XSI specification set.

zombie process

An inactive process that will be deleted at some later time when its parent process executes *wait*( ) or *waitpid*( ).

[n, m] and [n, m)

Notations denoting mathematical ranges. The square brackets [and] include the limit; the parentheses (and) exclude the limit; that is, if *x* is in [0, 1], it can be from 0 to 1 inclusive, but if *x* is in [0, 1), it can be from 0 up to but not including 1.

±0

The algebraic sign provides additional information about any variable that has the value zero. Although all precisions have distinct representations for +0, −0, +Inf, and −Inf, the signs are significant in some circumstances, such as division by zero, and not in others.

Appendix D

Referenced Documents

Open Group Documentation

How to Brand — What to Buy
The X/Open Branding Program, How to Brand — What to Buy, February 1995 (ISBN: 1-85912-084-9, X951).

Internationalization Guide, Version 2
Guide, July 1993, Internationalization Guide, Version 2 (ISBN: 1-859120-02-4, G304).

Programming Languages, Issue 3
Chapters 1 to 4 of X/Open Specification, 1988, 1989, February 1992, Programming Languages, Issue 3 (ISBN: 1-872630-39-1, C214); this specification was formerly X/Open Portability Guide, Volume 4, August 1988 (ISBN: 0-13-685868-6, XO/XPG/89/005).

X/Open Curses, Issue 4, Version 2
CAE Specification, May 1996, X/Open Curses, Issue 4, Version 2 (ISBN: 1-85912-171-3, C610).

XBD, Issue 4, Version 2
CAE Specification, August 1994, System Interface Definitions, Issue 4, Version 2 (ISBN: 1-85912-036-9, C434).

XBD, Issue 5
CAE Specification, January 1997, System Interface Definitions, Issue 5 (ISBN: 1-85912-186-1, C605).

XCU, Issue 4, Version 2
CAE Specification, August 1994, Commands and Utilities, Issue 4, Version 2 (ISBN: 1-85912-034-2, C436).

XCU, Issue 5
CAE Specification, January 1997, Commands and Utilities, Issue 5 (ISBN: 1-85912-191-8, C604).

XDSA-DCE
CAE Specification, February 1997, Distributed Software Administration — DCE Interoperability (ISBN: 1-85912-137-3, C430).

XNFS
CAE Specification, October 1992, Protocols for X/Open Interworking: XNFS, Issue 4 (ISBN: 1-872630-66-9, C218).

XNS, Issue 4
CAE Specification, August 1994, Networking Services, Issue 4 (ISBN: 1-85912-049-0, C438).

XNS, Issue 5
CAE Specification, February 1997, Networking Services, Issue 5 (ISBN: 1-85912-165-9, C523).

XSH, Issue 4, Version 2
: CAE Specification, August 1994, System Interfaces and Headers, Issue 4, Version 2 (ISBN: 1-85912-037-7, C435).

XSH, Issue 5
: CAE Specification, January 1997, System Interfaces and Headers, Issue 5 (ISBN: 1-85912-181-0, C606).

Standards Documentation

ANSI C
: American National Standard for Information Systems: Standard X3.159-1989, Programming Language C.

FIPS 151-2
: Federal Information Procurement Standards (FIPS) 151-2.

ISO/IEC 646
: ISO/IEC 646:1991, Information Processing — ISO 7-bit Coded Character Set for Information Interchange.

ISO C
: ISO/IEC 9899:1990: Programming Languages — C, including:
Amendment 1:1995 (E), C Integrity (Multibyte Support Extensions (MSE) for ISO C).

ISO POSIX-1
: ISO/IEC 9945-1:1996, Information Technology — Portable Operating System Interface (POSIX) — Part 1: System Application Program Interface (API) [C Language] (identical to ANSI/IEEE Std 1003.1-1996). Incorporating ANSI/IEEE Stds 1003.1-1990, 1003.1b-1993, 1003.1c-1995 and 1003.1i-1995.

ISO POSIX-2
: ISO/IEC 9945-2:1993, Information Technology — Portable Operating System Interface (POSIX) — Part 2: Shell and Utilities (identical to IEEE Std 1003.2-1992 as amended by IEEE Std 1003.2a-1992).

ISO/IEC 10646
: ISO/IEC 10646-1:1993, Information Technology — Universal Multiple-Octet Coded Character Set (UCS) — Part 1: Architecture and Basic Multilingual Plane.

ISO 6937
: ISO 6937:1983, Information Processing — Coded Character Sets for Text Communication.

ISO 8859-1
: ISO 8859-1:1987, Information Processing — 8-bit Single-byte Coded Graphic Character Sets — Part 1: Latin Alphabet No. 1.

ISO 9660
: ISO 9660:1988, Information Processing — Volume and File Structure of CD-ROM for Information Interchange.

POSIX.1
: IEEE Std 1003.1-1990, Standard for Information Technology — Portable Operating System Interface (POSIX) — Part 1: System Application Program Interface (API) [C Language].

POSIX.1b IEEE Std 1003.1b-1993, Realtime Extension

POSIX.1c IEEE Std 1003.1c-1995, Threads Extensions

POSIX.1d IEEE Draft Std P1003.1d/D8 (September 1993), Amendment d: Realtime Extension [C Language]

POSIX.1g IEEE Std 1003.1g-1996, Protocol Independent Interfaces (PII).

POSIX.1i IEEE Std 1003.1i-1995, Technical Corrigenda to Realtime Extension

POSIX.1j IEEE Draft Std P1003.1j/D5 (May 1995), Amendment j: Additional Realtime Extension [C Language]

POSIX.13
IEEE Draft Std P1003.13/D7 (February 1995), Standardized Application Environment Profile — POSIX Realtime Application Support (AEP)

POSIX.21LIS
IEEE Draft Std P1003.21LIS/D1.0 (September 1996), Amendment: Realtime Distributed Systems

POSIX.5b
IEEE Std 1003.5b-1996, Ada Language Interfaces — Part 1: Binding for System Application Program Interface (API) — Amendment 1: Realtime Extensions

POSIX.2
IEEE Std 1003.2-1992, Standard for Information Technology — Portable Operating System Interface (POSIX) — Part 2: Shell and Utilities.

POSIX-7.2
IEEE Std. 1387.2-1995, Information Technology — Portable Operating System Interface (POSIX) System Administration — Part 2: Software Administration.

Historical Documentation and Other Texts

- 4.3BSD: University of California at Berkeley — Computer Science Research Group, 4.3 Berkeley Software Distribution, Virtual VAX-11 Version, Berkeley CA: The Regents of the University of California, April 1986.
- *A Systematic Approach to Designing Distributed Real-Time Systems*, L. Sha and S.S. Sathaye, IEEE Computer 26, 9, 68-78.
- *Aperiodic Task Scheduling for Hard-Real-Time Systems*, B. Sprunt, L. Sha, and J. Lehoczky, Real-Time Systems 1, 1, 27-60.
- *Applying New Scheduling Theory to Static Priority Preemptive Scheduling*, N.C. Audsley, A. Burns, M.F. Richardson, K.W. Tindell, and A.J. Wellings, Software Engineering Journal 8, 5, 284-292.
- *Change Management and the Momentum of Open Systems*, C. Jacobs, M. Placko, March 1995, Published by The Open Group (ISBN: 1-85912-011-3, B006).
- *MVS/ESA: Planning: OpenEdition MVS*, SC23-3015-02.
- *On the Complexity of Fixed Priority Scheduling of Periodic, Real-Time Tasks*, J.Y.T. Leung and J.W. Whitehead, Performance Evaluation 2, 4, 237-250.
- *Open Comments*, Open Group Newsletters (1996-1997).
- *Priority Inheritance Protocols: An Approach to Real-Time Synchronization*, L. Sha, R. Rajkumar, and J.P. Lehoczky, IEEE Transactions on Computers 39, 1175-1185.
- *Programming with POSIX Threads*, David Butenhof, Addison Wesley Longman.

- *Pthreads Programming*, Nichols, Buttlar and Prouxl Farrell, published by O'Reilly.
- *Real-Time Scheduling Theory and Ada*, L. Sha and J.G. Goodenough, IEEE Computer 23, 4, 53-62.
- *Scheduling Algorithms for Multiprogramming in a Hard-Real-Time Environment*, C.L. Liu and J.W. Layland, Journal of the ACM 20, 1, 46-61.
- SVID: American Telephone and Telegraph Company, System V Interface Definition (SVID), Issues 2 and 3; Morristown, NJ, UNIX Press, 1986, 1989.
- *The Open Product Brand*, An Open Group White Paper, J.Hansen, G. Bird, January 1997.
- *Threads Primer*, Bill Lewis and Daniel J. Berg, published by SunSoft Press.
- *Threadtime*, Scott J. Norton and Mark D. Dipasquale, published by Prentice Hall.
- *U.S. Air Force Procurement Demands X/Open Brand Certification as Proof of Conformance to Open Systems*, Open Group Press Release, 29th January 1996.

Index